Equity Markets, Valuation, and Analysis

Founded in 1807, John Wiley & Sons is the oldest independent publishing company in the United States. With offices in North America, Europe, Australia and Asia, Wiley is globally committed to developing and marketing print and electronic products and services for our customers' professional and personal knowledge and understanding.

The Wiley Finance series contains books written specifically for finance and investment professionals as well as sophisticated individual investors and their financial advisors. Book topics range from portfolio management to e-commerce, risk management, financial engineering, valuation and financial instrument analysis, as well as much more.

For a list of available titles, visit our Web site at www.WileyFinance.com.

Equity Markets, Valuation, and Analysis

H. KENT BAKER

GREG FILBECK

HALIL KIYMAZ

WILEY

Published by John Wiley & Sons, Inc., Hoboken, New Jersey.
Published simultaneously in Canada.

For general information on our other products and services or for technical support, please contact our Customer Care Department within the United States at (800) 762-2974, outside the United States at (317) 572-3993, or fax (317) 572-4002.

Wiley publishes in a variety of print and electronic formats and by print-on-demand. Some material included with standard print versions of this book may not be included in e-books or in print-on-demand. If this book refers to media such as a CD or DVD that is not included in the version you purchased, you may download this material at http://booksupport.wiley .com. For more information about Wiley products, visit www.wiley.com.

Library of Congress Cataloging-in-Publication Data:
Names: Baker, H. Kent (Harold Kent), 1944- editor. | Filbeck, Greg, editor.
    | Kiymaz, Halil, 1964- editor.
Title: Equity markets, valuation, and analysis / H. Kent Baker, Greg
    Filbeck, Halil Kiymaz.
Description: Hoboken, New Jersey : Wiley, [2020] | Series: Wiley finance
    series | Includes index.
Identifiers: LCCN 2020021382 (print) | LCCN 2020021383 (ebook) | ISBN
    9781119632931 (cloth) | ISBN 9781119632948 (adobe pdf) | ISBN
    9781119632924 (epub)
Subjects: LCSH: Stock exchanges. | Valuation.
Classification: LCC HG4551 .E65 2020 (print) | LCC HG4551 (ebook) | DDC
    332.63/2042—dc23
LC record available at https://lccn.loc.gov/2020021382
LC ebook record available at https://lccn.loc.gov/2020021383

Cover Design: Wiley
Cover Image: © AnuStudio/Getty Images

Printed in the United States of America

SKY10020052_072420

Contents

CHAPTER 4
Securities Regulation   51
Douglas Cumming and Sofia Johan

CHAPTER 5
Investor Psychology and Equity Market Anomalies   63
Hunter M. Holzhauer

PART TWO

Valuation and Analysis

CHAPTER 6
Financial Statement Analysis and Forecasting   81
Somnath Das and Shailendra Pandit

Acknowledgments

A good editor is someone who cares a little less about the author's needs than the reader's.

Dene October

Bringing this book from the idea stage to publication was a team effort. We greatly appreciate the roles played by all participants – some more direct than others. We thank our chapter authors for sharing their knowledge. They painstakingly wrote and then revised each chapter multiple times without complaint. We edited your words but not your message. Without your dedication, this book would not exist.

We also thank the highly talented professionals at John Wiley & Sons, especially Bill Falloon (executive editor), Richard Samson (project editor), and Koushika Ramesh (production editor), for their guidance. We also thank everyone at Cape Cod Compositors, Inc. Additionally, we recognize the support provided by the Kogod School of Business at American University, the Behrend College at Penn State Erie, and the Crummer Graduate School of Business at Rollins College.

Finally, we express gratitude for our families, who have largely been our silent partners in this process. We dedicate this book to Linda and Rory Baker; Janis, Aaron, Andrea, Kyle, and Grant Filbeck; Nilgün and Tunc Kiymaz.

About the Editors

H. Kent Baker, CFA, CMA, is University Professor of Finance at the Kogod School of Business at American University. Professor Baker is an award-winning author/editor of 36 books, including *Debt Markets and Investments*; *Investment Traps Exposed: Navigating Investor Mistakes and Behavioral Biases*; *Financial Behavior: Players, Services, Products, and Markets*; *Investor Behavior: The Psychology of Financial Planning and Investing*; and *Survey Research in Corporate Finance*. He is also the editor of two book series: Financial Markets and Investments (Oxford University Press) and the H. Kent Baker Investments Series (Emerald Publishing). As one of the most prolific finance academics, he has published about 190 refereed academic journal articles and 125 practitioner-oriented articles appearing in such outlets as the *Journal of Finance*, *Journal of Financial and Quantitative Analysis*, *Financial Management*, *Journal of Corporate Finance*, *Financial Analysts Journal*, *Journal of Portfolio Management*, and *Harvard Business Review*. He has consulting and training experience with more than 100 organizations and has conducted more than 800 training programs in North America and Europe. He is the past president of the Southern Finance Association and its 2019 Distinguished Scholar. Professor Baker holds a BSBA from Georgetown University; an MEd, MBA, and DBA from the University of Maryland; and an MA, MS, and two PhDs from American University.

Greg Filbeck, CFA, FRM, CAIA, CIPM, PRM, is the Samuel P. Black III Professor of Finance and Risk Management at Penn State Behrend, and serves as the director for the Black School of Business. He formerly served as senior vice president of Kaplan Schweser and held academic appointments at Miami University and the University of Toledo, where he served as the Associate Director of the Center for Family Business. Professor Filbeck is an author/editor of 14 books and has published more than 100 refereed academic journal articles in the *Financial Analysts Journal*, *Financial Review*, and *Journal of Business, Finance, and Accounting*, among others. He is the former president of the CFA Society Pittsburgh. Professor Filbeck holds and conducts training worldwide for candidates for the CFA, FRM, and CAIA designations. Professor Filbeck holds a BS from Murray State University, an MS from Penn State University, and a DBA from the University of Kentucky.

Halil Kiymaz, CFA, is Bank of America Professor of Finance at the Crummer Graduate School of Business at Rollins College. Professor Kiymaz maintains an extensive research agenda focusing on international mergers and acquisitions, emerging capital markets, linkages among capital markets of developing economies, IPOs, and financial management of multinationals. Professor Kiymaz has authored or edited five books and has published more than 85 articles in scholarly and practitioner journals. His research has appeared in such outlets as the *Journal of Banking and Finance*,

Financial Review, Global Finance Journal, Journal of Applied Finance, Journal of Economics and Finance, Review of Financial Economics, and *Quarterly Journal of Business and Economics.* He is the recipient of several research awards, including the McGraw-Hill Irwin Best Paper Award and the Outstanding Research Award at the Global Conference on Business and Finance. Professor Kiymaz also serves on the editorial boards of *Journal of Emerging Markets* and *Journal of Economics, Business, and Finance.* He is the former president of the Academy of Financial Services and finance editor of the *International Journal of Emerging Markets.* Professor Kiymaz received a BS in business administration from the Uludag University, an MBA, an MA in economics, and a PhD in financial economics from the University of New Orleans.

About the Chapter Authors

Elif Akben-Selçuk is an Associate Professor of Finance at at Gebze Technical University in Kocaeli, Turkey. She teaches undergraduate and graduate courses in accounting and financial management. Professor Akben-Selçuk's research interests include corporate finance, mergers and acquisitions, corporate governance, emerging markets, personal finance, and financial literacy. Her research has appeared in such outlets as *Managerial Finance, International Journal of Bank Marketing, International Journal of Emerging Markets, Economics Bulletin,* and *Psychological Reports,* among others. Professor Akben-Selçuk received a BA in business administration, an MA in economics, and a PhD in finance from Bogazici University in Istanbul, Turkey.

Tom Barkley, CFA, FRM, CAIA, ERP, is a Professor of Finance Practice at the Whitman School of Management, Syracuse University, and the Director of the MS in Finance program. His teaching and research are in corporate finance and derivatives. He previously worked for Enron (Research Group) and the Risk Analytics Group at Florida Power & Light. In both cases, his work included pricing exotic options and structuring products for use in the energy markets. Other experience includes retail banking in the United Kingdom, teaching high school mathematics in the Bahamas, and general management of a family-run publishing company. He received an MBA from Thunderbird, the American Graduate School of International Management, and a PhD in finance from the University of Florida.

Christopher J. Barnes, CFA, is a vice president in Deutsche Bank's equity research group on its North America consumer staples team covering the beverages, household and personal care products, food, and tobacco industries. He has broad-based consumer sector experience assessing public equity securities. Before joining Deutsche Bank, he evaluated the hardlines, grocery, and broadlines retailing sectors, along with the media and entertainment sectors, at Telsey Advisory Group. He also analyzed the consumer leisure sector at Oppenheimer & Co. Mr. Barnes received a BBA in finance with high honors from Hofstra University.

Onur Bayar is an Associate Professor of Finance at the University of Texas at San Antonio. Professor Bayar's research interests are in corporate finance, entrepreneurial finance and venture capital, and market microstructure. He has published in *Journal of Financial Economics, Journal of Financial and Quantitative Analysis, Journal of Corporate Finance, Review of Corporate Finance Studies,* and *Financial Management,* among others. Professor Bayar received an MS in financial economics from Carnegie Mellon University and a PhD in finance from Boston College.

Nicholas Biasi is an independent financial consultant. Mr. Biasi was an analyst for the Student Management Investment Fund at Hofstra University, where he performed research on various asset classes and recommended investments to the Board of Directors. He is a CFA Level 2 candidate and is also pursuing an MS in finance. He holds a BS in finance from the Frank G. Zarb School of Business at Hofstra University.

Emmanuel Boutron is an Associate Professor of Finance at Paris Nanterre University and also at the École des Ponts ParisTech. His research focuses on the financing of growth firms, especially on initial public offerings of small and medium-sized firms. He has published in several academic journals and book chapters. Professor Boutron is involved in continuing education programs for managers at the Institute de Haute Finance in Paris. He holds an MS in finance from Lorraine University and received a PhD in finance from Paris Nanterre University.

Jay T. Brandi is a Professor and Chair of the Department of Finance at the College of Business, University of Louisville. Before beginning his academic career, he served as both the Assistant Director of Securities and Securities Investigation Supervisor for the Division of Securities. He also was a lobbyist for the Comptroller of the State of Florida. Professor Brandi's research primarily focuses on securities issues, investments, and portfolio management. His research appears in the *Journal of Legal Economics*, *Journal of International Finance*, *Journal of Investing*, *Labor Law Journal*, and *Journal of American Entrepreneurship*, among others. Professor Brandi has also authored finance texts, including *Corporate Finance: Foundations of Value Optimization and Survival*, *Essential Corporate Finance*, and *Money Management and Personal Finance*. He received a PhD in finance with a minor in law from the University of Arizona.

Alain Coën is a Professor of Finance at the Graduate School of Business (ESG) of the University of Québec in Montréal (UQÀM). Before joining ESG-UQÀM, he was an Associate Professor of Finance at the EDHEC School of Management. His research interests focus on asset pricing, international finance, hedge funds, real estate investment trusts, business cycles, and financial econometrics. Professor Coën has published in the *Journal of Banking and Finance*, *Journal of International Money and Finance*, *Journal of Empirical Finance*, *Journal of Financial Research*, *Economics Letters*, *Finance Research Letters*, and *Real Estate Economics*. He has also written a book in financial management. He holds an MA in economics from Laval University, a Master in Management from ESSCA and accreditations to supervise research (HDR in Management) from Paris Dauphine University and (HDR in Economics) from the University of Paris I Panthéon-Sorbonne. Professor Coën has a PhD in finance from the University of Grenoble and a PhD in economics from the University of Paris I Panthéon-Sorbonne.

Douglas Cumming, CFA, is the DeSantis Distinguished Professor of Finance and Entrepreneurship at the College of Business, Florida Atlantic University. He has published over 180 articles in leading refereed academic journals such as the *Academy of Management Journal*, *Journal of Financial Economics*, and *Review of Financial Studies*. Professor Cumming is the Managing Editor-in-Chief of the *Journal of Corporate Finance* (January 2018–December 2020), and the incoming Managing

Editor-in-Chief of the *British Journal of Management* (January 2020–December 2022). He is the Founding Editor of *Annals of Corporate Governance* (January 2016–current). Professor Cumming has published 18 academic books. His work has been reviewed in numerous media outlets, including the *Chicago Tribune, The Economist, The New York Times, The Wall Street Journal, The Globe and Mail, Canadian Business, National Post,* and *The New Yorker*. Professor Cumming holds a BCom in economics and finance from McGill University, an MA in economics from Queen's University, and a JD and PhD from the University of Toronto.

Somnath Das is Professor and Coordinator of the Doctoral Program in Accounting at the University of Illinois at Chicago. Previously, he was on the faculty at University of California–Berkeley's Haas School of Business. His research focuses on corporate disclosure, financial analysts, and firm performance. He has published in leading academic journals such as *The Accounting Review, Contemporary Accounting Research, Journal of Accounting and Economics,* and *Journal of Finance,* among others. His research has received coverage in the business press, including *The Wall Street Journal*. He teaches courses in financial and managerial accounting. Professor Das has a bachelor's degree in physics from St. Stephens College, Delhi, an MBA from the Indian Institute of Management, Ahmedabad, and a master's in public policy as well as a PhD from Carnegie Mellon University.

Xiaohua Diao is the Dean of the School of Finance at Chongqing Technology and Business University, China. He is a Professor of Finance at the Research Center for Economy of Upper Reaches of the Yangtse River of Chongqing Technology and Business University. His research primarily focuses on financial risk management. He has published in more than 20 peer-reviewed journals and received research grants from central and state governments. Dean Diao also served as a consultant of the China Development Bank and on independent boards of directors of several publicly traded firms in China. He holds a master's degree with a specialization in accounting from Xiamen University.

Shantanu Dutta is an Associate Professor of Finance and Telfer Fellow in Global Finance at the Telfer School of Management, University of Ottawa. Before beginning his academic career, he was a finance manager at Lafarge, a world leader in construction materials. Professor Dutta's research focuses on mergers and acquisitions, media coverage and financial decisions, corporate governance, and dividend policy. He has published in the *Review of Accounting Studies, Journal of Corporate Finance, Financial Management, Journal of Banking and Finance,* and *Journal of Business Finance & Accounting* among others. He is a recipient of the SSHRC grant and Barclays Global Investors Canada Research Award (2006) for the best paper on the Canadian security market. He also received the Literati Network Award for Excellence in 2009 and 2014 for articles in the *International Journal of Managerial Finance*. He holds a PhD in finance from Carleton University.

Aaron Filbeck, CFA, CAIA, CIPM, is the Associate Director of Content Development at CAIA Association. He is involved with the development of the CAIA Charter Program's curriculum, supports the Association's academic partnership program, and serves as Content Director and Assistant Editor of *Alternative Investment Analyst Review* (AIAR), a practitioner-focused journal published by the Association. Before joining CAIA, Mr. Filbeck was a portfolio manager for a registered investment adviser, where he oversaw portfolio construction and manager research efforts for high-net-worth individuals. He received a BS in finance with distinction and a Master of Finance from Pennsylvania State University.

Didier Folus is Professor of Finance at the Management School, Paris Nanterre University, and also teaches at Paris Dauphine University, École des Ponts ParisTech, and in MBA and executive master programs. His primary research interests are in the areas of long-term investment exposure to risks and insurance securitization in a risk management perspective. He has published in *Applied Economic Letters*, *Bankers, Markets & Investors*, and *Applied Economics*, among others, He has also written several book chapters. Professor Folus consults for institutional investors, insurance companies, and banks in the field of innovative financial products. He holds a master's degree in finance from Paris Dauphine University, an MS in actuarial science from ENSAE (Paris), and a PhD in finance from Paris Dauphine University.

Xudong Fu is an Assistant Professor of Finance at the College of Business, University of Louisville. His research focuses on various topics in corporate finance including mergers and acquisitions, equity offerings, corporate governance, debt contracts, insider trading, and corporate social responsibility. Professor Fu has published in such journals as *Financial Management*, *Journal of Banking and Finance*, *Journal of Corporate Finance*, and *Journal of Empirical Finance*. He received a PhD from the University of Alabama.

Gaurav Gupta, CFA, FRM, is an analytics consultant at SRNL International in New Jersey. Before joining SRNL International, he worked as an analyst at OpenLink Financial LLC. He also has experience in managing a secondary steel manufacturing plant in India, where he managed the production as well as purchase teams of the business. He obtained a BS in engineering from Panjab University and an MBA with a double major in finance and business analytics with distinction from Hofstra University.

Hunter M. Holzhauer is the Robert L. Maclellan and UC Foundation Associate Professor of Finance at the University of Tennessee Chattanooga. Professor Holzhauer is an award-winning professor in research, teaching, and service. He has taught various graduate and undergraduate classes, including corporate finance, intermediate finance, investments, financial analysis, behavioral finance, portfolio management, and derivatives. His financial industry experience includes positions as a credit analyst with Colonial Bank and a financial planner and fixed-income portfolio manager with AmSouth Bank. Since 2013, Professor Holzhauer has published 16 research papers and seven chapters on such topics as behavioral finance, alternative investments, socially responsible investing, financial risk tolerance, and hedge funds. His research has been published in the *Journal of Investing*, *Journal of Applied Finance*, *Journal of Risk Finance*, and *Journal of Behavioral and Experimental Finance*. Professor Holzhauer received a BS in business administration and biopsychology from Birmingham-Southern College, an MBA from Mississippi State University, and a PhD from the University of Alabama.

Tianqi Jiang is a PhD candidate in finance at the University of Rhode Island. Her research interests include the social network of sell-side analysts, corporate disclosure, venture capital, and corporate governance. She has presented papers at various conferences, including those of the American Accounting Association and European Financial Management Association. Ms. Jiang obtained a BS in finance from Donghua University, an MS in finance from Hofstra University, and an MS in economics from Florida Atlantic University.

Sofia Johan is an Assistant Professor of Finance at the College of Business, Florida Atlantic University. She is an Extramural Research Fellow at Tilburg University in The Netherlands. Professor Johan's research covers topics ranging from crowdfunding, securities regulation, stock exchange trading rules, mutual funds, hedge funds, venture capital, private equity, and sovereign wealth funds. She has published 51 articles in leading refereed academic journals in finance, management, and law and economics, such as the *American Law and Economics Review, Journal of Financial Economics,* and *Journal of International Business Studies.* She is the co-author of *Venture Capital and Private Equity Contracting* (Elsevier Academic Press, 2nd edition, 2013), *Hedge Fund Structure, Regulation and Performance around the World* (Oxford University Press, 2013), and *Crowdfunding: Fundamental Cases, Facts, and Insights* (Elsevier Academic Press, 2019). Professor Johan is a regular speaker at academic and industry conferences around the world. She earned a law degree from the University of Liverpool and an LL.M. in International Economic Law from the University of Warwick. She also holds a PhD in law and economics from Tilburg University.

Timothy A. Krause is an Assistant Professor of Finance and the Director of the Intrieri Family Student Managed Fund at the Black School of Business at Penn State Behrend. Before starting his academic career, he spent 20 years in the financial services industry as an investments professional and held management positions at Bank of America, BNP Paribas, Vector Capital Markets, and Zecco Trading, now part of Ally Financial. He previously taught undergraduate and MBA finance courses at the University of Texas at San Antonio, Pepperdine University, and St. Edward's University. His research and teaching interests include investments, derivatives, risk management, financial institutions, market microstructure, and general financial markets. He has published in the *Review of Quantitative Finance and Accounting, Journal of Derivatives, Applied Financial Economics, International Review of Economics and Finance, Journal of Asset Management,* and *International Review of Economics and Finance.* Professor Krause received a BA in government/economics and an MBA from Georgetown University, and a PhD in finance from the University of Texas at San Antonio.

Sang Hoon Lee is a Professor of Finance and Dean of BRAC University in Dhaka, Bangladesh. Professor Lee has considerable academic and private consulting experience. He held teaching positions in the United States and Kazakhstan and quasi-government and private sector executive positions in Korea. His research interests mainly focus on capital market development in emerging markets, and the topics of his publications include financial literacy, asset valuation, small business financing, and financial crises from emerging market perspectives. He has a PhD in financial economics from the University of New Orleans.

Yini Liu is a PhD student in finance at the University of Texas at San Antonio. Ms. Liu's primary research interests are in empirical corporate finance with a focus on private investments in public equity, reverse mergers, IPOs, and financial intermediation. She also has research interests in law and finance and labor economics. Ms. Liu has taught as an independent instructor at the University of Texas at San Antonio. She received the UTSA Keith Fairchild Teaching Excellence Award in 2019. Ms. Liu received a BA in economics and an MA in finance from Fudan University.

David Lundgren, CFA, CMT, is an Adjunct Professor at the Brandeis International Business School, Brandeis University. He teaches a class on the practical applications of technical analysis, which emphasizes the strong link between price trends and the fundamentals that drive them. Mr. Lundgren is also Director of Technical Research at Wellington Management in Boston, Massachusetts, where he manages client portfolios exclusively using technical analysis strategies. He also serves as a member of the Board of Directors of the Chartered Market Technicians Association and is the chair of its Advocacy Committee. Mr. Lundgren received a bachelor's degree in finance and investments from Babson College.

Joseph McBride, CFA, Head of Commercial Real Estate Finance at Trepp, is a key leader of the firm's product development and market research initiatives. He leads Trepp's Commercial Real Estate and Banking businesses that support clients who invest, lend, broker, value, and risk manage commercial real estate (CRE) assets. Mr. McBride works closely with clients and industry groups to build and enhance data, models, and analytics that drive client investment decisions and streamline their work. His market analysis is frequently cited in publications and other media that monitor the CRE market. Mr. McBride is often quoted in publications such as Crain's, *The Wall Street Journal,* and various regional business journals. Mr. McBride holds a BS and MBA with a concentration in finance and is an Adjunct Assistant Professor of Finance at Fordham University.

David Craig Nichols is an Associate Professor of Accounting at the Whitman School of Management, Syracuse University. He specializes in financial statement analysis, valuation, and financial modeling. His research appears in such journals as the *Journal of Accounting Research, Journal of Accounting & Economics, Review of Accounting Studies, Contemporary Accounting Research, Accounting Horizons,* and *Financial Analyst Journal.* He has a bachelor's degree in accounting and a master's degree in tax accounting from the University of Alabama as well as an MBA and PhD in accounting from Indiana University.

Ehsan Nikbakht, CFA, FRM, is the C. V. Starr Distinguished Professor of Finance and International Financial Services in the Frank G. Zarb School of Business at Hofstra University and previously served as department chair and Associate Dean. He served on the Advisory Board of the International Association of Financial Engineers and Chair of Derivatives Committee of the New York Society of Security Analysts. Professor Nikbakht currently is on the editorial board of *Global Finance Journal.* He has published in *Journal of Applied Finance, Financial Decisions, Global Finance Journal,* and other refereed journals, and also authored *Finance,* published by Barron's, and *Foreign Loans and Economic Performance.* Professor Nikbakht received a BA from the Tehran School of Business, an MBA from the Iran Center for Management Studies, and a DBA in finance from the George Washington University.

Randolph D. Nordby, CFA, FSA, is a Professional Lecturer in the Kogod School of Business at American University. He has more than 15 years of managing and monitoring investments, investment research, security valuation, economic analysis, preparing customized investment policy statements, and portfolio implementation. Professor Nordby previously served as a member of the CFA Society of Washington's Board of Directors and a subject matter expert for derivatives regulations at the Commodities Futures Trading Committee. He holds an MS in finance from American University, an MA in economics from George Mason University, and an MBA from Shenandoah University. He is currently pursuing a doctoral degree in finance at Temple University.

Michael Pain, CFA, CFP, has of over 15 years of financial advisory experience assisting family offices and high-net-worth individuals to identify, analyze, and select suitable investments. Mr. Pain has provided high-level supervisory and management oversight of registered representatives and their supervisors for a multinational bank. He has extensive experience in both the domestic U.S. markets and the international equity markets. Mr. Pain holds a B.Com in accounting from the University of Cape Town, South Africa, and an MBA with a concentration in finance from Brigham Young University.

Shailendra Pandit is an Associate Professor of Accounting at the University of Illinois at Chicago. Previously, he taught at The Ohio State University and Tulane University. His research interests include financial reporting, capital market intermediaries, and firm-level relationships. He has published in leading academic journals such as *The Accounting Review*, *Review of Accounting Studies*, and *Contemporary Accounting Research*. Professor Pandit's teaching interests include introductory and intermediate financial accounting and financial statement analysis. He received a BS in electronics engineering from Jiwaji University, India, an MBA in finance from the University of Indore, India, and a PhD in accounting with a minor in finance from the University of Rochester.

Dianna Preece, CFA, is a Professor of Finance at the University of Louisville. She has published in such journals as the *Journal of Banking and Finance* and *Financial Review,* co-authored two practitioner books on investments, and written book chapters on topics ranging from hedge fund performance to the future of private equity. Professor Preece also provides consulting and training to banking associations, including the American Bankers Association and the Kentucky Bankers Association. She holds a BBA and MBA from Marshall University and a DBA from the University of Kentucky.

Michael C. Sinodinos, CFA, works in wealth management and advises high-net-worth individuals, foundations, and institutions in financial planning, portfolio management, and investment strategy. Mr. Sinodinos and his team manage a total of $1.6 billion in assets for their clients. He is a member of the CFA Society of New York. He is also active in the community and works with high school students from low-income areas to ensure they graduate while providing guidance and academic assistance to mentees. Mr. Sinodinos earned a BS in business management from Stony Brook University.

Andrew Siwo is the Director of Sustainable Investments and Climate Solutions for the New York State Common Retirement Fund. He is charged with providing leadership and oversight of sustainable investment efforts across the Fund's $220 billion portfolio. Previously, Mr. Siwo was an Investment Director and Head of Mission-Related Investments at Colonial Consulting, an investment consultancy to over 150 leading foundations and endowments. Before joining Colonial Consulting, Mr. Siwo was a manager at the Global Impact Investing Networking (GIIN). In his capacity, he was responsible for the operation, sourcing, and development of ImpactBase, the largest platform of impact investment funds globally. Mr. Siwo also spent five years in the investment banking division at J.P. Morgan. He was a member of the Corporate Finance and Real Estate Strategy Group at Victoria's Secret, leading project finance initiatives. He holds a BA in accounting from Morehouse College and completed an MPA in finance and fiscal policy at Cornell University. He has held FINRA Series 7, 63, and 24 licenses.

Andrew C. Spieler, CFA, CAIA, FRM, is the Robert F. Dall Distinguished Professor of Business in the Frank G. Zarb School of Business at Hofstra University. He has published in *Real Estate Economics*, *Journal of Real Estate Finance and Economics*, *Journal of Real Estate Portfolio Management*, *Global Finance Journal*, *Journal of Applied Finance,* and other journals. He served as Chair of the Derivatives Committee at the New York Society of Securities Analysts. Professor Spieler is also the co-director of the annual real estate conference sponsored by the Wilbur F. Breslin Center for Real Estate Studies. He received undergraduate degrees in math and economics from Binghamton University (SUNY), an MS in finance from Indiana University, and an MBA and PhD from Binghamton University (SUNY).

Raisa Varejao works at a credit rating agency as an associate analyst in the Structured Finance, Residential Mortgage-Backed Securities group. She is a CFA Level III candidate and holds a BS in accounting and economics from the FUCAPE Business School (ES, Brazil) and an MS in finance from the McCombs School of Business at The University of Texas at Austin.

Zhao Wang is an Assistant Professor of Finance at the Capital University of Economics and Business in Beijing, China. Previously, Professor Wang was a quantitative analyst at a capital management company in New York and focused on mutual funds and hedge funds of funds. His research interests include capital market anomalies, analysts, and executive compensation. He received a BS in finance from Tianjin University of Finance and Economics, an MS in finance from Hofstra University, and a PhD in finance from the University of Rhode Island.

PengCheng (Phil) Zhu, CFA, is an Associate Professor of Finance at the School of Business, University of San Diego. His research primarily focuses on corporate mergers and acquisitions, top executives, and emerging markets. He has published in leading business journals including *Administrative Science Quarterly*, *Strategic Management Journal*, *Journal of Operations Management*, *Review of Accounting Studies,* and *Journal of Corporate Finance*. Before joining the faculty at the University of San Diego, Professor Zhu taught at the University of the Pacific and Carleton University. He also worked as a business analyst in a global management consulting firm in Canada. He holds a PhD in finance from Carleton University.

CHAPTER 1

Equity Markets, Valuation, and Analysis: An Overview

H. Kent Baker
University Professor of Finance, Kogod School of Business, American University

Greg Filbeck
Director and Samuel P. Black III Professor of Finance and Risk Management,
Black School of Business, Penn State Behrend

Halil Kiymaz
Bank of America Professor of Finance, Crummer Graduate School of Business,
Rollins College

INTRODUCTION

The earliest activity resembling a stock market system took place in the late thirteenth century in Antwerp, which served as the commercial center of Belgium. The history of equity markets dates back to the early seventeenth century with the launch of the Amsterdam Exchange. In 1602, the Dutch East India Company (VOC) became the first company to continuously trade. Although the creation of the London Stock Exchange (LSE) was in 1801, restrictions on companies issuing shares in Britain did not occur until 1825, which limited the effectiveness of the LSE. The New York Stock Exchange (NYSE) was formed in 1817 and quickly became the center of U.S. trade. Electronic trading debuted in 1971 with the creation of the NASDAQ market.

World equity markets have grown steadily since the 1980s. For example, world market capitalization of listed companies reached $79.121 trillion in 2017 from a low of $2.501 trillion in 1980 (World Bank 2018). During this period, it fluctuated dramatically, declining almost 50 percent during the global financial crisis of 2007–2008. Among the world stock exchanges, 16 have a market capitalization greater than $1 trillion, such as the NYSE, NASDAQ, LSE, Deutsche Böerse, Euronext, and Shanghai Stock Exchange. These 16 exchanges account for 87 percent of global market capitalization. North America leads other regions with a market capitalization of more than $28 trillion, representing 41 percent of the world total (Visual Capitalist 2016; World Federation of Exchanges 2019).

What is an equity market, and why is it important? An *equity market* is a market in which firms issue stocks to fund their operations. After issuance, investors trade shares on exchanges and over-the-counter (OTC) markets. Equity markets are an important part of a country's economy. Their primary function is to support the growth of business and industry by channeling funds from savers to firms. These markets not only provide firms with an opportunity to access capital and raise funds to grow their business but also give investors a chance to become shareholders.

Equity markets also serve the role of a common platform for the buyers and sellers of these listed public stocks. They can also include private stocks traded through the OTC market. Common and preferred stocks constitute the two main types of stock. *Common stock* represents residual ownership in a company. *Preferred stock* is a hybrid security that typically lacks voting rights but gives its shareholders a prior claim to receiving dividends before common stockholders. Companies may also create different classes of stocks to customize voting rights. For example, Class A shareholders may have multiple voting rights for each share, while second-class B shares may have only one vote per share.

How are activities of the equity market tracked? Overall, market changes over time can be tracked by using market indices. A *market index* is a weighted average of many stocks, which is computed using the prices of the stocks included in the index. The oldest U.S. stock market index – the Dow Jones Industrial Average (DJIA) – originated in 1885 as the Dow Averages. The DJIA consists of 30 large, influential U.S. companies. Another widely used market index – the Standard & Poor's 500 index – represents 500 large U.S. stocks. Investors can use these stock indices, as well as many others, to follow market trends and compare their portfolio performance.

Equity markets allow investors to buy and sell stocks. An important issue is how investors can determine the underlying value of shares to trade. Is valuation an art or science? Stock valuation is not a simple process. In fact, some contend that stock valuation is more of an art than a science. If so, what is needed to get a reasonable estimate of a stock's intrinsic value?

Valuation and analysis involve several steps. First, investors should have a good understanding of the market and the industry in which a firm operates. Market analysis involves determining the demand for a firm's products by using consumer demographics and trends in the firm's operating sector as well as the firm's competitive position. The purpose of market analysis is to determine the opportunities available regarding developing or improving products and services that would be accepted by a firm's customers. This analysis also provides an avenue for the firm's resource planning. Industry analysis helps investors to explore potential profit opportunities for the firm by analyzing external and internal factors. An expanding industry presents ample opportunity for a firm to improve its position. A declining or contracting industry, however, would force firms to search for opportunities elsewhere. Technological advances, innovation, and changes in regulation could make an industry attractive or unattractive. Industry analysis further helps a firm to understand its position relative to its major competitors in terms of both opportunities and threats.

Second, various ways are available to value a stock. An analyst should have a good understanding of how each valuation technique works and why it can lead to a different valuation.

- *Dividend discount method.* Dividend discount valuation uses the present value of future dividend payments to compute a stock's fundamental value. This model requires estimating the growth patterns for dividends, cost of capital, and the last dividend paid. Some models, such as the Gordon constant growth model, assume that the historical dividend growth rate continues in the future, whereas others make different assumptions.

- *Free cash flow method.* If a firm does not pay dividends, an alternative valuation technique, called free cash flow valuation, uses a firm's free cash flow, which is the cash flow available in a company after considering investment in fixed capital, working capital, and other expenses to keep the company going. Although positive free cash flow is desirable and an optimistic sign for a firm's financial health, negative free cash flow is not necessarily an unfavorable signal as it may indicate that a firm is making substantial investments.
- *Comparables method.* Market-based valuation focuses on comparing similar businesses to value a firm's stock. This valuation is known as comparables or comps valuation and can be based on the type of business, transaction, or industry averages. The key element of the approach is to find a value-based characteristic relative to the value of the business.
- *Other valuation methods.* Additional valuation techniques include residual income valuation, which focuses on excess income above the costs measured relative to the equity used, and technical analysis, which values a firm or stock using the data from trading activities, including price and volume changes.

Equity investment models and strategies also play an important role in investing activities and their success. An investor may choose active investing and try to time the market with an objective of short-term gains. A passive investor may choose to invest for the long term by tracking an index. This strategy reduces the risk through diversification. Furthermore, investors can strategically focus on certain types of stocks. For example, one may choose to invest in stocks whose earnings are expected to grow faster than others (growth strategy) or may look for undervalued stocks that are expected to increase in value (value strategy).

Equity markets also accommodate special cases of investing, including activist investing and socially responsible investing, as well as investing in emerging markets, private equity, and crowdfunding investments. For example, activist investors invest in companies to influence their activities through pressuring management with specific agenda items such as changing the compensation plans, forcing the firm to merge or divest certain assets, and changing a company's product lines. Socially responsible investing involves applying nonfinancial social screens to a universe of investment alternatives to identify investment candidates. A *social screen* is the expression of an investor's social, ethical, or religious concern in a form that enables an investment manager to apply it in the investment decision-making process, along with other screens.

ABOUT THIS BOOK

This section discusses the book's purpose, its distinguishing features, and its intended audience.

Purpose of the Book

The primary purpose of this book is to provide an objective look into the dynamic world of equity markets, valuation, and analysis. The coverage extends from discussing basic concepts and their application to increasingly intricate and real-world situations. This volume spans the gamut from theoretical to practical while attempting to offer a useful balance of detailed and user-friendly coverage. Discussion of relevant research permeates the books. Readers can gain an in-depth understanding about this subject from experts in the field, both academics and practitioners. Readers interested in a broad survey will benefit as will those looking for more in-depth presentations of specific areas within this field of study. In summary, this book provides a fresh look at this intriguing but often complex subject.

Distinguishing Features

Several features distinguish *Equity Markets, Valuation, and Analysis* from others in the market.

- The book provides an introduction to this broad, complex, and competitive field. It skillfully blends the contributions of a global array of academics and practitioners into a single review of some of the most important topics in this area. The varied backgrounds of the contributors assure different perspectives and a rich interplay of ideas. The book also reflects the latest trends and research in a global context and discusses several controversial issues as well as the future outlook for this field.
- While retaining the content and perspectives of the many contributors, the book follows an internally consistent approach in format and style. Similar to a choir that contains many voices, this book has many contributing authors, each with their separate voices. A goal of both a choir and this book is to have the many voices sing together harmoniously. Accomplishing this task for the book requires skilled editing by the co-editors to assure a seamless flow when moving from chapter to chapter. Hence, the book is collectively much more than a compilation of chapters from an array of different authors.
- The book presents theory without unnecessary abstraction, quantitative techniques using basic mathematics, and conventions at a useful level of detail. It also incorporates how investment professionals analyze and manage equity portfolios.
- The book places a strong emphasis on empirical evidence involving equity markets, valuation, and analysis. When discussing the results of various studies, the objective is to distill them to their essential content and practical implications so they are understandable to a wide array of readers.
- The end of each chapter contains four to six discussion questions that help to reinforce key concepts. The end of the book provides guideline answers to each question. This feature should be especially important to faculty and students using the book in classes.

Intended Audience

Given its broad scope, this practical and comprehensive book should be of interest to various groups. The primary market consists of academics, researchers, investors, and financial professionals/practitioners. Students, policymakers, libraries, and anyone curious about equity markets, valuation, and analysis make up the secondary market. For academics and researchers, the book provides the basis for gaining a better understanding of various aspects of equity markets, valuation, and analysis and as a springboard for future research. Academics can also use the book as a stand-alone or supplementary resource for advanced undergraduate or graduate courses in investments as well as a PhD seminar, given the book's research orientation. Investors, financial professionals, and practitioners should also find the book to be a valuable resource in gaining a better understanding of equity markets, valuation, and analysis. Students, policymakers, and libraries should find this book suitable as a reference. Thus, this book should be essential reading for anyone who wants a better understanding of these important topics.

STRUCTURE OF THE BOOK

The remainder of this book consists of 23 chapters divided into four main parts. A brief synopsis of each part and chapter follows.

Part One: Background

This part contains four chapters (Chapters 2–5) that provide important background information that sets the stage for the remaining sections. These chapters examine ownership structure and stock classes, equity markets and performance, securities regulation, and investor psychology and equity market anomalies.

Chapter 2 Ownership Structure and Stock Classes (Christopher J. Barnes, Ehsan Nikbakht, and Andrew C. Spieler) This chapter examines different ownership structures and stock classes. Several exceptions are available to the widely held belief that a share of common stock is the same as any other share. The most common exception is multiple-class common stock (dual-class stock), which offers some shareholders superior voting rights relative to shareholders in a separate class. Even for companies with only a single class of common stock, several types of shares may be available. For example, investors in tracking stock have no direct claim, as their investment targets the financial performance of a subdivision of a larger corporation. Cross-listings and depositary receipts each facilitate investment in corporations whose primary listings are in other countries. Although cross-listings represent a direct listing on a foreign stock exchange, depositary receipts are indirect ownership vehicles in which an intermediary institution holds shares directly and offers receipts certifying ownership for the investor. Another single-class ownership structure is that of dual-listed companies, which may arise when two companies combine business operations without merging the respective legal entities. This structure enables two separate and distinct classes of shares, and therefore shareholders, to survive the merger. These dual-listed companies try to equalize ownership such that a share of one twin equals a share in the other, but each twin's shares correspond to different underlying legal entities. Each of these structures falls under the umbrella of common stock but exemplifies the potential differences among shares of common stock from a single company.

Chapter 3 Equity Markets and Performance (Jay T. Brandi and Xudong Fu)   Equity markets and performance develop the connections among the economy, financial markets, employment, profitability, and the value of corporate securities – specifically equity securities. This chapter presents various approaches to segmenting the financial markets by issue type, issue size, and other characteristics and discusses using equity indices as economic indicators. It also discusses the efficient market hypothesis and its three forms along with the characteristics of marketability and liquidity and how they relate to the economy, financial markets, equity performance, and valuation.

Chapter 4 Securities Regulation (Douglas Cumming and Sofia Johan)   This chapter summarizes securities regulation pertaining to trading on stock exchanges in most countries around the world. It identifies different types of trading rules for different forms of misconduct, including but not limited to insider trading (such as front-running and client precedence), price manipulation (such as ramping/gouging and prearranged trades), volume manipulation (such as spoofing and switching), and broker-agency misconduct (such as violation of trade-through rules and know-your-client rules). The chapter reviews research on how cross-sectional and time-series differences in rules across countries and over time affects market liquidity. It also explains how rules are enforced with computerized surveillance technology and how differences in enforcement across countries and over time substantially affect market efficiency and integrity.

Chapter 5 Investor Psychology and Equity Market Anomalies (Hunter M. Holzhauer)   This chapter examines investor psychology and equity market anomalies. It begins with a brief synopsis of the differences between behavioral finance and traditional finance. It examines investor psychology using foundational ideas behind behavioral finance like bounded rationality and prospect theory to explore why investors are not always rational. Although these two foundational ideas are certainly related, they showcase several different issues and biases that are relevant to investors. The final section uses equity market anomalies to discuss different violations of the efficient market hypothesis. The chapter concludes by explaining the importance of behavioral finance and its role in investor psychology and choice behavior.

Part Two: Valuation and Analysis

This part consists of nine chapters (Chapters 6–14) dealing with valuation and analysis. This section begins with a discussion of financial statement analysis and forecasting followed by chapters on fundamentals of equity valuation, company analysis, and technical analysis. The discussion then turns to examining various valuation methods including discounted dividend valuation, free cash flow valuation, market-based valuation, residual income valuation, and private company valuation.

Chapter 6 Financial Statement Analysis and Forecasting (Somnath Das and Shailendra Pandit)
This chapter discusses using financial statements for forecasting in financial markets. Based on a common stock valuation formula, the chapter focuses on forecasting future stock prices and earnings for a business entity. Evidence on the predictability of stock prices or earnings has important implications for both asset pricing models and investment strategies. The chapter provides a brief survey of the literature on

using technical analysis, fundamental analysis, and time series analysis for forecasting stock prices and earnings while highlighting the challenges faced by forecasters as well as strategies for improving the forecasts. The discussion primarily focuses on forecasts, including a discussion of earnings forecasts, concerning U.S. firms using financial statements. The chapter also discusses some limitations of using financial statement analysis in forecasting.

Chapter 7 Fundamentals of Equity Valuation (Emmanuel Boutron, Alain Coën, and Didier Folus) Equity valuation refers to a key economic metric that represents a company's net worth. Numerous practitioners and academics use and study equity valuation. The main stakeholders involved in a company's net worth are stockholders, banks, and bondholders, who are directly interested in the company's intrinsic value. Financial executives and clients are indirectly concerned. Different approaches are available to evaluate a company's equity, including discounted cash flow (DCF)-based valuation, market-based valuation, and option-based valuation. The DCF approach is based on the firm's expected free cash flow or on futures dividends. Using the DCF approach implies using fundamental analysis of the company's business and financial statements to forecast its cash flow, which should be discounted at a risk-adjusted rate of return. Investors and analysts can use various asset pricing models, such as the capital asset pricing model, to calculate the required rate of return used in the equity valuation process. Practitioners often use market-based approaches, including multiples and ratios, because such approaches are cost-effective and enable making comparisons among companies. This chapter highlights the crucial role of equity valuation in modern finance for both academics and practitioners.

Chapter 8 Company Analysis (David Craig Nichols) Company analysis refers to the analysis of a company's financial statements and other information to better understand its profitability, growth, and risk. This chapter develops a company analysis in the context of a three-step framework for understanding the relation between business activities and stock prices. The first step maps business activities into financial statements through the financial reporting process. The second step maps financial statements into forecasts and estimates of share value through the fundamental analysis process. The third step maps equity values into share prices through the trading process. The chapter focuses on accounting analysis and ratio analysis, including profitability, growth, liquidity, solvency, and financial distress, but describes the role of financial statements in equity valuation more generally.

Chapter 9 Technical Analysis (David Lundgren) This chapter demonstrates the underappreciated philosophical link between technical analysis and fundamental analysis illustrated using Dow Theory. Specifically, the linkage between the two types of analysis on the relative performance of a company's share price is mainly dependent on the company's fundamental strength. This chapter also investigates several technical strategies, including trend following and cross-sectional momentum, used today by technical and fundamental investors alike, to improve their stock selection and timing decisions. Further, it also examines techniques for determining the health of broad market trends, thus equipping investors with the skills needed to assess the overall risk environment.

Chapter 10 Discounted Dividend Valuation (Elif Akben-Selçuk)   This chapter explores the dividend discount model (DDM), which defines the value of common stock as the present value of expected future dividend payments. It investigates both the constant growth model (also called the Gordon model), which assumes a steady-state rate for the firm forever. The chapter also examines multi-stage models, including the two-stage model, H-model, and three-stage model, which assume a multiple-stage growth for dividends and earnings. Besides these traditional models, the chapter considers binomial and trinomial stochastic DDMs and the uses of DDMs. Finally, it discusses the results of empirical studies testing the relevance and practical significance of DDMs.

Chapter 11 Free Cash Flow Valuation (Tom Barkley)   Valuation analysis lies at the heart of finance. It tries to ascertain the true worth of assets, securities, companies, and projects. Absolute valuation approaches rely on fundamental analysis to estimate a firm's intrinsic value based only on its characteristics. By contrast, relative valuation methods rely on multiples associated with comparable companies, based on a firm's characteristics relative to its peers. Regarding the former approaches, the most commonly used is a discounted cash flow (DCF) analysis, which forecasts a firm's future cash flows and discounts them at an appropriate rate to obtain their present values, whose sum is then the firm's value. This chapter highlights four special cases of DCF analysis: (1) the weighted average cost of capital approach; (2) the adjusted present value method; (3) the capital cash flow model; and (4) the free cash flow to equity technique.

Chapter 12 Market-Based Valuation (Sang Hoon Lee)   The purpose of this chapter is to introduce a valuation method using market-based multiples and discuss the advantages and challenges of using this method. Practitioners widely use market multiples such as equity-related or enterprise value (EV)-related multiples. This valuation method has distinctive benefits over the fundamental valuation approach, offering a potential reduction of biases from estimating future cash flows and discount rates. The rationale for using market multiples for valuation is the principle of substitution for equally valuable assets. Therefore, selecting comparable companies that closely match the target company is the key to success for improving valuation accuracy as the benchmark multiples are drawn from these companies. Since different multiples and value drivers produce dissimilar valuation estimates, choosing the most effective multiples or a combination of them with theoretically consistent measures in the composition of a multiple is essential. Equity researchers and practitioners often propose using a harmonic mean of different multiples to minimize valuation errors. Also, forward performance measures usually produce more accurate value estimates. However, controversy remains about the efficacy of various multiples.

Chapter 13 Residual Income Valuation (Shailendra Pandit and Somnath Das)   This chapter reviews the concept of residual income (RI) and its application in equity valuation. RI is surplus profits generated by a project after accounting for the cost of capital invested in the project. RI has its roots in the concept of opportunity cost: To create value for investors, an investment project must generate returns above the opportunity cost of the invested capital. From its roots in the emergence of modern economic thought, RI evolved as a formal valuation approach in the twentieth century. The impetus for broader adoption of RI came not only from accounting and finance scholars but also from valuation and strategy consultants who played a crucial role in popularizing the concept among business organizations. Computing RI involves using a clean surplus relation to adjust and remove potential biases from financial statement numbers, forecast growth in those amounts, and compute the opportunity cost of equity. Today, RI is widely used in capital budgeting, operational planning, performance evaluation, executive compensation, and equity valuation.

Chapter 14 Private Company Valuation (Onur Bayar and Yini Liu)   This chapter reviews the application of different valuation methods for evaluating investment opportunities in private companies. It focuses on the underlying fundamentals of each method, when each technique is appropriate, and how some applications differ between privately held and publicly traded companies. The chapter also discusses the following valuation methods in the context of private equity (PE): discounted cash flow, comparable firm valuation, the venture capital method, and option pricing. A thorough understanding of these methods enhances the ability to make value-increasing decisions in a PE setting. Although the chapter discusses some strengths and weaknesses of each method in private company valuation, it also highlights the connections among them and how they can complement each other to help entrepreneurs, investors, and analysts make better investment decisions and evaluations.

Part Three: Equity Investment Models and Strategies

This part consists of six chapters (Chapter 15–20) focusing on equity investments strategies including factor investing, smart beta versus alpha, activist and impact investing, and socially responsible investing. The final chapter in this section deals with pooled investment vehicles: open-end mutual funds, closed-end mutual funds, exchange-traded funds, and unit investment trusts.

Chapter 15 Equity Investing Strategies (Nicholas Biasi, Andrew C. Spieler, and Raisa Varejao) This chapter provides a discussion of popular and emerging trends in equity strategies. An entire spectrum of equity investing strategies is available, ranging from passive indexing to active management, stable income to growth, and everything in between. Value investing can trace its roots back to Benjamin Graham and seeks to identify companies that are trading a substantial discount to their intrinsic values. Conversely, growth investing involves identifying firms that have expected high earnings growth. Still other strategies are designed to provide stable income. A variety of exchange-traded fund (ETF) structures allow investors to design diversified equity portfolios to meet their desired risk and return characteristics. Quantitative strategies exploit computing power to identify trends or mispricings and thus remove human emotion from the trade. Options allow investors to increase, decrease, and tailor their exposure based on their view of the underlying equity position.

Chapter 16 Factor Investing (Aaron Filbeck)   This chapter reviews factor investing as an equity investment strategy. Factors are measurements of systematic risk used to explain returns for diversified portfolios. The chapter begins by providing a brief history of factor investing, starting with the capital asset pricing model. This single-factor model assumes that the market (beta) is the only factor affecting returns. Next, the chapter examines some other prominent factors, including value, size, momentum, low volatility, and quality/profitability. Finally, the chapter introduces some portfolio management considerations in practice, which include multi-factor portfolio construction and active management benchmarking.

Chapter 17 Smart Beta Strategies versus Alpha Strategies (Timothy A. Krause)   This chapter reviews the academic literature and articles in the financial press on the performance of this relatively new investment paradigm and provides an analysis of the empirical performance of these smart beta exchange-traded funds (ETFs). Smart beta investing strategies have gained increased attention from both academics and practitioners in recent decades. Between 2014 and 2018, growth in smart beta ETFs averaged almost 30 percent annually. These strategies are based on the concept of "factor" investing, which has existed for decades. Now, however, ETF providers use the term *smart beta* to indicate various factor-based strategies. The empirical evidence on smart beta performance is generally positive, but it does have its detractors. The empirical analysis in this chapter indicates that, in recent years, smart beta strategies outperform alpha-seeking strategies on both absolute and risk-adjusted-performance measures, but not passive capitalization- or equal-weighted indices.

Chapter 18 Activist and Impact Investing (Michael Sinodinos, Andrew Siwo, and Andrew C. Spieler) This chapter examines activist investing and impact investing. Activist investing is when an investor seeks to make changes to corporate strategies or policies by owning shares of a public company. Activists can be wealthy individuals, pension funds, hedge funds, or even gadflies. Activists may engage management privately, submit proposals via the proxy statement, engage in proxy fights, or seek board representation. Recent trends include increased hedge fund activism and coordinated efforts. Impact investing is when an investor seeks to make investments that have the objective of obtaining a social or environmental benefit alongside a financial return. The integration of environmental, social, and governance (ESG) factors into investing is an approach that has captured the attention of institutional investors globally and brings nonfinancial factors, such as diversity, carbon emissions, and board structure, to the fore.

Chapter 19 Socially Responsible Investing (Randolph D. Nordby)   Earning money while doing good for society is the typical goal for socially responsible investing (SRI). However, does achieving this goal require compromising financial returns? Can investors achieve their financial goals while still being true to their values and principles? SRI has become part of mainstream investing and is being integrated into the investment decision-making process at many firms. Yet, no single agreed-upon definition of SRI – or even a consensus on what constitutes best practices for using these factors to make informed investment decisions – exists. This chapter discusses the evolution of SRI investing into today's more traditional environmental, social, and governance (ESG) investing. It also explores the best practices being promoted by top global associations of investment professionals using ESG factors for equity valuation. From a practitioner's perspective, a critical challenge of using ESG data for asset valuation is properly integrating these nonstandardized factors into an asset's valuation process. This area has attracted much attention, but little clarity. Thus, this chapter focuses on providing both a better understanding of the multiple methods of SRI investing and an overview of the best practices for integrating ESG metrics into the equity valuation process.

Chapter 20 Pooled Investment Vehicles (Joseph McBride, Michael Pain, and Andrew C. Spieler)
This chapter discusses the four major pooled investment vehicles (PIVs) that dominate the market today: open-end mutual funds (MFs), closed-end mutual funds (CEFs), exchange-traded funds (ETFs), and unit investment trusts (UITs). It also discusses the overall structure and related benefits, drawbacks, and risks of each structure. Additional discussion focuses on the creation and redemption process, net asset value (NAV), premium/discount, tradability, liquidity attributes, tax efficiency, and leverage, as well as indirect and direct costs. The chapter also provides a brief history and general trends involving PIVs and the need to follow a disciplined investment process when evaluating these types of investments.

Part Four: Special Equity Topics

Part Four of the book contains four chapters (Chapters 21–24) that examine special equity topics. These issues include investing in private equity, investing in emerging markets, disclosure regulations in emerging economies, and equity crowdfunding investments.

Chapter 21 Investing in Private Equity (Gaurav Gupta, Tianqi Jiang, and Zhao Wang)   Private equity (PE) is an alternative asset class in which a direct investment exists in the equity of a private or a public company. Equities and bonds are traditionally traded in the secondary markets, whereas private equity is a private dealing between an investor or PE fund manager and the issuer company. The term *private* in PE signifies that the deal occurs in private rather than in public. The risk–reward profile of PE investments tends to be higher than for some other asset classes, resulting in potentially higher rewards. This chapter provides an overview of PE investments dealing with venture capital (VC) and buyouts as well as private investment in public entity (PIPE). It also discusses the long-term investment horizon, illiquidity, capital commitment, capital commitment period, capital call, portfolio diversification, performance, and risk factors involving PE investments.

Chapter 22 Investing in Emerging Markets (Xiaohau Diao, Shantanu Dutta, and Peng Cheng Zhu)
Emerging markets offer expanded investment opportunities for global investors. Although emerging market returns are becoming more correlated with developed market returns, reducing the attractiveness of the diversification rationale, emerging markets are still distinct enough to appeal to global investors. Emerging markets offer higher return potential. However, to realize better returns and manage associated risks, investors need to have coordinated investment strategies. They also need to understand various factors associated with capital flows to emerging markets, market characteristics, political dynamics, and valuation challenges. Further, investors should pay close attention to legal protection, asset valuation techniques, corporate governance, and the regulatory environment that may substantially affect

investment returns. The goal of this chapter is to examine issues related to capital market integration in an emerging market setup and to discuss various institutional strategies for making better investment decisions.

Chapter 23 Disclosure Regulations in Emerging Economies and Their Impact on Equity Markets (Xiaohau Diao, Shantanu Dutta, and Peng Cheng Zhu)   Corporate disclosure and financial reporting convey valuable information to shareholders and market participants. Although financial reporting is routinely done, mostly in a regular interval, according to regulatory requirements, corporate disclosures could be voluntary or mandatory depending on the nature of the information. This chapter focuses on emerging markets corporate disclosure-related regulations such as environmental and corporate social responsibility (CSR) disclosure, private meeting disclosure, and insider trading-related disclosure that attract interest among regulators, practitioners, and academics. The empirical evidence shows that implementing these regulations is not particularly effective. In many instances, authorities fail to identify or take adequate actions against violators. However, the regulatory bodies appear to have become more careful in recent years, which is likely to enhance the effectiveness of these disclosure regulations.

Chapter 24 Equity Crowdfunding Investments (Dianna Preece)   This chapter examines equity crowdfunding, which was an innovation introduced in the Jumpstart Our Business Startups (JOBS) Act of 2012 that many expected to be a boon for startups. Signed into law with bipartisan support, the JOBS Act intended to enable Americans to invest in new companies and their founders. However, the Securities and Exchange Commission (SEC) took years to create regulations to govern equity crowdfunding. After being launched in May 2016, equity crowdfunding has grown more slowly than expected. Early-stage investments are risky, and many nonaccredited investors may lack the sophistication to assess risks. JOBS 3.0 is expected to fix any existing problems but has yet to pass the U.S. Senate. Despite these roadblocks, equity crowdfunding is on the rise in both the United States and abroad, though investors are, so far, less plentiful than expected. Research on U.S. equity crowdfunding risks and returns is scant.

SUMMARY AND CONCLUSIONS

Equity securities are an important component in the portfolios of both individual and institutional investors. Including an equity component has several benefits, including portfolio diversification and potentially higher long-term returns in terms of capital gains and dividends. However, owning equity securities involves risk, given the volatility of these markets. To achieve their portfolio objectives, investors need to know how to analyze and value equity securities if they are selecting stocks themselves or how to select an appropriate pooled investment vehicle with professional managers. *Equity Markets, Valuation, and Analysis* provides the foundation for making sound investment decisions in equities. Contributions by both scholars and practitioners provide an in-depth survey of the role of equity securities, including the background of equity securities, an understanding of issues related to valuation and analysis, and various equity investment models and strategies, as well as special topics involving equity investments.

REFERENCES

Visual Capitalist. 2016. "All the World's Stock Exchanges by Size." Available at http://www
.visualcapitalist.com/all-of-the-worlds-stock-exchanges-by-size/.

World Bank. 2018. "Market Capitalization of Listed Domestic Companies." Available at
https://data.worldbank.org/indicator/CM.MKT.LCAP.CD?end=2017&start=1975.

World Federation of Exchanges. 2019. "Welcome to the Future of Markets." Available at
https://www.world-exchanges.org/.

Background

CHAPTER 2

Ownership Structure and Stock Classes

Christopher J. Barnes
Equity Research, Deutsche Bank AG,

Ehsan Nikbakht
C. V. Starr Distinguished Professor of Finance and International Financial Services
Frank G. Zarb School of Business Hofstra University

Andrew C. Spieler
Robert F. Dall Distinguished Professor of Business
Frank G. Zarb School of Business Hofstra University

INTRODUCTION

A commonly held view is that all common stock issues are the same. Although overwhelmingly true for most companies, several exceptions exist to this concept. The most apparent exception is multiple-class common stock, more commonly known as *dual-class stock*, which offers shareholders in one class of stock superior voting rights relative to shareholders in a separate class.

Before comparing single-class and dual-class common stock, single-class common stock can be divided into various structures. For example, besides the primary listing of a single class of common stock, a company may cross-list its shares on stock exchanges in other countries. Depositary banks may create an analogous share for investors to partake in ownership of a foreign listed company. Cross-listings and depositary receipts each facilitate investment in corporations whose primary listings are in other countries. Although cross-listings represent a direct listing on the foreign stock exchange, depositary receipts are indirect ownership vehicles, where an intermediary institution holds shares directly and offers receipts certifying ownership.

Tracking stock represents yet another type of single-class common stock. Unlike most cases of common stock where shares represent ownership claims on a corporation's assets, investors in tracking stock have no such claim, as their investment targets the financial performance of a subdivision of a larger corporation. Occasionally, companies may choose to merge business operations without effectuating a legal merger. This pseudomerger allows retaining two legal identities. These dual-listed companies try to equalize ownership such that a share of one twin equals a share in the other. Yet, each twin's shares correspond to different underlying legal entities and create some differences between shares.

This chapter presents an overview of these special instances of common stock. The remainder of the chapter is organized as follows. The next section describes several instances of single-class common equity by separating cross-listings, depositary receipts, tracking stock, and dual-listed companies. The subsequent section describes multiple-class common stock (dual-class stock). Finally, the chapter offers a summary and conclusions regarding single-class and dual-class common stock.

SINGLE-CLASS COMMON EQUITY

Equity represents the net value of a company's assets over its liabilities, which would be attributable to all company owners in the event of a liquidation. This net asset value can be further divided between the two primary forms of equity: common and preferred. Preferred equity has a more senior claim, relative to common equity, on the company's assets and receives priority when the company declares and pays dividends. However, this seniority typically results in limited or no voting rights for preferred shareholders. Conversely, common equity gives holders the right to vote on specific corporate issues, including the election of the board of directors, corporate objectives and policy, and acquisitions and divestitures. Shares of common equity represent fractional ownership interests of the company, entitling owners to the profits generated by the company remaining after making all contractual payments to senior capital providers. In the event of liquidation or dissolution, common equity holders only receive the remainder of funds, if any, after satisfying all other stakeholders with primacy on the company's assets. Although common stockholders elect the board of directors, the enfranchisement of common stock typically has little value, except in proxy contests for control because the board of directors makes most major corporate decisions or delegates them to company employees (Bainbridge 1991).

Although all forms of common stock share in a corporation's profits, common stock can be broadly categorized into two forms: single-class and dual-class. In a single-class equity structure, each share has an equivalent number of votes, conferring a manner of shareholder democracy as each share receives an equal degree of influence. To control a single-class company, one must amass a majority of shares, therefore tying economic performance with control. Voting rights and control represent the primary difference between single- and dual-class stocks. In the latter, shareholders can control companies while holding a disproportionate (typically small) economic interest in the company.

This section describes several different types of share structures. A *cross-listing* enables corporations to offer their shares on multiple exchanges, perhaps in different countries, while representing the same fundamental underlying ownership in the company. Depositary receipts and cross-listings share many characteristics, but the former represents an indirect ownership claim. *Dual listings* are a less frequent structure in which two companies merge operations but retain separately listed stocks in different countries. Finally, *tracking stock* is a special case of parent corporation stock whose value is linked to the financial performance of a subsidiary rather than the parent.

Cross-Listed Stocks

Increasing integration of global financial markets and globalization have contributed to more companies choosing to list their shares on other exchanges outside their domestic market. A cross-listed company offers its stock for trading directly on multiple exchanges, one on a domestic exchange and at least one other exchange located in a foreign market. Baker, Nofsinger, and Weaver (2002) find that international cross-listings on the New York Stock Exchange (NYSE) or London Stock Exchange (LSE) raise investor recognition significantly, while also reducing the cross-listed firm's overall cost of capital.

Cross-listed shares reduce existing market frictions, such as currency or custody requirements, associated with foreign ownership of common stock. For example, consider a U.S. incorporated multinational company that wants to broaden its investor base in Japan. This company could issue shares on the Tokyo Stock Exchange, which would trade in Japanese yen in the home market of Japanese investors, perhaps raising visibility with investors in a new market.

Like depositary receipts, which are described in the next subsection, cross-listed shares are fungible for the same company's shares on another exchange. Unlike a depositary receipt, which represents shares held by a custodian, cross-listings are direct ownership vehicles in the subject company. The local exchange may demand reporting and corporate governance obligations to qualify for trading and comply with local laws and regulations. According to Dobbs and Goedhart (2008), the idea that cross-listings create value is dated because capital markets have become more globalized and integrated. Additionally, trading liquidity in the cross-listed markets often pales in comparison to the primary market's. Therefore, the potential benefits do not justify the costs for compliance with additional exchange rules, notably for companies cross-listing into the United States. In contrast, Roosenboom and van Dijk (2009) conclude that a firm's cross-listing shares on developed market exchanges, such as the NYSE or LSE, do create shareholder value by way of bonding to heightened investor protection laws and increased information disclosure of the developed market. *Bonding* is the process by which companies located in countries with lax regulation align themselves with more stringent financial disclosure and corporate governance standards by cross-listing onto a developed market exchange.

Depositary Receipts

To facilitate the trading of internationally listed stocks for domestic investors, financial institutions created *depositary receipts* (DRs) because market frictions and structures prevent most investors from transacting easily across markets, due to differences in clearance, settlement, and currency denominations. When banks and brokers issue DRs to investors, the underlying stock remains held and deposited in the market of the foreign company. A Securities and Exchange Commission (SEC) (2012) bulletin explains DRs' ownership of the underlying foreign listed stock, but the DR may be sold as a multiple or fraction of the underlying shares. Although DRs represent indirect ownership for investors outside the company's home market, they are fungible, meaning the DR itself can be exchanged for the underlying shares in the company's home market.

The most common form of DR is the American depositary receipt (ADR), which enables U.S. investors to buy and sell shares of non-U.S. listed companies. These shares trade and settle in U.S. dollars and their prices fluctuate with movements in the underlying stock and changes in the exchange rate, as well as the local market (i.e., the United States) conditions such as ownership and trading volume. ADR facilities may be *sponsored*, which involves cooperation between the depositary and the company issuer, or *unsponsored*, which involves a bank or broker offering the ADR without the company's participation (Saunders 1993). Depending on the degree of access the foreign company has to the U.S. equity market, ADRs can also be classified into three levels (I, II, and III), which determine reporting requirements. Level I ADRs trade over the-counter (OTC), rather than on a U.S. exchange, and also have minimal reporting requirements but may not raise new capital via the ADR (JPMorgan 2008). Levels II and III have more stringent financial reporting requirements and trade on national U.S. exchanges (e.g., NASDAQ or NYSE), with the primary distinction between the two levels being that Level III can raise new capital via the ADR facility (Citi 2019).

Following the ADR, the second most common DR is a *global depositary receipt* (GDR), which is a generalized form of the ADR. For example, a Chilean company could offer shares to European investors in Europe by engaging a depositary bank to implement a GDR program. Likewise, a *European depositary receipt* (EDR) is a DR used for investors based in Europe. Other country-specific programs exist, such as CREST Depository Interests (CDIs) for U.K.-based investors and Transferable Custody Receipts (TraCRs) for Australia-based investors, each designed to conform with local regulations and norms.

DRs offer benefits for issuers and investors alike. For issuers, a DR is a useful tool to diversify the investor base beyond the home market, which contributes to increases in investor recognition of the company (Foerster and Karolyi 1999). Additionally, having new investors in the company also raises trading liquidity for the company's shares. In certain instances, companies may use DRs to raise capital or to fund cross-border merger or acquisition activity. Similarly, DRs facilitate stock ownership for employees in the company's overseas subsidiaries. For investors, globalizing a portfolio is simplified via DRs because they trade, clear, settle, and pay dividends in the investor's home currency and by its market conventions, eliminating foreign custody and safekeeping charges. When transacting in DRs, investors pay taxes only as levied by their home market. Moreover, depending on tax treaties between the home market and the market of the invested company, investors may receive dividends without foreign withholding taxes. For institutional investors whose charters prevent transacting in foreign securities, DRs may be recognized as local market stocks.

Alongside these benefits come certain disadvantages for DR issuers and investors. For the issuer, DRs can create direct listing costs and periodic fees charged by securities exchanges. Moreover, DRs may create reporting obligations, raising audit costs as a corollary, maintaining compliance with securities regulators in the overseas market (Doidge, Karolyi, and Stulz 2010). Failure to comply could result in fines and sanctions for the DR listing. For investors in DRs, despite being quoted and traded in a local currency, DRs fail to protect against risks from changes in exchange rates and inflation of the foreign currency, or changes in the political and regulatory environments of the overseas market. Although arguably simpler than investing directly in a foreign market, DRs still require coordination by the depositary bank, safekeeping by the custodian, and other services. These institutions typically pass the cost of these services through to investors in DRs, in some instances as a direct fee or as a deduction from the dividends paid by the company. Finally, investors may find DRs to be illiquid in their home market, despite adequate trading activity in the issuer's home market.

Dual Listings

Dual listings, also referred to as "Siamese twins" or "dual-headed" enterprises, are atypical, and ostensibly a vanishing corporate structure in which two legally distinct companies operate as if they were a single economic enterprise, retaining independent legal identities. A set of contractual agreements pool operations and link the cash flows and control of the dual-listed companies (DLCs) into a single entity. Profit-sharing and other arrangements associate rights, cash flows, and ownership of one entity of the pair to those of the other, based upon a predefined ratio, thereby implying that ownership in either of the pair should be equivalent to the other contractually. Because each pair's shares manifest ownership in a different company, shares between the pairs are not fungible. Unlike a cross-listing, which offers investors the same shares on multiple markets, a DLC's shares are associated with discrete underlying companies.

In most cross-border combinations, a single holding company combines the merging companies. Still, dual-listing transactions arose from a desire to merge business operations while retaining individual corporate identities. This separation permitted the involved companies to retain their respective tax jurisdictions, national identities, exchange listings, and distinct shareholder bases. The survival of the discrete legal entities likewise avoids unintended political or tax-related negative synergies that might arise following standard merger or acquisition transactions (U.K. Panel on Takeovers and Mergers 2002).

Although the DLC structure is not unique to specific industries or countries, most historically have involved a U.K.-domiciled pair. Current and historical examples of DLCs include Unilever, a consumer products manufacturer; Royal Dutch Shell, an oil and gas company; Carnival, a cruise line operator; and SmithKline Beecham, a pharmaceutical and consumer healthcare manufacturer (now part of GlaxoSmithKline). At one point in their respective histories, these four companies could be categorized into three forms of dual-listing structures: combined entities, separate entities, and stapled stock.

In the combined entities structure, Companies A and B form a new jointly owned company, which owns the assets of both A and B and subsequently pays dividends to each based on the equalization ratio, but A and B remain separately traded entities (Cleary Gottlieb Stein & Hamilton 2002). Although the businesses merge, legal identities remain independent, making this structure similar to a joint venture model. If a combined entity's structure is infeasible, for instance, due to financial, legal, or other constraints, A and B may choose to merge via a separate entity's structure. In this "synthetic merger," A and B retain ownership of their respective assets and maintain legal separation, but they operate as if they were a single company (Hancock, Gray, and Sommelet 2002). Finally, effecting a merger through a stapled stock structure involves combining the assets into a jointly held company while preserving A and B's listings (U.K. Panel on Takeovers and Mergers 2002). Unlike in the combined entities structure, the shares of A and B are stapled together and cannot be traded separately, minimizing the price variances that might arise if traded separately. Figure 2.1 distinguishes between simplified ownership structure charts existing for DLCs.

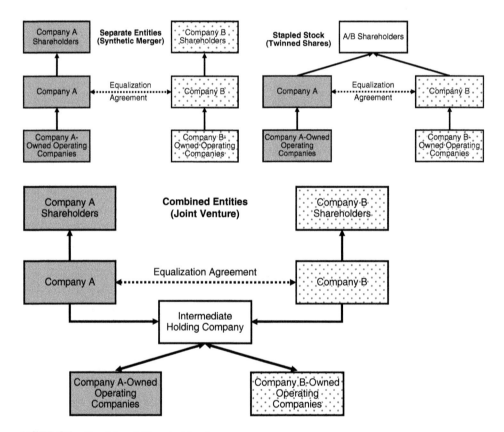

FIGURE 2.1 Dual-listed Shareholder Structures

This figure, modified from the U.K. Panel on Takeovers and Mergers (2002), portrays the three most frequent dual-list-company simplified corporate structures firms may adopt: separate entities, combined entities, and stapled stock. The separate entities and combined entities structures retain two independent shareholder bases, while the stapled stock structure amalgamates the two distinct shareholder bases into a single group.

Source: U.K. Panel on Takeovers and Mergers (2002).

In most DLCs, the two companies combine operationally into a single organization, giving the joint enterprise the same potential scale benefits as a traditional merger, such as purchasing power or vendor consolidation. Unlike in a traditional merger, the separate legal entities survive, preserving certain attributes, such as the source of dividends or domicile. These traits guard against potentially undesirable repercussions from merging. By retaining national identity and source of income, the company usually can maintain its listing on the national stock exchange and index constituency. For example, Unilever NV, a Dutch-registered company, and Unilever PLC, a U.K.-registered company, enjoy membership in both the Euro Stoxx 50 and FTSE 100 indexes. Without the DLC structure, PLC and NV together may not have qualified for membership in both indexes.

The agreements linking DLCs are understandably complex. In some instances, such as in Royal Dutch Petroleum and Shell Transport & Trading's DLC before its unification, the structure creates duplication and inefficiencies. Royal Dutch and Shell each had separate management teams and boards of directors. Even in cases where an identical board of directors manages the DLC, such as for Unilever, agency problems arise if shareholders in the individual parents have conflicting interests. The separate identities of DLCs often cause underrepresentation in value-weighted stock indexes because only one of the pair's market capitalization is considered. Although efficient capital markets suggest that twin share prices should be identical, a corollary of equalization arrangements, historically substantial price deviations occurred and persisted, even for extended periods (Rosenthal and Young 1990). Froot and Dabora (1999) present evidence purporting that DLC stocks exhibit excess comovement with the location at which the shares are traded, irrespective of implied equalization. Furthering this analysis, De Jong, Rosenthal, and van Dijk (2009) explore apparent arbitrage opportunities in 12 pairs of DLCs, determining that market participants cannot easily exploit mispricings due to unique risks of the DLC structure. Finally, equalization and other contractual agreements complicate using the stock as an acquisition currency (FTI Consulting 2018).

Since the early 2000s through 2019, a noticeable trend toward unification has emerged in the subset of DLCs on the market. Between 1990 and 2019, at least 16 companies were organized as multinational DLCs at some point, but only five remained in 2019: Unilever, Rio Tinto, BHP Billiton, Investec, and Carnival. Indeed, in 2017, activist investor Elliott Associates campaigned for BHP Billiton to unify its Anglo-Australian DLC, arguing that the structure is value destructive given the underperformance of the U.K. company (Elliott Associates 2017).

Equalization stipulates that any dividends declared be paid to both twins at the predetermined ratio. Because the U.K. firm's profitability and reserves came under pressure, the Australian firm was required to transfer funds to subsidize dividends to the U.K. shareholders, thus forfeiting an Australian "franking," or tax, dividend credit. Figure 2.2 provides a list of known firms operating as DLCs.

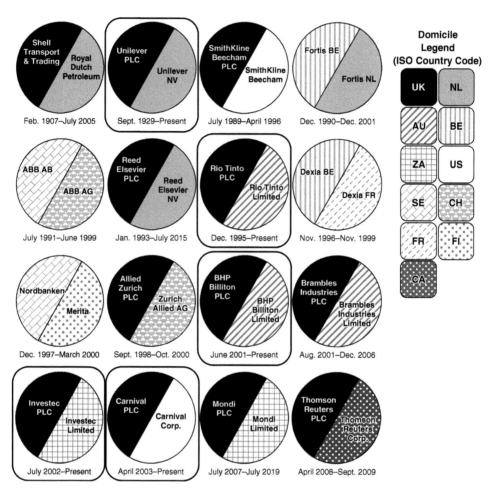

FIGURE 2.2 Cross-Border Dual-listed Companies

This figure provides a snapshot of 16 (5 current and 11 former) DLCs. While the 1990s experienced a rise in DLC formations, this complicated stock structure has since seemingly fallen out of favor alongside the trend toward "unification" or "simplification" of the corporate structure. Dates shown are the beginning and end dates for the inception and dissolution (if applicable) of the DLC structure.

Unilever Example To contextualize the properties of DLCs, consider Unilever, a transnational consumer goods company, which is the combination of Unilever PLC and Unilever NV, a U.K.- and Dutch-domiciled company, respectively. Unilever PLC's primary listing is on the LSE and Unilever NV's is on the Amsterdam Stock Exchange. Unilever is organized under the separate entities structure: The PLC and NV companies are legally distinct entities, which each fully own their respective operations. Equalization agreements between the two enable them to operate as a single economic entity. According to the Unilever Group (2019), "To avoid punitive taxation levies and the disruption to the business that would result from dividing integrated national companies into their component parts, both companies pooled their interests through a business merger as opposed to a legal merger." This structure enables non-Dutch investors to invest in Unilever shares without being penalized by Dutch withholding taxes. For example, a British investor is subject to a 15 percent withholding tax on dividends paid to NV shares, but not on dividends paid to PLC shares. Recall that gross dividends may be equalized (adjusted to foreign exchange rate movements), but a British investor in NV shares is disadvantaged relative to a Dutch investor in those same shares on an after-tax basis. The dual-listed structure of Unilever enables a British investor in PLC shares to receive dividends while avoiding the Dutch dividend withholding tax.

Tracking Stock

A *tracking stock* is a special type of equity in which a multidivisional corporation issues shares whose value is designed to reflect a specific subsidiary or business unit of the company, rather than the entire enterprise. Other names for these securities are "targeted stock," "lettered stock," and "alphabet stock." A tracking stock's value is intended to mirror the economic results of the subsidiary it targets. Still, tracking stock shareholders are shareholders in the parent corporation rather than in the tracked subsidiary. Therefore, shareholders do not have "direct ownership of the subsidiary to which their cash flows are tied" (Chemmanur and Paeglis 2005, p. 102). Corporations with tracking stocks report financials of the stand-alone business units for the tracking stock groups, reducing information asymmetry between insiders and the market. Although tracking stocks embody separate, tradeable assets, the parent corporation retains legal ownership and control of all assets and cash flows from which the tracking stock purportedly derives its value, suggesting that the intention to reflect subsidiary performance may not indicate economic reality. Tracking stock groups do not have a separate board of directors. Rather, the parent's board of directors sets capital allocation policies for the overall corporation in the interest of the parent, which may conflict with tracking stock group shareholders (Haas 1996).

Numerous corporate governance issues arise from the absence of legal ownership of assets. For companies with multiple tracking stocks in issue, the lack of a direct claim on assets has an interesting implication. By virtue of the parent's fundamental legal control, the value and price of one tracking stock group within a company may influence other tracking stock groups, despite theoretical independence. The returns for multiple classes of a single company's tracking stock may be interdependent, given the parent's discretion of cash flow allocation (Haas 1999).

Additionally, though the assets and liabilities are attributed to individual groups, all are ultimately owned and incurred by a consolidated entity. The obligations of any tracking stock group are thus shared by each of the other groups (Haas 1996). Although the earnings attributable to the tracking stock group should determine the dividends available to the group, the board of directors sets dividend policy and may determine to divert funds away from the profitable group toward less profitable groups in the best interest of the corporation as a whole (Logue, Seward, and Walsh 1996).

In relation to traditional stocks and bonds, tracking stocks are a relatively new development, first designed in 1984. Murphy (1989) offers a comprehensive analysis of General Motors Company's (GM) inaugural offering. This offering sought to provide investors with choice, aligned managerial incentives, and information via the separately traded security, while GM retained legal ownership of a newly acquired subsidiary's assets, and GM's board of directors made capital allocation decisions. The issuance of tracking stock is a form of corporate restructuring like a spin-off or equity carve-out in which shareholders in a tracking stock group do not have a legal claim on the underlying subsidiary assets it tracks (Danielova 2008). Tracking stocks also provide investors with an increased choice: Rather than investing in the conglomerate, investors may choose to invest in a corporation's tracking stock for a specific subsidiary, often faster-growing than the parent organization (Murphy 1989). Given that diversified firms tend to carry a discount to their theoretical value, tracking stocks are a corporate restructuring tool that attempts to unlock value by creating a pseudo pure-play company, without relinquishing control (Billett and Mauer 2000). Because of separate financial reporting for tracking stock groups, management may be compelled to improve operating decisions for the division more than would otherwise occur (Harper and Madura 2002).

DUAL-CLASS COMMON EQUITY

Dual-class structures separate economic ownership from control via the difference in voting rights for each share class. This wedge between the degree of economic interest and actual voting power to affect corporate changes has been subject to investor debate. Economic ownership and voting power are intrinsically linked for a single class of equity: one share equals one vote. However, dual-class equity structures give preferential voting rights to one class of stock. Holders of these super-voting classes then retain outsized influence per unit of economic ownership. With a dual-class structure, influence and control instead become independent from an economic interest in the company.

In a dual-class structure, the firm ascribes superior voting rights to one class and inferior voting rights to another. Generally, the share classes have equal rights in all other aspects, such as liquidation. Some corporations may offer other tangible benefits to holders of inferior voting shares, such as preferential dividends rights or the right to vote as a class to nominate a certain number of directors. Burkart and Lee (2008) present a comprehensive survey analyzing the impacts of deviations from the one-share-equals-one-vote structure.

In the past decade through 2019, the increase in the incidence of dual-class structures fueled immense criticism because such structures intrinsically violate one-share-equals-one-vote, disenfranchising certain shareholders. Over this period, several technology companies, such as Facebook, Snap Inc., Uber, and Lyft, in their initial public offerings (IPOs) raised equity capital in the public markets while concentrating control of the corporation with founders and other insiders. Although recent furor and press coverage generally discuss the use of dual-class stock by technology and media companies, the Council of Institutional Investors (CII), an influential association of investment firms focused on corporate governance, maintains a comprehensive list of over 250 U.S. incorporated companies with disparate voting rights (Council of Institutional Investors 2019). In 2018, the CII petitioned the NYSE and NASDAQ to prevent companies seeking new listings from going public with dual-class shares (Williams, Mahoney, and Bertsch 2018a, 2018b). Advocates against dual-class shares decry super-voting structures as anathema to shareholder democracy, the one-share-equals-one-vote principle recommending that influence and control be proportionate to economic interest. This shareholder structure has seen renewed interest to be more common as many closely held, founder-led technology companies seek to retain control while also raising equity capital in the public markets (Condon 2018).

Without an outright prohibition of dual-class shares, several opponents of dual-class stock suggest sunset clauses as potential remedies in cases of perpetual dual-class stock. Bebchuk and Kastiel (2017) agree that dual-class stock may be efficient for companies going public, but believe that efficiency declines over time, and therefore that sunset clauses empower shareholders to revisit and eliminate, if necessary, the dual-class structure. In response to the CII's petitions, Berger (2019) contends that does not only empirical evidence fail to support compulsory sunset provisions, but also, without dual-class stock, ownership of common stock for many companies has become concentrated in a few large institutional investors. Moreover, according to Burkart and Lee (2008), linking economic ownership with control is not optimal for widely held firms. Proponents of dual-class stock point to several economic benefits provided by this ownership structure. Dual-class shares permit management to focus on long-term value creation without preoccupation with short-term profits or demands of activist investors (Govindarajan and Srivastava 2018). For young founder-led dual-class firms, the economic wealth and reputation of the founders is highly correlated with the firm's value and performance, aligning incentives with inferior voting shareholders (Kim and Michaely 2019).

Discovery Inc.: A Case Study

Discovery, Inc. is a global media company incorporated in the United States whose share capital is divided into three series of common stock – Series A, B, and C – and two series of convertible preferred stock – Series A-1 and C-1. With Discovery's three classes of common stock, the economic interest varies substantially from the respective voting interest of the class. Discovery's Form 10-K filing with the SEC indicates that these three classes "have equal rights, powers and privileges, except as otherwise noted" (Discovery, Inc. 2019, p. 120), continuing to explain that the only material difference between the share classes is voting power attributed to each series of stock. Besides the three series of common stock, Discovery's share capital also includes two series of convertible preferred stock, Series A-1 and Series C-1, which are convertible into Series A and Series C common shares, respectively. Table 2.1 presents Discovery, Inc.'s common share structure, exemplifying the wedge between economic and voting interests among the share classes.

Discovery's wedge enables certain shareholders to exert outsized influence and control, despite minority economic interests in the enterprise. Table 2.2 lists Discovery's 10 largest beneficial shareholders, depicting the substantial voting power ascribed to certain shareholders without a corresponding economic interest.

TABLE 2.1 Discovery, Inc. Common Equity Share Class Structure

Class	Ticker	Price	Shares Out.	Market Cap.	Economic Interest	Voting Rights	Aggregate Vote	Voting Power
Series A	DISCA	$27.43	157.8	$4,327.6	23.0%	1.0	157.8	53.7%
Series B	DISCB	31.00	6.5	201.9	1.1	10.0	65.1	22.2
Series C	DISCK	25.90	360.5	9,337.9	49.6	0.0	0.0	0.0
Series A-1		27.43	70.7	1,938.6	10.3	1.0	70.7	24.1
Series C-1		25.90	116.5	3,018.1	16.0	0.0	0.0	0.0
Total Discovery, Inc. (As converted basis)				18,823.9	100.0		293.6	100.0

This table illustrates Discovery, Inc.'s share class structure, with three classes of common stock. Discovery is a global media company domiciled in the United States. The only material difference between the share classes is voting power attributed to each series of stock. Besides the three series of common stock, Discovery's share capital also includes two series of convertible preferred stock, Series A-1 and Series C-1, which are convertible into Series A and Series C common shares, respectively.
Price per share and shares outstanding as of March 15, 2019.
Shares outstanding, market capitalization, and aggregate vote are in millions.
The numbers are rounded.
Source: FactSet (2019).

TABLE 2.2 Discovery, Inc.'s Largest Beneficial Shareholders

	Largest Beneficial Shareholders	Economic Ownership (%)	Voting Power (%)
1	Advance/Newhouse Programming Partnership (ANPP)	26.3	24.1
2	The Vanguard Group, Inc.	7.3	5.8
3	BlackRock Inc.	4.8	3.7
4	Hotchkis & Wiley Capital Management, LLC	3.3	0.0
5	John C. Malone	2.6	21.4
6	Clearbridge Investments, LLC	2.5	5.8
7	FMR LLC	1.9	4.5
8	Capital Research Global Investors	1.7	4.0
9	JPMorgan Chase & Co.	1.3	3.0
10	David M. Zaslav	0.4	0.5
	Total top 10 beneficial shareholders	52.1	72.8
	ANPP + John C. Malone	28.9	45.5

This table lists the largest beneficial shareholders by economic ownership, and the corresponding voting power attributed to each of those beneficial shareholders. Because of Discovery's dual-class share structure, certain shareholders have disproportionate voting rights relative to their economic interest. The economic ownership and voting power columns of this table present the Series A-1 and Series C-1 shares on an "as converted" basis. Each Series A-1 share is convertible into nine shares of Series A stock, and each Series C-1 share is convertible into 19.3648 shares of Series C stock. Numbers are rounded for presentability.
Source: FactSet (2019).

SUMMARY AND CONCLUSIONS

Common stock represents residual claims to a corporation's profits after meeting other stakeholders' claims. The majority of companies link economic interest in the company with control, enabling one share to carry one vote for issues requiring shareholder approval. Although common stock generally is more homogenous than corporate debt issuances, several mechanisms are available for corporations to differentiate one class of stock from another.

Besides ordinary common stock, this chapter discusses several forms of more complicated share listings. For single classes of stock, these include cross-listings, depositary receipts, dual-listed companies, and tracking stock. Cross-listed shares enable domestic companies to trade in foreign markets. Depositary receipts similarly achieve this goal via a financial intermediary, both with and without the company's sponsorship. Dual-listed companies are a special instance of common stock. Found mostly in Europe, these listings represent two independent companies whose businesses are merged while retaining separate legal identities. Each twin's respective management team agrees to equalize each twin to a predetermined ratio via complex agreements, but the market of dual-listed company stocks exhibits mispricings from theoretical parity. Tracking stock is a less popular, arcane form of common stock of a corporation whose value theoretically targets the financial performance of only a subunit of the corporation.

Finally, dual-class common equity structures are a prevalent form of stock in which different voting arrangements offer certain shareholders superior voting rights. A wedge separates a shareholder's control from that owner's capital at risk. Dual-class common stock can permit overall control of the corporation without a controlling stake in the economic value of the enterprise.

DISCUSSION QUESTIONS

1. Compare and contrast depositary receipts and cross-listed stocks.
2. Discuss the benefits and drawbacks for investors in tracking stocks.
3. Explain the three types of dual-listed company structures.
4. Identify what motivates companies to offer dual-class equity structures.

REFERENCES

Bainbridge, Stephen. 1991. "The Short Life and Resurrection of SEC Rule 19C-4." *Washington University Law Review* 69:2, 565–634.

Baker, H. Kent, John Nofsinger, and Daniel Weaver. 2002. "International Cross-Listing and Visibility." *Journal of Financial and Quantitative Analysis* 37:3, 495–521.

Bebchuk, Lucian, and Kobi Kastiel. 2017. "The Untenable Case for Perpetual Dual-Class Stock." *Virginia Law Review* 103:4, 585–631.

Berger, David. 2019. "Why Dual-class Stock? A Response to CII's Petition to NASDAQ for Mandatory Sunset Provisions." Available at https://clsbluesky.files.wordpress.com/2019/03/here..pdf

Billett, Matthew, and David Mauer. 2000. "Diversification and the Value of Internal Capital Markets: The Case of Tracking Stock." *Journal of Banking and Finance* 24:9, 1457–1490.

Burkart, Mike, and Samuel Lee. 2008. "One Share – One Vote: The Theory." *Review of Finance* 12:1, 1–49.

Chemmanur, Thomas, and Imants Paeglis. 2005. "Why Issue Tracking Stock? Insights from a Comparison with Spin-Offs and Carve-Outs." *Journal of Applied Corporate Finance* 14:2, 102–114.

Citi. 2019. "American Depositary Receipts (ADRs): A Primer." Available at https://depositary receipts.citi.com/adr/common/file.aspx?idf=1248.

Cleary Gottlieb Steen & Hamilton. 2003. "Cross Border Mergers: The Cases for and against Dual Headed Structures." *European M&A Report*, October, 3–7.

Condon, Zoe. 2018. "A Snapshot of Dual-Class Share Structures in the Twenty-First Century: A Solution to Reconcile Shareholder Protections with Founder Autonomy." *Emory Law Journal* 68:2, 336–367. Available at http://law.emory.edu/elj/content/volume-68/issue-2/comments/dual-class-twenty-first-solution-protections-autonomy.html.

Council of Institutional Investors. 2019. "Dual-class Companies List." Available at https://cii.membershipsoftware.org/files/June%202019%20Dual%20Class%20List%20Upgrade%20w%20Lucy%20edits(2).pdf.

Danielova, Anna. 2008. "Tracking Stock or Spin-Off? Determinants of Choice." *Financial Management* 37:1, 125–139.

De Jong, Abe, Leonard Rosenthal, and Mathijs van Dijk. 2009. "The Risk and Return of Arbitrage in Dual-Listed Companies." *Review of Finance* 13:3:, 495–520.

Discovery, Inc. 2019. Form 10-K 2018. Available at https://ir.corporate.discovery.com/static-files/cdeb0ba2-e0a0-4f70-a74d-4b8f54d30f81.

Doidge, Craig, G. Andrew Karolyi, and René Stulz. 2010. "Why Do Foreign Firms Leave U.S. Equity Markets?" *Journal of Finance* 65:4, 1507–1553.

Dobbs, Richard, and Marc Goedhart. 2008. "Why Cross-listing Shares Doesn't Create Value." *McKinsey on Finance*, November. Available at https://www.mckinsey.com/business-functions/strategy-and-corporate-finance/our-insights/why-cross-listing-shares-doesnt-create-value.

Elliott Associates. 2017. "Elliott Sends Letter and Presentation to Directors of BHP Billiton Outlining Shareholder Value Unlock Plan." Available at https://www.prnewswire.com/news-releases/elliott-sends-letter-and-presentation-to-the-directors-of-bhp-billiton-outlining-shareholder-value-unlock-plan-618784104.html.

FactSet Data Systems. 2019. "FactSet Workstation."

Foerster, Stephen, and G. Andrew Karolyi. 1999. "The Effects of Market Segmentation and Investor Recognition on Asset Prices: Evidence from Foreign Stocks Listing in the United States." *Journal of Finance* 54:3, 981–1013.

Froot, Kenneth, and Emil Dabora. 1999. "How Are Stock Prices Affected by the Location of Trade?" *Journal of Financial Economics* 53:2, 189–216.

FTI Consulting. 2018. "Value Release from Unification at BHP." Available at https://www.fixingbhp.com/content/uploads/2018/03/FTI-Value-Release-from-Unification-at-BHP-Final.pdf.

Govindarajan, Vijay, and Anup Srivastava. 2018. "Reexamining Dual-Class Stock." *Business Horizons* 61:3, 461–466.

Hancock, Stephen, Maryse Gray, and Cécile Sommelet. 2002. "Dual-Headed Structures Revisited." Global Counsel. Available at https://uk.practicallaw.thomsonreuters.com/6-101-7959?

Harper, Joel, and Jeff Madura. 2002. "Sources of Hidden Value and Risk within Tracking Stock." *Financial Management* 31:3, 91–109.

Haas, Jeffrey. 1996. "Directorial Fiduciary Duties in a Tracking Stock Equity Structure: The Need for a Duty of Fairness." *Michigan Law Review* 94:7, 2089–2177.

Haas, Jeffrey. 1999. "How Quantum, DLJ and Ziff-Davis Are Keeping on Track with 'Tracking Stock': Part I." Working Paper, New York Law School. Available at https://papers .ssrn.com/sol3/papers.cfm?abstract_id=223633.

JPMorgan. 2008. "Depositary Receipts: Reference Guide."

Kim, Hyunseob, and Roni Michaely. 2019. "Sticking around Too Long?: Dynamics of the Benefits of Dual-Class Voting." *Swiss Finance Institute Research Paper Series* 19:9.

Logue, Dennis, James Seward, and James Walsh. 1996. "Rearranging Residual Claims: A Case for Targeted Stock." *Financial Management* 25:1, 43–61.

Murphy, J. Austin. 1989. "Analyzing Sub-Classes of General Motors Common Stock." *Financial Management* 18:1, 64–71.

Rosenthal, Leonard, and Colin Young. 1990. "The Seemingly Anomalous Price Behavior of Royal Dutch/Shell and Unilever NV/PLC." *Journal of Financial Economics* 26:1, 123–141.

Roosenboom, Peter, and Mathijs van Dijk. 2009. "The Market Reaction to Cross-Listings: Does the Destination Market Matter?" *Journal of Banking & Finance* 33:10, 1898–1908.

Saunders, Mark. 1993. "American Depositary Receipts: An Introduction to U.S. Capital Markets for Foreign Companies." *Fordham International Law Journal* 17:1, 48–83.

Securities and Exchange Commission. 2012. "Investor Bulletin: American Depositary Receipts." Available at https://www.sec.gov/investor/alerts/adr-bulletin.pdf.

U.K. Panel on Takeovers and Mergers. 2002. "Dual-listed Company Transactions and Frustrating Action." Available at http://www.thetakeoverpanel.org.uk/wp-content/uploads/2008/11/pcp11.pdf.

Unilever Group. 2019. "Unilever Shares – The Basics." Available at https://www.unilever.com/investor-relations/unilever-shares/about-shares/unilever-shares-the-basics/.

Williams, Ash, Jeff Mahoney, and Ken Bertsch. 2018a. "CII Petition to NYSE." Available at https://www.cii.org/files/issues_and_advocacy/correspondence/2018/20181024 %20NYSE%20Petition%20on%20Multiclass%20Sunsets%20FINAL.pdf.

Williams, Ash, Jeff Mahoney, and Ken Bertsch. 2018b. "CII Petition to NASDAQ." Available at https://www.cii.org/files/issues_and_advocacy/correspondence/2018/20181024 %20NASDAQ%20Petition%20on%20Multiclass%20Sunsets%20FINAL.pdf.

CHAPTER 3

Equity Markets and Performance

Jay T. Brandi
Professor of Finance, University of Louisville
Xudong Fu
Assistant Professor of Finance, University of Louisville

INTRODUCTION

A *market* is a place that facilitates a transaction between two parties for the exchange of tangible goods and services. A *financial market* is a market for trading financial assets or investments such as stocks and bonds. In a financial market, investors trade on claims: the claims to a company's ownership or claims to an entity's debt obligations. These claims are the connections between people who want to save and invest money for the future rather than current consumption and organizations that need money.

Financial markets provide savers – potential investors and users – individuals, companies, and government entities with mechanisms for making transactions to meet specific financial needs and objectives. Savers can earn returns from the financial markets, while users turn to the financial markets to obtain needed funds. Interestingly, a person or organization can be both a fund's saver and user at the same time. An individual can, for example, simultaneously invest monthly 401(k) contributions in the stock market as a saver and use mortgage financing for a home purchase as a user. Similarly, a business firm can both borrow money as a user for long-term projects and invest retained earnings in the Treasury market or other financial markets as a saver.

Financial markets can be classified in several ways. One way is to categorize them based on the maturity of the issues involved in transactions such as either the *money market* for short-term investments or the *capital market* for long-term investments. The money market is comprised of mainly debt securities maturing in one year or less. This category includes Treasury bills, short-term notes payable, banker's acceptances, commercial paper, and negotiable certificates of deposit. In contrast, the capital market includes issues such as common stock with no maturity or corporate bonds with a maturity greater than one year.

Another way to categorize capital markets is by *debt or equity* markets. Debt markets include long-term notes payables, bonds, and *debentures*, a debt instrument that is not secured by collateral and usually has a term greater than 10 years. Debt, such as bonds and debentures, are obligations of the issuer and provide a claim of liability for the investor. Equity markets include common stocks and preferred stocks. The equity market is one of the most important segments of the financial market, providing evidence of equity ownership claims for investors.

As Tables 3.1 and 3.2 show, the volume of corporate bonds issued is much greater than the issuance of corporate equity. The majority of equity issues are common stocks, with 92.4 percent of the equity issued in 2018. Secondary or follow-on offerings of previously issued shares totaled 74.5 percent of the equity issued in 2018.

TABLE 3.1 Issuance Volume of Equity Securities in Billions of Dollars

This table shows the yearly issuance volume of various types of equity in billions of dollars between 2014 and 2018.

Security	2018	2017	2016	2015	2014
Common stock	204.4	213.4	193.2	234.9	273.3
Preferred stock	16.8	26.1	24.8	32.1	38.5
Secondaries	164.8	173.7	172.5	202.5	179.3
Initial public offerings	50.6	39.8	20.8	32.4	93.9
Total equity issuance	221.2	239.5	218.1	267.1	311.8

Note: Securities firms, banks, and asset managers provide this information to SIFMA. Volume is defined as the volume traded on each exchange or by the listing exchange regardless of where traded.
Source: Securities Industry and Financial Markets Association (SIFMA) (2019).

TABLE 3.2 Issuance Volume of Corporate Bonds in Billions of Dollars

This table shows the yearly issuance volume of various corporate bonds in billions of dollars between 2014 and 2018.

Security	2018	2017	2016	2015	2014
Investment grade	1165.1	1368.2	1290.3	1232.9	1124.3
High yield	173.0	284.2	237.3	261.9	314.1
Callable – fixed rate	816.8	989.7	1020.6	997.2	863.8
Callable – floating rate	146.9	147.6	32.7	30.7	21.5
Non-callable – fixed rate	265.0	391.0	389.9	383.9	425.9
Non-callable – floating rate	109.5	124.2	84.3	83.0	127.2
Convertible	38.6	27.2	22.4	20.7	37.2
Total corporate bond issuance	1376.7	1679.6	1550.0	1515.5	1475.6

Note: SIFMA collects information from Bloomberg, Dealogic, Thomson Reuters Eikon SDC, the U.S. Treasury, Fannie Mae, Freddie Mac, Ginnie Mae, Farmer Mac, Farm Credit, and the FHLB in determining the volume of bonds issued over a stated period.
Source: Securities Industry and Financial Markets Association (SIFMA) (2019).

As Table 3.2 shows, the largest volume of bond issuance involves investment-grade bonds, accounting for 84.6 percent of the corporate bonds issued in 2018. Convertible bonds, which can be exchanged for the issuing firm's stock, amounted to only 2.8 percent of the total bond issuance in 2018. The differing maturity characteristics for equity and debt issues are substantial. Unlike debt issues such as bonds, equity investments have no maturity date, and thus the issuing firms have no obligation to repurchase them from investors. Therefore, for investors who want to sell shares of stocks, having an actively traded secondary market is crucial.

Except in the case of a firm choosing to repurchase shares or retire debt issues before maturity, neither buyers nor sellers of an issue are issuing firms. In the primary market, however, the seller is the issuing firm. Investors who want to buy a firm's securities when a primary offering is not extended must go to the secondary market to purchase the securities from another investor. Only a small number of investors participate in the primary market; most stock transactions occur in the secondary market. Trading in the secondary market sets the market price or value per share. A firm's management should theoretically try to maximize the market value of its shares. Therefore, a good secondary market is necessary for all marketable securities, not just stocks.

THE EQUITY MARKET AND THE ECONOMY

The equity market is important to the economy for several reasons.

- *Source of funding.* Stock markets provide a source of funding for business entities. When companies enter equity markets to issue new shares, they often cite "investment needs" as the reason for their new issues. In such cases, by selling equity (ownership) to incoming stockholders, firms obtain funding for their current and future business developments.
- *Facility for allocating money.* The equity market provides a great facility for allocating a scarce resource – money. In a well-functioning financial market, companies with the best performance and investment potential are likely receiving greater access to funding.

Imagine that investors face two stock investment options: Company A and Company B. Company A has outperformed the general equity market for the past 10 years and has a full pipeline of innovative projects and investments. Company B has underperformed the market for the past 10 years and has limited future potential. Of the two alternatives, most equity investors would choose Company A. This situation means that in equilibrium, Company A would receive more funding for the promising investment projects in its future. In contrast, the managers at Company B are likely to find obtaining funds both more difficult and expensive. Money flows to Company A because investors consider it a better alternative for obtaining future returns than Company B. However, in the real world, the choice is not just between Company A or B. Instead, the market provides investors with a wide array of other investments, allowing the allocation of funds to the industries, sectors, and businesses that investors find to be most appealing.

- *A way to send signals.* Equity markets send credible signals to the marketplace, which have real effects on a country's economy. If the economy is booming, most companies are likely to enjoy higher profits and cash flows. Because stock prices are forward-looking, future profits and cash flows that do better than expected generally increase a firm's stock price. The reason is that investors perceive that these firms are more likely to provide dividends and/or capital gains in the future. If the market perceives that a firm's performance may falter, resulting in lower earnings, its stock price generally falls.

As a result, market signals indicating stock performance are important to the financial market are thus also considered reliable economic indicators. Through their ongoing trades in the secondary market, investors reveal and produce information about their expectations of the future profitability of alternative investment opportunities. This information is likely to be reflected in market prices; if more investors like a stock, its price tends to increase.

Similarly, if a stock is not favored, its price typically falls. Stock prices guide business managers' investment decisions after incorporating information from investors. If a chief executive officer (CEO) sees a substantial increase in the company's stock price, this situation can indicate that investors view the firm's performance potential positively and therefore approve of its publicly known operations and investment plans. The stock market is also a predictor of the rate of corporate investment. When the stock market is on the rise as indicated by increasing stock prices, this situation indicates improved profitability and often provides firms with lower financing costs. Financing costs are the hurdle rates firms must meet or exceed to produce economic value. With lower financing costs, firms find themselves with more lucrative investment opportunities.

These investment opportunities are also an important driver in labor markets: firm managers, anticipating a favorable economic environment and ample investment opportunities, may accept more projects to maximize firm value. A byproduct of such managerial decisions is the necessity for additional employees to meet product demand. The competition for available workers also has the potential to provide increased wages for currently employed workers. The improved labor markets, as shown by lower unemployment rates and increased wages, give employees more purchasing power as consumers. Figures 3.1, 3.2, and 3.3 show the relation among industrial production, the accompanying decrease in unemployment, and the ultimate increase in consumer spending. These consumers can buy more products and services offered by firms, which in turn drive firm profits and stock prices even higher, as shown in Figure 3.4.

However, although the stock market is generally a leading indicator, signals from the stock market can also further deteriorate economic conditions. During the financial crisis of 2007–2008, after the stock market lost value due to failures in the financial markets, companies processed the signals of bleak future profitability and in turn, reduced investments. As a result of reducing the level of future investments, companies required fewer workers to meet the demand for products and services, leading to higher unemployment rates. Facing job difficulties, among other uncertainties, consumers spent less, especially on big-ticket items such as automobiles and appliances. Declining sales negatively affected firms' profitability and stock price.

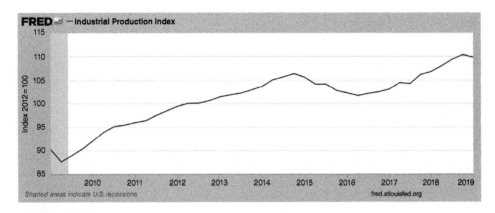

FIGURE 3.1   Industrial Production Index

This figure shows the trend of the Industrial Production Index in the United States between 2009 and 2019.

Note: The Industrial Production Index (INDPRO) is an economic indicator that measures real output for all facilities located in the United States manufacturing, mining, and electric and gas utilities, excluding those in U.S. territories.

Source: Board of Governors of the Federal Reserve System (U.S.) (2019).

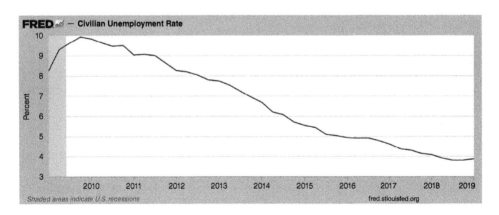

FIGURE 3.2   Unemployment Rate

This figure shows the unemployment trend in the United States between 2009 and 2019.

Note: The unemployment rate represents the number of unemployed as a percentage of the labor force.

Source: U.S. Bureau of Labor Statistics (2019).

Vehicle affecting government revenue. The stock market is also related to government revenue streams. As previously discussed, a booming stock market is generally associated with higher company profitability and worker income. Both of these factors are important sources of government tax revenues. Relative to the increasing corporate profitability and market returns between 2012 and 2019, Figure 3.5 shows the accompanying increase in government revenues over the same period.

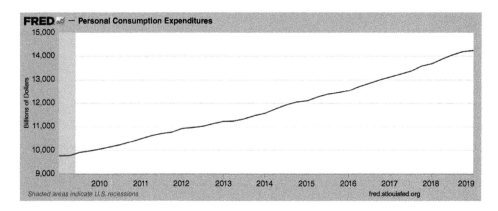

FIGURE 3.3 Personal Consumption Expenditures

This figure shows the trend of aggregate personal consumption expenditures in the United States between 2009 and 2019.

Note: As per the Bureau of Economic Analysis, consumer spending or personal consumption expenditures (PCEs) are the value of the goods and services purchased by or on the behalf of U.S. residents.

Source: U.S. Bureau of Economic Analysis (2019b).

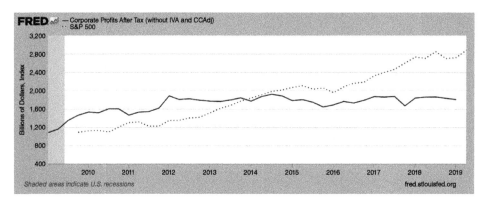

FIGURE 3.4 Corporate Profits versus Standard & Poor's 500 Index

This figure shows the relation between aggregate corporate profits and stock market as shown by S&P 500 Index level between 2010 and 2019.

Source: U.S. Bureau of Economic Analysis (2019a).

Economic improvement or trouble is accompanied by corporate securities issues increasing in good economic periods and decreasing when the economy faces a downturn. Business firms turn to the economy and the market for an indication as to whether they should increase production and require additional capital funding. Figure 3.6 provides insight into the relation between stock market capitalization and the economy, as evidenced by gross domestic product (GDP). Between 2012 and 2019, capitalization or firm value improved in line with the related improvements in the economic conditions in the United States, as shown in GDP.

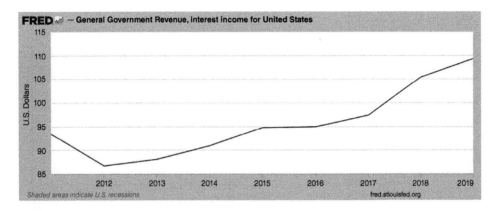

FIGURE 3.5 Government Revenues

This figure shows aggregate government revenues between 2011 and 2019.

Source: International Monetary Fund (2019).

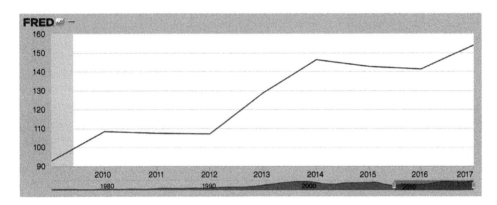

FIGURE 3.6 Stock Market Capitalization to GDP

This figure shows the ratio of stock market capitalization to GDP between 2009 and 2017.

Note: Data are defined as the total value of all listed shares in a stock market as a percentage of GDP.

Source: World Bank, Stock Market Capitalization to GDP for United States [DDDM01USA156NWDB] (2019).

MARKET INDICATORS

Many market indicators for the economy, including market indices, are available. A *market index* is a hypothetical portfolio of investment holdings representing a segment of the stock market. The change in the value of this portfolio can serve as an indicator of market movement. Calculating the index return involves summing the products of individual index component returns and weights.

Different index-weighting schemes are based on factors such as market capitalization (market-cap) and price. Two popular stock indices for tracking the

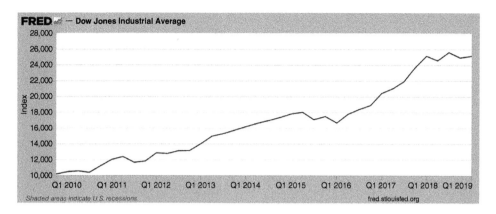

FIGURE 3.7 Dow Jones Industrial Average

This figure shows the Dow Jones Industrial Average index level between 2010 and 2019.

Source: S&P Dow Jones Indices LLC (2019b).

performance of the U.S. market are the Dow Jones Industrial Average (DJIA) and the Standard & Poor's 500 Index (S&P 500).

- *DJIA.* The DJIA is one of the oldest, most famous, and most frequently used indices in the world. It measures the stock performance of 30 large companies listed on U.S. stock exchanges. These companies are mature companies traditionally paying dividends over time. The DJIA represents about 25 percent of the total value of the U.S. stock market. Figure 3.7 shows the trendline of the DJIA between the first quarter (Q1) of 2010 and Q1 of 2019.
- *S&P 500 Index.* Another market indicator is the S&P 500 Index, which is an index of 500 of the largest companies in the U.S. market. Stocks are selected for this index mainly based on company size, which is measured by market capitalization, along with other factors such as *public float* (i.e., the number of a firm's shares available for trading in the market), financial stability, and the firm's historical record. The S&P 500 Index represents about 80 percent of the total value of the U.S. stock market, so it widely serves as an indication of the stock market and economy as a whole. Figure 3.8 illustrates the S&P 500's movement between Q1 2010 and Q1 2019.

GOOD MARKETS – LIQUIDITY

Liquidity and marketability are often used interchangeably. Although related, the two market characteristics differ. *Liquidity* refers to the speed with which an asset can be converted into cash without a loss of value. *Marketability* refers to the level of ease or the ability of buyers or sellers of a security to create and complete a transaction.

Generally speaking, securities with better marketability are more liquid than those with poor marketability. As a result, they trade more often. This high level of trading activity implies that the change in value from trade to trade is generally minimal relative to the changes in value for illiquid securities. This feature is important to investors: Illiquidity essentially measures one type of cost related to

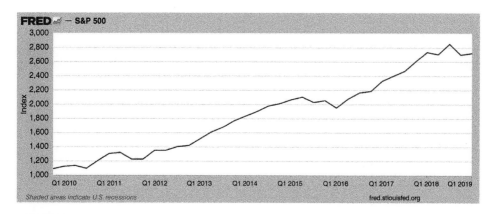

FIGURE 3.8 S&P 500 Index

This figure shows the S&P 500 Index level between 2010 and 2019.

Note: The S&P 500 is a gauge of the large-cap U.S. equities market. Since the S&P 500 is a price index and not a total return index, it does not contain dividends.

Source: S&P Dow Jones Indices (2019a).

stock trading and investing and is, therefore, a vital consideration for investors. Pastor and Stambaugh (2002a) show that stocks with higher sensitivity to liquidity have a higher required rate of return.

Market participants can easily buy and sell marketable securities, but nonmarketable securities are more challenging to trade. The shares of a privately held company, for example, are more difficult to sell and thus less marketable than shares in a publicly held company because they do not trade in the public secondary market. The presence of an actively traded secondary market improves a security's marketability. In summary, securities with poor marketability are less liquid (illiquid) than those with better marketability because they trade less often, implying that changes in their values from trade to trade are generally larger relative to the changes in value for liquid securities.

GOOD MARKETS – EFFICIENCY

One characteristic of a good market is *market efficiency*, which is an important component of a capitalist system. For efficient capital markets to function smoothly in allocating financial resources, the prices of company stocks must be reasonable, if not perfect, indicators of firm value.

The root market efficiency question hinges on both the type and amount of information available. Specifically, the type of information defines the three forms of the hypothesis: weak, semi-strong, and strong. Studies identify various anomalies in efficient markets.

Weak Form Efficiency

Weak form efficiency occurs if stock prices currently reflect all known market information, including stock prices and volume. In this market, stock prices adjust rapidly to existing market information. These adjustments occur so quickly that investors cannot expect to consistently make abnormally large returns based on new market information as it becomes known. For example, Kendall (1953) finds that stock prices do not show any predictable patterns. In other words, whether the stock prices go up or down on the previous day does not predict the stock price movement today.

Semi-Strong Form Efficiency

Semi-strong form efficiency occurs if stock prices currently reflect all known public information, including all market information. In a semi-strong form efficient market, stock prices also adjust rapidly to new public information. As with weak form efficiency, these adjustments occur so rapidly that investors cannot consistently earn abnormally large returns based on any new public information (Patell and Wolfson 1984). Two types of studies – event studies and mutual fund performance studies, show that markets are generally efficient in the semi-strong form. For example, Busse and Green (2002) use an event test to study the minute-by-minute stock prices of companies that are discussed on CNBC's segments. They show that stock prices move rapidly to new levels, depending on whether the reports they receive are positive or negative. Pastor and Stambaugh (2002b) find that mutual fund managers do not outperform their fund's benchmarks. These studies indicate that using public information in stock selections is unlikely to consistently lead to profits because stock prices have already incorporated this information.

Strong Form Efficiency

Strong form efficiency occurs if stock prices currently reflect all known information, including all public and private information. The additional information included at this level is private or inside information. If a market is strong form efficient, investors cannot expect to consistently make abnormally large returns based on any information, including private information. Another issue that exists with using private or inside information is that using inside information violates securities trading rules in the United States and other countries.

Studies and Implications Regarding Market Efficiency

Numerous studies show that markets with many profit-maximizing investors appear to be both weak form and semi-strong form efficient. Studies examining strong form efficiency generally indicate that these same marketplaces are not strong form efficient (Givoly and Palmon 1985; Jaffe 1974), even with prohibitive securities regulations. The fact that these markets are weak and semi-strong form efficient does not prohibit an investor from earning an acceptable return. Instead, the hypothesis merely clarifies that in an efficient market, investors cannot consistently earn abnormal returns as new market and/or other public information becomes available (Seyhun 1986).

Testing strong form efficiency presents various challenges. First, studying the efficiency of strong form markets requires using private data. Second, because the information is privately held, no competitive trading can take place on the information. Third, because the information is private and cannot be used competitively, government regulation is required to prevent insider trading on private information from occurring. Therefore, the markets cannot be strong form efficient in an otherwise efficient market such as that in the United States.

On average, in an efficient market, the returns earned should be commensurate with the level of risk taken. Over the long term, this risk–return tradeoff is critical to investors since, in an efficient market, shareholders should have the opportunity to receive a fair return relative to the risk they undertake. Without efficient markets, some investors could be consistent winners, but a larger portion of the investors, especially retail traders, are doomed to incur losses.

Good Markets – Trust and Confidence

Besides liquidity and market efficiency, another important requirement for a good market is investor trust and confidence. Others may overlook this issue, but not the U.S. Securities and Exchange Commission (SEC).

To illustrate the importance of investor confidence and trust, remember the old adage: fool me once, shame on you; fool me twice, shame on me. As related to market trading, investors are unlikely to trust people or organizations that trick them. Being tricked in the capital market means losing money. A lack of trust in the market and its integrity leads to fewer investors and less market efficiency and liquidity. However, Diamond (1989) notes that building a good reputation and trust with investors takes a long time.

INFORMATION DISCLOSURE

How can investor trust be earned and maintained? This task can be accomplished by providing adequate information disclosure. Ordinary investors do not have access to specific information about company operations, financing, and future plans. Instead, they must rely on information disclosure and announcements by those companies. To ensure fair disclosure of information, the SEC generally requires publicly traded companies to file updated information both annually and quarterly, and, when necessary, to provide timely announcements about important events. The SEC adopts new rules and regulations when necessary to improve the level and flow of information.

ENFORCEMENT

Besides information disclosure, enforcement, especially against insider trading, is another mechanism the SEC uses to preserve investor trust. In most insider trades, insiders have an informational advantage, and if they choose to exploit this advantage illegally, they can benefit at the cost of outside investors. The reason is simple – when an insider buys stock believing its price is about to increase, outside investors pay the price as the sellers of those shares. Similarly, when an insider sells knowing that stock price is likely to fall, outside investors are the ones who buy those shares.

By providing liquidity for these informed insider trades, outside investors are losers. Rational investors would never choose to trade against an insider exploiting an informational advantage. A market plagued with insider trades makes participating unappealing for ordinary investors simply due to the loss of money and, more importantly, confidence. The SEC continually enforces regulations to reduce illegal insider trading in the market, and its enforcement is effective in curbing insider trading with superior information.

MONETARY POLICIES

In some extreme cases, the government may use monetary policies to restore the stock market and investor confidence. After the Great Recession from 2007 to early 2009, central banks worldwide conducted several rounds of *quantitative easing* (QE), which generally means buying government bonds to make bonds less attractive to investors and to enable firms to receive cheaper funds for future projects. Although these QE policies have their fair share of critics, they boosted the stock markets and helped restore investor confidence. Consequently, with the improved stock market, firms began to invest more. Traditionally, an increase in business investments is associated with hiring additional employees and, therefore, an accompanying improvement in the job market.

INVESTMENTS: COMPARATIVE RISK AND RETURN

Focusing on investments from the perspectives of both return and risk is important. Although returns are an easy concept for investors to grasp, they are more likely to lack an understanding of the importance of accompanying risk.

Investment risks can be classified in various ways. One of the first issues to consider is asset class. Although other categories such as real estate are available in general, the most common investment assets are traditional investments, including stocks, bonds, or money market assets.

Firm size is another crucial issue. Although different ways are available to measure a company's size, such as its sales, assets, or even the number of employees, the most frequently used method is by market capitalization calculated as the product of the number of shares outstanding and the market value of each share. Consider, for example, that on August 16, 2019, the price of Apple Inc. stock closed at $206.50. At that time, the firm had 4.5 billion shares outstanding in the hands of investors. Combining the two values, on August 16, 2019, the market capitalization of Apple, Inc. was about $928.8 billion ($206.40 per share × 4.5 billion shares outstanding = $928.8 billion of market capitalization).

Different size categories of stock include large-cap (large-capitalization), mid-cap (mid-capitalization), small-cap (small-capitalization), micro-cap (micro-capitalization), or even nano-cap stocks. Nano is a prefix used to represent a one-billionth part of something – here, nano-capitalization stocks.

Although capitalization categories can differ substantially depending on the source, *large-cap* stocks are usually thought of as those with a capitalization of $10 billion or larger. For *mid-cap* stock, capitalizations generally lie in the $2 billion to $10 billion range, while *small-cap* stock capitalization definitions range from $300 million to $2 billion. Alternatively, some small-cap stocks have capitalizations greater than $500 million but less than $2,400 million. *Micro-* and *nano*-cap stocks are often defined as those whose market capitalizations are between $50 million and $300 million for micro-caps and less than $50 million for nano-cap stocks.

Collectively, large-cap companies may be considered the backbone of the U.S. economy. For example, the total market capitalization of the S&P 500 Index firms consists of roughly 80 percent of the market capitalization of the entire stock market. By comparison, small-capitalization and micro-capitalization firms are often young and focus on one or two niches of expertise.

Much like market-cap classes, debt issues can also be categorized by class. Bond categorization, however, is more likely to be by the identity of bond issuers and maturity than by size. Commonly used bond segments include classifications such as long-term corporate, long-term government, municipal issues, and short-term issues, which include U.S. Treasury bills.

As Table 3.3 shows, major differences exist in both the returns possible and the risk accepted by investing in different classes of stock and bonds. In general, stocks provide higher average returns than bonds, but they also involve a higher level of risk.

A review of the data shown in Table 3.3 provides good insight into the average returns and risks of basic asset classes over time. Based on their long-term geometric mean rate of return, large-capitalization stock investments provide at least four percentage points more annually on average over the long-term than long-term corporate bonds. This difference might look modest for one or two years, but it makes a big difference after accumulation over the years.

Consider that a $1 investment in large-cap stocks at 10 percent a year grows to $2.59 over 10 years, $45.25 in 40 years, and $2,048.40 in 80 years. Alternatively, investing $1 in long-term corporate bonds at 6 percent a year only returns $1.79 in 10 years, $10.29 in 40 years, and $105.78 in 80 years.

TABLE 3.3 Returns and Risk Between 1926 and 2018

This table shows the statistics of various classes of financial assets between 1926 and 2018.

Asset Classification	Geometric Mean Returns (%)	Arithmetic Mean Returns (%)	Standard Deviation of Returns (%)
Large-cap stocks	10.0	11.9	19.8
Long-term corporate bonds	5.9	6.3	8.4
Long-term government bonds	5.5	5.9	9.8
U.S. Treasury bills	3.3	3.4	3.1
Inflation	2.9	3.0	4.0

This example is both interesting and important to investors, especially those with long-term investment horizons. The four-percentage-point yearly difference between stocks and bonds may not initially appear large, but with time the difference increases substantially. Consider also the issue of *Treasury bills*, a short-term debt offered by the U.S. federal government. The long-term return from Treasury bills at only 3.3 percent a year is only slightly higher than the 2.9 percent long-term rate of inflation.

The substantially higher returns available over the long term with stock investments beg an important question: Why do investors hold bonds with lower returns or even Treasury bills with much lower returns? A partial answer may lie in the last column of Table 3.3, which shows the amount of risk quantified as the standard deviation of expected returns for the investment alternatives.

The standard deviations of stock classes are more than twice the standard deviation of bond classes. Note that an easy but often inaccurate way to interpret standard deviation is to consider that it quantifies the amount of a variation from the mean over time. For large stocks, a standard deviation of 19.8 percent suggests that while the average arithmetic return on those stocks was 11.9 percent between 1926 and 2018, that return had a range of returns between −7.9 percent and 31.7 percent, which is a spread of 39.6 percentage points. By comparison, long-term corporate bonds provided an average return of 5.9 percent with a standard deviation of only 8.4 percent over the same period, which equates to a possible range of returns from −2.5 percent to 14.3 percent, or a spread of only 16.8 percentage points, which is about 40 percent of the range of large-company stocks.

Although investors must still bear uncertainty with bond investments, the magnitude of accepted risk is much smaller than that of stock investments. Furthermore, the standard deviation of U.S. Treasury bills is only 3.1 percent, implying that for investors of Treasury bills, returns were much lower, but with an average return of only 3.3 percent, possible losses are low.

A further look into the various classes of equity provides a clear pattern of both returns and risk. The relative performance comparison between large and small companies has attracted interest from both finance scholars and practitioners. For example, Fama and French (1993) find that firm size is a key factor determining stock returns, as small firms outperform large firms in the long-term.

This difference can be explained from a risk perspective. Although large-cap stocks tend to be more stable than smaller stocks, as shown by their relatively lower standard deviation of returns, they also provide lower average returns. At the other end of the spectrum, micro-cap stocks, many of which are risky gambles with the potential for high levels of growth, also have a high potential for failure as evidenced by their long-term arithmetic average returns of 17.7 percent between 1926 and 2018 and their accompanying 38.5 percent standard deviation.

As Figure 3.9 shows, the DJIA, another proxy for the market in general, rose 11.67 percent annually on average between 2009 and 2019. This result suggests that while stock returns vary over time, the market's general long-term trend is up, not down. Although market returns periodically fall, these declines generally occur less frequently and for shorter durations than the rising movements.

In general, as Table 3.3 shows, an important axiom in finance is that an investment's expected return should be commensurate with its risk. The fundamental

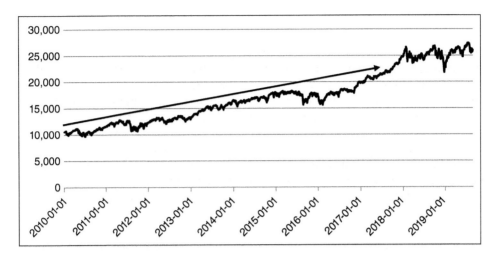

FIGURE 3.9   Recent Annual Returns on the Dow Jones Industrial Average

This figure shows the Dow Jones Industrial Average between 2010 and 2019.

Note: Daily returns between 2010 and 2019 are unadjusted for any seasonal effect and were last updated on August 28, 2019.

Source: S&P Dow Jones Indices LLC (2019b).

reason for this tradeoff is that most investors are risk-averse. The *risk aversion* of investors implies that they prefer less risk and choose the investment with the least risk if returns are comparable across investment options. For risk-averse investors to participate in risky investments, they must be rewarded with higher expected returns.

STOCKS VERSUS BONDS: THE ISSUER'S PERSPECTIVE

Up to this point, the chapter focuses on an equity investment from the investor's perspective. However, examining the implications of choosing stock (equity) financing or debt (bond) financing from a firm's perspective is also important. Stocks and bonds represent two distinct financing choices for firms.

When a firm sells equity to investors, it sells a firm's ownership and control, providing stockholders with ownership or an ownership claim on both the firm's assets and earnings. As owners, common stockholders have a right to some control over the organization as provided via their right to vote on important issues. Shareholders receive residual claims of assets and earnings after other stakeholders are paid.

Alternatively, debt interest and principal payments are legal obligations. If a firm fails to pay periodic interest or principal, it is technically in default of a contractual obligation and faces the possibility of bankruptcy or reorganization, a process in which the firm's ownership may be transferred from shareholders to debtholders by a court order.

SUMMARY AND CONCLUSIONS

To summarize, the financial markets and the economy differ but are closely related. The financial markets provide a place for both investing excess funds as well as obtaining funds to meet funding needs. Well-functioning secondary markets provide investors with information, low-cost trading, and liquidity. Without such markets, an economy would suffer because investors would be much less inclined to invest their money.

Equity investments provide investors with a claim of ownership and a residual claim on assets and cash flows. An efficient equity market enables firms to obtain funds at lower costs than in an inefficient market and to borrow funds at lower costs. Lower costs with fixed-cost debt financing can magnify earnings, thus providing even more economic benefit than possible with variable-cost equity funding.

When an economy is strong, the magnification of earnings can lead to more demand for products and services, which in turn leads to higher employment and, ultimately, greater consumer spending as well as consumer and business investment. Under these conditions, the economy continues to grow. When an economy is weak, leverage, which is a mechanism that magnifies gains in a boom and losses in a recession, can magnify losses through the following chain: demand for products and services falls, employment situations worsen, and both business and consumer investments decline as a result of less consumer spending.

In conclusion, the financial markets and the economy are related. Good economic conditions lead to investment and growth, while weak economies lead to reductions in investment funding and lower growth.

DISCUSSION QUESTIONS

1. Explain at least two ways to classify financial markets.
2. Discuss why the equity market is important to the economy.
3. Define and differentiate between at least two of the equity market indices used as market indicators.
4. Explain the difference between liquidity and marketability for a financial market.
5. Define financial market efficiency.
6. Define and differentiate among the weak form, semi-strong form, and strong form levels of market efficiency.

REFERENCES

Board of Governors of the Federal Reserve System (US), Industrial Production Index [INDPRO]. 2019. Available at https://fred.stlouisfed.org/series/INDPRO.

Busse, Jeffrey A., and Clifton T. Green. 2002. "Market Efficiency in Real Time." *Journal of Financial Economics* 65:3, 415–437.

Diamond, Douglas. 1989. "Reputation Acquisition in Debt Markets." *Journal of Political Economy* 97:4, 828–862.

Duff & Phelps, LLC. 2019. "2019 Cost of Capital: Annual U.S. Guidance and Examples." Chapter 2, Cost of Capital Navigator. Available at www.duffandphelps.com.

Fama, Eugene F., and Kenneth R. French. 1993. "Common Risk Factors in Returns on Stocks and Bonds." *Journal of Financial Economics* 33:1, 3–56.

Givoly, Dan, and Dan Palmon. 1985. "Insider Trading and Exploitation of Inside Information: Some Empirical Evidence." *Journal of Business* 58:1, 69–87.

International Monetary Fund. 2019. "General Government Revenue, Interest Income for United States [USAGGROPI]. Available at https://fred.stlouisfed.org/series/USAGGROPI.

Jaffe, Jeffrey T. 1974. "Special Information and Insider Trading." *Journal of Business* 47:3, 410–428.

Kendall, Maurice. 1953. "The Analysis of Economic Time Series, Part I: Prices." *Journal of the Royal Statistical Society* 116:1, 11–34.

NASDAQ OMX Group. 2019. "NASDAQ Composite Index [NASDAQCOM]." Available at https://fred.stlouisfed.org/series/NASDAQCOM.

Pastor, Lubos, and Robert F. Stambaugh. 2002a. "Liquidity Risk and Expected Stock Returns." *Journal of Political Economy* 111:3, 642–685.

Pastor, Lubos, and Robert F. Stambaugh. 2002b. "Mutual Fund Performance and Seemingly Unrelated Assets." *Journal of Financial Economics* 63:3, 315–349.

Patell, James, and Mark A. Wolfson. 1984. "The Intraday Speed of Adjustment of Stock Prices to Earnings and Dividend Announcements." *Journal of Financial Economics* 13:2, 223–252.

Securities Industry and Financial Markets Association. 2019. Thomson Reuters. Available at www.sifma.org.

Seyhun, H. Nejat. 1986. "Insiders' Profits, Costs of Trading and Market Efficiency." *Journal of Financial Economics* 16:2, 189–212.

S&P Dow Jones Indices LLC. 2019a. "Dow Jones Industrial Average (DJIA)." Available at https://fred.stlouisfed.org/series/DJIA.

S&P Dow Jones Indices LLC. 2019b. "S&P 500 (SP500)." Available at https://fred.stlouisfed.org/series/SP500.

U.S. Bureau of Economic Analysis. 2019a. "Corporate Profits after Tax (without IVA and CCAdj) (CP)." Available at https://fred.stlouisfed.org/series/CP.

U.S. Bureau of Economic Analysis. 2019b. "Personal Consumption Expenditures (PCEC)." Available at https://fred.stlouisfed.org/series/PCEC.

U.S. Bureau of Labor Statistics. 2019. "Civilian Unemployment Rate (UNRATE)." Available at https://fred.stlouisfed.org/series/UNRATE.

World Bank. 2019. "Stock Market Capitalization to GDP for United States (DDDM01USA156 NWDB)." Available at https://fred.stlouisfed.org/series/DDDM01USA156NWDB.

CHAPTER 4

Securities Regulation

Douglas Cumming
DeSantis Distinguished Professor of Finance and Entrepreneurship,
Florida Atlantic University

Sofia Johan
Assistant Professor of Finance, Florida Atlantic University

INTRODUCTION

Securities regulation is a diverse topic that covers many areas, including but not limited to the distribution of new securities (United States Securities Act of 1933), trading of securities, brokers, and exchanges (United States Securities Act of 1933), debt securities (United States Trust Indenture Act of 1939), mutual funds (Investment Company Act of 1940), and investment advisors (Investment Advisers Act of 1940). Given that the book's focus is on equity markets and valuation, this chapter focuses on trading securities on public stock exchanges.

According to Cumming and Johan (2019), some authors have written about the impact of securities regulation without even understanding that the source of regulatory change that they have studied involves exchange-trading rules. Two types of regulatory regimes are available: regulator-led and market-led. Hence, recognizing that trading rule sources are not always the same around the world is important. The source of securities regulations for trading on exchanges varies by country, and the source likewise varies over time. For example, in China, the rules pertaining to the trading of securities are found in the China Securities and Regulatory Commission rules. In the United States, the trading rules are listed on the stock exchange web pages. In Europe before 2004, the rules were likewise made available by the exchange or found on each exchange's web page, but thereafter these rules were harmonized and are now found in a set of pan-European wide directives. Collectively, they are called the *Lamfalussy Directives* – the Market in Financial Instruments Directive (MiFID), the Prospectus Directive, the Market Abuse Directive (MAD), and the Transparency Directive. The Lamfalussy Directives comprise a four-part system, where MAD is Part 3, and MiFID culminates in Part 4 with computer surveillance and enforcement (Cumming and Johan 2019).

This chapter consists of three main sections. The first part explains the meaning of different types of trading rules and the forms of market manipulation that the rules are intended to curtail. The second part reviews evidence on the impact of trading rules and enforcement on trading outcomes. The third part reviews evidence on the impact of trading rules and enforcement on real corporate outcomes.

TRADING RULES AND RULES PERTAINING TO BROKER-DEALER CONDUCT

Securities regulation governs the permitted conduct of brokers and other market participants on stock exchanges. At a broad level, most countries have a general rule that prohibits market misconduct in the form of manipulating share prices. However, what constitutes market manipulation is not always perfectly clear, and, as such, different countries have adopted more specific rules at different points in time. Rule specificity is not a trivial issue since more specific rules may signal to market participants that securities laws enumerate surveillance and enforcement of those prohibitive types of trading (Cumming, Johan, and Li 2011). A blanket rule or a general statement against market misconduct may not have the same effect.

The following explains the different types of trading rules that may be found in different countries around the world. Additionally, some evidence is presented on rule specificity in different countries.

The three main categories of trading rules are rules designed to: (1) mitigate insider trading, (2) lessen market manipulation, and (3) curtail broker-agent conflicts. Each is described, followed by an explanation of how the rules pertain to broker-dealer conduct.

Insider Trading Rules

Insider trading involves market participants who trade on material nonpublic information. The general public is likely more familiar with insider trading cases involving company directors or managers, although insider trading may involve any market participant, such as brokers. Although rules prohibiting insider trading, in general, are commonplace around the world, enforcement is less common.

The specific regulations as to what exactly constitutes insider trading vary across exchanges. Securities regulations may specify exactly what constitutes material nonpublic information, such as whether the information was from a client order, possibly giving rise to a client precedence violation or a front-running violation.

Client Precedence   *Client precedence* refers to brokers violating the time priority of client orders. A client precedence rule is violated during insider trading when a broker initiates a trade on his or her own account shortly before executing a client's order, with the client's trade being executed at a worse price. Brokers, acting either independently or in collusion, carry out violations of client preference, which requires trade execution and a change in beneficial ownership. Violations of client precedence, by definition, violate price/time priority but do not by themselves give rise to a manipulated price or volume.

Front Running *Front running* refers to brokers trading ahead of clients' orders. In the case of front running, upon receipt of a large client order, a broker trades shortly before executing a client's order with the expectation that the client's order is likely to move the price. Front running can also involve brokers that, after receiving a client's order, take the opposite position to the client's order in the market without the client's knowledge and then, immediately thereafter, the same broker crosses with the same client off-market at a profit. Front running is independently initiated by brokers and requires trade execution and a change in beneficial ownership. Front running violates price/time priority. Brokers benefit from front running by trading before executing another trade, but front running itself does not give rise to a misleading price and volume. Lewis (2014) identifies another front run, which shows high-frequency trading (HFT) algorithms using the information of any (nonclient) order and trading in advance of that order by virtue of the speed associated with HFT.

Other Forms of Insider Trading Other forms of insider trading can involve using material nonpublic information about the company being traded. Trading rules can mitigate the presence of this form of insider trading by prohibiting trading ahead of the public release of research reports created by brokerages, and the separation of research and trading departments at brokerages (commonly referred to as a "Chinese wall"). Trading ahead of research reports is independently carried out by brokers and requires trade execution and a change in beneficial ownership. Trading ahead of research reports possibly violates price/time priority. Brokers benefit by trading before the release of material nonpublic information, but trading ahead of research reports by itself does not give rise to a misleading price and volume.

Trading rules may limit affiliation between exchange members and member companies, or between members and their investment company securities, to mitigate the flow of information that might be material and nonpublic. Rules can also provide details with respect to the nature of communication between brokerages and the public by regulating how the flow of material nonpublic information is released. Further, trading rules sometimes limit brokerage ownership, the extent to which brokerages can influence or reward employees of others, or ban anti-intimidation and/or coordination activities (e.g., to stop people from reporting illegal activities). These restrictions can limit the flow of material nonpublic information.

Market Manipulation Rules

Market manipulation rules encompass price manipulation, volume manipulation, spoofing, and disclosure manipulation.

Price Manipulation Rules Price manipulation can be carried out in many different ways and take various forms. One common way is when a client, broker, or colluding brokers enter purchase orders at successively higher prices to create the appearance of active interest in a security, which is also termed *ramping/gouging*. For example, in a pump-and-dump scheme, the manipulator generates a substantial increase in price and volume for a security, carries out a quick flip, and then sells the security often to retail customers at the higher prices. Clients may initiate intraday ramping/gouging, possibly independently or in collusion. Ramping/gouging requires trade execution. Ramping/gouging does not require a change in beneficial ownership or a violation of price/time priority. The manipulator benefits by misleading the stock's price and volume.

Another similar type of price manipulation is *prearranged trading*, which involves colluding parties simultaneously entering orders at an identical price and volume. Prearranged trading generally harms the marketplace because two specific parties benefit from the liquidity event without allowing other market participants to potentially participate in the transaction. Prearranged trades are initiated by brokers, require trade execution, involve a change in beneficial ownership, and violate price/time priority. Prearranged trades benefit all of the colluding brokers and may or may not give rise to misleading prices and volumes.

Price manipulation can be carried out through domination and control, and can take the form of corners or squeezes in cross-market activity. Corners and squeezes involve shortages in one market that can affect the price of a cross-market security. A *corner* involves securing control of the bid or demand side of both the derivative and the underlying asset, and the dominant position can be exploited to manipulate the price of either. A *squeeze* involves taking advantage of a shortage in an asset by controlling the demand side and exploiting market congestion during such shortages in a way that creates artificial prices. Another related form of manipulation includes *mini-manipulations*, whereby trading in the underlying security of an option is carried out in order to manipulate its price so that the options will become in-the-money (Merrick et al. 2005).

Domination and control may be initiated by a client or a company and may be carried out independently or in collusion with others. Domination/control requires a change in beneficial ownership but does not violate price/time priority. The client/company benefits through misleading price and volume. Price manipulation can also be carried out to take advantage of market setting, whereby brokers cross-order at the short-term high or low to affect the volume-weighted average price, or to set the price in one market for a cross in another market.

Clients or brokers may initiate market-setting manipulation, but it requires colluding brokers to carry out market setting. *Market setting* involves a broker crossing a client order to a price to execute the trade at the short-term high or low. Market setting is distinct from prearranged trades because the price level is manipulated before the matching of orders. Market setting can be detected by pattern activity and by observing an effect on the volume-weighted average price of the manipulated security.

Three different forms of price manipulation refer to a specific time period: (1) marking the open with regard to the market's opening, (2) marking the close with regard to the market's closing, and (3) trading to manipulate prices at the end of the month/quarter/year. The opening session can be subject to particular types of manipulation subject to the rules for entering bids and asks in the preopening session. Similarly, end-of-day trades may be geared toward manipulating the security's closing market price, and exchanges often specifically prohibit this type of act. Financial record-keeping among companies provides incentives to manipulate share prices around the end of the month/quarter/year that depends on the governance specific to the company.

Volume Manipulation Rules   Volume manipulation can take two primary forms: churning and wash trading. *Churning* refers to the excessive trading of a stock to inflate its volume, thereby giving rise to the false impression that positive investor sentiment exists for the stock. Churning of client accounts may be carried out by traders and/or brokers to generate commission fees. Churning of principal positions gives the appearance of enhancing volume and may also be used to give the false appearance that a broker has a greater market share.

Churning of both client positions and principal positions is initiated by the broker and requires trade execution. A change in beneficial ownership occurs in churning of client positions and possibly in the case of churning of principal positions. Price/time priority is violated in the case of churning client positions. The broker benefits in the case of churning client positions, and possibly the underlying company also benefits in the case of churning of principal positions. Churning inflates volume and may or may not give rise to misleading prices.

Wash trading, another form of volume manipulation, means having the same client reference on both sides of a trade. Although no beneficial change occurs in ownership, wash trades have the effect of creating a misleading appearance of an active interest in a stock. With the appearance of a higher volume, wash trading allows brokers to take their clients out of a position at a potentially higher price.

Brokers initiate wash trades either in collusion or independently. Wash trades require client execution. No change in beneficial ownership occurs with wash trades, and wash trades do not violate price/time priority. Wash trades inflate volume to the benefit of the trading parties. Wash trades may also mislead price.

Spoofing Manipulation Rules   *Spoofing*, also known as *painting the tape*, is a form of market manipulation that involves actions taken by market participants to give an improper or false impression of unusual activity or price movement in a security. Some exchange-trading rules have general statements of prohibition toward actions that give rise to a false appearance. Other exchanges more explicitly indicate ways of creating a false appearance, including entering fictitious orders, giving up priority, having switches, and layering of bid/asks.

- *Entering fictitious orders* involves entering orders on one side of the market, then completing orders on the other side of the market and deleting the original order after the trade occurs.
- *Giving up priority* refers to deleting orders on one side of the market as they approach priority and then entering the order again on the same side of the market. Giving up priority may be initiated by brokers or clients, and independently without collusion. Giving up priority does not result in trade execution or a change in beneficial ownership, but may violate price/time priority. Giving up priority benefits the broker and/or client through misleading the order book and therefore misleading both price and volume.
- *Having switches*. Switches involve both sides of the market, unlike giving up priority, which is on one side of the market. *Switches* involve deleting orders on one side of the market as they approach priority and then entering the order again on the opposite side of the market. These distinctions are somewhat subtle but some exchange-trading rules explain these different scenarios in detail. Similar to giving up priority, switches are initiated by brokers or clients independently.

Switches do not require trade execution. No change in beneficial ownership occurs, but a violation of price/time priority may take place. The broker and/or client benefits by misleading price and volume due to misleading the order book.

■ *Layering of bid/asks. Layering of bid/asks* refers to traders or brokers who stagger orders from the same client reference at different price and volume levels to give the misleading impression of greater interest in the security from a more diverse set of exchange participants. This act might be viewed as being carried out for manipulation. Layering of bid/asks is initiated by a broker or client and can be done independently without colluding with others. It does require trade execution and a change in beneficial ownership, and possibly violates price/time priority. Brokers/clients benefit by misleading price, but not volume.

False Disclosure Rules

False disclosure rules are distinct from insider trading rules and may or may not be specifically enumerated in securities laws and/or within an exchange's rule book. For instance, market participants might actively distribute false or misleading information that has the effect of distorting the marketplace. False disclosure can be carried out by a broker or client independently and does not require trade execution or a change in beneficial ownership. It does not violate price/time priority but does mislead price and volume.

Parking or *warehousing* refers to the failure to disclose information, such as the mandatory disclosure of ownership interests above a certain threshold level, which is typically set at 5 percent in many countries around the world, by having third parties controlled by an individual or associates trading in their names. Clients initiate parking/warehousing, but it may be done in collusion with a broker. Parking/warehousing requires trade execution but it does not require a change in beneficial ownership or violate price/time priority. Clients benefit from parking/warehousing, but it does not directly affect price or volume.

Overall, this section refers to trading rules on price manipulation, volume manipulation, spoofing, and false disclosure as the market manipulation rules. Cumming, Johan, and Li (2011) aggregate these rules to form separate indices for each, which they call subcomponent indices. They then combine them in their sum total to form the Market Manipulation Rules Index. These indices are considered separately from insider trading rules and broker-agency conflict rules, which form the other two primary indices.

Broker-Agency Conflict Rules

Brokers act on behalf of clients but can do so in ways that are against client interests. This type of principal-agent problem may arise from a broker's failure to obtain the best price for a client, which is commonly known as a *breach of a trade through obligation*; brokers may favor trades with affiliated brokers, the broker charging excessive fees (improper execution at unreasonable costs) or acting in ways that are generally detrimental to client interests such as by investing in securities that do not match the client's risk/return profile, which is referred to as breach of the *know-your-client rule.* Trade-throughs are initiated by colluding brokers, where trades involve a beneficial change in ownership and a violation of price/time priority. The broker benefits, but no direct adverse price of volume impact takes place. Improper execution is initiated by independent brokers, not necessarily colluding, where trades involve a beneficial change in ownership but without necessarily violating price/time priority. Here, the broker benefits, but no direct adverse price or volume impact occurs. Brokers might also use the exchange's name improperly in marketing their services or carry out other forms of improper or unethical sales and marketing efforts. For broker-agency conflict rules, Cumming et al. (2011) use information explicitly indicated in the rules of the exchange, and not guidelines from professional associations such as the Chartered Financial Analysts' ethics guidelines and the like.

Cumming et al. (2011) summarize all the different types of manipulation described in stock exchange trading rules. The trading rules for a stock exchange are drafted with varying degrees of specificity as they outline the exchange membership requirements, listing requirements, trading rules and regulations, and especially prohibited trading practices.

Each of the different rules for insider trading, market manipulation, and broker-agency conflict described in the exchanges' trading rules are weighted equally in the indices reported in Cumming et al. (2011). The Insider Trading Rules Index comprises 10 items. The Market Manipulation Rules Index encompasses a total of 14 items, which include price manipulation (seven items), volume manipulation (two items), spoofing (three items), and false disclosure (two items). The Broker-Agency Conflict Rules Index comprises five items. The indices in Cumming et al. summarize the degree of regulation in a country before and after the changes brought about in Europe with the Lamfalussy Directives, which encompass both MAD and MiFID.

Cumming et al. (2011) find evidence consistent with the view that more detailed trading rules are associated with greater market liquidity, in the spirit of early work ranking the quality of exchanges around the world (Aitken and Siow 2003). Cumming et al. use an international sample of countries, including some but not all in Europe, and use the pan-European wide regulatory change as a natural experiment to study the effect of a securities regulatory change on liquidity. They find strong evidence of a positive impact of the market abuse rules enumerated earlier.

Christensen, Hail, and Leuz (2016) study the same regulatory change as in Cumming et al. (2011), even though email correspondence with Cumming et al. shows that Christensen et al. did not realize that the regulatory change they examined involved changes in trading rules. Cumming and Johan (2019) document their lack of understanding about the regulatory change, among other things. Christensen et al. use a set of European-only countries, and likewise show a positive effect of the regulatory change on market liquidity. They also use slightly different dates than Cumming and Johan in their contribution to the literature.

Similar to work showing that trading rules improve liquidity, other research is likewise consistent with the view that stronger trading rules, surveillance, and enforcement affect the trading location of cross-listed stocks (Cumming, Hou, and Wu 2018) and curtail suspected insider trading activity (Aitken, Cumming, and Zhan 2015a) and end-of-day manipulation (Aitken, Cumming, and Zhan 2015b, 2017).

SURVEILLANCE

A necessary first step toward enforcement of securities laws is surveillance (Domowitz 2012). Put differently, without surveillance, no enforcement of trading rules occurs. *Surveillance* refers to automated computer algorithms that are used to detect manipulative trading patterns identified earlier. Surveillance algorithms send messages called "alerts" to staff that work at securities commissions or the authority that governs the particular stock exchange. The alerts are in real time, meaning that market abuse is detected immediately. With one-time behavior, a manipulation might lead a surveillance authority to call the trader(s) involved for an explanation. Normally traders have an "alternative plausible explanation" (APE) to explain why they executed the trades in question. However, with repeated pattern behavior, the surveillance authority can more easily prove misconduct and pursue a legal remedy.

Computer software providers, such as SMARTS Group, Inc., had provided software to over 50 exchanges around the world before being acquired by NASDAQ in 2010. Such software customizes its system to manage the type of alerts provided to surveillance staff. Such customization is necessary as each exchange or securities commission around the world differs in scope and requirements for surveillance. The set of alerts in conjunction with manipulative practices depicted in Cumming et al. (2011) is comprehensive for most surveillance systems. These alerts apply to both single-market manipulations and cross-market manipulations. *Cross-market surveillance* refers to surveillance across different products, such as equity and a related option on the same underlying equity, and across markets or different exchanges or different countries. Cross-market surveillance is much more technical to perform and execute in terms of computing power.

Moreover, cross-market surveillance requires information-sharing agreements across exchanges. Cumming and Johan (2008) present evidence from 25 markets around the world, showing that many exchanges in Europe did not have effective market surveillance at the time of the national implementation of MAD. However, such surveillance was in place around the time of MiFID. As such, Cumming and Johan (2019) are highly critical of derivative work (Christensen et al. 2016) that replicates earlier studies of the impact of market trading rules on market liquidity (Cumming et al. 2011) using MAD adoption dates and not MiFID adoption dates.

The effectiveness of the surveillance systems in different jurisdictions around the world depends on various factors (Cumming and Johan 2008).

- Alerts should minimize false positives and maximize true positive manipulative practices. To be able to do this, the surveillance system needs to ascertain normal trading activity to set the abnormal alert parameters. For example, normal price and volume measures need to be set for typical trading ranges for a particular exchange-traded product.
- A surveillance department should be able to reconstruct all trading activity to replay the full order/quote schedule. Market surveillance should also identify the activity of each market participant.
- The surveillance staff should be versed on the issues that need to be investigated. A surveillance system's quality depends on the quality of the software used and the degree to which the surveillance staff are educated and trained on using the information provided in the alerts.

- The effectiveness of a surveillance system also depends on the degree to which market participants are informed about the surveillance activities.
- For cross-market surveillance, surveillance effectiveness depends to a large degree on the extent to which information is shared across jurisdictions.
- The efficiency of the surveillance system depends on the regulatory framework. In many jurisdictions around the world, the exchanges themselves are self-regulatory organizations (SROs) that establish their own listing standards and monitor and discipline market participants for violation of their rules of operation. In other jurisdictions, the securities commission has a greater role in setting listing standards and trading rules.

ENFORCEMENT

Cumming, Groh, and Johan (2018) examine enforcement cases that involve detected market abuse, not actual (unobserved) fraud or suspected market abuse. They present data that suggest massive differences in enforcement despite similar rules across European countries. They also show that the data are consistent with the view that countries with more capital market activity are more likely to detect market abuse. Similarly, the data highlight that the legal quality in a country, with respect to the protection of shareholders and lenders, mitigates infringement activity. Also, the data suggest that enforcement authorities are more vigorous in detecting and reporting fraud when minimum pecuniary fines are higher.

Cumming et al. (2018) offer several policy implications based on their analyses. Legal enforcement of market abuse comes in three primary forms: (1) direct expenditures on enforcement officers, (2) quality of surveillance through information sharing and cooperation, and (3) rules pertaining to deterrence. Their data show that each of these three mechanisms is extremely important for detecting and deterring fraud. Expenditures on enforcement officers, surveillance, and enforcement rules are effective mechanisms to fight fraud in financial markets and to increase investor confidence in the existence of sound capital markets.

IMPACT OF TRADING RULES AND SURVEILLANCE ON CORPORATE OUTCOMES

Market manipulation rules, surveillance, and enforcement can have implications that extend beyond market efficiency outcomes, such as liquidity. This section provides a brief discussion of two examples of the effect of trading manipulation on corporate outcomes: mergers and acquisitions (M&As) and innovation.

Market Manipulation and M&As

Cumming, Ji, Johan, and Tarsalewska (2019) consider the possibility that stocks are manipulated before M&As to influence the likelihood of, and the terms of, an M&A transaction. End-of-day (EOD) prices, for example, can influence the price at which acquisition occurs. Cumming et al. (2019) examine M&As from over 45 countries between 2003 and 2014 and show that the presence of EOD target price manipulation before M&As increases the probability of an M&A deal withdrawal, and decreases the premium paid. More detailed exchange-trading rules that govern manipulation across countries and over time lower the probability of withdrawal mitigate the negative impact of EOD manipulation on withdrawal and raise premiums paid. Finally, they show that although fewer cases of acquirer price manipulations occur before M&As, acquirer price manipulation in share M&As also increases the probability of deal withdrawal.

Market Manipulation and Innovation

Cumming, Ji, Peter, and Tarsalewska (2018) examine EOD price manipulation in relation to patent activity. They contend that EOD manipulation gives rise to short-termism in managerial planning, which is inconsistent with long-term value maximization. Moreover, EOD manipulation causes long-term harm to a firm's equity values, and thereby reduces incentives for employees to innovate. Insider trading, by contrast, enables innovators to achieve exacerbated profits from innovation by insider trading on the knowledge of an impending patent not yet publicly announced. Using a sample of suspected manipulation events based on intraday data for all stocks from nine countries over eight years, Cumming et al. (2018) find evidence consistent with these real impacts of market manipulation on innovation, particularly regarding EOD manipulation. They explain that their findings are not attributable to "bad" firms innovating less and manipulating more, since the average firm subjected to manipulation in the sample is more innovative during the premanipulation period. Trading rules that curtail EOD manipulation, therefore, have an additional benefit of ensuring more innovative firms in the marketplace.

SUMMARY AND CONCLUSIONS

This chapter focused on one type of securities regulation that is pertinent to equity markets and valuation: trading rules. It explained that the different types of trading rules are designed to curtail a wide array of different types of market abuse. It further explained that trading rules do not operate in isolation. Without computerized surveillance and not merely single-market surveillance but more importantly cross-product and cross-market surveillance, trading rules are unenforceable and, therefore, meaningless. Finally, the chapter showed that despite similarities in trading rules across some countries, large differences exist in actual enforcement that is attributable to differences in expenditures on enforcement and information sharing across exchanges.

Securities regulation clearly improves measures of market efficiency, such as liquidity. Securities regulation likewise improves other corporate outcomes such as M&As and innovation. Further work on the causes and consequences of different types of securities regulation and different types of outcomes would help guide academics, practitioners, and regulators alike.

DISCUSSION QUESTIONS

1. Explain the nature and function of trading rules on stock exchanges.
2. Differentiate between trading rules and surveillance.
3. Identify the criticisms and benefits of securities regulation.
4. Discuss how trading rules differ across countries.
5. Discuss how trading rules and surveillance affect firm outcomes such as M&As and innovation.

REFERENCES

Aitken, Michael, Douglas J. Cumming, and Feng Zhan. 2015a. "Exchange Trading Rules, Surveillance, and Suspected Insider Trading." *Journal of Corporate Finance* 34:C, 311–330.

Aitken, Michael, Douglas J. Cumming, and Feng Zhan. 2015b. "High Frequency Trading and End-of-Day Price Dislocation." *Journal of Banking and Finance* 59:C, 330–349.

Aitken, Michael, Douglas J. Cumming, and Feng Zhan. 2017. "Trade Size, High-Frequency Trading, and Colocation around the World." *The European Journal of Finance* 23:7–9, 781–801.

Aitken, Michael, and Audris Siow. 2003. "Ranking Equity Markets on the Basis of Market Efficiency and Integrity." In *Hewlett-Packard Handbook of World Stock, Derivative & Commodity Exchanges*, edited by Herbie Skeete, pp. xlix–lv. London: Mondo Visione Ltd.

Christensen, Hans B., Luzi Hail, and Christian Leuz. 2016. "Capital-Market Effects of Securities Regulation: Prior Conditions, Implementation, and Enforcement." *Review of Financial Studies* 29:11, 2885–2924.

Cumming, Douglas J, Alexander Groh, and Sofia A. Johan. 2018. "Same Rules, Different Enforcement: Market Abuse in Europe." *Journal of International Financial Markets Institutions & Money* 54:1, 130–151.

Cumming, Douglas J., Wenxuan Hou, and Eliza Wu. 2018. "Exchange Trading Rules, Governance, and the Trading Location of Cross-Listed Stocks." *European Journal of Finance* 24:16, 1453–1484.

Cumming, Douglas J., Shan Ji, Sofia A. Johan, and Monika Tarsalewska. 2019. "End-of-Day Price Manipulation and M&As." *British Journal of Management*, forthcoming.

Cumming, Douglas J., Shan Ji, Rejo Peter, and Monika Tarsalewska. 2018. "Market Manipulation and Innovation."

Cumming, Douglas J., and Sofia A. Johan. 2008. "Global Market Surveillance." *American Law and Economics Review* 10:2, 454–506.

Cumming, Douglas J., and Sofia A. Johan. 2019. "Capital-Market Effects of Securities Regulation: Prior Conditions, Implementation, and Enforcement Revisited." *Finance Research Letters*, forthcoming.

Cumming, Douglas J., Sofia A. Johan, and Dan Li. 2011. "Exchange Trading Rules and Stock Market Liquidity." *Journal of Financial Economics* 99:3, 651–671.

Domowitz, Ian. 2012. *Market Abuse and Surveillance.* London: Foresight, Government Office for Science. Available at https://www.gov.uk/government/uploads/system/uploads/attachment_data/file/289053/12-1076-eia17-market-abuse-and-surveillance.pdf/.

Lewis, Michael. 2014. *Flash Boys.* New York, NY: W. W. Norton & Company.

Merrick, John J., Narayan Y. Naik, and Pradeep K. Yadav. 2005. "Strategic Trading Behavior and Price Distortion in a Manipulated Market: Anatomy of a Squeeze." *Journal of Financial Economics* 77:1, 171–218.

CHAPTER 5

Investor Psychology and Equity Market Anomalies

Hunter M. Holzhauer
Robert L. Maclellan and UC Foundation Associate Professor of Finance,
University of Tennessee Chattanooga

INTRODUCTION

Richard Thaler, a founding father of behavioral finance, notes: "You assume that the agents in the economy are as smart as you are, and I assume that they are as dumb as me" (Harford 2019, p. 1). Thaler directed his comment to traditionalist Robert Barro during a National Bureau of Economic Research (NBER) conference. The quote perfectly contrasts the irrationality of investor decision-making explored in behavioral finance with the more rational framework of traditional finance models. However, behavioral finance is often and wrongly viewed as a direct competitor to traditional established theories like expected utility theory (EUT) (Bernoulli 1738; Neumann and Morgenstern 1944), modern portfolio theory (MPT) (Markowitz 1952), and the efficient market hypothesis (EMH) (Fama 1970, 1991). The most logical but false reason that many view behavioral finance as the polar opposite of traditional finance is that these well-established traditional theories assume that investors are always rational. Thus, many books erroneously claim that behavioral finance assumes that investors are always irrational. This assumption is simply not valid. Instead, behavioral finance assumes that investors are human but not always rational. This clarification is important because behavioral finance is not necessarily a substitute for traditional finance, but a complement. The two approaches are not mutually exclusive.

Instead, behavioral finance merely attempts to explain what traditional finance theories do not explain. In some cases, investors incorporate behavioral finance concepts into investment strategies that mostly disagree with traditional finance. However, the most basic tenets of behavioral finance aim to build on the existing foundation built by traditional finance. In other words, if traditional finance reveals most of the rational pieces of the market puzzle, behavioral finance attempts to reveal the final irrational missing pieces. Thus, any discussion on behavioral finance should begin with the understanding that most research in behavioral finance assumes that the market can be partially efficient, that investors can be partially rational, and that traditional finance theories do a remarkably accurate job of explaining a substantial portion of market behavior. In short, the bulk of behavioral finance explains why traditional finance theories do not always get market behavior right.

Having provided a brief synopsis on the relation between behavioral finance and traditional finance, the next two sections of this chapter focus primarily on investor psychology. More specifically, the following sections use two foundational concepts of behavioral finance – bounded rationality and prospect theory – as frameworks to provide reasons investors may not always be rational. The final section uses equity market anomalies as evidence for a detailed discussion on the limits of efficient markets. The chapter concludes by explaining why behavioral finance plays an important role in investor psychology and choice behavior.

INVESTOR PSYCHOLOGY: BOUNDED RATIONALITY

Much debate surrounds whether investors are rational. One concept that provides a logical framework for examining investor rationality is bounded rationality. *Bounded rationality* states that investor behavior may lead to mispriced stocks because investors are limited by the information they have, their cognitive abilities, and the time they have to make a decision (Simon 1978).

Information Limitations

Investors may have incomplete or inaccurate information. This ignorance gap can decrease the tractability of an investor's decision problem. For example, Baker and Nofsinger (2010) and Nofsinger (2018) discuss various biases that might create information limitations, including contamination bias, confirmation bias, omission bias, selection bias, sample size bias, and even time period–specific biases.

Cognitive Limitations

Even if the information is correct, investors may have cognitive limitations. Baker and Nofsinger (2010) and Nofsinger (2018) include different biases that indicate cognitive limitations, including framing, hindsight bias, memory recall issues, and cognitive dissonance. Other cognitive issues such as overconfidence can lead to scapegoating, the winner's curse, and the hot-hand illusion. Humans are also imperfect calculators. For example, they repeatedly make mistakes when calculating probabilities for two-stage problems, as highlighted by issues such as the isolation effect, the conjunction fallacy, and the gambler's fallacy.

Time Limitations

Even if the information is correct and processed correctly, investors may still behave irrationally, especially given a time constraint. Bounded rationality implies that investors have limited attention and use *heuristics* or mental shortcuts, which may lead to suboptimal-choice behavior. Baker and Nofsinger (2010) and Nofsinger (2018) discuss some of the more well-known heuristics, including affect, representativeness, availability, familiarity, ambiguity aversion, mental accounting, and anchoring and adjusting. Time limitations also create various inertia biases such as conservatism, normalcy bias, the ostrich effect, regret aversion, and the endowment effect. An example of an inertia bias is *status-quo bias,* which is a preference for the current state of affairs. This bias is important, especially in terms of retirement and health insurance planning, because it shows a tendency for individuals to stick with the default choice. Thus, authors such as Thaler and Sunstein (2009) recommend improving retirement planning by making automatic enrollment the default choice for pension plans and 401(k) plans rather than voluntary enrollment. Finally, all of these previously mentioned investor limitations, biases, and heuristics are relevant to investor psychology and merit additional discussion. However, for the sake of brevity, the following subsection uses prospect theory as a logical framework to focus on a few key issues that are extremely pertinent for investor psychology.

INVESTOR PSYCHOLOGY: PROSPECT THEORY

The basis of most traditional economic and financial models, such as the previously mentioned EUT, MPT, and EMH, is the assumption, or at least the implication, that investors are rational and, given choices, seek to maximize their utility. According to Kahneman and Tversky (1979, 1984), this primary assumption is flawed. Hence, they propose an alternative model called *prospect theory* (PT). PT assumes that investors value potential losses and gains differently, and maintains that investors' choices should be viewed more as a function of subjective decision weights than objective mathematical probabilities.

When Kahneman and Tversky (1979, 1984), introduced PT, it changed the way many investors and academics thought about choice behavior. First, academics often consider the PT approach more rigorous than its predecessor, namely, Simon's (1978) bounded rationality approach. Moreover, PT has stood the test of time and even paved the way for newer behavioral finance theories. Two notable theories include *behavioral capital asset pricing theory* (Shefrin and Statman 1994) and *behavioral portfolio theory* (Shefrin and Statman 2000). Behavioral capital asset pricing theory focuses primarily on the interaction between noise traders who commit cognitive errors and information traders who are free of cognitive errors. Behavioral portfolio theory suggests that a wide range of goals motivates investors, and these goals are not limited to simply maximizing the value of their portfolios. With respect to these newer theories and a growing stream of research in behavioral finance, PT remains the conventional wisdom for how to approach choice behavior. Thus, the final part of this section discusses PT and a few of its main contributions.

Reference Wealth

From a return perspective, a fundamental principle behind PT is that investors do not make decisions based on their potential gain or loss from a prospect (i.e., gamble), but rather on how their wealth may change compared to their *reference wealth.* In other words, PT assumes that choice decisions are based on a subjectively determined benchmark or reference wealth. However, EUT has no reference point. EUT assumes choices are independent of a reference wealth. In PT, the changes in wealth and not the level of end wealth matter. For example, given the same $1 million investment opportunity, a billionaire and a millionaire may behave differently because gaining or losing $1 million is unlikely to affect the billionaire's reference wealth as dramatically as it would the smaller reference wealth for the millionaire. Assume they both chose the investment but at different times. The millionaire goes first and doubles his wealth to $2 million. The billionaire goes second but loses $1 million. The millionaire is happier due to having a greater increase in utility than the billionaire, given this outcome. However, the billionaire is still better off financially. Thus, PT states that the change in wealth is more important for choice behavior than the final total amount of wealth. PT does not dispute that using end wealth is more rational, but rather, PT maintains that investors are not always rational, are often more short-term focused, and typically behave in terms of deviations from a reference point.

Risk versus Certainty

From a risk perspective, much of PT is based on the concept of *risk aversion*, which is the tendency to reduce or avoid uncertainty. Most investors are risk-averse, which means that they would rather avoid a loss than receive an equivalent gain. Risk aversion also helps explain the *certainty effect*, which states that investors often overweigh probable outcomes, especially small to medium probabilities of winning. Allais (1953) first notes the certainty effect when he coined the *Allais paradox*, which explains that investors' actual observed choices can violate the predictions of EUT. To illustrate both the certainty effect and the Allais paradox, assume an investor has to choose between a 100 percent chance of winning $25,000 or a 50 percent chance of winning $50,000. Although the expected payouts of these two gambles are equal, the certainty effect says a higher percentage of investors would choose the 100 percent or certain payout of $25,000.

Moreover, considering most investors are risk-averse, they would probably take even less than $25,000, such as $20,000, to avoid the risk involved in the 50 percent chance of winning $50,000. In this case, the utility of a certain payoff is higher for the investor than the uncertain payoff with a higher expected monetary value. However, if a certain payoff of $20,000 became an uncertain payoff (e.g., an 80 percent chance of winning $25,000), investors may now choose the 50 percent chance of winning $50,000 because neither choice provides the higher utility associated with certainty.

Other Effects of Prospect Theory

As further evidence of the subjective nature of investors, Kahneman and Tversky (1979, 1984) discuss two other pervasive effects that violate traditional theories like EUT: the reflection effect and the disposition effect. PT is largely based on the *reflection effect*, which explains that investors may have different preferences for gambles depending on the sign of the outcome (i.e., whether the outcome is a loss or a gain). In other words, investors are more likely to be risk-averse when they have something to gain and more likely to be risk-seeking when they have something to lose. The reflection effect may help explain the disposition effect. Two golden rules of investing from the well-known seventeenth-century economist David Ricardo are to cut short your losses and let your profits run (Zweig 2017). The opposite is the *disposition effect*, which is the tendency for investors to cut short their profits and to let their losses run (Shefrin and Statman 1985). Kahneman and Tversky (1979) explain the disposition effect in terms of risk aversion in that investors dislike losing much more than they enjoy winning. In other words, investors tend to sell assets that have increased in value because they do not want to experience the chance of the asset losing value. Likewise, they tend to hold on to assets that have dropped in value too long because they do not want to realize the loss. In short, PT presents many issues of why investors may be irrational. The next section looks at specific violations of the EMH.

EQUITY MARKET ANOMALIES: VIOLATIONS OF THE EMH

One of the more important concepts in finance is the *efficient market hypothesis* (EMH), which implies that stock prices fairly and accurately reflect all information available to investors (Fama 1970, 1991). The EMH has a heralded history of academic support (Kendall and Hill 1953; Cootner 1964; Fama 1965; and Malkiel 1973). Malkiel (1973, 2003), in particular, contends that stock prices evolve according to a *random walk*, which means price changes are random and cannot be predicted. Malkiel went as far as to say that "a blindfolded chimpanzee throwing darts at the *Wall Street Journal* could select a portfolio that would do as well as the experts." That said, not everyone agrees. A growing list of EMH critics exists, such as Lo (1999), Lo and MacKinlay (2002), and Bhargave (2014), who present evidence of nonrandom trends in the stock market that suggest the stock market is somewhat predictable. One area of behavior finance in particular – equity market anomalies – provides abundant evidence that markets are not entirely efficient. Thus, the following section describes the limits of the EMH with a particular focus on market anomalies and how they violate the different forms of the EMH.

Fama (1970) proposes three forms or different views of the EMH: weak form, semi-strong form, and strong form.

1. The *weak form EMH* asserts that the market has already incorporated all past trading (market) information such as price and volume into current stock prices. It also implies that investors cannot consistently outperform the market using *technical analysis*, which charts statistical trends in past trading behavior and forms trading strategies based on recurrent and predictable patterns in stock prices and volume levels.

2. The *semi-strong form EMH* asserts that the market has not only priced in all past trading (market) information but has also incorporated all publicly available information. The added implication with the semi-strong EMH is that investors cannot consistently outperform the market using *fundamental analysis*, which analyzes all publicly available information, including financial statements, to measure a firm's intrinsic value based on relevant qualitative and quantitative factors.

3. The *strong form EMH* asserts that the market has already incorporated all relevant information, including not only past and public information but also private information. Thus, the strong form implies that investors cannot consistently outperform the market even through *insider trading*, which is the usually illegal practice of trading a firm's stock based on access to private or material nonpublic information about the firm.

TABLE 5.1 Usefulness of Market Information for Different Views of Market Efficiency

Different Views of the Efficient Market Hypothesis (EMH)	Usefulness of Different Sources of Market Information and Analysis		
	Past Information and Technical Analysis	Public Information and Fundamental Analysis	Private Information and Insider Trading
Not efficient	Yes	Yes	Yes
Weak form EMH	No	Yes	Yes
Semi-strong form EMH	No	No	Yes
Strong form EMH	No	No	No

This table breaks down the usefulness of different sources of market information and analysis based on increasing views of market efficiency. "Yes" means that this information and analysis may be useful because the market has not fully priced this information into stock prices. "No" means that this information and analysis is not useful because the market has already fully priced this information into stock prices.

Table 5.1 lists these different views of the EMH and which types of market information or analysis might be helpful to investors based on these respective views. In Table 5.1, "Yes" indicates that the market may not respond to this information in an accurate or timely manner and investors may be able to use the information or analysis to outperform the market consistently. Conversely, "No" indicates that the market has already incorporated this information into current security prices and investors are unable to use the information to outperform the market consistently. For example, look at the two extreme views. Table 5.1 shows that no market information or analysis is useful for outperforming the market in the strong form of EMH because the market has already priced this information into stock prices. However, if the market is inefficient, then technical analysis, fundamental analysis, and insider trading may all be useful because the market has not fully priced past, public, or private information into stock prices.

Violations of the Weak Form EMH

Having reviewed the different forms of the EMH, violations of each form are explored next. The weak form EMH involves several important violations: the momentum effect, the reversal effect, and calendar-related anomalies. The latter violation is a broad category of anomalies that focuses on different time periods associated with recurring patterns in stock prices. However, this section starts with a discussion of the first two violations, which are often incorporated into technical analysis and are essentially two different types of *serial correlation*.

Serial Correlation *Serial correlation*, sometimes called *autocorrelation*, is the relation or correlation between a variable and its lagged version at different time intervals. According to Bodie, Kane, and Marcus (2013), a serial correlation for stock market returns is the tendency for current stock market returns to be related to past stock market returns.

The two types are a *positive serial correlation,* as seen with the *momentum effect,* and a *negative serial correlation,* as seen with the *reversal effect.* Positive serial correlation implies a direct relation, meaning that positive stock returns tend to follow positive stock returns. For example, the *momentum effect* is the tendency for a stock's recent performance, good or bad, to continue in that same direction in the following period. Conversely, negative serial correlation implies an inverse relation, meaning that positive stock returns tend to follow negative stock returns. For example, the *reversal effect* is the tendency for a stock's recent performance, good or bad, to reverse or correct itself in the following period.

An important deviator between these two effects is time horizons. Research attributes the momentum effect to returns over short-term horizons and the reversal effect to returns over long-term horizons (DeBondt and Thaler 1985). For example, Jegadeesh and Titman (1993) investigate abnormal stock returns over 3- to 12-month holding periods and find evidence of both short- and intermediate-horizon price momentum. As for the long-term horizon, the authors rank-order stock returns over five years and compare their "loser" portfolio of the bottom 35 stocks with their "winner" portfolio of the 35 top stocks. They find significant negative autocorrelation as the loser portfolio outperformed the winner portfolio by an average of 25 percent cumulative return in the following three-year period. One behavioral explanation for both of these effects is that short-term momentum is often the result of temporary overreactions by investors, which may lead to a long-term reversal as investors over time recognize and correct past pricing mistakes.

Short-Term Calendar-Related Anomalies   The final weak form EMH violation is calendar-related anomalies. Several short-term anomalies include weather patterns (Saunders 1993; Hirshleifer 2001; Hirshleifer and Shumway 2003), seasonality patterns (Kamstra, Kramer, and Levi 2003; Garrett, Kamstra, and Kramer 2004), daylight savings patterns (Kamstra, Kramer, and Levi 2000; Singal 2004), and holiday effects (Zweig 1986; Lakonishok and Smidt 1988; Ariel 1990). Academics have even examined the investment adage *sell in May and go away,* also known as the *Halloween effect,* which instructs investors to sell on the first trading day in May and buy on the sixth trading day before the end of October (Gultekin and Gultekin 1983; Keim and Ziemba 2000; Bouman and Jacobsen 2002; Doeswijk 2005). Dzhabarov and Ziemba (2011) provide evidence that using a sell-in-May-and-go-away strategy can offer superior returns compared to a standard buy-and-hold strategy. Interestingly, the reasons for this abnormal performance, and abnormal performance in most other calendar-related patterns, tend to focus on time period–specific differences in trading volume, investor mood, and market uncertainty.

Another example of a calendar-related anomaly that fits into this category is the *weekend effect* or *day-of-the-week effect.* This anomaly refers to the tendency of stock prices to decrease on Mondays and increase the most on Wednesdays and Fridays. Another, more substantiated, calendar-related anomaly is the *turn-of-the-month effect,* which is based on the tendency of stock prices to rise on the last trading day of the month and the first three trading days of the next month. The main explanation for this anomaly is that these four days represent the vast majority of monthly and quarterly announcements by firms and government reporting agencies. These four days also likely capture the bulk of trading activity regarding required portfolio rebalancing. Finally, perhaps the most significant and most substantiated calendar-related anomaly is the *turn-of-the-year effect*, which describes a pattern of increased trading volume and higher stock prices in the last week of December and the first two weeks of January.

Small-Firm-in-January Effect   Some academics attribute the bulk of the turn-of-the-year effect to the *small-firm-in-January effect*. In other words, after breaking down the turn-of-the-year effect into different asset classes and time periods, one asset class and time period stands out in terms of abnormal returns – small-firm stocks in the first two to three weeks of January. The *January effect* is one of the most well-known anomalies, and certainly the most researched calendar-related anomaly, in financial markets. It is characterized by a seasonal increase in stock prices, especially for small firms, during January, with the bulk of the rally occurring primarily in the first two weeks of the month. Wachtel (1942) first documented the January effect with Banz (1981), adding the *small-firm effect*, which states that stocks of small firms earned abnormal risk-adjusted returns. As evidence, Bodie et al. (2013) stratify all New York Stock Exchange (NYSE) firms into 10 portfolios according to their size. They show that NYSE firms in the smallest-size decile outperformed the NYSE firms in the largest-size decile by 8.8 percent, on average, annually between 1926 and 2010. Later research by Reinganum (1983), Blume and Stambaugh (1983), and Keim (1993) provides conclusive data that the small-firm effect is restricted almost entirely to January. Both the January and small-firm effects are often combined and labeled as the small-firm-in-January effect.

Several important and potential explanations are available for the January effect. Some investors believe the January effect is a product of year-end bonuses, which allow investors to put large volumes of cash into the market. January is also a great time of the year from an investor psychology perspective to start new investment programs or to begin new investment-related New Year's resolutions. Another reason for the January effect could be "window dressing," which entails portfolio managers selling lesser-known and underperforming small firms at the end of each year so that these firms do not appear on year-end reports. In other words, from an optics perspective, portfolio managers may prefer for their year-end statements to list larger and overperforming firms that their clients might recognize and consider as safer and more prudent investments. Although these rationales have some merit, most analysts and academics focus on taxes as the main reason for the January effect. They contend that many investors embrace tax-loss harvesting in December to offset any realized capital gains for the year.

Long-Term Calendar-Related Anomalies   Finally, some investors may look for time-related patterns that stretch beyond the calendar year such as political effects or anomalies including the *presidential premium*, which suggests that the average stock market returns are significantly higher under Democratic presidential administrations compared to Republican presidential administrations (Santa-Clara and Valkanov 2003). However, investors should be careful using the presidential premium as an investment guide because several statistical issues need to be addressed. For example, Campbell and Li (2004) take a different statistical approach that controls for market volatility. They find that neither risk nor return is significantly different for Republican or Democrat presidential cycles. Statistically, many other inherent flaws need to be controlled when examining the presidential premium, including limited sample size, lag effects, announcement effects, and expectation effects of different administrations. Even measuring the actual impact of any president on the stock market is complicated. Thus, like many other calendar-related anomalies, research has explored some issues, but others remain a mystery. The only consistent theme is that both the predictability and the reasoning behind many of these anomalies remain highly debatable.

Violations of the Semi-Strong Form EMH

The semi-strong form EMH states that investors cannot consistently outperform the market using either past or publicly available information. However, when examining publicly available information, researchers find several noteworthy anomalies, including outperformance by stocks with high dividend yields, low price-to-earnings (P/E) ratios, and low price-to-book (P/B) ratios. Some of the most interesting anomalies are related to announcement effects, including initial public offerings, seasoned equity offerings, debt issuances, share repurchases, and dividend changes (Cohen, Lys, and Zach 2011). Three important announcement-related anomalies are linked respectively to firms' announcements of earnings, stock splits, and mergers and acquisitions (M&As).

Post-Earnings-Announcement Price Drift   In a truly efficient market, a firm's stock price should immediately reflect any information or surprise concerning an earnings announcement. Much evidence indicates that stock prices respond immediately to earnings surprises. Nevertheless, after earnings announcements and the immediate market response, the firm's stock price tends to continue to drift in the same direction as the earnings surprise for days, weeks, and even months after the announcement (Ball and Brown 1968). For example, Foster, Olsen, and Shevlin (1984) show that firms with extreme positive and negative quarterly earnings surprises have average stock returns of 3.23 percent and −3.09 percent, respectively, for the 60 trading days following the announcement. Bernard and Thomas (1989) also document this post-earnings-announcement price spread. They find a spread of 4.20 percent for the same 60-day post-earnings trading period. Moreover, both studies find that this effect is far more prominent among smaller firms than larger firms. Thus, the market appears to continue to gradually adjust to the earnings surprise by creating a sustained period of abnormal returns, especially for smaller firms.

Stock Splits   Another announcement-related anomaly is the *stock-split effect*. Theoretically, stock splits are merely a cosmetic change to the firm's stock price that should not affect the company's overall value. Still, empirical studies link significant price reaction directly to splits (Grinblatt, Masulis, and Titman 1984; Lamoureux and Poon 1987). According to Ikenberry, Rankine, and Stice (1996), investors use stock splits as signals. They find a 3.38 percent post-split announcement return for two-for-one stock splits. Strikingly, they maintain that this return is a market underreaction. In the subsequent one-year and three-year periods, these same stocks continue to earn post-split excess returns of 7.93 percent and 12.15 percent, respectively. The authors suggest that managers' decisions to split usually align with their expectations for higher future performance.

Interestingly, professional investors do not seem to agree with these managers. Dhar, Goetzmann, Shepherd, and Zhu (2005) find that individual investors make a higher percentage of post-split trades, whereas professional investors reduce their buying activity. Thus, stock splits may simply attract new and perhaps less sophisticated investors.

Mergers and Acquisitions   Unlike stock splits, M&As represent important events that should affect a firm's value. Merger arbitrage involves trading stocks in companies that are subject to mergers or acquisitions. When firms announce a merger or takeover, the target firm's value being acquired tends to rise while the value of the bidding firm tends to fall. Arbitragers attempt to take advantage of the difference between the premium price the bidding firm is offering and the target firm's true intrinsic value. Research over various periods shows that after a merger, acquiring firms earn an average return of −7.00 percent for the following year (Schwert 1996), −4.00 percent for the following three years (Rau and Vermaelen [1998], and −10.26 percent for the subsequent five years following the merger (Agrawal, Jaffe, and Mandelker 1992). According to Schwert, this underperformance mainly results from abnormal outperformance by bidding firms in the years before the mergers.

Violations of the Strong Form EMH and Other Critiques of the EMH

The strong form EMH states that not only should all of the previous weak form and semi-strong form violations not exist, but that investors should also be unable to profit from insider trading. However, much research suggests that insider trading may represent the most profitable of all stock market anomalies and has delivered abnormal returns for insiders for the past 50 years (Lorie and Niederhoffer 1968; Jaffe 1974; Givoly and Palmon 1985; Seyhun 1988; Jeng, Metrick, and Zeckhauser 2003). Moreover, politicians seem to outperform even corporate insiders when it comes to insider trading. Ziobrowski, Cheng, Boyd, and Ziobrowski (2004) show that U.S. senators' stock purchases between 1993 and 1998 beat the market by 85 basis points per month while their stock sales lagged the market by 12 basis points per month.

Semi-Efficient Market Hypothesis   Another competing idea with the EMH is the *semi-efficient market hypothesis* (SEMH), which is the idea that some stocks or areas of the market are priced less efficiently than the more recognized stocks found on the largest stock exchanges. Some examples of equities that are less covered by traditional research analysts include international stocks, small-cap stocks, and emerging markets. One anomaly that lends credence to the SEMH is the *neglected-firm effect*, which is the tendency for lesser-known firms to outperform more well-known firms. Arbel and Strebel (1983) use the neglected-firm effect as an interpretation of the previously mentioned small-firm effect. They propose that smaller firms – in contrast with larger firms – are less monitored and more neglected by large institutional investors, resulting in less publicly available information about smaller firms. This increased uncertainty about smaller firms makes them riskier investments that command higher returns.

Other Critiques of EMH   In short, many different recurring violations of the EMH are available. Some investors even view stock market bubbles and infrequent events such as the 2000 dot-com bubble and the 2008 housing crisis as evidence that markets are not always efficient. Perhaps the most confirmative evidence for market inefficiency is that even Fama, the originator of the EMH, agrees that markets are not always efficient (Fama and Thaler 2016). He states that the EMH is just a model. The real issue is not whether markets are inefficient but rather how inefficient they are. Although market inefficiency is challenging to measure, anomalies do present empirical results that reflect either inefficiency in the market or inadequacies in the underlying asset pricing model.

Critiques of Anomalies   The amount of research supporting anomalies varies dramatically, as does their timing, consistency, significance, magnitude, and robustness. Little evidence is available that investors can consistently profit from exploiting anomalies. First, considering that anomalies should decrease in efficient markets as arbitragers take advantage of them, no certainty exists that the past performance of anomalies has any predictive power regarding future performance. In other words, Fama (1998) maintains that if behavioral finance is real, it is insignificant and primarily based on data mining. He goes further to suggest that most long-term anomalies are fragile at best and that most short-term anomalies are simply due to chance, resulting from either short-term overreactions or underreactions. Second, if behavioral finance is real, Fama believes investors should be able to leverage these market anomalies into superior returns. However, many anomaly-based trading strategies are no longer profitable once returns are adjusted for trading costs and taxes. Third, researchers have examined few anomalies from a risk-adjusted return perspective, which would shed much-needed light on whether anomalies outperform relative to the market, their benchmark, or a model of "normal" return behavior.

SUMMARY AND CONCLUSIONS

Thaler states, "When an economist says the evidence is 'mixed,' he or she means that theory says one thing and data says the opposite" (Batista 2014, p. 42). The evidence and arguments for and against behavioral finance are certainly "mixed." Interestingly, Thaler's quote could be taken in two different ways. For example, Thaler could argue that the evidence for efficient markets is "mixed" because EMH says one thing and data like anomalies says the opposite. On the other hand, others could counter that evidence for behavioral finance theories is also "mixed," with theories like PT saying one thing and evidence against it saying the opposite (Levy and Levy 2002a, 2002b).

Furthermore, even if investors are irrational, do irrational investors lead to inefficient markets? Not necessarily. Rau (2010) lists three conditions needed for market inefficiency: (1) investors cannot always be rational, (2) their irrational biases must be correlated because random biases would effectively cancel each other out, and (3) arbitragers must be somewhat limited and cannot fully take advantage of these correlated biases. In other words, even if the first condition is assumed, the necessity of all three conditions for market inefficiency appears to support market efficiency. However, Schoenhart (2008) and Rau (2010) discuss several reasons for the prevalence of the latter two conditions, including herding effects among investors and additional risks and implementation costs for arbitragers.

In conclusion, even with only "mixed" support, behavioral finance continues to gain traction as an important field of finance that attempts to explain the many facets of investor psychology and to provide explanations for market inefficiencies like equity market anomalies. Such concepts as bounded rationality and PT are clearly contrary to more traditional finance ideas that assume investors are rational. Behavioral finance maintains that investors are not computers that can perfectly weigh expected probabilities. Even if investors properly use computers to make the best mathematical choices, limitations still exist involving available information and time constraints. Thus, investors' decisions are often biased, irrational, and driven by motivations other than maximizing their utility. Although behavioral finance is not meant to replace traditional finance, it is needed because it offers practical benefits. That is, behavioral finance is simply more adaptive for a real world with irrational investors and complex choice behavior than traditional finance. In the end, the goal of behavioral finance is to build better bridges from the theoretical world to the real world.

DISCUSSION QUESTIONS

1. Discuss three conditions needed for market inefficiency and whether bounded rationality may address these conditions.
2. List three different effects that relate to PT and how each effect can cause investors to make irrational decisions.
3. List three violations of the weak form EMH and explain how they differ.
4. List three announcement-related violations of the semi-strong form EMH and explain how they differ.

REFERENCES

Agrawal, Anup, Jeffrey Jaffe, and Gershon Mandelker. 1992. "The Post-merger Performance of Acquiring Firms: A Re-Examination of an Anomaly." *Journal of Finance* 47:4, 1605–1621.

Allais, Maurice. 1953. "Le Comportement de l'Homme Rationnel devant le Risque: Critique des Postulats et Axiomes de l'Ecole Americaine." *Econometrica* 21:4, 503–546.

Arbel, Avner, and Paul Strebel. 1983. "Pay Attention to Neglected Firms." *Journal of Portfolio Management* 9:2, 37–42.

Ariel, Robert. 1990. "High Stock Returns Before Holidays: Existence and Evidence on Possible Causes." *Journal of Finance* 45:5, 1611–1626.

Baker, H. Kent, and John Nofsinger. 2010. *Behavior Finance: Investors, Corporations, and Markets.* Hoboken, NJ: John Wiley & Sons.

Ball, Ray, and Philip Brown. 1968. "An Empirical Evaluation of Accounting Income Numbers." *Journal of Accounting Research* 6:2, 159–178.

Banz, Rolf. 1981. "The Relationship Between Return and Market Value of Common Stock." *Journal of Financial Economics* 9:1, 3–18.

Batista, José. 2014. *Burn, Baby, Burn: Money & Markets Most Outrageous, Funny and Witty Quotes, Sayings and Stories.* Scotts Valley, CA: Createspace Independent Pub.

Bernard, Victor, and Jacob Thomas. 1989. "Post-earnings-announcement Drift: Delayed Price Response or Risk Premium?" *Journal of Accounting Research* 27(Supplement): 1–36.

Bernoulli, Daniel. 1738. "Specimen Theoriae Novae de Mensura Sortis (Exposition of a New Theory on the Measurement of Risk)." *Commentarii Academiae Scientiarum Imperialis Petropolitanae (Papers of the Imperial Academy of Sciences in Petersburg)* 5, 175–192.

Bhargave, Alok. 2014. "Firms' Fundamentals, Macroeconomic Variables and Quarterly Stock Prices in the US." *Journal of Econometrics* 183:2, 241–250.

Blume, Marshall, and Robert Stambaugh. 1983. "Biases in Computed Returns: An Application to the Size Effect." *Journal of Financial Economics* 12:3, 387–404.

Bodie, Zvi, Alex Kane, and Alan Marcus. 2013. *Essentials of Investments*, 9th ed. New York, NY: McGraw-Hill.

Bouman, Sven, and Ben Jacobsen. 2002. "The Halloween Indicator, 'Sell in May and Go Away': Another Puzzle." *American Economic Review* 92:5, 1618–1635.

Campbell, Sean, and Canlin Li. 2004. "Alternative Estimates of the Presidential Premium." Finance and Economics Discussion Series (FEDS) Federal Reserve Board Working Paper No. 69.

Cohen, Daniel, Thomas Lys, and Tzachi Zach. 2011. "Net Stock Anomalies." In *The Handbook of Equity Market Anomalies: Translating Market Inefficiencies into Effective Investment Strategies*, edited by Leonard Zacks, 129–146. Hoboken, NJ: John Wiley & Sons.

Cootner, Paul. 1964. *The Random Character of Stock Market Prices*. Cambridge, MA: MIT Press.

DeBondt, Werner, and Richard Thaler. 1985. "Does the Stock Market Overreact?" *Journal of Finance* 40:3, 793–808.

Dhar, Ravi, William Goetzmann, Shane Shepherd, and Ning Zhu. 2005. "The Impact of Clientele Change: Evidence from Stock Splits." Working Paper, Yale University and University of California.

Doeswijk, Ronald. 2005. "The Optimism Cycle: Sell in May." *De Economist* 156:2, 175–200.

Dzhabarov, Constantine, and William Ziemba. 2011. "Seasonal Anomalies." In *The Handbook of Equity Market Anomalies: Translating Market Inefficiencies into Effective Investment Strategies*, edited by Leonard Zacks, 205–264. Hoboken, NJ: John Wiley & Sons.

Fama, Eugene. 1965. "Random Walks in Stock Market Prices." *Financial Analysts Journal* 21:5, 55–59.

Fama, Eugene. 1970. "Efficient Capital Markets: A Review of Theory and Empirical Work." *Journal of Finance* 25:2, 383–417.

Fama, Eugene. 1991. "Efficient Capital Markets II." *Journal of Finance* 46:7, 1575–1618.

Fama, Eugene. 1998. "Market Efficiency, Long-term Returns, and Behavioral Finance. *Journal of Financial Economics* 49:3, 283–306.

Fama, Eugene, and Richard Thaler. 2016. "Are Markets Efficient?" *Chicago Booth Review*, June 30. Available at https://review.chicagobooth.edu/economics/2016/video/are-markets-efficient.

Foster, George, Chris Olsen, and Terry Shevlin. 1984. "Earnings Releases, Anomalies, and the Behavior of Security Returns." *The Accounting Review* 59:5, 574–603.

Garrett, Ian, Mark Kamstra, and Lisa Kramer, 2004. "Winter Blues and Time Variation in the Price of Risk." *Journal of Empirical Finance* 12:2, 291–316.

Givoly, Dan, and Dan Palmon. 1985. "Insider Trading and Exploitation of Inside Information: Some Empirical Evidence." *Journal of Business* 58:1, 69–87.

Grinblatt, Mark, Ronald Masulis, and Sheridan Titman. 1984. "The Valuation Effects of Stock Splits and Stock Dividends." *Journal of Financial Economics* 13:4, 461–490.

Gultekin, Mustafa, and N. Bulent Gultekin. 1983. "Stock Market Seasonality: International Evidence." *Journal of Financial Economics* 12:4, 469–481.

Harford, Tim. 2019. "Richard Thaler: 'If You Want People to Do Something, Make It Easy.'" *Financial Times*, August 2. Available at https://www.ft.com/content/a317c302-aa2b-11e9-984c-fac8325aaa04.

Hirshleifer, David. 2001. "Investor Psychology and Asset Pricing." *Journal of Finance* 56:4, 1533–1597.

Hirshleifer, David, and Tyler Shumway. 2003. "Good Day Sunshine: Stock Returns and the Weather." *Journal of Finance* 58:3, 1009–1032.

Ikenberry, David, Graeme Rankine, and Earl Stice. 1996. "What Do Stock Splits Really Signal?" *Journal of Financial and Quantitative Analysis* 31:3, 357–375.

Jaffe, Jeffrey. 1974. "Special Information and Insider Trading." *Journal of Business* 47:3, 410–428.

Jegadeesh, Narasimhan, and Sheridan Titman. 1993. "Returns to Buying Winners and Selling Losers: Implications for Stock Market Efficiency." *Journal of Finance* 48:1, 65–91.

Jeng, Leslie, Andrew Metrick, and Richard Zeckhauser. 2003. "Estimating the Returns to Insider Trading: A Performance-Evaluation Perspective." *Review of Economics and Statistics* 85:2, 453–471.

Kahneman, Daniel, and Amos Tversky. 1979. "Prospect Theory: An Analysis of Decision Under Risk." *Econometrica* 47:2, 263–291.

Kahneman, Daniel, and Amos Tversky. 1984. "Choices, Values, and Frames." *American Psychologist* 39:4, 341–350.

Kamstra, Mark, Lisa Kramer, and Maurice Levi. 2000. "Losing Sleep at the Market: The Daylight Saving Anomaly." *American Economic Review* 90:4, 1005–1011.

Kamstra, Mark, Lisa Kramer, and Maurice Levi. 2003. "Winter Blues: A SAD Stock Market Cycle." *American Economic Review* 93:1, 324–343.

Keim, Donald. 1993. "Size Related Anomalies and Stock Return Seasonality: Further Empirical Evidence." *Journal of Financial Economics* 12:1, 13–32.

Keim, Donald, and William Ziemba. 2000. *Security Market Imperfections in World Wide Equity Markets*. Cambridge, UK: Cambridge University Press.

Kendall, Maurice, and A. Bradford Hill. 1953. "The Analysis of Economic Time-Series-Part 1: Prices." *Journal of the Royal Statistical Society: Series A* 116:1, 11–34.

Lakonishok, Josef, and Seymour Smidt. 1988. "Are Seasonal Anomalies Real? A Ninety-year Perspective." *Review of Financial Studies* 1:4, 403–425.

Lamoureux, Christopher, and Percy Poon. 1987. "The Market Reaction to Stock Splits." *Journal of Finance* 42:5, 1347–1370.

Levy, Haim, and Moshe Levy. 2002b. "Experimental Test of the Prospect Theory Value Function." *Organizational Behavior and Human Decision Processes* 89:2, 1058–1081.

Levy, Moshe, and Haim Levy. 2002a. "Prospect Theory. Much Ado About Nothing." *Management Science* 48:10, 1334–1349.

Lo, Andrew. 1999. *A Non-Random Walk Down Wall Street*. Princeton, NJ: Princeton University Press.

Lo, Andrew, and Archie MacKinlay. 2002. *A Non-Random Walk Down Wall Street*, 5th ed. Princeton, NJ: Princeton University Press.

Lorie, James H., and Victor Niederhoffer. 1968. "Predictive and Statistical Properties of Insider Trading." *Journal of Law and Economics* 11:1, 35–51.

Malkiel, Burton. 1973. *A Random Walk Down Wall Street*, 6th ed. New York, NY: W. W. Norton & Company, Inc.

Malkiel, Burton. 2003. "The Efficient Market Hypothesis and Its Critics." CEPS Working Paper No. 91.

Markowitz, Harry. 1952. "Portfolio Selection." *Journal of Finance* 7:1, 77–91.

Neumann, John von, and Oskar Morgenstern. 1944. *Theory of Games and Economic Behavior*. Princeton, NJ: Princeton University Press.

Nofsinger, John. 2018. *The Psychology of Investing*, 6th ed. New York, NY: Routledge.

Rau, Raghavendra. 2010. "Market Inefficiency." In *Behavior Finance: Investors, Corporations, and Markets*, edited by H. Kent Baker and John Nofsinger, 331–350. Hoboken, NJ: John Wiley & Sons.

Rau, Raghavendra, and Theo Vermaelen. 1998. "Glamour, Value and the Post-acquisition Performance of Acquiring Firms." *Journal of Financial Economics* 49:2, 223–253.

Reinganum, Marc. 1983. "The Anomalous Stock Market Behavior of Small Firms in January: Empirical Tests for Tax-Loss Effects." *Journal of Financial Economics* 12:1, 89–104.

Santa-Clara, Pedro, and Rossen Valkanov. 2003. "The Presidential Puzzle: Political Cycles and the Stock Market." *Journal of Finance* 58:5, 1841–1872.

Saunders, Edward, Jr. 1993. "Stock Prices and Wall Street Weather." *American Economic Review* 83:5, 1337–1345.

Schoenhart, Michael. 2008. *Behavioral Finance and Market Anomalies: An Academic Review.* Saarbrücken, Germany: Verlag Dr. Müeller.

Schwert, G. William. 1996. "Markup Pricing in Mergers and Acquisitions." *Journal of Financial Economics* 41:1, 153–192.

Seyhun, H. Nejat. 1988. "The Information Content of Aggregate Insider Trading." *Journal of Business* 61:1, 1–24.

Shefrin, Hersh, and Meir Statman. 1985. "The Disposition to Sell Winners Too Early and Ride Losers Too Long: Theory and Evidence." *Journal of Finance* 40:3, 777–790.

Shefrin, Hersh, and Meir Statman. 1994. "Behavioral Capital Asset Pricing Theory." *Journal of Financial and Quantitative Analysis* 29:3, 323–349.

Shefrin, Hersh, and Meir Statman. 2000. "Behavioral Portfolio Theory." *Journal of Financial and Quantitative Analysis* 35:2, 127–151.

Simon, Herbert. 1978. "Rationality as a Process and as a Product of Thought." *American Economic Review* 70:1, 1–16.

Singal, Vijay. 2004. *Beyond the Random Walk: A Guide to Stock Market Anomalies and Low Risk Investing.* New York, NY: Oxford University Press.

Stout, 2010. "Trust Behavior: The Essential Foundation of Financial Markets." In *Behavior Finance: Investors, Corporations, and Markets*, edited by H. Kent Baker and John Nofsinger, 513–522. Hoboken, NJ: John Wiley & Sons.

Thaler, Richard, and Cass Sunstein. 2009. *Nudge: Improving Decisions About Health, Wealth, and Happiness.* New Haven, CT: Yale University Press.

Wachtel, Sidney. 1942. "Certain Observations on Seasonal Movements in Stock Prices." *Journal of Business* 15:2, 184–193.

Ziobrowski, Alan, Ping Cheng, James Boyd, and Brigitte Ziobrowski. 2004. "Abnormal Returns from the Common Stock Investments of the U.S. Senate." *Journal of Financial and Quantitative Analysis* 39:4, 661–676.

Zweig, Jason. 2017. "Economist David Ricardo – One of the Most Successful Quants in History." *Wall Street Journal.* May 26. Available at https://blogs.wsj.com/moneybeat/2017/05/26/economist-david-ricardo-one-of-the-most-successful-quants/.

Zweig, Martin. 1986. *Winning on Wall Street.* New York, NY: Warner Brooks.

PART TWO

Valuation and Analysis

CHAPTER 6

Financial Statement Analysis and Forecasting

Somnath Das
Professor of Accounting, University of Illinois at Chicago
Shailendra Pandit
Associate Professor of Accounting, University of Illinois at Chicago

INTRODUCTION

Financial statement analysis is the process of reviewing and analyzing a company's financial statements with the intent of making better economic decisions. *Forecasting* is using public information – typically, past historical data – to make predictions. More broadly, forecasting is any analysis aimed at aiding and improving decision-making. Hence, any examination of the role of financial statement analysis in forecasting necessarily begs questions such as "forecasting what?" "forecasting for whom?" "which decisions?" or "which decision-makers?" For the purposes of this chapter, decision-making is limited to financial market participants making asset allocation decisions. From a practitioner's standpoint, asset allocation requires forecasts of stock returns that can lead to improved investment performance. Toward this end, the discussion of financial statement analysis for forecasting primarily includes firm valuation, which also encompasses stock prices. A widely accepted view is that stock prices and hence firm value represent the present value of the business entity's future cash flows. Therefore, an investor's principal challenge is to predict an entity's future cash flows. This chapter examines approaches to forecast future cash flows with a particular focus on using financial statements.

The chapter has the following structure. The next section provides a brief historical background and then reviews the literature on time series–based forecasting, followed by a literature review on financial statement analysis and how it can be used for forecasting. Then, the chapter reviews the literature on analyst earnings forecasts, focusing on their forecast properties and performance relative time series models. The final section reviews the literature on analysts using financial statement analysis and concludes with a discussion of some limitations.

BACKGROUND

Historically, practitioners in the financial sector of the economy have employed various approaches in an attempt to forecast asset prices. During the latter part of the nineteenth century, Charles Dow, the founder of the Dow Jones index, reportedly used past prices to predict stock prices. Some records suggest that Muneisha Homma, a rice merchant from Sakata, Japan, used "candlestick charts" to trade in the rice futures market in the eighteenth century (Nison 1991). In recent years, the task of forecasting has become more systematic. For example, Gordon's (1959) constant growth model has become a common way to forecast among investors and financiers and remains the premise behind the discussion in this chapter. Hence, the chapter begins by specifying Gordon's model, as shown in Equation 6.1:

$$P_t = \sum_{z=1}^{\infty} R_D^{-z} E_t(d_{(t+z)}|Z_t) \tag{6.1}$$

where P_t denotes a security's price at time t; R_D is 1 plus the discount rate for the firm; $E_t(.)$ represents the expectation at time t; d_{t+z} indicates dividends at time $t + z$; and Z_t = information at time t over which the expectation is conditioned. Equation 6.1 is also in the spirit of the dividend capitalization formula of Williams (1938) that had a major influence on fundamental analysis.

If investors can predict the future stream of dividends, then they can easily calculate current prices. Indeed, investors are assessing the future stream of dividends using the information set Z_t to arrive at a price P_t. Much of the research in financial accounting assumes dividends equal earnings (i.e., the payout ratio of 100 percent). Feltham and Ohlson (1995), Ohlson (1995), and Ohlson and Juettner-Naurath (2005) provide equivalent representations of Equation 6.1 in terms of earnings using the accounting identity, which requires that the book value in period t equals the book value in period $t - 1$ plus period t earnings less dividends paid in period t (i.e., $BV_t = BV_{t-1} + X_t - D_t$). In accounting parlance, this relation is commonly referred to as the *clean surplus equation*. Rearranging the above relation yields: $D_t = BV_{t-1} + NI_t - BV_t$ or $D_t = \Delta BV_t + NI_t$. Substituting the dividend stream, D_t in Equation 6.1 and under certain assumptions about what contributes to changes in book value, yields a valuation formula that depends on expected values of future earnings (NI_t), where earnings and net income are equivalent and interchangeable. Hence, the above valuation framework provides the backdrop for focusing on forecasting earnings. This characterization of earnings is also consistent with how this valuation framework is often used in practice (Koller, Goedhart, and Wessels 2015).

As Cottle, Murray, and Block (1988, p. 533) note,

> *The concept of earning power has a definite place in investment theory. It combines a statement of actual earnings performance – over a period of years – with a reasonable expectation that the past level or trend will be approximated in the future unless extraordinary conditions supervene. The performance may be measured in terms of either (1) the earnings per share of common stock or (2) the rate of return covered on common stock equity.*

Forecasting earnings can be both fascinating and frustrating. Because earnings inherently contain a sizable unpredictable component, the best forecasting models can explain only a relatively small part of future earnings.

TECHNICAL ANALYSIS–BASED FORECASTING

Despite the valuation formula, many academics and practitioners continue to focus on stock prices. They use technical analysis, which relies on using statistical techniques and approaches to analyze past stock prices to predict future stock price movements. In its simplest form, technical analysis involves using time series analysis of stock prices (Chavarnakul and Enke 2009; Teixeira and Oliveira 2010) and trading volume. Charles Dow, the founder of the Dow Jones index and the father of modern technical analysis, was reportedly one of the earliest users of a chart-and-figure system of daily stock prices. Finance academics are also interested in forecasting stock returns since the ability to forecast returns has important implications for testing market efficiency and producing more realistic asset pricing models. Perhaps the earliest academic exposition of technical analysis can be traced to Cowles (1933). The underlying tenet of this approach is that past trends are predictive of the future, particularly to the extent of fitting appropriate time series models. Indeed, this approach has gained additional momentum in recent years with "program trading," "high-frequency trading," and "big data" trading.

TIME SERIES–BASED FORECASTING

Time series is a type of technical analysis because it uses past data to predict a variable's future value. Hence, technical analysis led finance academics and practitioners to generate a huge body of work predicting stock prices. The random walk model of Malkiel (2011) became widely popular. Rapach and Zhou (2013) and Nazario, Silva, and Sobreiro (2017) provide excellent literature reviews on stock return forecasting and technical analysis in stock markets.

Aside from relying on a purely technical analysis of stock prices, some work focuses on forecasting earnings using traditional, well-established statistical time series. These studies rely on long historical (past) earnings patterns to form expectations about future realizations of the underlying variable, such as earnings. Although some view using historical time series as part of technical analysis, others view it as a primitive use of financial statement analysis in forecasting future earnings. Both academics and practitioners now acknowledge earnings as a summary statistic of a firm's financial performance.

Besides the random walk, autoregressive, integrated, moving average (ARIMA) models have generally been the staple of time series–based models used in the extant literature. An ARIMA model is a mixed model that integrates an autoregressive model with a moving average model. An autoregressive model of order p, often referred to as AR(p) model, can generally be written as Equation 6.2:

$$Y_t = c + \phi_1 Y_{t-1} + \phi_2 Y_{t-2} + \cdots + \phi_p Y_{t-p} + \varepsilon_t \qquad (6.2)$$

where ε_t is white noise. Equation 6.2 is similar in spirit to a multiple regression analysis with lagged values of the dependent variable Y_t as its predictors. In contrast, a moving average model, often referred to as an MA(q) model, uses past forecast errors in a regression, instead of past values as in an AR(p) model, and hence is generally expressed as Equation 6.3:

$$Y_t = c + \varepsilon_t + \theta_1 \varepsilon_{t-1} + \theta_2 \varepsilon_{t-2} + \cdots + \theta_q \varepsilon_{t-q} \qquad (6.3)$$

where ε_t is white noise. Since ε_t is not observed, each value of Y_t can be thought of as a weighted moving average of the past forecast errors. Thus, combining differencing with the AR(p) model and the MA(q) model yields the nonseasonal ARIMA (p,d,q) model expressed in Equation 6.4:

$$y'_t = c + \phi_1 y'_{t-1} + \cdots + \phi_p y'_{t-p} + \theta_1 \varepsilon_{t-1} + \cdots + \theta_q \varepsilon_{t-q} + \varepsilon_t \qquad (6.4)$$

where y'_t is the differenced series and the right-hand side predictors comprise both lagged values of y_t and lagged errors. Equation 6.4 is referred to as an ARIMA(p,d,q) model, where p denoted the order of the autoregressive part, d is the degree of first differencing involved, and q represents the order of the moving average part.

Any model is only worth how well it performs. Hence, model specification and selection must be evaluated for its performance. For time series models, two fundamental approaches are available: one assesses in-sample performance and the other assesses out-of-sample performance. Hence, analysts can use several basic approaches to evaluate the performance of the underlying model, which include examining in-sample performance using (1) mean absolute prediction error (MAPE) or (2) root mean square error (RMSE) using out-of-sample concurrence. Brooks and Buckmaster (1976) examine the time-series properties of accounting income, as do several other early researchers (Ball and Watts 1972; Albrecht, Lookabill, and McKeown 1977; Watts and Leftwich 1977) who document the superiority of the random walk model for predicting next-period earnings. As Kothari (2001, p. 145) notes, "A large body of evidence suggests a random walk with drift is a reasonable description of the time-series properties of annual earnings." Bradshaw, Drake, Myers, and Myers (2012) draw a similar inference. The predictability of time series models is, to a certain degree, a function of the underlying firm-specific characteristics and the earnings-generating function.

Independent of how well technical analysis does from a forecasting accuracy/efficiency perspective, both proponents and critics agree that a fundamental limitation of technical analysis is that it ignores the fundamentals. In other words, critics view this method as forecasting in a vacuum. The natural questions are: "What is the alternative?" "Does the alternative provide superior forecasting?" and "Can some combination of both technical and alternative forecasting approaches improve on the forecast?"

Given that these time series forecasts primarily focus on earnings implies that analysts were ignoring much information that underlies earnings, which is only a "summary statistic" of current period performance. Indeed, analysts were ignoring not only income statement items but also information in the balance sheet, statement of cash flows, and statement of retained earnings. Assuming that earnings is a sufficient statistic and given that the dividend discount model (DDM) is a straightforward metric that can be used by assuming a 100 percent payout was convenient for forecasters. However, one question continued to haunt academics and practitioners alike: Can earnings forecasts, and by implication, price forecasts be improved by going beyond earnings and stock prices?

FUNDAMENTAL ANALYSIS–BASED FORECASTING

Forecasting studies mainly focused on earnings. Forecasting earnings assumes that earnings are a sufficient statistic representing all information contained in financial statements. An alternative approach to forecasting earnings is using financial statement analysis that relies on a broader range of information than just past earnings. Financial statement analysis, also referred to as fundamental analysis, involves analyzing the information contained in financial statements that analysts use to forecast future performance. A key distinction is to identify value independent of price. Fundamental analysis assumes that careful investigation facilitates identifying under- and overvalued common stocks used to make investment decisions. This approach attempts to find a security's *intrinsic value* based on the facts, including its assets, earnings, dividends, and prospects (Cottle, Murray, and Block 1988). This approach uses information from all financial statements and places greater reliance on accounting information.

PROCESS OF ANALYZING FINANCIAL STATEMENTS

Financial statement analysis involves using and extracting information from financial statements to understand not only current and past performance but also to forecast future performance. Major financial statements include the (1) income statement, (2) balance sheet, (3) statement of cash flows, and (4) statement of retained earnings. Typically, each statement is accompanied by both mandatory and voluntary notes and disclosures that provide additional information. Since the typical manager would want to report what is mandatory and necessary and exclude anything vital and not required, the task of financial statement analysis is to unravel the hidden truths using disclosed information.

Financial statement analysis may involve identifying something as basic as the amount of cash collected from customers, which is typically unreported but can be inferred by reconstructing the accounts receivable account. However, identifying the sources of a firm's profitability could be more interesting. For example, are the profits generated by operating or non-operating activities? Thus, consider the following relations:

Return on equity (ROE) = Operating return + Nonoperating return

Net income/Average equity = Return on net operating assets RNOA

+ Financial leverage × Spread

Where

$$RNOA = \frac{\text{Net operating profit after taxes NOPAT}}{\text{Average net operating assets}}$$

Net operating assets NOA = Operating assets less operating liabilities

Financial leverage = Net nonoperating obligationsNNO

= Nonoperating liabilities less nonoperating assets

Net nonoperating expenseNNE = NOPAT − Consolidated net income

Net nonoperating expense percent NNEP = NNE/Average NNOSpread

= RNOA–NNEP

Thus, the ROE equation can be reframed into the following expression:

ROE (Net income/Average equity) = RNOA + NNO × (RNOA − NNEP)

The preceding analysis and expression are similar to the more commonly known *DuPont analysis*, popularized by the DuPont Corporation as an approach to understanding the fundamentals of firm performance by decomposing the ROE into its component drivers (Penman 2013, p. 374). This simple disaggregation permits examining the sources of profitability, which analysts can then use to forecast earnings from core activities. Practitioners often use NOPAT as a measure of earnings (Koller, Goedhart, and Wessels 2015). Indeed, Soliman (2008) documents that elements of the DuPont analysis incrementally predict future earnings. Nissim and Penman (2001, 2003) provide additional insights into applications of fundamental analysis in practice.

EVIDENCE ON THE USEFULNESS OF FINANCIAL STATEMENT ANALYSIS

A critical piece of financial statement information is the current ROE. Several studies show that ROE is useful in predicting future earnings changes. Beaver (1970) and Lookabill (1976) demonstrate the time-series property of mean reversion in ROE and hence its usefulness in predicting earnings changes. Board and Walker (1990) also report positive correlations between "unexpected" ROE and "abnormal" stock returns. However, they use a random walk expectation in measuring unexpected ROE, which may be an improper characterization given the observed mean reversion in ROE.

From a conceptual standpoint, Freeman, Ohlson, and Penman (1992) represent an early attempt to empirically document the role of financial statement analysis in forecasting, using line items other than earnings. They use accounting rates of return to predict the direction of subsequent period earnings change. Their research represents a response to establishing the information content of earnings, independent of stock prices, since up until then, the primary focus was on inferring the information content of accounting numbers via observed prices (Ball and Brown 1968; Beaver 1968). Implicit in this stock price–based inference procedure are two key assumptions: (1) market participants correctly price a firm based on all available information (market efficiency), and (2) market participants and analysts use a "black box" that transforms accounting information into observed prices. Recent evidence questions both assumptions.

Subsequently, Penman (1991, p. 253), who examines ROE as a measure of risk and profitability, concludes that "ROE is best interpreted as a profitability measure and not a risk measure." According to Penman (1992a, p. 480), "The key to the analysis of book value premiums is the determination of this rate of mean reversion, that is, how representative current ROE is of future ROE." Manegold (1981) compares the predictive ability of models based on components such as interest expense, depreciation expense, operating income before depreciation, and interest expense with models based on aggregate earnings only. The results, however, could not support the possible superiority of a component-based earnings prediction model, thus leading to a setback for fundamental analysis.

Subsequent research in Ou and Penman (1989) expands the information set to include further line items and shows that such information is useful in predicting the direction of subsequent period earnings changes and stock returns. They develop a measure using financial statement information that is useful in taking investment positions. Specifically, using a logit specification, the authors create a measure called *Pr*, a probability metric that is indicative of the direction of future earnings changes. However, a key limitation of the *Pr* measure is that it only distinguishes between increasing and decreasing earnings if they involve earnings reversals and that it does not forecast the magnitude of the earnings change. In other words, *Pr* can identify the mean-reverting property of ROE in the cross-section but is unable to identify the positive serial correlation property of ROE.

Moreover, as Penman (1992b, p. 577) notes, *Pr* provides

> ... *an* ex ante *indicator of earnings persistence and recognizes non-stationarity in persistence and the use of financial statement information to track the variation. This measure is based on one-year ahead earnings changes only, and earnings persistence refers to earnings over a longer horizon. Because it is estimated from pooled cross-sectional data, it does not allow for variation in the relationship between financial statement items and future earnings over firms.*

The implication is to distinguish between currently transitory high (low) earnings from growth (declining) conditions. However, little evidence is available about the extent and degree of persistence in earnings in the cross-section. So, while Ou and Penman (1989) was a big leap forward toward using financial statement analysis in forecasting earnings, it has its limitations.

Subsequent work extended the results in Ou and Penman (1989). For example, Holthausen and Larcker (1992) use the *Pr* measure to predict stock returns directly and show that it did not perform well after 1983, perhaps due to the overfitting of the data. Greig (1992) uses a more direct approach and finds that the positive association between the *Pr* measure and subsequent stock returns becomes insignificant and even negative when controlling for size. Greig concludes that Ou and Penman's results are another manifestation of the size effect rather than new evidence of market inefficiency.

Following a somewhat different approach, Lev and Thiagarajan (1993) use an analyst's perspective to identify relevant variables that are likely to be useful in forecasting. Their guided search approach contrasts with Ou and Penman's (1989) statistical approach. Lev and Thiagarajan identify 12 signals: (1) inventories, (2) accounts receivable, (3) capital expenditures, (4) research and development (R&D), (5) gross margin, (6) selling and administrative (S&A) expenses, (7) provision for doubtful receivables, (8) effective tax rate, (9) order backlog, (10) labor force, (11) last-in, first-out (LIFO) earnings, and (12) audit qualification. Examining the association of the 12 signals with annual returns, they find that only inventories, accounts receivable, capital expenditure, gross margin, S&A expenses, and order backlog signals have statistically significant associations.

Abarbanell and Bushee (1997) criticize Ou and Penman (1989) because their choice of variables is not grounded in conceptual arguments, and many of their variables do not follow from a business-economic logic. The critical insight gained is that the fundamental signal has incremental predictive power relative to current-year earnings. In other words, this signal does better than the random walk. More recently, Piotroski (2000) argues that the *Pr* measure has severe shortcomings. Criticizing Ou and Penman (1989) and Holthausen and Larcker (1992) for using a vast amount of historical accounting information, Piotroski documents that a simple financial statement analysis using nine binary accounting variables capturing profitability (measured by return on assets, change in return on assets, cash from operations, and accruals), leverage, liquidity, sources of funds, and operating efficiency (measured by change in gross margin and change in asset turnover), enables discriminating between value stocks with a low and high future return. Specifically, Piotroski computes an F-Score, which is the sum of the nine binary accounting signals.

Consequently, companies with a high (low) F-Score are characterized by a broad improvement (decline) in financial performance during the previous fiscal year. Several practitioners find that F-Score is useful in their investment strategies. In a similar vein, Beneish, Lee, and Tarpley (2001) and Mohanram (2005) provide evidence on using financial statement analysis to pick winners and losers in the stock market. In related literature, Dickinson and Sommers (2012) provide evidence on how financial statement information captures measures of competition. Fairfield and Yohn (2001) supply evidence on using asset turnover ratios and profit margins to forecast changes in firm profitability.

In summary, ample evidence is available on the usefulness of financial statement analysis in forecasting future earnings. Richardson, Tuna, and Wysocki (2010) offer an extensive literature review on fundamental analysis focusing on investment strategies and stock market anomalies, including summary data from a survey of practitioners and their use of fundamental analysis.

SECURITY ANALYSTS AND FINANCIAL STATEMENT ANALYSIS

The role of financial statement analysis is to identify value independent of prices. Among the most pervasive users of financial statements in identifying and predicting firm values are financial analysts associated with brokerage houses. In this sense, financial analysts are major consumers of financial statement information because they generate reports containing forecasts of target prices, cash flow forecasts, revenue forecasts, stock recommendations, and long-term growth forecasts, among others. Some consider forecasting future earnings as the *raison d'être* of security analysts, and both academics and practitioners focus on the properties of their earnings forecasts. Therefore, a natural place to begin investigating the strength of financial statement analysis is to document the extent to which analysts use such analysis when predicting earnings and making stock recommendations.

This section provides a literature review of the properties of analyst forecasts of earnings. This review discusses both the performance of analyst forecast relative to time series models and analysts' use or lack of use of financial statements in their forecast of earnings. The primary focus of this review concerns the role of financial statement analysis in forecasting. Thus, the review excludes the vast literature on earnings forecasting by financial analysts, which is available in Schipper (1991), Brown (1993), Ramnath, Rock, and Shane (2008), and Bradshaw, Ertimur, and O'Brien (2016).

Some criticize the analysts' forecasting process involving earnings, revenues, cash flows, and target prices as being a "black box" because the process is mostly unobservable (Schipper 1991). According to Malkiel (2011, p. 161), "Security analysts have enormous difficulty in performing their basic function of forecasting earnings prospects for the companies they follow. Investors who put blind faith in such forecasts in making their investment selections are in for some rude disappointments." However, one can make inferences about analysts' forecasting process, particularly about using financial statement analysis via inferences based on actual forecast outcomes. Indeed, a natural place to begin investigating the strength of financial statement analysis is to document the extent to which analysts use financial statements to predict earnings and make stock recommendations. This section offers a literature review that examines whether and to what extent analysts make full and rational use of financial statement information in predicting earnings.

In early work, Govindarajan (1980) finds that security analysts use earnings rather than cash flows in their reports, suggesting a limited role for line items other than earnings. However, in a survey of British and German financial analysts, Pike, Meerjanssen, and Chadwick (1993) find that next to a discussion with company personnel and in-company presentations such as press conferences, analysts find published annual reports and associated financial statements to be the most relevant source of information for predicting earnings. Soliman (2008) also shows that the DuPont analysis of ROE is positively associated with analyst forecast revisions, suggesting that they use some level of financial statement analysis.

Several researchers investigate the performance of alternative sources of earnings forecasts in terms of earnings prediction accuracy and as a measure of market expectations of earnings. Generally, they find that the level of forecast accuracy by financial analysts (Brown, Griffin, Hagerman, and Zmijewski 1987; Brown, Hagerman, Griffin, and Zmijewski 1987) and security price (Collins, Kothari, and Rayburn 1987) are based on a broader information set that is superior to forecasts based solely on the historical earnings series (i.e., time-series forecasts).

Abarbanell and Bernard (1992) document early evidence examining analysts' use of prior information such as past earnings, stock prices, and forecast errors. Abarbanell and Bushee (1997) document that several of the fundamental signals in their study are associated with analysts' one-year-ahead earnings forecasts and five-year earnings growth forecasts, suggesting that analysts may be using such information. Abarbanell and Bushee (1997) also examine whether analysts use the fundamental variables in Lev and Thiagarajan (1993) that had incremental explanatory power for returns to revise their forecasts. Abarbanell and Bushee (1997, p. 22) conclude with the puzzling statement: "We also found that analysts' forecasts do not completely impound the information that investors perceive is contained in the fundamental signals. Because analysts' forecast revisions are strongly associated with many of these signals in the same way as returns, a question arises as to why these revisions fail to subsume value-relevant information." In general, the evidence suggests that analysts do not make full and rational use of all available information (Easterwood and Nutt 1999). Thus, finding evidence of analysts using financial statement information involving line items is difficult.

Ali, Klein, and Rosenfeld (1992) find that analysts incorporate a permanent and transitory component of earnings as measured by P/E ratio in predicting next-period earnings. Prior studies also attempt to address whether financial statement analysis-based investment strategy can outperform an investment strategy based on analysts' recommendation of an earnings increase or decrease. Stober (1992), for example, demonstrates that analyst forecast–based strategy does better than the Ou and Penman (1989) *Pr* strategy only when they confirm the direction of earnings change predicted by each other. Stober's results imply that analysts' forecasts do not necessarily incorporate information contained in financial statement analysis. The predictive ability comparisons of analysts' forecasts with Ou and Penman's *Pr* in Stober (pp. 360–361) using a bivariate analysis show that the "analysts' forecasts are marginally superior to *Pr* as predictors of the signs of one-year-ahead EPS changes." Nonetheless, several researchers attempt to examine analysts' use of financial statement information in their forecast. Wahlen and Wieland (2010) also examine using financial statement analysis and document that their parsimonious model of earnings increases performs better than analysts' stock recommendations, suggesting that analysts do not fully incorporate the information in financial statements.

LIMITATIONS OF USING FINANCIAL STATEMENT ANALYSIS IN FORECASTING

Although financial statement analysis appears to add value in forecasting future earnings and hence a firm's future value, it has its limitations. A key factor in financial statement analysis is its reliance on the reported values in the Securities and Exchange Commission (SEC)-mandated financial statements, namely, the income statement, balance sheet, statement of cash flows, and statement of retained earnings. Since these statements are required to be prepared following the reporting and recognition standards (rules and principles) set forth by the Financial Accounting Standards Board (FASB), they are geared toward comparability and standardization, which may restrict certain firm-specific information. These limitations raise concerns about whether the information reported in the financial statements fully reflects the economics of the underlying transactions.

For example, expenditures for R&D, which are required to be expensed immediately in the income statement but whose benefits likely span several years into the future, suggest that a potential asset is not reported in the balance sheet. Not all R&D expenses are likely to be future assets, as only the successful efforts bear fruit, and may result in a collateral loss. This particular distortion is an increasing concern as the size and composition of business entities shift toward a knowledge-based economy from brick-and-mortar-based, and the relative proportion of tangible versus intangible asset shifts. Similarly, financial statements do not reflect other intangible assets, such as brands and patents. How to incorporate such information in forecasting remains a daunting task.

Another limitation of financial statement analysis–based forecasting involves measurement concerns such as accruals (Dechow, Ge, and Schrand 2010), real earnings management (Roychowdhury 2006), and conservatism in reported numbers (Basu 1997). The fact that reported numbers in financial statements are not completely unbiased also has implications for prediction performance.

Furthermore, competition among traders and investment banks implies that once analysts identify a successful forecasting model, others readily adopt it. The widespread adoption of successful forecasting models can then cause stock prices to move in a manner that eliminates the models' forecasting ability (Lo 2005; Timmermann and Granger 2004; Timmermann 2008). Indeed, the extensive use of earnings surprise–based trading strategies in practice has since eliminated the trading profits. In contrast to earnings prediction, rational asset pricing theory posits that stock return predictability can result from exposure to time-varying aggregate risk. To the extent that successful forecasting models consistently capture this time-varying aggregate risk premium, they are likely to remain successful over time. This latter element associated with the inherent difficulty of capturing time-varying risk makes earnings prediction more difficult. Hence, a continuing demand exists to search for newer prediction or forecasting models of future earnings.

A relatively unexplored avenue is the effectiveness of combining multiple forecasts. Bates and Granger (1969) show that a combination of forecasts usually outperforms the best individual forecast. Since technical analysis ignores firm fundamentals other than historical earnings, and fundamental analysis relies mostly on the most recent realizations, both methods exclude some information. Similarly, Hutton, Lee, and Shu (2012) document that security analysts are better at incorporating industry and macroeconomic factors in their forecasts that both technical and fundamental analysis largely ignore. This discussion suggests that a potential avenue for future exploration is how to combine technical analysis and fundamental analysis with analysts' forecasts.

SUMMARY AND CONCLUSION

This chapter provides an overview of using financial statement analysis in forecasting, primarily focusing on earnings. Although evidence shows that financial statement analysis can be useful in forecasting future earnings, limited evidence is available on whether such analysis is superior to either technical analysis (time series)–based forecasts or security analysts' forecasts of earnings. Hence, academics and practitioners should consider exploring approaches that combine multiple forecasts. Additionally, measurement concerns associated with reported numbers in financial statements suggest that any forecast must recognize the underlying contextual settings, such as the level of firm-specific or macroeconomic uncertainty.

DISCUSSION QUESTIONS

1. Explain the difference between forecasting based on technical analysis and fundamental analysis.
2. Discuss whether security analysts typically use information in financial statements in making their forecasts.
3. Discuss how analysts can use financial statements to improve their forecasts.
4. Discuss the limitations of using financial statements for purposes of forecasting and how forecasters can overcome such limitations.
5. Discuss whether technical and fundamental analysis can be combined to achieve superior forecasting.

REFERENCES

Abarbanell, Jeffery S., and Victor L. Bernard. 1992. "Tests of Analysts' Overreaction/Underreaction to Earnings Information as an Explanation for Anomalous Stock Price Behavior." *Journal of Finance* 47:3, 1181–1207.

Abarbanell, Jeffery S. and Brian J. Bushee. 1997. "Fundamental Analysis, Future Earnings, and Stock Prices." *Journal of Accounting Research* 35:Spring, 1–24.

Albrecht, W. Steve, Larry L. Lookabill, and James C. McKeown. 1977. "The Time-series Properties of Annual Earnings." *Journal of Accounting Research* 15:2, 226–244.

Ali, Ashiq, April Klein, and James Rosenfeld. 1992. "Analysts' Use of Information about Permanent and Transitory Earnings Components in Forecasting Annual EPS." *The Accounting Review* 67:1, 183–198.

Ball, Raymond, and Paul Brown. 1968. "An Empirical Evaluation of Accounting Income Numbers." *Journal of Accounting Research* 6:2, 159–178.

Ball, Raymond, and Ross Watts. 1972. "Some Time Series Properties of Accounting Income." *Journal of Finance* 27:3, 663–681.

Basu, Sudipta. 1997. "The Conservatism Principle and the Asymmetric Timeliness of Earnings." *Journal of Accounting and Economics* 24:1, 3–37.

Bates, John M., and Clive W. J. Granger. 1969. "The Combination of Forecasts." *Operations Research Quarterly* 20:4, 451–468.

Beaver, William H. 1968. "The Information Content of Annual Earnings Announcements." *Journal of Accounting Research* 6:Supplement, 67–92.

Beaver, William H. 1970. "The Time Series Behavior of Earnings." *Journal of Accounting Research* 8:Supplement, 62–99.

Beneish, Messod D., Charles M. C. Lee, and Robin L. Tarpley. 2001. "Contextual Fundamental Analysis Through the Prediction of Extreme Returns." *Review of Accounting Studies* 6:2–3, 165–189.

Board, John L. G., and Martin Walker. 1990. "Intertemporal and Cross-Sectional Variation in the Association Between Unexpected Accounting Rates of Return and Abnormal Returns." *Journal of Accounting Research* 28:1, 182–192.

Bradshaw, Mark T., Michael S. Drake, James N. Myers, and Linda A. Myers. 2012. "A Re-examination of Analysts' Superiority over Time-series Forecasts of Annual Earnings." *Review of Accounting Studies* 17:4, 944–968.

Bradshaw, Mark T., Yonca Ertimur, and Patricia O'Brien. 2016. "Financial Analysts and Their Contribution to Well-functioning Capital Markets." *Foundations and Trends in Accounting.* 11:3, 119–191.

Brooks, LeRoy D., and Dale A. Buckmaster. 1976. "Further Evidence on the Time Series Properties of Accounting Income." *Journal of Finance* 31:5, 1359–1373.

Brown, Lawrence D. 1993, "Earnings Forecasting Research." *International Journal of Forecasting* 9:3, 337–342.

Brown, Lawrence D., Paul A. Griffin, Robert L. Hagerman, and Mark E. Zmijewski. 1987. "Security Analyst Superiority Relative to Univariate Time-Series Models in Forecasting Quarterly Earnings." *Journal of Accounting and Economics* 9:1, 61–87.

Brown, Lawrence D., Robert L. Hagerman, Paul A. Griffin, and Mark E. Zmijewski. 1987. "An Evaluation of Alternative Proxies for the Market's Assessment of Unexpected Earnings." *Journal of Accounting and Economics* 9:2, 159–193.

Chavarnakul, Thira, and David Enke. 2009. "A Hybrid Stock Trading System for Intelligent Technical Analysis-Based Equivolume Charting." *Neurocomputing* 72:16–18, 3517–3528.

Collins, Daniel W., Sriprakash Kothari, and Judy D. Rayburn. 1987. "Firm Size and the Information Content of Prices with Respect to Earnings." *Journal of Accounting and Economics* 9:2, 111–138.

Cottle, Sidney, Roger F. Murray, and Frank E. Block. 1988. *Graham and Dodd's Security Analysis.* New York, NY: McGraw-Hill.

Cowles, Alfred. 1933. "Can Stock Market Forecasters Forecast?" *Econometrica* 1:3, 309–324.

Dechow, Patricia, Weili Ge, and Catherine Schrand. 2010. "Understanding Earnings Quality: A Review of the Proxies, Their Determinants and Their Consequences." *Journal of Accounting and Economics* 50:2–3, 344–401.

Dickinson, Victoria, and Gregory A. Sommers. 2012. "Which Competitive Efforts Lead to Future Abnormal Economic Rents? Using Accounting Ratios to Assess Competitive Advantage." *Journal of Business Finance and Accounting* 39:3–4, 360–398.

Easterwood, John, and Stacey R. Nutt. 1999. "Inefficiency in Analysts' Earnings Forecasts: Systematic Misreaction or Systematic Optimism?" *Journal of Finance* 54:5, 1777–1797.

Fairfield, Patricia M., and Teri L. Yohn. 2001. "Using Asset Turnover and Profit Margin to Forecast Changes in Profitability." *Review of Accounting Studies* 6:4, 371–385.

Feltham, Gerald A., and James A. Ohlson. 1995. "Valuation and Clean Surplus Accounting for Operating and Financial Activities." *Contemporary Accounting Research* 11:2, 689–731.

Freeman, Robert, James A. Ohlson, and Stephen H. Penman. 1982. "Book Rate-of-return and Prediction of Earnings Changes: An Empirical Investigation." *Journal of Accounting Research* 20:2, 639–653.

Gordon, Myron J. 1959. Dividends, Earnings and Stock Prices." *Review of Economics and Statistics* 41:2, 99–105.

Govindarajan, Vijay G. 1980. "The Objectives of Financial Statements: An Empirical Study of the Use of Cash Flows and Earnings by Security Analysts." *Accounting, Organizations, and Society* 5:4, 383–392.

Greig, Anthony C. 1992. "Fundamental Analysis and Subsequent Stock Returns." *Journal of Accounting and Economics* 15:2–3, 413–442.

Holthausen, Robert W., and David F. Larcker. 1992. "The Prediction of Stock Returns Using Financial Statement Information." *Journal of Accounting and Economics* 15:2–3, 373–411.

Hutton, Amy P., Lian Fen Lee, and Susan Z. Shu. 2012. "Do Managers Always Know Better? The Relative Accuracy of Management and Analyst Forecasts." *Journal of Accounting Research* 50:5, 1217–1244.

Koller, Tim, Marc Goedhart, and David Wessels. 2015. *Valuation: Measuring and Managing the Value of Companies,* 6th ed. . Hoboken, NJ: John Wiley & Sons.

Kothari, Sriprakash. 2001. "Capital Market Research in Accounting." *Journal of Accounting and Economics*, 31:1–3, 105–231.

Lev, Baruch, and S. Ramu Thiagarajan. 1993. "Fundamental Information Analysis." *Journal of Accounting and Research* 31:2, 190–215.

Lo, Andrew W. 2005. "Reconciling Efficient Markets with Behavioral Finance: The Adaptive Markets Hypotheses." *Journal of Investment Consulting* 7:2, 21–44.

Lookabill, Larry L. 1976. "Some Additional Evidence on the Time Series Properties of Accounting Earnings." *The Accounting Review* 51:4, 724–738.

Malkiel, Burton G. 2011. *A Random Walk Down Walk Street*, rev. ed. New York, NY: W. W. Norton.

Manegold, James G. 1981. "Time-Series Properties of Earnings: A Comparison of Extrapolative and Component Models." *Journal of Accounting Research* 19 (2): 360–373.

Mohanram, Partha S. 2005. "Separating Winners from Losers among Low Book-to-Market Stocks Using Financial Statement Analysis." *Review of Accounting Studies* 10 (2–3): 133–170.

Nazario, Rodolfo Toribio Farias, Jessica L. E. Silva, and Vinicius A. Sobreiro. 2017. "A Literature Review of Technical Analysis on Stock Markets." *Quarterly Review of Economics and Finance* 66:C, 115–126.

Nison, Steve. 1991. *Japanese Candlestick Charting Techniques: A Contemporary Guide to the Ancient Investment Technique of the Far East*. New York, NY: New York Institute of Finance, Simon & Schuster.

Nissim, Doron, and Stephen H. Penman. 2001. "Ratio Analysis and Equity Valuation: From Research to Practice." *Review of Accounting Studies* 6:1, 109–154.

Nissim, Doron, and Stephen H. Penman. 2003. "Financial Statement Analysis of Leverage and How It Informs about Profitability and Price-to-Book Ratios." *Review of Accounting Studies* 8:4, 531–560.

Ohlson, James A. 1995. "Earnings, Book Values, and Dividends in Equity Valuation." *Contemporary Accounting Research* 11:2, 661–687.

Ohlson, James A., and Beate E. Juettner-Nauroth. 2005. "Expected EPS and EPS Growth as Determinants of Value." *Review of Accounting Studies* 10:2–3, 349–365.

Ou, Jane A., and Stephen H. Penman. 1989. "Financial Statement Analysis and the Prediction of Stock Returns." *Journal of Accounting and Economics* 11:4, 295–329.

Penman, Stephen H. 1991. "An Evaluation of Accounting Rates of Return." *Journal of Accounting, Auditing and Finance* 16:2, 233–255.

Penman, Stephen H. 1992a. "Return to Fundamentals." *Journal of Accounting, Auditing and Finance* 7:4, 465–483.

Penman, Stephen H. 1992b. "Financial Statement Information and the Pricing of Earnings Changes," *The Accounting Review* 67:3, 563–577.

Penman, Stephen H. 2013. *Financial Statement Analysis and Security Valuation*, 5th ed. New York, NY: McGraw-Hill.

Pike, Richard, Johannes Meerjanssen, and Leslie Chadwick. 1993. "The Appraisal of Primary Shares by Investment Analysts in the UK and Germany." *Accounting and Business Research* 23:92, 489–499.

Piotroski, Joseph D. 2000. "Value Investing: The Use of Historical Financial Statement Information to Separate Winners from Losers." *Journal of Accounting Research* 38: Supplement, 1–41.

Ramnath, Sundaresh, Steven Rock, and Philip B. Shane. 2008. "Financial Analysts' Forecasts and Stock Recommendations: A Review of the Research." *Foundations and Trends in Finance* 2:4, 311–421.

Rapach, David, and Guofu Zhou. 2013. "Forecasting Stock Returns." *Handbook of Economic Forecasting* 2, 328–338.

Richardson, Scott, İrem Tuna, and Peter Wysocki. 2010. "Accounting Anomalies and Fundamental Analysis: A review of recent research advances." *Journal of Accounting and Economics* 50:2–3, 410–454.

Roychowdhury, Sugato. 2006. "Earnings Management Through Real Activities Manipulation." *Journal of Accounting and Economics* 42:3, 335–370.

Schipper, Katherine. 1991. "Analysts' Forecasts." *Accounting Horizons* 5:4, 105–121.

Soliman, Mark T. 2008. "The Use of DuPont Analysis by Market Participants." *The Accounting Review* 83:3, 823–853.

Stober, Thomas. 1992. "Summary Financial Statement Measures and Analysts' Forecasts of Earnings." *Journal of Accounting and Economics* 15:2–3, 347–372.

Teixeira, Lamartine A., and Adriano L. I. D. Oliveira. 2010. "A Method for Automatic Stock Trading Combining Technical Analysis and Nearest Neighbor Classification." *Expert Systems with Applications* 37:10, 6885–6890.

Timmermann, Allan. 2008. "Elusive Return Predictability." *International Journal of Forecasting* 24:1, 1–18.

Timmermann, A., and Clive W. J. Granger. 2004. "Efficient Market Hypothesis and Forecasting." *International Journal of Forecasting* 20:1, 15–27.

Wahlen, James, and Matthew M. Wieland. 2011. "Can Financial Statement Analysis Beat Consensus Analysts' Recommendations?" *Review of Accounting Studies* 16:1, 89–115.

Watts, Ross L., and Richard W. Leftwich. 1977. "The Time Series of Annual Accounting Earnings." *Journal of Accounting Research* 15:2, 253–271.

Williams, John. B. 1938. *The Theory of Investment Value.* Cambridge, MA: Harvard University Press.

CHAPTER 7

Fundamentals of Equity Valuation

Emmanuel Boutron
Associate Professor of Finance, University Paris Nanterre
Alain Coën
Professor of Finance, Université du Québec à Montréal
Didier Folus
Professor of Finance, University Paris Nanterre

INTRODUCTION

Equity valuation is a central topic in finance because it lies at the cornerstone of the relationships among a firm's stakeholders, including investors, lenders, and employees. Since seminal studies in the early 1930s, equity valuation methods stand among the main topics in the finance literature. These methods highlight the importance of both the value of time and price risk in the investment process, often using the discounting of expected future cash flows. This context calls for defining a required rate of return or hurdle rate. Valuing equity is critical in finance because any corporate decision related to investment, financing, or dividend policy should be made according to the value-maximizing principle. Thus, valuation methods help managers in decision-making. The different approaches developed by academics and practitioners can be divided into three main categories: (1) asset-based valuation, (2) market-based valuation, and (3) other valuation approaches. This chapter's primary goal is to present the fundamentals of equity valuation.

This chapter is organized as follows. The next section defines equity valuation and highlights its crucial role in modern finance for academics and practitioners. The following three sections examine free cash flow–based valuation, dividend-based valuation, and market-based valuation. The subsequent section presents the modeling of the required rate of return used in the equity valuation process. Option theory–based valuation is discussed before concluding the chapter.

WHAT IS EQUITY VALUATION?

Equity valuation (EV) is an important finance topic that has received the attention of both academics and practitioners. It is a key economic metric that represents a company's net worth. Thus, many stakeholders study and use EV. *Equity valuation* refers to identifying equity value and calculating the intrinsic value of a company's equity or stock. EV is based mainly on a company's fundamental analysis as well as the need to understand its financial statements and to grasp its economic and regulatory environment.

Fundamental Analysis

Fundamental analysts seek to determine the intrinsic value of a company's stock, focusing primarily on a quantitative analysis of its financial statements. By looking at revenues, expenses, assets, liabilities, and other relevant financial data, analysts expect to gain insight into a company's future performance. Less tangible firm characteristics can also influence its future performance. Therefore, a qualitative analysis complements the quantitative one. A fundamental analyst has to consider both quantitative and qualitative information to estimate future cash flows that underlie a pricing model.

Understanding Financial Statements

A large part of fundamental analysis involves analyzing financial statements, which represent a type of report card of a company's business. Analysts measure a company's value creation, commonly through financial ratios, and determine the appropriate risk level to calculate a target risk-adjusted return or value for the company's stock.

Understanding Economic and Regulatory Environment

Analysts should have a solid understanding of the market structure, including major players, main customers, suppliers, and a company's market share and growth rate projections for the market. They must also identify the firm's competitive advantages to measure the sustainability of its value creation.

Specific industries are more heavily regulated than others due to their importance or nature of their products or services. For example, before a newly developed aircraft model enters operation, it must obtain a certificate from the responsible aviation regulatory authority, which is the Federal Aviation Agency in the United States and the European Union Aviation Safety Agency in Europe. This certificate gives a competitive advantage for insider aircraft makers. For example, Airbus taking a majority stake in Bombardier Inc.'s C Series aircraft program in 2018 (now Airbus A220) illustrates how a company can manage its certifications.

Equity Valuation Objectives

Equity valuation uses different measures – return, volatility, and dividends – as well as different metrics – present value, multiples, and ratios – to determine the intrinsic value and to advise stakeholders such as investors, investment funds managers, lenders, and brokers. Traditionally, a stock's market price should converge to its intrinsic value. In practice, that convergence is not guaranteed because discrepancies appear between the market price and intrinsic value. That is, the market return is not perfectly correlated with analyst assumptions about the different model parameters. Overvaluation or undervaluation frequently occurs.

Who Is Interested in Equity Valuation?

Numerous internal and external stakeholders are interested in equity valuation.

- *Shareholders.* A company's owners or shareholders are interested in equity valuation for purposes of portfolio decision-making (selling or buying).
- *Investment fund managers.* Investment fund managers make buying or selling securities decisions and rebalance their portfolios, which requires conducting valuations. For example, the manager of a value-style oriented fund wants to buy underpriced securities and to sell overpriced ones to create value for clients.
- *Financial institutions.* Financial institutions are interested in equity valuation because they have to comply with prudential rules. In particular, banks and insurance companies must have equity amounts that reach regulatory targets, those being partially related to the value of the held securities.
- *Financial executives.* A company's financial executives are interested in equity valuation for three reasons. First, they must identify and select investment opportunities and business developments that increase shareholder equity value. Second, they face agency conflicts between shareholders and lenders that can have a costly impact on equity value. Third, they receive incentives via products like stock options, whose value is linked to the equity value.
- *Lenders.* Company's lenders such as bondholders and banks are involved in equity valuation in two ways. First, the debt-to-equity ratio is a criterion that lenders typically examine before deciding to lend to the company. Second, the value of complicated products such as subordinated loans or convertible bonds are contractually related to the issuing company's equity value.
- *Clients.* The company's providers and clients are indirectly involved in equity valuation, especially when the commercial relation is business to business. A high equity value reduces the cost of financial distress and offers the possibility of financing the business by buyer credit or supplier credit. Moreover, the company's employees' unions are supposed to defend the employees' jobs, interests, and benefits.

Equity Valuation Paradigm

Discounted cash flow (DCF) embodies the equity valuation paradigm. According to this concept, the current value of company equity is equal to the present value of its future cash flows that are attributable to shareholders.

Denoting CF_t as the company cash flow in year t, with r being the discount rate, Equation 7.1 shows the calculation of a stock's intrinsic value:

$$V_0 = \frac{CF_1}{(1 + r)^1} + \frac{CF_2}{(1 + r)^2} + \dots + \frac{CF_T}{(1 + r)^T} \qquad (7.1)$$

Analysts and investors compare this theoretical value to the current stock price to determine whether the company's stock is properly valued. If not, the stock provides either buying or selling opportunities depending on whether the stock is under- or overvalued, respectively. In practice, the DCF method requires estimating and using three major inputs: (1) expected future cash flows CF_1, CF_2, CF_3, ..., CF_n, (2) an investment horizon of time T, and (3) an appropriate discount rate r.

Analysts estimate future cash flows through an in-depth analysis of a company's assets and its competitive position in the market. Analysts choose an investment time horizon depending on the client and their ability to calculate futures cash flows. Individuals investing for a private pension face a several-decade investment horizon, whereas a private equity fund usually invests for three to five years before exiting. The investment risk–reward is related to the time the money remains invested, according to the mean reversion argument that a stock's price tends to move to the average price over time (Campbell and Shiller 2001). Finally, analysts must calculate and adjust the discount rate for the risk taken.

Equity Valuation Approaches

Analysts traditionally use three major approaches to value equity: (1) the DCF approach, (2) the market-based approach, and (3) the asset-based approach.

DCF Approach The present value of future cash flow models differs based on the type of cash flow used in the analysis. The cash flows can include free cash flow to firm (FCFF), free cash flow to equity (FCFE), and dividends.

Although the DCF model focuses on the dividends the company pays to shareholders, the free cash flow models look at the cash flows that can be paid to shareholders after paying all expenses, reinvesting in the business to maintain capacity or firm competitiveness, and repaying debt. Analysts must anticipate these streams of cash flows, making certain assumptions about the firm's business, such as competitive position and return on assets, as well as its economic and financial environment, including such variables as interest rates, inflation, and the economy's growth rate. Analysts then compute the present value of the future cash flow using a discount rate reflecting the firm's riskiness.

Market-Based Valuation Market-based valuation (MBV) consists of various metrics using a mix of a company's financial statements data and market data. MBV often takes the form of a multiple or a ratio. *Financial ratios* are mathematical calculations using data mainly from the financial statements that analysts can use to evaluate a company's valuation and financial performance. A common market multiple is the price-to-earnings (P/E) ratio. Some other well-known valuation ratios include Tobin's q (Kaldor 1966; Dybvig and Warachra 2015) and the price-to-book (P/B) ratio.

For example, the P/B ratio compares the price per share to the company's book value per share. Suppose a company has an equity book value of $100 million and a market capitalization of $300 million; the P/B ratio equals 3. On an absolute basis, this ratio indicates that the company's shares trade at a higher value than their book value. Comparing the ratio on a relative basis provides useful insights on the share "value" or "growth" profile.

Analysts can also calculate other ratios or multiples to be compared with threshold values (absolute basis) or historical values of the ratio for the company, along with comparisons to competitors and the overall market itself. Analysts use the calculations produced by the valuation ratios to gain some understanding of a company's value.

Asset-Based Valuation   Asset-based valuation computes a company's net asset value (NAV), which is the difference between its total assets and total liabilities. Analysts have to determine which assets and liabilities to include in the valuation. Each asset or liability has a book value, but analysts are likely to adjust the value to consider a market value if possible, embody goodwill or price-intangible assets such as patents and trademarks. Asset-based valuation is especially suitable for private companies, nonlisted companies, or when a company's equity is not divided into shares because of a lack of information about the market sentiment, stock price history, or appropriate risk-adjusted discount rate.

Other Approaches   Among other approaches, *residual income* (RI) is calculated as the difference between the firm-generated net income and an equity charge (i.e., total equity capital multiplied by the required rate of return). Also, the real options approach is an alternative framework that is based on option theory.

Pinto, Robinson, and Stowe (2019) survey professional practices involving the use of equity valuation approaches. Their findings show that 92.8 percent of respondents use market multiples, followed by 78.8 percent using a DCF approach and 61.4 percent using option-based valuation. Survey results further show that a large percentage of respondents use all approaches with mean conditional frequencies of 68.6 percent and 59.5 percent, respectively (i.e., the percentage of cases in which a given approach is reported to be used, given that the analyst uses the approach). Analysts appear to use market multiples and DCF approaches as general tools, whereas asset-based (mean frequency of 36.8 percent) and especially option-based valuation (mean frequency of 20.7 percent) appear to be useful tools for more specialists. So, the primary findings show that survey respondents apply market multiples and DCF approaches with average frequencies of 64 percent and 47 percent, respectively. The corresponding frequencies for asset-based and option-based valuation approaches are roughly 23 percent and 1 percent, respectively. With this survey, two-thirds of the respondents are from the Americas.

In a similar survey, Bancel and Mittoo (2014) survey 356 valuation experts across 10 European countries with the CFA designation or an alternative designation to explore their valuation practices. Among the findings, relative valuation models (multiples and ratios) and DCF (mainly the FCFF approach) are equally popular, used by about 80 percent of respondents; 67 percent of them combine the two approaches. These results are consistent with those reported in the Pinto et al. (2019) survey. The prominence of those two approaches probably reflects their dominance in academic and practitioner textbooks. According to Bancel and Mittoo's survey, experts also use various methods to estimate the model inputs, such as the growth rate, risk premium, and terminal value, leading to different estimates, which illustrates a gap between the theoretical framework and its practical implementation.

FREE CASH FLOW–BASED VALUATION

A free cash flow (FCF)–based valuation approach can use FCFF and FCFE models. The first model values the entire firm, while the second one assesses the value of the shareholders' equity directly.

Free Cash Flow to the Firm Model

FCFF is based on the principle that an asset's value is equal to the present value of its expected future cash flows. Assets refer to a firm's present and future operating assets. These operating assets consist of long-term assets, including intangibles, fixed assets, and noncash working capital, which are frequently called *capital employed*.

The next step is to calculate the cash flows the firm generates. *FCFF* is an after-tax operating cash flow less the amount reinvested in the capital employed to fuel its growth. More precisely, FCFF equals the operating income earned from the capital employed (earnings before interest and taxes, or EBIT), from which tax (t) is deducted and depreciation (*Dep.*), a noncash expense, is added to derive the cash flow generated by the operations. Next, the capital expenditure (CAPEX) and the change in noncash working capital (ΔWC) are subtracted to obtain the FCFF, as shown in Equation 7.2.

$$FCFF = EBIT \times (1 - t) + Dep. - \Delta WC - CAPEX \qquad (7.2)$$

FCFF does not consider extraordinary items. Its estimate reflects the cash generated under normal/usual economic business conditions. It does not account for interest expenses because the cost of debt appears in the discount rate. FCFF is the cash left over to compensate those who finance the capital employed, including shareholders and creditors or bondholders. Hence, the discount rate that reflects their expectations about time and risk is the weighted average cost of capital (WACC). Analysts often use models such as the capital asset pricing model (CAPM), the arbitrage pricing model (APT), or the Fama-French three-factor model to estimate the cost of equity (k_e). The cost of debt is the after-tax cost of debt to account for the tax deductibility of the interest expenses. The interest rate should reflect the risk borne by the debt- or bondholders at the time of the valuation. The weights of equity (E) and debt (D) in the financial structure depend on the financial structure objective and are typically measured using the market value, which measures the current/actual cost of raising funds. Equation 7.3 shows the calculation of WACC:

$$WACC = k_e \times \frac{E}{E + D} + k_d \times \frac{D}{E + D} \qquad (7.3)$$

Equation 7.4 presents a firm's value (V_{Firm}) over a period of N years using the FCFF model:

$$V_{Firm} = \sum_{i=1}^{N} \frac{FCFF_i}{(1 + WACC)^i} \qquad (7.4)$$

Given the firm's value, the next step is to derive the value of the shareholders' equity by deducting the market value of debt from the firm value and adding back the cash and the market value of marketable securities whose impact on the FCFF has not been taken into account during the first step. Equation 7.5 gives the equity value.

$$V_{Equity} = V_{Firm} - V_{Debt} + V_{Cash \ and \ marketable \ securities} \qquad (7.5)$$

Two versions of the general model can be derived depending on whether the company is mature or growing rapidly. For mature companies whose cash flow is growing at a low but constant rate (g) toward infinity (the growth rate should be equal or lower than the expected growth of the economy) and provided that the WACC is greater than g, Equation 7.5 shows the valuation model specific to mature firm:

$$V_{Firm} = \frac{FCFF_1}{(WACC - g)} \qquad (7.6)$$

For example, Garmin is listed on the NASDAQ and operates in the consumer electronics sector. Many analysts considered Garmin to be a stable growth firm. At the end of 2018, the company had an FCFF of $430 million, expected to grow at 4.5 percent (approximated by average growth of its FCFF over the last five years) in the long term. Its cost of equity was 7.58 percent, the pretax cost of debt was 4 percent, and the corporate tax rate was 21 percent. The market value of its equity and debt was $15,300 and $60 million, respectively. Garmin had $190 million shares outstanding and $1,060 million of cash and marketable securities.

$$WACC = 7.58 \times \frac{15,300}{15,300 + 60} + (1 - 21\%) \times \frac{60}{15,300 + 60} = 7.56\%$$

The value of the firm is:

$$V_{Garmin} = \frac{\$430.5(1 + 4.5\%)}{7.47\% - 4.5\%} = \$14,688.51$$

The shareholders' equity is equal to $V_{Equity} = \$14,688.51 - \$60.00 + \$1,060.00 = \$15,688.51$. Finally, its value per share is $\frac{\$15,688.51}{190} = \$82.57$. When the firm announced its 2018 results and the earning guidance for 2019, its stock surged from $71.00 to $82.00.

The following model shown in Equation 7.7 is suitable for companies expecting to face an N-year period of high growth, followed by an indefinite period of low and stable growth.

$$V_{Firm} = \sum_{i=1}^{N} \frac{FCFF_i}{(1 + WACC)^i} + \frac{FCFF_{N+1}/(WACC-g)}{(1 + WACC)^N} \qquad (7.7)$$

The first element at the right-hand side of the equals sign is the present value of the FCFF during the high-growth period. The second element is the present value of the firm's terminal value.

Using FCFF models to assess the value of the firm and its equity requires forecasting the components of the FCFF, its growth rate, duration of the high-growth period if any, and WACC. Using historical data implies that the future is expected to be similar to the past. This assumption might be correct for mature firms but not for young companies. The firm or its environments, such as financial analysts and industry syndicate, can provide analysts with estimates, but they might be biased. When no data are available, using a sample of listed comparable firms might also be helpful. The number of years of the high-growth period depends on a firm's characteristics (e.g., young, competitive advantage, or with patents) and the market in which it operates (e.g., emergence and duration of the business cycle). No one best solution exists.

However, the FCFF approach helps to value non-dividend-paying firms or firms with negative net income. It also requires analysts to consider the firm's business model to make accurate assumptions. It further accounts for the advantages and drawbacks of debt financing that come with estimating the cost of capital.

Free Cash Flow to Equity Models

The FCFE model is an intermediate model between FCFF and DDMs. Similar to DDMs, the FCFE model directly assesses the shareholders' equity. Although the FCFE model directly estimates the shareholders' equity, as do DDMs, it does not consider the expected dividends but the amount the firm could pay out after having fulfilled its financial obligations and investment needs (CAPEX and ΔWC). Moreover, this is where the main advantage of the model originated, since the tendency of executives to curb dividend growth does not affect the value of equity. The consequence is that no cash remains on the balance sheet, and therefore, no income can be derived from it. Another advantage to the FCFE model is that it can be negative and as such, accounts into the value of equity, the likely dilution of any new stock issues. Equation 7.8 shows the FCFE model.

$$FCFE = NI + Dep. - \Delta WC - CAPEX + \Delta Debt \tag{7.8}$$

The main drawback of the FCFE model compared to the FCFF model is that it requires assessing the amount of debt redeemed and issued each year in addition to capital expenditures and new working capital needs.

DIVIDEND-BASED VALUATION

The dividend-based valuation model assumes that an investor who buys a share of the company's stock earns the annual dividend D_t paid by the company on date t, plus a sale price P_T when liquidating the position on a future date T. Over a holding period of T years, the investor would agree to invest the present value of those future earnings. Thus, Equation 7.1 becomes Equation 7.9, where $r = k$ = company's cost of equity:

$$V_0 = \frac{D_1}{(1+k)^1} + \frac{D_2}{(1+k)^2} + \dots + \frac{D_T + P_T}{(1+k)^T} \tag{7.9}$$

Because the stock is a transferable security, it theoretically has an infinite maturity date. Thus, P_T can be assimilated into the intrinsic value V_T, which is equal to the present value of future dividends D_{T+1}, D_{T+2}. As a result, Equation 7.9 becomes Equation 7.10:

$$V_0 = \frac{D_1}{(1+k)^1} + \frac{D_2}{(1+k)^2} + \dots + \frac{D_\infty}{(1+k)^\infty} \tag{7.10}$$

According to Equation 7.10, the intrinsic stock value equals the present value of all expected future dividends into perpetuity. Capital gains are embedded in the equation through future dividend expectations. Equation 7.10 requires estimating the future dividends chain D_1 to D_∞, estimating the cost of capital k, and calculating the sum. Analysts forecast future dividends and estimate the cost of capital using CAPM or another model (Folus 1997).

The Constant-Growth DDM

Gordon and Shapiro (1956) popularize a didactic version of the DDM, introducing a constant dividend growth rate g to simplify the modeling of future dividend patterns. Denoting D_0 as the observed current dividend, expected future dividends follow a geometric sequence: $D_1 = D_0(1 + g)$, $D_2 = D_0(1 + g)^2$, and the like. So, Equation 7.10 becomes Equation 7.11.

$$V_0 = \frac{D_0(1 + g)}{(1 + k)^1} + \frac{D_0(1 + g)^2}{(1 + k)^2} + \ldots + \frac{D_0(1 + g)^\infty}{(1 + k)^\infty} \qquad (7.11)$$

Under the condition that $g < k$, Equation 7.11 can be simplified as Equation 7.12 (Bodie, Kane, and Marcus 2018).

$$V_0 = \frac{D_0(1 + g)}{k - g} \qquad (7.12)$$

For example, consider the case of Nike Inc., which paid an annual dividend of \$0.88 in 2019. The financial analysts' consensus expects a growth rate of $g =$ 7.50 percent (perpetual). The company's beta is equal to 1.10, the risk-free rate is 2.00 percent (10-year T-bond yield), and the market risk premium is 6.00 percent. Applying the CAPM provides $k = 8.60$ percent $= 2.00$ percent $+ 1.10$ (6.00 percent).

Applying Equation 7.5 leads to $V_0 = \$86.00$, close to the Nike Inc. stock quote \$87.50 (NYSE on July 29, 2019). If the consensus were $g = 7.0$ percent, the intrinsic stock value would be \$58.85; in the same way, any variation of k markedly affects the intrinsic value.

Finally, the intrinsic value is highly sensitive to the Gordon model parameters, mainly because the model has a restrictive underlying hypothesis, particularly the constant-growth rate. A more realistic approach is a multistage growth DDM.

Multistage Growth DDM

A firm rarely has a constant dividend growth rate. Firms pass through business cycles and have life cycles. A company could, for example, cut its current dividend to save cash to finance a new investment that offers an attractive return. Later, if the business earnings grow, the company may adjust its payout ratio and dividend level. Such a context explains why financial analysts, investment bankers, or brokers develop pricing models that use flexible state patterns for growth.

Another reason to introduce flexibility in the model comes from the fact that financial analysts are accountable for customer advice. Because the Gordon model is highly sensitive to the growth rate, a client could view the calculated intrinsic value and the following advice as unrealistic.

To illustrate the idea of a flexible growth rate, consider a two-stage model. An analyst expects a growth rate g for years 1 to 3, and a lower growth rate g' from year 4 ($g' < g$). Equation 7.11 becomes Equation 17.13:

$$V_0 = \underbrace{\frac{D_0(1+g)}{(1+k)^1} + \frac{D_0(1+g)^2}{(1+k)^2} + \frac{D_0(1+g)^3}{(1+k)^3}}_{\text{High-growth stage}} + \underbrace{\frac{D_3(1+g')^1}{(1+k)^4} + \ldots + \frac{D_3(1+g')^\infty}{(1+k)^\infty}}_{\text{Low-growth stage}}$$

(7.13)

where $D_3 = D_0(1+g)^3$. Applying the Gordon model to the low-growth stage terms, Equation 7.13 becomes Equation 7.14:

$$V_0 = \frac{D_0(1+g)}{(1+k)^1} + \frac{D_0(1+g)^2}{(1+k)^2} + \frac{D_0(1+g)^3}{(1+k)^3}\frac{(1+k)}{(k-g')}$$

(7.14)

Returning to the Nike Inc. case, assume an analyst expects a $g = 10.00$ percent short-term growth rate, and a $g' = 7.50$ percent long-term growth rate. As previously mentioned, the annual dividend is $D_0 = \$0.88$ and the cost of capital is $k = 8.60$ percent. Based on these assumptions and implementing Equation 7.14 with the numerical value of each parameter, the intrinsic value would equal 92.08, indicating that the stock is underpriced compared to the market price of $87.50.

Finally, all DDM models assume that analysts can forecast futures dividends or future growth rates. Although this assumption may be valid for mature, blue-chip companies, it probably is not the case for small caps with less certain future cash flows or companies developing new businesses. In the latter case, MBV using multiples or ratios could be more useful.

MARKET-BASED VALUATION: MULTIPLES AND RATIOS

According to Pinto et al. (2019), multiples approaches are the most popular ways to value firms. The frequent use of this method is mainly due to its simplicity and speed of implementation.

Analysts typically use two types of ratios for market-based ratios. The first type directly gives the value of the shareholders' equity, namely price-to-earnings (P/E), which is the most common, price-to-cash flow (P/CF), price-to-sales (P/S), and price-to-book value of equity (P/B). The second type assesses a firm's value, and then deducting the market value of debt gives the value of shareholders' equity: enterprise value to sales (EV/Sales), enterprise value to EBITDA (EV/EBITDA), and enterprise value to EBIT (EV/EBIT).

Contrary to using cash flow or dividend valuation methods, the market-based approach does not estimate an asset's intrinsic value but tells how much the market is ready to pay for a similar asset. As such, it incorporates market sentiment.

Valuing stock using multiples involves four steps:

1. *Identify a sample of comparable listed firms.* To select a list of comparable firms, financial analysts usually choose firms in the same geographical area (e.g., emerging versus developed countries), which operate in the same sector and whose fundamentals (e.g., growth, risk, and return) are similar to those of the firm being valued.
2. *Gather information on the multiples of the panel firms.* When computing the multiples of the panel of comparable firms, many questions arise about the market value taken as the numerator (a current price or average price over a defined period) or the value of the denominator (e.g., last available value, last or next 12-month value). If too much variability exists in the data, then using the median value, instead of the mean, might be more appropriate because, unlike the mean, the median is unaffected by outliers.
3. *Choose the appropriate result of the company to be valued.* This metric could be net income for the P/E or EBITDA for the EV/EBITDA. The result of the company being valued should not only be consistent with the multiple chosen but also reflect the expected result under normal business conditions. Using a normalized result might be the solution, especially for cyclical firms.
4. *Compute the value of equity.* Accomplishing this task involves multiplying the average value of the multiples of the sample by the estimated value of the result of the firm under scrutiny.

Using the P/E is infeasible when the company being valued displays negative earnings. To overcome this problem, one solution is to rely on a cash flow measure such as FCFE. If FCFE is also negative, then using the P/B may be the next solution because the book value of equity is more stable than earnings or FCFE. However, even the book value of equity can be negative. The only ratio left is the P/S, whose denominator is always positive. However, this solution requires carefully controlling for costs and profit margin when selecting comparable firms.

Cimarex Energy Co. operates as an independent oil and gas exploration and production company in the United States. Its last 12-month diluted earnings per share (EPS) before extraordinary items is around $6.15 and is supposed to double next year. A set of comparable firms with a lower expected growth displays an average P/E of 12.8. The expected price per share of Cimarex Energy Co. should be at least equal to 12.8 × $6.15 = $78.72. At the end of August 2019, its price was around $40, leaving room for considerable appreciation.

Equity multiples require carefully examining the financial structure of the comparable firms, as debt increases risk borne by shareholders. Using firm multiples avoids this situation. Those ratios value the entire company's worth and, as such, do not depend on a firm's capital structure. Additionally, those ratios might also be used for loss-making companies.

Instead of valuing stocks, investors can extract the underlying market expectations of fundamentals (e.g., growth, risk, and return) from multiples, and compare these expectations with information disclosed by the company and/or its environment. Although the market-based approach does not require formulating explicit hypotheses about fundamentals such as in cash flow valuation models, multiples are based on the same fundamentals (Damodaran 2010). For instance, in Equation 7.15 the one-period DDM is transformed to make the P/E multiple and the parameters, on which it depends, appear:

$$V_0 = \frac{D_0 \times (1+g)}{k-g} = \frac{(1-d) \times EPS_0 \times (1+g)}{k-g} = \frac{(1-d) \times EPS_1}{k-g}$$

$$\frac{V_0}{EPS_1} = \frac{(1-d)}{k-g} \qquad\qquad (7.15)$$

where V_0 = value of one share, EPS_1 = earning per share in year 1, d = payout ratio, and k = cost of equity.

Equation 7.16 assumes that earnings growth (g) depends on the amount of earnings reinvested $(1 - d)$ in the business, where d is the dividend payout ratio, and the return on equity (ROE). It is also what is called the endogenous rate of growth. Therefore, the PE ratio is indeed a function of growth, risk, and return.

$$g = (1 - d)ROE \qquad\qquad (7.16)$$

Investors use the P/E value and Equation 7.15 to infer market expectations of the dividend payout ratio (d), required rate of return (k), growth rate (g), or return on equity (ROE), assuming that three out of the four parameters aforementioned are known. For instance, investors might compare the P/E implied earnings growth (respectively PE implied ROE) of Company ABC with the actual or anticipated growth (respectively ROE) to judge whether the stock is under- or overvalued. Company ABC has the following characteristics: P/E = 10, k = 15 percent, and d = 20 percent. Using Equation 7.15, the P/E implied earnings growth or the market expectations about earnings growth are equal to a 7 percent growth rate in earnings. If ABC's ROE has a good chance to level off at 15 percent, then its endogenous growth rate of earnings is equal to 12 percent (using Equation 7.16), which is considerably higher than the market's anticipation.

Using Equation 7.16, a P/E implied earnings growth of 7 percent and a 20 percent payout ratio are equivalent to a market-expected ROE of 8.75 percent, well below the 15 percent the firm is supposed to achieve. Both results converge, leading to the conclusion that ABC stock is undervalued and, as such, is a good bargain.

Apart from selecting sample firms, a market-based approach is a relatively easy method to assess the value of listed and nonlisted companies. As this approach relies on the same fundamentals as the cash flow methods, analysts can also use it to confront market expectations with actual or anticipated values of those fundamentals.

MODELING THE REQUIRED ASSET RETURN

The required rate of return or hurdle rate is usually defined by linear asset pricing models. The standard model is the CAPM, as introduced by Sharpe (1964).

The CAPM is a market equilibrium model that evaluates the price of risk. At equilibrium, all investors hold the same portfolio for risky assets – the market portfolio. It contains all traded assets, and the proportion of each asset is its market value as a percentage of the total market value.

The risk for a financial asset has two dimensions: idiosyncratic (unsystematic) and systematic. The idiosyncratic risk is the specific risk (endogenous risk) for a firm, while the systematic risk is the market risk (exogenous risk). Through diversification, investors can avoid idiosyncratic risk. Thus, only systematic market risk is profitable and should be priced.

The basic CAPM equation shown in Equation 7.17 indicates that the expected return of a financial asset $E[R_i]$ (the required rate of return) is the sum of two components: (1) the risk-free rate R_f and (2) the market risk premium $(E[R_m] - R_f)$ multiplied by the asset's beta. *Beta* is defined as the covariance of returns for the single asset and the returns of the market portfolio, divided by the variance of the returns of the market portfolio.

$$E[R_i] = R_f + \beta_i(E[R_m] - R_f) \tag{7.17}$$

For an asset, only its participation in the market risk is priced, and its beta measures this participation. The CAPM and linear asset pricing models presented here are developed ex-ante. In practice, they are used ex-post.

The CAPM is one of the most established models in modern financial theory, but it has serious drawbacks. Following Basu (1977) and Banz (1981), Fama and French (1992, 1993) introduce a three-factor asset pricing model to account for anomalies observed in financial markets: size effect (SMB) and book-to-market effect (HML). Carhart (1997) proposes a momentum factor (UMD) to augment the Fama and French asset pricing model. More recently, Fama and French (2015) develop a five-risk-factor model with two new risk premia related to profitability (RMW) and conservatism (CMA) in investment choice. The risk factors used in a linear asset pricing model to compute the required rate of return are MKT (market risk premium), SMB (size factor), HML (book-to-market factor), UMD (momentum factor), RMW (profitability factor), CMA (conservatism factor), and LIQ (liquidity factor). Details of computing these risk factors are available on Kenneth French's website and the Pastor and Stambaugh (2003) website for the specific illiquidity premium. Equation 7.18 gives the expected required rate of return for multi-factor asset pricing models, including APT models with K risk factors, where $E[F_k]$ is the expected return of the risk factor k:

$$E[R_i] = R_f + \sum_{k=1}^{K} \beta_{ik}E[F_k] \tag{7.18}$$

As mentioned earlier, the assumptions underlying the CAPM's validity are highly restrictive. Ross (1976) introduces a multifactor linear asset pricing model based on the APT. The three no-arbitrage conditions are translated in econometrics as orthogonality conditions introducing a dynamic and stochastic risk factors basis. These econometric conditions should be observed to test the APT model empirically in practice but are rarely validated.

Chen, Roll, and Ross (1986) test the empirical APT model. In this linear asset pricing model, they report six risk factors: R_m (the return on a value-weighted index of NYSE-listed stocks), MP (the monthly growth rate in U.S. industrial production), DEI (the change in inflation, measured by the U.S. consumer price index), UI (the difference between actual and expected levels of inflation), UPR (the unanticipated change in the bond credit spread [Baa yield – R_f]), and UTS (the unanticipated term structure shift [long-term less short-term R_f]).

Financial analysts and portfolio managers can also use BARRA risk factors. In practice, when using a multi-factor linear asset pricing model is not relevant, applying an ad hoc approach to define the required rate of return is possible. More precisely, a global risk premium is added to a risk-free rate (or equivalent). As an example, for a small unlisted firm, an ad hoc risk premium of three to four percentage points may be added to the global cost of debt to valuate the required rate of return. This ad hoc risk premium may be much higher for venture capital or private equity.

OPTION THEORY–BASED VALUATION

Classic valuations based on DCFs are static approaches that ignore the flexibility that firms or projects have in the real world. This flexibility may be measured by options, more precisely by real options. Bachelier (1900) initially develops option theory for financial markets. Later, Merton (1973) and Black and Scholes (1973) generalize and apply option theory. Myers (1977) adapts and applies this methodology to corporate finance decisions. He suggests decomposing a firm into two components: the value of assets in place and the value of opportunities (especially growth opportunities considered as real options). In this case, Equation 7.19 shows a firm's market value (MV) may be computed as the sum of the net present value of DCFs (PV(DCF)) without options plus the value of the managerial options (Opt) or real options implicit in the firm.

$$MV = PV\,(DCF)\,+\,Opt \qquad (7.19)$$

This technique is particularly relevant for firms with major investment, financing, or flexibility opportunities such as energy, commodities, high-tech, raw materials, mining industry, and startups. Among the different options that apply are growth options (call), expand options (call), delay options (call), or abandon options (put). Real options are priced using and applying the methodology introduced by Black and Scholes (1973) to value call and put options for investment and corporate decisions. The put–call parity condition applies. As well acknowledged, the values of a call and a put (European options) are, respectively, given by the following relations shown in Equation 7.20 and 7.21, respectively:

$$Call = SN(d1) - Ke^{-rt}N(d2) \qquad (7.20)$$

$$Put = -SN(d1) + Ke^{-rt}N(-d2) \qquad (7.21)$$

where $d1 = \dfrac{ln\left(\frac{S}{K}\right)+\left(r+\frac{\sigma^2}{2}\right).t}{\sigma\sqrt{t}}$ and $d2 = d1 - \sigma\sqrt{t}$, in which S = underlying asset's value; K = option's strike; σ = underlying asset's variance; r = riskless interest rate corresponding to the option's life; t = option's time to expiration; and $N(.)$ = standard normal cumulative distribution function.

SUMMARY AND CONCLUSIONS

Fundamental analysis focuses on equity valuation and intrinsic value estimation. Its objective is to identify under- and overpriced securities. If the estimated value exceeds the market price, analysts infer that the security is undervalued. Conversely, if the estimated value is less than the market price, analysts infer that the security is overvalued. Three major approaches to equity valuation are available: DCF models, market-based models, and asset-based valuation models. Recent academic studies suggest that practitioners mainly use relative value and DCF approaches. The choice of an approach depends on the availability of input data and the analyst's confidence in both the information and the model's appropriateness, which helps to explain why equity valuation suffers disparities in practice. More standardization in key valuation parameters calculation could improve the equity "fair value" estimation.

DISCUSSION QUESTIONS

1. Describe the major categories of equity valuation models and discuss the pros and cons of each.
2. Assume a stock is priced at $100; calculate its intrinsic value based on the Gordon growth DDM, with the following assumptions: $D_0 = \$3$, $g = 6$ percent, and $k = 10$ percent. Indicate whether investors should buy, hold, or sell the stock. Indicate your recommendation if $g = 7$ percent.
3. Explain the rationale for using price multiples to value equity, how the P/E and P/B multiples relate to fundamentals, and using multiples based on comparable firms.
4. Explain why FCFF is discounted at the WACC.
5. Explain the main limitation of the P/E ratio.

REFERENCES

Bachelier, Louis. 1900. "Theory of Speculation." *Annales Scientifiques de l'École Normale Supérieure* 3:17, 21–86.

Bancel, Franck, and Usha R. Mittoo. 2014. "The Gap between the Theory and Practice of Corporate Valuation: Survey of European Experts." *Journal of Applied Corporate Finance*, 26:4, 106–117.

Banz, Rolf W. 1981. "The Relationship between Return and Market Value of Common Stocks." *Journal of Financial Economics* 9:1, 3–18.

Basu, Suleiman. 1977. "Investment Performance of Common Stocks in Relation to Their Price-Earnings Ratios: A Test of the Efficient Market Hypothesis." *Journal of Finance* 32:3, 663–682.

Black, Fischer, and Myron Scholes. 1973. "The Pricing of Options and Corporate Liabilities." *Journal of Political Economy* 81:3, 637–654.

Bodie, Zvi, Alex Kane, and Alan J. Marcus. 2018. *Investments and Portfolio Management*, 10th ed. New York, NY: McGraw-Hill.

Campbell, John Y., and Robert J. Shiller. 2001. "Valuation Ratios and the Long-run Stock Market Outlook: An Update." NBER Working Paper, National Bureau of Economic Research.

Carhart, Mark M. 1997. "On Persistence in Mutual Fund Performance." *Journal of Finance* 52:1, 57–82.

Chen, Nai-Fu, Richard Roll, and Stephen A. Ross. 1986. "Economic Forces and the Stock Market." *Journal of Business* 59:3, 383–403.

Damodaran, Aswath. 2010. *The Dark Side of Valuation: Valuing Young, Distressed, and Complex Businesses*, 2nd ed. Upper Saddle River, NJ: FT Press.

Dybvig, Philip H., and Mitch Warachra. 2015. "Tobin's q Does Not Measure Firm Performance: Theory, Empirics, and Alternatives." Working Paper, SSRN. Available at https://ssrn.com/abstract=1562444.

Fama, Eugene F., and Kenneth R. French. 1992. "The Cross-Section of Expected Stock Returns." *Journal of Finance* 47:2, 427–465.

Fama, Eugene F., and Kenneth R. French. 1993. "Common Risk Factors in the Returns on Stocks and Bonds." *Journal of Financial Economics* 33:1, 3–56.

Fama, Eugene F., and Kenneth R. French. 2015. "A Five-Factor Asset Pricing Model." *Journal of Financial Economics* 116:1, 1–22.

Folus, Didier. 1997. "Actions: Modélisation, Evaluation, Gestion." In *Encyclopédie des Marchés Financiers*, edited by Yves Simon, 1–25. Paris: Economica.

Gordon, Myron J., and Eli Shapiro. 1956. "Capital Equipment Analysis: The Required Rate of Profit." *Management Science* 3:1, 102–110.

Kaldor, Nicholas C. 1966. "Marginal Productivity and the Macro-Economic Theories of Distribution: Comment on Samuelson and Modigliani." *Review of Economic Studies* 33:4, 309–319.

Merton, Robert C. 1973. "Theory of Rational Option Pricing." *Bell Journal of Economics and Management Science* 4:1, 141–183.

Myers, Stewart C. 1977. "Determinants of Corporate Borrowing." *Journal of Financial Economics* 5:2, 147–175.

Pastor, Lubos, and Robert Stambaugh. 2003. "Liquidity Risk and Expected Stock Returns." *Journal of Political Economy* 111:3, 642–685.

Pinto, Jerald E., Thomas R. Robinson, and John D. Stowe. 2019. "Equity Valuation: A Survey of Professional Practice." *Review of Financial Economics* 37:2, 219–233.

Ross, Stephen A. 1976. "The Arbitrage Theory and Capital Asset Pricing." *Journal of Economic Theory* 13:3, 343–362.

Sharpe, Williams F. 1964. "Capital Asset Prices: A Theory of Market Equilibrium under Conditions of Risk." *Journal of Finance* 19:3, 425–442. Available at https://mba.tuck.dartmouth.edu/pages/faculty/ken.french/data_library.html.

CHAPTER 8

Company Analysis

David Craig Nichols
Associate Professor of Accounting, Syracuse University

INTRODUCTION

This chapter introduces company analysis in the context of a three-step framework linking business activities to share prices. The origin of this framework is Nichols, Wahlen, and Wieland (2017) and Nichols and Wahlen (2020). The financial reporting process captures information on a company's underlying business activities, aggregates the information into financial reports, and communicates that information to investors (step 1). The financial statements provide crucial input for fundamental analysis, from which analysts and investors develop cash flow expectations and estimates of share value (step 2). In the final step, traders act on their information and value estimates, and these trading activities incorporate investor information about a company's business activities into the price (step 3).

This chapter focuses on company analysis, encompassing step 1 and the fundamental analysis part of step 2. The next section of this chapter describes each of these steps in more detail. The chapter then discusses accounting analysis, followed by fundamental analysis, before concluding.

THREE STEPS LINKING BUSINESS ACTIVITIES TO EQUITY PRICES

The relation between current accounting information and current stock prices depends on three steps, as depicted in Figure 8.1. Step 1 is the financial reporting process. In this process, the accounting system captures information about a company's transactions, events, and business activities. The accounting system aggregates this information into financial statements that reflect a company's performance for the period (income statement) and its financial position as of the end of the period (balance sheet), as well as notes and other disclosures to aid in interpreting the information in the basic financial statements. This process renders much of a company's private information about its activities publicly available to investors.

Step 2 is the fundamental analysis and valuation process. In this process, investors, analysts, and others use the information in financial statements to evaluate a company's profitability, growth, and risk. These parties use the results of their financial statement analysis as well as other publicly available information to develop

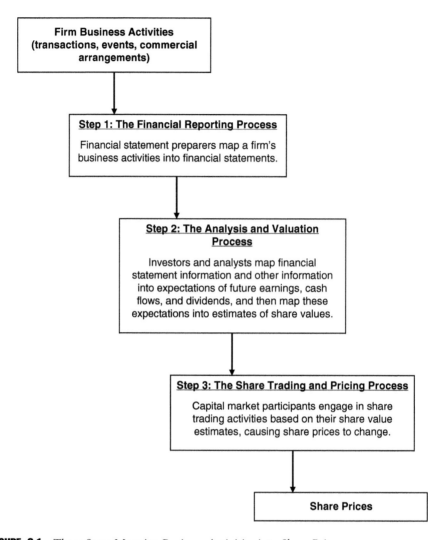

FIGURE 8.1   Three Steps Mapping Business Activities into Share Prices

This figure describes the three-step framework from Nichols, Wahlen, and Wieland (2017) mapping firm business activities into share prices.

expectations of future cash flows. With expectations of cash flows and assessments of risk in hand, investors and analysts estimate the value of a share of stock.

Step 3 is the equity trading process. In this process, investors trade on their information and estimates of share value, optimizing their holdings for their desired risk–return tradeoff. When share prices deviate from fundamental values, the equity trading process aids in (ultimately) eliminating the difference. Step 3 assumes share trading is informed by accounting information, and analysts' and investors' share value estimates. Trading often occurs for many other reasons, which creates slippage in step 3. Slippage can arise from, for example, liquidity trading (e.g., selling shares to meet cash needs), noise trading (e.g., trading on rumors), market frictions (e.g., wide bid–ask spreads or short-sale restrictions), and market sentiment (e.g., bubbles and crashes), which can lead to temporary departures of share prices from fundamental values, even in highly efficient markets. Furthermore, trading constraints can also prevent trading activities from eliminating departures of price from the fundamental value (e.g., Beneish, Lee, and Nichols 2015).

This chapter illustrates the operation of the three links with an analysis of the correlation between stock prices and accounting fundamentals. The analysis estimates annual regressions of stock prices on operating income, other income, the book value of equity, and dividends (all on a per-share basis). This analysis implements Ohlson (1995), a classic valuation theory paper linking current prices to currently observable fundamental accounting measures.

The sample includes all stocks in the intersection of Compustat and CRSP with sufficient data for inclusion in the sample from 1982 to 2018. Variables are trimmed at 0.5 percent and 99.5 percent to eliminate outliers. The R^2 from these annual regressions measures the proportion of variance in price captured by the accounting fundamentals, thus measuring the extent of value-relevant information captured by the accounting system (step 1), used for valuation (step 2), and incorporated into price through trading (step 3). Figure 8.2 presents the results.

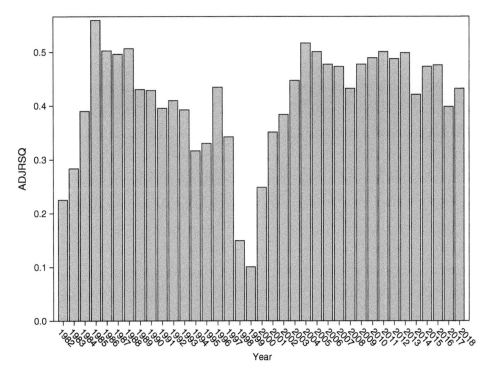

FIGURE 8.2 Adjusted R^2 from Annual Regressions of Prices on Accounting Fundamentals between 1982 and 2018

This figure plots adjusted R^2 (ADJRSQ) from annual regressions of prices on book value, net income, and dividends between 1982 and 2018. All data with available observations are collected from Compustat and CRSP. Observations are trimmed at 0.5 percent and 99.5 percent to eliminate outliers.

The average annual R^2 value is 0.409, indicating that fundamental summary accounting measures capture a substantial proportion of the value-relevant information in stock prices. Large temporal variation exists in the value relevance of accounting fundamentals. The value relevance of accounting information weakened between 1998 and 1999, a period marked by a stock price bubble during which prices decoupled from accounting fundamentals. Value relevance returned to normal levels by 2003 and remained steady over the remainder of the sample period.

The part of price that remains unexplained by current accounting fundamentals reflects expectations of future cash flows to equity holders. Companies pay cash flows to equity holders out of earnings. Thus, stronger (weaker) expected cash flows imply stronger (weaker) future earnings. Based on these observations, high (low) residuals from regressions of current prices on current accounting fundamentals should portend high (low) future earnings. To test this relation, the subsequent analysis sorts residuals from each annual cross-sectional regression into deciles. The next period's operating income (scaled by assets to create a version of return on assets, or ROA) for the highest (lowest) deciles are then averaged each period, and the spread is plotted in Figure 8.3.

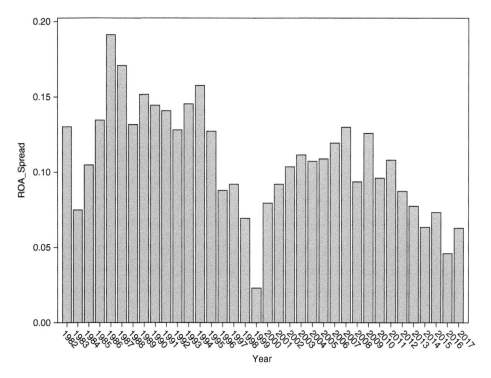

FIGURE 8.3 Spread in ROA to High and Low Deciles of Unexpected Price between 1982 and 2017

This figure plots the difference in the next-period operating income to total assets (ROA spread) between the highest and lowest deciles of unexplained price between 1982 and 2017. Unexplained price is the residual from a regression of price on book value, net income, and dividends. All data with available observations are collected from Compustat and CRSP. Observations are trimmed at 0.5 percent and 99.5 percent to eliminate outliers.

The results confirm that the other value-relevant information in price not captured by current accounting fundamentals relates to future accounting earnings. Stocks with higher (lower) prices than expected given current accounting fundamentals have high (low) future earnings. The spread in future earnings between the highest and lowest deciles of unexpected price averages 10.8 percent of total assets each year. Again, Figure 8.3 shows a temporal variation in the result over time, most notably in 1999. Consistent with a decoupling of price from fundamentals, not only did fundamentals poorly explain prices in 1999, but unexplained prices in 1999 possessed a weak relation with future earnings.

The results in this section confirm that fundamental accounting measures capture a substantial fraction of the value-relevant information impounded in price. Therefore, financial statements provide a useful starting point for understanding a firm's business activities. The first step in using the financial statements to understand a firm's story involves comprehending the language in which the story is told. The next section discusses this process, known as accounting analysis.

ACCOUNTING ANALYSIS

Slippage in step 1 can occur because financial statements are constrained in the information they can capture. Financial statements serve a unique role in capital markets as the premier source of externally verified information about a company's business activities. External verification limits the information that the accounting system can capture and convey to outsiders. Consequently, financial reporting is primarily limited to past transactions and events that auditors can verify. Yet, accounting systems generally require a higher level of verifiability to recognize good news than bad news, a feature of accounting called conditional (on the sign of the news) conservatism (Basu 1996; Watts 2003a, 2003b; Ball and Shivakumar 2006; Nichols, Wahlen, and Wieland 2009). Financial reporting also incorporates unconditional conservatism for highly uncertain cash flows, such as expenditures for research and development (R&D), advertising, and investments in organizational capital. To the extent these expenditures create future economic benefits, total assets from the balance sheet will understate the value of a company's economic resources and overstate profitability. Failure by analysts to recognize these effects can lead to unrealistic expectations and value estimates (slippage in step 2).

Analysts should review a company's accounting policies and identify areas of discretion in applying those policies. Accounting rules allow managers to express their private information about the firm through discretion over many areas of the financial reporting process. Managers who exercise discretion in this manner improve the tightness of step 1. Nevertheless, managers may employ discretion opportunistically or for reasons other than to facilitate the operation of the financial reporting process. Such activities decouple financial reporting from the underlying business activities. This process not only reduces the tightness of step 1 but also increases the risk of unrealistic forecasts and valuations (step 2).

The manager's financial reporting incentives provide the context for interpreting the exercise of discretion over financial reporting. In a survey of top-level managers at publicly traded companies, Graham, Harvey, and Rajgopal (2005) find that managers view earnings as the most important measure of firm performance communicated to parties outside the firm. Among the benefits of meeting earnings benchmarks, managers mention increased stock prices, stronger credibility, and higher managerial reputation. Consequences of missing earnings benchmarks include higher uncertainty and the concern by outsiders that previously unknown problems exist within a company.

Burgstahler and Dichev (1997) provide evidence that managers manage earnings to avoid losses and earnings declines. Specifically, the distributions of earnings and earnings changes show a pronounced discontinuity at the benchmark, with too few observations reporting a small loss or small earnings decline and too many observations reporting a small profit or small earnings increase. Yet, Burgstahler and Chuk (2015, 2017) as well as Nichols and Wahlen (2020) show that the discontinuity has become less pronounced in recent periods, possibly due to regulatory changes such as SEC Staff Accounting Bulletin 99 (SAB 99). SAB 99 holds that auditors should consider an accounting error material if the error allows a company to meet its earnings benchmarks. Degeorge, Patel, and Zeckhauser (1999) show that too many stocks meet or barely beat analyst forecasts and too few barely miss them than would be expected by chance. Many companies, however, have a policy of issuing earnings guidance, which can help explain this result.

Many other incentives for earnings management exist, but the strongest and most pervasive seem to arise from capital markets and management compensation. Salary is negatively associated with the intensity of earnings management (Gao and Shrieves 2002) and with the likelihood of fraud (Erickson, Hanlon, and Maydew 2006). The intensity of earnings management is positively associated with stock options (Gao and Shrieves 2002). Firms that restate and commit fraud have higher option compensation (Burns and Kedia 2006; Erickson et al. 2006; Efendi, Srivastava, and Swanson 2007). Managers manage earnings down before option grants (Baker, Collins, and Reitenga 2003; Balsam, Chen, and Sankaraguruswamy 2003) but up before option exercises (Safdar 2003; Bartov and Mohanram 2004; Bergstresser and Philippon 2006).

Capital markets also influence reporting decisions. Managers understate earnings in the context of management buyouts (Perry and Williams 1994; Wu 1997; Marquardt and Wiedman 2004). Initial public offerings (IPOs) and seasoned equity offerings (SEOs) provide incentives to overstate (Aharony, Lin, and Loeb 1993; Friedlan 1994; Teoh, Welch, and Wong 1998a, 1998b; Teoh, Wong, and Rao 1998). Nonetheless, exceptions exist to earnings overstatement at the time of the IPO. If the IPO is part of a plan that includes subsequent SEOs, managers tend to understate or "hoard" earnings at the IPO (Chaney and Lewis 1998).

Quantitative tools also exist to aid in detecting earnings manipulation. For example, Beneish (1999) uses financial statement characteristics to distinguish between fraud and nonfraud firms. His approach allows analysts to quantify the likelihood of earnings overstatement based on a company's financial statement profile. Beneish, Lee, and Nichols (2013) show that the model works well in identifying ex-ante highly publicized fraud cases and is useful in predicting stock returns. Dechow, Ge, Larson, and Sloan (2011) follow a similar approach to Beneish (1999), but they use a different set of financial statement characteristics and a much larger sample of misreporting stocks.

In summary, accounting analysis provides the analyst with a better understanding of the relation between a company's business activities, transactions, and events and its financial reports. Analysts should identify the natural limitations in financial reporting germane to the company (e.g., intellectual property rights for a research-intensive company and internally generated brand value for a consumer products company), as well as limitations potentially created by the managers to achieve financial reporting objectives. Analysts should evaluate financial reporting choices in the context of the manager's incentives, especially regarding compensation and capital markets. Analysts should also become acquainted with quantitative tools to help identify earnings manipulation, such as the Beneish (1999) M-Score and the Dechow et al. (2011) F-Score.

FUNDAMENTAL ANALYSIS

Financial statement analysis places structure on the financial statements to better understand a company's profitability, growth, and risk. Various financial statement ratios can aid analysts in evaluating a company's fundamental health and forecasting future profitability and growth.

Profitability

Return on equity (ROE) provides the broadest summary ratio of a firm's profitability for owners. ROE measures how managers use the capital invested by the owners to generate a return to benefit the owners. To better understand ROE, analysts can decompose ROE into measures that reflect the performance of the business and the use of leverage. Figure 8.4 provides a common decomposition, along with interpretation and calculation details.

Disaggregating ROE aids in forecasting. For example, a disaggregated forecasting approach along the dimensions of (1) operating versus financing and (2) persistent earnings versus unusual and/or infrequent items generates the best out-of-sample ROE forecasts (Esplin, Hewitt, Plumlee, and Yohn 2014).

Fairfield, Ramnath, and Yohn (2009) show that analyzing firms by industry improves forecasts of growth and profitability overusing large sample averages. Vorst and Yohn (2018) employ the Dickinson (2011) life cycle classification scheme to show that analyzing firms by life cycle stage improves out-of-sample accuracy of profitability and growth. Cantrell and Dickinson (2020) examine the industry-adjusted life cycle, finding that industry laggards earn higher returns and tend to employ differentiation strategies.

Economics of Profitability

Analysts should be familiar with economics shaping business profitability (i.e., ROA). Figure 8.5 shows ROAs by profit margins and asset turnovers across industries. Creating this graph involved collecting all companies in the Compustat database between 1982 and 2018 with sufficient data to calculate the ratios in any given year. Companies were assigned to industries based on primary SIC code. ROA, profit margin, and asset turnover were computed each year for each company. The median profit

Ratio	Computation	Interpretation
Return on equity (ROE = ROA × EL × AL)	$\frac{\text{Net income}}{\text{Avg shareholder equity}}$	Profitability for equity holders. ROE is a function of business profitability and leverage. The decomposition allows analysts to distinguish the performance of the business from choices in how the business is financed. Average equity is computed as the beginning period balance plus the ending period balance divided by 2.
Return on assets (ROA = PM × ATO)	$\frac{EBI}{\text{Avg total assets}}$	Profitability of the business. Reflects the operating and investing activities, and is the source of value creation. Average assets is computed as the beginning period balance plus the ending period balance divided by 2. Earnings before interest (EBI) is defined below.
Profit margin (PM)	$\frac{EBI}{\text{Sales}}$	Return to capital providers from each dollar of sales. As a measure of a company's operating activities, this ratio focuses on the cost structure. Analysts can decompose PM using a common-size income statement in which each line item is expressed as a percentage of sales. Analysts can find more information about each line item in Item 7 of the Form 10-K.
Asset turnover (ATO)	$\frac{\text{Sales}}{\text{Avg total assets}}$	Sales generated by each dollar of assets. As a measure of a company's investing activities, this ratio focuses on the productivity of the asset base. Analysts can decompose ATO with a common-size (percent of sales) balance sheet.
Earnings leverage (EL)	$\frac{\text{NI}}{\text{EBI}}$	The return to equity (net income, NI) as a percentage of the return to all capital providers (EBI). This ratio indicates how equity and debt investors share the total return generated during the period.
Asset leverage	$\frac{\text{Avg Total assets}}{\text{Avg shareholder equity}}$	The dollar of assets employed in the business per dollar of equity. This ratio is a function of invested debt capital (e.g., long-term debt) and operating liabilities (e.g., payables).
Earnings before interest (EBI)	NI − Int. exp. × 1 − Tax rate	Measure of the business performance to benefit all providers of capital. EBI estimates the earnings if the company had no debt. The tax adjustment reflects the tax shield on the debt. For example, $1 of interest with a tax rate of 25 percent reduces net income by only $0.75. Estimating earnings if a company had no debt requires a $0.75 add-back to net income. The purpose of EBI is to distinguish business performance from financing decisions.

FIGURE 8.4 Common Profitability Ratios

This figure provides computation and interpretation details for basic profitability ratios.

margin and asset turnover were computed each year for each industry. The industry was then plotted in the figure based on the time-series average of the median profit margin and asset turnover. The solid lines, called isoquants, indicate the combinations of turnover and margin that yield an ROA of 4.5 percent or an ROA of 7.5 percent.

The underlying economics of the industry and features of the competitive environment shape the location of industries in Figure 8.5. For example, the typical utility

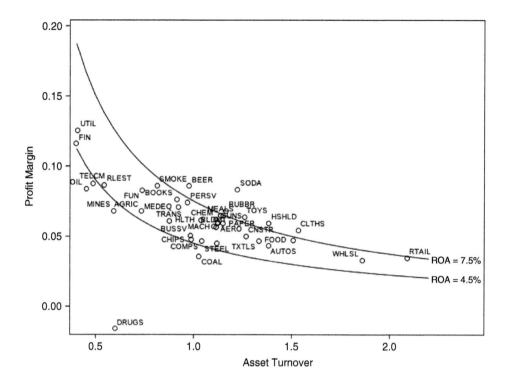

FIGURE 8.5 ROA by Profit Margin and Asset Turnover Across U.S. Industries between 1982 and 2018

This figure plots industries using profit margin and asset turnover between 1982 and 2018. All data with available observations are collected from Compustat. Observations are sorted into industries each year. Median profit margins and asset turnovers are computed each year. The average of the yearly medians is then plotted in the figure.

Source: Author's computation using data provided by Compustat.

company has an ROA similar to most other industries but composed of high margins and low turnovers. Utilities require a tremendous investment in the asset base resulting in low turnovers.

Conversely, most utilities have a monopoly over their geographic region as part of the regulations governing the industry. This situation allows utilities to generate a high (but capped by regulation) margin, providing a competitive rate of return on capital. In contrast, retailing is an industry with low capital requirements, low barriers to entry, and intense competition. Retailers have high turnovers but low margins as a result.

Some industries appear to provide abnormally high ROAs. The beverage industry, for example, has an industry ROA that is considerably above the 7.5 percent isoquant. Two possible explanations exist. First, two major competitors dominate the industry. Competition in this industry has evolved to focus on elements other than price, such as brand recognition and loyalty. That is, Coca-Cola and Pepsi intensely compete for supremacy of the beverage industry, but both competitors recognize that competing on price likely harms the margins of both players. Thus, Coca-Cola and Pepsi maintain high margins and, therefore, high ROA by implicitly agreeing to compete on other dimensions in the industry. An abnormally high (low) profitability relative to a competitive return on capital is termed *economic rent.*

In contrast, Coca-Cola and Pepsi are two of the most valuable brands in the world. They have cultivated their brands over the decades through continuous investment in brand equity. These companies generally expense the efforts and expenditures related to building these brands as incurred. Consequently, these firms exclude the most valuable economic assets in the beverage industry from the capital base used to calculate profitability. Thus, the ROA for a particular year for Coca-Cola or Pepsi vastly overstates the company's real economic performance in that year. That is, the stream of sales and earnings generated in the current period is, in part, merely the realization of value created by these companies in the previous years by cultivating their brands, which is a form of slippage in step 1.

The preceding discussion developed the economic intuition governing profitability in the cross-section. Yet, the intuition also extends to the evolution of ROA over time, as shown in Figure 8.6. ROAs exhibit wide dispersion in year 0 (the sort year). Over the next 10 years, the differences largely evaporate, yielding a much tighter distribution at the end of the horizon. Competition wears away abnormal

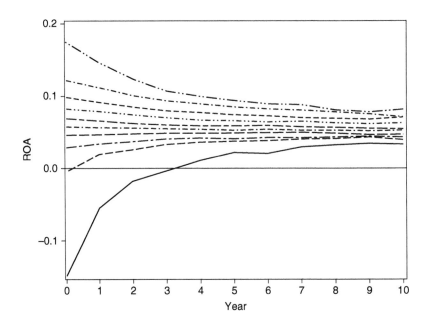

FIGURE 8.6   Return on Assets for U.S. Companies between 1982 and 2018

This figure reports return on assets (ROA) by decile over time between 1982 and 2018. Data are collected from Compustat. ROA is calculated for each firm-year observation. Observations are then grouped into 10 portfolios based on current-year ROA, and the median ROA of each portfolio is then tracked for the next 10 years. This procedure is repeated each year, and the average across yearly trials is then plotted in the figure.

Source: Author's computation using data provided by Compustat.

performance, driving ROAs toward the cost of capital. The median ROA across deciles in year 10 is approximately 6 percent, the midpoint of the isoquants in Figure 8.1.

Xie (2001) and Sloan (1996) show that the persistence of ROA depends on the relative mix of cash from operations and accruals. By contrast, Fairfield, Whisenant, and Yohn (2003) suggest that the accrual effect is a growth effect driven by the denominator of ROA. The persistence of ROA also varies with the earnings component. Disaggregating earnings into operating earnings, nonoperating earnings and taxes, and special items improves forecasts of future profitability (Fairfield, Sweeney, and Yohn 1996).

In sum, at the conceptual level, ROA and the other measures of return on capital reflect three broad influences: (1) the expected return on capital defined by the opportunity cost of the capital base, (2) the abnormal return on capital, reflecting the degree of under- or overperformance of a company (whether by windfall or successful execution of a winning strategy), and (3) the measurement error from using limited accounting constructs in developing profitability measures. Analysts should keep these influences in mind when interpreting profitability measures across firms, over time, or relative to the cost of capital benchmark.

Other Profitability Components

Other profitability components assist analysts in understanding recent trends in ROE and ROA and in forecasting future profitability. Changes in profit margin and asset turnover aid in forecasting changes in ROA (Fairfield and Yohn 2001; Soliman 2008). Industry-based analyses of profitability and profitability components provide superior profitability forecasts than do economy-wide averages (Fairfield et al. 2009). Nissim and Penman (2001) show that leverage ratios possess high persistence. Once a company reaches its equilibrium target capital structure, it generally maintains that structure with little change over time. Mean reversion in ROA implies mean reversion in ROE, but the mean or norm for ROE is higher due to persistent leverage ratios. Figure 8.7 confirms the mean reversion in ROE.

Growth

Besides profitability, analysts should evaluate recent growth trends and develop growth expectations. Sales growth summarizes the expansion of a company's business activities and is a key determinant of growth in the asset base and the potential need for external capital. Over the near term, the firm's specific investments shape its sales growth. For example, sales can climb when a manufacturer opens a new factory, when an airline adds new routes, or when a retailer opens new locations. Over the longer term, primarily industry and macroeconomic trends drive sales growth. Consequently, extreme sales growth rates driven by firm-specific actions revert to normal levels relatively quickly, where "normal" is governed by industry growth and macroeconomic growth rates.

As Figure 8.8 shows, extreme growth rates do not persist for long. The substantial differences in sales growth apparent in year 0 mostly vanish by year +3, and the

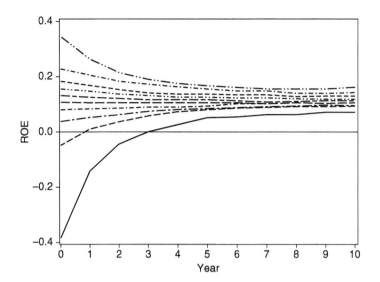

FIGURE 8.7 Return on Equity for U.S. Companies between 1982 and 2018

This figure reports return on equity (ROE) by decile over time. For each year between 1982 and 2018, all observations with sufficient data to calculate all basic ratios are collected from Compustat. ROE is calculated for each firm-year observation. Observations are then grouped into 10 portfolios based on current-year ROE, and the median ROE of each portfolio is then tracked for the next 10 years. This procedure is repeated each year, and the average across yearly trials is then plotted in the figure.

Source: Author's computation using data provided by Compustat.

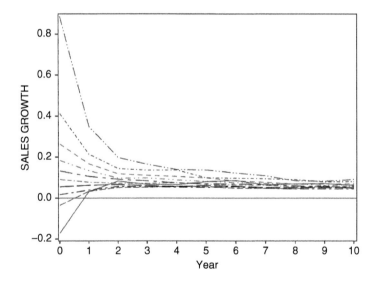

FIGURE 8.8 Sales Growth for U.S. Companies between 1982 and 2018

This figure reports sales growth by decile over time. For each year between 1982 and 2018, all observations with sufficient data to calculate all basic ratios are collected from Compustat. Sales growth is calculated for each firm-year observation. Observations are then grouped into 10 portfolios based on current-year sales growth, and the median sales growth of each portfolio is then tracked for the next 10 years. This procedure is repeated each year, and the average across yearly trials is then plotted in the figure.

Source: Author's computation using data provided by Compustat.

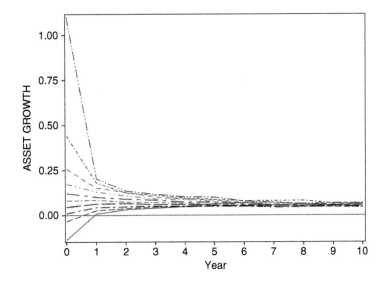

FIGURE 8.9 Asset Growth for U.S. Companies between 1982 and 2018

This figure reports asset growth by decile over time. For each year between 1982 and 2018, all observations with sufficient data to calculate all basic ratios are collected from Compustat. Asset growth is calculated for each firm-year observation. Observations are then grouped into 10 portfolios based on current-year asset growth, and the median asset growth of each portfolio is then tracked for the next 10 years. This procedure is repeated each year, and the average across yearly trials is then plotted in the figure.

Source: Author's computation using data provided by Compustat.

growth rates tightly cluster by year +10. Moreover, the norm around which growth rates cluster in year +10 is about 5 percent, the average nominal GDP growth rate for the U.S. economy between 1982 and 2018. The growth in the economy forms a ceiling on the long-term growth of any company operating within that economy.

Business growth drives the need for capital. Indeed, Nissim and Penman (2001) find that past sales growth provides a better predictor of future equity growth than does past equity growth. Thus, growth in assets (as shown in Figure 8.9) and growth in equity (as shown in Figure 8.10) also display sharp mean-reverting patterns. Moreover, both growth rates tightly cluster around 5 percent in year +10.

Liquidity, Solvency, and Financial Distress

Besides a company's profitability and growth fundamentals, analysts should also evaluate its liquidity, solvency, and financial distress. Liquidity ratios aid in evaluating a company's short-term risk. For example, the ratio of current assets to current liabilities (current ratio) compares a company's liabilities that will come due over the next year to the resources available to pay on those liabilities. Yet, companies typically pay their payables in the next 30–60 days, whereas many current assets (notably inventory) may not convert to cash during that time frame. The quick ratio compares the most liquid assets (cash, marketable securities, and receivables) to the current liabilities for this reason.

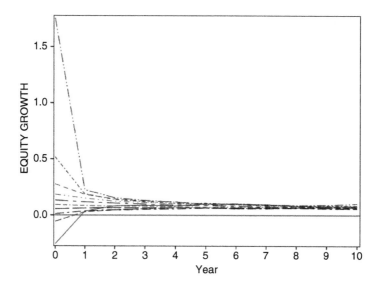

FIGURE 8.10 Book Value of Equity Growth for U.S. Companies between 1982 and 2018

This figure reports equity growth by decile over time. For each year between 1982 and 2018, all observations with sufficient data to calculate all basic ratios are collected from Compustat. Equity growth is calculated for each firm-year observation. Observations are then grouped into 10 portfolios based on current-year equity growth, and the median equity growth of each portfolio is then tracked for the next 10 years. This procedure is repeated each year, and the average across yearly trials is then plotted in the figure.

Source: Author's computation using data provided by Compustat.

Solvency analysis takes a longer-term perspective on a company's ability to service liabilities. Ratios of debt to assets or debt to equity provide potential insights into unused debt capacity and the possibility of financial distress, especially when compared to industry averages. Interest coverage ratios, such as earnings before interest and taxes (EBIT) as a multiple of the interest expense, indicate a company's margin of safety with interest. Concerns about the ability to service debt rise as these ratios decline toward one, and ratios of less than one (or negative) can portend imminent financial distress.

Accounting fundamentals provide much information useful for predicting financial distress and bankruptcy. Altman (1968) offers a well-known bankruptcy prediction model that investors and analysts continue to use. The Altman Z-score includes measures of liquidity (net working capital to assets), past profitability (retained earnings to assets), current profitability (EBIT to assets), asset turnover, and leverage (market value to total liabilities). Altman reports a 95 percent accuracy rate one year before the bankruptcy, with a false positive (Type I) error rate of 6 percent and false negative (Type II) error rate of 3 percent. The two-year-ahead accuracy rate was 83 percent. Although the ratios differ, Ohlson (1980) develops a similar bankruptcy model that is still in use today.

More recent attempts to develop bankruptcy or business failure prediction models include Shumway (2001) and Campbell, Hilscher, and Szilagyi (2008). Equity market measures feature prominently in these models. As previously noted, prices and returns reflect a rich set of information about a company's past and anticipated business outcomes. Thus, these models exploit this information to develop superior predictors of business failure.

SUMMARY AND CONCLUSIONS

This chapter introduced a framework for understanding how accounting information relates to share price using a three-step process. First, the accounting system captures information about a company's business activities. The accounting system aggregates and summarizes this information into financial statements. Second, investors and equity analysts analyze financial statements and other information to develop expectations and form value estimates. Third, trading activities incorporate investor expectations and value estimates into the share price. Company analysis refers to the process of analyzing a company's financial statements and other information for purposes of developing expectations and forming estimates of share value.

Analysis of a company's accounting policies provides analysts with an understanding of step 1 in the three-step framework. Analysis of a company's fundamentals through a ratio analysis of the financial statements forms a key element of step 2. An understanding of a company's fundamentals equips analysts to forecast future performance (Chapter 6) and estimate share value (Chapters 10 through 13), completing step 2. Part Three of this book explores investor trading on these issues, completing step 3.

DISCUSSION QUESTIONS

1. Describe the three steps linking business activities to equity prices.
2. Discuss why the analysis of a company's accounting policies is an important part of company analysis.
3. Explain how risk, economic rents, and accounting distortions affect ROA.
4. Discuss how ROA relates to ROE.

REFERENCES

Aharony, Joseph, Chan-Jane Lin, and Martin P. Loeb. 1993. "Initial Public Offerings, Accounting Choices, and Earnings Management." *Contemporary Accounting Research* 10:1, 61–81.

Altman, Edward I. 1968. "Financial Ratios, Discriminant Analysis and the Prediction of Corporate Bankruptcy." *Journal of Finance* 23:4, 589–609.

Baker, Terry, Denton Collins, and Austin Reitenga. 2003. "Stock Option Compensation and Earnings Management Incentives." *Journal of Accounting, Auditing & Finance* 18:4, 557–582.

Ball, Ray, and Lakshmanan Shivakumar. 2006. "The Role of Accruals in Asymmetrically Timely Gain and Loss Recognition." *Journal of Accounting Research* 44:2, 207–242.

Balsam, Steven, Lucy Huajing Chen, and Srinivasan Sankaraguruswamy. 2003. "Earnings Management Prior to Stock Option Grants." Working Paper, Temple University.

Bartov, Eli, and Partha Mohanram. 2004. "Private Information, Earnings Manipulations, and Executive Stock-Option Exercises." *Accounting Review* 79:4, 889–920.

Basu, Sudipta. 1997. "The Conservatism Principle and the Asymmetric Timeliness of Earnings." *Journal of Accounting and Economics* 24:1, 3–37.

Beneish, Messod D. 1999. "The Detection of Earnings Manipulation." *Financial Analysts Journal* 55:5, 24–36.

Beneish, Messod D., Charles M. C. Lee, and D. Craig Nichols. 2013. "Earnings Manipulation and Expected Returns." *Financial Analysts Journal* 69:2, 57–82.

Beneish, Messod Daniel, Charles M. C. Lee, and D. Craig Nichols. 2015. "In Short Supply: Short-Sellers and Stock Returns." *Journal of Accounting and Economics* 60:2–3, 33–57.

Bergstresser, Daniel, and Thomas Philippon. 2006. "CEO Incentives and Earnings Management." *Journal of Financial Economics* 80:3, 511–529.

Burgstahler, David, and Elizabeth Chuk. 2015. "Do Scaling and Selection Explain Earnings Discontinuities?" *Journal of Accounting and Economics* 60:1, 168–186.

Burgstahler, David, and Elizabeth Chuk. 2017. "What Have We Learned About Earnings Management? Integrating Discontinuity Evidence." *Contemporary Accounting Research* 34:2, 726–749.

Burgstahler, David, and Ilia Dichev. 1997. "Earnings Management to Avoid Earnings Decreases and Losses." *Journal of Accounting and Economics* 24:1, 99–126.

Burns, Natasha, and Simi Kedia. 2006. "The Impact of Performance-Based Compensation on Misreporting." *Journal of Financial Economics* 79:1, 35–67.

Campbell, John Y., Jens Hilscher, and Jan Szilagyi. 2008. "In Search of Distress Risk." *Journal of Finance* 63:6, 2899–2939.

Cantrell, Brett W., and Victoria Dickinson. 2020. "Conditional Life Cycle: An Examination of Operating Performance for Leaders and Laggards." *Management Science* 66:1, 433–451.

Chaney, Paul K., and Craig M. Lewis. 1995. "Earnings Management and Firm Valuation under Asymmetric Information." *Journal of Corporate Finance* 1:3–4, 319–345.

Dechow, Patricia M., Weili Ge, Chad R. Larson, and Richard G. Sloan. 2011. "Predicting Material Accounting Misstatements." *Contemporary Accounting Research* 28:1, 17–82.

Degeorge, François, Jayendu Patel, and Richard Zeckhauser. 1999. "Earnings Management to Exceed Thresholds." *Journal of Business* 72:1, 1–33.

Dickinson, Victoria. 2011. "Cash Flow Patterns as a Proxy for Firm Life Cycle." *Accounting Review* 86:6, 1969–1994.

Efendi, Jap, Anup Srivastava, and Edward P. Swanson. 2007. "Why Do Corporate Managers Misstate Financial Statements? The Role of Option Compensation and Other Factors." *Journal of Financial Economics* 85:3, 667–708.

Erickson, Merle, Michelle Hanlon, and Edward L. Maydew. 2006. "Is There a Link Between Executive Equity Incentives and Accounting Fraud?" *Journal of Accounting Research* 44:1, 113–143.

Esplin, Adam, Max Hewitt, Marlene Plumlee, and Teri Lombardi Yohn. 2014. "Disaggregating Operating and Financial Activities: Implications for Forecasts of Profitability." *Review of Accounting Studies* 19:1, 328–362.

Fairfield, Patricia M., Sundaresh Ramnath, and Teri Lombardi Yohn. 2009. "Do Industry-Level Analyses Improve Forecasts of Financial Performance?" *Journal of Accounting Research* 47:1, 147–178.

Fairfield, Patricia M., Richard J. Sweeney, and Teri Lombardi Yohn. 1996. "Accounting Classification and the Predictive Content of Earnings." *Accounting Review* 71:3, 337–355.

Fairfield, Patricia M., J. Scott Whisenant, and Teri Lombardi Yohn. 2003. "Accrued Earnings and Growth: Implications for Future Profitability and Market Mispricing." *Accounting Review* 78:1, 353–371.

Fairfield, Patricia M., and Teri Lombardi Yohn. 2001. "Using Asset Turnover and Profit Margin to Forecast Changes in Profitability." *Review of Accounting Studies* 6:4, 371–385.

Friedlan, John M. 1994. "Accounting Choices of Issuers of Initial Public Offerings." *Contemporary Accounting Research* 11:1, 1–31.

Gao, Pengjie, and Ronald E. Shrieves. 2002. "Earnings Management and Executive Compensation: A Case of Overdose of Option and Underdose of Salary." Working Paper, University of Tennessee, Knoxville.

Graham, John R., Campbell R. Harvey, and Shiva Rajgopal. 2005. "The Economic Implications of Corporate Financial Reporting." *Journal of Accounting and Economics* 40:1–3, 3–73.

Marquardt, Carol A., and Christine I. Wiedman. 2004. "How Are Earnings Managed? An Examination of Specific Accruals." *Contemporary Accounting Research* 21:2, 461–491.

Nichols, D. Craig, and James M. Wahlen. 2020. "The Essential Role of Accounting Information in the Capital Markets: Updating Seminal Research Results with Current Evidence." Working Paper, Syracuse University.

Nichols, D. Craig, James M. Wahlen, and Matthew M. Wieland. 2009. "Publicly Traded Versus Privately Held: Implications for Conditional Conservatism in Bank Accounting." *Review of Accounting Studies* 14:1, 88–122.

Nichols, D. Craig, James M. Wahlen, and Matthew M. Wieland. 2017. "Pricing and Mispricing of Accounting Fundamentals in the Time-Series and in the Cross Section." *Contemporary Accounting Research* 34:3, 1378–1417.

Nissim, Doron, and Stephen H. Penman. 2001. "Ratio Analysis and Equity Valuation: From Research to Practice." *Review of Accounting Studies* 6:1, 109–154.

Ohlson, James A. 1980. "Financial Ratios and the Probabilistic Prediction of Bankruptcy." *Journal of Accounting Research* 18:1, 109–131.

Ohlson, James A. 1995. "Earnings, Book Values, and Dividends in Equity Valuation." *Contemporary Accounting Research* 11:2, 661–687.

Perry, Susan E., and Thomas H. Williams. 1994. "Earnings Management Preceding Management Buyout Offers." *Journal of Accounting and Economics* 18:2, 157–179.

Safdar, Irfan. 2003. "*Stock Option Exercise, Earnings Management, and Abnormal Stock Returns.*" Working Paper, Widener University.

Shumway, Tyler. 2001. "Forecasting Bankruptcy More Accurately: A Simple Hazard Model." *Journal of Business* 74:1, 101–124.

Soliman, Mark T. 2008. "The Use of DuPont Analysis by Market Participants." *Accounting Review* 83:3, 823–853.

Sloan, Richard G. 1996. "Do Stock Prices Fully Reflect Information in Accruals and Cash Flows about Future Earnings?" *Accounting Review* 71:3, 289–315.

Teoh, Siew Hong, Ivo Welch, and Tak Jun Wong. 1998a. "Earnings Management and the Long-Run Market Performance of Initial Public Offerings." *Journal of Finance* 53:6, 1935–1974.

Teoh, Siew Hong, Ivo Welch, and Tak Jun Wong. 1998b. "Earnings Management and the Underperformance of Seasoned Equity Offerings." *Journal of Financial Economics* 50:1, 63–99.

Teoh, Siew Hong, Tak J. Wong, and Gita R. Rao. 1998. "Are Accruals During Initial Public Offerings Opportunistic?" *Review of Accounting Studies* 3:1–2, 175–208.

Vorst, Patrick, and Teri Lombardi Yohn. 2018. "Life Cycle Models and Forecasting Growth and Profitability." *Accounting Review* 93:6, 357–381.

Watts, Ross L. 2003a. "Conservatism in Accounting Part I: Explanations and Implications." *Accounting Horizons* 17:3, 207–221.

Watts, Ross L. 2003b. "Conservatism in Accounting Part II: Evidence and Research Opportunities." *Accounting Horizons* 17:4, 287–301.

Wu, Y. Woody. 1997. "Management Buyouts and Earnings Management." *Journal of Accounting, Auditing & Finance* 12:4, 373–389.

Xie, Hong. 2001. "The Mispricing of Abnormal Accruals." *Accounting Review* 76:3, 357–373.

CHAPTER 9

Technical Analysis

David Lundgren
Adjunct Professor, Brandeis University

INTRODUCTION

Despite ample academic studies and real-life examples of the efficacy of both the technical and fundamental philosophies of investing, practitioners of each style have historically shown little acknowledgment of each other's process. This unfortunate tension ignores the fact that the two investment approaches share similar philosophical beliefs. Both schools of thought agree that fundamentals are paramount, markets are both efficient in the long term and random in the short term, and behavioral biases are a key determinant in security pricing.

Technical and fundamental investors both recognize that any item whose price is determined by the free-market forces of supply and demand typically trends in the direction of the greater of those two forces. These investors agree that changes in fundamentals are likely to cause changes in supply and demand dynamics, and hence the direction of the trend for a company's share price. Although both types of investors are trying to capture the same fundamentally driven trend change, the fundamental process focuses on forecasting that change, while the technical process instead waits for concrete evidence, in the form of price, that it has indeed changed.

This chapter provides a discussion of the practical application of technical analysis. The following section offers background on technical analysis, including the underappreciated link between the technical and fundamental philosophies of investing. It then examines the primary tenets of technical analysis, including some core technical analysis tools such as trend following, momentum, and relative performance, all of which are successfully used by both technical and fundamental investors today. The last section summarizes and concludes the chapter.

BACKGROUND

This section explores the important connection between technical analysis and fundamental analysis. Both are rooted in the same core philosophical belief that fundamental trends drive price trends. The difference lies in the process used by each practitioner. Technicians invest in the direction of the established trend on the premise that the trend is happening for fundamental reasons identified vis-à-vis the market's collective wisdom. Fundamental investors search for trends that they believe are disconnected from their own fundamental assessment.

Link Between Technical and Fundamental Investment Philosophies

According to Bachelier (1900), markets behave in an unpredictable random fashion. This view set the stage for various research papers and books published during the 1960s advocating that markets were unpredictable and, therefore, unbeatable. This theory ultimately became known as the *random walk hypothesis*, with contributions from many giants of economics including Cootner (1964), Fama (1965), and Malkiel (1973).

The idea that markets are random can be explained using a dice analogy:

- Yesterday's price action does not influence today's price action, much like how rolling a pair of dice does not influence the next roll.
- Today's price action (dice roll) does not influence tomorrow's price action (dice roll).
- Finally, one investor's actions (dice roll) do not influence another investor's actions (dice roll).

In other words, investors are rational, unemotional, and act in their own best interests. Therefore, as with rolling dice, price action is normally distributed around a central mean tendency. Interestingly, Samuelson (1948) appeared to struggle with the idea that markets are truly random by noting that a bull market creates its own hopes. That is, if people buy thinking stocks will rise, this behavior leads to increasing stock prices, which causes another round of buying.

Samuelson's (1948) view recognizes that investor behavior may not be random at all. An investor's actions today may be influenced by what the market, other investors, and perhaps the investor did yesterday. In his description of how markets "really" work, Samuelson reveals a belief that, unlike rolling dice, investors are influenced by their prior actions, as well as the actions of their peers, thereby resulting in predictable, nonrandom, and ultimately trending market behavior.

The underpinnings of the random walk hypothesis are consistent with the *efficient market hypothesis* (EMH), which several academics developed in the 1960s to further explain why markets are random, unforecastable, and ultimately unbeatable. The EMH states that asset prices reflect all available information. For example, Fama (1970) offers a review of the EMH, which includes his pioneering explanation of three forms of financial market efficiency:

1. *Weak form efficiency* states that investors cannot use historical information such as price and volume to predict future prices. This hypothesis directly attacks technical analysis, which, at its core, studies past price behavior to predict future prices. However, various academic studies of the momentum factor such as Berger, Israel, and Moskowitz (2009) demonstrate that analysts can use past price behavior to predict future price behavior. According to Fama, price momentum is the biggest embarrassment for efficient markets (White 2015).

2. *Semi-strong form efficiency* states that, in addition to past information, investors cannot use current public information to beat the market because it responds too quickly to the new information, thereby preventing them from profiting from it. An entire field of study called *behavioral economics*, spearheaded by such luminaries as Kahneman, Slovic, and Tversky (1982) and Thaler (2016), contends that various behavioral biases all combine to prevent investors from rationally responding to new information, thereby resulting in inefficient markets.

3. *Strong form efficiency* states that besides being unable to benefit from all public information, investors also cannot use private or insider information to beat the market. The Securities Exchange Act of 1934 made trading on insider information illegal in the United States. Many offenders have since gone to jail for violating this act, but not without first handily outperforming the market, and some making millions of dollars for their efforts. Hence, the rule of law, not efficient markets, prevents investors from being able to beat the market with insider information.

As the random walk hypothesis and EMH achieved broad acceptance within academic circles, the support for technical analysis faded. Fortunately, with the ascension of behavioral economics, which has shed ample scientific light on the non-rational behavior of most investors (Hens and Meier 2015), coupled with the empirical success of trend following and momentum investing over decades, technical analysis has received added attention in the investment industry (Bouchaud, Lemperiere, Deremble, Seager, and Potters 2014).

Dow Theory: A Foundation

Lo and Hasanhodzic (2010) provide a comprehensive historical review of technical analysis, delving as far back as ancient Rome to unearth evidence of individuals recording price activity with the intent of using that information to help inform important business and investment decisions. Charles H. Dow was a pioneer of modern technical analysis in the late 1800s. Despite having a strong appreciation for fundamental and economic data and analysis, Dow also recognized that the market itself possessed the collective wisdom of all its participants, including both the well-informed and the misinformed. By tracking trends in the overall market, Dow believed that one could glean important predictive information about individual stocks, broader markets, and the economy itself. To this end, Dow developed the Dow Jones Industrial Average (DJIA) and the Dow Jones Transportation Average (DJTA) in 1896, later recording his techniques for interpreting trends in his new stock market averages in a series of editorials in the *Wall Street Journal* (*WSJ*) until his death in 1902. William Peter Hamilton, who became *WSJ*'s editor after Dow's death, wrote *The Stock Market Barometer* (Hamilton 1922), in which he identified the six primary tenets of Dow's investing philosophy.

First Tenet: The Market Discounts Everything According to Rhea (1932, p. 19), "It cannot too often be said that the stock market reflects absolutely all everybody knows about the business of the country." This core tenet of Dow theory seems to have served as a basis for the EMH many years later. As Rhea (p. 20) notes, both Dow and Hamilton believed that "consciously or unconsciously, the movement of prices reflects not the past, but the future." For instance, during a prolonged bear market, when economic conditions are at their worst and pessimism is at its peak, the market seems to reach bottom, to the amazement of most onlookers. Dow would argue that the market has not only discounted all the current information but has also begun to identify degrees of improvement too difficult to detect by individual investors so early in the process. Rhea (p. 41) also comments that "The stock market has considered all these things, with sources of information far more exhaustive than these critics can possibly possess." The Conference Board later validated Dow's intuition when it included the S&P 500 index as one of 10 components in its index of leading economic indicators.

Second Tenet: The Three Simultaneous Time Frames of Trend   Dow observed that market trends contain three magnitudes of movement, all unfolding simultaneously. He used the ocean to describe what can at times be a confusing task of imagining three trends all occurring at the same time:

1. *Primary trend.* Dow referred to this trend as the "tide," since it was the most powerful and influential of the three. Trends in fundamental data drive this time frame, and as such, can last for more than a year. Importantly, like the tides of the ocean, one individual or entity cannot alter these trends any more than even the largest of ships can redirect the tides. If the underlying fundamental trends are positive, the corresponding stock or market will advance in time, despite whatever efforts bearish investors might exert to the contrary.

2. *Secondary trend.* Dow recognized that even the most powerful trends do not unfold linearly. Rather, the *primary trend* unfolds in an alternating sequence of advances and declines, which Dow referred to as *secondary trends* or *waves.* Both fundamental trends and investor emotional responses to those trends, including greed and fear, drive the secondary trend. During secondary advances, investors can become overly optimistic, while secondary declines can drive investors to become overly pessimistic. Secondary trends tend to last for months and can be manipulated or altered for brief periods, either by controversial news items or large, albeit temporary, flows of capital. In a bullish primary trend, secondary advances tend to rise at a slower pace than the secondary declines fall, reflecting the difference between greed, which takes time to build, and fear, which can be immediate. Secondary declines typically retrace one-third to two-thirds of the last secondary advance and can be so dramatic at times that investors often mistake them for the start of the next multiyear, primary bear market.

3. *Minor trend.* Secondary trends also consist of a series of alternating advances and declines, each lasting days or weeks. Dow referred to these short-term movements as *minor trends* or "ripples," invoking the image of small drops of water flittering randomly about along the surface of the waves (secondary trend), pushed back and forth by the constantly shifting winds of investor emotions of hope, fear, and greed. Capital flows, news, and rumors can easily alter the minor trend.

Of the three magnitudes of trend, the primary trend is the most important to identify correctly. When the market's primary trend is bullish, most stocks are rising and systemic risk is reduced. As such, investors can focus more on stock selection and less on macro conditions. However, when the market's primary trend is bearish and systemic risk is higher, most stocks will be falling, requiring investors to focus more on risk management and safety.

This foundational philosophy of technical analysis finds healthy respect for the importance of fundamental trends, as well as a clear acknowledgment of the short-term impact of random investor behavior on securities prices. The longer the investment time horizon, the more efficient is the market, whereas the shorter the time horizon, the more random and noisier is its behavior. Therefore, the more a technical investor focuses on capturing minor short-term trends, the more that effort is subjected to the vagaries of irrational market behavior. Conversely, the more a technical investor attempts to capture the longer-term primary trend, the more that effort is likely to benefit from the tailwinds of the more deterministic force of the underlying fundamental trends.

Nearly 50 years after Dow used his ocean analogy to explain how markets behave, Samuelson (1948) expressed a similar sentiment, noting that a competitive market in equilibrium is constantly being disturbed but is always reforming itself, similar to the ocean's surface. Benjamin Graham, widely acknowledged to be the grandfather of value investing and mentor to famed value investor Warren Buffett, also conceded that the market is simultaneously random and efficient. According to Graham ([1949] 1986), the market in the short run is a voting machine, but a weighing machine in the long run. Again, Dow outlined this philosophical perspective from one of the great value managers of our time nearly 50 years earlier, when he distinguished between short-term fluctuations and long-term trends.

Third Tenet: Primary Trends Unfold in Three Phases   According to Dow theory, multiyear primary bull and bear trends each pass through three distinct phases. In the later stages of a primary bear market, when valuations are inexpensive, pessimism is at an extreme, and the economy is fragile, the market begins to trade sideways in a range, or a line, ignoring the continued negative news. Dow referred to this first phase of a new primary bull market as *accumulation*, when more knowledgeable investors begin to buy stocks in anticipation of improving economic trends. At this point, according to Rhea (1932, p. 45), "The market is a dragging affair with but little public participation. Some important companies are usually in financial difficulties, and a certain amount of political unrest is generally apparent."

When the DJIA and DJTA both move decisively above their respective upper barriers, investors should begin positioning for *public participation*, the second, and typically longest, phase of the new primary bull market. During this phase, investors recognize that economic trends are improving, further fueling their desire to own equities.

During the third and final phase of a primary bull market, which Dow theorists refer to as the *speculative phase*, stocks begin to rapidly advance based on forecasts of continued economic expansion into the future, resulting in high valuations and excessive optimism. During the public participation and speculative phases of the primary bull market, each secondary advance exceeds the highest point achieved during the preceding secondary advance, and each successive secondary decline terminates at a level that is higher than the low point of the preceding secondary decline. This combination, depicted in Figure 9.1, is referred to as *higher highs and higher lows*, which defines a bullish trend outlined by Dow.

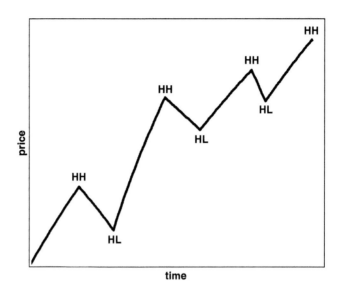

FIGURE 9.1   Higher Highs (HH) and Higher Lows (HL) Define an Uptrend

This figure demonstrates the meaning of "higher highs and higher lows."

This unbridled enthusiasm for equities plants the seeds for *distribution*, the first phase of the sure-to-follow primary bear market, as more informed investors begin selling shares they accumulated at much lower prices. The initial secondary decline of the new primary bear market is indistinguishable from all the other secondary declines that happened during the accumulation, public participation, and speculation phases of the preceding primary bull market. However, unable to forge higher despite continued good news and heightened optimism, the market begins to form yet another line, or sideways price range.

When the DJIA and DJTA each trade decisively below their respective support areas, investors should then begin to position for *liquidation*, the second phase of the primary bear market. At this point, the investing public finally understands that the economy is weakening and begins to sell their holdings.

As conditions continue to deteriorate, the primary bear trend transitions to its third and final stage – panic. As Rhea (1932, p. 37) notes, the market experiences "distressed selling of sound securities, regardless of their value, by those who must find a cash market for at least a portion of their assets." Just as investors projected unending prosperity during the final speculative phase of the last primary bull market, they now project never-ending economic malaise. During the liquidation and panic phases, both indices persistently record lower lows and lower highs, as shown in Figure 9.2, confirming the existence of bearish trends. Eventually, new lines will form in preparation for the next primary bull market.

Fourth Tenet: Indices Must Confirm Each Other   Dow believed that the DJIA and DJTA should trend together, consistent with the general direction of economic trends. Dow observed that when these two indices began trending in opposite directions—referred to as a *divergence*—the market, through its collective wisdom, was warning investors that economic conditions might be changing. At the end of a primary bull market,

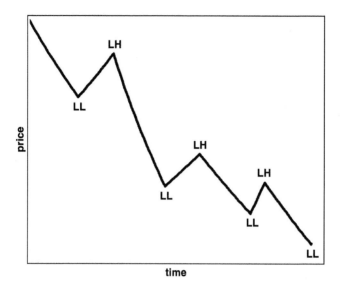

FIGURE 9.2 Lower Lows (LL) and Lower Highs (LH) Define a Downtrend

This figure demonstrates the meaning of "lower lows and lower highs."

when only one index is left making new highs, a bearish divergence has formed. A similar condition at the end of a primary bear market, when one index goes into a "line" while the other continues to make new lows, is referred to as a *bullish divergence*.

Importantly, Dow stressed the need for investors to wait for both indices to begin trending in the same direction before reacting. Due to the emotionally charged nature of minor and secondary price trends, during a secondary decline in a primary bull market, one index often records a lower low, while the other index holds above its own former low, only to have the weaker index suddenly reverse upward again to a new high. This situation is an example of how investors can often confuse a secondary decline for the start of a new primary bear trend, and the only protection against that faulty interpretation is to wait for both indices to confirm each other.

After a primary bear market, as both indices finally begin trading sideways in a line, a Dow theory buy signal is registered when both indices begin recording higher highs, each by trading through the upper band of their respective lines. The new highs from each index do not have to be recorded at the same time, nor does it matter which index records new highs first. What is most important is that they both begin trending upward together.

A Dow theory sell signal is recorded after a primary bull market when both indices break downward from their respective lines. As with Dow theory buy signals, the indices do not have to break down at the same time, nor does it matter which index breaks down first. The signal is simply confirmed when the second index breaks downward from its own line.

Fifth Tenet: The Importance of Volume   Intuitively, according to Dow theory, *volume*, which is the number of a company's outstanding and freely floating shares traded on a given day, should increase as price moves in the direction of the primary trend and decrease during secondary and minor reactions or declines. At major turning points, proponents of Dow theory believed that volume would begin to expand during declines as part of a topping process and expand during advances as part of a bottoming process. Ultimately, however, neither Dow nor Hamilton put much credence in the importance of volume, as they felt that even transaction activity itself fell under the guiding principle of the first tenet: The market discounts everything, including the intensity of market volume.

Sixth Tenet: Dow Theory Is Fallible   Dow also warned that his approach to investing in the equity markets was fallible, meaning it was not a guaranteed path to beating the market. Rhea (1932, p. 26) summarizes this point in Dow theory as follows: "Its successful use as an aid in speculation requires serious study, and the summing up of evidence must be impartial. The wish must never be allowed to father the thought." Rhea's observation reveals how the early thought leaders of the technical community endorsed what later became the foundational principles of behavioral finance.

Dow, Hamilton, and Rhea all understood how important maintaining an awareness of one's own biases was for successful investing. If investors are not careful, they are likely to be prone to seeing what they want to see from the fundamental data, as opposed to seeing what the data are actually revealing. All three relied on the trend-following strategies of Dow theory to protect them against their own behavioral biases.

Finally, Brown, Goetzman, and Kumar's (1998) study of the performance of Dow theory reveals market-like returns, but with an improved Sharpe ratio due to a significant reduction in volatility. Thus, Brown et al. (p. 1331) conclude "In broader terms, it also suggests that the empirical foundations of the efficient market theory may not be as firm as long believed."

PULLING IT ALL TOGETHER: FUNDAMENTALS, BIASES, AND TRENDS

Fundamental performance is what drives changes in share values over time. Strong earnings trends beget strong price trends, and vice versa. Importantly, starting valuation levels can have a magnifying effect on these stock price movements. Starting at a low valuation when fundamental trends begin to improve results in more rapid share appreciation than if valuations start at a high level, all else being equal.

However, behavioral biases prevent investors from efficiently responding in a timely manner to changes in underlying fundamental data. For instance, *belief perseverance* occurs when an investor clings to a bearish view about a company's fundamental prospects despite new information that firmly contradicts it, such as substantial earnings surprises, new product success, or management change.

This delayed response to changing fundamentals is why securities prices trend over time, as investor attitudes slowly morph from denial and underappreciation in the beginning stages of a trend change to acceptance and exuberance in the latter stages, as per the third tenet, primary trends unfold in three phases.

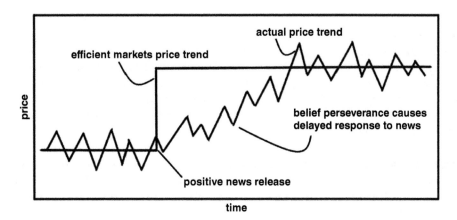

FIGURE 9.3 Prices Trend Slowly to Fair Value Due to Investor Behavioral Biases

This figure illustrates how behavioral biases cause prices to trend over time to fair value.

Trend Following

According to Dow theory, the market is typically engaged in multiple trends simultaneously across three distinct time frames: primary, secondary, and minor. For instance, the market may be in a primary uptrend, a secondary downtrend, and a minor uptrend, all at once. To help bring some order to the otherwise chaotic interaction of these multiple time frames of price action, Dow theory offers a few general guidelines:

- Structure. A *positive trend* is identified by a series of higher highs and higher lows, while a *negative trend* is identified by a series of lower lows and lower highs.
- Time. Primary trends can last for many months, sometimes years, while secondary trends can last for many weeks, often many months. Minor trends can last for days and sometimes weeks.
- Volatility. If both the DJIA and DJTA experience sideways price movement that extends for two to three weeks or longer, during which period the price variation of both averages moves within a range of about 5 percent, the market is said to be in a *line* (Rhea 1932). Any fluctuations encompassing lesser time or volatility should be considered of secondary or even minor degree.

Fortunately, with the advent of computers, more systematic and less discretionary tools are available to help determine the direction of the market's trend over these three time frames.

Moving Averages

This chapter focuses on how best to use a moving average to determine the existence of either a trend or a range, particularly as it relates to Dow theory. A *moving average* is used to smooth out the volatility of a price series and is calculated by summing the prices over a selected lookback window and dividing that sum by the number of periods in that lookback window.

Tracking the long-term primary trend requires focusing on a moving average calculated with a sufficient lookback period to capture multi-month, if not multiyear, trends such as a 200-day simple moving average. To capture the secondary trend, which can last for months, analysts can use a more intermediate-term 50-day simple moving average. Finally, the more random and volatile *minor trend* is best captured using a shorter-term 15-day simple moving average.

The slope of each of these averages can provide an effective guide for determining the direction of each time frame of a trend. For instance, Figure 9.4 shows the DJIA, along with its 15-day, 50-day, and 200-day averages. This figure reveals that all three averages are declining—that is to say, the primary, secondary, and minor trends are all negative or bearish. Figure 9.4 also shows how the primary bear trend that unfolded throughout 2008 (declining 200-day average) was composed of a series of alternating secondary and minor bull and bear trends.

Furthermore, analysts can use moving averages to help properly label the minor, secondary, and primary highs and lows being recorded during primary trends. As a general rule, during a bullish primary trend, a decline from the high of a bullish trend that only intersects with the 15-day average should be considered minor. If the decline is substantial enough to intersect with the 50-day average, but not the 200-day average, it should be considered secondary. Of course, if it intersects with the 200-day average, it should be considered primary.

FIGURE 9.4 Dow Theory Trend Change Confirmed by Bearish Moving Average Configuration

This figure illustrates how Dow theory and moving averages can be used together to identify major trend changes in the market.

Source: Metastock and David Lundgren.

Having labeled these highs and lows enables identifying higher highs and higher lows of varying time frames while they each unfold within the context of each other. Finally, combining the violation of these highs and lows with the changing slopes of the various averages allows for more confident identification of when a trend changes in the three time frames.

Importantly, tracking the progress and direction of each of these trends separately allows an investor to better maintain a proper perspective. If an investor identifies the primary trend as being bearish, as shown in Figure 9.4, occasional bullish trends in the secondary and minor time frames can be understood to be running contrary to the dominant bearish trend, and not the start of a new primary bull trend. This interpretation allows an investor to maintain short exposure, or perhaps even increase it, as the secondary and minor trends play out counter to the dominant bearish primary trend.

From the perspective of Dow theory, the DJIA's primary trend turned lower in early 2008 when the index broke through the August 2007 primary low, the bottom of the price range it had been in for the prior seven months. This break of support resulted in the first lower primary low in many months, meeting Dow theory's definition of a new downtrend. At the same time, the index broke below the bottom of the range. Note how the 200-day average, the mechanical representation of the primary trend, also began turning lower, confirming the traditional Dow theory indication of a downtrend. Also, the 50-day average (secondary trend) and 15-day average (minor trend) were already declining, leaving all three time frames in bear trends in early 2008.

Figure 9.5 shows how the DJIA and DJTA indices began trading in a line in late 2007, with a bearish divergence forming when the transports failed to record a new primary trend higher high in October, resulting in a bearish divergence with the higher high recorded by the DJIA. The DJTA then broke downward from its own line in November, a bearish signal that was not confirmed by the DJIA until January 2008, when it also traded below its own line. By this time, the 200-day averages of both indices were declining, providing a more mechanical confirmation of that traditional Dow theory sell signal.

Livermore (1940) observed that all stocks go down in a bear market and all stocks go up in a bull market. In other words, once determining the direction of the market's primary trend, investors should then use the same process to identify stocks that are trending in the same direction. While the market is in a primary bull trend, investors are better served by looking for stocks to buy that are also in a primary bull trend, and vice versa.

Wang (2009) finds that both market- and sector-level variance influences individual stock variance, confirming the importance of first identifying the direction of the primary trends of both the market and a stock's sector before investing. Doing so is likely to increase the accuracy of an investor's stock selection.

Momentum Investing

Once an investor has identified that the market is in a bullish primary trend, and further isolated those sectors and stocks that are also in primary bull trends, the next

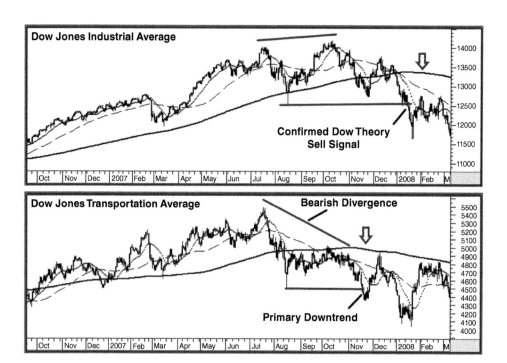

FIGURE 9.5 Dow Theory Sell Signal

This figure demonstrates the process by which the market tends to register a Dow theory sell signal at major market tops.

Source: Metastock and David Lundgren.

step is to narrow the list of ideas to a final portfolio. Relative performance is an effective input for reducing an extensive list of candidates to those with the highest odds of future market-beating performance.

Relative Strength Comparative   Two general techniques are available for measuring the strength of one stock relative to the market or some other group of stocks: *relative strength comparative* and *cross-sectional momentum*. In the former, a stock's relative performance trend is presented as a chart and is calculated by dividing the stock's price by the price of an index, sector, or another stock. When a stock's relative performance trend is rising, as defined by Dow theory, the stock is outperforming the market, while a falling relative performance trend indicates that the stock is underperforming the market.

Therefore, in a bull market, a rising relative performance trend means that the outperforming stock (numerator) is advancing faster than the market (denominator). By contrast, in a bear market, a rising relative performance trend means the outperforming stock (numerator) is falling slower than the market (denominator). In both cases, the rising relative performance line indicates superior performance.

Investors can use the same Dow theory trend identification techniques outlined here for absolute price trends to determine a stock's primary, secondary, and minor

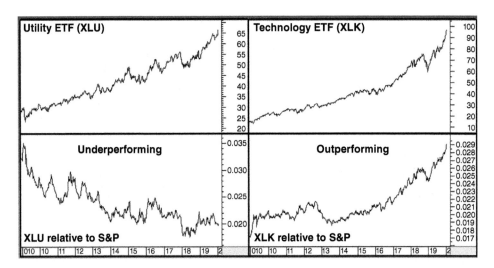

FIGURE 9.6 Using Relative Strength Comparative to Distinguish between Absolute Trends

This figure demonstrates how relative performance can be used to distinguish the strength of one trend relative to another.

Source: Metastock and David Lundgren.

relative price trends. For instance, Figure 9.6 shows the 20-year absolute price trends of the XLU Utilities Sector ETF (top left panel) and the XLK Technology ETF (top right panel). A simple visual inspection yields little differentiation between these two charts. Both are clearly in primary bull trends.

Yet, comparing the performance of each of these two ETFs to the market itself (lower two panels) results in a meaningfully different outcome. The case of the Utility ETF (XLU) on the left shows a relative underperformance trend with a series of lower highs and lows since 2008 when the global financial crisis reached its peak. On the other hand, the Technology ETF (XLK) shows a relative outperformance trend with a series of steadily rising higher highs and higher lows since 2008.

In comparison, although both absolute price charts are in healthy primary trends (top panels), the XLU is in a primary time frame bearish trend relative to the market, while the XLK is in a bullish primary trend, both absolute and relative to the market. As an investor whose objective is to outperform the market, focusing exposure in the technology sector would, therefore, present higher odds of achieving that goal, as that sector is outperforming the broader market, while utilities are lagging the broader market.

Cross-sectional Momentum The above-described technique is more in keeping with how Livermore (1940) used the concept of relative strength to ensure buying the strongest stocks in the strongest industries. Cross-sectional momentum, first explored by Cowles and Jones (1937), and later by Jagadeesh and Titman (1993), and more recently by Asness, Frazzini, Israel, and Moskowitz (2014), does not involve a visual inspection of charts. Instead, the investor merely sorts the universe of stocks according to their historical performance and then buys the stocks with top-decile performance and shorts the stocks with bottom-decile performance.

For instance, at the end of a calendar month, an investor would sort the constituents of the S&P 500 index according to their performance over the past 12 months, then buy the 50 stocks in the top-performing decile and short the 50 stocks in the bottom-performing decile. Going forward, this process would be repeated at the end of each month, with no effort to further refine the selection process using fundamental analysis or any other input.

The chart in Figure 9.7 demonstrates how each decile of prior 12-month performance has performed since 1927 (French 2019). As can be seen, stocks in the top-performance decile ("1st Dec") tend to perform best over time, while stocks in the bottom-performance decile ("10th Dec") perform worst.

A starker comparison in performance would be between "1st Dec" and "10th Dec" specifically, which is featured in Figure 9.8. In essence, this chart uses the relative performance trend concept described in the prior section, only comparing the best momentum stocks ("1st Dec" in the numerator) with the worst momentum stocks ("10th Dec" in the denominator) since 1927.

Fundamental investors can use these technical analysis strategies in conjunction with traditional fundamental analysis to potentially improve their stock selection efforts. For instance, Fisher, Shah, and Titman (2016, p. 33) explore the idea of combining momentum with value and discover that a strategy that "simultaneously incorporates both value and momentum outperforms a strategy that combines pure-play value and momentum portfolios that are formed independently."

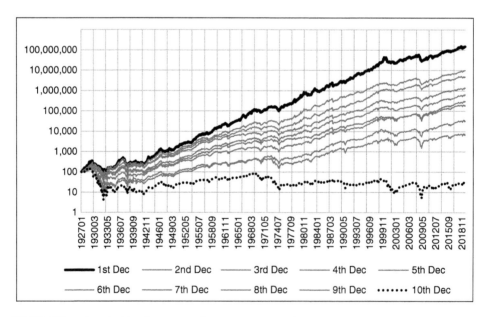

FIGURE 9.7 Historical Performance of Momentum Deciles

This figure shows the performance of the 10 deciles of cross-sectional momentum since 1927.

Source: Kenneth French and David Lundgren.

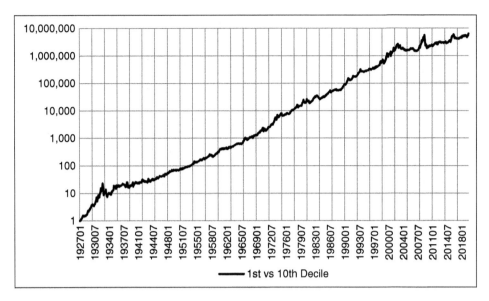

FIGURE 8.8 Historical Performance of Top Decile versus Bottom Decile Momentum

This figure demonstrates the relative performance between the top and bottom deciles of cross-sectional momentum since 1927.

Source: Kenneth French and David Lundgren.

SUMMARY AND CONCLUSIONS

This chapter examines the underappreciated overlap between the technical and fundamental philosophies of investing, particularly their deep mutual appreciation for the importance of trends in fundamental data. The main difference between technical and fundamental investors is not philosophy, but process. A fundamental investor builds a process designed to forecast the change in fundamentals, and, by design, the change in price trend, before it happens. By contrast, the technical investor waits for a trend to change before investing, assuming that the trend is changing for fundamental reasons. In either case, both investors are attempting to capture the same fundamentally driven price trends.

This chapter also stresses the importance of properly defining the primary trend for the market since the opportunity for profitable stock selection is the greatest while in a bull market, and the risk of the substantial capital loss is greatest during a primary bear market. A comprehensive discussion of Dow theory provides several techniques for defining the primary trend.

Finally, the chapter introduces several technical concepts, including trend following, relative strength, and cross-sectional momentum, which technical and fundamental investors alike can use to help reduce a broad list of securities to a narrower list of stocks with the most attractive technical characteristics. The chapter stresses owning the strongest stocks in the strongest industries while in a primary bull market. It also emphasizes the importance of protecting capital during primary bear markets, either by raising cash or buying defensive stocks observing positive relative performance trends.

DISCUSSION QUESTIONS

1. Discuss the philosophical link between technical and fundamental investment strategies.
2. Explain the importance of properly defining the market's primary trend as a first step toward building a portfolio.
3. Identify the three phases that both primary bull and bear markets undergo and explain how changing economic and fundamental trends and investors' behaviorially biased perceptions of them are driving forces.
4. Discuss the similarities and differences between trend following and cross-sectional momentum strategies.

REFERENCES

Asness, Cliff S., Andrea Frazzini, Ronen Israel, and Tobias J. Moskowitz. 2014. "Fact, Fiction and Momentum Investing." *Journal of Portfolio Management* 40:5, 75–92. Available at https://pdfs.semanticscholar.org/5dee/b75a0f2c290031a4aca4957c24ad4d9a299e.pdf?_ga=2.12.

Bachelier, Louis. 1900. "The Theory of Speculation." Available at https://pdfs.semanticscholar.org/bba7/101ed8278893a5bd205614fce948628af8e3.pdf.

Berger, Adam L., Ronen Israel, and Tobias J. Moskowitz. 2009. "The Case for Momentum Investing." Working Paper, AQR Capital Management.

Bouchaud, Jean-Phillippe, Yvet Lempérière, Cyril Deremble, Philip Seager, and Marc Potters. 2014. "Two Centuries of Trend Following." Working Paper, Capital Fund Management. Available at https://arxiv.org/pdf/1404.3274.pdf.

Brown, Stephen J., William N. Goetzman, and Alok Kumar. 1998. "The Dow Theory: William Peter Hamilton's Track Record Reconsidered." *Journal of Finance* 53:4, 1311–1333.

Cootner, Paul. 1966. "The Random Character of Stock Market Prices." *Journal of Business* 39:4, 532–535.

Cowles, Alfred 3rd, and Herbert E. Jones. 1937. "Some a Posteriori Probabilities in Stock Market Action." *Econometrica* 5:3, 280–294. Available at https://doi.org/0012-9682 (193707)5:3<280:SAPPIS>2.0.CO;2-Q.

Fama, Eugene F. 1965. "The Behavior of Stock Market Prices." *Journal of Business* 38:1, 34–105.

Fama, Eugene F. 1970. "Efficient Capital Markets: A Review of Theory and Empirical Work." *Journal of Finance* 25:1, 383–417.

Fisher, Gregg, Ronnie Shah, and Sheridan Titman. 2016. "Combining Value and Momentum." *Journal of Investment Management* 14:2, 33–48.

French, Kenneth. 2019. Website. Available at http://mba.tuck.dartmouth.edu/pages/faculty/ken.french/data_library.html#Research.

Graham, Benjamin. (1949) 1986. *The Intelligent Investor*. 4th rev. ed. New York, NY: Harper & Row.

Hamilton, William Peter. 1922. *The Stock Market Barometer*. New York, NY: John Wiley & Sons.

Hens, Thorsten, and Anna Meier. 2015. "Behavioral Finance: The Psychology of Investing." Working Paper, Behavioral Finance Solutions GmbH, Credit Suisse, University of Zurich.

Jagadeesh, Narasimhan, and Sheridan Titman. 1993. "Returns to Buying Winners and Selling Losers: Implications for Stock Market Efficiency." *Journal of Finance* 48:1, 65–91.

Kahneman, Daniel, Paul Slovic, and Amos Tversky. 1982. *Judgment Under Uncertainty: Heuristics and Biases*. New York, NY: Cambridge University Press.

Livermore, Jesse, and Richard Smitten. 1940. *How to Trade in Stocks*. New York, NY: McGraw-Hill.

Lo, Andrew, and Jasmina Hasanhodzic. 2010. *The Evolution of Technical Analysis: Financial Prediction from Babylonian Tablets to Bloomberg Terminals*. New York, NY: Bloomberg Press.

Malkiel, Burton. 1973. *A Random Walk Down Wall Street: The Time-tested Strategy for Successful Investing*. New York, NY: W.W. Norton & Company.

Rhea, Robert. 1932. *The Dow Theory*. New York, NY: Barron's.

Samuelson, Paul. 1948. *Economics*. New York, NY: McGraw Hill Book Company.

Thaler, Richard. 2016. *Misbehaving: The Making of Behavioral Economics*. New York, NY: W.W. Norton & Company.

Wang, Hoaming. 2009. "Impact of Sector and Market Variance on Individual Equity Variance." Honors Thesis, Duke University.

White, Amanda. 2015, "Investors from the Moon: Fama." Top1000Funds.com, December 11. Available at https://www.top1000funds.com/2015/12/investors-from-the-moon-fama/.

CHAPTER 10

Discounted Dividend Valuation

Elif Akben-Selçuk
Associate Professor, Gebze Technical University

INTRODUCTION

The dividend discount model (DDM), initially developed by Gordon and Shapiro (1956) and Gordon (1959, 1962), is one of the oldest and simplest models to estimate the value of a company's outstanding stock. In basic terms, the model defines the value of common stock as the present value of future dividend payments, assuming that the company has a perpetual life. Although many analysts consider the model to be outdated, it is still intuitively appealing and remains a useful tool for specific company types (Damodaran 2012; Pinto, Henry, Robinson, and Stowe 2015).

This chapter provides a detailed discussion of the DDM. It has the following organization. The next section provides a general statement of the DDM and then discusses the simplest version of the model, the constant growth or Gordon model. The following section investigates multistage models, including the two-stage model, the H-model, and the three-stage model, followed by binomial and trinomial stochastic DDMs. The chapter then examines the uses of DDMs and the results from studies testing the model's relevance. The last section summarizes and concludes the chapter.

THE GENERAL MODEL

In markets with rational investors, the value of any asset is defined as the present value of the cash flows that it is expected to provide, discounted at a rate appropriate for their risk level. In other words, investors "get what they pay for" (Drake 2015). The DDM applies this principle to common stock. With common stock, the two cash flows are the dividends expected to be paid and the stock's price when it is sold. Since the price itself is also determined by expected dividends in the future, the common stock's value (or price) per share becomes the present value of dividends up to infinity (Damodaran 2012). This price is referred to as the *fair value* or *intrinsic value* because it is the stock's perceived value based on all the available information

(Drake 2015). The stock's intrinsic value based on the DDM can be calculated using Equation 10.1:

$$\text{Value per share of common stock} = \sum_{t=1}^{t=\infty} \frac{E(DPS_t)}{(1 + k_r)^t} \qquad (10.1)$$

where DPS_t denotes expected dividends per share at the end of period t and k_r indicates the required rate of return.

Getting the common stock's value from Equation 10.1 requires estimating two variables: (1) the required rate of return, which depends on the investor's riskiness and can be estimated using different asset pricing models in finance, and (2) the expected dividends. Since estimating an infinite series of dividends is practically impossible, assumptions about the growth rate of dividends are needed. Based on these various assumptions, academics and practitioners have developed different versions of the DDM, which are discussed in the next section.

CONSTANT GROWTH OR GORDON MODEL

The Gordon constant growth model assumes that dividends grow at a constant rate g forever. When applying this assumption to the general form of the DDM, Equation 10.1 simplifies to Equation 10.2:

$$\text{Value per share of common stock} = \frac{DPS_0\,(1 + g)}{(k_e - g)} = \frac{DPS_1}{(k_e - g)} \qquad (10.2)$$

where DPS_0 denotes the last dividend per share paid; DPS_1 is the next expected dividend; k_e indicates the cost of equity; and g represents the expected growth rate of dividends.

A company's sustainable growth rate can be calculated by multiplying its return on equity by its *retention ratio*, which is the percentage of net earnings not distributed as dividends. For example, if dividends on a stock are $3 per share today, the cost of equity is 8 percent, and dividends are expected to grow at a rate of 5 percent forever, the value per share of common stock, V_0, can be calculated as follows:

$$V_0 = \frac{\$3(1 + 0.05)}{(0.08 - 0.05)} = \$105$$

Theoretically, the model can also be used if dividends are expected to decrease in the future. For example, consider a share of common stock that currently pays dividends of $3, and whose dividends are expected to decrease at a rate of 2 percent each year forever. Assuming a cost of equity of 8 percent, the value per share of common stock, V_0, can be calculated as follows:

$$V_0 = \frac{\$3(1 - 0.02)}{(0.08 - (-0.02))} = \$2.40$$

Finally, the model can be used if dividends are expected to remain the same. For example, if a share of common stock currently pays dividends of $3, which are expected to remain constant, and the cost of equity is 8 percent, V_0 can be calculated as follows:

$$V_0 = \frac{\$3}{0.08} = \$37.50$$

This simple version of the DDM model is generally appropriate for mature companies that have reached a steady rate of growth and have well-established and predictable dividend policies (Damodaran 2012). The cost of equity and growth rate in the model should reflect long-term prospects about the company (Pinto et al. 2015).

Moreover, the growth rate used in this model should be less than or equal to the growth rate of the economy in which the firm is operating, which is usually measured by the percentage change in gross domestic product (GDP). If the growth rate is higher, it is likely to slow down in the future once the company ages and matures (Damodaran 2012; Pinto et al. 2015). When using the Gordon model, keep in mind that it is susceptible to assumptions about the growth rate and cost of equity, and hence, sensitivity analysis could be useful. Finally, for the model to work, the growth rate must be less than the cost of equity. Otherwise, the calculated share price would be negative, which makes no sense. For many companies, the simplifying assumption of a single future growth rate in the Gordon model is unrealistic, and growth can be expected to follow multiple stages based on the life-cycle stage of a given company. These multistage models are the focus of the next section.

MULTISTAGE MODELS

Molodovsky, May, and Chottiner (1965) modify the DDM to allow for multiple growth phases that better reflect the life cycle of companies. The life cycle of many companies tends to follow three phases (Pinto et al. 2015). The first one is the "growth phase," in which companies experience a rate of growth in their earnings that is faster than that of the economy. Since companies in this stage have high levels of investment to finance growth, they tend to pay no or low dividends. For example, automobile firms in the 1920s, software firms in the 1990s, or technology firms in the 2000s would constitute examples for this first stage and are called "supernormal" or "growth" firms (Brealey, Myers, Allen, and Mohanty 2012). Following this first stage is the "transition phase," in which the growth rate starts to decrease, funds needed for investments decline, and dividend payments begin to increase. The final stage is the "mature phase," in which the growth rate and dividends reach their long-term growth levels, and thus the Gordon model discussed earlier can be appropriately employed to find the value of common stock (Pinto et al. 2015). These growth phases are the basis of multiple-stage DDMs: the two-stage model, the H-model, and the three-stage model.

The Two-Stage Model

The classic version of the two-stage model has two phases: an initial high-growth phase lasting n year where dividends grow at an above-normal rate of g_a and a

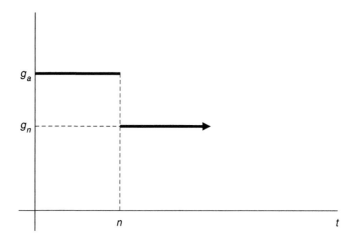

FIGURE 10.1   Two-Stage

Model

This figure illustrates the two phases of growth in the two-stage model of discounted dividend valuation. The growth rate is at an above-normal rate of g_a for n years and then abruptly decreases to a normal rate g_n and remains there indefinitely.

second phase where dividends are expected to grow at a steady-state rate of g_n forever. Figure 10.1 shows this growth pattern.

Equation 10.3 gives the expected value per share of common stock, V_0.

$$V_0 = \sum_{t=1}^{t=n} \frac{DPS_0(1+g_a)^n}{(1+k_e)^n} + \frac{P_n}{(1+k_e)^n}$$

and

$$P_n = \frac{DPS_{n+1}}{k_e - g_n} \tag{10.3}$$

where DPS_t denotes the dividend per share paid at the end of period t; k_e is the cost of equity; P_n represents the price per share of common stock at the end of year n (terminal value); g_a signifies the above-normal growth rate in the first phase; and g_n stands for the steady-state growth rate that lasts from year n to infinity.

For example, consider a share of common stock currently paying dividends of $3, which are expected to grow at a rate of 10 percent for two years and a rate of 5 percent afterward. If the cost of equity is 8 percent, the value per share V_0 can be calculated as follows:

$$V_0 = \frac{\$3(1.10)}{(1+0.08)} + \frac{\$3(1.10)^2}{(1+0.08)^2} + \frac{P_2}{(1+0.08)^2} \text{ and}$$

$$P_2 = \frac{\$3(1.10)^2(1.05)}{(0.08 - 0.05)} = \$127.05$$

$$V_0 = \frac{\$3.3}{1.08} + \frac{\$3.63}{1.1664} + \frac{\$127.05}{1.1664} = \$115.09$$

This model is appropriate for companies that are experiencing high growth, but the sources of this growth are expected to disappear in the future (Damodaran 2012). Examples of this scenario could be having a patent, first-mover advantage, or barriers to entry into the industry (Damodaran 2012; Pinto et al. 2015). A potential limitation of this model is that the decrease from the above-normal growth rate in the first phase to the steady-state growth rate in the second phase occurs suddenly. Although such abrupt changes in growth rates are possible, it would be much more realistic to assume that a gradual shift would be more realistic (Damodaran 2012). Additionally, determining the length of the high-growth period and estimating growth rates are crucial in obtaining successful estimates from the two-stage model (Pinto et al. 2015).

The H-Model

The H-model is another version of the two-stage DDM first presented in Fuller and Hsia (1984). Although the first version two-stage DDM discussed in the previous section assumes that the growth rate changes from one period to the next in an abrupt manner, the H-model assumes that the growth rate decreases from its current level to its steady-state level in a linear manner. Figure 10.2 illustrates this growth pattern. The growth rate starts at an above-normal level g_a and decreases linearly to a normal level g_n over $2H$ years. The growth rate g_n is then expected to be sustained forever. The H-model also assumes that the dividend payout ratio and the cost of equity are constant over time.

In this model, Equation 10.4 gives the expected value per share of common stock (V_0) in which the first part represents the value resulting from normal growth and

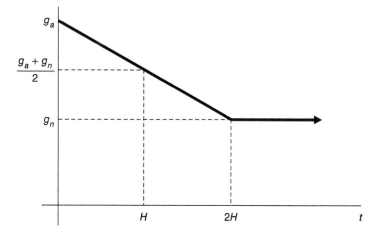

FIGURE 10.2 H-model

This figure illustrates the two phases of growth in the H-model of discounted dividend valuation. The growth rate decreases from an above-normal rate g_a to a normal rate g_n linearly over $2H$ years and remains there indefinitely.

Source: Fuller and Hsia (1984).

the second part represents the incremental value from above-normal growth.

$$V_0 = \frac{DPS_0(1 + g_n)}{k_e - g_n} + \frac{DPS_0 H(g_a - g_n)}{k_e - g_n} \qquad (10.4)$$

where DPS_0 denotes the last dividend paid; k_e reflects the cost of equity; H is the halfway point of the above-normal growth phase, which lasts $2H$ years; g_a signifies the growth rate of dividends in the above-normal growth phase; and g_n indicates the growth rate of dividends in the normal growth phase.

For example, consider a share of common stock currently paying dividends of $3 and whose growth rate of dividends is expected to decrease linearly from 10 percent to 5 percent over four years. If the cost of equity is 8 percent, the value per share V_0 can be calculated as follows:

$$V_0 = \frac{\$3(1.05)}{(0.08 - 0.05)} + \frac{(\$3)(2)(0.10 - 0.05)}{(0.08 - 0.05)} = \$105 + \$10 = \$115.00$$

In this example, $105 of the value is due to normal growth, while $10 is due to abnormal growth.

This model is appropriate for companies that are experiencing a high rate of growth, but whose rate of growth is expected to gradually decline over time as the firm becomes larger and its competitive advantage starts to disappear (Damodaran 2012). Although the model overcomes the limitation of the previous two-stage model resulting from an abrupt decrease in the growth rate, it also has limitations: First, the growth rate needs to follow the exact linear decrease assumed by the model. Second, the dividend payout ratio must remain constant in both phases, which limits the model's applicability (Damodaran).

The Three-Stage Model

The three-stage DDM is a combination of the Gordon model, the two-stage model, and the H-model previously discussed and aims to overcome some limitations of these formulas by incorporating elements from all three models. The three-stage DDM starts with an initial period of high growth lasting n years as the firm expands its operations by offering new products or entering new market segments. This phase is followed by a gradual decline over the second phase, which lasts $2H$ years, which then stabilizes to a steady-state value in the third period (Drake and Fabozzi 2012). Figure 10.3 shows this growth pattern.

Equation 10.5 provides the expected value per share of common stock, V_0, in the three-stage DDM.

$$V_0 = \sum_{t=1}^{t=n} \frac{DPS_0(1 + g_a)^n}{(1 + k_e)^n} + \frac{P_n}{(1 + k_e)^n}$$

where

$$P_n = \frac{DPS_{n+1} + DPS_n H(g_a - g_n)}{k_e - g_n} \qquad (10.5)$$

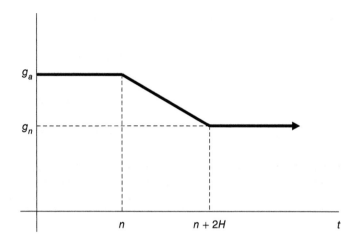

FIGURE 10.3 Three-Stage Model

This figure illustrates the three phases of growth in the three-stage model of discounted dividend valuation. The growth rate is an above-normal rate of g_a for n years and then decreases to a normal rate g_n linearly over $2H$ years and remains at that rate indefinitely.

where DPS_0 denotes the last dividend paid; k_e is the cost of equity; n signifies the number of years in the initial high-growth phase; H indicates the halfway point of the second (transition) phase, which lasts $2H$ years; g_a represents the growth rate of dividends in the first stage; and g_n symbolizes the growth rate of dividends in the third growth phase.

For example, consider a share of common stock currently paying dividends of $3, which are expected to grow at a rate of 10 percent for two years. Then, the growth rate of dividends is expected to decrease linearly from 10 percent to 5 percent over a period of four years. If the cost of equity is 8 percent, the value per share V_0 can be calculated as follows:

$$V_0 = \frac{\$3(1.10)}{(1 + 0.08)} + \frac{\$3(1.10)^2}{(1 + 0.08)^2} + \frac{P_2}{(1 + 0.08)^2}$$

$$\text{and } P_2 = \frac{\$3(1.10)^2(1.05) + \$3(1.10)^2(2)(0.10 - 0.05)}{(0.08 - 0.05)} = \$139.15$$

$$V_0 = \frac{\$3.30}{1.08} + \frac{\$3.63}{1.1664} + \frac{\$139.15}{1.1664} = \$125.47$$

The advantage of the three-stage model is that it captures all three life-cycle stages of a firm. Moreover, the three-stage DDM is the most general and least restrictive of all DDMs because it does not require any assumptions about payout ratios (Damodaran 2012).

STOCHASTIC MODELS

Both the constant growth model and multistage DDMs operate in a deterministic setting. Stochastic DDMs that allow for probabilities are also available and are especially appropriate for companies with unpredictable and volatile dividend payment patterns. Two versions of the stochastic DDM are the binomial and trinomial models.

Binomial Model

Hurley and Johnson (1998) first suggested stochastic DDMs. In their model, they assume dividends follow a simple Markov process. In other words, firms either increase dividends by a specified amount or keep them constant based on some predefined probabilities. This model is called a binomial stochastic DDM because two possibilities for dividends may occur. However, two versions of the binomial stochastic model are available: the additive version in which dividends increase by a specified dollar amount and the geometric version in which dividends increase at a predetermined rate of growth. The additive version can be modeled, as shown in Equation 10.6:

$$D_{t+1} = \begin{cases} D_t + C \text{ with probability } p \\ D_t \text{ with probability } 1 - p \end{cases} \quad \text{for } t = 1, 2, \dots \qquad (10.6)$$

where D_t denotes the dividend paid at the end of period t; D_{t+1} indicates the dividend paid at the end of period $t + 1$; C is the dollar amount of a dividend increase; and p specifies the probability of a dividend increase.

The stock's theoretical value, V_0, in the additive binomial stochastic model can be calculated using Equation 10.7:

$$V_0 = \frac{D_0}{k_e} + \left[\frac{1}{k_e} + \frac{1}{k_e^2} \right] Cp \qquad (10.7)$$

where k_e denotes the cost of equity; C is the dollar amount of a dividend increase; and p represents the probability of a dividend increase.

For example, if dividends are $3 today, the additive growth rate is $0.25 per year, the probability of a dividend increase is 70 percent, and the cost of equity is 8 percent, the value per share V_0 can be calculated as follows:

$$V_0 = \frac{\$3}{0.08} + \left[\frac{1}{0.08} + \frac{1}{(0.08)^2} \right] (\$0.25)(0.7)$$

$$= \$37.50 + 168.75(\$0.25)(0.70) = \$67.03$$

In the geometric version of the binomial model, dividends are assumed to increase at a rate of g and this can be modeled as Equation 10.8:

$$D_{t+1} = \begin{cases} D_t(1 + g) \text{ with probability } p \\ D_t \text{ with probability } 1 - p \end{cases} \quad \text{for } t = 1, 2, \dots \qquad (10.8)$$

The stock's theoretical value, V_0, in the geometric binomial stochastic model can be calculated using Equation 10.9:

$$V_0 = \frac{D_0(1 + pg)}{k_e - pg} \qquad (10.9)$$

For example, if dividends are $3 today, the growth rate is 5 percent, the probability of a dividend increase is 70 percent, and the cost of equity is 8 percent, the value per share V_0 can be calculated as follows:

$$V_0 = \frac{\$3(1 + 0.70(0.05))}{0.08 - 0.70(0.05)} = \$69.00$$

Trinomial Model

Unlike the binomial model that only allows dividends to increase or to remain constant, the trinomial stochastic DDM derived by Yao (1997) allows for the probability of dividend cuts, which are common for many firms, at least temporarily (Drake and Fabozzi 2012).

The additive version of the trinomial stochastic DDM can be written as Equation 10.10:

$$D_{t+1} = \begin{cases} D_t + C \text{ with probability } p_u \\ D_t - C \text{ with probability } p_d \\ D_t \text{ with probability } 1 - p_u - p_d \end{cases} \qquad \text{for } t = 1, 2, \ldots \qquad (10.10)$$

where D_t denotes the dividend paid at the end of period t; D_{t+1} indicates the dividend paid at the end of period $t + 1$; C is the dollar amount of a dividend increase; p_u specifies the probability of a dividend increase; and p_d represents the probability of a dividend decrease.

The stock's theoretical value, V_0, in the geometric binomial stochastic model can be calculated using Equation 10.11:

$$V_0 = \frac{D_0}{k_e} + \left[\frac{1}{k_e} + \frac{1}{k_e^{\,2}} \right] C(p_u - p_d) \qquad (10.11)$$

where D_0 denotes the last dividend paid; k_e represents the cost of equity; C is the dollar amount of a dividend increase; p_u indicates the probability of a dividend increase; and p_d connotes the probability of a dividend decrease.

For example, if dividends are $3 today, the additive growth rate is $0.25 per year, the probability of a dividend increase is 70 percent, the probability of a dividend decrease is 10 percent, and the cost of equity is 8 percent, the value per share V_0 can be calculated as follows:

$$V_0 = \frac{\$3}{0.08} + \left[\frac{1}{0.08} + \frac{1}{(0.08)^2} \right] (\$0.25)(0.70 - 0.10)$$

$$= \$37.50 + 168.75(\$0.25)(0.60) = \$62.81$$

In the geometric version of the trinomial model, dividends are allowed to increase or decrease at a rate of g. The geometric trinomial model can be written as Equation 10.12:

$$D_{t+1} = \begin{cases} D_t(1+g) \text{ with probability } p_u \\ D_t(1-g) \text{ with probability } p_d \qquad \text{for } t = 1, 2, \ldots \\ D_t \text{ with probability } 1 - p_u - p_d \end{cases} \qquad (10.12)$$

Equation 10.13 provides the stock's value, V_0.

$$V_0 = \frac{D_0[1 + (p_u + p_d)g]}{k_e - (p_u - p_d)g} \qquad (10.13)$$

For example, if dividends are \$3 today, the growth rate is 5 percent, the probability of a dividend increase is 70 percent, the probability of a dividend decrease is 10 percent, and the cost of equity is 8 percent, the value per share V_0 can be calculated as follows:

$$V_0 = \frac{\$3[1 + (0.70 + 0.10)(0.05)]}{0.08 - (p_u - p_d)(0.05)} = \$62.40$$

Stochastic DDMs are useful in overcoming a major limitation of traditional models such as constant growth or multistage models in which the analysts can estimate a stock's value, but they cannot specify their degree of confidence in their estimation. However, stochastic models allow analysts to generate a probability distribution for the stock's value, which reflects the degree of confidence in the estimation (Drake and Fabozzi 2012).

USES OF DDMS

Previous sections focused on calculating the intrinsic or fair value based on expected dividends, growth rates, and the cost of equity appropriate for the company's riskiness. Investors can then compare the value calculated from the model to the actual stock's price to identify overvalued (the implied price is less than the actual price) or undervalued (the implied price is more than the actual price) stocks and appropriate action to buy or sell the stock can be taken.

Another way of using the DDM is to calculate expected returns. The *expected return* is the discount rate that equates the present value of the expected future dividends with the stock's actual price. The mathematical equation to calculate expected returns can be generated by replacing the value per share of common stock in Equation 10.1 with the stock's actual price. The cost of equity in the equation then becomes the expected return as Equation 10.14:

$$P_A = \sum_{t=1}^{t=\infty} \frac{E(DPS_t)}{(1 + ER)^t} \qquad (10.14)$$

where DPS_t denotes expected dividends per share at the end of period t; P_A is the stock's actual price; and ER signifies the expected return.

Comparing the expected return obtained from Equation 10.14 to the required return given the company's riskiness (calculated by using the CAPM or other asset pricing models) enables identifying mispriced stocks. If the expected return is more than the required return, then the stock is considered undervalued; if it is less than the required return, then the stock is considered overvalued.

Although Equation 10.14 uses the general form of the DDM to derive expected returns, applying the same logic to any version of the model is also possible. This approach is especially simple and commonly used for the Gordon model given by Equation 10.2. Rearranging the terms of Equation 10.2, Equation 10.15 gives the expected return.

$$ER = \frac{DPS_1}{P_A} + g \tag{10.15}$$

The first part of Equation 10.15 is the part of the return coming from expected dividends and is called "dividend yield." The second part is known as "capital gains yield."

For example, if dividends on a stock are $3 per share today, the actual price per share is $50 and dividends are expected to grow at a rate of 5 percent forever, the expected return (ER) can be calculated as follows:

$$ER = \frac{\$3(1 + 0.05)}{\$50} + 0.05 = 11.30 \text{ percent}$$

Besides the calculation of fair prices and expected returns, DDMs can also be used to relate stock prices and price multiples to a company's fundamental characteristics (Drake 2015). For instance, an investor can relate a company's price-to-earnings (P/E) ratio, which is the ratio of price per share of common stock to the earnings per share (EPS), to its dividend payout, expected growth rate, and required rate of return using the Gordon model. Taking Equation 10.2 and dividing both sides of the equation by EPS, E_0, results in Equation 10.16, which expresses P/E ratio in terms of dividend payout, growth rate, and required rate of return.

$$\frac{P_0}{E_0} = \frac{\frac{DPS_0}{E_0}(1 + g)}{k_e - g} = \frac{\text{Dividend payout ratio}(1 + g)}{k_e - g} \tag{10.16}$$

Equation 10.16 suggests that the P/E ratio is positively related to dividend payout ratio and growth rate and negatively related to the required rate of return.

The DDM also allows relating the stock price and the *price-to-book value ratio*, which is the price per share divided by book value per share, dividend payout, and return on equity (ROE). Since return on equity (ROE_0) can be calculated by dividing earnings per share (E_0) to book value per share (B_0), E_0 can be replaced by $B_0(ROE_0)$ and the Gordon model can be rearranged as Equation 10.17:

$$P_0 = \frac{DPS_0 (1 + g)}{(k_e - g)} = \frac{\left[\frac{DPS_0}{E_0} E_0\right](1 + g)}{(k_e - g)} = \frac{\frac{DPS_0}{E_0} B_0 ROE_0 (1 + g)}{(k_e - g)} \tag{10.17}$$

Equation 10.17 suggests that price per share is positively related to the dividend payout ratio, growth rate, book value per share, and return on equity and negatively related to the cost of equity.

Dividing both sides of Equation 10.17 by B_0 results in Equation 10.18, which suggests that price-to-book value ratio is positively related to the dividend payout, return on equity, and growth rate and negatively related to cost of equity.

$$\frac{P_0}{B_0} = \frac{\frac{DPS_0}{E_0} ROE_0(1+g)}{(k_e - g)} \qquad (10.18)$$

EMPIRICAL TESTS OF THE DIVIDEND DISCOUNT MODEL

Testing the DDM involves comparing a stock's intrinsic or fair value predicted by the model to the stock's actual price (Damodaran 2012). Many empirical studies test the effectiveness of DDMs in forecasting stock prices and in identifying overvalued or undervalued stocks (Sorensen and Williamson 1985; Hickman and Petry 1990; Yao 1997; Jacobs and Levy 1988; Penman and Sougiannis 1998; Francis, Olsson, and Oswald 2000; Foerster and Sapp 2005; Bujang and Nassir 2007; Larrain and Yogo 2008; Drake and Fabozzi 2012; McLemore, Woodward, and Zwirlein 2015; Mugosa and Popovic 2015).

In one of the earliest and simplest tests of the DDM, Sorensen and Williamson (1985) use the model to value 150 stocks in December 1980. They compare their results to the actual market price at that time to form five portfolios based on the degree of over- or undervaluation of each stock. To conduct the analysis, the authors use the EPS of the previous five years as the current EPS, assuming a dividend payout ratio of 45 percent and a stable growth rate of 8 percent for all stocks. Sorensen and Williamson assume an extraordinary growth period of five years and use the CAPM to calculate the cost of equity. The authors then estimate the returns of these five portfolios for the two years between January 1981 and January 1983. Their results show that compared to the S&P 500 index, the portfolio most overvalued by the DDM had a negative excess return of 15 percent, while the most undervalued portfolio had a positive excess return of 16 percent. This finding indicates the model's usefulness in assessing stock value.

In another study, Foerster and Sapp (2005) evaluate the DDM using data from a single stock, the Bank of Montreal, over 120 years. Their results show that the model performed reasonably well in explaining actual prices over the study period. In their study of 199 public European companies, Mugosa and Popovic (2015) compare the prices estimated using the constant growth DDM to the actual stock prices between 2010 and 2013. Their results show that the model is a reliable estimator of stock prices even in a period strongly affected by the global financial crisis. In an emerging market context, Bujang and Nassir (2007) test the Gordon constant growth model on selected stocks listed on Bursa Malaysia. Their results show that the model was relevant in assessing stock value and had practical significance.

In contrast to these studies documenting the usefulness of DDMs, many others find that such models are unsuccessful in explaining equity value. In one such study,

Francis et al. (2000) use a sample of 2,907 firm-year observations ranging from 554 to 607 publicly traded firms each year and find that the median of the forecast errors using DDMs was 69 percent. Other studies, including Hickman and Petry (1990), Penman and Sougiannis (1998), and Larrain and Yogo (2008) compare actual prices and implied values from the DDMs and report similar significant forecast errors. Similarly, Jacobs and Levy (1988) find that selecting stocks with low P/E ratios adds 0.92 percent to quarterly returns, while further screening based on the DDMs only provides a marginal addition of 0.06 percent.

More recently, McLemore et al. (2015) investigate prediction errors in the DDMs using data on firms that consistently paid dividends between 1989 and 2008. Depending on the length of the time period employed to estimate the model, they report prediction errors ranging from 2 percent to 55 percent. The evidence shows that shorter time periods in the model result in lower prediction errors.

To test the stochastic DDMs, Yao (1997) applies such models to stocks of utility companies. The results show that stochastic models work well in estimating stock prices and that the trinomial model provides better estimates than the binomial model. Drake and Fabozzi (2012) conduct a similar analysis using updated data on five electric utility companies and compare the stock prices calculated using the binomial stochastic DDM, the stochastic trinomial model, and the constant growth model. In three of the five cases, the binomial model resulted in the closest estimation of the stock price to the actual price. In the remaining two stocks, the trinomial model provided the best estimation. In none of them did the constant growth model provide the closest estimation of the stock value.

SUMMARY AND CONCLUSIONS

Discounted valuation analysis is a useful tool to value companies for which future dividends can be predicted with some degree of certainty. When investors buy stock in a public company, the only cash flow they receive is dividends. Based on this basic idea, DDMs suggest that a common stock's value is equal to the present value of all future dividends discounted at a rate appropriate for the company's riskiness. Since forecasting all future dividends is practically impossible, academics and practitioners have developed different versions of the DDM based on various assumptions about future growth. The simplest one, called the Gordon model, assumes constant growth into perpetuity. Several multistage models are available. The classical two-stage model assumes a high growth rate for a limited period that then suddenly drops to its steady-state value. With the H-model, the growth rate drops from its current value to its steady-state level in a linear fashion. The three-stage model assumes three different growth phases. Finally, more complex stochastic DDMs allow for introducing probabilities when calculating value.

DDMs are highly popular in corporate finance to value common stock. They are theoretically sound models based on the premise that the value of any asset can be calculated as the present value of the cash flows that investors can expect to receive in the future (McLemore et al. 2015). However, as several empirical studies point out, forecast errors can be large when applying a specific method in practice. As a result, anyone using DDMs for valuation purposes should be aware of their limitations.

DISCUSSION QUESTIONS

1. Discuss the advantages and limitations of the Gordon model.
2. Explain the life-cycle stages followed by firms constituting the basis of multistage DDMs.
3. Identify in which company types the classical two-stage DDM is likely to work best to estimate common stock value.
4. Explain the basic features of stochastic DDMs and compare them to traditional constant growth and multistage models.
5. Discuss the uses of DDMs.

REFERENCES

Brealey, Richard A., Stewart C. Myers, Franklin Allen, and Pitabas Mohanty. 2012. *Principles of Corporate Finance*. New York, NY: McGraw-Hill Education.

Bujang, Imbarine, and Annuar Md Nassir. 2007. "The Relevance of Gordon's Model and Earnings Multiplier Approaches in Emerging Stock Market: Test with Appropriate Refinements." *Journal of International Research Journal of Finance and Economics* 7:1, 140–152.

Damodaran, Aswath. 2012. *Investment Valuation: Tools and Techniques for Determining the Value of Any Asset*. Hoboken, NJ: John Wiley & Sons.

Drake, Pamela P. 2015. "Dividend Valuation Models." Available at https://educ.jmu.edu/~drakepp/FIN362/resources/dvm.pdf.

Drake, Pamela P., and Frank J. Fabozzi. 2012. "Dividend Discount Models." In *Encyclopedia of Financial Models II*, edited by Frank J. Fabozzi, 3–14. Hoboken, NJ: John Wiley & Sons.

Foerster, Stephen R., and Stephen G. Sapp. 2005. "The Dividend Discount Model in the Long-run: A Clinical Study." *Journal of Applied Finance* 15:2, 55–75.

Francis, Jennifer, Per Olsson, and Dennis R. Oswald. 2000. "Comparing the Accuracy and Explainability of Dividend, Free Cash Flow, and Abnormal Earnings Equity Value Estimates." *Journal of Accounting Research* 38:1, 45–70.

Fuller, Russell J., and Chi-Cheng Hsia. 1984. "A Simplified Common Stock Valuation Model." *Financial Analysts Journal* 40:5, 49–56.

Gordon, Myron J. 1959. "Dividends, Earnings, and Stock Prices." *Review of Economics and Statistics* 41:2, 99–105.

Gordon, Myron J. 1962. *The Investment, Financing, and Valuation of the Corporation*. Homewood, IL: Richard D. Irwin.

Gordon, Myron J., and Eli Shapiro. 1956. "Capital Equipment Analysis: The Required Rate of Profit." *Management Science* 3:1, 102–110.

Hickman, Kent, and Glenn H. Petry. 1990. "A Comparison of Stock Price Predictions Using Court Accepted Formulas, Dividend Discount, and P/E Models." *Financial Management* 19:2, 76–87.

Hurley, William J., and Lewis D. Johnson. 1998. "Generalized Markov Dividend Discount Models." *Journal of Portfolio Management* 25:1, 27–31.

Jacobs, Bruce I., and Kenneth N. Levy. 1988. "Disentangling Equity Return Regularities: New Insights and Investment Opportunities." *Financial Analysts Journal* 44:3, 18–43.

Larrain, Borja, and Motohiro Yogo. 2008. "Does Firm Value Move Too Much to Be Justified by Subsequent Changes in Cash Flow?" *Journal of Financial Economics* 87:1, 200–226.

McLemore, Ping, George Woodward, and Thomas Zwirlein. 2015. "Back-tests of the Dividend Discount Model Using Time-varying Cost of Equity." *Journal of Applied Finance* 25:2, 1–20.

Molodovsky, Nicholas, Catherine May, and Sherman Chottiner. 1965. "Common Stock Valuation: Principles, Tables, and Application." *Financial Analysts Journal* 21:2, 104–123.

Mugosa, Ana, and Sasa Popovic. 2015. "Towards an Effective Financial Management: Relevance of Dividend Discount Model in Stock Price Valuation." *Economic Analysis* 48:1–2, 39–53.

Penman, Stephen H., and Theodore Sougiannis. 1998. "A Comparison of Dividend, Cash Flow, and Earnings Approaches to Equity Valuation." *Contemporary Accounting Research* 15:3, 343–383.

Pinto, Jerald E., Elaine Henry, Thomas R. Robinson, and John D. Stowe. 2015. *Equity Asset Valuation*. Hoboken, NJ: John Wiley & Sons.

Sorensen, Eric H., and David A. Williamson. 1985. "Some Evidence on the Value of Dividend Discount Models." *Financial Analysts Journal* 41:6, 60–69.

Yao, Yulin. 1997. "A Trinomial Dividend Valuation Model." *Journal of Portfolio Management* 23:4, 99–103.

CHAPTER 11

Free Cash Flow Valuation

Tom Barkley
Professor of Finance Practice, Syracuse University

INTRODUCTION

Discounted cash flow (DCF) analysis is probably the most commonly used approach to equity analysis. This type of analysis estimates the value of a company's equity on an absolute basis, rather than providing a valuation relative to other firms in the same industry. The versatility of the DCF method allows for explicit assumptions about various line items from the financial statements to be built into the model, whether these items are expressed as growth rates or specific monetary values. Although the DCF approach is useful in valuing entire companies, whether public or private, analysts also use it for specific projects that a corporation or government sector entity might undertake. These analysts then employ capital budgeting tools, such as net present value (NPV) and internal rate of return (IRR), to decide whether to undertake the project.

Gordon (1959) introduces the constant growth dividend discount model (DDM) as a valuation technique based on future cash dividend payments or share repurchases made by a company. Chapter 10 describes these techniques. A challenge of using these techniques is that they are limited in scope to those firms that make regular distributions to shareholders. To be used to value non-dividend-paying firms or those with an irregular dividend pattern, analysts must make assumptions about (1) when the firm is likely to pay dividends, (2) the size of the dividends, and (3) the growth rate associated with future dividends beyond the first payment. Although analysts make these assumptions when using DDMs, uncertainty in the assumptions can lead to substantial errors in estimating a company's equity value. In the case of privately held firms, obtaining nonpublic information about distributions to owners may be challenging.

Free cash flow (FCF) valuation analysis also involves assumptions, which are more closely tied to current and historic observable trends. FCFs rely on cash generated and used by the firm, rather than cash paid explicitly to shareholders. Typically, these cash flows are "free" to be used at management's discretion after considering all needed investments to be made to keep the business going. The principal requirement for using this type of model is for the business to generate stable, positive, and predictable FCFs. Thus, the analysis is best suited for valuing mature firms that are beyond their initial start-up phase.

When making assumptions about the accounts on the firm's financial statements, a common approach is to begin at the top of the income statement. For instance, analysts can model growth rates in sales by averaging the growth rate over the past three years or so, considering macroeconomic factors affecting the industry's growth over the medium term, or estimating the demand for products/services from existing and new customers. Analysts can assume that many accounts on the firm's income statement and balance sheet grow at the sales growth rate if they are expected to remain as a fixed proportion of sales. The company's cost of goods sold and gross profit, for example, may remain at a fixed proportion of its sales. Alternatively, if analysts expect operating efficiency to improve gradually over time, the gross profit margin is likely to increase, and they can build this change into the model. Analysts may also need to adapt the model when forecasting levels of fixed assets if growth tends to vary substantially. Constructing a new factory or acquiring a building means that fixed assets do not grow gradually over time. Instead, the firm may have excess capacity relative to its production of goods and services, necessitating substantive and periodic increases in fixed assets.

This chapter's goal is to illustrate the methodology for using several FCF valuation models, making comparisons between them to demonstrate their usefulness in various settings. The remainder of the chapter is organized as follows. The next section presents a general approach to FCF models, beginning with a more comprehensive explanation of how to calculate FCFs. The following section discusses four special cases, highlighting the most relevant and appropriate uses of each one. Finally, the chapter concludes by referencing other equity valuation approaches to be discussed in later chapters.

GENERAL APPROACH TO FCF ANALYSIS

Some key features of any DCF analysis include: (1) estimating the expected cash flows, determining their growth pattern, (2) using an appropriate discount rate, and (3) calculating a horizon (or terminal) value. After obtaining the value of a firm's operations, an analyst can make necessary adjustments to find the value of a firm's equity and, finally, its price per share. This chapter illustrates these steps using a simple example after making some terminology more explicit.

Before proceeding with estimating the expected cash flows, defining the term "free cash flow" is necessary. *Free cash flow* is the amount of cash generated from a firm's operations that is available for a company's use, after deducting investments to sustain its ongoing operations, both long-term (fixed assets) and short-term (working capital). Strictly speaking, this definition refers to "free cash flow to the firm" (FCFF), representing cash that could be distributed to a firm's investors, such as shareholders and creditors. The term can also refer to "free cash flow to equity" (FCFE), which reflects FCF adjusted for changes in debt and after-tax interest expenses. Another distinction to be made is between unlevered and levered cash flows: the former represents how much cash a business has before it has to meet its financial obligations, while the latter represents the amount of money a firm has after it pays for those obligations. The next section uses these definitions when considering special cases of DCF models.

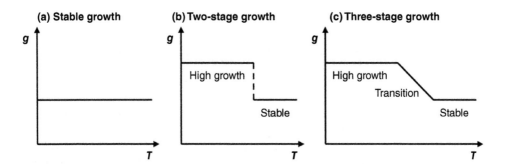

FIGURE 11.1   Growth Patterns for FCFs

This figure shows three different growth patterns for modeling FCFs: (a) stable growth,
(b) two-stage growth, and (c) three-stage growth.

Consider a general DCF model in which a firm has a known FCF in Year 0.
A growth pattern for future expected FCFs is anticipated to follow one of three forms,
as shown in Figure 11.1. The simplest form is to assume a constant growth rate over
time. In this case, the growth rate (g) must be less than the appropriate discount rate
(r) used to find present values of the cash flows. This assumption does not mean,
however, that growth rates can never be higher than the discount rate, only that
they cannot persist at a higher level indefinitely. In two-stage and three-stage growth
patterns, the growth rate is assumed to be high in the near term (possibly higher than
the discount rate) but dropping to a level below the discount rate in the longer term.
A two-stage growth pattern assumes a sudden drop from a high growth rate to a
stable one, while a three-stage growth pattern assumes that a smoother transition
takes place between the short-term and long-term rates.

Once the analyst estimates expected cash flows up to the horizon in which a stable long-term growth rate is forecasted, the second step to consider is choosing an
appropriate discount rate to be used in the valuation model. Analysts may use different discount rates depending on the special case chosen. The next section discusses
these cases in more detail. Analysts often assume that the discount rate is constant
over time, although this assumption does not have to be the case. In more complex
models, the discount rate may vary from one year to the next, although this chapter
does not demonstrate such an approach.

The third step in this general approach is to calculate the firm value at the point
in which the cash flows begin to grow at a stable rate. This value, known as the
horizon value or *terminal value*, represents the present value of all future cash flows
discounted back to that horizon point. One way to calculate the horizon value is to
assume that a price-to-cash-flow multiple can be applied to the cash flow in Year
N, the horizon year, thus obtaining the value of all future cash flows at that point.
Another way to calculate the terminal value is to assume that the cash flows grow
forever at a constant rate (the stable growth rate, g), and then to use the growing
perpetuity formula given in Equation 11.1 with a discount rate r:

$$TV_N = \frac{FCF_{N+1}}{r - g} = \frac{FCF_N(1 + g)}{r - g} \tag{11.1}$$

where FCF denotes the free cash flow; r indicates the required rate of return; and g represents the constant growth rate. Note that the terminal value (TV) in Year N is calculated using the next year's FCF (i.e., in Year $N + 1$, not in Year N).

By summing the present values of all expected future FCFs, including the present value of the horizon value, an analyst obtains the company's value of operations. If the firm has nonoperating assets, such as excess cash, marketable securities, and short-term investments, then analysts should add these assets to the value of operations to get the total value. Finally, calculating a company's common equity occurs by subtracting any debt and/or preferred stock from the total firm value. Dividing the value of common equity by the number of shares outstanding results in a share price.

To illustrate this generalized approach, consider the following example incorporating a three-stage growth pattern in the cash flows. A company generates $100 million in FCF during its most recent fiscal year. For the next six years, analysts expect its cash flows to grow at 20 percent per year, then decrease uniformly over the following four years to a long-term stable growth rate of 4 percent per year from Year 10 forward. The company has $250 million in short-term investments; it also has $1.5 billion of debt and $300 million of preferred stock making up its long-term liabilities. The firm has 80 million shares of common equity outstanding. Table 11.1 shows the DCF model.

TABLE 11.1   General Approach to FCF Valuation

This table provides an example of valuing a company using a general DCF model, with a three-stage growth pattern for the FCFs.

Discount rate	10%											
Year	0	1	2	3	4	5	6	7	8	9	10	11
Growth rate		20%	20%	20%	20%	20%	20%	16%	12%	8%	4%	4%
Free cash flow	$100	$120	$144	$173	$207	$249	$299	$346	$388	$419	$436	$453
Terminal value											$7,553	
Discount factor		0.909	0.826	0.751	0.683	0.621	0.564	0.513	0.467	0.424	0.386	
PV of free cash flow		$109	$119	$130	$142	$155	$169	$178	$181	$178	$3,080	
Value of operations	$4,439											
Short-term investments	$250											
Value of firm	$4,689											
Debt	$1,500											
Preferred stock	$300											
Common equity	$2,889											
Shares outstanding	80											
Price per share	$36.11											

TABLE 11.2 Sensitivity Analysis for FCF Valuation

This table presents a sensitivity analysis for a company valuation using the general DCF model. More specifically, a two-way table is presented showing the values of a company's price per share for different discount rates and long-term stable growth rates.

		Long-term growth rate				
		2%	3%	4%	5%	6%
	8%	$42.64	$52.59	$67.53	$92.42	$142.18
	9%	$32.57	$39.26	$48.64	$62.69	$86.12
Discount rate	10%	$25.07	$29.80	$36.11	$44.94	$58.18
	11%	$19.29	$22.76	$27.22	$33.17	$41.49
	12%	$14.71	$17.32	$20.60	$24.80	$30.41

Using Equation 11.1, TV in Year 10 is $7,553 million. This terminal value, along with the FCFs from Years 1 to 10, is discounted back to the present using the discount factors shown. These are present value interest factors (PVIFs), which are calculated using Equation 11.2:

$$PVIF_t = \frac{1}{(1 + r)^t} \tag{11.2}$$

The sum of all the present values results in the company's value of operations ($4,439 million) and adding the $250 million of nonoperating assets gives a total firm value of $4,689 million. Subtracting the debt and preferred stock leaves the value of common equity ($2,889 million). Finally, dividing by the 80 million shares outstanding results in a price per share of $36.11.

Although calculating the stock price is the primary goal of the analysis, considering the sensitivity of this price to the input variables is also essential. Sensitivity analysis examines how the share price changes when the initial FCF changes, discount rate is altered, initial high growth rate is modified, and long-term growth rate is increased or decreased. Table 11.2 illustrates a two-way sensitivity analysis where the price per share increases substantially for higher long-term growth rates and lower discount rates.

Note the relative size of the discounted terminal value to the company's value of operations. In this example, the discounted terminal value is $2,912 million (= $7,553 million × $PVIF_{10}$), and this total represents 65.6 percent of the value of operations. The horizon value is often a large percentage of a firm's value, indicating the importance of accurately estimating the long-term growth rate. Small changes in this stable growth rate can substantially affect firm value and correspondingly the price per share. This issue arises in all FCF valuation approaches and also affects DDMs. Analysts usually assume that the FCFs have the same long-term growth rate as that of a company's industry or the gross domestic product (GDP) growth rate for the country where a firm primarily operates.

Another issue that arises with all equity valuation approaches is whether a company's capital structure changes over the forecast horizon. In some instances, the assumption is that a company's debt-to-equity ratio remains constant over time, so that debt and equity grow at the same rate. In other situations, analysts assume that debt levels can be forecast more easily so that the proportion of debt and equity varies over time. Although accurately forecasting long-term growth rates can be challenging, several alternative methods are available to value companies based on assumptions related to their capital structure changes. The next section describes four of these methods.

FOUR SPECIAL CASES OF FCF VALUATION APPROACHES

This section considers four methods, each with features that are useful in specific valuation scenarios. These methods are the (1) weighted average cost of capital (WACC) approach, (2) adjusted present value (APV) method, (3) capital cash flow (CCF) model, and (4) free cash flow to equity (FCFE) technique. The first three methods value the whole firm, while the fourth only values a firm's equity. Each subsection provides a discussion of other differences and their relevant usage. Fernandez (2019) describes 10 methods and 9 theories, but some of these methods and theories represent only minor variations on those described here. All four of these approaches assume an "anchor" value of zero, meaning that they value a firm's equity based only on discounted FCFs. In Chapter 13, residual income valuations assume an anchor corresponding to the book value of equity and then discount differences between the forecasted expected returns on equity and the book value returns on equity.

The following examples use data for Lowe's Companies, Inc. (NYSE: LOW). Tables 11.3 and 11.4 show some key figures from the firm's financial statements. Table 11.5 provides additional information necessary for the valuations.

TABLE 11.3   Income Statement for Lowe's

This table reproduces the Consolidated Statements of Earnings for Lowe's Companies, Inc. (in millions, except per share and percentage data).

Fiscal years ended on	02/01/19	02/02/18	02/03/17	01/29/16
Net sales	$71,309	$68,619	$65,017	$59,074
Cost of sales	$48,401	$46,185	$43,343	$38,504
Gross profit	$22,908	$22,434	$21,674	$20,570
Expenses:				
Selling, general, and administrative	$17,413	$14,444	$14,375	$14,105
Depreciation and amortization	$1,477	$1,404	$1,453	$1,494
Earnings before interest and tax	$4,018	$6,586	$5,846	$4,971
Interest expense (net)	$624	$633	$645	$552
Loss on extinguishment of debt	$0	$464	$0	$0
Earnings before tax	$3,394	$5,489	$5,201	$4,419
Income tax expense	$1,080	$2,042	$2,108	$1,873
Net income	$2,314	$3,447	$3,093	$2,546

Source: Company's 10-K filings with the SEC on 04/02/19, 04/02/18, 04/04/17, and 03/29/16.

TABLE 11.4 Balance Sheet for Lowe's

This table reproduces the Consolidated Balance Sheets for Lowe's Companies, Inc. (in millions, except par value).

Fiscal years ended on	02/01/19	02/02/18	02/03/17	01/29/16
Assets				
Current assets:				
Cash and cash equivalents	$511	$588	$558	$405
Short-term investments	$218	$102	$100	$307
Inventory	$12,561	$11,393	$10,458	$9,458
Other current assets	$938	$689	$884	$391
Total current assets	**$14,228**	**$12,772**	**$12,000**	**$10,561**
Property, less accumulated depreciation	$18,432	$19,721	$19,949	$19,577
Long-term investments	$256	$408	$366	$222
Deferred income taxes (net)	$294	$168	$222	$241
Goodwill	$303	$1,307	$1,082	$154
Other assets	$995	$915	$789	$511
Total assets	**$34,508**	**$35,291**	**$34,408**	**$31,266**
Liabilities and shareholders' equity				
Current liabilities:				
Short-term borrowings	$722	$1,137	$510	$43
Current maturities of long-term debt	$1,110	$294	$795	$1,061
Accounts payable	$8,279	$6,590	$6,651	$5,633
Accrued compensation and employee benefits	$662	$747	$790	$820
Deferred revenue	$1,299	$1,378	$1,253	$1,078
Other current liabilities	$2,425	$1,950	$1,975	$1,857
Total current liabilities	**$14,497**	**$12,096**	**$11,974**	**$10,492**
Long-term debt, excluding current maturities	$14,391	$15,564	$14,394	$11,545
Deferred revenue (extended protection plans)	$827	$803	$763	$729
Other liabilities	$1,149	$955	$843	$846
Total liabilities	**$30,864**	**$29,418**	**$27,974**	**$23,612**
Shareholders' equity:				
Common stock	$401	$415	$433	$455
Capital in excess of par value	$0	$22	$0	$0
Retained earnings	$3,452	$5,425	$6,241	$7,593
Accumulated other comprehensive income/(loss)	($209)	$11	($240)	($394)
Total shareholders' equity	**$3,644**	**$5,873**	**$6,434**	**$7,654**
Total liabilities and shareholders' equity	**$34,508**	**$35,291**	**$34,408**	**$31,266**

Source: Company's 10-K filings with the SEC on 04/02/19, 04/02/18, 04/04/17, and 03/29/16.

TABLE 11.5 Additional Information Related to Lowe's

This table provides additional information related to Lowe's Companies, Inc. on April 2, 2019, when the company filed its 10-K with the Securities and Exchange Commission (SEC). The estimated number of shares outstanding and the market capitalization are in millions.

Risk-free rate	2.5%
Market risk premium	5.5%
Levered company beta	1.05
Levered cost of equity	8.3%
Cost of debt	3.6%
Marginal tax rate	25.8%
Target debt-to-equity ratio	21.3%
Weighted average cost of capital	7.3%
Short-term high growth rate	15.9%
Long-term stable growth rate	1.9%
Closing price per share	$108.32
Number of shares outstanding	796
Market capitalization	$86,218

Sources:
(i) The risk-free rate is the 10-year Treasury rate obtained from the Daily Treasury Yield Curve Rates on the U.S. Department of the Treasury website on 04/02/19 (https://www.treasury .gov/resource-center/data-chart-center/interest-rates/pages/TextView.aspx?data=yieldYear& year=2019).
(ii) The equity market risk premium is the U.S. median estimate from Fernandez, Martinez, and Acin (2019).
(iii) The levered company beta is estimated from a linear regression of daily returns for Lowe's against daily returns of the S&P 500 (04/04/16 to 04/02/19), where the returns are computed from adjusted closing prices from Yahoo! Finance.
(iv) The levered cost of equity is calculated using the CAPM model, as shown in Equation 11.6.
(v) The company's cost of debt is estimated as the weighted average interest rate of its most recently issued bonds (May 2017), as found on p. 66 of its 10-K filing.
(vi) The marginal tax rate is the 2018 statutory federal income tax rate (21.0 percent) plus the 2018 state income tax rate, net of federal tax benefit (4.8 percent), as found on p. 72 of its 10-K filing.
(vi) The target debt-to-equity ratio is the author's estimate based on an average of the company's debt-to-equity ratio over the years between 2016 and 2019.
(vii) The WACC is calculated using Equation 11.5.
(viii) The short-term high growth rate is obtained from Aswath Damodaran's website at NYU Stern for expected growth in EPS over the next five years for the Retail Building Supply sector (http://pages.stern.nyu.edu/~adamodar/New_Home_Page/datafile/histgr.html).
(ix) The long-term stable growth rate is estimated as the implied growth rate that results from the GDP long-term forecast for the United States in 2060 from the OECD Data website (https:// data.oecd.org/gdp/gdp-long-term-forecast.htm).
(x) The closing price per share is obtained from historical data on Yahoo! Finance.
(xi) The number of shares outstanding is the value on 03/29/19, as on p. 2 of its 10-K filing.
(xii) The market capitalization is the closing price per share multiplied by the number of shares outstanding.

Weighted Average Cost of Capital (WACC)

This approach, also called FCFF valuation, is the most frequently used in DCF analysis. Empirical evidence by Marsh (1982) and Hovakimian, Opler, and Titman (2001) shows that financial managers often tend to think in terms of target debt-to-equity ratios, and this approach adapts well to such cases. It allows analysts the flexibility to make assumptions about a company's growth in revenues, expenses, current assets and current liabilities, and investments in fixed assets. Analysts generally assume that the discount rate for these cash flows—the weighted average cost of capital—remains constant over the forecasting horizon, but this relation does not have to be the case. The model works best when a company's target debt-to-equity ratio is known and assumed to be constant in the future (through continuous rebalancing). Conversely, if a firm rebalances its capital structure only once a year, Miles and Ezzell (1980) demonstrate how to adjust the unlevered cost of equity.

A firm's cash flows are forecasted under the assumption that its capital structure consists entirely of equity (i.e., unlevered cash flows are computed). Analysts estimate these cash flows as the net operating profit after taxes (NOPAT) minus the net investment in operating capital (NIOC), as Equation 11.3 shows:

$$FCFF = NOPAT - NIOC \tag{11.3}$$

Considering the profit that is generated before interest and tax expenses are paid as being the net operating profit, then analysts can estimate NOPAT as earnings before interest and taxes (EBIT) multiplied by $(1 - T_c)$, where T_c is the firm's marginal tax rate. Additionally, the gross investment in operating capital is the sum of any investment in fixed assets and working capital. As a result, NIOC recognizes that depreciation expense is incurred and must be subtracted from the gross investment. Thus, Equation 11.4 provides a means of calculating FCFF:

$$FCFF = EBIT(1 - T_c) - (CapEx + \Delta NWC - Depn)$$
$$= EBIT(1 - T_c) + Depn - \Delta NWC - CapEx \tag{11.4}$$

where T_c is the marginal corporate tax rate for the firm; *Depn* is the depreciation and amortization expense for the year; ΔNWC is the change in net working capital; and *CapEx* represents the capital expenditures for the year.

Some analysts choose a simpler approach, which is not followed here, that approximates FCFF by only referring to the statement of cash flows: they estimate FCFF as the cash flow from operations (CFFO) minus the cash flow from investing (CFFI). Equation 11.4 is used for the analysis described in this chapter.

The *weighted average cost of capital* (WACC) estimates the cost associated with a firm raising long-term capital from the markets by issuing debt, equity, and other securities. It weights the required return for each type of security by the market value of that security in a firm's capital structure. Jagannathan, Liberti, Liu, and Meier (2017) note that the true cost of capital is unobservable and that firms use hurdle rates as proxies. Nevertheless, analysts often estimate WACC by using the relative market weights of debt and equity (D/V, E/V) multiplied by the after-tax cost of debt (r_D) and cost of equity (r_E), respectively, as shown in Equation 11.5:

$$r_{WACC} = r_D(1 - T_c)\left(\frac{D}{V}\right) + r_E\left(\frac{E}{V}\right) \tag{11.5}$$

The tax rate (T_c) is the firm's marginal corporate tax rate—the tax that a firm would pay on the next dollar earned. Similarly, the cost of debt is the marginal cost—typically estimated as the coupon rate on new bonds that a company might issue today. Finally, analysts often estimate the cost of equity using the capital asset pricing model (CAPM), shown in Equation 11.6, where the expected return on equity (r_E) from an investor's perspective is measured as the risk-free rate (r_f) plus the firm's beta multiplied by the market risk premium (RP_m), where $RP_m = (r_m - r_f)$:

$$r_E = r_f + \beta_E(RP_m) = r_f + \beta_E(r_m - r_f) \tag{11.6}$$

The equity beta, β_E, in Equation 11.6 is a levered beta, generally found by relevering an unlevered industry beta using a firm's debt-to-equity ratio. The industry beta can proxy for a firm's asset beta, β_A, which represents its business risk without including the effects of leverage. Hamada (1972) proposes the relation between a levered beta and an unlevered beta as that given by Equation 11.7, and Taggart (1991) extends it to a more comprehensive framework.

$$\beta_E = \beta_A + (1 - T_c)(\beta_A - \beta_D)\left(\frac{D}{E}\right) \tag{11.7}$$

Returning to the example of Lowe's valuation, Table 11.6 shows the DCF analysis. More details are provided here than in the general DCF approach in Table 11.1, as the FCFs are modeled using some explicit assumptions that deviate from simple calculations. For instance, the change in net working capital in 2018 should be calculated as noncash current assets minus spontaneous current liabilities (i.e., excluding current interest-bearing liabilities). This approach would result in a value of –$583 million, a substantial reduction in the company's invested working capital. Instead, recognizing that this decrease in net working capital might be a singular event and modeling Lowe's change in net working capital as the average of the changes over the past three years results in an estimate of $124 million as the change for 2018. The second instance of an explicitly changed assumption is based on the note in the company's 10-K filings that states the forecast capital expenditures for 2019 are about $1.6 billion—a 33.3 percent growth over the $1.2 billion in 2018. The model results in a price of $107.31 per share, which is less than 1 percent away from the actual adjusted closing price per share of $108.32 on April 2, 2019.

Adjusted Present Value (APV)

This method of DCF analysis values a firm in a piecewise manner. The basic piece is firm value, as though it were an all-equity firm. Then, if a company has debt, a piece must be added to capture the present value of tax shield benefits; if a risk of financial distress exists due to high levels of debt, the analyst should subtract the present value of financial distress costs; if value arises from real options that a firm has, their present value needs to be added; and so forth. Equation 11.8 summarizes this approach.

Value of a firm = PV(Unlevered cash flows) $+ PV(Tax$ shield benefits of debt)

$- PV$(Financial distress costs associated with debt) $+ PV$(Real options) $+ \ldots$

$$\tag{11.8}$$

TABLE 11.6 Valuation of Lowe's Using the WACC Approach

This table illustrates the valuation of Lowe's Companies, Inc., on April 2, 2019, using the WACC approach with a two-stage growth pattern for earnings (in millions, except per share and percentage data). Earnings before interest and taxes (EBIT), net operating profit after taxes (NOPAT), depreciation expenses, and changes in net working capital (NWC) all grow at the high growth rate in the first stage of the five years shown. Capital expenditures of $1.2 billion (actual) in 2018 and $1.6 billion (forecast) in 2019 are as found on page 31 of the company's 10-K filing; they grow at the high growth rate for the remaining four years of the period as shown. The change in NWC in 2018 is estimated as the average of the changes in NWC over the previous three years. Net debt is computed as the company's long-term debt, including current maturities plus short-term borrowings minus cash and cash equivalents.

Discount rate (WACC)	7.3%

Marginal tax rate	25.8%

Fiscal year	2018	2019	2020	2021	2022	2023	2024
Growth rate		15.9%	15.9%	15.9%	15.9%	15.9%	1.9%
Earnings before interest and taxes (EBIT)	$4,018	$4,657	$5,397	$6,255	$7,250	$8,403	$8,563
Net operating profit after taxes (NOPAT)	$2,981	$3,455	$4,005	$4,642	$5,380	$6,235	$6,353
Depreciation expense	$1,477	$1,712	$1,984	$2,299	$2,665	$3,089	$3,148
Change in net working capital (NWC)	$124	$144	$167	$194	$224	$260	$265
Capital expenditures	$1,200	$1,600	$1,854	$2,149	$2,491	$2,887	$2,942
Free cash flow	$3,134	$3,423	$3,967	$4,598	$5,329	$6,177	$6,294
Terminal value						$116,822	
Discount factor		0.932	0.869	0.810	0.755	0.703	
PV of free cash flow		$3,191	$3,447	$3,723	$4,022	$86,527	
Value of operations	$100,910						
Short-term investments	$218						
Value of firm	$101,128						
Net debt	$15,712						
Common equity	$85,416						
Shares outstanding	796						
Price per share	$107.31						

Although Myers (1974) introduces the APV method, he primarily emphasizes the first two components of Equation 11.8. The method is most suitable for valuation when a company's debt levels are known for the years in the forecasting horizon, as this allows explicitly calculating interest expenses and associated tax shields. Of particular relevance are valuations involving leveraged buyouts (LBOs), where debt financing is prominent, and the levels of debt can be forecast reasonably well while it is being paid down. Luehrman (1997) expands on the financing side effects to tailor the analysis to fit managers' needs.

Suppose that Lowe's plans to reduce its level of net debt at the same rate as from 2017 to 2018 for the next five years (a growth rate of −4.5 percent per year). To value the firm in this case, the APV method requires two separate DCF analyses: one requires discounting its FCFs at the unlevered cost of equity, r_A; the other requires discounting its interest tax shields at the appropriate cost of capital, r_{ITS}. Equation 11.7 shows how to obtain the company's unlevered equity beta, resulting in a value of 0.91. The unlevered cost of equity is then computed using Equation 11.6, resulting in a value of 7.5 percent. The interest expenses can be calculated each year by multiplying the debt level by the cost of debt; then interest tax shields are obtained by multiplying the interest expenses by the marginal tax rate.

A much-debated issue is what the appropriate discount rate should be for these interest tax shields. As Ehrhardt and Daves (2002, p. 31) note, Modigliani and Miller (1958, 1963) (M&M) and Hamada (1972) "assume that the interest tax shield should be discounted at the cost of debt," but their models assume a zero-growth firm. Ehrhardt and Daves (p. 31) explain how their results accommodate the assumption of discounting interest tax shields at a higher rate, and "express the value-risk relationships as explicit functions of leverage, growth, and an arbitrary discount rate for the interest tax shield. The M&M/Hamada analyses, the adjusted present value (APV) model of Myers (1974), and the compressed adjusted present value (CAPV) model of Kaplan and Ruback (1995, 1996) are all special cases" of their results. Ehrhardt and Daves (p. 32) also note that "if a firm maintains a constant capital structure, then the amount of debt will depend on the value of the firm. Thus, Miles and Ezzell (1980) and Ezzell and Miles (1983) argue that the tax shield is as risky as the underlying assets and should be discounted at the unlevered cost of equity." Exhibit 1 of Ehrhardt and Daves (2002) and Appendix D of Koller, Goedhart, and Wessels (2005) each provide excellent summaries of the possible alternatives: if debt is a constant proportion of enterprise value, then debt must grow at the same rate as the business, as $r_{ITS} = r_A$; on the other hand, if the interest tax shields are assumed to have the same risk as the firm's debt, then $r_{ITS} = r_D$.

Opting for the second assumption, the valuation of Lowe's using the APV method results in a price of $110.92 per share, as shown in Table 11.7. Although this valuation is close to the actual adjusted closing price, using the unlevered cost of equity to discount the tax shields results in an even better estimate of $107.94 per share (not shown).

TABLE 11.7   Valuation of Lowe's Using the APV Approach

This table illustrates the valuation of Lowe's Companies, Inc., on April 2, 2019, using the adjusted present value (APV) approach with a two-stage growth pattern for earnings (in millions, except per share and percentage data). Earnings before interest and taxes (EBIT), net operating profit after taxes (NOPAT), depreciation expenses, and changes in net working capital (NWC) all grow at the high growth rate in the first stage of the five-year period shown. Capital expenditures of $1.2 billion (actual) in 2018 and $1.6 billion (forecast) in 2019 are as found on page 31 of the company's 10-K filing; they grow at the high growth rate for the remaining four years of the period as shown. Debt is assumed to decrease in level at a constant rate over the five-year period. The change in NWC in 2018 is estimated as the average of the changes in NWC over the previous three years. Net debt is computed as the company's long-term debt, including current maturities plus short-term borrowings minus cash and cash equivalents.

Discount rate (unlevered cost of equity, r_A)	7.5%						
Cost of capital for interest tax shields (r_{ITS})	3.6%						
Marginal tax rate	25.8%						
Fiscal year	2018	2019	2020	2021	2022	2023	2024
Growth rate		15.9%	15.9%	15.9%	15.9%	15.9%	1.9%
Earnings before interest and taxes (EBIT)	$4,018	$4,657	$5,397	$6,255	$7,250	$8,403	$8,563
Net operating profit after taxes (NOPAT)	$2,981	$3,455	$4,005	$4,642	$5,380	$6,235	$6,353
Depreciation expense	$1,477	$1,712	$1,984	$2,299	$2,665	$3,089	$3,148
Change in net working capital (NWC)	$124	$144	$167	$194	$224	$260	$265
Capital expenditures	$1,200	$1,600	$1,854	$2,149	$2,491	$2,887	$2,942
Free cash flow	$3,134	$3,423	$3,967	$4,598	$5,329	$6,177	$6,294
Terminal value						$112,659	
Discount factor		0.930	0.866	0.805	0.749	0.697	
PV of free cash flow		$3,185	$3,434	$3,703	$3,993	$82,826	
Value of (unlevered) operations (A)	$97,140						
Fiscal year	2018	2019	2020	2021	2022	2023	2024
Growth rate		−4.5%	−4.5%	−4.5%	−4.5%	−4.5%	1.9%
Debt	$16,223	$15,486	$14,783	$14,111	$13,470	$12,858	$13,103
Interest expense		$554	$528	$504	$482	$460	$468
Interest tax shield		$143	$136	$130	$124	$119	$121
Terminal value						$7,215	
Discount factor		0.965	0.932	0.900	0.869	0.839	
PV of interest tax shield		$138	$127	$117	$108	$6,152	
Value of all interest tax shield benefits (B)	$6,642						
Short-term investments (C)	$218						
Value of firm (A + B + C)	$104,001						
Net debt	$15,712						
Common equity	$88,289						
Shares outstanding	796						
Price per share	$110.92						

Capital Cash Flow (CCF)

Ruback (2002, p. 85) describes this model by noting that, although the WACC approach is the most commonly used for valuing risky cash flows, it "poses several implementation problems in highly leveraged transactions, restructurings, project financings, and other instances in which capital structure changes over time." A CCF model, like the APV method, is best suited for instances when the company's debt levels are known for the forecasting years. In this case, the cash flows include all of the cash available to capital providers (debtholders and shareholders), including the interest tax shields. A revised version of Equation 11.4 must be used in such a model, which produces Equation 11.9:

$$CCF = FCFF + \text{Interest } tax \text{ shield} \tag{11.9}$$

Additionally, the appropriate discount rate to be used is a before-tax rate because the interest tax shields are part of the cash flows. The pre-tax WACC that is used corresponds to the unlevered cost of equity that is used in the APV method, as shown in Equation 11.10:

$$\textit{Pre-tax } WACC = r_A = r_D \left(\frac{D}{V} \right) + r_E \left(\frac{E}{V} \right) \tag{11.10}$$

As Table 11.8 shows, the valuation of Lowe's using a CCF model results in a price of \$108.76 per share. In this illustration, the debt is not decreasing in value over time but is growing at the same rate as earnings.

Free Cash Flow to Equity (FCFE)

In this fourth and final technique, referred to as the "free cash flow to equity" model or "equity residual" model, the value of a company's equity is calculated directly. As mentioned previously, FCFE is the cash flow available for distribution only to common shareholders. It is a levered cash flow calculated as FCFF adjusted for changes in debt and after-tax interest expenses. Equation 11.11 shows the relevant adjustments:

$$\begin{aligned} FCFE &= (EBIT - r_D D)(1 - T_c) - (CapEx + \Delta NWC - Depn) + \Delta D \\ &= EBIT(1 - T_c) + Depn - \Delta NWC - CapEx - r_D D(1 - T_c) + \Delta D \\ &= FCFF - r_D D(1 - T_c) + -D \end{aligned} \tag{11.11}$$

where D is the face value of the firm's debt and ΔD is the change in the level of that debt.

These cash flows should be discounted using the estimated levered cost of equity obtained using the WACC approach. Similar to that approach, this technique tends to work well when a company's target debt-to-equity ratio is known and assumed to be constant over the valuation horizon. Table 11.9 shows that the valuation of Lowe's using the FCFE technique results in a price per share of \$112.04.

TABLE 11.8 Valuation of Lowe's Using the CCF Approach

This table illustrates the valuation of Lowe's Companies, Inc., on April 2, 2019, using the capital cash flow (CCF) approach with a two-stage growth pattern for earnings (in millions, except per share and percentage data). Earnings before interest and taxes (EBIT), net operating profit after taxes (NOPAT), depreciation expenses, changes in net working capital (NWC), and debt all grow at the high growth rate in the first stage of the five-year period shown. Capital expenditures of $1.2 billion (actual) in 2018 and $1.6 billion (forecast) in 2019 are as found on page 31 of the company's 10-K filing; they grow at the high growth rate for the remaining four years of the period as shown. The change in NWC in 2018 is estimated as the average of the changes in NWC over the previous three years. Net debt is computed as the company's long-term debt, including current maturities plus short-term borrowings minus cash and cash equivalents.

Discount rate (pre-tax WACC, r_A)	7.5%						
Cost of debt (r_D)	3.6%						
Marginal tax rate	25.8%						

Fiscal year	2018	2019	2020	2021	2022	2023	2024
Growth rate		15.9%	15.9%	15.9%	15.9%	15.9%	1.9%
Earnings before interest and taxes (EBIT)	$4,018	$4,657	$5,397	$6,255	$7,250	$8,403	$8,563
Net operating profit after taxes (NOPAT)	$2,981	$3,455	$4,005	$4,642	$5,380	$6,235	$6,353
Depreciation expense	$1,477	$1,712	$1,984	$2,299	$2,665	$3,089	$3,148
Change in net working capital (NWC)	$124	$144	$167	$194	$224	$260	$265
Capital expenditures	$1,200	$1,600	$1,854	$2,149	$2,491	$2,887	$2,942
Debt	$16,223	$18,802	$21,792	$25,257	$29,273	$33,927	$34,572
Interest expense		$672	$779	$903	$1,047	$1,213	$1,236
Interest tax shield		$173	$201	$233	$270	$313	$319
Capital cash flow	$3,134	$3,597	$4,168	$4,831	$5,599	$6,490	$6,613
Terminal value						$118,366	
Discount factor		0.930	0.866	0.805	0.749	0.697	
PV of free cash flow		$3,346	$3,608	$3,890	$4,195	$87,023	
Value of operations	$102,062						
Short-term investments	$218						
Value of firm	$102,280						
Net debt	$15,712						
Common equity	$86,568						
Shares outstanding	796						
Price per share	$108.76						

TABLE 11.9 Valuation of Lowe's Using the FCFE Approach

This table illustrates the valuation of Lowe's Companies, Inc., on April 2, 2019, using the free cash flow to equity (FCFE) approach with a two-stage growth pattern for earnings (in millions, except per share and percentage data). Earnings before interest and taxes (EBIT), net operating profit after taxes (NOPAT), depreciation expenses, and changes in net working capital (NWC) all grow at the high growth rate in the first stage of the five-year period shown. Capital expenditures of $1.2 billion (actual) in 2018 and $1.6 billion (forecast) in 2019 are as found on page 31 of the company's 10-K filing; they grow at the high growth rate for the remaining four years of the period as shown. The change in NWC in 2018 is estimated as the average of the changes in NWC over the previous three years. Debt is computed as the company's long-term debt, including current maturities plus short-term borrowings.

Discount rate (levered cost of equity, r_E)	8.3%						

Cost of debt (r_D)	3.6%
Marginal tax rate	25.8%

Fiscal year	2018	2019	2020	2021	2022	2023	2024
Growth rate		15.9%	15.9%	15.9%	15.9%	15.9%	1.9%
Earnings before interest and taxes (EBIT)	$4,018	$4,657	$5,397	$6,255	$7,250	$8,403	$8,563
Net operating profit after taxes (NOPAT)	$2,981	$3,455	$4,005	$4,642	$5,380	$6,235	$6,353
Depreciation expense	$1,477	$1,712	$1,984	$2,299	$2,665	$3,089	$3,148
Change in net working capital (NWC)	$124	$144	$167	$194	$224	$260	$265
Capital expenditures	$1,200	$1,600	$1,854	$2,149	$2,491	$2,887	$2,942
Debt	$16,223	$18,802	$21,792	$25,257	$29,273	$33,927	$34,572
After-tax interest expense	$580	$672	$779	$903	$1,047	$1,213	$1,236
Change in debt	-$772	$2,579	$2,990	$3,465	$4,016	$4,654	$645
Free cash flow to equity	$1,782	$5,330	$6,178	$7,160	$8,299	$9,618	$5,703
Terminal value						$89,455	
Discount factor		0.924	0.853	0.788	0.728	0.672	
PV of free cash flow to equity		$4,923	$5,270	$5,641	$6,038	$66,575	
Value of operations (to equity holders)	$88,447						
Cash and cash equivalents	$511						
Short-term investments	$218						
Common equity	$89,176						
Shares outstanding	796						
Price per share	$112.04						

SUMMARY AND CONCLUSIONS

The DCF analyses presented in this chapter make assumptions about the forecasted cash flows and the applicable discount rates to be used. Table 11.10 shows these key aspects.

These DCF models all focus on firm valuation based on fundamental analysis, seeking to estimate the intrinsic value of a firm's equity based on its characteristics. During a general business cycle, occasions may occur when an entire industry or sector is over- or undervalued. In those cases, valuing a firm relative to its peers may be more appropriate, and market-based valuations using multiples should be employed as described in Chapter 12. Damodaran (2002) provides a detailed perspective on fundamental principles of relative valuation using earnings multiples, book value multiples, revenue multiples, and sector-specific multiples.

A final aspect of DCF models should be noted. Analysts can sometimes use them to reverse engineer certain inputs to the model. For instance, if an analyst assumes a firm's current observed market stock price is consistent with reality, but a firm's WACC is unknown, then the analyst could use a DCF model to back out a firm's WACC. Similarly, if an analyst assumes a firm's WACC and stock price are known and accurate, then the analyst could use a DCF model to estimate a firm's long-term growth rate.

TABLE 11.10 Summary of Key Features of Valuation Approaches

This table summarizes the major features of four DCF valuation approaches: (1) weighted average cost of capital (WACC) or free cash flow to the firm (FCFF); (2) adjusted present value (APV); (3) capital cash flow (CCF); and (4) free cash flow to equity (FCFE). The first three methods value the whole firm, while the fourth only values the firm's equity.

Method	Cash flows	Discount rate
WACC	Unlevered free cash flows: $FCFF = EBIT(1 - T_c) + Depn - \Delta NWC - CapEx$	$r_{WACC} = r_D(1 - T_c)(D/V) + r_E(E/V)$
APV	(i) Unlevered free cash flows: $FCFF = EBIT(1 - T_c) + Depn - \Delta NWC - CapEx$	$r_A = r_D(D/V) + r_E(E/V)$
	(ii) Interest tax shields: $ITS = r_D D T_c$	r_{ITS} (equal to either r_D or r_A)
CCF	Capital cash flows: $CCF = FCFF + ITS$	Pre-tax WACC $= r_A$
FCFE	Levered free cash flows: $FCFE = FCFF - r_D D(1 - T_c) + \Delta D$	$r_E = r_A + (1 - T_c)(r_A - r_D)(D/E)$

DISCUSSION QUESTIONS

1. Articulate the advantages and disadvantages of FCF valuation analysis relative to DDM analysis.
2. Define what is meant by FCFF and FCFE.
3. Explain why growth patterns are important in modeling FCFs.
4. Discuss the choice of FCF method that would be most suitable for the valuation of: (1) a venture capital investment, (2) a mature manufacturing firm, (3) an acquisition through an LBO, and (4) a commercial bank.
5. Summarize the alternative uses of a DCF model besides valuing a company.

REFERENCES

Damodaran, Aswath. 2002. *Investment Valuation: Tools and Techniques for Determining the Value of Any Asset*, 2nd ed. New York, NY: John Wiley & Sons.

Ehrhardt, Michael C., and Phillip R. Daves. 2002. "Corporate Valuation: The Combined Impact of Growth and the Tax Shield of Debt on the Cost of Capital and Systematic Risk." *Journal of Applied Finance* 12:2, 31–38.

Ezzell, John R., and James A. Miles. 1983. "Capital Project Analysis and the Debt Transaction Plan." *Journal of Financial Research* 6:1, 25–31.

Fernandez, Pablo. 2019. "Valuing Companies by Cash Flow Discounting: Ten Methods and Nine Theories." *Valuation and Common Sense, Chapter 4.* IESE Business School, University of Navarra. Available at http://ssrn.com/abstract=256987.

Fernandez, Pablo, Mar Martinez, and Isabel F. Acin. 2019. "Market Risk Premium and Risk-Free Rate Used for 69 Countries in 2019: A Survey." Available at http://ssrn.com/abstract=3358901.

Gordon, Myron J. 1959. "Dividends, Earnings, and Stock Prices." *Review of Economics and Statistics* 41:2, 99–105.

Hamada, Robert S. 1972. "The Effect of a Firm's Capital Structure on the Systematic Risk of Common Stocks." *Journal of Finance* 27:1, 435–452.

Hovakimian, Armen, Tim Opler, and Sheridan Titman. 2001. "The Debt-Equity Choice." *Journal of Financial and Quantitative Analysis* 36:1, 1–24.

Jagannathan, Ravi, José Liberti, Binying Liu, and Iwan Meier. 2017. "A Firm's Cost of Capital." *Annual Review of Financial Economics* 9, 259–282.

Kaplan, Steven N., and Richard S. Ruback. 1995. "The Valuation of Cash Flow Forecasts: An Empirical Analysis." *Journal of Finance* 50:4, 1059–1093.

Kaplan, Steven N., and Richard S. Ruback. 1996. "The Market Pricing of Cash Flow Forecasts: Discounted Cash Flow vs. the Method of 'Comparables.'" *Journal of Applied Corporate Finance* 8:4, 45–60.

Koller, Tim, Marc Goedhart, and David Wessels. 2005. *Valuation: Measuring and Managing the Value of Companies*, 4th ed. *McKinsey & Company.* Hoboken, NJ: John Wiley & Sons.

Luehrman, Timothy A. 1997. "Using APV: A Better Tool for Valuing Operations." *Harvard Business Review* 75:3, 145–154.

Marsh, Paul. 1982. "The Choice Between Equity and Debt: An Empirical Study." *Journal of Finance* 37:1, 121–144.

Miles, James A., and John R. Ezzell. 1980. "The Weighted Average Cost of Capital, Perfect Capital Markets, and Project Life: A Clarification." *Journal of Financial and Quantitative Analysis* 15:3, 719–730.

Modigliani, Franco, and Merton H. Miller. 1958. "The Cost of Capital, Corporation Finance, and the Theory of Investment." *American Economic Review* 48:3, 261–297.

Modigliani, Franco, and Merton H. Miller. 1963. "Corporate Income Taxes and the Cost of Capital: A Correction." *American Economic Review* 53:3, 433–443.

Myers, Stewart C. 1974. "Interactions of Corporate Financing and Investment Decisions – Implications for Capital Budgeting." *Journal of Finance* 29:1, 1–25.

Ruback, Richard S. 2002. "Capital Cash Flows: A Simple Approach to Valuing Risky Cash Flows." *Financial Management* 31:2, 85–103.

Taggart, Robert A. Jr., 1991. "Consistent Valuation and Cost of Capital Expressions with Corporate and Personal Taxes." *Financial Management* 20:3, 8–20.

CHAPTER 12

Market-based Valuation

Sang Hoon Lee
Professor of Finance, BRAC University

INTRODUCTION

Financial asset valuation is generally based on the principle of substitution under an "arbitrage-free" condition. The broad premise for this principle is an efficient market for economic transactions. This condition implies that two identical assets or perfect substitutes should be priced equally, assuming no market frictions such as transaction costs.

An asset's price may deviate from its equilibrium price if market frictions are sufficiently high or the market is inefficient, even if the assets are close to being perfect substitutes. Although some believe in efficient markets, they may not be ready to take an asset's daily fluctuating market price as a long-term equilibrium value due to asset-specific noises. Nonetheless, academics and practitioners have developed and applied various valuation methods in equity research practices. Some widely used methods include intrinsic valuation, such as the discounted cash flow (DCF) approach; current valuation, using market-based multiples; asset valuation, mainly for liquidation purposes; and real option valuation, incorporating option values of future decision-making in a project. As Yee (2004) notes, however, no single valuation technique has shown absolute superiority in accuracy according to previous empirical research. As a result, analysts jointly use several alternatives and practical valuation methods to increase the confidence of valuation predictions.

Valuation using the multiples method is based on directly applying the principle of substitution. It assumes an efficient market and the ability to estimate a target asset's value by relating to the publicly traded values of other similar companies or of previous acquisition transactions. Therefore, the multiples method relies on actual prices of real firms rather than estimated cash flows and discount rates as required in the DCF approach. However, these multiples are drawn from the same principles used in the DCF approach, such as a positive relation with future payoffs and a negative relation with risk. The multiples method is particularly useful when the target asset is a nonpublic company about to set an offer price for an initial public offering (IPO), a closely held business for determining gift and estate taxes, a spinoff project through restructuring, or a company with negative cash flows or earnings.

Obtaining a robust set of similar companies or transactions is often challenging. In general, analysts determine the similarity of comparable companies by the industry to which the selected company belongs and to similar operational and financial characteristics. Having defined a set of comparable firms and transactions, analysts usually acquire valuation multiples calculated by taking a ratio of a company's value measure to its performance measure from a portfolio of comparable companies and transactions. Then, they estimate the target's value by multiplying the calculated multiple to a measure of the target's performance that is used to calculate the multiple. Analysts use this estimated price as a basis for a merger negotiation or for determining whether the asset or transaction is correctly valued in the market.

Comparable transactions are acquisitions of similar companies that were completed within a few years so that all relevant information is not too outdated. Typically, the comparable transaction method provides a higher range of multiples because the transaction value potentially includes control and acquisition premiums. Analysts often use the estimates from multiple valuation methods for calibrating those estimates from other valuation approaches and, in combination, through calculating a weighted average value. In this way, analysts can draw a reasonably fair value range of a target asset. Analysts also use the multiple valuation approach to complement the permanent (constant) growth model in calculating the terminal value for the DCF approach.

This chapter presents an overview of various market multiple valuation methods. The next section examines the types and uses of multiples and discusses cautions when using these methods. The following two sections review issues in selecting comparable firms and the efficacy of using different multiples in previous valuation studies. The next section empirically identifies potential factors determining the values of various multiples. The final section provides a summary and conclusions.

WIDELY USED VALUATION MULTIPLES AND VALUATION STEPS

Analysts often use two groups of multiples. Although the choice may depend on industry characteristics, the most popular set of multiples for valuing companies includes the following:

- *Equity-related multiples.* Price-to-earnings per share (P/E), price-to-book value per share (P/B), price-to-sales per share (P/S), and price-to-cash flows per share (P/CF).
- *Enterprise value (EV)-related multiples.* EV-to-earnings before interest and tax (EV/EBIT), EV-to-earnings before interest, tax, depreciation, and amortization (EV/EBITDA), EV-to-sales (EV/Sales), and EV-to-cash flows (EV/CF).

Besides these common market multiples, analysts frequently use industry-specific multiples such as EV/Access lines for the communication industry and EV/EBITDAX (i.e., EV/earnings before interest, tax, depreciation, depletion, amortization, and exploration) or EV/reserves for oil and mineral exploration industries.

The following example summarizes the valuation steps for a target firm in the industrial equipment supplier industry using multiples of comparable firms. This example excludes the P/CF and EV/CF multiples because the valuation mechanism is the same as other multiples, but a separate free cash flow needs to be estimated for the multiples.

First, five comparable companies are selected from publicly listed companies based on key financial and operational characteristics that closely match the target firm's characteristics. Then, financial statements of comparable and target firms are adjusted by excluding nonoperating and extraordinary items. If the valuation is performed in the middle of the accounting period, all financial statements should be reconstructed to make the last-twelve-months (LTM) statements. Table 12.1 provides key financial information for comparable firms.

Based on this information, earnings per share (EPS), book value per share (BPS), and sales per share (SPS) are calculated. Also, the EVs are computed by summing the market value of equity and net debt for comparable firms. In the net debt calculation, the market value of debt should be used if available. However, corporate debt is not

TABLE 12.1   Key Financial Information for Comparable Companies and the Target Company

This table shows key financial information collected for the target and comparable firms from their last-twelve-months (LTM) statements. This information can be used to assess similarities of comparable firms to the characteristics of the target firm and future steps of target valuation.

| Key Financial Information | Comparable Companies | | | | | Target Company |
	W. W. Grainger	Rockwell Automation	General Dynamics	Stanley Black & Decker	Ingersoll-Rand	
Closing stock price ($/share)	293.20	189.50	182.40	147.50	113.40	187.60
Long-term debt ($ million)	2,090.0	1,225.2	11,444.0	3,819.8	3,740.7	4,755.0
Equity (book value, $ million)	4,141.0	3,393.7	24,149.0	12,034.6	11,114.0	16,527.0
Cash and cash equivalent ($ million)	528.6	790.0	5,615.8	3,477.0	5,156.0	2,480.0
Sales ($ million)	11,221.0	6,720.2	36,193.0	13,982.4	15,668.2	27,058.0
EBITDA ($ million)	1,459.0	1,450.4	5,220.0	2,391.5	2,373.1	5,106.0
EBIT ($ million)	1,205.0	1,285.8	4,457.0	1,885.0	2,011.6	4,538.0
Net income ($ million)	776.2	1,037.4	3,052.5	1,380.1	2,350.2	3,278.2
Number of shares outstanding (in millions)	55.4	119.5	288.8	151.4	242.2	280.2
Average sales growth rate (% per year)	4.0%	1.8%	4.8%	7.8%	5.6%	5.2%

usually traded in the public market, and market values may be unavailable. In this case, analysts typically substitute the book value for the market value, assuming that firms are conservative and frequently mark-to-market these debts in their financial statements. Ingersoll-Rand has more cash and cash equivalents than long-term debt, and therefore, its net debt becomes negative, and the market value of equity becomes higher than its enterprise value. Also, the target company's key financial and operational information are collected. This information includes earnings, EBIT, EBITDA, sales, long-term debt, book value of equity, and number of shares outstanding. In this example, the target company is relatively larger in terms of its book value of equity and earnings. Table 12.2 shows the value drivers (denominators of the multiples) and EVs of the target and comparable companies.

The next step is calculating the valuation multiples. In this example, six multiples (P/E, P/B, P/S, EV/EBIT, EV/EBITDA, and EV/Sales) are calculated for the five comparable firms. Then, a normalization process is performed for these multiples using the harmonic mean, arithmetic mean, and median values. To minimize valuation errors, equity researchers and practitioners often recommend using the harmonic mean and forward valuation metrics such as forward EPS, forecasted sales, and forward EBITDA. The *harmonic mean* is the value obtained by summing the reciprocals of the comparable ratios, averaging the sum by dividing it by the number of comparable firms and then taking the reciprocal of the average. This approach tends to penalize large values of multiples caused by weak transitory earnings or CF (the denominator of the P/E or P/CF multiple), but at the same time, it may aggravate the bias from small values. Since only positive values of multiples are used to calculate the normalized multiple, the harmonic mean could be a better fit than other choices. The forward metrics and market consensus values for the public companies are available in various equity research reports such as Bloomberg, Capital IQ, Google Finance, Yahoo! Finance, and IBES. Table 12.3 shows the calculated values of six multiples for each comparable firm and the harmonic and arithmetic means as well as the median values. The harmonic mean is always smaller than the arithmetic mean since

TABLE 12.2 Calculations of Value Drivers and EVs

This table shows the value drivers (denominators of equity-related multiples) such as EPS, BPS, and SPS for all firms, and the enterprise values for comparable firms.

Per Share Price and EV	W. W. Grainger	Rockwell Automation	General Dynamics	Stanley Black & Decker	Ingersoll-Rand	Target Company
EPS ($)	14.00	8.70	10.60	9.10	9.70	11.70
BPS ($)	74.70	28.40	83.60	79.50	45.90	59.00
SPS ($)	202.40	56.20	125.30	92.40	64.70	96.60
Market equity ($ million)	16,255.6	22,647.6	52,663.0	22,317.6	27,462.0	To be estimated
EV ($ million)	17,817.0	23,082.8	58,491.2	22,660.4	26,046.6	To be estimated

The table header "Comparable Companies" spans the W. W. Grainger, Rockwell Automation, General Dynamics, Stanley Black & Decker, and Ingersoll-Rand columns.

TABLE 12.3 Calculations of Multiples and the Average and Median Values

This table shows six multiples from the five comparable firms as well as a harmonic mean, arithmetic mean, and median values for each multiple.

Multiple	W. W. Grainger	Rockwell Automation	General Dynamics	Stanley Black & Decker	Ingersoll-Rand	Harmonic Mean	Arithmetic Mean	Median
P/E	20.9	21.8	17.3	16.2	11.7	16.7	17.6	17.3
P/B	3.9	6.7	2.2	1.9	2.5	2.8	3.4	2.5
P/S	1.4	3.4	1.5	1.6	1.8	1.7	1.9	1.6
EV/EBIT	14.8	18.0	13.1	12.0	12.9	13.9	14.2	13.1
EV/EBITDA	12.2	15.9	11.2	9.5	11.0	11.6	12.0	11.2
EV/Sales	1.6	3.4	1.6	1.6	1.7	1.8	2.0	1.6

an observation's weight is inversely proportional to its magnitude in calculating the weighted average for the harmonic mean.

In this example, the valuation for the target firm is performed using the harmonic means of multiples. The target firm's EPS, BPS, SPS, EBIT, EBITDA, and sales value, respectively, are multiplied to these harmonic means of six multiples to estimate the target's stock price and enterprise value. The stock price can be directly estimated using the equity-related multiples. However, the EV-related multiples require two-step procedures to estimate target's stock price: (1) estimate the target's EV using EV/EBIT, EV/EBITDA, or EV/Sales, and (2) estimate the target's market value of equity by subtracting net debt from the EV. Then, the estimate of stock price can be computed by dividing the equity value by the target's number of shares outstanding. If the target firm is an acquisition target, then the fully diluted number of shares should be used instead by incorporating potential dilution effects from stock options and convertible bonds.

The estimates of the target's stock price range from \$163.20 (minimum) to \$216.80 (maximum), as indicated in Tables 12.4 and 12.5. The average value is \$185.70 and the median value is \$181.90 (\$168.10 + \$195.70)/2). In fact, the target's financial information is extracted from the financial statements of Raytheon

TABLE 12.4 Target Valuation Using Equity-related Multiples

This table shows the stock price estimates of the target using P/E, P/B, and P/S multiples ranging from \$163.20 to \$195.70.

Metric (Value Driver)	Target Company (\$ Per Share)	Multiple (Harmonic Mean)	Estimated Share Price for Target
Earnings	\$11.70	16.7	\$195.70
Book value	\$59.00	2.8	\$163.20
Sales	\$96.60	1.7	\$168.10

TABLE 12.5 Target Valuation Using EV-related Multiples

This table shows the stock price estimates of the target using EV/EBIT, EV/EBITDA, and EV/Sales multiples range from $166.90 to $216.80. (in millions, except multiple and per-share price)

Metric (Value Driver)	Target Company ($ mil)	Multiple (Harmonic Mean)	Estimated Enterprise Value for Target	Less: Net Debt	Estimated Equity Value for the Target	Fully Diluted Shares	Estimated Share Price for Target
EBIT	$4,538.0	13.9	$63,036.4	($2,275.0)	$60,761.4	280.2	$216.80
EBITDA	$5,106.0	11.6	$59,287.6	($2,275.0)	$57,012.6	280.2	$203.50
Sales	$27,058.0	1.8	$49,048.6	($2,275.0)	$46,773.6	280.2	$166.90

Company, and the stock's actual market price at the time after collecting all information for comparable firms was $187.60 per share. The average estimate of the target's value deviates less than $2.00 (about 1 percent) from the actual market price.

SELECTING COMPARABLE FIRMS

The multiple approach of valuation can be highly effective for a target valuation if closely matching comparable firms, or similar previous transactions, are available. Furthermore, the usefulness of a valuation multiple depends on the nature of the operational and financial differences between the target and comparable firms and the sensitivity of the multiples to these differences. Obtaining a robust set of comparable companies is often challenging due to a lack of perfect substitutes among the companies. For a public firm, its past multiples could be the closest substitutes for the current multiples, assuming that past performance may repeat in the future. However, retrieving records of private firms and start-ups may be difficult. Therefore, judiciously selecting comparable firms from publicly listed companies is the key to minimizing valuation errors. Although the approach is highly subjective, practitioners focus on the similarities of operational and financial profiles such as industry, size, future growth rate, profitability, capital structure, and cost of capital in selecting comparable firms.

Analysts may question the degree of dispersion among the multiples of comparable firms due to the sensitivity of the average to extreme values. The outliers may represent recording errors. Alternatively, an extreme value may be a legitimate value but from a different population. The most common approaches to avoid reaching a misleading average are excluding outliers in calculations or taking the median value.

Alford (1992) asserts that firms in the same industry are expected to be similar in terms of risk and earnings growth, as well as accounting methods. In his analysis, similar accuracy occurs when using the risk, as measured by firm size, and earnings growth together to construct portfolios of comparable firms. No improvement results in adjusting P/E based on differences in leverage across comparable firms. Besides, the efficacy of selecting comparable firms based on the industry is higher for large firms than for small firms.

Baker and Ruback (1999) and Liu, Nissim, and Thomas (2002) use firms in the same industry and match historical earnings growth to reduce valuation errors using the E/P ratio. Baker and Ruback contend that comparable firms should be selected based on measures that minimize the spread across multiples within the industry since the underlying value drivers differ across industries. Nevertheless, Kim and Ritter (1999) propose leaving the task of selecting comparable firms in IPO valuation to investment bankers, recognizing their insights in canvassing market demand before setting a final offer price of IPO firms. Bhojraj and Lee (2002), however, propose a "warranted multiple" for each target firm. A warranted multiple is derived through regression analysis incorporating cross-sectional variations of profitability, growth, and risk characteristics. They suggest choosing comparable firms as those having the closest warranted multiple of the target firm.

In summary, academic researchers and practitioners agree that comparable firms should be selected from the same industry as the target firm. The main variables of interest in selecting comparable firms in the same industry may include but are not limited to company size (e.g., sales revenue or market capitalization), average growth rate and profitability (e.g., return on asset and return on equity) for at least the past three years, capital structure (e.g., debt ratio and debt-to-equity ratio), and credit rating. If available, professional equity research reports and consensus estimates on earnings and other profit margins are particularly useful in selecting comparable firms and analyzing various ratios.

THE EFFICACY OF DIFFERENT MULTIPLES IN VALUATION

A multiple calculated from various companies is likely to produce a different valuation for a target. Differing value drivers also yield dissimilar value estimates. This difficulty worsens if a large portion of assets are intangibles. In other words, much room exists for judgment and subjectivity in selecting the types of multiples with different performance measures or value drivers. An arbitrary choice of specific multiples or value drivers or some type of a weighted average of them may lead to an incorrect decision.

No particular multiple dominates the others in all criteria of valuation accuracy. An industry multiple may be a useful benchmark since it is calculated by including all firms in an industry. Baker and Ruback (1999) analyze industry multiples drawn from a simple mean, harmonic mean, value-weighted mean, and median value for their performances in predicting value. They find that the harmonic mean minimizes valuation errors. Baker and Ruback also recommend using multiples that use EBITDA rather than EBIT or revenue to minimize valuation errors. Similarly, Liu, Nissim, and Thomas (2002, 2007) propose using a harmonic mean to improve prediction performance. They suggest using the forward EPS as a value driver since a professional consensus estimate is likely to mitigate the effect of transitory low earnings and, therefore, an unusually high P/E ratio.

Yee (2004) suggests taking advantage of diversification benefits by incorporating as many bona fide value estimates as possible. He concludes, however, that choosing the optimal weights for different valuation estimates remains context-specific.

Chan (2016) shows substantial improvement in valuation using a composite of P/E and P/B ratios over a single multiple. The weights for combining these ratios are determined through regression analysis using firm-specific characteristics.

The value estimates from multiple methods need further adjustments when the target firm is a subject of an acquisition by a strategic buyer or a private company not traded in a public exchange. As Finnerty and Emery (2004) note, the value determined by the multiples assumes estimating the target's stock price traded in a public exchange, which does not include a control or acquisition premium. Therefore, valuation multiples, if they are being used to value a firm that is changing control, must be adjusted for the value of corporate control or calculated using the matched comparable transaction method in which a change of control exists. Furthermore, the estimated price from multiple valuations is drawn from listed prices of public firms, which may reflect a large liquidity premium. This liquidity premium may be irrelevant to a target valuation if it is a private firm. More critically, the market values of those comparable firms may be subject to specific time-dependent market conditions or irrational investor sentiment. Multiple valuations are unlikely to help determine a target's fundamental value if an entire industry is overvalued or undervalued. Therefore, an appropriate adjustment is needed, which considers market conditions.

Academic researches provide some evidence of the valuation accuracies of multiples. Liu et al. (2002) examine the valuation performance of a comprehensive list of multiples with different value drivers. They find the following relative performance rankings: multiples derived from forward earnings perform the best, followed by historical earnings, then cash flow and book value are tied for third, and finally, multiples based on sales perform the worst. These overall rankings are observed consistently for almost all industries examined.

Liu et al. (2007) extend their 2002 study by analyzing valuation in the international market setting. They find that forward earnings are a superior value driver than forecasted cash flows when comparing valuation errors between P/E and P/CF multiples. Lie and Lie (2002) report that asset multiples (unadjusted EV or adjusted EV-to-book value of assets) generally yield better estimates than do sales and earnings multiples, and using forecasted earnings improves the estimates using P/E ratio. Additionally, the EBITDA multiple usually provides better estimates than does the EBIT multiple. Finnerty and Emery (2004) also support using EBITDA for valuation.

Leibowitz (2002) finds a significant negative impact of leverage on the P/E ratio. As the debt ratio increases, the given levered return on equity (ROE) implies an ever-lower fundamental unlevered return on assets (ROA). The result is a lower economic value and hence, uniformly lowers the theoretical P/E ratios. Therefore, market analysts should pay careful attention to a company's debt structure when trying to determine the appropriate theoretical P/E for valuation purposes.

In general, an IPO involves young firms for which forecasting future cash flows may be difficult. Kim and Ritter (1999) use various multiples such as P/E, P/B, P/S, EV/Sales, and EV/Operating cash flow ratios for valuing IPOs and find that the equity-related multiples have only modest predictive ability without further adjusting the historical accounting numbers. Industry multiples do not capture many idiosyncratic factors without making various adjustments for differences in growth and profitability. When using forward earnings, however, the accuracy of P/E multiple valuations improves substantially. Gilson, Hotchkiss, and Ruback (2000) compare the multiple valuation methods with intrinsic valuation (capital cash flow approach) to value bankrupt firms. They use an industry median EV/EBITDA multiple drawn from the first-year projected EBITDA, assuming the comparable industry firms, on average, match the bankrupt companies' growth and risk. The authors find that the median valuation error is less than 5 percent, although the valuation errors have a wide range. Conversely, the estimates from other valuation methods are not statistically different from those of the multiple methods. Gilson et al. also show that using a single-year EBITDA does not distort the results.

In another stream of academic studies, researchers analyze multiples to test market efficiency. These studies show why some multiples are relevant in valuation. Basu (1977) examines the investment performance of common stocks in its relation to P/E (or E/P) ratios under the efficient market framework. He shows that low-P/E stocks tend to outperform high-P/E stocks and earn a superior return on a risk-adjusted basis. Beaver and Morse (1978), however, assert that the persistently deviating P/E ratios from expectations based on risk and growth are due to differing accounting methods. A conservative accounting method would tend to generate higher P/E ratios than a less conservative accounting method. This result indicates that analysts using P/E ratios for valuation should carefully consider the adjustments of different accounting methods in generating EPS.

By contrast, Ou and Penman (1989) explain that the P/E anomaly indicates the market's underutilization of current accounting information in financial statements. The authors assert that price changes predict earnings changes relatively poorly since price changes reflect transitory elements of current earnings change. The P/E ratio, rather than price, leads both prices and earnings since it measures risk related to future returns.

Analysts can use a P/B or P/S multiple when the earnings amount is negative. Researchers often analyze a P/B ratio in an inverse form, such as a B/P ratio. An aggregated form of the market value of equity-to-book value of equity (ME/BE) or an inverse form of it can also be used. Studies such as Lakonishok, Shleifer, and Vishny (1994) report that value stocks, which have relatively low P/B ratios, have higher average returns than growth stocks, which have relatively high P/B ratios in many countries.

As Fama and French (1992, 1993, 1995) show, the combination of size and the B/P ratio consistently helps to explain the cross-section of stock returns. The smaller the size (measured by market equity) and the higher the B/P (i.e., value stock), the higher is the stock return. Fama and French explain that high B/P stocks are fundamentally riskier and therefore require a higher return.

In contrast, Lakonishok et al. (1994) explain that value strategies, such as investing in high B/P stocks, produce superior returns because they are contrarian to naive strategies followed by other investors. These naive strategies may include extrapolating past performance too far into the future, overreacting to good or bad news, or equating a sound investment with a good company irrespective of price. The overreaction of investors and agency problems of institutional investors who tend to tilt toward glamour stocks (e.g., low-B/P stocks or growth stocks) are possible reasons explaining the overpricing of glamour stocks compared to value stocks.

As Penman, Richardson, and Tuna (2007) show, the B/P ratio is determined by both an operation component and a financing activity component. The operation component of B/P has a positive relation with future stock returns. The leverage component of B/P is represented by the net debt-to-market equity ratio and is negatively associated with future stock returns. This negative relation is robust across different specifications and controls for known factors that may influence returns.

Billings and Morton (2001) investigate the ability of the B/P multiple to predict future returns. They decompose the B/P ratio into a more persistent, biased accounting recognition component and a transitory delayed accounting recognition component. The authors find that although both components are related to analyst expectations of future earnings, the delayed recognition component in B/P attributable to past price changes is the dominant factor capturing the inverse relation between B/P and future returns and systematic stock price reversals.

Wilcox (1984) finds a direct relation between the P/B ratio and ROE based on the cross-section of firms in different industries and markets. He regressed log(P/B) on actual ROE as an empirical proxy for the expected ROE and finds that it explains current prices of stocks based on historical data. The P/B-ROE model offers a more accurate estimate than the P/E model.

Regarding the P/B-ROE relation, Fairfield (1994) shows that the P/B ratio correlates positively with future ROE. Also, P/E is a positive function of earnings growth. Together, the ratios reveal information about expected future profitability relative to current profitability. Penman (1996) shows a similar result that the P/B ratio is positively determined by the projection of future ROE. For a given projection, the P/E ratio is determined by comparing current (negatively related) and future ROE (positively related). He concludes that because P/B reflects future profitability and is unaffected by current profitability unless serially correlated, it is a more appropriate indicator of a firm's earnings growth and a better valuation method.

Analysts use the difference in accounting methods to explain an anomalous P/B multiple. Cole, Helwege, and Laster (1996) observe that the P/B ratio of the S&P Industrials was substantially higher in the early 1990s compared to the historical average of 2.0. Yet, they are unable to explain the high ratio even after adjusting the book value of equity with the addition of liabilities implemented by Financial Accounting Standards (FAS) No. 106 for retiree health benefits. Cole et al. predict that the market is overvalued based on the substantially high P/B ratio. Conversely, Saunders (1996) explains why the overvalued P/B ratio in Cole et al. can be sustainable. Given that P/B is a product of P/E and E/B (i.e., ROE), a high P/B may come from a high ROE if P/E is stable. ROE can be permanently high due to a high return on previously committed assets, downsizing or restructuring of equity due to booked losses, and a high growth rate in the knowledge industry, which usually carries the intangibles at book value. Therefore, P/B is an irrelevant indicator if P/E is appropriate.

In recent times, P/S has become well accepted among practitioners for valuing the service industry if the asset weight is relatively low. Earnings may fluctuate without the changes in a company's core performance measures. The timing of capital expenditure or research and development (R & D) investment is likely to affect the accounting period's earnings substantially. A more stable indicator of a firm's performance may be sales and its trend. Besides, analysts often consider sales to be less subjective to management manipulation than earnings. However, sales represent income for both equity and debt holders, whereas stock price is relevant for equity holders. Therefore, the P/S ratio may be inconsistent since it is a ratio with two different characteristics.

Although empirical studies on the efficacy of EV-related multiples are scant, these multiples may produce fewer valuation errors than equity-related multiples. EV multiples are likely to be more robust when companies being compared have differences in leverage. Penman et al. (2007) show a negative relation between leverage and stock return. Leibowitz (2002) also explains that leverage negatively affects the P/E ratio. Therefore, the impact on the EV-related multiples of leverage is less than on the equity-related multiples since EV is the total capital a company uses and is capital structure–neutral.

A logical multiple using sales as a value driver is EV/Sales. Kim and Ritter (1999) report that, using historical accounting information and controlling for leverage effects, the EV/Sales ratio works reasonably well for both young and old firms. Additional adjustments that reflect differences both in sales growth rates and in profitability per dollar of sales improve the fit even more.

Liu et al. (2002) explain that sales, EBITDA, and EBIT should be associated with enterprise value, rather than equity alone, and those value drivers can be considered with EV-related multiples. Many researchers recommend EBITDA rather than EBIT in EV-related multiples since EV is the present value of free cash flows to the firm and depreciation and amortization are not cash flows. This rationale is also relevant for sales, which is a measure inclusive of the cost of operation and noncash charges. Sales are free from the differences in accounting of, for example, inventory and depreciation.

COMMON FACTORS DETERMINING DIFFERENT MULTIPLES

This section attempts to identify some common factors and their sensitivities to determine different multiples using firms contained in the S&P 500 based on 2018 financial statements. The following tables present correlations among different multiples. The analysis excludes firms with negative earnings, missing values, and extreme values. The equity-related multiples are calculated from 440 firms, which include 338 New York Stock Exchange (NYSE)-listed and 102 National Association of Securities Dealers Automated Quotations (NASDAQ)- and Chicago Board Options Exchange (CBOE)-listed firms. The EV-related multiples are also calculated from a different group of 440 firms consisting of 321 NYSE-listed and 119 NASDAQ- and CBOE-listed firms. Table 12.6 shows correlations among equity-related multiples for NYSE- and NASDAQ/CBOE-listed firms.

All averages of equity-related multiples in NYSE-listed firms are lower than those of NASDAQ- and CBOE-listed firms. The P/E multiple has relatively lower correlations with both P/B and P/S multiples, whereas P/B and P/S have higher positive correlation.

Will listing on NASDAQ have any beneficial impact on valuation? In most cases, intangibles, which are not carried on the books at market value, determine the values of high-technology and start-up companies. Therefore, the average P/B multiple of NASDAQ-listed firms may be higher than that of NYSE-listed firms. Besides, the growth rate of the technology sector and start-ups has been substantially higher than that of mature firms. NASDAQ contains a relatively large number of technology firms and start-ups. Assuming a positive relation between growth and value, the multiples for NASDAQ-listed companies may show higher values than those of NYSE-listed firms.

TABLE 12.6   Correlations among Equity-related Multiples

This table shows the linear association between two equity-related multiples, which are estimated for both NYSE-listed and NASDAQ/CBOE-listed firms. In general, equity multiples of NASDAQ/CBOE-listed firms are higher than those of NYSE-listed firms. In both exchanges, the correlations for P/E with other multiples are substantially lower compared to the correlation between P/B and P/S. Correlations with less than a 0.05 significance level are in bold numbers.

	NYSE-listed Firms ($N = 338$)					NASDAQ and CBOE-listed Firms ($N = 102$)			
	Average	P/E	P/B	P/S		Average	P/E	P/B	P/S
P/E	12.64	1.000			P/E	13.19	1.000		
P/B	2.40	0.213	1.000		P/B	4.31	0.014	1.000	
P/S	3.20	0.238	0.356	1.000	P/S	4.71	0.048	**0.553**	1.000

Earnings management is common for many firms, and the S&P 500 firms are no exception. For this reason, the EPS may show substantial differences, even if two firms are identical. Although distortions in book value and sales amount may exist, the degree of distortions should be less than that of EPS among firms. This reason partially explains the low correlations for P/E with other multiples. Further, the correlations for P/E with other multiples in NASDAQ-listed firms are lower than those in NYSE-listed firms. The earnings accounting method seems more diversified among NASDAQ-listed firms than NYSE-listed firms. Therefore, the value estimate from P/E should substantially differ from those estimated from other multiples, and these deviations could be more severe in NASDAQ-listed firms.

In EV-related multiples, the averages for NASDAQ-listed firms are higher than for NYSE-listed firms. The correlations are significantly higher among EV-related multiples than equity-related multiples. Notably, the correlation between EV/EBIT and EV/EBITDA is strong (0.787 for NYSE and 0.814 for NASDAQ firms). The target value estimates from EV-related multiples could be more consistent than those estimated from equity-related multiples. As in equity-related multiples, the average values of EV-related multiples are higher in NASDAQ-listed firms. According to the information in both Tables 12.6 and 12.7 alone, NASDAQ listing could be advantageous, as indicated in high values of all six multiples.

Various factors affect the values of different multiples. Previous studies identify growth in sales and cash flows and risk factors such as market beta and leverage ratio. Table 12.8 shows regression analyses of the multiples against the independent variables such as market beta, growth rate of sales, size represented by sales amount (for P/E and P/B multiples) and market equity (for P/S and EV-related multiples), debt-to-equity ratio, and dummy variables representing the stock exchange listing (NYSE = 0, NASDAQ = 1) and industry that companies belong to (Industrial = 0, Financial = 1). Also, the regressions include the compounding effects of the exchange dummy and other variables.

TABLE 12.7 Correlations among EV-related Multiples

This table shows the linear association between two EV-related multiples estimated for both NYSE-listed and NASDAQ/CBOE-listed firms. In general, EV multiples of NASDAQ/CBOE-listed firms are higher than those of NYSE-listed firms. Correlations with less than a 0.05 significance level are in bold numbers.

NYSE-listed Firms (321)

	Average	EV/EBIT	EV/EBITDA	EV/Sales
EV/EBIT	18.96	1.000		
EV/EBITDA	12.59	0.787	1.000	
EV/Sales	3.69	0.662	0.687	1.000

NASDAQ and CBOE-listed Firms (119)

	Average	EV/EBIT	EV/EBITDA	EV/Sales
EV/EBIT	23.16	1.000		
EV/EBITDA	16.48	0.814	1.000	
EV/Sales	4.80	0.560	0.682	1.000

In most cases, the market beta negatively affects all these multiples for NYSE-listed firms. Higher market beta could naturally reflect negatively in equity price or enterprise value. Alternatively, statistically significant positive relations occur for size (measured by market equity), leverage, and the growth rate on specific multiples. NASDAQ listing status itself is not the reason to have higher values of multiples observed for NASDAQ and CBOE firms. Instead, it may have a negative impact on P/E and EV/Sales multiples since the coefficients for the exchange dummy show significant negative effects.

Then again, the compounding variable for the market beta and NASDAQ listing shows a significantly positive impact on all multiples except P/E. This finding means that the market beta may not be a significant factor in determining multiples for NASDAQ-listed firms since the sum coefficient would offset the negative effect. Also, the impact of market beta on these multiples may not necessarily be linear. The D/E ratio of NASDAQ-listed firms has a stronger impact on P/E but a lesser impact on the P/B multiple compared to the P/E and P/B ratios of NYSE-listed firms. The higher P/E and EV/Sales ratios of NASDAQ-listed firms are not due to the listing status but to a stronger positive impact of leverage (in P/E) and a less negative impact of market beta (in EV/Sales). One result that still needs to be explained is the negative impact of sales on the P/B multiple. Higher sales might have carried much higher expenses or increased more of the book value than the amount that could be matched to the stock price increase due to the increase in sales during this period for the S&P 500 index firms.

TABLE 12.8   Regression Analysis for Multiples on Various Potential Factors

This table shows six multiples in log form and regressed against three-year average market beta, three-year geometric average sales growth rate, log value of previous year's sales or year-end market equity, year-end debt-to-equity ratio, and dummy variables representing stock exchange and industry. Also, the regression includes the compounding effects of exchange listing and other independent variables. The p-values are shown in parentheses.

	Dependent Variable					
	Equity Multiples ($N = 440$ firms)			EV Multiples ($N = 440$ firms)		
	Ln(P/E)	Ln(P/B)	Ln(P/S)	EV/EBIT	EV/EBITDA	EV/Sales
Constant	2.205 ***	1.777 ***	−0.833 *	2.738 ***	1.988 ***	−0.371
	(0.000)	(0.000)	(0.100)	(0.000)	(0.000)	(0.424)
Market Beta	−0.243 ***	−0.162 *	−0.472 ***	−0.286 ***	−0.253 ***	−0.478 ***
	(0.006)	(0.063)	(0.000)	(0.000)	(0.000)	(0.000)
Growth rate	0.834	0.857 *	1.137 **	0.366	0.339	0.827 *
	(0.113)	(0.097)	(0.038)	(0.272)	(0.256)	(0.092)
Ln(Sales)	0.015	−0.123 ***				
	(0.682)	(0.001)				
Ln(Market Equity, ME)			0.179 ***	0.031	0.061 **	0.149 ***
			(0.000)	(0.292)	(0.019)	(0.001)
D/E ratio	0.157	0.427 ***	0.200	−0.004	0.070	0.256 **
	(0.252)	(0.002)	(0.161)	(0.964)	(0.353)	(0.039)
ExchangeXBeta	−0.062	0.316 *	0.524 ***	0.182 *	0.244 ***	0.507 ***
	(0.712)	(0.058)	(0.003)	(0.061)	(0.005)	(0.000)
ExchangeX-Growth rate	0.008	−0.978	−0.031	0.310	−0.071	0.177
	(0.992)	(0.192)	(0.969)	(0.490)	(0.860)	(0.790)
ExchangeXD/E ratio	0.009 ***	−0.006 *	−0.005	0.000	0.001	−0.001
	(0.009)	(0.092)	(0.143)	(0.939)	(0.272)	(0.547)
ExchangeXSales or ME	0.201 ***	0.017	0.054	−0.014	−0.018	−0.007
	(0.009)	(0.823)	(0.538)	(0.771)	(0.678)	(0.926)
Dummy (Industry)	0.075	−0.731 ***	0.468 ***	0.243 ***	0.209 ***	0.843 ***
	(0.416)	(0.000)	(0.000)	(0.000)	(0.000)	(0.000)
Dummy (Exchange)	−1.445 *	0.274	−0.471	0.074	0.205	−0.079 ***
	(0.052)	(0.707)	(0.616)	(0.890)	(0.669)	(0.920)
Adjusted R^2	0.050	0.222	0.206	0.117	0.144	0.287

Note: *, **, *** represent statistical significance at the 0.10, 0.05, and 0.01 level, respectively.

For valuing financial firms, analysts widely use equity-related multiples due to the ambiguities of the definitions of inventory, accounts receivable, and long-term debt. The average P/B multiple for financial firms is substantially lower than that of industrial firms. However, the P/S and EV-related multiples are higher in financial firms. Book value of equity for financial firms is more frequently updated compared to industrial counterparts under the capital adequacy regulation. Therefore, it can grow faster compared to industrial firms with the same level of revenue growth. Additionally, valuation for the financial industry may be higher than that of the industrial industry at a given sales or profit margin for the S&P 500 firms.

In summary, industry (financial firms) and exchange listing (NASDAQ listing) have positive relations on the values of multiples, either directly or indirectly. The market beta has a significantly negative impact on the multiples for NYSE-listed firms. Size, leverage ratio, and growth rate generally have positive impacts on the values of multiples.

SUMMARY AND CONCLUSIONS

Analysts widely use market-based multiples in valuing assets and testing market efficiency in industry practices and academic studies. Nevertheless, the efficacy of this valuation method in estimating a target's value depends heavily on the degree of similarity of comparable firms and their benchmark multiples. Previous studies recommend selecting comparable firms from the same industry to which the target firm belongs. A harmonic mean of multiples drawn from different comparable firms can reduce valuation errors. The forward value drivers, such as forward EPS and forecasted EBITDA, can minimize valuation errors by avoiding distortions from transitory earnings shock or margin variation. The numerator and denominator of a multiple should follow a consistent concept, both representing either leverage-free variables or equity-related variables. Some common factors determining the multiples are industry classification, market beta, size, growth rate, and the leverage ratio.

DISCUSSION QUESTIONS

1. Give several examples of widely used valuation multiples and discuss how to estimate the target's value using these multiples.
2. Identify the main factors proposed in academic research to determine the values of different multiples.
3. Discuss the major advantages and disadvantages of using the multiple valuation method.
4. Discuss the main reasons that researchers and practitioners use forecasted values rather than historical values for the value drivers.
5. Discuss using the harmonic mean as a normalizing method for different multiples drawn from different comparable firms.

REFERENCES

Alford, Andrew W. 1992. "The Effect of the Set of Comparable Firms on the Accuracy of the Price-Earnings Valuation Method." *Journal of Accounting Research* 30:1, 94–108.

Baker, Malcolm, and Richard Ruback. 1999. "Estimating Industry Multiples." Working Paper, Harvard Business School, 1–30.

Basu, Suleiman. 1977. "Investment Performance of Common Stocks in Relation to Their Price-Earnings Ratios: A Test of the Efficient Market Hypothesis." *Journal of Finance* 32:3, 663–682.

Beaver, Williams, and Dale Morse. 1978. "What Determines Price-Earnings Ratios?" *Financial Analysts Journal* 34:4, 65–76.

Bhojraj, Sanjeev, and Charles Lee. 2002. "Who Is My Peer? A Valuation-Based Approach to the Selection of Comparable Firms." *Journal of Accounting Research* 40:2, 407–439.

Billings, Bruce K., and Richard M. Morton. 2001. "Book-to-Market Components, Future Security Returns, and Errors in Expected Future Earnings." *Journal of Accounting Research* 39:2, 197–219.

Chan, Kelly. 2016. "Equity Valuation Using Benchmark Multiples: An Improved Approach Using Regression-Based Weights." *Corporate Ownership and Control* 13:4, 483–496.

Cole, Kevin, Jean Helwege, and David Laster. 1996. "Stock Market Valuation Indicators: Is This Time Different?" *Financial Analysts Journal* 52:3, 56–64.

Fairfield, Patricia M. 1994. "P/E, P/B, and the Present Value of Future Dividends." *Financial Analysts Journal* 50:4, 23–31.

Fama, Eugene F., and Kenneth R. French. 1992. "The Cross-Section of Expected Stock Returns." *Journal of Finance* 47:2, 427–465.

Fama, Eugene F., and Kenneth R. French. 1993. "Common Risk Factors in the Returns on Stocks and Bonds." *Journal of Financial Economics* 33:1, 3–56.

Fama, Eugene F., and Kenneth R. French. 1995. "Size and Book-to-Market Factors in Earnings and Returns." *Journal of Finance* 50:1, 131–155.

Finnerty, John D., and Douglas Emery. 2004. "The Value of Corporate Control and the Comparable Company Method of Valuation." *Financial Management* 33:1, 91–99.

Gilson, Stuart C., Edith S. Hotchkiss, and Richard S. Ruback. 2000. "Valuation of Bankrupt Firms." *Review of Financial Studies* 13:1, 43–74.

Kim, Moonchul, and Jay R. Ritter. 1999. "Valuing IPOs." *Journal of Financial Economics* 53:3, 409–437.

Lakonishok, Josef, Andrei Shleifer, and Robert Vishny. 1994. "Contrarian Investment, Extrapolation, and Risk." *Journal of Finance* 49:5, 1541–1578.

Leibowitz, Martin L. 2002. "The Leverage P/E Ratio." *Financial Analysts Journal* 58:6, 68–77.

Lie, Erik, and Heidi J. Lie. 2002. "Multiples Used to Estimate Corporate Value." *Financial Analysts Journal* 58:2, 44–54.

Liu, Jing, Doron Nissim, and Jacob Thomas. 2002. "Equity Valuation Using Multiples." *Journal of Accounting Research* 40:1, 135–172.

Liu, Jing, Doron Nissim, and Jacob Thomas. 2007. "Is Cash Flow King in Valuations?" *Financial Analysts Journal* 63:2, 56–68.

Ou, Jane A., and Stephen H. Penman. 1989. "Accounting Measurement, Price-Earnings Ratio, and the Information Content of Security Prices." *Journal of Accounting Research* 27: Supplement, 111–144.

Penman, Stephen H. 1996. "The Articulation of Price-Earnings Ratios and Market-to-Book Ratios and the Evaluation of Growth." *Journal of Accounting Research* 34:2, 235–259.

Penman, Stephen H., Scott A. Richardson, and Irem Tuna. 2007. "The Price-to-Book Effect in Stock Returns: Accounting for Leverage." *Journal of Accounting Research* 45:2, 427–467.

Saunders, Howard M. 1996. "Valuation Indicators." *Financial Analysts Journal* 52:6, 85–87.

Yee, Kenton K. 2004. "Combining Value Estimates to Increase Accuracy." *Financial Analysts Journal* 60:4, 23–28.

Wilcox, Jarrod W. 1984. "The P/B-ROE Valuation Model." *Financial Analysts Journal* 40:1, 58–66.

CHAPTER 13

Residual Income Valuation

Shailendra Pandit
Associate Professor of Accounting, University of Illinois at Chicago
Somnath Das
Professor of Accounting, University of Illinois at Chicago

INTRODUCTION

The modern corporation operates on the principle of shareholder value maximization. To create wealth for its owners, a firm must earn more on its invested capital than the cost of that capital. Firm stakeholders evaluate a firm's financial performance using various measures, such as revenues, earnings, cash flows, and return on investment. Residual income (RI) is a commonly used metric that captures the net surplus generated by the firm. RI and accounting-based net income (NI) share some similarities in that both RI and NI subtract operating expenses and taxes from revenues to arrive at profits. However, RI differs from NI in a crucial aspect: whereas NI defines profits net of interest expense, RI measures profits net of the cost of both debt and equity capital. Thus, RI accounts for the opportunity cost of the total capital employed in the business (Biddle, Bowen, and Wallace 1997, 1999).

Current accounting rules do not permit reflecting the cost of equity in reported income. Therefore, proponents of RI advocate adjusting reported income by subtracting an additional charge for the cost of equity. In combining income and opportunity cost, RI contrasts the factual course of action with the counterfactual course of action (Magni 2009). Since RI measures a firm's profit above the normal return required by investors, analysts and investors can use RI to determine whether managerial decisions generate positive economic value. Consistent with this notion, various parties use RI in equity valuation, capital budgeting, performance measurement, executive compensation, and tax planning. This chapter discusses the historical evolution and computation of RI, its application to equity valuation, and scholarly and practitioner critiques of the concept.

HISTORY AND FOUNDATIONS OF RESIDUAL INCOME

The concept of opportunity cost underpins modern economic theory. *Opportunity cost* is the potential gains or benefits that are forgone when a decision maker chooses one alternative over another. In more formal terms, a resource's opportunity cost is the value of the next-highest-valued alternative use of that resource. Deploying capital in an investment project results in a loss of profits that could have been earned had the capital been employed in an alternative investment opportunity. An investment opportunity must earn returns above its opportunity cost of capital to generate incremental value for the investor. This idea is the foundation of RI.

The concept of net surplus generated after accounting for the opportunity cost of capital is not new. Marshall (1890) discusses the notion of excess profit, likely motivated by Hamilton (1777), who, in turn, appears to have been influenced by Smith (1776). Therefore, RI can be traced back to the beginning of modern economic thought. Scholars in the late nineteenth and early twentieth centuries, such as Ladelle (1890), Leake (1921), Canning (1929), and Preinreich (1936, 1937, 1938), contributed to the development of the concept. In particular, Preinreich (1938) develops an analytical framework in which a project's capital value equals the sum of a project's current book value and discounted future excess profits. In this framework, *excess profits* are the difference between profit per unit of capital investment less interest per unit of capital investment. This concept is similar to the modern notion of RI.

Moreover, in a foreshadowing of the valuation application of RI, Preinreich (1938) discusses reconciling accounting numbers with capital values, as do Edwards and Bell (1961), Solomons (1965), and Peasnell (1982). In a related vein, Hicks (1946) develops the idea of "economist's income," which focuses on the value of future cash flows after imposing an interest charge. In parallel with these academic developments, corporations such as General Motors, DuPont, and General Electric began adopting forms of RI for internal evaluation and control purposes (Lewis 1955; Solomons 1965).

Although RI attracted management accountants because of its use in performance evaluation and compensation, the concept did not initially draw much attention in valuation research. Seminal work by Ohlson (1991, 1995) and Feltham and Ohlson (1995, 1996, 1999) reintroduced RI to valuation scholars. Finance and valuation experts widely use the discounted dividends model (DDM) in which current equity value equals the discounted present value of expected dividends. Ohlson (1995) sought to draw a direct link between RI and the DDM so that accounting-based valuation could be grounded in finance theory. Feltham and Ohlson (1995) and Ohlson (1995) develop the "clean surplus relation" (CSR) in which changes in the book value of equity are set equal to earnings minus dividends, net of capital contributions. This assumption permits replacing dividends with earnings and book values in the traditional DDM. In the Ohlson (1995) framework, equity value is expressed as a weighted average of capitalized current earnings (adjusted for dividends) and current book value, thus giving a prominent role to RI in valuation.

Subsequent studies offered refinements to Ohlson's (1995) RI framework. For example, Feltham and Ohlson (1999) relax assumptions about investors' risk-bearing preferences and interest rates and provide a generalized version of the RI valuation model. Myers (1999) stresses using a linear information model, while Biddle et al. (2001) introduce capital investment dynamics, which set up net capital investment to be a function of current profitability and thereby influence future profits. O'Hanlon and Peasnell (2002) and Pfeiffer and Schneider (2007) are other examples of extensions and refinements to the RI framework. Along with the valuation role of RI, scholars also studied the incentive effects of RI. For example, Rogerson (1997) models the effect of different investment allocation rules on managers' investment incentives when basing managerial compensation on the income that includes allocations for investment expenditures. Rogerson shows that an allocation rule based on RI or economic value added induces managers to choose the most efficient investment level.

Similar to its slow acceptance in the academic community, and despite early enthusiasm among the business community, practitioners used RI on a limited basis in the early to mid-twentieth century. Surveys from the 1980s suggest that only about 10 percent of large corporations in the United States and the United Kingdom used some version of RI in investment selection and performance evaluation (Bromwich and Walker 1998). RI saw a revival in the business community in the 1990s, in part due to its promotion by Stern Stewart & Co., which developed its version of excess profits called economic value added (EVA) (Stewart 1991). Stern Stewart & Co. aggressively promoted EVA, claiming that EVA-based financial management systems had the potential to motivate the entire organization and not just senior management (Stern, Stewart, and Chew 1995; Stern, Shiely, and Ross 2001). Because computing RI requires many adjustments to reported financial accounting numbers, practitioners developed several versions of RI. For example, consulting firms such as McKinsey (economic profit), Boston Consulting Group (total business return or TBR), and A.T. Kearney (economic earnings) proposed their own sets of accounting adjustments with claims of making accounting numbers better measures for performance measurement and valuation.

In sum, RI has undergone a gradual yet substantial transformation from its early roots in classical economic theory to its current status, where practitioners widely apply RI not only to valuation but also to project planning, budgeting, performance measurement, and compensation.

COMPUTING RESIDUAL INCOME

Measurement of RI involves adjustments to accounting earnings reported in the firm's financial statements. Under generally accepted accounting principles (GAAP), the cost of debt financing is charged to earnings in the form of interest expense. However, GAAP does not allow any corresponding expense for equity financing. Therefore, some scholars and practitioners contend that reported earnings are an incomplete measure of the return on invested capital (ROIC), which includes both debt and equity. For example, if a project generates returns that exceed the cost of debt, then it can increase reported earnings while still reducing shareholder wealth unless the returns are more than the opportunity cost of equity capital. RI is designed to address such issues.

A key input to computing RI is net operating profits after tax (NOPAT), defined as earnings before interest and taxes (EBIT) adjusted for taxes. EBIT subtracts the cost of debt and taxes from net income (NI), which are then accounted for explicitly in computing RI. The other required input is the *weighted average cost of capital* (WACC), which is a weighted average of the costs of debt and equity, respectively, with the amounts of debt and equity acting as the respective weights. The cost of debt is computed on a post-tax basis. The sum of debt and equity constitutes the firm's total invested capital (TIC). Then, RI for period t is defined as in Equation 13.1:

$$RI_t = NOPAT_t - (WACC_t \times TIC_{t-1}) \tag{13.1}$$

where TIC (debt plus equity) equals a firm's total assets. Therefore, NOPAT can be alternatively expressed as return on assets (ROA) times TIC. Thus, Equation 13.1 can be expanded, as shown in Equation 13.2:

$$RI_t = (ROA_t \times TIC_{t-1}) - WACC_t \times TIC_{t-1}] \tag{13.2}$$

Rearranging Equation 13.2 yields Equation 13.3:

$$RI_t = (ROA_t - WACC_t) \times TIC_{t-1} \tag{13.3}$$

Equation 13.3 implies that the rate of return on TIC must be greater than the WACC to result in a positive RI. In other words, a project must have a positive "spread" between the return from the project and the cost of capital to generate incremental shareholder value.

Drawing a direct correspondence between RI and the traditional accounting NI is possible by noting that Equation 13.3 can be alternatively expressed as Equation 13.4:

$$RI_t = NI_t - (k_t \times BV_{t-1}) \tag{13.4}$$

where BV is the book value of equity and k is the cost of equity. Since NI already accounts for the cost of debt, subtracting the cost of equity from NI yields RI (Biddle et al. 1999).

Practitioners maintain that inputs into the RI calculation, such as accounting earnings and book value, suffer from biases and need adjustments before using them when computing RI. However, disagreement exists about the needed adjustments. For example, Stern Stewart's EVA calls for several steps such as capitalization and amortization of research and development (R&D) expenditures, adding back accounting depreciation and instead subtracting "economic" depreciation, capitalizing operating leases, adding back noncash expenses, and accounting for income taxes on a cash basis rather than accrual basis as required under GAAP. Because different versions of RI require different adjustments, a more tractable conceptual approach is to start from NOPAT, as in Equation 13.1.

Accounting earnings under GAAP have certain advantages that could be lost when adjusting NI or NOPAT when computing RI. Accounting earnings are based on accruals, or accounting adjustments, that reflect managers' expectations of future performance. Past studies such as Bowen, Burgstahler, and Daley (1986) and Finger (1994) show that reported earnings are better predictors of firm performance compared with cash flows that are stripped of accruals. Even if certain adjustments to reported earnings are warranted, investors may use a different set of adjustments than those recommended under a given variant such as EVA. Further, the market may use the cost of capital estimates that differ from those chosen by a specific user. Finally, the market may not recognize the incremental information contained in RI. Although this lack of recognition could result in valuation estimates that differ from the current market values, it could also create profitable investment opportunities for savvy investors.

EQUITY VALUATION USING RESIDUAL INCOME

The DDM is the bedrock of modern valuation theory. Ohlson (1995) relates this valuation theory to accounting by proposing that net equity value at any point in time should reconcile with the creation and distribution of shareholder value as captured by the accounting system. This idea stems from a "clean surplus relation" (CSR) in which all changes in equity value are reflected through the income statement and dividends. The Ohlson (1995) framework assumes away "dirty surplus," which covers changes in equity that bypass the income statement and appear directly in the shareholders' equity account in the balance sheet. For example, the dirty surplus may include items contained in other comprehensive income (OCI) such as gains and losses on pensions and foreign currency translation adjustments. Ohlson defines RI as earnings minus a charge for using capital, measured as beginning-of-period book value multiplied by the cost of capital. In this framework, equity value is the sum of the current book value and capitalized future RI.

To reconcile RI-based valuation with the traditional DDM, recall that DDM expresses the market value of equity as the net present value (NPV) of future dividends as shown in Equation 13.5:

$$V_t = \sum_{n=1}^{\infty} D_{t+n}/(1 + k)^n \tag{13.5}$$

where V_t is the market value of equity at time t; D_{t+n} signifies the cash dividend paid out at future date n period ahead; and k represents the discount rate used to calculate the present value of dividends (i.e., the cost of equity). The key to forging a link between RI valuation and the DDM is to transform dividends as a function of accounting constructs such as book value of equity. To do so, Ohlson's (1995) CSR assumption implies that changes in the book value of equity are solely a function of net income and dividends. Specifically, CSR implies Equation 13.6:

$$BV_t = BV_{t-1} + NI_t - D_t \tag{13.6}$$

which can be rearranged to yield Equation 13.7:

$$D_t = BV_{t-1} + NI_t - BV_t \tag{13.7}$$

Further, net income can be expressed as a function of RI, book value of equity, and the cost of equity by rearranging the definition of RI in Equation 13.4 to produce Equation 13.8:

$$NI_t = RI_t + (k_t \times BV_{t-1}) \tag{13.8}$$

Substituting the above value of NI_t into Equation 13.7 and rearranging terms leads to the following expression for dividends in Equation 13.9:

$$D_t = RI_t + (1 + k) \times BV_{t-1} - BV_t \tag{13.9}$$

Substituting the value of dividends thus obtained back into the DDM valuation Equation 13.5 leads to Equation 13.10:

$$V_t = \sum_{n=1}^{\infty} \{RI_{t+n} + (1 + k)BV_{t+n-1} - BV_{t+n}\}/(1 + k)^n \tag{13.10}$$

This seemingly complicated expression can be simplified by recognizing that discounted present values decrease in magnitude rather quickly by projecting sufficiently far into the future. In other words, assuming that $BV_{t+n}/(1 + k)^n$ gets close to zero as n approaches ∞, then Equation 13.10 becomes Equation 13.11:

$$V_t = BV_t + \sum_{n=1}^{\infty} RI_{t+n}/(1 + k)^n \qquad (13.11)$$

This equation is the familiar formulation in Ohlson (1995), which states that the current equity value is a sum of the current book value of equity and capitalized future RI. A conceptual problem with this approach is that while the current book value of equity is observable, expected RI in future periods is unknown. To solve this problem, Feltham and Ohlson (1996) propose that future RI is related to current RI via a stochastic process termed *linear information dynamics* (LID). This evolutionary path for RI simplifies the valuation process by expressing current firm value as a weighted average of current book value and capitalized current earnings (adjusted for dividends). This extension makes mapping Ohlson's (1995) RI framework into reality easier. Computing RI and its use to value the market value of equity is illustrated next using a numerical example.

NUMERICAL EXAMPLE

As discussed earlier, computing RI involves subtracting the opportunity cost of capital from profits, which can be done in two ways. One way is to subtract the opportunity cost of equity capital from NI, which already accounts for the cost of debt. The other way is to subtract the weighted average cost of total capital, which includes both debt and equity, from NOPAT. The following numerical example illustrates the two approaches.

Suppose P&D Inc. has total invested capital of $10 million, consisting of $6 million in debt and $4 million in equity (i.e., the debt-to-total capital ratio is 0.60). The cost of debt is 6 percent and the opportunity cost of equity is 10 percent. For the year under review, assume that EBIT is $1,200,000 and the tax rate is 40 percent.

Approach 1. Subtract a charge for equity capital from NI

EBIT	$1,200,000
Less: Interest ($6,000,000 × 6%)	360,000
Income before income tax	840,000
Less: Income tax ($840,000 × 40%)	336,000
Net income	504,000
Less: Cost of equity ($4,000,000 × 10%)	400,000
Residual income	$ 104,000

Approach 2. Subtract the weighted average cost of total capital
from NOPAT

EBIT	$1,200,000
Less: Income tax ($1,200,000 × 40%)	480,000
Net operating profit after tax	720,000
Less: Weighted average cost of capital ($10,000,000 × 6.16%*)	616,000
Residual income	$ 104,000

* WACC = [(After-tax cost of debt × Debt) + (Cost of equity × Equity)]/(Debt + Equity) = [(6% × (1 − 40%) × $6,000,000) + 10% × $4,000,000)]/($6,000,000 + $4,000,000) = [3.6% × $6,000,000 + 10% × $4,000,000]/$10,000,000 = 6.16%.

This value of RI can be substituted into the valuation equation (13.11) to obtain the firm's market value. For simplicity, assume no growth in RI over time (i.e., current and future RI values are constant at $104,000). As discussed earlier, the market value of the firm's equity can be expressed as the sum of the current book value of equity ($4,000,000) and the present value of the stream of future RIs ($104,000) discounted at the cost of equity (10 percent). Therefore:

$$\text{Market value of equity} = \$4 + \$104,000/(1 + 10\%)^1$$
$$+ \$104,000/(1 + 10\%)^2 + \$104,000/(1 + 10\%)^3 + \$104,000/(1 + 10\%)^4 + \dots$$

Simplifying the summation of the infinite stream of discounted annuity:

$$\text{Market value of equity} = \$4 + (104,000)/(0.1) = \$4 + 1$$
$$\text{Therefore, market value of equity} = \$5.$$

APPLYING RI TO EQUITY VALUATION

Soon after the publication of Ohlson (1995), scholars and practitioners began to evaluate the model's validity, as well as ways to estimate it empirically. For example, Frankel and Lee (1998) use analyst earnings forecasts to operationalize expected future income to compute expected RI. They examine the usefulness of RI for predicting cross-sectional stock returns and find positive correlations between such earnings estimates and contemporaneous stock prices. Moreover, the authors also find that the value-to-price ratio based on RI estimates is a good predictor of long-horizon returns. However, tests of the LID inherent in Ohlson do not always yield consistent results. For example, Dechow, Hutton, and Sloan (1999) report evidence consistent with a mean-reverting RI process but note that LID is not necessarily superior to simply capitalizing one-period-ahead earnings in explaining equity values. Similarly, Myers (1999) examines several formulations of LID to find that none outperformed the book value of equity alone. Such inconsistencies led to scholars such as Verrecchia

(1998), Beaver (1999), Lee (1999), and Lo and Lys (2000) to call for a theory-based exploration of factors that influence RI and situations in which the Ohlson model would be applicable.

In response, several studies tried to address the model's potential limitations by infusing it with "real-life" dynamics. For example, Baginski and Wahlen (2003) adapt the model to situations where obtaining the cost of capital estimates is difficult because market-based risk measures are unavailable. Cheng (2005) examines how economic rents and conservative accounting affect RI and develops a measure of abnormal return on equity (ROE). He then examines whether integrating the determinants of abnormal ROE into the RI valuation model can improve its ability to explain the firm value. Heinrichs, Hess, Homburg, Lorentz, and Sievers (2013) extend the RI valuation model to incorporate real-world factors such as dirty surplus accounting and examine the consequences for terminal value modeling. They report that their extended model significantly improves the valuation accuracy of the RI model.

Overall, despite limitations, practitioners use Ohlson (1995) and Feltham and Ohlson (1996) for equity valuation in various settings. For example, besides the studies discussed previously, which generally focus on industrial firms, Begley, Chamberlain, and Li (2006) and Stoughton and Zechner (2007) apply RI valuation techniques to financial institutions, including banks. Balachandran and Mohanram (2012) decompose earnings growth into growth in RI, growth in invested capital, and other components. They then use this decomposition to explain the observed stock returns. The authors claim that their approach is superior for explaining stock returns compared with a simple regression of stock returns on accounting earnings. In an applied valuation setting, Knauer, Silge, and Sommer (2018) focus on applying value-based management, which is a variation on the RI model, to mergers and acquisitions (M&As), and report that the market responds more positively to acquisition announcements by firms that implement value-based metrics. The breadth and depth of the applications discussed earlier suggest that the RI valuation model is a useful framework for linking accounting numbers with firm value and thus provides a direct link between accounting numbers and finance theory.

EVALUATION AND CRITIQUE OF RESIDUAL INCOME

Scholars and practitioners criticized RI even before academic research such as Ohlson (1995) and consulting firms such as Stern, Stewart, & Co. popularized the concept. Academic critiques of RI are related to construct validity and the correspondence with other valuation frameworks such as the DDM, while practitioners raised concerns over implementation aspects such as using an appropriate cost of capital estimate and the accounting adjustments necessary to compute a reliable RI measure. *Construct validity* refers to the degree to which a test measures what it purports to measure.

As discussed previously, the Ohlson (1995) model was initially met with enthusiasm. Early empirical research, including Bernard (1995), Penman and Sougiannis (1998), and Francis, Olsson, and Oswald (2000), finds that the model explained stock prices better than alternative valuation models based on dividends and cash flows. As Frankel and Lee (1998) note, the Ohlson model provides a comprehensive and rigorous theory-based valuation approach. However, subsequent examinations point out its shortcomings. For example, consistent with Ohlson's information dynamics, Dechow et al. (1999) find that RI follows a mean-reverting process, which is reflected in stock prices, implying that the book value of equity conveys additional information over earnings in explaining contemporaneous stock prices. However, they also find that the RI model provides only minor improvement in explanatory power over the traditional valuation approaches such as the DDM. According to Lee (1999), the main challenge in valuation is forecasting future earnings. The Ohlson model does not offer much guidance in this aspect since it does not directly relate financial statement numbers to firm value. Key inputs to RI valuation, such as future expected abnormal earnings, are forecasts, not actual realizations of earnings, and the CSR link among dividends, book value, and earnings are insufficient to implement RI valuation. Bernard (1995) discusses how a second link between current accounting numbers and future RI is an essential part of fundamental analysis, which is missing in RI valuation. To overcome this problem, Ohlson introduces the idea of LID, which assumes a stochastic process for future abnormal earnings and nonaccounting information based on their historical realizations. However, the extent to which this theoretical assumption plays out in real-world data is an empirical question.

Another issue with Ohlson (1995) is that the model assumes unbiased accounting, implying that historical earnings are a reliable predictor of future earnings. If accounting systems are biased due to GAAP requirements or because of managerial discretion, then average abnormal earnings will be nonzero. Given conservative accounting, reliably predicting future growth in book value becomes a critical component of the model. Lee (1999) observes that Feltham and Ohlson (1995, 1996) modify the original LID assumptions to allow current book value to provide information about future RI. However, these simplifications and additional assumptions do not necessarily reflect reality. Myers (1999) further points out that empirical studies making ad hoc modifications to the linear information models contain internal inconsistencies and violate the no-arbitrage assumption. Myers also reports that the Ohlson (1995) and Feltham and Ohlson (1995) models provide equity value estimates that are no better than book value alone.

Lo and Lys (2000) echo some of these sentiments in discussing the logical and empirical challenges in RI valuation. For example, similar to Myers (1999), they note that many empirical studies implement the model without the information dynamics that are the key feature of the framework. Lo and Lys also show that RI valuation imposes data requirements that are difficult to meet in actual empirical settings. As a result, tests of RI valuation require approximating the model's requirements. However, the consequences of such approximations on the model's predictions are difficult to assess. As a result, rejecting RI valuation can lead to concluding that the test approach is flawed or the data are bad, but not that the model is wrong.

Lundholm and O'Keefe (2001) compare the traditional DCF model and RI valuation framework, which yield different estimates of equity value in prior studies. This finding is puzzling since both DCF and RI models are derived from the same underlying assumptions (i.e., that stock price is the present value of expected future net dividends discounted at the cost of equity capital). As Lundholm and O'Keefe note, most studies divide the valuation exercise into two periods: (1) a finite period, where various line items in financial statements are forecasted and each year's valuation metric (free cash flow or RI) is separately discounted; and (2) a terminal period, where the financial statement forecasts and valuation metrics are represented as a summary measure (e.g., growth at a constant rate in perpetuity). Ali, Hwang, and Trombley (2003) offer a similar view.

Lundholm and O'Keefe (2001) identify several errors with actually implementing this approach. Some studies assign incorrect amounts to the perpetuity of valuation metrics, leading to inconsistent forecast errors. The DCF and RI models reflect these errors in different ways, causing divergence in value estimates. The second type of implementation error is the incorrect discount rate error. This error arises from a potentially faulty approach in which first the value of the whole firm is computed by discounting firm-level CF or RI using the WACC. Then the analyst backs out the value of equity by subtracting the value of debt from total firm value. However, the correct discount rate is a weighted average of the cost of equity and the cost of debt with carefully chosen weights. Violating this condition can result in a discount rate that is inconsistent with the DDM, causing differences in the estimated values generated by the DCF and the RI frameworks. Another type of error, called the *missing cash flow error*, occurs when the financial statement forecasts do not satisfy CSR (i.e., when net income minus net dividends does not equal the change in shareholders' equity). The existence of dirty surplus can cause a divergence between future dividends implied by the RI model and those forecasted in the DCF model. As Lundholm and O'Keefe note, many empirical studies suffer from one or more of these errors, leading to internally inconsistent and inaccurate value estimates.

Although some scholars criticize the RI valuation model on theoretical and practical grounds, others defend the model and point out its relative advantages in specific settings. For example, Jiang and Lee (2005) discuss attributes of the RI model that make it suitable for equity valuation, particularly for studying stock price volatility. In the DDM approach, stock prices are a function of discounted expected dividends. However, cash dividend levels tend to be constant and sticky, and therefore have limited explanatory power for the observed volatility in stock prices. The RI valuation model is derived from the DDM by replacing dividends with earnings and book value, which are inherently more volatile when compared with dividends and hence provide a natural link to stock price volatility. Another advantage of using accounting numbers rather than dividends is that many firms, especially high-tech and growth firms, do not pay cash dividends, at least in the early stages of their life cycle. Therefore, although the DDM may not apply to such firms, the RI model can still be implemented as long as the current book value and future RI estimates are available. The CSR underpinning the RI model takes a broader view of dividends as the difference between earnings and changes in the book value. Therefore, the RI model can more easily reflect changes in share repurchases and other forms of cash payouts by way of the change in book value. Such transactions cannot be easily accommodated in the DDM.

According to Jiang and Lee (2005), the biggest strength of the RI model is that it shifts the focus away from the distribution of wealth (i.e., dividends) to the creation of wealth (i.e., book value and abnormal earnings). A firm's operations drive wealth creation as opposed to the firm's financing choices. The RI framework can naturally integrate dividend policy irrelevance. Since the firm pays dividends out of book value, not current earnings, RI is invariant to changes in the dividend policy. Jiang and Lee suggest that the RI model performs as well as the DDM, and is superior in some settings, in explaining stock price volatility. On the whole, although the criticisms of the RI valuation model highlight its conceptual and practical shortcomings, some scholars believe that the RI model is a superior valuation technique in some settings.

SUMMARY AND CONCLUSIONS

RI is the net surplus generated by an investment project after accounting for the opportunity cost of invested capital. For a project to have a positive RI and create value for the owners, it must generate returns that exceed its cost of capital. Accounting rules allow for charging the cost of debt to income in the form of interest expense. However, GAAP does not allow subtracting the cost of equity as an expense, leaving accounting net income as a potentially incomplete measure of the return on investment. Some scholars and practitioners contend that net income also suffers from other biases due to the prevailing accounting rules such as expensing R&D and the treatment of one-time charges and discontinued items. Therefore, advocates of RI recommend adjusting the accounting net income to remove potential biases and then subtracting the cost of equity to arrive at a more appropriate measure of performance. Since RI measures profits above the required rate of return, it can be used to evaluate value creation through managerial decisions. Accordingly, practitioners use RI for equity valuation, project management, budgeting, performance measurement, executive compensation, and tax planning.

Despite its apparent strengths as a measure of value, RI is subject to criticism for its potential theoretical inconsistencies and practical limitations. Prior studies find that the RI valuation model provides only minor improvement in explaining firm value over accounting numbers such as book value or the traditional DDM. A major issue is that key inputs to RI valuation, such as future expected abnormal earnings, are forecasts that are unavailable from a firm's financial statements. The real challenge in valuation is accurately forecasting future performance, where the RI model does not offer much help. Practically implementing the RI model involves adjusting accounting earnings for potential biases. However, ad hoc modifications can be internally inconsistent. Another practical challenge is selecting an appropriate cost of equity, which is difficult to estimate. Due to these limitations, the RI valuation model can generate estimates that are inaccurate and different from estimates generated by traditional valuation methods, such as the DDM.

Despite these criticisms, the RI model has certain advantages. For example, it can be applied to firms that do not pay dividends, which makes applying the DDM impractical. Another strength of the RI model is that it focuses on RI, which measures the creation of wealth, rather than on dividends, which represent the distribution of wealth. This characteristic makes the RI framework particularly suitable for operational planning, performance management, and compensation, besides its valuation role. Also, the DDM has limited explanatory power regarding stock price volatility because cash dividends are generally stable and persistent over time. Therefore, scholars and practitioners should evaluate the relative advantages and disadvantages of different valuation techniques, including RI, and choose the one that is best suited for the task at hand.

DISCUSSION QUESTIONS

1. Define RI and discuss how to measure it.
2. Discuss the types of adjustments to reported financial statement numbers needed when calculating RI, and why such adjustments are needed.
3. Discuss how RI is applied to equity valuation.
4. Explain the advantages of RI valuation over traditional approaches such as the DDM.
5. Explain the disadvantages of RI valuation compared with traditional approaches such as the DDM.

REFERENCES

Ali, Ashiq, Lee-Seok Hwang, and Mark A. Trombley. 2003. "Residual-income-based Valuation Predicts Future Stock Returns: Evidence on Mispricing vs. Explanations." *Accounting Review* 78:2, 377–396.

Baginski, Stephen P., and James M. Wahlen. 2003. "Residual Income Risk, Intrinsic Values, and Share Prices." *Accounting Review* 78:1, 327–351.

Balachandran, Sudhakar V., and Partha Mohanram. 2012. "Using Residual Income to Refine the Relationship between Earnings Growth and Stock Returns." *Review of Accounting Studies* 17:1, 134–165.

Beaver, William. 1999. "Comments on an Empirical Assessment of the Residual Income Valuation Model." *Journal of Accounting and Economics* 26:1, 35–42.

Begley, Joy, Sandra l. Chamberlain, and Yinghua Li. 2006. "Modeling Goodwill for Banks: A Residual Income Approach with Empirical Tests." *Contemporary Accounting Research* 23:1, 31–68.

Bernard, Victor L. 1995. "The Feltham-Ohlson Framework: Implications for Empiricists." *Contemporary Accounting Research* 11:2, 733–747.

Biddle, Gary C., Robert M. Bowen, and James S. Wallace. 1997. "Does EVA® Beat Earnings? Evidence on Associations with Stock Returns and Firm Values." *Journal of Accounting and Economics* 24:3, 301–336.

Biddle, Gary C., Robert M. Bowen, and James S. Wallace. 1999. "Evidence on EVA." *Journal of Applied Corporate Finance* 12:2, 69–79.

Biddle, Gary C., Peter Chen, and Guochang Zhang. 2001. "When Capital Follows Profitability: Non-linear Residual Income Dynamics." *Review of Accounting Studies* 6:2–3, 229–265.

Bowen, Robert M., David Burgstahler, and Lane A. Daley. 1986. "Evidence on the Relationships between Earnings and Various Measures of Cash Flow." *Accounting Review* 61:4, 713–725.

Bromwich, Michael, and Martin Walker. 1998. "Residual Income Past and Future." *Management Accounting Research* 9:4, 391–419.

Canning, John B. 1929. *The Economics of Accountancy: A Critical Analysis of Accounting Theory*. New York, NY: The Ronald Press.

Cheng, Qiang. 2005. "What Determines Residual Income?" *Accounting Review* 80:1, 85–112.

Dechow, Patricia M., Amy P. Hutton, and Richard G. Sloan. 1999. "An Empirical Assessment of the Residual Income Valuation Model." *Journal of Accounting and Economics* 26:1, 1–34.

Edwards, Edgar O., and Philip W. Bell. 1961. *The Theory and Measurement of Business Income*. Berkeley, CA: University of California Press.

Feltham, Gerald A., and James A. Ohlson. 1995. "Valuation and Clean Surplus Accounting for Operations and Financial Activities." *Contemporary Accounting Research* 11:2, 689–731.

Feltham, Gerald A., and James A. Ohlson. 1996. "Uncertainty Resolution and the Theory of Depreciation Measurement." *Journal of Accounting Research* 34:2, 209–234.

Feltham, Gerald A., and James A. Ohlson. 1999. "Residual Earnings Valuation with Risk and Stochastic Interest Rates." *Accounting Review* 74:2, 165–183.

Finger, Catherine A. 1994. "The Ability of Earnings to Predict Future Earnings and Cash Flow." *Journal of Accounting Research* 32:2, 210–223.

Francis, Jennifer, Per Olsson, and Dennis R. Oswald. 2000. "Comparing the Accuracy and Explainability of Dividend, Free Cash Flow and Abnormal Earnings Equity Valuation Estimates." *Journal of Accounting Research* 38:1, 45–70.

Frankel, Richard, and Charles M. C. Lee. 1998. "Accounting Valuation, Market Expectation, and Cross-sectional Stock Returns." *Journal of Accounting and Economics* 25:3, 283–320.

Hamilton, Robert. 1777. *An Introduction to Merchandize.* Edinburgh: J. Hunter.

Heinrichs, Nicolas, Dieter Hess, Carsten Homburg, Michael Lorenz, and Soenke Sievers. 2013. "Extended Dividend, Cash Flow, and Residual Income Valuation Models: Accounting for Deviations from Ideal Conditions." *Contemporary Accounting Research* 30:1, 42–79.

Hicks, John. 1946. *Value and Capital: An Inquiry into Some Fundamental Principles of Economic Theory.* Oxford, UK: Clarendon Press.

Jiang, Xiaoquan, and Bon-Soo Lee. 2005. "An Empirical Test of the Accounting-based Residual Income Model and the Traditional Dividend Discount Model." *Journal of Business* 78:4, 1465–1504.

Knauer, Thorsten, Lisa Silge, and Friedrich Sommer. 2018. "The Shareholder Value Effects of Using Value-based Performance Measures: Evidence from Acquisitions and Divestments." *Management Accounting Research* 41:1, 43–61.

Ladelle, Oscar G. 1890. "The Calculation of Depreciation." *Accountant.* November 29, 659.

Leake, Percy D. 1921. *Commercial Goodwill: Its History, Value and Treatment in Accounts.* London, UK: Pitman and Sons Ltd.

Lee, Charles M. C. 1999. "Accounting-based Valuation: Impact on Business Practices and Research." *Accounting Horizons* 13:4, 54–68.

Lewis, Robert W. 1955. *Planning, Managing and Measuring the Business: A Case Study of Management Planning and Control at the General Electric Company.* New York, NY: Controllers Institute Research Foundation (now the Financial Executives Research Foundation).

Lo, Kin, and Thomas Z. Lys. 2000. "The Ohlson Model: Contributions to Valuation Theory, Limitations, and Empirical Applications." *Journal of Accounting, Auditing & Finance* 15:3, 337–367.

Lundholm, Russell, and Terry O'Keefe. 2001. "Reconciling Value Estimates from the Discounted Cash Flow Model and the Residual Income Model." *Contemporary Accounting Research* 18:2, 311–335.

Magni, Carlos A. 2009. "Splitting Up Value: A Critical Review of Residual Income Theories." *European Journal of Operation Research* 198:1, 1–22.

Marshall, Alfred. 1890. *Principles of Economics.* London, UK: MacMillan.

Myers, James N. 1999. "Implementing Residual Income Valuation with Linear Information Dynamics." *Accounting Review* 74:1, 1–28.

O'Hanlon, John, and Ken Peasnell. 2002. "Residual Income and Value-creation: The Missing Link." *Review of Accounting Studies* 7:2–3, 229–245.

Ohlson, James A. 1991. "The Theory of Value and Earnings, and an Introduction to the Ball-Brown Analysis." *Contemporary Accounting Research* 8:1, 1–19.

Ohlson, James A. 1995. "Earnings, Book Values, and Dividends in Equity Valuation." *Contemporary Accounting Research* 11:2, 661–687.

Ohlson, James A. 1996. "Accounting Earnings, Book Value and Dividends: The Theory of the Clean Surplus Equation (Part I)." In *Clean Surplus: A Link Between Accounting and Finance*, edited by Richard Brief and Kenneth Peasnell, 167–227. New York, NY: Garland Publishing.

Peasnell, Kenneth V. 1982. "Some Formal Connections between Economic Values and Yields and Accounting Numbers." *Journal of Business Finance and Accounting* 9:3, 361–381.

Penman, Stephen H., and Theodore Sougiannis. 1998. "A Comparison of Dividend, Cash Flow, and Earnings Approaches to Equity Valuation." *Contemporary Accounting Research* 15:3, 343–383.

Pfeiffer, Thomas, and Georg Schneider. 2007. "Residual Income-Based Compensation Plans for Controlling Investment Decisions Under Sequential Private Information." *Management Science* 53:3, 495–507.

Preinreich, Gabriel A. D. 1936. "The Fair Value and Yield of Common Stock." *Accounting Review* 11:2, 130–140.

Preinreich, Gabriel A. D. 1937. "Valuation and Amortization." *Accounting Review* 12:3, 209–226.

Preinreich, Gabriel A. D. 1938. "Annual Survey of Economic Theory: The Theory of Depreciation." *Econometrica* 6:1, 219–241.

Rogerson, William P. 1997. "Intertemporal Cost Allocation and Managerial Investment Incentives: A Theory Explaining the Use of Economic Value Added as a Performance Measure." *Journal of Political Economy* 105:4, 770–795.

Smith, Adam. 1776. *An Inquiry into the Nature and Causes of the Wealth of Nations.* Oxford, UK: Clarendon Press.

Solomons, David. 1965. *Divisional Performance: Measurement and Control.* Homewood, IL: Richard D. Irwin.

Stern, Joel M., G. Bennett Stewart, and Donald H. Chew, Jr. 1995. "The EVA® Financial Management System." *Journal of Applied Corporate Finance* 8:2, 32–46.

Stern, Joel M., John S. Shiely, and Irwin Ross. 2001. *The EVA Challenge: Implementing Value-Added Change in an Organization.* New York, NY: John Wiley & Sons.

Stewart, G. Bennett. 1991. *The Quest for Value.* New York, NY: HarperCollins Business.

Stoughton, Neal M., and Josef Zechner. 2007. "Optimal Capital Allocation Using RAROC™ and EVA™." *Journal of Financial Intermediation* 16:3, 312–342.

Verrecchia, Robert E. 1998. "Discussion of Accrual Accounting and Equity Valuation." *Journal of Accounting Research* 36:Supplement, 113–115.

CHAPTER 14

Private Company Valuation

Onur Bayar
Associate Professor of Finance, University of Texas at San Antonio
Yini Liu
PhD Candidate, University of Texas at San Antonio

INTRODUCTION

Private company valuation is a challenging and often subjective exercise. Unlike publicly traded companies, a private company has no observable stock price to serve as an objective measure of the intrinsic value of its equity. Since no readily available market value exists for either a private firm's debt or equity, any valuation method inputs that require them, such as debt ratios for computing the firm's cost of capital, are harder to estimate. Similarly, risk measures based on market prices, such as beta and bond ratings, also are unavailable for private companies. Another challenge faced when valuing private companies is that their financial statements are likely to go back only a few years and have much less detail compared to publicly traded companies, which increases the difficulty of forecasting cash flows.

Private equity (PE) managers such as venture capitalists, entrepreneurs, investment bankers, and other outside investors use valuation methods to evaluate privately held companies as an investment opportunity. Damodaran (2018) describes three broad scenarios in private company valuation:

1. Private-to-private transactions, in which a private company is valued for sale by one individual to another.
2. Private-to-public transactions, in which a private firm is valued for an initial public offering (IPO) or sale (acquisition) to a publicly traded firm.
3. Private-to-venture capital-to-public transactions, in which a private firm is expected to raise venture capital on its path to going public.

This chapter focuses on private company valuation in the last two scenarios. Finally, the valuation methods discussed in this chapter are also used in highly leveraged public-to-private transactions such as leveraged buyouts (LBOs).

The next section describes discounted cash flow (DCF) valuation techniques in the setting of a private company valuation. The following two sections deal with how analysts and others use the comparable firms approach and the venture capital (VC) method to value private companies, respectively. After these sections is a brief discussion of the application of option pricing techniques in PE. The final section offers a summary and conclusions.

DCF VALUATION METHODS FOR PRIVATE COMPANIES

This section starts by discussing two approaches to DCF analysis in private company valuation: (1) the capital cash flow (CCF) method of Ruback (1995a, 1995b, 2002), which is a variation of the adjusted present value (APV) method of Myers (1974), and (2) the free cash flow (FCF) method. All DCF methods start by determining a private firm's FCF. Equation 14.1 shows the calculation of a firm's FCF in year t:

$$FCF_t = EBIT_t(1 - \tau) + Depreciation_t - CAPEX_t - \Delta NWC_t \qquad (14.1)$$

where *EBIT* denotes earnings before interest and taxes; τ is the corporate tax rate; *Depreciation* represents depreciation and amortization expense; *CAPEX* signifies capital expenditures; and ΔNWC stands for changes in net operating working capital.

In Equation 14.1, the first term, *EBIT*, is the accounting measure that forms the base for all cash flow calculations. For an all-equity firm without nonoperating income or expenses, *EBIT* equals pre-tax net income. In this case, the term $EBIT(1 - \tau)$ represents the total after-tax operating income produced by the firm's operating assets. Analysts make cash flow adjustments to this first term to transform the accounting recognition of receipts and expenses into cash flows. These adjustments include adding depreciation and subtracting both capital expenditures and changes in net operating working capital. The *EBIT* measure includes some noncash expenses but excludes some cash expenditures. The included noncash expenses are depreciation and amortization, which reduce *EBIT* on the income statement but do not require any direct cash outflows by the firm. Thus, one adds back depreciation and amortization expenses (*Depreciation*) in Equation 14.1. In contrast, analysts should not treat capital expenditures (i.e., investments by the company in plant and equipment) as an accounting expense on the income statement but do count cash outflows. Thus, one subtracts capital expenditures (*CAPEX*) in Equation 14.1. In a high-growth private firm, capital expenditures most likely exceed depreciation, so that the increase in a firm's net fixed assets (*CAPEX − Depreciation*) is positive in a given year. Finally, analysts should subtract the change in net operating working capital (ΔNWC), in Equation 14.1 to transform the sales into cash receipts and inventory and payables into cash expenses.

FCFs are independent of a firm's capital structure. They measure the cash flows generated by the firm's operating assets regardless of the types of claims issued on those assets. In particular, FCF calculations do not incorporate the benefit of tax shields from tax-deductible interest payments. According to Metrick and Yasuda (2011), when valuing VC-backed private firms, a reasonable approach is to abstract from the actual capital structure and assume that the firm is all-equity financed. They report that the median debt percentage in the capital structure of a VC-backed IPO firm is 1.2 percent at the time of the IPO and 2.8 percent two years after the IPO.

The Capital Cash Flow Method

The capital cash flow (CCF) method of valuation takes estimates of future FCFs and separates firm value into two components: (1) the value of the firm's operating assets V_u, which equals the firm value for an all-equity financed (unlevered) firm, and (2) the value V_{ts} of interest tax shields (ITS) that arise from debt financing. Thus, the CCF method first calculates the value of the unlevered (all-equity) firm. The value of ITS from debt financing is calculated separately and then added to the unlevered firm value to find the total firm value as shown in Equation 14.2:

$$V = V_u + V_{ts} \tag{14.2}$$

The CCF method also adds other elements of value associated with the capital structure if they are present, such as the present value of investment tax credits, distress costs, and issue costs.

To estimate the value V_u of the unlevered firm, the first step is to forecast a firm's future FCFs from Equation 14.1. Analysts usually make explicit FCF forecasts for the next 5 to 10 years. T denotes the ending year of this explicit forecast horizon. After obtaining FCF forecasts for periods 1 to T, a terminal value (TV) is calculated. After year T, the firm's future FCFs flows are assumed to grow forever at a stable (terminal) growth rate of g, and the appropriate discount rate for the unlevered firm is determined by the riskiness of the firm's assets, k_a. Hence, using the formula for the present value of a growing perpetuity, Equation 14.3 gives a firm's estimated TV at time T:

$$TV_T = \frac{FCF_T(1+g)}{k_a - g} \tag{14.3}$$

Estimating the TV is important in private company valuation because the majority of a private company's value, especially one in an early-stage setting, may come from the TV. Valuations in which the TV represents a substantial majority of the value are likely to be sensitive to small changes in growth rate assumptions (Lerner and Willinge 2002; Gompers 2015; Damodaran, 2018). Therefore, checking the reality of the growth rate assumption is essential. When using nominal discount rates, the terminal growth rate should reflect assumptions about the expected inflation rate. Analysts often assume a growth rate slightly higher than the expected inflation rate to compensate for faster growth now but zero real growth in the future. In the long run, most firms probably grow at a rate between the inflation rate and the overall growth rate of the economy (nominal GDP). If forecasts indicate that the cash flow is likely to be constant in inflation-adjusted dollars, analysts should use a terminal growth rate equal to the inflation rate.

Given the terminal value TV_T in Equation 14.3, Equation 14.4 gives the estimated value of the firm's operating assets:

$$V_u = \frac{FCF_1}{(1+k_a)} + \cdots + \frac{FCF_T + TV_T}{(1+k_a)^T} \tag{14.4}$$

Finally, Equation 14.5 gives the estimated value V_{ts} of the firm's interest tax shields (ITS):

$$V_{ts} = \frac{ITS_1}{(1+k_{ts})^1} + \cdots + \frac{ITS_t}{(1+k_{ts})^t} + \cdots \tag{14.5}$$

where ITS_t denotes the interest tax shield in year t and k_{ts} is the appropriate discount rate that reflects the riskiness of a firm's ITS. The ITS_t in any year t is equal to the product of the marginal corporate tax rate τ and the interest expense Int_t of a firm in year t: $ITS_t = \tau \times Int_t$.

To estimate the unlevered firm value V_u in Equation 14.4, the CCF method discounts projected FCFs at the cost of assets k_a, which is also known as the cost of unlevered equity. Assuming a company's debt grows proportionally with firm value, Ruback (1995a, 1995b, 2002) shows that the systematic risk of ITS is the same as the systematic risk of operating assets. This outcome means that the rate k_{ts} used to discount the ITS is equal to k_a, the cost of unlevered equity, or the cost of assets. Setting k_{ts} equal to k_a reveals that the levered equity cost of capital of the firm k_e is given by Equation 14.6 (Ruback 2002; Koller, Goedhart, and Wessels 2010):

$$k_e = k_a + \frac{D}{E}(k_a - k_d) \qquad (14.6)$$

where D is the market value of a firm's debt and E is the market value of a firm's equity. Note that $V = D + E$. After rearranging this equation, the cost of unlevered equity or the cost of assets can then be expressed as Equation 14.7:

$$k_a = \left(\frac{D}{D+E}\right)k_d + \left(\frac{E}{D+E}\right)k_e \qquad (14.7)$$

For expositional simplicity, the assumption here is that the capital asset pricing model (CAPM) holds as the model for estimating the cost of capital. In the CAPM framework, Equation 14.7 is equivalent to Equation 14.8:

$$\beta_a = \left(\frac{D}{D+E}\right)\beta_d + \left(\frac{E}{D+E}\right)\beta_e \qquad (14.8)$$

For private firms, the quantities on the right-hand side of Equations 14.7 and 14.8 are unobservable. Given the empirical evidence that high-growth private firms carry low amounts of debt in their capital structure (Metrick and Yasuda 2011), a reasonable simplifying assumption is that the debt is risk-free so that the beta of debt, β_d, is zero. In this case, Equation 14.8 simplifies to Equation 14.9:

$$\beta_a = \left(\frac{E}{D+E}\right)\beta_e \qquad (14.9)$$

Estimating the asset beta (the unlevered equity beta) of a private company involves the following steps:

1. Identify a set of comparable public companies that have similar assets and activities to those of the desired private company to value.
2. Estimate the levered equity beta β_e for each comparable public company.
3. Given the levered equity beta β_e, compute the asset beta β_a of each comparable public company using Equation 14.9. The market values of equity (E) and debt (D) are observable for public companies.
4. Compute the average of these asset betas and use this average as the estimated asset beta of the desired private company to value.
5. Use the CAPM to estimate the private company's cost of assets k_a.

The last step applies the CAPM to calculate the cost of unlevered equity, as shown in Equation 14.10:

$$k_a = r_f + \beta_a(E[r_m] - r_f) \tag{14.10}$$

where r_f is the risk-free rate and $(E[r_m] - r_f)$ is the market risk premium. Lerner and Willinge (2002) and Gompers (2015) suggest that when determining the appropriate risk-free rate (r_f), analysts should attempt to match the maturity of the investment project with that of the risk-free rate. Since most private companies resemble long-term investment projects, this approach implies that the appropriate risk-free rate is the yield on a long-term Treasury bond. Consistent with recent surveys and studies about the equity risk premium, Gompers suggests that, as a general rule, a market risk premium estimate of between 5 percent and 6 percent would be a reasonable choice.

The Adjusted Present Value Method

The CCF method and Myers' (1974) adjusted present value (APV) method are closely related. Essentially, both methods use the same logic in implementing Equation 14.2, as shown in Equation 14.11:

$$V = PV(\text{FCFs discounted at } k_a) + PV(\text{ITS discounted at } k_{ts}) \tag{14.11}$$

For both methods, the discount rate for the FCFs is the cost of assets k_a, which is generally computed using the CAPM with the beta of an unlevered firm, as described earlier.

Interest tax shields that are discounted by the cost of assets k_a in the CCF method are discounted by the cost of debt k_d in the APV method. The APV method results in higher firm value than the CCF method because it treats the ITS as being less risky than the firm as a whole on account of the level of debt being implicitly assumed to be a fixed dollar amount. As a result, a tax adjustment is made when unlevering an equity beta to calculate an asset beta. In contrast, the CCF method, like the FCF method, assumes that debt is proportional to value so that the risk of the ITS, therefore, matches the risk of the assets.

The Free Cash Flow Method

The FCF method, which is also known as the weighted average cost of capital (WACC) method, discounts the firm's future FCFs at the firm's WACC. It starts with the same projections of future FCFs and estimates of asset betas with which the CCF method starts. The difference between the two methods is where the tax advantages of debt come into the calculation. Although the CCF method estimates and values the tax shield effects of debt financing as cash flows separately (distinct from FCFs), the FCF method excludes ITS from cash flow calculations and includes the effect of tax-deductible interest payments in the after-tax WACC as shown in Equation 14.12:

$$k_{\text{WACC}} = \left(\frac{D}{D+E}\right) k_d(1 - \tau) + \left(\frac{E}{D+E}\right) k_e \tag{14.12}$$

where k_d is the firm's before-tax cost of debt and k_e is the firm's cost of levered equity. Thus, the WACC-based FCF method adjusts the before-tax cost of debt k_d by the factor $(1 - \tau)$ to reflect the tax shield effect of debt financing in the discount rate k_{WACC}.

When estimating a private firm's cost of levered equity, k_e, to calculate its WACC, relevering the estimated asset beta is necessary, using the firm's target debt-to-equity ratio to estimate the firm's levered equity beta, as shown in Equation 14.13:

$$\beta_e = \left(1 + \frac{D}{E}\right)\beta_a \tag{14.13}$$

Equation 14.14 gives the cost of levered equity:

$$k_e = r_f + \beta_e(E[r_m] - r_f) \tag{14.14}$$

Finally, Equation 14.15 gives a firm's estimated value:

$$V = \frac{FCF_1}{(1 + k_{WACC})} + \cdots + \frac{FCF_T + TV_T}{(1 + k_{WACC})^T} \tag{14.15}$$

where the terminal value TV_T is estimated as $TV_T = \frac{FCF_T(1+g)}{k_{WACC}-g}$.

Ruback (1995a, 2002) shows that both the FCF and CCF methods give identical answers to firm valuation when using the same assumptions (i.e., when debt is proportional to total firm value). However, as Ruback (2002), Lerner and Willinge (2002), and Gompers (2015) note, both the CCF and APV methods are easier to apply than the FCF method under circumstances in which (1) a firm's capital structure changes over time or when debt is forecasted in dollar amounts over time and (2) a company's effective tax rate changes over time.

Scenario Analysis in DCF Valuation Methods

In private company valuation, one of the most important steps is to obtain unbiased estimates of expected FCFs. Lerner and Willinge (2002) point out that, given the many assumptions and estimates made during the valuation process, arriving at a single or "point" firm value is unrealistic. They suggest estimating different cash flows under "best," "most likely," and "worst" case assumptions. Using sensitivity analysis, the cash flows under these different scenarios should then be discounted using a range of discount rates (e.g., the cost of assets and the WACC) and the terminal growth rate (g) to give a likely range of values. Assigning probabilities to each scenario enables determining a firm's expected value as a weighted average.

THE COMPARABLE FIRMS APPROACH IN PRIVATE COMPANY VALUATION

The comparable company valuation method is popular in PE settings. This method enables practitioners such PE investors, investment bankers, and others to assess a private company's value by comparing it to similar companies that: (1) are publicly traded (trading multiples) and (2) have been a takeover target or received financing from PE investors such as venture capitalists in a recent transaction (transaction multiples). Analysts often use the comparable company valuation method to complement DCF analysis (absolute valuation). The main idea is to get the market's opinion about a private company by using information from the relative values of comparable companies at similar stages (relative valuation).

First, the method entails finding a comparable company or a set of comparable companies. The comparable companies are as similar as possible to the private company that is to be valued. Typical dimensions used to gauge comparability in terms of fundamentals include industry, past performance, size, growth rates, and the business model. Second, analysts pick an appropriate performance metric and calculate valuation multiples for each of the comparable companies. A *valuation multiple* is a ratio of company value (measured in different ways) to a performance measure. Next, analysts weigh and average these multiples across all comparable companies and adjust the calculated average multiple (if appropriate). Finally, analysts multiply this average multiple by the specified performance measure for the private company of interest to derive a valuation estimate of that private company.

For example, suppose that a venture capitalist wants to estimate an exit valuation for PrivateCo. After some preliminary analysis during due diligence and investment screening, the venture capitalist estimates that a successful case for PrivateCo would be $55 million of sales revenue in seven years. The venture capitalist also observes that the public companies in PrivateCo's industry have enterprise values about six times sales on average. By applying this same multiple to PrivateCo, the venture capitalist estimates an exit valuation of $330 million.

Metrick and Yasuda (2011) indicate that, among venture capitalists, comparables analysis is the most popular method of exit valuation. Some empirical support is available for this popularity, as comparables seem to drive IPO valuation more than DCF analysis does (Kim and Ritter 1999). Similarly, the corporate finance literature shows that the comparable firms valuation approach generates more reliable valuation estimates for late-stage companies and LBOs (Kaplan and Ruback 1995; Baker and Ruback 1999; Chaplinsky, 2018). However, in many cases, a careful analysis that combines both DCF and comparables analysis can yield insights into valuation anomalies. The outcome's reasonableness with a DCF valuation can be assessed using a thoughtful comparable company's valuation, and vice versa. The next subsection covers the steps necessary to perform a more careful comparable analysis.

The Choice of Valuation Metrics in the Comparable Firms Approach

To form a valuation multiple, analysts need both numerators and denominators. The two numerators most often used in comparables analysis are enterprise value (EV) and market value of equity (MVE). The most intuitive denominators are proxies for cash flow. If investors perceive some usefulness in a multiple's denominator as a driver of future sales and future cash flows, it can be predictive for valuing a comparable company. Some commonly used valuation multiples in private company valuation follow:

1. *EV/EBIT.* EV is the total market value of all company securities including common stock, straight debt, and preferred stock. The denominator, earnings before

interest and taxes (EBIT), may be viewed as proportional to a steady-state cash flow measure, in which case the EV/EBIT ratio has an intuitive interpretation as the ratio of firm value to cash flow.

2. *EV/EBITDA*. Like EBIT, some analysts view EBITDA as a firm's cash flow measure in the short run, in which capital expenditures used to replace depreciated equipment can be delayed. EBITDA can be particularly useful for evaluating industries having a wide variation in their depreciation practices.

3. *EV/(EBITDA – CAPEX)*. According to Ivashina and Boe (2017), this ratio is the second-most-common metric among PE investors. This measure adjusts for capital intensity.

4. *EV/Sales*. This valuation ratio is particularly useful for firms in high-growth industries favored by venture capitalists. In these industries, many companies have negative EBIT and EBITDA, which makes forming reasonable multiples for those measures impossible. Because sales (revenue) are never negative, the EV/Sales multiple is always available.

5. *Price/Earnings*. With company-level data, computing the P/E ratio requires dividing the market value of the firm's equity by the net income (earnings).

6. *Price/Book*. The price-to-book (P/B) ratio is equal to the market value of the firm's equity divided by the shareholder's equity on the balance sheet (market-to-book ratio). An enterprise-level equivalent of P/B would divide the book value of all assets into the EV.

7. *EV/Employees*. Metrick and Yasuda (2011) point out that the number of employees is the fastest-moving measure of potential firm size, so even if all other accounting-based ratios are lagging, the EV/Employee ratio might still provide some insights.

If the denominator of the valuation multiple is an enterprise-level quantity (e.g., EBIT, EBITDA, Sales, or Employees), then the EV is the correct numerator. If the denominator represents some quantity that only accrues to equity holders (e.g., net income or book value of equity), then the market value of equity is the correct numerator.

Analysts should heed several caveats when using multiples of comparable firms for private companies. First, finding out what valuations have been assigned to other privately held companies is difficult. Second, because accounting and other performance information on private companies are often unavailable, key ratios of comparable private companies may be impossible to calculate. Therefore, analysts may have to use the trading multiples of comparable public companies only. Finally, the valuations assigned to comparable firms in financing rounds or exit transactions (IPOs or acquisitions) may take place at prices that may seem unjustifiable on a cash flow basis for the private company valued by analysts. According to Schoar (2011), this situation may be the case because high multiples for firms that enter the market during a hot IPO market need not apply for firms that go public in a few years (mean reversion and market timing effects). Similarly, IPO multiples may overstate short-term valuation gains at the expense of IPO companies' long-term performance. Purnanandam and Swaminathan (2004) document that IPO firms are overvalued relative to matched seasoned firms. Bayar and Chemmanur (2011, 2012) show that after controlling for the long-run expected payoff from an IPO exit, the IPO valuation premium over acquisitions largely vanishes.

Lerner and Willinge (2002) maintain that accounting-based comparables may be less suitable in a PE setting in which companies are often unprofitable and experiencing rapid growth. Therefore, they advocate using industry-specific operational performance metrics that are positively associated with firm value. For example, in an internet or media business, a good indicator of value may be the number of subscribers enrolled in the company. A valid proxy for the value of a biotechnology firm may be the number of patents awarded or the number of scientists employed by the firm.

Kim and Ritter (1999) report that accounting-based multiples of comparable firms such as the price-to-earnings, market-to-book, price-to-sales, EV-to-sales, and EV-to-EBITDA ratios have only modest predictive ability without further adjustments for differences in growth rates, profitability, and earnings quality. This situation is mainly due to the wide variation of these ratios for young firms within an industry. Kim and Ritter conclude that the difficulty of using comparable firm multiples for valuing IPOs, without further adjustments, leaves a major role for investment bankers in valuing IPOs.

The Choice of Comparable Companies

When choosing comparable companies, understanding the connection between comparables analysis and DCF analysis is essential. As Metrick and Yasuda (2011) and Gompers (2015) note, most valuation ratios have some connection to DCF formulas. Consider a firm with steady-state growth. Then, the firm EV would be given by Equation 14.16:

$$EV = \frac{FCF}{k - g} = \frac{FCF}{(k - ROIC \times IR)} \tag{14.16}$$

where g is the perpetual growth rate of cash flows; k denotes the discount rate; IR represents the firm's investment rate (plowback rate); $ROIC$ signifies the return on invested capital; and FCF stands for the forecasted FCF in the next period.

The formula in Equation 14.16 is essentially the same valuation formula for terminal value TV_T given in Equation 14.3. One can start by defining the EV to FCF multiple as shown in Equation 14.17.

$$\frac{EV}{FCF} = \frac{1}{(k - ROIC \times IR)} \tag{14.17}$$

Next, note that the FCF in the next period can be expressed as Equation 14.18:

$$FCF = EBIT(1 - \tau)(1 - IR) \tag{14.18}$$

Substituting Equation 14.18 into Equation 14.16 and dividing both sides by EBIT (or $NOPAT = EBIT(1 - \tau)$) yields Equation 14.19:

$$\frac{EV}{EBIT} = \frac{(1 - \tau)(1 - IR)}{(k - ROIC \times IR)}, \frac{EV}{NOPAT} = \frac{(1 - IR)}{(k - ROIC \times IR)} \tag{14.19}$$

For a comparable firm with no debt, the $EV/NOPAT$ ratio is identical to the P/E ratio. Substituting $EBIT = Sales \times Margin$ into Equation 14.19 yields Equation 14.20:

$$\frac{EV}{Sales} = \frac{Margin(1 - \tau)(1 - IR)}{(k - ROIC \times IR)} \tag{14.20}$$

Thus, to find comparable companies for P/E or EBIT ratios, an analyst must search for companies with similar steady-state levels for investment opportunities (for $ROIC$ and IR), discount rates, and (for EBIT) tax rates. If the private firm's current operating margins are not yet at their steady levels, then analysts might be better off using an EV/Sales multiple and identifying comparable companies with stable operating margins.

THE VENTURE CAPITAL METHOD FOR HIGH-GROWTH PRIVATE COMPANIES

The venture capital (VC) method is a valuation tool commonly used by venture capitalists in the PE industry. As discussed previously, PE investments are often characterized by negative cash flows and earnings and highly uncertain but potentially substantial future rewards. The VC method accounts for this cash flow profile by estimating a private company's value at a time in the future when it is projected to have achieved positive cash flows and/or earnings. In practice, this value typically coincides with the exit valuation for the company when the venture capitalist expects to exit an investment in the company through an IPO or acquisition (a successful exit). This "exit value" is then discounted back to the present using a high discount rate, typically between 40 and 80 percent. Next, the VC method uses the discounted exit value of the private company and the size of the required investment to calculate the venture capitalist's desired equity stake in the company. The application of the standard VC valuation method consists of the following four steps.

Exit Valuation

First, the VC method starts by estimating a company's exit valuation at the time of a successful exit, where a successful exit is an IPO or an acquisition (sale) that is competitive with an IPO. The exit value is usually calculated using the comparable firms approach, as previously discussed. For example, a P/E ratio may be multiplied by the projected net income in the exit year. The exit value can also be calculated using other techniques, including DCF methods. Furthermore, analysts can look at the average valuation for recent successful exits in the same industry as a benchmark. The estimated time to a successful exit, T, can vary, typically between 2 and 8 years, depending on the private company's life-cycle stage at the time of the VC financing round.

Target Rate of Return and Discounted Exit Valuation

In the second step, venture capitalists determine the company's discounted exit value by discounting the exit value calculated in the first step. Instead of using a traditional cost of capital as the discount rate, venture capitalists typically use a high "target rate of return" in the range of 40 to 80 percent. The target rate of return r_{target} is the annualized yield the venture capitalist thinks is required to justify the risk and effort of the particular investment. The discounted exit value of the private company is calculated as shown in Equation 14.22:

$$Discounted\ exit\ valuation = \frac{Exit\ value}{(1 + r_{target})^T} \qquad (14.22)$$

Venture capitalists justify using high target rates of returns (discount rates) in the application of the VC method for three main reasons. First, they contend that using high discount rates compensates for the illiquidity of private firms. Second, venture capitalists are active investors who invest much of their time monitoring portfolio companies. They provide reputation, access to skilled managers, industry contacts, networks, and other resources to private companies. A high discount rate crudely compensates the VC for this investment of time and resources. Finally, venture capitalists may believe that financial projections presented by entrepreneurs are overly optimistic. High discount rates supposedly compensate for these inflated projections.

The Venture Capitalist's Expected Retention Ratio

In the VC method, one must usually account for negative cash flows, which then require further rounds of investment and a dilution in the ownership percentage for previous investors. To compensate for the effect of dilution from future rounds of financing, the venture capitalist needs to calculate the expected retention ratio, which quantifies the expected dilutive effect of future rounds of financing on the venture capitalist's ownership. Equation 14.23 provides the private company's post-money valuation at the current round of financing:

$$Post - Money\ valuation = Discounted\ exit\ valuation \times Expected\ retention\ ratio \qquad (14.23)$$

The Venture Capitalist's Required Equity Stake

In the last step of the VC method, the required current percent ownership necessary for the venture capitalist to realize its target rate of return is then calculated using Equation 14.24:

$$Required\ current\ ownership\ \frac{Investment}{Post - Money\ valuation} \qquad (14.24)$$

As an example, suppose that the VC firm HiTech Ventures is considering a $5 million investment in BiotechCo in a first-round (Series A) financing. The current number of shares outstanding before the financing is 500,000. The venture capitalist's target rate of return is 50 percent per year. The projected net income of BiotechCo at the time of a successful exit seven years from now is $20 million. The average P/E ratio of profitable biotech firms is 15. Assume that the expected retention rate for the first-round investment in this industry is 70 percent.

In this case, the company's value in a successful exit is 15($20 million) = $300 million. Then, the company's discounted exit valuation is ($300 million)/1.50^7 = $17.56 million. Thus, the post-money valuation of BiotechCo after the current round of financing is $17.56 million(0.70) = $12.29 million. Finally, the venture capitalist's required equity stake in the Series A round is $5/$12.29 = 0.4068 = 40.68 percent. This calculation means that the number of new shares issued to HiTech Ventures in the Series A round is [(500,000)(0.4068)]/(1 − 0.4068) = 342,886. The implied share price in the first financing round is $5 million/342,886 = $14.58. The implied pre-money valuation of the company is $12.29 million − $5 million = $7.29 million.

OPTION VALUATION FOR PRIVATE COMPANIES

Many private companies have growth opportunities that can be appropriately valued by using option pricing techniques. As Lerner and Willinge (2002) point out, option pricing is useful in situations where the flexibility exists to wait, learn more about the proposed investments' prospects, and then decide whether to invest. Dixit and Pindyck (1994) provide a detailed technical analysis of real options. Flexibilities for private company managers include the ability to change the production rate, delay investment and development, or abandon a project. The ability to make follow-on investments in a private company is a form of flexibility that is of particular interest to venture capitalists. The value of these "real options" that affect a private company's value cannot be accurately measured using DCF techniques. Therefore, investment opportunities that incorporate flexibility are undervalued using traditional DCF methods.

Analysts can use the Black-Scholes model to value European options using five variables as inputs. For an option on a stock, these inputs are the (1) exercise price (X), (2) stock price (S), (3) time to expiration (T), (4) standard deviation (or volatility) of returns on the stock (σ), and (5) risk-free rate (r_f). Using these variables enables valuing the right to buy a share stock at some future point. Similarly, analysts can evaluate a private company's decision to invest in a project using the Black-Scholes model of option pricing. In the case of a real option to delay investment, the equivalency between financial option variables and real option variables are as follows:

X. The exercise price of a real option in firm valuation can be viewed as the present value of the expenditures required to undertake the project.

S. The stock price of a real option in firm valuation can be viewed as the present value of the project's expected cash flows.

T. Time to expiration is the length of time that the investment decision can be delayed.

σ. Standard deviation of returns is the volatility of the cash flows from the project's underlying assets.

r_f. The risk-free rate of return is the rate of return of a hypothetical investment with no risk of financial loss, over a given period of time.

After estimating these input variables for a project of a private company, the value of this real option to delay investment can be calculated using the Black-Scholes formula. Other similar real options relevant to private companies include call options such as the option to expand plant/equipment capacity and the option to extend an existing brand/product's life and put options such as the option to abandon a new project and the option to reduce plant/equipment capacity.

Finally, option pricing finds many useful applications in the pricing of securities issued by private companies to PE investors. These PE securities include warrants issued to VC investors as deal sweeteners, redeemable preferred stock, convertible preferred stock, participating convertible preferred stock, and participating convertible preferred stock with a cap. The carried interest compensation of the general partners of a VC fund can also be modeled as a call option. *Carried interest* is a share of any profits that the general partners of private equity and hedge funds receive as compensation regardless of whether they contribute any initial funds. Further, many private companies award stock options to their employees as incentive compensation. The underlying asset value in these applications of option pricing in VC financing is the private portfolio company's value at the time of a successful exit, such as an IPO or an acquisition. Metrick and Yasuda (2011) and Gornall and Strebulaev (2020) develop option pricing–based valuation models, which correct for using convertible preferred securities in VC financing contracts to estimate the implied value of VC-backed private companies. The main concern associated with using option pricing methodology in private company valuation is that its complexity requires a higher level of technical expertise compared to simpler valuation methods discussed earlier.

SUMMARY AND CONCLUSIONS

Entrepreneurs and investors need a thorough understanding of different valuation methods to make value-increasing decisions in a PE setting. Although each valuation method has its strengths and weaknesses, this chapter discusses the important links that connect them and how they can complement each other to help improve valuing private companies.

The review of DCF valuation techniques in this chapter emphasizes the importance of obtaining unbiased expected cash flow estimates through scenario analysis. Further, estimating a firm's TV is especially important because the majority of a private company's value, especially one in an early-stage setting, may come from the TV. The analysis of the link between comparable firms approach and DCF valuation suggests that analysts look to firms in the same industry, facing similar investment opportunities, with similar long-run margins and productivity when searching for comparable firms in private company valuation. The VC method provides a synthesis of DCF methods and the comparable firm approach in private company valuation. Although identifying the real option aspects of investment opportunities may be challenging for PE investors and entrepreneurs, it is critical for valuing private companies because a large component of their value derives from future growth opportunities.

DISCUSSION QUESTIONS

1. Discuss some limitations of DCF valuation methods and the comparable firm valuation method in private company valuation.

2. Discuss the justifications for using high target rates of returns (discount rates) in the VC valuation method.
3. Discuss the accuracy of calculating the post-money valuation in the VC method as an estimate of the implied enterprise value of a private company.
4. Identify the role of capital structure in private company valuation.

REFERENCES

Baker, Malcolm, and Richard Ruback. 1999. "Estimating Industry Multiples." Working Paper, Harvard University. Available at https://pdfs.semanticscholar.org/714f/60b51594d9e9d652b5b5daaad2b242466843.pdf?_ga=2.18211003.304620190.1577817992-2071943875.1577817992.

Bayar, Onur, and Thomas J. Chemmanur. 2011. "IPOs versus Acquisitions and the Valuation Premium Puzzle: A Theory of Exit Choice by Entrepreneurs and Venture Capitalists." *Journal of Financial and Quantitative Analysis* 46:6, 1755–1793.

Bayar, Onur, and Thomas J. Chemmanur. 2012. "What Drives the Valuation Premium in IPOs Versus Acquisitions? An Empirical Analysis." *Journal of Corporate Finance* 18:3, 451–475.

Chaplinsky, Susan. 2018. "Valuing Late-Stage Companies and Leveraged Buyouts." University of Virginia, Darden Business Publishing, UV7578.

Damodaran, Aswath. 2018. *The Dark Side of Valuation.* Upper Saddle River, NJ: Prentice-Hall.

Dixit, Avinash, and Robert Pindyck. 1994. *Investment under Uncertainty.* Princeton, NJ: Princeton University Press.

Gompers, Paul. 2015. "A Note on Valuation in Private Equity." Harvard Business School Note 9-213-034.

Gornall, Will, and Ilya Strebulaev. 2020. "Squaring Venture Capital Valuations with Reality." *Journal of Financial Economics* 135:1, 120–143.

Ivashina, Victoria, and Henrik Boe. 2017. "Primer on Multiples Valuation and Its Use in Private Equity Industry." Harvard Business School Note 9-218-017.

Kaplan, Steven, and Richard Ruback. 1995. "The Valuation of Cash Flow Forecasts: An Empirical Analysis." *Journal of Finance* 50:4, 1059–1093.

Kim, Moonchul, and Jay R. Ritter. 1999. "Valuing IPOs." *Journal of Financial Economics* 53:3, 409–437.

Koller, Tim, Marc Goedhart, and David Wessels. 2010. *Valuation: Measuring and Managing the Value of Companies.* Hoboken, NJ: John Wiley & Sons.

Lerner, Josh, and John Willinge. 2002. "A Note on Valuation in Private Equity Settings." Harvard Business School Note 9-297-050.

Metrick, Andrew, and Ayako Yasuda. 2011. *Venture Capital and the Finance of Innovation.* Hoboken, NJ: John Wiley & Sons.

Myers, Stewart C. 1974. "Interactions of Corporate Financing and Investment Decisions. Implications for Capital Budgeting." *Journal of Finance* 29:1, 1–25.

Purnanandam, Amiyatosh K., and Bhashkaran Swaminathan. 2004. "Are IPOs Really Underpriced?" *Review of Financial Studies* 17:3, 811–848.

Ruback, Richard S. 1995a. "Technical Note for Capital Cash Flow Valuation." Harvard Business School Case No. 295-069.

Ruback, Richard S. 1995b. "Technical Note for Introduction to Cash Flow Valuation Methods." Harvard Business School Case No. 295-155.

Ruback, Richard S. 2002. "Capital Cash Flows: A Simple Approach to Valuing Risky Cash Flows." *Financial Management* 31:2, 85–103.

Schoar, Antoinette. 2011. "New Venture Valuation." MIT Sloan School of Management Lecture Note 15.431.

Equity Investment Models and Strategies

Equity Investing Strategies

Nicholas Biasi
Independent Financial Consultant
Andrew C. Spieler
Robert F. Dall Distinguished Professor of Business,
Frank G. Zarb School of Business, Hofstra University
Raisa Varejao
Structured Finance Associate

INTRODUCTION

Investors must decide on their broad asset class exposures and weightings. They use a strategy called *strategic asset allocation* to set target allocations for various asset classes and rebalance periodically. Investors should have diversified portfolios that include some weighting to equities. The specific weighting depends on several factors, including the investor's time horizon, risk tolerance, and income needs. Investors must also decide on the tactical asset allocation within the equity asset class.

Tactical asset allocation is a decision to deliberately deviate from the strategic asset allocation, which is constructed from the risk and return objectives of an investment policy statement (IPS) to add value to the portfolio. An important part of this decision is based on choosing the appropriate investing style(s). This chapter provides a discussion of the prominent and emerging trends in equity investing strategies. Furthermore, security selection is a more deliberate strategy than tactical asset allocation. This process involves putting more weight on securities that investors believe are likely to outperform a specified benchmark. The benchmark may be the sector benchmark for that specific security, or it could be the return on the market as a whole such as the S&P 500 index, which is a stock market index that measures the stock performance of 500 large companies listed on stock exchanges in the United States.

Since Benjamin Graham introduced value investing in the early 1900s, other investment strategies have evolved. The goal of the strategies discussed in this chapter remains the same: to achieve appropriate returns. However, the tenets underlying each strategy differ. For example, value investing focuses on finding stocks trading at a discount relative to their fundamental value, whereas growth investing channels its capital toward stocks that are expected to grow at a higher earnings rate relative to their industry or the market. Furthermore, growth at a reasonable price (GARP) investing attempts to combine both value and growth strategies to achieve excess returns. Technical analysis focuses on historical trends and patterns, not fundamental value, to predict future price movements. Income investing concentrates on increasing portfolio returns with steady streams of payments. Perhaps the most complicated strategy is quantitative analysis, which uses complex models and algorithms to predict patterns and exploit arbitrage opportunities. *Arbitrage* is the practice of buying an asset in one market at a lesser price and then selling it in the other market at a higher price. A recent trend within equity investing is environmental, social, and governance (ESG) investing, which concentrates primarily on ethical investing and considers both financial return and social/environmental considerations to encourage social change. All of these equity investing strategies have both potential merits and drawbacks.

The chapter is organized as follows. First, it begins by discussing value, growth, GARP, and income investing strategies using equities. The chapter also summarizes such recent trends as indexing and quantitative trading strategies, including algorithmic trading and high-frequency trading (HFT). Next, it describes the basic principles of ESG investing. The final section offers a summary and conclusions.

VALUE INVESTING

The concept of value investing originated with Benjamin Graham and David Dodd more than 75 years ago with the publication of their seminal book on security analysis, first released in 1934 (Graham and Dodd 1996). Despite the passage of time and fundamental changes in financial markets, investors still find their concepts appealing. The main idea behind value investing is that a security's price and its intrinsic value are two distinct concepts. In short, *price* is what an investor pays, and *value* is what an investor receives. A financial asset's price is subject to many factors that may not necessarily affect its intrinsic value. Value investors look for securities that are substantially *undervalued*, meaning that the security's current price may not correctly reflect its intrinsic value.

Investors can easily observe market prices by looking at a stock's current trading price. In contrast, various ways are available to assess value. Value can be measured by simple multiples such as price-to-earnings (P/E) and price-to-book (P/B) ratios or by a more bottom-up approach via discounted cash flow (DCF) valuation. Thus, the goal of value investors is to buy a stock with a below-average P/E or P/B ratio with the expectation that the price will increase and reach the industry average, eventually leading to a profitable trade. The same idea applies using the DCF valuation approach—purchase a stock with a market price below its intrinsic value calculated via a DCF model.

A value investor is not overly concerned about short-term price movements. A security's fundamental value ultimately results from a company's ability to generate free, unencumbered cash flows. This analysis includes qualitative factors such as management's ability to improve efficiency, adapt to market competitors, differentiate its products and services, and employ an appropriate capital structure. Macro factors, including industry dynamics and exposure to international markets, also affect a company's long-term operations. Another common qualitative analysis to assess industry profitability is Porter's five forces. Porter (1979) identifies the following factors as contributors to an industry's future growth: (1) degree of competition between rivals, (2) bargaining power of suppliers, (3) bargaining power of buyers, (4) potential for new entrants, and (5) threat of substitutes.

After evaluating a company's fundamental value drivers, if the market price is substantially lower than its fundamental value, then the company is a good target for investment. Graham and Dodd (1996) call the gap between a company's fundamental value and its trading price the *margin of safety*. They believe that the margin of safety should be about 50 percent but no less than one-third of the market price. Although market participants can observe differences between price and value, the empirical results do not suggest that a value investment strategy provides a higher return. For example, Damodaran (2012) compares value mutual fund returns to small-, mid-, and large-cap index returns. Empirically, value mutual funds generally perform worse than indices with a few notable exceptions, such as between 2007 and 2011 for large- and small-cap stocks. Damodaran believes that the difference in returns between value mutual funds and indexes is not due to the negative returns of a few "bad" funds. Among all the value funds in his study, 55 percent of large-cap value fund managers, 64 percent of mid-cap value fund managers, and 56 percent of small-cap value fund managers underperformed their respective indices between 2002 and 2011. Even between 2007 and 2011, the most favorable period in the comparison, using the median return rather than the average return across value funds yields negative excess returns.

However, several notable outliers exist regarding value investors, including Warren Buffett's Berkshire Hathaway. Between 1965 and 2014, Berkshire Hathaway's stock price increased by more than 1,800,000 percent. Its performance far exceeded that of the S&P 500 index, which increased by about 11,000 percent over the same period, including dividends (Munger 2014).

Value investors must also be wary of a common pitfall called the *value trap*, which suggests that a company appears to be currently trading at a discount but might not rebound. This relation can happen due to several factors such as an inability to innovate and consequently losing market share, operational inefficiencies, which normally result in lower free cash flows (FCFs), lower growth rates, or poor allocations of deployed capital. Such outcomes can lower multiples and generate large returns.

GROWTH INVESTING

Unlike value investing, in which investors buy securities they believe the market undervalues, growth investing is an investment strategy that focuses on the growth of an investor's capital. Growth investors typically invest in growth stocks or companies whose earnings are expected to grow at an above-average rate compared to their industry or the market.

Philip Fisher and Thomas Owen Price Jr. are likely the two individuals most associated with the emergence of growth investing as a valid and important investment strategy. Investors have considered Microsoft, Apple, Amazon, or Facebook as growth stocks at some point. In some cases, growth stocks have the potential to increase dramatically in a relatively short time, but they can trade at a discount due to their underlying expected future cash flows. Metaphorically, a growth stock can be described as "a first-round draft pick in the NFL or NBA" (Longo 2016, p. 67).

These stocks have high expectations and are in relatively high demand, so they usually sell at a high price multiple or high price relative to earnings.

Two common measures used to differentiate growth stocks from value stocks are P/E and P/B ratios. A *P/E ratio* is a stock's market price per share divided by a company's annual earnings per share. For example, if a company's current market value per share is $25 with its last reported annual earnings as $5, the stock's P/E ratio is 5.0 times. A *P/B ratio* is the ratio of a stock's market price per share divided by its book value per share. Book value is not the same as market value, but rather an accounting value on the balance sheet, which is a company's total assets minus its total liabilities on a per-share basis. A high P/B ratio could indicate a growth stock because valuation is partly based on its future potential. By contrast, a low P/B ratio could indicate a value stock that could be undervalued relative to its intrinsic worth. To distinguish growth from value stocks, analysts look at the market's average valuation. For these two measures, any ratio above the current market average results in a classifying a stock as growth, while any ratio measure below the average results in classifying a stock as value. For example, if the market P/E ratio is currently at 15.0, any stock with a P/E ratio of less than 15.0 could be considered a value stock, while a P/E ratio higher than 15.0 could be considered a growth stock.

As previously noted, growth stocks can turn into value stocks and vice versa. For example, consider a high-growth technology company that has made numerous innovations. Initially, the company's stock had a market value (price) of $300 per share and annual earnings of $12 per share. Thus, the stock is trading at a P/E ratio of 25.0 compared to the average market P/E ratio of 18.0. Now suppose that this company underwent a period of slow growth and financial distress. As a result, its market value dipped to $185 per share, with a P/E ratio of 15.4, while the market P/E ratio remained at 18.0. If investors believe the company can innovate, reduce expenses, and generate sufficient cash flow, then they might view this company as a value stock. Similarly, a value stock has the potential to transform into a growth stock if the undervalued stock ends up rallying in price based on greater market recognition.

Fisher was one of the first well-known investors to conduct fundamental analysis. As Longo (2016, p. 70) notes, Fisher called this approach the "scuttlebutt method or business grapevine." The scuttlebutt method involved analyzing factors beyond the company's financial statements, such as corporate governance, management, suppliers, competitors, and macroeconomic environments. Fisher identified a few key tenets when screening for growth companies. Primarily, he looked for companies with the potential to substantially grow sales for several years into the future. After assessing the quality of a firm's sales potential, he believed that having a particular firm's sales grow at a faster rate than the industry or sector as a whole is a good sign.

Fisher looked beyond the current product mix for the company's ability to maintain its growth even when product cycles reached their end. Thus, quality management was an important qualitative factor. In other words, even when a company's product has fully saturated the market, the company may be able to make the product better or make new products that can capture sales from competitors to sustain sales growth. Another critical factor Fisher examined was the company's research and development (R&D) activities. As Longo (2016, p. 78) notes, Fisher questioned, "Did a significant part of a company's sales come from new products? Or was the company a one-trick pony ... ?" Fisher liked to invest in companies that were not one-trick ponies. That is, the company could maintain strong sales by generating new product features and new market opportunities through quality management and a focused and productive R&D department.

GROWTH AT A REASONABLE PRICE

Growth at a reasonable price (GARP) investing is a strategy that balances both value and growth investing. The basic principle is to find stocks that lie somewhere between General Electric (GE)-like value traps—cheap stocks with a bleak future—and overhyped and overvalued growth stocks reminiscent of Amazon (Rabener 2019). Historically, the earnings growth of GARP stocks is considerably above that of the broad market. Performance metrics of GARP stocks can vary but are generally based on the price/earnings (P/E)-to-growth ratio, referred to as the PEG ratio, which divides the P/E ratio by the expected growth rate in earnings. Stocks exhibiting a PEG ratio below one are classified as GARP stocks. However, PEG ratios greater than one may be breaching the line between GARP and growth, which requires further analysis. Analysts can use publicly available data from the company's annual report or the Securities and Exchange Commission (SEC) filing (10-K) to retrieve the fiscal year ending basic earnings per share, along with the closing stock price the same day (or the day after) the filing was released. If the company pays a consistent dividend, then the long-term sustainable growth rate can be calculated as one minus the dividend payout ratio (retention ratio) multiplied by the company's return on equity (ROE). If the company has stable shareholders' equity, then using the reported year-ending value is appropriate. If it seemingly has a volatile and fluctuating ending shareholders' equity, then an analyst can take the arithmetic mean of the current year's shareholders' equity and the prior years and apply it to the ROE.

This process helps identify stocks with growth potential that are trading at reasonable prices. However, as with any ratio, the accuracy of the PEG ratio depends on the inputs used. The quality of the inputs is critical and must be scrutinized thoroughly from public sources. Using historical growth rates may provide an inaccurate PEG ratio if an analyst expects future growth rates to deviate from a company's historical growth. The ratio can be calculated using one-year, three-year, or five-year expected growth rates. Before applying a growth rate, analyzing a company's financial performance is beneficial. Once an investor has an established a PEG ratio, several ways are available to determine whether the stock is undervalued. For example, an investor could buy the stock if it trades at a P/E ratio that is less than the expected growth rate. Although little evidence shows that the strategy discussed here earns excess returns, it seems to have gained popularity as a viable strategy among some investors. Nonetheless, it is a risky strategy and not highly recommended because external factors could influence or distort the PEG ratio. For example, in a high-interest-rate environment, a stock may seem to be undervalued but is still risky due to other factors.

A motive for fusing the metrics and principles of both value stocks and growth stocks is to take the best (or worst) of both worlds to try and outperform the market. GARP stocks exhibit outperformance since 1989, but this result can be explained in part by simply excluding stocks with negative earnings. The PEG ratio calculation requires stocks to have positive earnings, which is another limitation of the ratio. After filtering out negative earnings stocks, GARP stock outperformance declines substantially (Rabener 2019).

INCOME INVESTING

Aside from value, growth, and GARP strategies, some investors primarily invest to generate income, a strategy known as *income investing*. Income investors search for securities that generate a steady, predictable income; capital gains and price appreciation are of lesser importance. More specifically, income investing focuses on dividend-paying equity securities and interest-paying fixed income securities. Generally, individuals earn most of their income through employment income. However, disciplined saving and investment in the financial markets can grow modest savings into large investment portfolios, yielding an investor a substantial annual investment income stream over time.

Dividends

A *dividend* is the proportionate distribution of firm earnings to its shareholders. Dividends may differ based on the class of investors such as common or preferred shareholders. The board of directors technically declares dividends in line with the firm's strategic objectives and growth opportunities. Dividends are most commonly issued as cash payments that are taxable to shareholders but can also be issued as shares of stocks (stock dividends) or property. U.S. companies generally pay cash dividends quarterly, but other payment schedules are possible.

Income investors add stocks to their portfolios that consistently pay dividends because dividends boost holding period returns (HPRs) and total returns. Dividends also dampen the drag on poor equity performance. That is, if an investor experiences a capital loss or depreciation in a stock's market value, the loss may be offset or lessened if the stock pays a dividend. For a company to pay a consistent dividend or even increase dividend payments to shareholders, it must be able to generate high and sustainable income. A company with a high payout ratio implies that it pays out a large amount of its earnings to shareholders. High-dividend-paying firms may or may not exhibit sustainable EPS growth, whereas a company with a higher retention ratio and a lower payout ratio generally has more sustainable EPS growth. Additionally, paying dividends is a rough measure of cash flow capacity. To consistently pay higher dividends, the firm must generate sustainable free cash flows.

INDEX INVESTING

Index investing, also known as passive equity investing, produces returns that closely follow a specific index, which is often a broad market index. Index investing is a channel by which investors can gain exposure to index performance that is usually less risky than the underlying asset or asset classes it tracks. The primary method to invest is via an exchange-traded fund (ETF). Popular ETFs include "SPY," which tracks the

S&P 500, "EEM," which tracks emerging markets, and "QQQ" or Invesco QQQ, which tracks the NASDAQ 100. Although similar to open-end mutual funds, ETFs have some subtle differences in share creation and redemption.

The main advantage of investing in ETFs is the low transaction costs of trading ETFs relative to the underlying basket of assets. ETFs also have two major tax advantages compared to mutual funds. Due to structural differences, mutual funds typically incur more capital gains taxes than ETFs. Moreover, investors incur a capital gains tax on an ETF only upon its sale, whereas mutual funds pass on capital gains taxes to investors through the investment's life even when shares are not sold. Chapter 20 discusses ETFs in more detail.

ETFs generally offer low-cost exposure to certain industries, subsectors, asset classes, and geographical regions. They also play a role in risk management for portfolios. Investors may want to quickly gain portfolio exposure to specific sectors, styles, industries, or countries but do not have the expertise and/or in-depth knowledge in those areas. Given the wide variety of sectors as well as style, industry, and country categories available, ETF shares can provide investors easy exposure to a specific desired market segment or asset classes (Carrel and Ferri 2011). Moreover, recent ETFs can match specific investment strategies. For example, through ETFs, an investor can buy or sell stock market volatility or invest in the highest-yielding currencies in the world. In terms of liquidity, investors can trade ETFs in secondary markets (Hill, Nadig, and Hougan 2015). Investors can also buy ETFs on *margin* (leveraged purchase), and short the securities. Investors can tailor ETFs to trading strategies just like an individual stock.

QUANTITATIVE TRADING

Quantitative trading is an investment strategy that includes mathematical modeling and data analysis. A few examples of quantitative trading strategies are algorithmic trading, high-frequency trading (HFT), and statistical arbitrage.

- *Algorithmic trading. Algorithmic trading* (algo-trading) is trading based on a set of rules to generate buy and sell decisions. A challenge of manual trading is that human behavior can affect returns. In contrast, a computer-based algorithm eliminates those biases because its decision is strictly based on objective data and computer-based rules. The data used for the algorithms come from several different sources, including market data, fundamental data, macroeconomic data, news and press releases, HFT data, and alternative data such as social media.
- *High-frequency trading. High-frequency trading* is a type of algorithmic trading that uses powerful computers to place orders in a fraction of a second. Those trades are built through a machine learning algorithm that analyzes massive amounts of data, normally trading data. The program learns to optimize the trade and execute it. HFT has several popular strategies. For example, statistical arbitrage exploits temporary deviation in the price of securities. Similarly, news-based HFT is based on alternative sources such as news websites, Bloomberg, and social media feeds. The algorithm analyzes keywords and executes the trade based on alternative sources of information. Another common HFT strategy is *momentum ignition*. In this strategy, the goal is to buy

the stock to induce other high-frequency traders to do the same and then sell it and profit based on the movement in price caused by the increase in demand.

■ *Statistical arbitrage. Statistical arbitrage* is a technique of exploiting mispricing of similar securities and holding a long and short position of the paired assets. Statistical arbitrage started in the 1980s, but it became more sophisticated in recent years. The strategy can be implemented in several different asset classes. A common approach from a statistical arbitrage fund is to select two sets of similar securities, highly correlated or cointegrated. When these two sets are trading at a spread above the historical average, the investor buys the security that is decreasing in price, or not increasing as much, and sell the security that is appreciating more. Now those trades are automated and quant funds may execute these trades in high frequency (Smietana 2019).

TECHNICAL ANALYSIS

In contrast to fundamental analysis in which analysts or investors conduct in-depth financial statement analysis to identify value or growth stocks, technical analysis does not require company financial statements or detailed analysis into the company's industry, competitors, multiples, and free cash flows. Instead, its central tenet is to analyze market data to detect trends. Market data include all past, observable market variables such as prices, volume, spreads, and other similar factors. In short, technical analysts believe that analyzing historical trends can help them predict future prices via chart analysis. Among the most common charting techniques include candlesticks (a simple and easy-to-visualize technique that provides information about open, close, high, and low prices), head and shoulders (a chart formation that normally appears when a pattern reversion exists), and Bollinger bands (bands drawn around a price structure consisting of a middle band that is the moving average and an upper and lower band indicating whether prices are high or low). Chapter 9 contains a more detailed discussion of technical analysis.

According to Murphy (1999), technicians base their analysis on three core premises: (1) the markets reflect all relevant information; hence, everything that can affect the stock price is already affecting its current price; (2) prices move in trends; and (3) history repeats itself. Investors use many technical indicators when making investment decisions. For example, a popular technical indicator is a *moving average*, which is the average price of a security over a defined previous period. Normally an analyst plots different moving averages on a graph and identifies turning points in which the moving averages intersect.

An example is the 4-9-18 day moving average, which technical analysts widely use. In an uptrend, the 4-day moving average will be higher than the 9-day moving average, followed by the 18-day moving average. In a downtrend, the order reverses. Murphy (1999) explains that a buy signal occurs when the 4-day moving average crosses above the 9-day moving average and the 18-day moving average. A confirmed signal would be when the 9-day moving average also crosses above the 18-day moving average.

Other widely used technical tools include support and resistance levels, which act like a floor and ceiling, respectively. If the price breaks through its ceiling (resistance), then the prior resistance becomes the next support. The opposite also holds: if the price falls below its support, then the prior support becomes the new resistance.

Besides moving averages and support/resistance levels, technical analysts also consider the *relative strength index* (RSI), which indicates whether the security is oversold or overbought. The indicator ranges from 0 to 100, where 30 and 70 signify thresholds indicating oversold and overbought status, respectively. An RSI below 30 indicates the security is oversold and signals a buying opportunity. Similarly, an RSI above 70 indicates the security is overbought, resulting in an expected reversal generating a sell signal. Although technical analysis includes many other indicators, discussing them is beyond the scope of this chapter.

OPTIONS STRATEGIES

An option is a type of derivative that gives the holder the right to buy (long call) or sell (long put) a security at a set price (strike price) on or before a predetermined expiration date. Conversely, if the investor is short the stock option, the investor has an obligation to buy or sell the security.

Investors can implement many strategies using options ranging from being long a call, if the investor is bullish, or long a put if the investor is bearish to more sophisticated strategies using only options or a mix of options and the underlying asset. The following discussion includes a few examples of options strategies.

- A *covered call* is a pure option strategy in which the investor is long the underlying asset and short a call option on the same asset. This strategy is successful when an investor does not believe that the price is going to move much, so the investor can still earn the premium of the call that the investor wrote.
- A *protective put* is another common option strategy in which the investor is long the underlying asset and long a put option. Investors normally use this strategy when they expect the stock price to fall. If the price goes down, the put acts as insurance, and it can be exercised to protect the long position.
- A *bull call spread* is a strategy that can be implemented with options only by going long a call with a lower stock price and short a call with a higher stock price with the same expiration date. The idea is to profit from a limited increase in price. The gains and losses are limited due to the upper and lower strike prices.

  An example of a bull call spread is buying a company ABC 100 call for $10 and selling the 105 call for $8. This operation starts with a net cost of $2, and the maximum profit is $3, which is the difference between the strike price of $5 ($105 – $100) minus the cost of the operation of $2 ($8 – $10). An investor achieves the maximum profit if the stock price is at or above the strike price of the short call on the expiration day.
- A *calendar spread* consists of options of the same security with the same strike price but different expiration dates. An investor can construct a calendar spread with all calls or all puts. The calendar spread provides an opportunity to trade differences in volatility levels at two points in time and to benefit from the increasing rate of time decay as the option gets closer to expiration. An investor can build a *neutral calendar call spread* by buying long-term calls and writing

the same amount of short-term calls at-the-money or slightly out-of-the-money with the same strike price.

For instance, a trader thinks that the market is likely to trade sideways for the upcoming months, and the stock ABC is expected to follow the market. This trader can write 100 short-term calls and buy 100 longer-term calls. Normally in this type of operation, an initial outflow occurs. However, as the expiration of the short-term call grows near (assuming the underlying asset keeps trading around the same price), it expires worthless and the trader earns a profit. In this case, the result of this trade would be a profit from the option that the trader wrote initially plus the value of the longer-term calls that he bought minus the initial outflow from the call premiums.

■ A *diagonal spread* is a more complicated option strategy involving purchasing the same number of options of the same underlying asset with different strike prices and different expiration months. The diagonal spread is similar to a calendar spread in the sense that it takes advantage of the faster time decay when an option is about to expire. However, in the diagonal spread period, the trader has a slightly more bullish/bearish view.

For instance, an investor can construct a diagonal call spread by being long in a longer-term call with a lower strike price, assuming a strike price of $45.00 for $10.00, and writing a shorter-term call with a higher strike price of $50 for $7.50. The strategy starts with an outflow of $2.50 as the short-term option gets closer to expiration; its price decreases until it becomes worthless at expiration day. An investor incurs the maximum profit if, at expiration day, the stock price equals the strike price of the shorter-term call of $50. In this case, the profit is $7.50 from the call that the investor wrote and the value of the long call option. In this case, the stock price went up, and the option in which the investor is long is in the money, so it loses a little bit of value due to time decay but not as much as in the calendar spread. Thus, the profit is higher. An *in-the-money call option* means the option holder can buy the security below its current market price. An investor can use the Black-Scholes option pricing formula to estimate the call's value.

In summary, many different options strategies are available based on underlying equity positions, including option-only positions as well as combinations of options and stocks. However, many other option strategies exist but are beyond the scope of those covered in this section.

ESG INVESTING

Environmental, social, and governance (ESG) investing is also called *sustainable investing, socially responsible investing, mission-related investing,* and *screening.* The popularity of ESG investing has increased in recent years and has attracted both asset managers and company executives. In 2006, the United Nations launched the Principles for Responsible Investment (PRI) (2019). According to the PRI website, at the time of formation, 63 investment companies consisting of asset owners, asset managers, and service providers with $6.5 trillion in assets under management (AUM) signed a commitment to incorporate ESG issues into their investment decisions. By 2019, the number of signatories had grown to 2,372 and represented $86.3 trillion in AUM. Many market observers expect this explosive growth to continue.

There are several reasons for the rapid rise in including ESG factors in investment decisions (Tidd and Subramanian 2019). The world is changing, and so is the type of risk for investors. For instance, sustainability challenges, such as flood risk and increases in sea levels, privacy and data security, demographic shifts, and regulatory pressures, provide new risk factors that investors may not have considered previously. Additionally, investors are changing, and so are their investment objectives. In the coming decades, millennials are going to invest several trillion dollars, and they have expressed different preferences for their investments than those of previous generations. For many millennials, their collective objective function involves not only a monetary return but also the investment's impact on society (societal return).

An argument against implementing ESG scores into investment decisions is the potential to affect returns negatively. However, according to MSCI researchers, this concern is not warranted. According to Giese, Lee, Melas, Nagy, and Nishikawa (2019), a link exists between ESG information and a company's valuation and performance. Specifically, ESG ratings affect a company's valuation and performance by lowering its systematic risk, which implies a lower cost of capital and, consequently, a higher valuation. Besides, higher ESG scores tend to be correlated with lower idiosyncratic risk, which translates into higher profitability and reduced exposure to tail risk.

Although many asset managers and investors now consider ESG factors, they face several drawbacks. Currently, no standard regulation exists for environmental and social disclosures, and an auditing process is unavailable to verify the data. A logical size bias also exists in which higher-market-cap companies can invest more in ESG and its disclosures, so they tend to have a higher score compared to mid-size and small businesses. This size bias can partially explain the lower risk (lower cost of capital). A geographical bias also exists in which regulatory reporting requirements of each region can influence the ESG score. Some inconsistencies also occur among rating agencies. ESG funds tend to have higher fees that decrease investor returns. Despite the challenges to ESG ratings and standardization, ESG strategies are an important topic that investors should incorporate into their decision-making process. Chapter 19 provides more details on socially responsible investing.

SUMMARY AND CONCLUSIONS

This chapter provides an overview of different equity investment strategies. It covers fundamental analysis, technical analysis, quantitative investing, options strategies, and ESG investing. It begins by discussing fundamental analysis in which the investor conducts in-depth financial statements analysis to identify stocks that may generate above-average returns. Several strategies fall under the rubric of fundamental analysis, including value, growth, and income investing. Unlike fundamental analysis, technical analysis does not require any financial statement analysis. Instead, the investor analyzes past market data to predict future prices. In quantitative trading, an investor often uses algorithms that can incorporate information from several different sources including financial statements, trading data, and even alternative sources like social media. The option strategy section describes a mix of options and stock and option-only strategies. ESG has become increasingly popular with asset managers and asset owners.

DISCUSSION QUESTIONS

1. Explain how technical analysis and fundamental analysis differ.
2. Describe how to assess a stock's intrinsic value.
3. Identify some key characteristics of growth stocks.
4. Discuss the basics of income investing using equities.
5. Describe the trend in ESG investing.

REFERENCES

Carrel, Lawrence, and Richard A. Ferri. 2011. "Benefits of ETFs." Available at www.fidelity .com/learning-center/investment-products/etf/benefits-of-etfs.

Damodaran, Aswath. 2012. "Value Investing: Where Is the Beef?" June. Available at https:// aswathdamodaran.blogspot.com/2012/06/value-investing-where-is-beef.html.

Giese, Guido, Linda-Eling Lee, Dimitris Melas, Zoltan Nagy, and Laura Nishikawa. 2019. "Foundations of ESG Investing: How ESG Affects Equity Valuation, Risk and Performance." *Journal of Portfolio Management* 45:5, 1–15.

Graham, Benjamin, and David Dodd. 1996. *Security Analysis: The Classic 1934*. New York, NY: McGraw-Hill Professional Publishing.

Hill, Joanne M., Dave Nadiq, and Matt Hougan. 2015. *A Comprehensive Guide to Exchange-Traded Funds (ETFs)*. Charlottesville, VA: CFA Institute Research Foundation.

Longo, John M. 2016. *The Art of Investing: Lessons from History's Greatest Traders*. Chantilly, VA: The Teaching Company.

Munger, T. Charles 2014. "Berkshire Hathaway Letter to Shareholders." Available at http:// www.berkshirehathaway.com/letters/2014ltr.pdf.

Murphy, John J. 1999. *Technical Analysis of the Financials Markets*. New York, NY: New York Institute of Finance.

Porter, Michael E. 1979. "How Competitive Forces Shape Strategy." *Harvard Business Review* 57:2, 137–145.

Principles for Responsible Investment (PRI). 2019. "About the PRI." Available at https://www .unpri.org/pri/about-the-pri.

Rabener, Nicolas. 2019. "GARP Investing: Golden or Garbage?" *CFA Institute Enterprising Investor*. August 19. Available at blogs.cfainstitute.org/investor/2019/03/11/garp-investing-golden-or-garbage/.

Smietana, Frank. 2019. "What Are the Different Types of Quant Funds?" Available at https:// www.quantstart.com/articles/what-are-the-different-types-of-quant-funds.

Tidd, Diana, and Raman Aylur Subramanian. 2019. "ESG Is Here to Stay." February. Available at https://www.msci.com/www/blog-posts/esg-investing-is-here-to-stay/01251377498.

CHAPTER 16

Factor Investing

Aaron Filbeck, CFA, CAIA, CIPM
Associate Director of Content Development,
CAIA Association

INTRODUCTION

This chapter is an overview of factor investing. A *factor* is a measurement of systematic risk used to explain returns for most diversified portfolios. Although not new to the academic literature, factor investing has become popular in mainstream practice to target specific risk drivers and expected returns.

Many traditional active managers are directly or indirectly factor investors through their stock selection. By simply isolating the underlying factors in an active manager's portfolio, investors can often partially or fully explain that manager's performance. Thus, factors are a useful tool for active management benchmarking and/or full replication.

This chapter has three major sections. The first section offers a brief history of factor investing, starting with the capital asset pricing model (CAPM), which is a single-factor model. The second section provides a more in-depth look at some other most prominent factors besides the market, including value, size, and momentum, as well as some more recent discoveries such as low volatility and quality/profitability. The third section introduces some portfolio management considerations in practice, including multi-factor portfolio construction and active management benchmarking.

Other chapters in this book explore additional investment strategies such as fundamental active and quantitative equity investing. This chapter notes the relation between the fundamental active manager's intuition and the quantitative manager's implementation. A factor investment strategy attempts to use the best of both worlds by identifying long-term pervasive drivers of stock returns while systematically constructing a portfolio to gain exposure to those drivers. By doing so, a factor investor may lower turnover and transaction costs, while also avoiding potential mistakes due to emotional or cognitive biases.

HISTORY

Before the CAPM, market participants often believed that stock-picking ability completely drove a portfolio manager's performance. Market participants measured performance on an absolute basis, rather than relative to a broad index, and the idiosyncratic risk was the primary driver of this performance. Then, in 1964, William Sharpe introduced the concept of systematic risk, incorporated in a model known as the CAPM (Sharpe 1964). This model changed how market participants measure investment performance.

The CAPM measures a stock's sensitivity to systematic (nondiversifiable) risk, known as the stock's *beta*, and uses it to project future returns relative to a broadly diversified market index, which has a beta of 1.0. For example, if a stock has a beta of 1.5 relative to a broad index, an investor should expect the stock's future performance to equal 150 percent of that broad index. If another stock has a beta of 0.8, the investor should expect the stock's future performance to equal 80 percent of that broad index. The model assumes that beta is the only systematic driver of performance, which is unrealistic.

The market excess return in CAPM is the original equity factor, introducing a concept known as the *market risk premium* or the *market factor*. The idea behind this factor is that if investors buy stocks over a long period, they should be compensated for taking on the risk of owning equities relative to a riskless asset, such as a 3-month Treasury bill. Additionally, the model states that investors should be rewarded only for taking on systematic risk, as idiosyncratic or diversifiable risk is not rewarded because it can be diversified away. Although stock selection is unlikely to add value over the long term, investors can increase or decrease their expected return by investing in higher or lower beta portfolios.

For years, many academics and practitioners accepted the CAPM as the explanation of returns. Researchers regressed long-only active and passive portfolios that "the market" typically proxied using a market capitalization-weighted index such as the S&P 500 index. According to prevailing theory, a portfolio's "market beta" could almost entirely explain a portfolio's over- or underperformance.

Although the CAPM is simple to understand and easy to implement, academics and practitioners criticized it mainly because of its unrealistic assumptions. For example, the CAPM assumes that all investors have access to the same information and are entirely rational when, in practice, some market participants may have access to better information and others are subject to behavioral biases. The CAPM also assumes that risk is static. In other words, betas remain constant and returns are normally distributed. However, over time, empirical researchers began to find "alternative betas" that account for flaws in the CAPM and help to better explain performance.

According to Fama and French (1992), two factors besides the market (beta) help to explain the divergences in diversified portfolio performance. By combining the already existing market factor (i.e., the CAPM), stocks with a high book value of equity to the market value of equity (book-to-market) ratios, and stocks with smaller capitalizations, Fama and French could explain about 90 percent of performance dispersion across diversified portfolios. By contrast, the CAPM could only explain roughly 70 percent.

Jegadeesh and Titman (1993) investigate stocks with recent 12-month performance minus the most recent month. By buying recent winners and shorting recent losers, they discover the existence of a premium, which became known as the *momentum factor*. Carhart (1997) confirmed this finding, and market participants began incorporating the momentum factor into a four-factor model. Incorporating momentum into a portfolio introduced the idea that "buy high, sell higher" was a viable investment strategy. This premise was counter to the value premium, which is captured by going long on cheap companies and shorting expensive ones. The combination of value and momentum could help a portfolio avoid value traps (cheap stocks that only get cheaper) and bubble-like stocks (extremely expensive stocks with unjustifiable valuations).

These discoveries affected how practitioners measure performance. In terms of regression analysis, systematic beta exposures were the explanatory variables, while alpha was the error term or unexplanatory variable. As researchers discovered more explanatory variables (systematic risks), the error term continued to shrink. This finding proposed a controversial idea that traditional, long-only active equity managers were mainly free-loading on these "alternative betas" rather than generating alpha using their skills and insights. This relation between alpha and beta over time can be stylized, as shown in Figure 16.1.

Before the CAPM, many believed that 100 percent of performance resulted from manager skill, essentially measuring performance on an absolute basis or relative to that of peers. For example, a manager's 10 percent total return was 10 percent alpha. With the introduction of the CAPM, academics discovered that managers earned a large portion of that alpha just by being invested in stocks. For example, investors believed that a 10 percent total return meant that 7 percentage points could be explained by the market beta and 3 percentage points by alpha. This discovery was not an unrealistic proposition for active managers because they were still adding

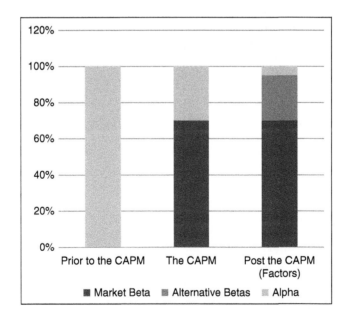

FIGURE 16.1 The Evolution of Alpha

This figure illustrates the decomposition of a portfolio's performance over different time periods. As more research identified risk premia, a larger piece of the portfolio's returns could be attributable to these premia. As a result, assumed alpha went from 100 percent of returns to a small fraction of returns.

Source: Author's calculations.

value that differentiated themselves from the broader market. However, the introduction of additional factors, such as value, size, and momentum, took an even bigger slice of perceived alpha. A combination of the CAPM market beta and other systematic factors could explain greater than 90 percent of the return. This fact meant that a 10 percent total return could be broken down in the following manner: 7.0 percentage points by the market beta, 2.0 to 2.5 percentage points by other factor betas, and 0.5 to 1.0 percentage points being unexplainable.

FACTORS OF PROMINENCE

This section describes some prominent factors, including value, size, momentum, low volatility, and profitability. This list covers only selective factors because researchers have identified several hundred others. However, these factors tend to be robust because they have been observed over multiple market and economic cycles. After defining each factor, a risk-based explanation or a behavioral-based explanation follows.

Value

Fama and French (1992) first incorporated the value factor into their three-factor model. Value can best be described as the tendency for relatively cheap stocks to outperform relatively expensive stocks. The term *cheap* refers to a stock's relative value. Fama and French define a company's relative cheapness by comparing its market value of equity to the book value of equity on its balance sheet. Over time, they discovered that stocks with low market-to-book value of equity ratios outperformed those stocks with the high market-to-book value of equity ratios.

In practice, factor investors have also used other measures of value. Although the concept is similar to that proposed by Fama and French, an investor can measure a stock's relative cheapness by comparing its market price to other fundamental values. For example, an investor might use a stock's price-to-earnings (P/E), price-to-free-cash flow (P/CF), or dividend yield (D/P) ratio. Taking this concept a step further, an investor might even combine multiple ratios or apply different ratios to different sectors.

A risk-based explanation for value contends that value companies are riskier than core or growth companies. Thus, the market prices of these companies with low relative valuations reflect this risk. Companies with relatively low valuations could be under financial distress or experiencing cyclical or secular disruption, leading market participants to bid down their stock prices to reflect this risk. Therefore, an investor who holds these stocks should earn a higher return if the prospect for these companies improves. The investor earns a higher return than the broader market because these companies are riskier than the broader market.

Behavioral finance proponents such as Lakonishok, Schleifer, and Vishny (1994) and Piotroski and So (2012) believe that the value premium results from investor forecasting errors. When forecasting a company's growth prospects, analysts often extrapolate past performance into the future. Since many value companies have suffered recent drawdowns in the market, analysts tend to expect this pattern to continue in the future, meaning market participants sell and price the stock accordingly. By taking the other side of this trade, called a contrarian position, the holder of a value stock would earn a risk premium if and when analysts recognize they have made this mistake.

Table 16.1 shows the value premium (high book-to-market minus low book-to-market) returned 4.29 percent between January 1, 1927, and June 30, 2019. In other words, cheap stocks outperformed expensive stocks by an annualized rate of 4.29 percent. The value premium (HML) was negative over a rolling 1-, 3-, 5-, 10-, and 15-year period. Measuring a 20-year rolling return, the premium is positive. *HML* stands for "high minus low" and refers to the returns of high book-to-market stocks minus those of low book-to-market stocks. This information represents a snapshot in time, and recent performance can influence rolling returns. In the most recent decade, the value premium experienced some of its worst drawdowns in history.

Table 16.2 displays the annual returns for value since 2000, displaying more clearly the cyclicality of the value factor over time. Since the financial crisis of 2007–2008, value (HML) as a factor has struggled. Notice, however, its precrisis performance. This cyclicality is not new to the value factor, and these painful drawdowns are what make factor-based investing work. By taking the other side of the trade and bearing the risk for it, investors are likely to experience periods of poor performance.

TABLE 16.1 Value Premium Performance as of June 30, 2019

This table shows that as of June 30, 2019, the value premium (HML) was negative over a rolling 1-, 3-, 5-, 10-, and 15-year period. However, over a 20-year rolling return, the premium was positive. It takes a 20-year rolling period to produce a positive premium return. However, longer-term performance has produced a premium return of 4.29 percent.

Performance Period	Value (%)
1 year	−11.95
3 years	−4.77
5 years	−5.23
10 years	−1.62
15 years	−1.00
20 years	1.39
Since 1927	4.29

Source: Publicly available at Kenneth R. French's Data Library at http://mba.tuck.dartmouth.edu/pages/faculty/ken .french/data_library.html.

TABLE 16.2 Annual Value (HML) Factor
Returns Between 2000 and 2018

This table shows that since the financial crisis
of 2007–2008, value (HML) as a factor has
struggled despite superior pre-crisis
performance.

Year	Value Premium Return (%)
2000	39.74
2001	19.48
2002	7.46
2003	5.33
2004	8.07
2005	8.31
2006	14.10
2007	−14.69
2008	0.81
2009	−9.16
2010	−5.30
2011	−8.45
2012	9.73
2013	1.50
2014	−1.64
2015	−9.61
2016	22.89
2017	−13.86
2018	−9.40

Source: Publicly available at Kenneth R.
French's Data Library at http://mba.tuck
.dartmouth.edu/pages/faculty/ken.french/
data_library.html.

Size

Banz (1981) observes the size premium, showing that smaller firms tend to have
higher returns than larger firms after controlling for market risk. Fama and French
(1992) also include the size premium in their three-factor model. The size premium
is often stylized as small minus big (SMB).

Several potential explanations exist for the size premium. Many smaller companies are in earlier stages of their life cycle compared to larger companies, meaning
they carry a higher level of business risk. Additionally, these companies may have
greater financial leverage and be more sensitive to economic growth and activity.

Kim and Burnie (2002) find that small companies tend to grow faster than larger companies during economic expansions but contract more than large companies in economic contractions, sometimes ending in bankruptcy. An investor bearing this risk earns a size risk premium.

From a structural standpoint, small-cap stocks have historically been less liquid than large-cap stocks, suggesting investors could earn a slight illiquidity premium for holding them. However, more recently, this argument appears to only apply to microcap stocks, defined by the Securities and Exchange Commission (SEC) as stocks with market capitalizations of $50 million to $300 million, suggesting a size premium may exist within the smallest part of the small-cap universe (Fama and French 2008).

Some detractors question the size premium. One reason for this resistance is that the return profile for the size premium is "lumpy," meaning the premium does not pay off for extended periods. For example, Alquist, Israel, and Moskowitz (2018) maintain that the size premium may have declined since its discovery. When the authors measure SMB, the return premium essentially remains flat after the 1980s. Furthermore, Fama and French (2012) find that a size premium did not exist when measured from 1990 to 2010, a 20-year time horizon.

Table 16.3 shows that between January 1, 1927, and June 30, 2019, the size premium (SMB) was 2.50 percentage points per year, indicating that small stocks outperformed large stocks by an annualized rate of 2.50 percentage points. Similar to value, the size premium has not experienced high returns in recent periods. As of June 30, 2019, the size premium (SMB) was negative over a rolling 1-, 3-, 5-year period, generating slightly positive returns over a 10- and 15-year rolling period. When measuring a 20-year rolling return, the premium was positive. These findings represent a snapshot in time, and recent performance can influence rolling returns.

TABLE 16.3   Size Premium Performance

This table shows that as of June 30, 2019, the size premium (SMB) was negative over a rolling 1-, 3-, 5-year period, slightly positive returns over a 10- and 15-year rolling period, and positive over a 20-year rolling return.

Performance Period	Size (%)
1 year	−12.01
3 years	−0.08
5 years	−1.54
10 years	0.43
15 years	0.65
20 years	3.48
Since 1927	2.50

Source: Publicly available at Kenneth R. French's Data Library at http://mba.tuck.dartmouth.edu/pages/faculty/ken.french/data_library.html.

In the most recent decade, the size premium has not performed as well as long-term performance suggests.

Table 16.4 displays the annual returns for value since 2000. The size factor returns have varied year by year, with recent annual performance being negative. Similar to the value factor's performance, the size factor has suffered more recently, due to large and relatively expensive stocks outperforming small and relatively cheap stocks.

The argument for and against the size premium is likely to persist. The size premium could be experiencing a cyclical downturn, similar to value, or other factors

TABLE 16.4   Annual Size Premium Performance Between 2000 and 2018

This table shows the annual returns of the size premium between 2000 and 2019. It shows that the performance of this premium has not produced consistent returns from year to year. Additionally, the table shows that since the financial crisis of 2007–2008, the size premium has only occasionally enhanced returns.

Year	Size Premium Return (%)
2000	−1.56
2001	18.08
2002	4.71
2003	26.17
2004	4.90
2005	−1.96
2006	0.24
2007	−7.18
2008	3.20
2009	9.23
2010	13.8
2011	−6.01
2012	−1.15
2013	7.27
2014	−8.08
2015	−4.05
2016	6.60
2017	−4.77
2018	−3.31

Source: Publicly available at Kenneth R. French's Data Library at http://mba.tuck.dartmouth.edu/pages/faculty/ken .french/data_library.html.

could be at play. Unlike the value premium, which is measured on a relative cheapness scale, the size premium compares big companies with small companies. As capital markets have evolved and matured, today's "small" companies are probably not comparable to "small" companies 30 years ago.

Momentum

Momentum is the tendency for assets exhibiting relatively good or poor performance to continue to demonstrate good or poor performance. As previously noted, Jegadeesh and Titman (1993) first observed this anomaly and Carhart (1997) incorporated momentum into the Fama-French three-factor model. Momentum is typically defined as the last 12 months of returns, excluding the most recent month, and is usually stylized as "up minus down" (UMD). Momentum is different from a trend: the former is cross-sectional whereas the latter is a time series. In other words, momentum is a relative measure, similar to value, in that it measures relative winners and losers.

Behavioral-based theorists appear to support momentum for two reasons: anchoring bias and the "herd mentality." Proponents of anchoring bias, such as Moskowitz (2010) and Da, Gurun, and Warachka (2014), claim that market participants tend to underreact to gradual changes in information, such as earnings or company news, resulting in market prices not fully reflecting new information. Da et al. use the analogy of a "frog in the pan." The phrase comes from the idea that a frog placed in a hot cooking pan will immediately jump out of it but will not react to being placed in a pan where the temperature is gradually increased until it is too late.

Let us compare two hypothetical stocks. The first stock had an excellent earnings quarter, beating market expectations by a wide margin; the second stock marginally beat earnings expectations, but has consistently done so for the previous four quarters. In an informationally efficient market, in which market participants are fully rational, both stocks would immediately move to their respective equilibrium prices. However, Da et al. (2014) imply that this may only happen for the first stock because its news is exciting and is likely to attract considerable analyst and media coverage. The other stock is less attractive to media pundits and analysts and, over the next several months, slowly moves to its equilibrium price. The second stock is an example of a successful momentum trade.

Proponents of the "herding mentality," such as Hurst, Ooi, and Pedersen (2013), claim that momentum works because investors experience a fear of missing out (FOMO) on future gains. Look no further than the late 1990s when investors eagerly bought technology stocks. Even though many of these companies were unprofitable and lacked viability, investors bought them. Between January 1, 1927, and June 30, 2019, the momentum premium returned 7.86 percent, meaning that recent winners outperformed recent losers by an annualized rate of 7.86 percent.

Unlike the value and size premia, momentum has experienced a strong near-term performance, as evidenced in Table 16.5. As of June 30, 2019, the momentum period generated a positive return over a rolling 1-, 3-, 5-, 10-, 15-, and 20-year period. Although this finding is encouraging, momentum experienced some extreme drawdowns over this period, such as in 2009 and 2016, when the premium experienced a −82 percent and −20 percent drawdown, respectively. Figure 16.2 displays the annual returns for momentum since 2000.

TABLE 16.5   Momentum Premium Performance

This table shows that as of June 30, 2019, momentum
generated a positive return over a rolling 3-, 5-, 10-, 15-, and
20-year period.

Performance Period	Momentum (%)
1 year	−0.83
3 years	0.28
5 years	3.42
10 years	2.19
15 years	1.28
20 years	4.03
Since 1927	7.86

Source: Publicly available at Kenneth R. French's Data
Library at http://mba.tuck.dartmouth.edu/pages/faculty/ken
.french/data_library.html.

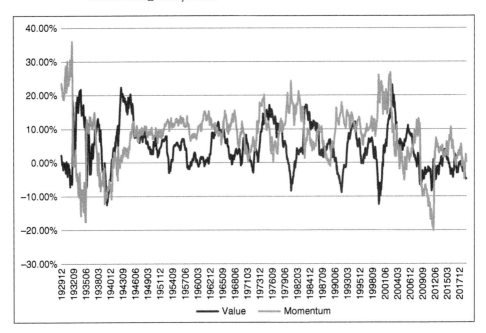

FIGURE 16.2   Rolling Three-Year Returns of Value and Momentum between 1927 and June
30, 2019

This figure illustrates the rolling three-year returns of the value and momentum factors since
1927. The figure shows how value and momentum have historically worked over different
periods, even though both have produced positive premia returns.

Source: Publicly available at Kenneth R. French's Data Library at http://mba.tuck.dartmouth
.edu/pages/faculty/ken.french/data_library.html and author's calculations.

TABLE 16.6   Annual Momentum Premium Performance
Between 2000 and 2018

This table shows the annual returns of the momentum
premium, indicating that momentum produced attractive
returns pre- and post-crisis with a few exceptions associated
with substantial market drawdowns.

Year	Momentum Premium Return (%)
2000	15.40
2001	4.31
2002	25.63
2003	−24.5
2004	−0.44
2005	14.87
2006	−7.80
2007	21.65
2008	13.17
2009	−82.23
2010	6.00
2011	7.37
2012	1.39
2013	7.88
2014	1.65
2015	20.70
2016	−20.38
2017	5.01
2018	9.28

Source: Publicly available at Kenneth R. French's Data
Library at http://mba.tuck.dartmouth.edu/pages/faculty/ken
.french/data_library.html.

Table 16.6 shows the performance of the momentum factor. Annual performance
figures show that momentum generated positive performance in most calendar years,
but tends to suffer sharp drawdowns in other years, such as 2000, 2007, and 2016.

RECENT FACTOR DISCOVERIES

Although researchers have identified hundreds of observed factors in equity markets, value, size, and momentum are well-documented factor premia that have been
repeatedly tested. Over time, academics have claimed to observe other factor premia,

but many of these are unexploitable in practice or are quickly arbitraged away. This section focuses on two recent factor premia that have come to the forefront of the academic literature: low volatility and profitability (i.e., quality).

Low Volatility

Ang, Hodrick, Xing, and Zhang (2006) find that companies with stock prices exhibiting lower volatility outperform companies with high-volatility stock prices. This phenomenon became known as the *low-volatility factor*, in which an investor buys the stocks with the lowest volatility and shorts those with the highest volatility. This concept is counterintuitive to most economic theories stipulating that assets with high systematic risks should be rewarded with high expected returns.

The risk-based argument for low-volatility stocks outperforming high-volatility stocks is that high-volatility stocks reflect higher economic, operational, or business risk. In other words, stocks that may experience higher variations in their underlying earnings or cash flows may have a higher risk of suffering permanent losses. In fact, contrary to research in support of this factor, Fama and French (2016) contend that the low-volatility factor can be explained by incorporating other previously discovered factors into a multi-factor model. In their five-factor model, which includes market, value, size, profitability, and investment (which measures the relative aggressiveness of a firm's capital expenditures), they find that low-volatility stocks tend to behave similarly to companies with high profitability and low investment. In other words, companies that maintain high levels of profitability and operate their businesses conservatively tend to outperform those with low levels of profitability but operate their businesses aggressively.

Another argument for the low-volatility factor is structural. Many large institutions are either subject to leverage constraints or are unwilling to take on leverage in their portfolios for various reasons. Nonetheless, many institutions have high return targets, forcing them to take on additional risk in their equity portfolios. This relation means they are more prone to buying high-beta/volatility stocks for the possibility of achieving their return targets, while altogether avoiding low-beta/volatility stocks, pushing down their valuations. Therefore, an investor who buys low-volatility stocks has the opportunity to earn a risk premium.

Preston (2019) finds that lower-volatility stocks outperformed a traditional capitalization-weighted index, using the S&P 500 Low Volatility Index and the S&P 500 Total Return Index as proxies, respectively. Table 16.7 details the results of this study.

Using these data, volatility stocks have historically outperformed traditional cap-weighted stocks since 1972. The more recent performance also supports this conclusion despite a shrinking premium, which Table 16.8 details using annualized returns.

What is interesting about this premium is its risk-adjusted nature. Low-volatility stocks have historically outperformed high-volatility stocks on both an absolute and risk-adjusted basis. Even given a shrinking premium, that relation has remained. If a low-volatility investor were to invest today, and the premium went to zero and matched the market's returns, that investor would likely still experience a better risk-adjusted experience.

TABLE 16.7 Monthly Performance of Low-Volatility Stocks Between 1972 and 2019

This table shows the returns of low-volatility stocks between 1972 and May 2019. It also shows the up and down capture of low-volatility stocks relative to the S&P 500 Total Return Index, and the beta of low-volatility stocks to the S&P 500 Total Return Index.

	February 1972 to May 2019	
	S&P 500 Low Volatility Index (%)	S&P 500 Total Return Index (%)
Average return (monthly)	1.03	0.92
Average return (up)	2.73	3.42
Average return (down)	−1.85	−3.33
Upside capture	79.82	100.00
Downside capture	55.49	100.00
Beta	0.68	1.00

Source: S&P Dow Jones Indices.

TABLE 16.8 Annual Performance of Low-Volatility Stocks Between 1972 and 1990 and 1990 and 2019

This table displays how the relative performance of the S&P 500 Low Volatility Index versus the S&P 500 Total Return Index has changed over time. Since 1990, low-volatility stocks still have outperformed with less risk, but the magnitude of outperformance has shrunk.

	February 1972–November 1990			December 1990–May 2019		
	Annualized Return (%)	Risk (%)	Return to Risk	Annualized Return (%)	Risk (%)	Return to Risk
S&P 500	10.72	16.39	0.65	10.08	14.12	0.71
S&P 500 Low Volatility	14.00	14.25	0.98	11.16	10.84	1.03

Source: S&P Dow Jones Indices.

Profitability (Quality)

The profitability factor is the tendency for more profitable firms, a measure of company quality, to do better than less profitable firms. The term *profitability* has often been used interchangeably with the term *quality*. Fama and French (2006) investigate the impact of company profitability on stock returns and discover that highly profitable companies have higher subsequent returns after controlling for other factors such as value.

Novy-Marx's (2013) looks at profitability in a different way. He finds that firms with high gross profits-to-assets ratios outperform firms with low gross profits-to-assets ratios. However, highly profitable firms tend to have higher valuations and tend to be growth stocks. Additional research into quality and profitability looks at management decision-making. For example, Titman, Wei, and Xie (2004)

TABLE 16.9 Factor Spreads for Quality/Profitability

This table shows the return differences between companies with different quality screens. "Top" refers to the highest-quality companies while "Bottom" refers to the lowest-quality companies. The difference is the "spread" to which high-quality companies have outperformed low-quality companies.

	Russell 1000 (1980–2018)			MSCI World ex US (1997–2018)		
	Top (%)	Bottom (%)	Difference (%)	Top (%)	Bottom (%)	Difference (%)
ROE	15.50	13.30	2.20	7.90	7.40	0.50
ROE variability	14.50	14.90	−0.40	7.10	8.70	−1.60
ROIC	15.50	13.60	1.90	8.10	7.60	0.50
Gross profitability	16.50	12.20	4.30	8.60	7.30	1.30

Source: Northern Trust Asset Management.

find that companies participating in "empire building" (i.e., making nonstrategic acquisitions) underperform companies that are less aggressive in their expansionary efforts.

The explanation for the profitability premium has support from risk-based and behavioral-based academics. From a risk-based perspective, Lam, Wang, and Wei (2016) find that a partial explanation of this premium is the fact that many profitability measures lend themselves favorably to growth firms. This relation occurs because most profitability ratios favor companies that are less capital-intensive, whereas value firms tend to be more capital-intensive. Yet, growth firms are subject to expected cash flows being further out in the future relative to value firms. An investor who purchases a firm with high profitability metrics bears the uncertainty of these cash flows. From a behavioral standpoint, many investors underappreciate high quality and sustainable earnings and are attracted to low quality and unsustainable earnings (Perotti and Wagenofer 2014).

Performance for quality/profitability may vary depending on the definition. In fact, in a white paper from Northern Trust Asset Management (2016), the firm's engineered equity team analyzes the performance of various definitions across some of the largest factor managers and find a wide dispersion. Additionally, Hundstad and Lehner (2019) examine market-neutral returns of various quality and profitability metrics, which are detailed in Table 16.9. Over this period, most of the quality/profitability metrics generated a positive spread. Still, performance depends on the definition.

PORTFOLIO IMPLEMENTATION CONSIDERATIONS

Chapter 17 provides a discussion of the evolution of factor-based application strategies, known as "smart betas." This section examines multiple considerations investors should contemplate when either measuring factor premia or trying to implement factor premia strategies in a portfolio.

Factor Definitions

One of the trickiest starting points when creating a factor portfolio to test and implement is defining the portfolio. For example, Fama and French (1992) define value stocks as publicly traded companies with price-to-book (P/B) ratios in the bottom 30 percent of the sample.

Although some may accept the intuition underlying the notion that "cheap stocks outperform expensive stocks," how research defines "cheap" or "expensive" might differ substantially. For example, "value" could be defined as price-to-earnings (P/E), price-to-cash flow (P/CF), or enterprise value-to-EBITDA (EV/EBITDA), causing premia returns to differ substantially.

Sector or Industry Weights

Another consideration when testing and implementing factor portfolios is how a portfolio manager selects stocks to create a portfolio. Using momentum as an example, does the portfolio manager select the absolute winners within a broad-based index or relative winners and losers when controlling for sectors and industries? The latter approach would allow the portfolio returns to rely solely on stock selection relative to the former approach, in which certain sectors such as long technology and short energy could dominate the long and short portfolios.

Multi-factor Portfolios

Two major approaches are available when creating factor portfolios. The first approach merely recreates a factor portfolio using a single factor, known as a single-factor strategy. This approach provides the most targeted exposure to one individual factor but is also highly exposed to the cyclicality of when the individual factor is in favor. The second approach combines multiple factors into a single portfolio. By doing this, a portfolio is exposed to multiple systematically rewarded factor premia but also benefits from diversification among the factors. Remember, other premia should be unable to explain factor premia portfolios, which make them a unique risk driver.

Value and momentum, which are negatively correlated, are an excellent example of a multi-factor diversification benefit. This relation should make intuitive sense because value stocks tend to be falling, and cheap and momentum stocks tend to be rising and more expensive. That is, these two factors are moving independently of one another. Figure 16.3 displays the return relation between value and momentum and the correlation between the two since 1926. Both use three-year returns on a monthly basis.

As previously noted, the value and momentum premia have generated positive returns over time but have performed well in different periods. Both figures show the association between their performance since 1927, as well as their correlations. Although the correlations shift over time, most of the observations show a negative correlation. In fact, the long-term correlation between value and momentum is −0.41 between January 1, 1927, and June 30, 2019. This example uses U.S. data, but the relation between value and momentum holds up across various markets and asset classes (Asness, Moskowitz, and Pederson 2013). As a result, combining value and momentum can potentially bring substantial diversification benefits to a factor portfolio.

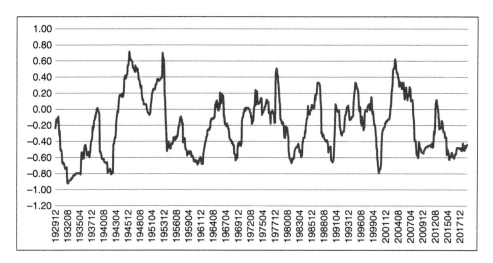

FIGURE 16.3 Rolling Three-Year Correlation Between Value and Momentum: 1927–June 30, 2019

This figure illustrates the rolling three-year returns of the value and momentum factors since 1927. The figure shows how value and momentum have historically worked over different periods, even though both have produced positive premia returns.

Source: Publicly available at Kenneth R. French's Data Library at http://mba.tuck.dartmouth .edu/pages/faculty/ken.french/data_library.html and author's calculations.

Top-down versus Bottom-up Multi-factor Construction

Two main methods are available to create a multi-factor portfolio. The first option is a top-down multi-factor method, which effectively combines two single-factor portfolios to create a portfolio. Using value and momentum as an example, a top-down approach might call for a portfolio of 60 percent value and 40 percent momentum. A multi-factor portfolio would be created by weighing 60 percent of the value portfolio and 40 percent of the momentum portfolio together. A benefit of the top-down approach is that it is simpler to understand and easier to control the factor exposures from an asset-weighting perspective. A major drawback of this approach is that the resulting portfolio suffers from a lack of position netting. Since these portfolios do not interact with one another, one portfolio may be buying a stock that another is selling or shorting, potentially canceling economic exposures and increasing transaction costs.

A second option is a bottom-up approach. Rather than combining two single-factor portfolios, this method starts at the individual stock level. A bottom-up approach would go stock-by-stock and rank each one for every factor in the portfolio using a factor score, which would be totaled using a combined score. In other words, a value and momentum portfolio would rank every stock based on its value and momentum characteristics and choose the stocks with the most attractive weighted-average rankings. A key benefit to this approach is that it solves the issue of a lack of netting from the top-down approach.

Additionally, a bottom-up approach can help limit exposures to extremes such as distressed companies that have become value traps or recent winners with bubble-like valuations. Still, this approach does not necessarily provide the most targeted individual exposure to factor premia because stocks are selected based on a weighted average score. For example, a value momentum portfolio using the bottom-up approach would provide exposure to cheap companies.

From Theory to Practice

Potentially hundreds of premia are available, but these discoveries do not always work in practice. High turnover, illiquidity, taxes, and transaction costs can diminish return premia to a point where they are not viable investment strategies. For example, some assume momentum to be a high turnover strategy in theory, which can prove challenging to implement in practice. In theory, a momentum portfolio may be rebalanced every month or quarter, with position weights changing or being removed altogether. In practice, such rebalancing can increase transaction costs and decrease after-tax returns to the investor due to capital gains taxes.

Another example is the size factor. Especially in smaller and foreign markets, a strategy created to take advantage of a size premium can be challenging to implement due to low levels of illiquidity. This situation is especially true if an investor is trying to create a long/short portfolio to gain pure exposure to the premium. Low liquidity can increase borrowing costs, which can decrease net returns to the investor.

Much of the academic literature accounts for neither real-world costs nor the management fees of fund managers. The next chapter more extensively covers smart-beta strategies, which are a way of applying factor investing.

SUMMARY AND CONCLUSIONS

Despite a recent surge in popularity, factor investing is not a new concept. As the academic literature continues to uncover empirical and theoretical factor premia, it will become increasingly important to ask the following questions as discoveries surface:

1. Is this factor pervasive? In other words, does the factor exist cross-sectionally across equity markets, and does it work during multiple periods and under different economic conditions?
2. Does an economic or behavioral rationale exist for this factor? Decades ago, the notion of economic rationality dominated the literature, but more recently, behavioral finance has become an increased area of study for many academics and practitioners.
3. Is this factor investible? Again, some factor premia may not be implementable due to illiquidity, transaction costs, or management fees substantially decreasing returns.

This chapter has covered the history of equity factor investing and some of the more well-regarded factors, as well as portfolio management considerations investors should contemplate when implementing a factor strategy. Some later chapters examine the history and current state of implementation, such as "smart-beta" strategies.

Finally, factor investing is simply a way of measuring performance and systematically implementing the underlying strategies. Therefore, it is dependent on the investment strategies of market participants, which are subject to change over time and may cause factor premia to be out of favor or disappear altogether.

DISCUSSION QUESTIONS

1. Define the term *factor*.
2. Identify and discuss the four most prominent factors in academic literature.
3. Identify and discuss two distinct arguments for why factor performance is robust over time.
4. Discuss why combining multiple factors into a portfolio can be beneficial to investors.
5. Discuss how and why an investor could use factors to benchmark fundamental active managers.

REFERENCES

Alquist, Ron, Ronen Israel, and Tobias Moskowitz. 2018. "Fact, Fiction, and the Size Effect." *Journal of Portfolio Management* 45:1, 3–31.

Ang, Andrew, Robert Hodrick, Yuhang Xing, and Xiaoyan Zhang. 2006. "The Cross-section of Volatility and Expected Returns." *Journal of Finance* 61:1, 259–299.

Asness, Clifford, Tobias Moskowitz, and Lasse Heje Pedersen. 2013. "Value and Momentum Everywhere." *Journal of Finance* 68:3, 929–985.

Banz, Rolf W. 1981. "The Relationship between Return and Market Value of Common Stocks." *Journal of Financial Economics* 9:1, 3–18.

Carhart, Mark M. 1997. "On Persistence in Mutual Fund Performance." *Journal of Finance* 52:1, 57–82.

Da, Zhi, Umit Gurun, and Mitch Warachka. 2014. "Frog in the Pan: Continuous Information and Momentum." *Review of Financial Studies* 27:7, 2171–2218.

Fama, Eugene F., and Kenneth R. French. 1992. "The Cross-Section of Expected Stock Returns." *Journal of Finance* 47:2. 427–465.

Fama, Eugene F., and Kenneth R. French. 2006. "Profitability, Investment and Average Returns." *Journal of Financial Economics* 82:3, 491–518.

Fama, Eugene F., and Kenneth R. French. 2008. "Dissecting Anomalies." *Journal of Finance* 63:4, 1653–1678.

Fama, Eugene F., and Kenneth R. French. 2012. "Size, Value, and Momentum in International Stock Returns." *Journal of Financial Economics* 105:3, 457–472.

Fama, Eugene F., and Kenneth R. French. 2016. "Dissecting Anomalies with a Five-Factor Model." *Review of Financial Studies* 29:1, 69–103.

Jegadeesh, Narasimhan, and Sheridan Titman. 1993. "Returns to Buying Winners and Selling Losers: Implications for Stock Market Efficiency." *Journal of Finance* 48:1, 65–91.

Hundstad, Michael, and Robert Lehner. "Foundations in Factors." Northern Trust Asset Management White Paper. Available at https://www.northerntrust.com/united-states/insights-research/2019/investment-management/foundations-in-factors.

Hurst, Brian, Yao Hua Ooi, and Lasse Heje Pedersen. 2013. "Demystifying Managed Futures." *Journal of Investment Management* 11:3, 42–58.

Kim, Moon K., and David A. Burnie. 2002. "The Firm Size Effect and the Economic Cycle." *Journal of Financial Research* 25:1, 111–124.

Lam, F. Y. Eric, Shujing Wang, and K. C. John Wei. 2016. "The Profitability Premium: Macroeconomic Risks or Expectation Errors?" Available at https://papers.ssrn.com/sol3/papers.cfm?abstract_id=2479232.

Lakonishok, Josef, Andrei Shleifer, and Robert W. Vishny. 1994. "Contrarian Investment, Extrapolation, and Risk." *Journal of Finance* 49:5, 1541–1578.

Moskowitz, Tobias. 2010. "Explanations for the Momentum Premium." AQR Capital Management White Paper. Available at https://www.aqr.com/Insights/Research/White-Papers/Explanations-for-the-Momentum-Premium.

Novy-Marx, Robert. 2013. "The Other Side of Value: The Gross Profitability Premium." *Journal of Financial Economics* 108:1, 1–28.

Northern Trust Asset Management. 2016. "A Superior Approach to Quality." Northern Trust Asset Management White Paper. Available at https://www.northerntrust.com/documents/white-papers/asset-management/what-is-quality.pdf?bc=25251323.

Perotti, Pietro, and Alfred Wagenhofer. 2014. "Earnings Quality Measures and Excess Returns." *Journal of Business Finance and Accounting* 41:5–6, 545–571.

Piotroski, Joseph D., and Eric C. So. 2012. "Identifying Expectation Errors in Value/Glamour Strategies: A Fundamental Analysis Approach." *Review of Financial Studies* 25:9, 2841–2875.

Preston, Hamish. 2019. "Four Decades of the Low Volatility Factor." S&P Dow Jones Indexology Blog. Available at https://www.indexologyblog.com/2019/06/11/four-decades-of-the-low-volatility-factor/.

Sharpe, William F. 1964. "Capital Asset Prices: A Theory of Market Equilibrium under Conditions of Risk." *Journal of Finance* 19:3, 425–442.

Titman, Sheridan, K. C. John Wei, and Feixue Xie. 2004. "Capital Investments and Stock Returns." *Journal of Financial and Quantitative Analysis* 39:4, 677–700.

Smart Beta Strategies versus Alpha Strategies

Timothy A. Krause
Assistant Professor of Finance,
Penn State Behrend,
Faculty Advisor, Intrieri Family Student Managed Fund

INTRODUCTION

The concept of "smart beta" has attracted increased interest in recent years as investors seek superior investment performance based on a factor investing approach. Chapter 15 discusses the history of factor investing going back decades to the early 1970s to BARRA Advisors (now a part of Morgan Stanley Capital International, MSCI) (MSCI 2019) and in the academic literature provided by Fama and French (1993) and Haugen and Baker (1996, 2010). This phenomenon has now been actualized in the retail investor market for exchange-traded funds (ETFs) with the advent of smart beta ETFs. According to FTSE Russell (2018), global smart beta assets under management (AUM) grew from $280 billion in 2012 to $999 billion in 2017, a compound annual growth rate of 29 percent. Of these assets, 51 percent went to ETFs, with the remainder going to managed accounts and mutual funds. These investments focus on factors related to stock performance and weighting schemes that are not based on market capitalizations, which studies show have provided superior equity market returns historically (Haugen and Baker 1996; Amenc and Goltz 2013; Glushkov 2015; Arnott, Beck, Kalesnik, and West 2016). Smart beta is distinguished from pure factor investing because it is generally a long-only investment approach, while factor investing typically adopts a long/short strategy (Carlson 2018). The first description of such long/short factor investment strategies in the academic literature appears in the factor portfolios of Fama and French (1993), as detailed in Chapter 15. Additionally, factor investing is generally benchmarked to a value-weighted index (Carlson 2018), and this study demonstrates the differences in relative performance that depend on the benchmarking scheme.

Nielson, Nielsen, and Barnes (2016) identify five prevalent factors that can lead to outperforming portfolios: size, value, momentum, quality, and low volatility. Although many possible iterations of factor investing exist, the term *smart beta* has essentially become a marketing term that is applied to investment vehicles, especially ETFs, to attract investor interest (Kirlin 2018). Winther and Steenstrup (2016, p. 85) describe smart beta as "the flavor of the decade in the investment world." In distinguishing factor investing from smart beta, de Martel (2018, p. 1) states "Investors now see 'factor' as the preferred term for the overall philosophy of systematic investing strategies, and terms such as 'smart beta' and 'active quant' as subsidiary product terms." Asness and Liew (2014, p. 1) support this assertion, stating, "Let's be blunt. Smart Beta is mostly re-packaged re-branded quantitative management."

This chapter reviews the academic literature and articles in the financial press on the performance of this relatively new investment paradigm and provides an analysis of the empirical performance of these smart beta ETFs. The study also analyzes return and variance characteristics for similar funds that attempt to provide "smart alpha" between 2009 and 2018, as well as two passive value- and equal-weighted S&P 500 indices. Each of these ETF classes requires "active" management, as opposed to most ETFs, which traditionally track a benchmark index to measure relative performance. According to www.etfdb.com, its database contains 904 smart beta ETFs out of 2,284 ETFs. Moreover, www.etf.com identifies 122 "alpha-seeking" ETFs in their database of 2,276 ETFs.

Broadly, smart beta ETFs fall into one of two subcategories. First, one-factor ETFs (e.g., iShares Russell 1000 Growth ETF and Invesco S&P 500 Low Volatility ETF) focus on a single factor such as value, growth, equal weighting, or low volatility. The other subcategory of smart beta ETFs (e.g., Hartford Multifactor Developed Markets (ex-U.S.) ETF and iShares Edge MSCI Multifactor International ETF) focuses on several factors, such as price-to-book ratio, debt-to-equity ratio, quality, and value. These multi-factor portfolios can be constructed and optimized based on a combination of several factors.

Many articles appear in the popular press and industry publications about smart beta with widely varying opinions. For example, de Martel (2018) concludes that factor investing has historically met or exceeded expectations overall. Regarding the exponential growth in smart beta ETFs, Roy (2016, p. 1) comments that "Factor investing is all the rage today." According to van Gelderen and Huij (2014), mutual funds that adopt factor investing strategies achieve added value for investors. According to Kim (2018), interest in these products may be fading. Kirlin (2018) also discusses the recent decline in investor interest in this sector. As Whyte (2019) notes, 2018 witnessed 49 percent fewer factor-based ETFs being launched as compared to 2017, which is an indicator of potential market saturation. Moreover, Segal (2019) documents that many investment institutions are not receiving the types of returns they anticipated, while also bearing unanticipated risks of currency, country, and sector allocations.

For these reasons, opinions are not universally positive about smart beta strategies. After studying more than 500 research papers, Arnott et al. (2016) conclude that the newly popular smart beta strategies only work because investors bought into the strategy and thus bid up stocks with high exposures to certain factors. Authers (2016) and Hecht and Du (2016) express similar skepticism and question statistical evidence about these strategies, suggesting that historical outperformance cannot continue *ad infinitum* and that historical backtests have produced positive results only due to data mining. John Bogle, one of the founders of the index fund industry, once said that "Smart beta is stupid … " (Jaffe, 2016, p. 1). Finally, Pappas and Dickson (2015) maintain that market-cap-weighted indices are still the best starting point for portfolio construction, contradicting factor-based and smart beta strategies.

Other authors, including Jacobs (2015), O'Shaughnessy (2016), and Winther and Steenstrup (2016), express a preference for smart alpha over smart beta. The number of alpha-seeking ETFs has grown but remains relatively small. These strategies performed poorly during the financial crisis of 2007–2008, losing much interest from institutional investors. However, as Orr (2019, p. 1) notes, they seem to be making a comeback even though these strategies "blew up so frequently during the financial crisis." Such cautionary examples include the Alberta Investment Management Company and the Missouri State Employees' Retirement System.

Quantilia (2019) suggests the concept of "portable alpha," which uses an alpha overlay in conjunction with a smart beta strategy to enhance returns. Parker and Steele (2019) describe portable alpha further as a strategy that allocates a portion of a portfolio to a market index via derivatives and a portion to active managers who attempt to generate alpha that is uncorrelated with the index beta. Clarke, de Silva, and Thorley (2016, p. 9) offer a similar approach to include index futures in combination with individual stock selection, suggesting that long-only factor investing is "not a mean-variance efficient way to capture expected factor returns." Jacobs and Levy (2014) provide a concise analysis of the differences between smart beta and smart alpha strategies. They note that smart beta seeks exposure to factor risks that generate excess returns, while smart alpha focuses on active stock selection and portfolio optimization.

WHAT IS SMART BETA?

Although various definitions of smart beta are available, this chapter defines it as a long-only factor strategy as applied to ETFs. According to Rob Arnott, founder and chairman of Research Affiliates, the London-based consulting firm Towers Watson coined the term *smart beta* in 2007, inspired by fundamental weighting (Carlson 2018). Although Research Affiliates is a pioneer in popularizing these strategies, the retail investment market has not widely used these strategies until recently, with the advent of smart beta ETFs. Alternative names for this general strategy include alternative beta, exotic beta, risk factor, style premia, and risk premia investing. Simply put, smart beta is the implementation of factor investing via ETFs that tilt portfolio weights toward equities that have higher exposures to certain factors that have outperformed historically. It is fundamentally related to the BARRA (now MSCI) factor investing approach and to the seminal academic papers on the topic by Fama and French (1993) and Haugen and Baker (1996, 2010).

Haugen (2010) describes the evolution of finance going from the "old finance" of financial statement analysis through the "modern finance" era of the capital asset pricing model (CAPM), all the way to the "new finance" of quantitative investing that includes factor investing and smart beta. He describes several fundamental mistakes that investors make involving risk, return, and volatility. He also demonstrates how investors can use factor models to mitigate risks and increase expected returns.

Kahn and Lemmon (2015) provide a framework to optimize the blend of smart beta and traditional investment strategies. Hsu, Kalesnik, and Li (2012) provide a concise summary of smart beta strategies that discusses their merits relative to active management and traditional passive index strategies. They present evidence that smart beta strategies result in superior performance relative to traditional capitalization-weighted indexes. Further, Hsu, Kalesnik, and Viswanathan (2015) provide a paradigm to assess the efficacy of equity factors that can be employed in smart beta strategies.

Figure 17.1 shows that investment firms use many style strategies. The most popular strategies, as described in Nielson et al. (2016), are size, value, momentum, quality, and low volatility. Other categories of smart beta strategies are also represented, including fundamental strategies such as revenue weighting, earnings weighting, high-dividend yields, and equal-weighted portfolios.

Fama and French (1993) and Haugen and Baker (1996) provide guidance regarding a specific approach to factor investing. This approach can be implemented using the following paradigm to estimate future returns based on historical data:

1. Measure the regression coefficients for a particular security using factors for a specific sample period.
2. Estimate the risk premium for each factor by forming "high vs. low" portfolios and measuring the difference in average returns.
3. Multiply each of the regression coefficients by its respective risk premium for each factor and add them up to calculate expected returns.
4. Select the securities that have the highest expected returns and Sharpe ratios for the portfolio.

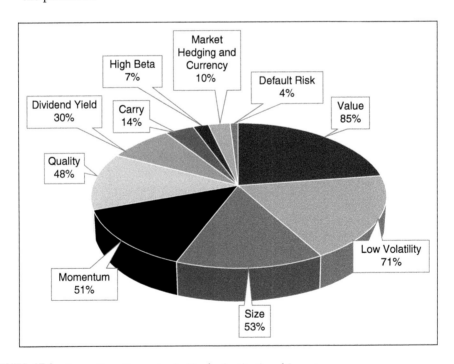

FIGURE 17.1   Smart Beta Strategies in Use by Institutional Investors

This graph shows the most popular factor investing strategies employed by institutional investors. The total percentages do not sum to 100 because a single institution may use multiple strategies. de Martel (2018) provides the data used to create the graph.

An alternative methodology is to measure factor exposures in standard deviations from the cross-sectional mean. Additionally, investors often use *t*-statistics for the regression coefficients to adjust factor weightings.

Various academic papers and books contain further details and refinements to the smart beta factor investing approach. AlMahdi (2015) describes a dynamic approach to portfolio optimization that achieves superior returns in which portfolio managers can adjust factor weightings in an attempt to time the market. Amenc, Ducoulombier, Esakia, Goltz, and Sivsubramanian (2017) document cross-factor interactions that may affect performance based on "top-down" versus "bottom-up" factor analysis. Amenc and Goltz (2013) implement an approach to "smart beta 2.0" that seeks to control the risks of smart beta investing. Bender, Briand, Melas, and Subramanian (2013) identify six equity risk premia factors that contribute to portfolio outperformance but note that factor performance is cyclical. Arnott, Harvey, Kalesnik, and Linnainmaa (2019) provide similar evidence, noting that factor-based portfolios sometimes experience larger than expected downside losses when factors become correlated. Bender, Briand, Melas, Subramanian, and Subramanian (2013) support a three-step approach to factor investing, emphasizing multi-factor index allocations. The three steps in their approach are to:

1. Assess the institution's objectives and constraints – What is the role of factor investing in the institution's overall investment strategy?
2. Select candidate factors – Does the institution believe that the outperformance of each factor is likely to persist over time?
3. Decide how to structure the implementation – What are the proper number and combinations of factors given the institution's objectives and constraints?

Hsu et al. (2015) suggest a comprehensive strategy to implement a framework for implementing a factor-based approach to investing that assesses the persistence of factor outperformance over extended time frames. Blitz (2015, p. 43) provides evidence that "the amount of factor exposure provided by smart beta strategies differs significantly," revealing that these factors are not "as straightforward as one might think." He adds two additional factors – operating profitability and investment – to the Fama-French five-factor model along with an assessment of size, factor timing, and long-short portfolio construction. Fung and Hsieh (2001) offer additional trend-following and credit spread factors that may add value to the analysis. Finally, Philips, Bennyhoff, Kinniry, Schlanger, and Chin (2015) provide a practical guide to evaluating smart beta strategies by assessing the relevance of risk factor exposures.

EMPIRICAL EVIDENCE FROM FACTOR INVESTING AND SMART BETA STUDIES

In their seminal academic study of factor investing spanning 1979 to 1993, Haugen and Baker (1996, p. 401) purport to reveal a major failure in the efficient market hypothesis (EMH), given that "stocks with higher expected returns and realized rates of return are *unambiguously* lower in risk than stocks with lower returns." They also demonstrate that common equity factors determine the expected stock returns. In their comprehensive follow-up study, Haugen and Baker (2010) provide evidence of "risk-loving" in the cross-section of equities and the continued persistence of factor investing outperformance, reflecting a link to the literature on behavioral finance. Chapter 15 provides more information about the link between factor investing and behavioral finance, which provides interpretations of factor outperformance based on behavioral theory. Fama and French (2012) offer more recent evidence that their proposed factors are still useful in building outperforming portfolios of stocks in *global* markets. Additionally, Blitz (2015) reports that the Fama-French factors continue to be relevant for out-of-sample performance, while also examining several further dimensions of factor investing, including factor timing, long-only versus long/short portfolios, international evidence, and factor investing in asset categories outside of equities.

Kim, Kim, and Fabozzi (2017) document that factor models are invaluable in constructing portfolios since risk factors are critical for managing investment risk, emphasizing the importance of robust factor investing models that account for worst-case scenarios. Melas (2016) contends that smart beta strategies are critical for investor success and compares the strategy to current technological improvements in digital devices. Hsu et al. (2012) provide early evidence specific to smart beta investing. Table 17.1 shows data obtained from their study that examines smart beta strategy performance between 1967 and 2010. These strategies could be called "naive" smart beta strategies, since the term smart beta was not in popular use during most of their study. As is evident, the smart beta strategies consistently outperform the S&P 500 Index on an absolute and risk-adjusted basis during this period.

More recent evidence by Hsu (2014) finds that value investing strategies based on smart beta perform better than traditional value style investing. Amenc, Goltz, and Lodh (2016) provide additional support for this assertion, finding that factors other than style and size are essential in assessing investment performance. Angelidis and Tessaromatis (2017) conduct a study of a global allocation strategy that can be implemented using ETFs or index futures. They find significant outperformance relative to the stock-based global factor portfolios of Fama and French (2012) and

TABLE 17.1   Performance of Smart Beta Strategies between 1967 and 2010

This table contains some early results for naive smart beta strategies, given that the term smart beta was not commonly used during this period.

Strategy	Total Return (%)	Volatility (%)	Sharpe Ratio	Relative Return (%)
S&P 500	9.86	15.52	0.28	–
Equal-weighted	11.96	17.81	0.36	2.10
Fundamental index	12.06	15.82	0.41	2.20
Minimum variance	11.61	12.10	0.50	1.75

Source: Hsu, Kalesnik, and Lei (2012).

the world market capitalization portfolio, even after accounting for transaction costs. Hecht and Du (2016) examine the process of backtesting that has been applied to factor investing to demonstrate outperformance. Their results show that data mining can likely taint results from backtests, and their historical outperformance may not be as high as sometimes promoted. Additionally, Hecht and Du point out that some studies show that factor investing provides some outperformance, but investors may soon be able to arbitrage away these factor effects.

Although the theoretical framework of factor investing suggests a long/short strategy, Huij, Lansdorp, Blitz, and van Vliet (2014) offer evidence that a long-only strategy provides superior performance, supporting the assertion that smart beta ETFs offer a valuable service. However, they also note that the increased transaction costs of the long/short strategy may offset any increase in investment performance. Although Ratcliffe, Miranda, and Ang (2017) demonstrate that smart beta may afford superior returns, they also show that factor strategies achieve results that may eventually become attenuated due to increased investor attention and AUM devoted to each factor strategy. However, the authors estimate factor capacity for multiple strategies, concluding that room is still available to grow in this investment space. Staal, Corsi, Shorres, and Woida (2015) extend the factor investing approach to fixed income markets, outlining factors related to the slope of the yield curve and credit spreads, besides the dominant factor of long-term interest rates. They do not conduct an empirical analysis of how these factors relate to performance, but rather suggest that this approach may become more widely used in the future. Podkaminer (2017) shows that this approach can be extended to other asset classes since they share many of the same macro- and style-factor exposures.

Although substantial evidence favors smart beta strategies, a lack of unanimity of opinion exists among academics. Various researchers express skepticism about the prior empirical results as well as the ability of smart beta to produce superior investment results in the future. In his presidential address to the American Finance Association in 2011, Cochrane (2011) describes the proliferation of potential factors in equity investing as a "factor zoo." Several follow-up papers examine this assertion, such as Hsu and Kalesnik (2014, p. 1), who suggest that "the proliferation of factors is deeply troubling." Further, Harvey and Liu (2019, p. 1) conclude that "the academic research is out of control." They provide a comprehensive census of over 400 factors documented in academic studies and propose that many of the positive findings are merely random. Despite this evidence, Mooney (2017) notes that the popularity of these strategies has led to a growth in this sector that approaches $1 trillion in AUM. She also notes several academic papers supporting the efficacy of such strategies.

A series of three 2016 articles co-authored by one of its main progenitors, Rob Arnott, provides perhaps the most convincing evidence against smart beta. Arnott et al. (2016a) document significant outperformance from smart beta strategies in a study of over 500 papers on the topic. However, the authors are unconvinced that the factors themselves drive the performance but may instead result from data mining and rising valuations as investors poured capital into these strategies. According to Arnott et al. (p. 1), "many investors are performance chasers who in pushing prices higher create valuation levels that inflate past performance, reduce potential future performance, and amplify the risk of mean reversion to historical valuation norms. We foresee the reasonable probability of a smart beta crash as a consequence of the soaring popularity of factor-tilt strategies." Arnott et al. (p. 2) assert that "The unsurprising reality is that many of the new factors deliver 'alpha' only because they've grown more expensive." Huang, Song, and Xiang (2019) offer additional support for the opinion that fund flows are largely responsible for the outperformance of factor-based strategies. Krkoska and Schenk-Hoppe (2019) provide further evidence of investor "herding" into these strategies.

Relative to these findings, Arnott, Beck, and Kolesnik (2016a, p. 1) state that "valuation factors are overvalued based on the newly popular factor style of investing" and demonstrate that "almost all of the eight factors and eight smart beta strategies we study exhibit a negative relationship between starting valuation and subsequent five-year performance." In the final article of the series, Arnott, Beck, and Kolesnik (2016b) posit that investors should use only smart beta strategies and factors that appear to be relatively undervalued to form portfolios designed to deliver superior performance.

The assertions of Arnott, Beck, and Kalesnik (2016a, 2016b) and Arnott et al. (2016) do not remain unchallenged. For example, Cliff Asness, the founder of AQR Capital Management, states that his firm takes extensive efforts to minimize the effects of data mining (Institutional Investor 2017). Besides, he claims that the Research Affiliates publications on factor investing contain a "plethora of mostly inapplicable, exaggerated, and poorly designed tests that also flout research norms" (Institutional Investor 2017, p. 1). In a preview of this debate, Asness (2006) states that smart beta or fundamental investing is simply a restatement of value investing that does not benchmark to traditional value-weighted indices. Also, in a follow-up interview, Asness describes smart beta as a "catchy label that can help people get to the right thing" (Ang, Asness, and Bender 2015, p. 4), which supports the previous statements in this chapter that the nomenclature of smart beta is simply a marketing strategy for factor investing. This dispute harkens back to the question of "What is smart beta?" Although Arnott and his colleagues dispute the efficacy of the strategies that they have profitably employed, Asness and Liew (2014) maintain that smart beta is simply a remarketing strategy of fundamental investing strategies that have been successful for many years.

In another critical analysis of smart betas, Glushkov (2015) finds that although 60 percent of smart beta categories outperform their passive benchmarks, no conclusive empirical evidence proves that smart beta ETFs outperform risk-adjusted benchmarks. However, Hsu and Kalesnik (2014) observe that traditional value-based index returns have not been significantly different from the S&P 500 Index, but that fundamentally weighted indices have outperformed the S&P 500 Index by more than two percentage points annually over the 30-year period ending on December 31, 2013. In contrast, the S&P 500 Value Index lagged the S&P 500 Index by 18 basis points annually. They also report superior Sharpe ratios for smart beta strategies.

Still, the argument does not end there. Jacobs (2015, p. 2) states that "In short, smart beta is not a good alternative to active, dynamic, multifactor portfolio management." This view seems to reconcile the arguments of others that the smart beta approach may be valuable, but it cannot be implemented without review, *ad infinitum*. AlMahdi (2015) and Amenc et al. (2016) provide additional support for this opinion. Finally, Malkiel (2004), a chief proponent of the EMH, acknowledges that certain smart beta ETFs have beaten the market during their lifetimes. However, he provides a caveat to this statement by asserting that these funds may have assumed higher levels of risk and supports the notion that smart beta is more of a marketing strategy than an investment strategy.

RECENT EMPIRICAL EVIDENCE FROM THE U.S. ETF MARKET

Thus far, evidence on the performance of smart beta versus alpha strategies has been mixed but mostly positive, despite a relatively robust and continual debate. To provide further evidence, this section discusses a brief empirical study that examines these phenomena in the U.S. ETF market in recent years.

Data

Data for 904 smart beta ETFs are obtained from www.etfdb.com and 122 alpha-seeking ETFs from www.etf.com. For each ETF, monthly returns are obtained from the Center for Research in Securities Prices (CRSP) monthly security file database. For comparative purposes, monthly returns are also obtained for the value-weighted S&P 500 Index ETF (symbol SPY) and the equal-weighted S&P 500 Index ETF (RSP). The data span from January 2009 to December 2018. Table 17.2 contains summary statistics for these ETFs.

As is evident in Table 17.2, many funds are classified as smart beta, even though they may not promote their products using this particular marketing strategy. On average, about 400 smart beta funds are available with usable monthly return observations. The number of observations in the smart beta ETF database dwarfs those of the alpha-seeking ETFs, as well as the S&P 500 Index ETFs. The mean monthly returns for the smart beta ETFs are similar to the value- and equal-weighted S&P 500 Index, albeit slightly higher. The equal-weighted S&P 500 Index, one of the simplest smart beta strategies, outperforms its value-weighted counterpart, which researchers often use as a performance benchmark for diversified portfolios. Performance of the alpha-seeking ETFs lags the others during this period, while an opposite pattern applies when observing the standard deviations of these groups. The following analysis examines whether these differences are statistically significant.

TABLE 17.2 Summary Statistics of ETF Mean Returns between 2009 and 2018

This table provides summary statistics for mean monthly return observations for smart beta ETFs and alpha-seeking ETFs, as well as the S&P 500 value-weighted (SPY) and equal-weighted (RSP) indices. The study period is between January 1, 2009, and December 31, 2018.

	n	Mean	Standard Deviation	Minimum	Maximum
Smart beta	48,889	0.01286	0.05026	−0.0852	1.83916
SPY	120	0.01101	0.03923	−0.1074	0.10915
RSP	120	0.01256	0.04510	−0.1125	0.18692
Alpha-seeking	2,891	0.00394	0.08089	−0.5048	1.82452

Pairwise Comparisons of Mean Returns and Sharpe Ratios

The first step in the analysis is to compare the mean monthly returns of the funds among the funds using pairwise statistical tests of means. Table 17.3 reports the results of this analysis.

The results are presented such that the differences are expressed as the funds in the rows' average monthly returns minus the column funds' average returns. For instance, the difference between smart beta funds' mean returns minus the alpha-seeking funds' mean returns is 0.009, or 0.9 percent, which translates to an annual return difference of 11.35 percent when it is compounded monthly. This finding provides strong statistical evidence of a difference in the returns at the 1 percent level during the sample period. Alternatively, no statistically significant difference exists among the smart beta funds and the two S&P 500 Index ETFs. Further, in the second row of Table 17.3, the alpha-seeking ETFs also underperform the two ETF benchmarks at about the same level, although with slightly lower statistical significance.

To further analyze the data, an analysis of variance (ANOVA) test is conducted and the results appear in Table 17.4.

Strong evidence suggests that the variances of each of the fund categories are not equal. However, the significantly higher standard deviation of the alpha-seeking funds, as first shown in Table 17.2, entirely drives this difference. Additionally, unreported tests among the smart beta ETFs and the two S&P 500 Index funds demonstrate no statistically significant difference in variance. However, statistically significant differences exist between the returns of smart beta ETFs and the alpha-seeking funds.

The final analysis in the study combines the prior results with an examination of the funds' Sharpe ratios. Table 17.5 includes the results of this analysis.

These results include a pairwise comparison of Sharpe ratio means for the funds, which vary slightly from the initial pairwise comparison of return means in Table 17.3. The previously documented outperformance of the smart beta funds is

TABLE 17.3 Pairwise Comparison of Mean Returns

This table presents the results of pairwise comparisons of average means among the different classes of funds in the sample. The results are presented such that the differences are expressed as the funds in the rows' average returns minus the column funds' average returns.

Row minus Column Mean Monthly Return Contrast	Smart Beta	Alpha-Seeking	SPY (Value-Weighted)	RSP (Equal-Weighted)
Smart beta	–	0.009	0.002	0.060
	–	(8.768)***	(0.648)	(0.476)
Alpha-seeking	–	–	−0.007	−0.009
	–	–	(−1.428)*	(−1.742)**
SPY	–	–	–	0.002
	–	–	–	(0.227)

***, **, * indicates statistical significance at the 0.01, 0.05, and 0.10 level, respectively.*

TABLE 17.4 Analysis of Variance (ANOVA) among the Fund Categories

This table provides evidence about the ANOVA among the ETF classes. Although the analysis indicates significant differences in variance, the much higher variance of the alpha-seeking funds drives these results. In unreported results, no statistically significant difference exists in the mean variance of the smart beta funds and SPY or RSP.

Source	Partial SS	df	MS	F-stat	p-value
Model	45.905	4	11.476	4065.16	0.000
Residual	153.173	54,258	0.003		
Total	199.078	54,262	0.004		

TABLE 17.5 Pairwise Comparison of Mean Sharpe Ratios

This table presents the results of pairwise comparisons of average Sharpe ratios among the different classes of funds. The differences are expressed as the funds in the rows' average returns minus the column funds' average returns.

Row minus Column Mean Monthly Sharpe Ratio	Smart Beta>	Alpha-Seeking	SPY (Value-Weighted)	RSP (Equal-Weighted)
Smart beta	–	0.207	−0.025	−0.744
	–	(10.276)***	(−0.398)	(−7.732)***
Alpha-seeking	–	–	−0.232	−0.951
	–	–	(−2.36)***	(−9.70)**
SPY	–	–	–	−0.719
	–	–	–	(−5.29)***

*** and** indicate statistical significance at the 0.01, 0.05, and 0.10 level, respectively

confirmed in the comparison of Sharpe ratios of the alpha-seeking funds at a high level of statistical significance.

Additionally, the second row of Table 17.5 is consistent with the underperformance of the alpha-seeking funds in previous results. The table offers two new pieces of information. First, in the fourth column of the first row, the smart beta ETFs underperform the equal-weighted S&P 500 Index ETF on a risk-adjusted basis. The fourth column in the third row demonstrates that the equal-weighted tracking ETF also outperforms the value-weighted ETF. Naturally, this outperformance is related to the tilt toward smaller-cap stocks when compared to a value-weighted index, and small stocks have traditionally outperformed larger stocks (Fama and French 1993) and may entail a higher level of risk. Therefore, considering this simple strategy may be worthwhile instead of paying the higher fee structure entailed in buying an actively managed smart beta fund. This evidence also suggests that relative performance measures highly depend on the benchmark index that is used.

SUMMARY AND CONCLUSIONS

The smart beta approach to investing has been profitable in the past, but no guarantee exists about future results. As existing fund managers and investors attempt to exploit these inefficiencies, they may disappear. Mean returns for naive factor-based strategies between 1967 and 2010 are significantly higher than those of the value-weighted S&P 500 Index. Although the returns between 2009 and 2018 are not statistically different, they do outperform alpha-seeking strategies on every measure studied in this chapter. Recent returns from smart beta do not differ statistically from those that could be obtained by a simple strategy of investing in a value- or equal-weighted index or ETF, and smart beta underperforms on a risk-adjusted basis relative to the equal-weighted index. This evidence is consistent with the recent empirical findings of Segal (2019) and Harvey et al. (2019). Investors should critically evaluate any claims about future performance because the performance assessment highly depends on the benchmark used and the factors involved in investment process decisions.

DISCUSSION QUESTIONS

1. Distinguish between factor investing and smart beta.
2. Differentiate between smart beta and alpha-seeking strategies.
3. Explain the performance of smart beta strategies between 1967 and 2010 and between 2009 and 2018.
4. Discuss whether the various investment strategies described in this chapter experience similar levels of volatility between 2009 and 2018.

REFERENCES

AlMahdi, Saud. 2015. "Smart Beta Portfolio Optimization." *Journal of Mathematical Finance* 5:2, 202–211.

Amenc, Noël, Frédéric Ducoulombier, Mikheil Esakia, Felix Goltz, and Sivagaminathan Sivasubramanian. 2017. "Accounting for Cross-Factor Interactions in Multifactor Portfolios without Sacrificing Diversification and Risk Control." *Journal of Portfolio Management* 43:5, 99–114.

Amenc, Noël, and Felix Goltz. 2013. "Smart Beta 2.0." *Journal of Index Investing* 4:3, 15–23.

Amenc, Noël, Felix Goltz, and Ashish Lodh. 2016. "Smart Beta Is Not Monkey Business." *Journal of Index Investing* 6:4, 12–29.

Ang, Andrew, Clifford Asness, and Jennifer Bender. 2015. "Practical Applications of Alpha, Beta, and the Blend." *Institutional Investor Smart Beta Special Issue*, November, 1–7.

Angelidis, Timotheos, and Nikolaos Tessaromatis. 2017. "Global Equity Country Allocation: An Application of Factor Investing." *Financial Analysts Journal* 73:4, 55–73.

Arnott, Robert D., Noah Beck, and Vitali Kalesnik. 2016a. "Timing 'Smart Beta' Strategies? Of Course! Buy Low, Sell High!" Working Paper, Research Affiliates.

Arnott, Robert D., Noah Beck, and Vitali Kalesnik. 2016b. "To Win with 'Smart Beta' Ask if the Price Is Right." Working Paper, Research Affiliates.

Arnott, Robert D, Noah Beck, Vitali Kalesnik, and John West. 2016. "How Can 'Smart Beta' Go Horribly Wrong?" Working Paper, Research Affiliates.

Arnott, Robert D, Campbell R. Harvey, Vitali Kalesnik, and Juhani T. Linnainmaa. 2019. "Alice's Adventures in Factorland: Three Blunders That Plague Factor Investing." Working Paper, Research Affiliates.

Asness, Cliff. 2006. "The Value of Fundamental Indexing." *Institutional Investor.* Available at https://www.institutionalinvestor.com/article/b150nsjcm4ph3y/the-value-of-fundamental-indexing.

Asness, Cliff, and John W. Liew. 2014. "Smart Beta: Not New, Not Beta, Still Awesome." *Institutional Investor.* Available at https://www.aqr.com/Insights/Research/Interviews/Smart-Beta-Not-New-Not-Beta-Sill-Awesome-Supplement.

Authers, John. 2016. "Smart Beta Not Quite as Clever as Marketed." *Financial Times,* March 25. Available at https://www.ft.com/content/66c7c616-f234-11e5-aff5-19b4e253664a.

Bender, Jennifer, Remy Briand, Dimitris Melas, and Raman A. Subramanian. 2013a. "Foundations of Factor Investing." Working Paper, MSCI. Available at https://www.msci.com/documents/1296102/1336482/Foundations_of_Factor_Investing.pdf/004e02ad-6f98-4730-90e0-ea14515ff3dc.

Bender, Jennifer, Remy Briand, Dimitris Melas, Raman A. Subramanian, and Mandu Subramanian. 2013. "Deploying Multi-Factor Index Allocations in Institutional Portfolios." Working Paper, MSCI. Available at https://www.msci.com/documents/10199/9c4fd1ca-867d-49cd-baec-2e96510dc204.

Blitz, David. 2015. "Factor Investing Revisited." *Journal of Index Investing* 6:2, 7–17.

Carlson, Debbie. 2018. "Smart Beta vs. Factor Funds: What's the Difference?" Available at https://www.etf.com/sections/features-and-news/smart-beta-vs-factor-funds-whats-difference?nopaging=1.

Clarke, Roger, Harindra de Silva, and Steven Thorley. 2016. "Fundamentals of Efficient Factor Investing" (Corrected May 2017). *Financial Analysts Journal* 72:6, 9–26.

Cochrane, John H. 2011. "Presidential Address: Discount Rates." *Journal of Finance* 66:4, 1047–1108.

de Martel, Vincent. 2018. "Invesco Global Factor Investing Study 2018." White Paper, Invesco. Available at https://www.invesco.com/static/us/investors/contentdetail?contentId=9e57efcb8b1d6610VgnVCM1000006e36b50aRCRD.

Fama, Eugene F., and Kenneth R. French. 1993. "Common Risk Factors in the Returns on Stocks and Bonds." *Journal of Financial Economics* 33:1, 3–56.

Fama, Eugene F., and Kenneth R. French. 2012. "Size, Value, and Momentum in International Stock Returns." *Journal of Financial Economics* 105:3, 457–472.

FTSE Russell. 2018 "Smart Beta: 2018 Survey Findings from US, Canadian, and UK Financial Advisors." Working Paper, FTSE Russell.

Fung, William, and Hsieh, David A. 2015. "The Risk in Hedge Fund Strategies: Theory and Evidence from Trend Followers." *Review of Financial Studies* 14:2, 313–341.

Glushkov, Denys. 2015. "How Smart Are "Smart Beta" ETFs? Analysis of Relative Performance and Factor Exposure." Available at https://papers.ssrn.com/sol3/papers.cfm?abstract_id=2594941.

Harvey, Campbell R., and Yan Liu. 2019. "A Census of the Factor Zoo." Available at https://papers.ssrn.com/sol3/papers.cfm?abstract_id=3341728.

Haugen, Robert A. 2010. *The New Finance: Overreaction, Complexity, and Their Consequences.* Boston, MA: Prentice Hall.

Haugen, Robert A., and Nardin L. Baker. 1996. "Commonality in the Determinants of Expected Stock Returns." *Journal of Financial Economics* 41:3, 401–439.

Haugen, Robert A., and Nardin L. Baker. 2010. "Case Closed." In *Handbook of Portfolio Construction: Contemporary Applications of Markowitz Techniques,* edited by John B. Guerard, 601–620. New York, NY: Springer.

Hecht, Peter, and Zhenduo Du. 2016 "Smart Beta, Alternative Beta, Risk Factor, Style Premia, and Risk Premia Investing: Data-Mining, Arbitraged Away, or Here to Stay?" Working Paper, Evanston Capital Management.

Hsu, Jason C. 2014. "Value Investing: Smart Beta vs. Style Indices." *Journal of Indexes* 5:1, 121–126.

Hsu, Jason, and Vitali Kalesnik. 2014. "Finding Smart Beta in the Factor Zoo." Working Paper, Research Affiliates.

Hsu, Jason, Vatali Kalesnik, and Feifei Li. 2012. "An Investor's Guide to Smart Beta Strategies." *AAII Journal* 12:2012, 11–16.

Hsu, Jason, Vitali Kalesnik, and Vivek Viswanathan. 2015. "A Framework for Assessing Factors and Implementing Smart Beta Strategies." *Journal of Index Investing* 6:1, 89–97.

Huang, Shiyang, Yang Song, and Hong Xiang. 2019. "Fragile Factor Premia." Available at https://papers.ssrn.com/sol3/papers.cfm?abstract_id=3312837.

Huij, Joop, Simon Lansdorp, David Blitz, and Pim van Vliet. 2014. "Factor Investing: Long-Only Versus Long-Short." Available at https://papers.ssrn.com/sol3/papers.cfm?abstract_id=2417221.

Institutional Investor. 2017. "Cliff Asness Blasts Rob Arnott on Factor Timing." Institutional Investor, March 16. Available at https://www.institutionalinvestor.com/article/b1505qjg9dyd03/cliff-asness-blasts-rob-arnott-on-factor-timing#.WO-TSVMrLq0.

Jacobs, Bruce I. 2015. "Is Smart Beta State of the Art?" *Journal of Portfolio Management* 41:5, 1–3.

Jacobs, Bruce I., and Kenneth N. Levy. 2014. "Smart Beta Versus Smart Alpha." *Journal of Portfolio Management* 40:4, 4–7.

Jaffe, Charles. 2016. "Jack Bogle Says 'Smart Beta' Funds Are 'Stupid.'" *Daytona Beach News-Journal*, December 23. Available at https://www.news-journalonline.com/news/20161224/jack-bogle-says-smart-beta-funds-are-stupid.

Kahn, Ronald N., and Michael Lemmon. 2015. "Smart Beta: The Owner's Manual." *Journal of Portfolio Management* 41:2, 76–83.

Kim, Crystal. 2018. ""Smart Beta" ETFs Were All the Rage. Now Some Are Disappearing." *Barron's*, September, 271.

Kim, Jang Ho, Woo Chang Kim, and Frank J. Fabozzi. 2017. "Robust Factor-Based Investing." *Journal of Portfolio Management* 43:5, 157–164.

Kirlin, Ryan. 2018. "Smart Beta Is Officially Dead, but Not Forgotten." September. Available at https://alphaarchitect.com/2018/09/06/what-is-smart-beta/.

Krkoska, Eduard, and Klaus R. Schenk-Hoppé. 2019. "Herding in Smart-Beta Investment Products." *Journal of Risk and Financial Management* 12:1, 1–14.

Malkiel, Burton G. 2014. "Is Smart Beta Really Smart?" *Journal of Portfolio Management* 40:5, 127–134.

Melas, Dimitris. 2016. "Power to the People: The Profound Impact of Factor Investing on Long-Term Portfolio Management." *Journal of Portfolio Management* 42:2, 6.

Mooney, Attracta. 2017. "Smart Beta Funds Stalked by Chaotic 'Factor Zoo.'" *Financial Times*, July 9. Available at https://www.ft.com/content/828ee964-617e-11e7-91a7-502f7ee26895.

Morgan Stanley Capital International (MSCI). 2019. "Elements of Performance: Factors by MSCI." July. Available at https://www.msci.com/factor-investing.

Nielson, Darby, Frank Nielsen, and Bobby Barnes. 2016. "An Overview of Factor Investing." Fidelity Investments. Available at https://www.fidelity.com/bin-public/060_www_fidelity_com/documents/brokerage/overview-factor-investing.pdf.

O'Shaughnessy, Patrick O. 2016. "Alpha or Assets? – Factor Alpha vs. Smart Beta." White Paper, O'Shaughnessy Asset Management. Available at https://www.osam.com/pdfs/research/_23_Commentary_AlphaOrAssets_FactorAlphaVersusSmartBeta_April-2016.pdf.

Orr, Leanna. 2018. "Why Is Portable Alpha Coming Back? Because It's Working." *Institutional Investor*, April 6. Available at https://www.institutionalinvestor.com/article/b17nhz6r4zlgsn/why-is-portable-alpha-coming-back-because-it%E2%80%99s-working.

Pappas, Scott N., and Joel M. Dickson. 2015. "Factor-Based Investing." Vanguard Research. Available at https://personal.vanguard.com/pdf/ISGFBI_042015_Online.pdf.

Parker, Tom, and Shawn Steel. 2019. "Portable Alpha Strategies." White Paper, BlackRock. Available at https://www.blackrock.com/institutions/en-us/insights/portfolio-design/by-the-numbers-portable-alpha-strategies.

Philips, Christopher B., Donald G. Bennyhoff, Francis M. Kinniry Jr., Todd Schlanger, and Paul Chin. 2015. "An Evaluation of Smart Beta and Other Rules-Based Active Strategies." Vanguard. Available at https://personal.vanguard.com/pdf/ISGSBA.pdf.

Podkaminer, Eugen. 2017. "Smart Beta Is the Gateway Drug to Risk Factor Investing." *Journal of Portfolio Management* 43:5, 130–134.

Quantilia. 2019. "Evolution of the Smart Beta Strategy: Is Smart Alpha Next?" Quantilia. Available at https://www.quantilia.com/smart-alpha-strategy/.

Ratcliffe, Ronald, Paolo Miranda, and Andrew Ang. 2017. "Capacity of Smart Beta Strategies: A Transaction Cost Perspective." Working Paper, Columbia Business School.

Roy, Sumit. 2016. "What You Should Know About Factor ETFs." May 25. Available at https://www.etf.com/sections/features-and-news/good-bad-factor-etfs.

Segal, Julie. 2019. "Why Factor Investing Isn't Working" *Institutional Investor*. Available at https://www.institutionalinvestor.com/article/b1flwrdtv24qzp/Why-Factor-Investing-Isn-t-Working.

Staal, Arne, Marco Corsi, Sara Shores, and Chris Woida. "A Factor Approach to Smart Beta Development in Fixed Income." *Journal of Index Investing* 6:1, 98–110.

van Gelderen, Eduard, and Joop Huij. 2014. "Academic Knowledge Dissemination in the Mutual Fund Industry: Can Mutual Funds Successfully Adopt Factor Investing Strategies?" *Journal of Portfolio Management* 40:4, 157–167.

Whyte, Amy. 2019. "Smart Beta Slows Down." *Institutional Investor*. Available at https://www.institutionalinvestor.com/article/b1f3vlr56s67yf/Smart-Beta-Slows-Down.

Winther, Kenneth, and Søren Steenstrup. 2016. "Smart Beta or Smart Alpha?" *Journal of Investing* 25:1, 85–94.

CHAPTER 18

Activist and Impact Investing

Michael Sinodinos
Independent Financial Consultant
Andrew Siwo
Director of Sustainable Investments and Climate Solutions,
New York State Common Retirement Fund
Andrew C. Spieler
Robert F. Dall Distinguished Professor of Business,
Frank G. Zarb School of Business, Hofstra University

INTRODUCTION

This chapter discusses the fundamentals of activist and impact investing. Activism and what is often referred to as socially responsible investing in the United States can trace its roots back to the early 1800s when the Religious Society of Friends, more commonly known as the Quakers, banned investments in slavery, war, and other areas unaligned with their religious values. This action essentially credited the religious organization with arguably making the first socially responsible investment. Specifically, this chapter examines the various techniques used by modern activists and the various outcomes that result from activist campaigns. The motives of activist investors range from gaining board control to changing corporate policy. Activist investors (hereafter "activists") have grown to include public pension funds, hedge funds, and individual "gadfly" investors, reflecting the changing tactics of activists over the past 30 years (Ponomareva 2018).

The landscape for activist investing has experienced dramatic changes since its modest beginnings. Activists attempt to influence management policy and strategy by obtaining board seats or through other methods. Their end goal is to bring about change in the target company. Activists generally believe that the target company has not reached its maximum value and has underperformed due to changeable factors. These reasons often involve inefficient use of corporate assets. Thus, intervention by an agitator can potentially reshape the target as a more efficient and profitable company.

Not surprisingly, management is often unresponsive or annoyed by activist campaigns. Target companies need to have a plan for responding to activists before negative publicity ensues. Management teams should realize that activists generally seek change in areas perceived to be value increasing. Historically, a limitation of activism is the relatively short time frame in which results are sought and expected.

Understandably, management teams of target companies tend to align better with investors whose interests are similar to their own and could conflict with those that may prioritize a single issue that often has no simple solution or a solution that is better achieved through actions that will exhibit longer-term results. For example, cutting costs by laying off lower-wage workers is more likely to generate negative media headlines than laying off highly paid executives.

METHODS OF ACTIVISM

Activists employ several techniques to gain attention and influence policy, often by contacting management privately to communicate concerns. If management is unreceptive, activists may turn to other tactics. For example, activists may submit shareholder proposals through a proxy statement, stage a proxy fight, or publicly shame a company.

Shareholder Proposals

Activists generally use shareholder proposals as their primary tool. A *shareholder proposal* is a formal document submitted by an activist investor to the target company recommending changes. According to SEC Rule 14a-8, a shareholder owning more than $2,000 of a company's stock or 1 percent of outstanding shares can submit a shareholder proposal. Ultimately, a shareholder proposal typically appears on the proxy statement for a shareholder vote if the activist follows corporate policies for timely submission to the corporate secretary. However, the SEC balances the desire for shareholder input and change with the potential interruption of business strategy to install a compromise: shareholder voting is advisory and nonbinding. Therefore, even with a majority vote favoring a shareholder proposal, management can legally ignore the voting result and maintain the status quo.

Public Attacks

The adage that "the pen is mightier than the sword" is appropriate for activists. Some campaigns can become visible to the public when an activist openly criticizes a company it is targeting, such as when Nelson Peltz publicly rebuked DuPont, a corporate giant, in 2015 (Gandel 2015). Another example is the California Public Employees Retirement System (CalPERS), the largest public pension fund in the United States, with $378 billion in assets under management (AUM) as of September 2019 (Jacobius 2019). CalPERS has been historically active in monitoring management and pursuing corporate and social agendas. Since the early 1990s, CalPERS has published a list of the "worst companies," which highlights what it believes to be corporate laggards (Mulligan 1994).

Proxy Fights

A *proxy fight* is a method by which a single shareholder or multiple shareholders target a company via a proxy ballot. By law, shareholders have the right to vote their shares, which is usually one vote per share, unless other provisions exist such as dual-class shares. Shareholders also have the right to transfer their votes via a proxy to a third party. In a proxy fight, the activist solicits other shareholders for collective proxy votes to garner additional board seats. After securing board representation, the shareholders can take an active role in effecting the desired change. The activist bears 100 percent of the cost of the proxy fight but only receives a percentage of any gains proportionate to their ownership stake. The advantage is heavily skewed toward the target firm, since a corporation typically has greater disposable resources to contest a proxy campaign.

Private Negotiation (Jawboning)

Although activists generally desire to negotiate with a target company privately rather than resorting to a public dispute, garnering media attention through a public dispute can be a powerful tool used to bring attention to a specific issue as well as a particular company. For the proxy year 2018, Sawyer, Boehmke, and Ludwig (2019) reported 268 activist campaigns, which is close to the average of the previous five years. However, the number of private negotiations is unknown, as the target's goal is generally to avoid public discussion or disclosure.

INSTITUTIONAL ACTIVISTS

Activists can also be institutions, which play an important role in shaping the activism landscape. These large investors have an economic incentive to expend resources to monitor management and attempt to effectuate value-increasing changes.

Public Pension Funds

Public pension funds are among the largest asset owners in the United States and globally. As of 2019, CalPERS and the New York State Common Retirement Fund have approximately $590 billion in AUM combined (Jacobius 2019; Office of the State Controller 2019). Although large pension funds own considerable positions in publicly traded companies and can engage in shareholder activism, their degree of public activism varies. Between 2006 and 2015, New York City pension funds launched 161 shareholder proposals, while CalPERS sponsored only 13 at large companies. The subject matter of these proposals varies greatly. The issues include employment rights, political spending or lobbying, human rights, the environment, proxy access, and executive compensation. The two most common subjects, comprising 34 percent of proposals, were employment rights and political spending or lobbying. Given the historically activist role of CalPERS, much of the activism is likely to occur behind closed doors (Copeland 2015).

Insurance Companies, Banks, and Mutual Funds

Insurance companies, banks, and mutual funds are asset owners that also engage in activist campaigns. A notable development has risen in shareholder activism from large institutional investors. Institutional investors, such as Vanguard and BlackRock, have grown tremendously from the popularity of passive investing, resulting in massive inflows into exchange-traded funds (ETFs) that track major indexes such as the S&P 500. Vanguard and BlackRock have become the *de facto* largest shareholders of many U.S. companies (DePillis 2019). These institutional investors have little choice but to purchase shares of companies as constituents of major equity indices. The focus on activism has increased dramatically because substantial shareholders have limited ability to "vote with their feet."

Hedge Funds

Hedge funds also have activist investing approaches. Some activist hedge funds include Pershing Square Capital, Trian Partners, and Icahn Enterprises. Several activist investing strategies are available to hedge funds. Examples of popular strategies are as follows:

- *Engage management.* The hedge fund directly communicates changes it believes are necessary to management.
- *Capital structure.* The hedge fund proposes changes to the target company's capital structure, such as retiring debt, selling assets, declaring special dividends, or repurchasing shares.
- *Corporate governance.* The hedge fund attempts to change the target company's management or its board of directors.
- *Business strategy.* The hedge fund pushes for a sale of a non-essential part of the business, merger, or spinoff.
- *Asset sale.* The hedge fund attempts to influence the company to sell off some assets.
- *Block merger.* The hedge fund attempts to block a merger that it views as a bad business decision.
- *Financing and bankruptcy.* The hedge fund provides financing for a company in distress and often takes an active management or operational role.

Ackman-Herbalife Nutrition   Bill Ackman founded Pershing Square Capital, a hedge fund with more than $8 billion in AUM. The fund frequently engages in activist investing campaigns. A notable activist campaign was when Mr. Ackman and Pershing Square Capital targeted Herbalife Nutrition, a global, multi-level marketing corporation that develops, markets, and sells dietary and weight-management supplements, and personal-care products.

In 2012, Ackman took a public stance that Herbalife is nothing more than a pyramid scheme (La Monica 2018). Pershing Square Capital took a $1 billion bet on the company, which was trading around $45 per share at the time of disclosure. Mr. Ackman and Pershing Square took a publicly known short position. Investors who short a stock believe the security is overvalued and likely to revert to its true price. Soon after disclosing his hedge fund's short position, Mr. Ackman engaged in a televised argument with Carl Icahn, another famous activist investor. The two verbally attacked each other; Icahn bet that the stock would rise, and Ackman maintained his view that Herbalife's price would fall. Icahn was one of the largest shareholders of Herbalife at the time of the argument. Mr. Ackman eventually conceded and closed his short position in 2017, losing about $1 billion.

Vulture Funds   Another type of activist investor is a *vulture fund*, which is a fund that buys securities of companies that are experiencing difficulties or on the verge of bankruptcy. Vulture funds seek companies whose share prices are unjustifiably low relative to the firm's intrinsic value. Vulture investors can alter or influence firm policy by their large shareholdings. In contrast, small shareholders must take a "buy and hold" approach in distressed investments. If such investors can identify a company whose shares are trading at a price higher or lower than its intrinsic value, but the rest of the market does not recognize this dynamic, they are unlikely to achieve their goal expediently.

The investment strategy differs when activists focus on the firm's debt. If the debt of a distressed company is trading at a substantial discount, investors should theoretically be able to buy the debt at a low price. If the company can pay interest and principal when the bonds mature, the investor is likely to generate outsized returns.

INDIVIDUAL ACTIVISTS

An *individual activist* is an investor who generally can acquire and influence a company's decisions and activities. Theoretically, those on the *Forbes* list of the wealthiest families or individuals have significant assets to deploy. They also face fewer institutional constraints and are less scrutinized by investing individual or family wealth. Some activists are small shareholders or represent coordinated shareholder efforts due to the ease of proxy access.

High Profile Activists

Some activists like Carl Icahn and the late T. Boone Pickens launched their own highly visible campaigns. Other investors may have much less capital or name recognition, but use the proxy process to their advantage to influence management behavior.

Carl Icahn   Carl Icahn is the founder and controlling shareholder of Icahn Enterprises, which had a market capitalization of about $14.9 billion on June 30, 2019 (Icahn Enterprises 2019). Icahn is one of the best-known individual activist investors. He gained notoriety as a prolific activist investor in the 1980s with the hostile takeover of TWA, a struggling U.S. airline (Grant 2006). Icahn quietly bought 20 percent of the company's stock and then promised that he would reverse the company's fortunes and restore profitability. He then took the company private and sold off most of its prized assets, generating almost $500 million for himself. However, Icahn was unable to fulfill his promise to TWA management. After years of financial difficulties, TWA filed for bankruptcy multiple times before eventually being acquired by American Airlines in 2001. Icahn is known for targeting companies that are inefficiently managing and using resources. He would often air his views in the media to obtain public and then reluctant management support.

T. Boone Pickens   T. Boone Pickens was chairman of hedge fund BP Capital Management and was a strong proponent and supporter of shareholder activism. Pickens specialized in the oil industry and had amassed a personal fortune of $500 million at the time of his death in 2019. Pickens was a firm believer in proper corporate governance, which he believed would unlock value in target companies for shareholders. He often employed the "greenmail" tactic, where BP would quietly acquire a large stake in the target before publicly announcing his ownership stake, and then attempted to negotiate the target company buying back his position at a substantial premium. Pickens also had a strong belief in sustainable energy and advocated for U.S. independence for energy (Butera 2019).

Gadflies

A *gadfly* is a small investor who uses the proxy process. Gadflies draw attention to their cause or disagreement with management by submitting shareholder proposals to be included at annual meetings. They also often ask pointed questions of the management team at the annual meeting.

Gilbert Brothers   Lewis and John Gilbert are relatively unknown in the investing world despite their success as influential investors. The Gilbert brothers are among the earliest activists and of the first investors to urge companies to put women on boards. They began investing in stocks before the Great Depression but did not engage in shareholder activism until the 1930s. The Gilbert brothers boasted that they "never sold a share" of any company they owned and considered themselves to be shareholders for life.

The Gilbert brothers would attend board meetings and ask questions, a rare practice at the time. They attended as many as 150 shareholder meetings per year. At each meeting, they came prepared with ideas and suggestions about how the company could and should improve. Their emphasis usually involved board composition and governance. Although decades passed before their style of activism attracted attention, the Gilbert brothers identified a method for engaging companies that still resonates and continues today (Hagberg 2016).

Evelyn Davis   Evelyn Davis was a Holocaust survivor from the Netherlands. She traveled around the United States to attend numerous shareholder meetings every year and was determined to gain the attention of executives. In the 1970s, Davis attended an AT&T annual meeting dressed as a construction worker to obtain press coverage and voiced her opinion on the changes she felt were necessary for AT&T. She frequently fought for individual investors as she felt that institutional investors had more influence and individual investors lacked the voice they deserved. Davis was an advocate for corporate governance and board accountability. She was never a large shareholder in a single company like Icahn or Pickens. Still, her passion and desire for corporations to behave responsibly allowed her to be recognized and appreciated by many (Smith 2018).

IMPACT INVESTING

Impact investing is an investing approach that involves making investments to generate both a financial return and positive, measurable social and/or environmental benefits. In its 2019 annual report, the Global Impact Investing Network (GIIN) estimates the impact investing market at just over $500 billion. During the 2010s, the size of assets directed toward impact investments proliferated. One reason for this growth is the wealth transfer to millennials, many of whom desire to invest their assets much differently than previous generations, being more conscious of the role that capital can play in addressing intractable problems (Global Impact Investing Network 2019).

In 2015, the United Nations launched the Sustainable Development Goals (SDGs), which are 17 goals set by the United Nations Generally Assembly to be achieved by 2030. The SDGs include goals such as ending poverty, combating climate change, and ensuring equitable education. Requisite in any impact investment is the desire and ability to measure and report the impact generated; this makes the SDGs useful metrics for asset owners and asset managers seeking to target specific sectors. Each impact investor should be able to describe (1) the problem being addressed, (2) the metrics being used to measure the problem being addressed, and (3) the approach being used to generate investment profits.

The inability to measure or identify an apparent problem being addressed can raise doubts about an impact investment's legitimacy, also referred to as "impact washing." Impact investments typically comprise private equity and private debt vehicles, but increasingly have surfaced in publicly traded vehicles containing rigorous impact measurement mechanisms. Impact investments can take place in either developed or emerging markets and exhibit a range of returns from the market rate to concessionary (i.e., capital not intended to achieve market-rate outcomes) (United Nations Development Programme 2019).

A growing appetite exists to extend the impact moniker to public equity portfolios. Public equities are often excluded from the impact investing conversation partly because intentionality and measurement are challenging to capture from the buying and selling of the publicly traded equity of a company. Market participants understand that alternative investments, including private equity, venture capital, and real estate, are asset classes that dominate the agreeable forms of impact investing. A growing acceptance exists for public equity portfolios that can demonstrate impact partly by selecting companies in which a majority of revenues can be tied to impactful activities. A case can also be made where activists file shareholder resolutions that influence companies to address social and environmental issues, such as inequality or climate change.

ESG Principles

The premise behind the environmental, social, and governance (ESG) approach to investing is that companies that display positive ESG attributes are better positioned to outperform. Much debate surrounds ESG attributes, given that effective integration of ESG factors in investment selection in some studies has shown a positive correlation to stock price, but far from demonstrating causation. ESG ratings are generated by data providers, such as MSCI, which rate thousands of publicly traded companies. Environmental factors can include energy usage, carbon emissions, waste, and recycling. Social factors can consist of health and safety, human rights, and diversity issues. Governance factors can include shareholder rights, board structure/size, and executive compensation. ESG ratings are challenging to compare across company sizes and industries. For example, the carbon emissions of a car manufacturer would be much different from those of an internet company. For these reasons, ESG ratings have a low correlation among ESG data providers, which detracts from the investment value of ESG ratings. and are not heavily relied on for specific investment action (Forum for Sustainable and Responsible Investment 2018).

According to the Forum for Sustainable and Responsible Investment (2018), sustainable investment assets account for about $12 trillion, nearly 25 percent of total AUM in the United States. Several organizations have contributed to advocating for ESG practices in investment management, such as the United Nations Principles for Responsible Investment (UN PRI). The set of six principles set forth by the UN PRI are voluntary guidelines developed to encourage integrating ESG factors into the investment selection process:

> **Principle 1.** We will incorporate ESG issues into investment analysis and decision-making processes.
>
> **Principle 2.** We will be active owners and incorporate ESG issues into our ownership policies and practices.
>
> **Principle 3.** We will seek appropriate disclosure on ESG issues by the entities in which we invest.
>
> **Principle 4.** We will promote acceptance and implementation of the Principles within the investment industry.
>
> **Principle 5.** We will work together to enhance our effectiveness in implementing the Principles.
>
> **Principle 6.** We will each report on our activities and progress toward implementing the Principles.

Since the launching of the UN PRI principles in April 2016 at the New York Stock Exchange (NYSE), the number of signatories has grown to over 2,000 investment firms. These firms disclose their investment policies and practices by annually submitting their information in the form of transparency reports that are publicly available online (Principles for Responsible Investments 2018).

Claims by investment managers of integrating ESG have received a mixed reception among regulators. In April 2018, the U.S. Department of Labor (2018, p. 2) issued guidance cautioning fiduciaries to "not too readily" treat ESG factors as economically relevant to the particular investment choice at issue when making a decision. The guidance is wary of the presumption that integrating ESG factors is inherently accretive. This caution is not a departure from the general performance aspiration of investment managers to outperform a benchmark. However, such regulatory pushback could present a challenge to investment managers incapable of illustrating how integrating ESG factors adds economic value (U.S. Department of Labor 2018).

Several approaches are available for investors to integrate ESG factors into their investment selection process, such as assessing company ESG ratings or actively engaging with management. Companies that rely less on fossil fuels often focus more on their efforts in manufacturing quality products and maintaining a sound corporate structure that is positioned to outperform their peers. Challenges exist in attributing causation of economic performance entirely to these nonfinancial factors and calling into question the financial claims of investment managers that offer such strategies. Since ESG ratings are generally unverifiable, unauditable, self-reported, and lack direct comparability, this regulatory caution is appropriate. Investors and advisors should evaluate ESG factors to understand the economic value intended to be achieved and separate material from nonmaterial factors.

Effectiveness of Impact Investing

Not all problems have a solution that can be addressed through impact investing, and not all impact investments have solutions that can generate superior risk-adjusted financial returns. Concessionary capital can often be a better solution for some social or environmental challenges. Impact investments have a dual objective of simultaneously achieving both a positive financial return and social/environmental benefits. This uniqueness causes major complexities when determining the effectiveness of impact investments, partly because of the lack of universally quantifiable impact metrics. Performance is not straightforward and the definition of an impact fund tend to vary and hard to broadly validate.

Concessional capital is often found in program-related investments (PRI), which is a term from the Internal Revenue Service (IRS) for investments that prioritize a charitable goal or purpose. A point of contention that remains in impact investing is the lack of a standardized mechanism for measuring impact. Assessing impact tends to be empirically challenging. Analysts and investors often use well-known financial benchmarks to measure financial success. However, financial returns are only part of the story for *double bottom line* investments, which produce both social/environmental impact and financial returns. Investors should resist the temptation to evaluate success of impact funds solely in terms of financial performance. In a traditional investment program, defining an objective is standard practice and clear, which is to outperform a benchmark. However, in an impact program, beating a financial benchmark is not enough. Impact investing is also about providing capital that advances solutions to problems. Without a thoughtful method for assessing social/environmental success, how can one determine whether a program embodies the dual characteristics of an impact investment? The ambiguity of making investments believed to have more than financial goals necessitate a clearly defined objective around how success should be assessed. A mission statement can help inform the types of managers sought, as well as the degree in which a portfolio is achieving its social/environmental objectives. The less precise the goal, the more difficult the task of quantifying success (Internal Revenue Service 2019).

Measuring success is one of the more challenging elements of making impact investments. While measuring investment performance can be straightforward, developing, for example, a reliable method that quantifies the amount of net CO_2 emissions avoided by the companies in a portfolio is not. How does one quantify all the materials recovered through recycling programs, or the amount of waste treated, or the amount of renewable energy generated? The answers are unclear. However, the Sustainability Accounting Standards Board (SASB), a nonprofit organization, is attempting to bring greater clarity to companies' social and sustainability performance.

SASB has provided a solution meant to solicit and include market feedback to methods for quantifying sustainability metrics. The Sustainable Accounting Standards Board (2019, p. 2) "develops and maintains robust reporting standards which enable businesses around the world to identify, manage, and communicate financially-material sustainability information to their investors. SASB standards are evidence-based, developed with broad market participation, and designed to be cost-effective for companies and decision-useful for investors." SASB is attempting to understand, interpret, and measure relevant sustainability issues at the industry level so that the ESG performance of companies within these industries can be measured, managed, and disclosed, in the same way that financial metrics are measured, managed, or disclosed. A company, thus, can be judged not only on financial performance but also on sustainability performance, as reflected in its 10-K filing. SASB actively solicits input from companies within the industries it follows to create a set of standards allowing investors to assess a company's sustainability commitment and then compare companies within the same sector (Sustainable Accounting Standards Board 2019).

Social Impact Bonds

Although social impact bonds (SIBs) are a popular form of impact investments, they are not bonds as the name suggests. Instead, they are contingent claims similar to a forward contract: two parties decide on terms, and the contract is monitored for a specified period ending in a binary outcome where payment is determined by the success or failure of a service being delivered. To illustrate, an investor is "long" on addressing a social or environmental issue, while the government is "short." If the metrics of the service being delivered are not met, the investor loses capital that would be paid to a service provider tasked with executing the delivery of a specified service, and the government would lose nothing. If the metrics are met, the investor gains a specified return, which the government would have otherwise spent for achieving predetermined goals.

SIBs, also known as "Pay for Success," are contracts that attract socially motivated investors and like-minded organizations to provide public services that would otherwise be underfunded. SIBs are an emerging tool facilitating the government's use of private capital to target and fund high-impact social programs. Two popular U.S.-based SIBs have had unfortunate and controversial results. Bloomberg Philanthropies and Goldman Sachs participated in a SIB to address recidivism at Riker's Island for youthful offenders. Ultimately, the investor lost $1.2 million because the service provider did not reduce the number of inmates returning to jail (Liang, Mansberger, and Spieler 2014). Another U.S.-based SIB focused on improving early childhood education in Utah for at-risk preschoolers. Some accused this SIB of overstating the effect that its investments had achieved in helping young children avoid special education. Although the data and useful lessons learned have some value, the financial losses were disheartening to investors (Popper 2015). Based on a small sample, the main lesson is that impact investments cannot solve all problems effectively and possibly are not the best cures to problems that are better addressed by other solutions.

Green Bonds

Green bonds are bonds whose proceeds are used to address climate change solutions. These bonds fund environmentally friendly projects, which can include themes such as energy efficiency, pollution prevention, and sustainable agriculture and water management. According to the Municipal Securities Rulemaking Board (2018), the three components of a green bond are (1) use of proceeds, (2) a process for project evaluation and selection, and (3) management of proceeds and reporting. Green bonds operate just like a typical bond, offering a stated return and commitment to using the proceeds for new or existing sustainable projects. Moody's and S&P have methodologies for sourcing and scoring green bonds. The ratings for green bonds, however, are unlike traditional bonds (credit ratings); they are forward-looking viewpoints of the issuers' ability to manage and administer green bonds proceeds. Not applying proceeds to environmental issues is known as *greenwashing* (Municipal Securities Rulemaking Board 2018).

SUMMARY AND CONCLUSIONS

Activist and impact investing are important investment activities that have become mainstream. These investing styles involve various approaches for changing corporate behavior and influencing investment decisions. Impact investing focuses on the dual objective of generating profits while achieving social and environmental benefits. ESG complements an investor's pursuit of superior financial outcomes by integrated ESG-related factors during investment selection. Activist investing can amplify investors' voices and increase the power of their votes to bring about change. The growth of ESG and impact assets globally attests to the growing interest of investors to integrate their values both individually and at an institutional level.

DISCUSSION QUESTIONS

1. Discuss the effectiveness of activist investing and identify its limitations.
2. Describe the different hedge fund activist approaches.
3. Describe the key differences between individual and institutional activists.
4. Compare and contrast the differences among SRI, ESG, and impact investing approaches and the asset classes that they are more likely to be found.
5. Discuss the challenges in measuring impact, ESG, and the tools that are currently being used.

REFERENCES

Butera, Chris. 2019. "The Co-Founder of Shareholder Activism Is Dead, but His Cause Is Thriving." Available at: http://www.ai-cio.com/news/shareholder-activist-oil-tycoon-t-boone-pickens-dies/.

Copeland, James R. 2015. "Special Report: Public Pension Funds' Shareholder-Proposal Activism." Available at https://www.proxymonitor.org/Forms/2015Finding3.aspx.

DePillis, Lydia. 2019. "Shareholder Activism Is on the Rise, but Companies Are Fighting Back." CNN Business. Available at https://www.cnn.com/2019/01/30/investing/activist-shareholders/index.html.

The Forum for Sustainable and Responsible Investment. 2018. "Naylor Association Management Software." Naylor Association Management Software. Available at www.ussif.org/trends.

Gandel, Stephen. 2015. "How DuPont Went to War with Activist Investor Nelson Peltz." *Fortune*, May 11. Available at https://fortune.com/2015/05/11/how-dupont-went-to-war/.

Global Impact Investing Network (GIIN). 2019. "Annual Impact Survey." Available at https://thegiin.org/assets/GIIN_2019%20Annual%20Impact%20Investor%20Survey_webfile.pdf.

Grant, Elaine X. 2006. "TWA – Death of a Legend." *St. Louis Magazine*, June 28. Available at https://www.stlmag.com/TWA-Death-Of-A-Legend/.

Hagberg, Carl. 2016. "The Original 'Shareholder Activists' and the Founders of the Modern Corporate Governance Movement." Available at https://optimizeronline.com/the-original-shareholder-activists-and-the-founders-of-the-modern-corporate-governance-movement/.

Icahn Enterprises. 2019. "Welcome." Available at https://www.ielp.com/home.

Internal Revenue Service. 2019. "Program-related Investments." Available at http://www.irs.gov/charities-non-profits/private-foundations/program-related-investments.

Jacobius, Arleen. 2019. "CalPERS Allots $5.4 Billion to Real Assets, Looks to Revise Investment Policy." *Pensions & Investments*, September 11. Available at https://www.pionline.com/searches-and-hires/calpers-allots-54-billion-real-assets-looks-revise-investment-policy.

La Monica, Paul R. 2018. "Bill Ackman's Herbalife Disaster Is Finally Over." CNN Business, May 1. Available at https://money.cnn.com/2018/03/01/investing/herbalife-bill-ackman-carl-icahn/index.html.

Liang, Max, Brian Mansberger, and Andrew C. Spieler. 2014. "An Overview of Social Impact Bonds." *Journal of International Business and Law* 13:2, 267–282.

Mulligan, Thomas S. 1994. "CalPERS Report Card Raps Some Knuckles: Shareholders: Pension Fund Issues Grades to Top Corporations after Asking about the Independence of Their Boards of Directors." *Los Angeles Times*, October 8. Available at https://www.latimes.com/archives/la-xpm-1994-10-08-fi-47865-story.html

Municipal Securities Rule Making Board. 2018. "About Green Bonds." Available at http://www.msrb.org/~/media/Files/Resources/About-Green-Bonds.ashx.

Office of the State Controller. 2019. "New York State Retirement Fund." Available at https://www.osc.state.ny.us/pension/.

Ponomareva, Yuliya. 2018. "Shareholder Activism Is on the Rise: Caution Required." *Forbes*, December 10. Available at https://www.forbes.com/sites/esade/2018/12/10/shareholder-activism-is-on-the-rise-caution-required/#3e72ad3d4844.

Popper, Nathaniel. 2015. "Success Metrics Questioned in School Program Funded by Goldman." *New York Times*, November 4. Available at http://www.nytimes.com/2015/11/04/business/dealbook/did-goldman-make-the-grade.html.

Principles for Responsible Investments (UN PRI). 2018. "Annual Report." Available at https://www.unpri.org/Uploads/g/f/c/priannualreport_605237.pdf.

Sawyer, Melissa, Lauren S. Boehmke, and Nathaniel R. Ludwig. 2019. "Review and Analysis of 2018 U.S. Shareholder Activism." Available at: https://corpgov.law.harvard.edu/2019/04/05/review-and-analysis-of-2018-u-s-shareholder-activism/.

Smith, Harrison. 2018. "Evelyn Y. Davis, Activist Shareholder and 'Queen of the Corporate Jungle,' Dies at 89." *The Washington Post*, November 5. Available at http://www.washingtonpost.com/local/obituaries/evelyn-y-davis-activist-shareholder-and-queen-of-the-corporate-jungle-dies-at-89/2018/11/05/b95f82c6-e10e-11e8-8f5f-a55347f48762_story.html.

Sustainable Accounting Standards Board. 2019. "Engagement Guide." February. Available at https://www.sasb.org/wp-content/uploads/2019/08/SASB-EngagementGuide2-1.pdf?__hstc=105637852.5aad9a46cb4b59571cc1c4e09111c37e.1572268995089.1572268995089.1572268995089.1&__hssc=105637852.30.1572268995089.

U.S Department of Labor. 2018. "Interpretive Bulletins 2016-01 and 2015-01." Available at https://www.dol.gov/sites/dolgov/files/ebsa/employers-and-advisers/guidance/field-assistance-bulletins/2018-01.pdf/

United Nations Development Programme. 2019. "The Sustainable Development Goals Report." Available at https://unstats.un.org/sdgs/report/2019/The-Sustainable-Development-Goals-Report-2019.pdf.

CHAPTER 19

Socially Responsible Investing

Randolph D. Nordby
Professional Lecturer American University

INTRODUCTION

The importance of socially responsible investing (SRI) has increased substantially in recent years. Top analysts at leading investment firms often grapple with the complicated process of integrating nonstandardized corporate environmental, social, and governance (ESG) data into their investment decision-making process. The recent emphasis on sustainability has brought major obstacles for practitioners, regulators, investors, and corporations regarding reporting and using sustainability data.

Despite the lack of a clear SRI definition, nonstandardized ESG reporting by corporations, and mixed academic results on the potential portfolio benefits from ESG investing, many investors are still interested in sustainable investments. Morgan Stanley (2018) estimates that more than $22.8 trillion is invested globally in sustainable investments, representing more than 24 percent of funds currently under professional management. SRI has been growing as an investment factor over the past few decades and has gone by many names, including SRI, responsible investing (RI), social investing, socially conscious investing, religious investing, green investing, values-based investing, and environmental, social, and governance (ESG) investing. The broadest term is *sustainability*. To emphasize the integration of sustainability data into the investment decision-making process, rather than the previously used exclusionary screening traditionally associated with historical SRI investment, this chapter refers to the current method of SRI investing as ESG investing. Another subset of SRI, called impact investing, emphasizes an investment's social impact and financial returns. Chapter 18 covers impact investing.

SRI participants frequently attempt to promote societal changes and address relevant social topics, such as environmental welfare concerns (e.g., global warming and carbon footprint), consumer product safety, human rights, and racial/gender diversity topics that may influence the actions of business. Also, SRI proponents may even avoid businesses that they perceive as having adverse social effects on society, such as alcohol, weapons, religion, tobacco, climate change, gambling, sex, and fossil fuel production. SRI is one of several related concepts and approaches that influence and, in some cases, even mandate how portfolio managers construct and monitor their investment portfolios.

The remainder of the chapter offers a brief history of SRI in the United States, discusses the growth of ESG investing in mutual funds and exchange-traded funds (ETFs), and explores the increased use of ESG factors in portfolio selection by institutional investors such as endowments and foundations. Finally, the chapter examines the lack of guidelines regarding voluntary nonfinancial ESG disclosure methods for operationalizing ESG factors and best practices for ESG integration for equities.

A BRIEF HISTORY OF SRI IN THE UNITED STATES

According to Schueth (2003), SRI can be traced back hundreds of years in the United States and even longer in other countries. Some estimate that the Methodists have been managing money in the United States using "social screens" for more than 200 years. For example, early Methodist leaders urged their followers to avoid investments in alcohol, tobacco, and gambling, which they thought hurt their neighbors. Going back even further to biblical times, Jewish law directed investors to invest for good by investing ethically. Finally, religious scholars around the world have called on investors for generations to avoid investing in goods and services that benefit from harming humans and society. A popular form of traditional SRI portfolio construction involves avoiding "sin stocks," including topics such as tobacco, alcohol, and weapons manufacturing.

SRI proponents cite the modern roots of the current U.S. sustainability movements to the turbulent 1960s, which brought about shifts in ways of thinking about the world in general for an entire generation associated with Vietnam, Woodstock, and civil rights. The number of socially concerned investors dramatically increased during the 1980s from collective protest movements against perceived injustices such as South Africa's previous apartheid policies and environmental disasters such as Chernobyl and the *Exxon Valdez*.

Recently, interest in a new adaptation of SRI – ESG investing – has seen even more growth since the financial crisis of 2007–2008 as investors and practitioners began to search for a better understanding of corporate risk that was either absent in financial statements or ignored in financial valuation best practices. For example, the safety record of British Petroleum (BP) in the years preceding the *Deepwater Horizon* oil spill was much worse than that of its peers. Analysts could have forecasted a potential severe oil spill if they had focused on the many egregious Occupational Safety and Health Administration (OSHA) violations leading up to the accident.

Understanding current sustainability issues requires reviewing a brief history of U.S. environmental regulatory policies explicitly involving the manufacturing industry. U.S. manufacturing did not face substantial environmental requirements until the creation of the Environmental Protection Agency (EPA) in 1970. Before the EPA, U.S. corporations had considerable immunity from environmental and health constraints. Unfortunately, during this time, Heim (2018) finds that many executives and investors deemed environmental management as a substantial nondiscretionary expense with no return on investment. Over the next several decades, company management transformed the U.S. economy by moving manufacturing overseas to countries that emphasized low operating costs and even less environmental regulation, benefiting from the global "urbanization" trend occurring in developing markets. Heim also finds that that contempt about the burdensome environmental regulations continues to be entrenched in political discussions in 2019 as U.S. President Trump and the Republicans rolled back environmental, health, safety, and corporate governance regulations that they consider burdensome to business.

Urbanization also continues to have a substantial impact on some developing economies, predominately where business and culture are forming sizeable global supply chains. As poorer and less educated citizens leave agriculture jobs to work in industrial cities, multi-national firms learned that they could substantially reduce human capital costs by sending their manufacturing processes to regions that paid reduced wages and lower benefits for their workers. Unfortunately, as discovered through investigative reporting and social media, some firms (e.g., Foxconn and Apple) were taking advantage of workers, who were working in substandard work environments that were discovered to be dangerous and inhumane, resulting in increased event risk for such firms.

Since the early 2000s, SRI has become predominately defined as promoting environmentally sustainable development. Many investors, including millennials, consider global climate change to be an important global, business, and investment risk. Heim (2018) finds that under the Obama administration, the EPA's scope increased to include a broader area of interlocking topics including air, emergency management, land and cleanup, pesticides, toxic substances, waste removal, and clean water. In contrast, the Trump administration created new mandates to curtail EPA's increased power by attempting to increase the use of fossil fuel such as coal and soften environmental regulations. As SRI becomes more mainstream and continues to evolve into an increasingly popular method for evaluating risk, many traditional investors are likely to look toward ESG factors to increase returns and reduce risk in their portfolios, not necessarily only to make changes to society or support specific causes.

ESG GROWTH IN POOLED INVESTMENT VEHICLES

According to Presler (2019), ESG funds continued a record six-year run with increasing annual net inflows, with 40 percent of these inflows going to ETFs. The number of sustainable investment funds increased by nearly 50 percent in 2018 to 351, with total assets of $161 billion by the end of 2018. Also, a record number of those funds started in 2018, and more existing funds added ESG criteria to their prospectuses. These changes mean more choices for investors to build both sustainable and diversified portfolios.

Individual investors still face the challenge of making money day trading or concentrating their portfolio in a few individual stocks. Contrary to some research about the death of diversification after the financial crisis of 2007–2008, practitioners continue to recommend that individual investors build diversified portfolios. If individual investors prefer to construct equity portfolios from individual stocks, experts recommend that they should hold about 30 stocks in different industries. However, many individual investors do not have the necessary financial resources to purchase so many shares of individual securities. Therefore, SRI investors should strongly consider investing in mutual funds and ETFs that are designed to invest sustainably. Mutual funds and ETFs, focused on ESG factors, allow socially responsible investors to benefit from diversification with relatively low amounts of money. These pooled investment vehicles also offer benefits for investors with more extensive investable portfolios. Chapter 20 includes more information on the basics of mutual funds and ETFs.

RESPONSIBLE INVESTING GROWTH BY INSTITUTIONAL INVESTORS

Institutional investors are clearly the leaders in sustainable investing, as measured by assets under management (AUM). Institutional investors such as banks, insurance companies, endowments, and pension funds are currently using ESG factors in their portfolio management decisions. In a recent survey of 118 institutional investors, Morgan Stanley (2018) reports that two factors are driving the use of sustainable investing in investment decisions: (1) the potential for better risk management and (2) increased return potential. This survey also reports that 84 percent of institutional investors are pursuing or considering pursuing ESG integration, with 60 percent of these firms incorporating ESG investing practices starting in 2014.

Although ESG practitioners often cite risk management and increased returns as essential drivers for pursuing ESG investing, little academic evidence is available on ESG's ability to provide either improved return or lower risk in portfolios. Thus, more research is needed to explore the relation between ESG investing and risk/return. The next section provides a brief overview of some important academic studies on the performance of integrating sustainability into the equity valuation process, both in the United States and globally.

Although many practitioners use ESG in their investment decision-making process, institutional investors continue to note that showing superior financial performance is still the number-one challenge that they face with incorporating sustainability metrics into their valuation models. Morgan Stanley (2018) finds that fewer than half of institutional asset managers believe that they have adequate tools to assess sustainable investments. Surprisingly, the lack of evidence involving ESG's impact on risk management and returns has not prevented institutional investors from incorporating ESG methods into their investment portfolios. Without evidence that ESG investing increases returns or improves portfolio risk management, ESG investing could become another "popular flavor" investing method that seems to be based more on marketing than on sound investment theory grounded by academic rigor.

THE PERFORMANCE OF SUSTAINABLE INVESTMENTS

Traditional finance focuses on risk and return using mean-variance optimization (MVO), while SRI considers other nonfinancial factors (ESG metrics). A question that often arises is whether making ethical investment decisions is financially beneficial. The debate on this issue is still ongoing.

The prior academic literature on the performance implications of sustainability investments reflects several different viewpoints and reports mixed results. In particular, SRI funds either (1) underperform conventional funds, (2) outperform conventional funds, or (3) result in no difference in performance versus conventional funds. For example, Margolis, Elfenbein, and Walsh (2008) find that trying to connect social responsibility with firm profitability is a popular undertaking. If a business case can be made for doing the right things, everybody wins – employees, stakeholders, shareholders, and society at large. However, academic researchers have struggled for decades to determine whether any link exists between increasing ESG factors and corporate financial returns. After analyzing 167 studies spanning 36 years, Margolis et al. find no statistically significant link between firms with strong ESG factors and increased stock returns. Interestingly, the firm's doing good does not seem to destroy shareholder value either. In summary, they report only a low correlation between strong ESG performance and sound financial results.

In another study, Humphrey and Tan (2014) simulate portfolios designed to mimic typical equity mutual funds' holdings while removing confounding influences of differences due to portfolio manager's skill, costs, and fees so they could test the effects of positive and negative screening on portfolio performance. Similar to Margolis et al. (2008), Humphrey and Tan find that a typical socially responsible fund neither gains nor loses from screening its portfolio.

In another study, Khan, Serafeim, and Yoon (2016) find that firms with good ratings on "material" sustainability issues significantly outperform firms with poor ratings on these issues. Also, firms with good ratings on immaterial sustainability issues do not significantly outperform firms with poor ratings on the same issues.

Filbeck, Filbeck, and Zhao (2019) investigate investment results further by isolating one specific ESG factor at a time, rather than looking at all ESG factors together, to identify ESG factors that significantly influence stock returns. They find that the U.S. stock market appears to value the governance (G) component of ESG investing as more important than both the environmental (E) and social (S) components for predicting future stock performance.

Additional research on the performance of ESG metrics for firms outside the United States has also received considerable attention. For example, a meta-analysis study by Lu and Taylor (2016) reviews 198 studies and find that sustainability performance likely increases a firm's financial performance, especially in the long run. They also find ESG outperformance is more significant for accounting-based measures (e.g., return on equity (ROE) and earnings per share (EPS)) versus market-based measures (e.g., market value, market return, and Tobin's q). More importantly, they also find that non-U.S. firms seem to show a stronger relation between ESG and financial performance compared to U.S. firms.

Akben-Selçuk (2019) finds that corporate social responsibility had a positive association with financial performance, rejecting the neoclassical view that suggests the relation between CSR and financial performance is negative because of the increased costs for the firm from diverting scarce resources from more profitable opportunities creating opportunity costs. Laskar (2018) examines the level of sustainability disclosure on firm performance in Asia. The regression results support a significant positive relation between sustainability reporting and a firm's performance. The study also finds that financial performance is better for developed countries (e.g., Japan and South Korea) versus developing countries in Asia (e.g., India and Indonesia).

Finally, Wiengarten, Lo, and Lam (2015) make an important contribution to the study of ESG metrics by researching the role that the newly created chief sustainability officer (CSO) has on a firm's performance after the CSO is added to a firm's top management team. The authors find that U.S. firms adding a CSO in the United

States increase financial performance and these benefits are even more pronounced if the CSO is female.

LACK OF GUIDELINES ON VOLUNTARY NONFINANCIAL DISCLOSURE

According to the Investor Responsibility Research Center Institute (IRRCi) (2013), Regulation S-K of the Securities Exchange Act of 1934 requires U.S. publicly traded companies to file an annual report (10-K) with the Securities and Exchange Commission (SEC). This filing includes the company's audited financial statements, description of business lines, organizational structure and history, material risk factors, and a management discussion and analysis (MD&A) section on the state of the business. Amel-Zadeh and Serafeim (2018) find the requirements for voluntary sustainability reporting by the firm are ambiguous to many asset managers and about 40 percent of them find ESG information disclosed by firms as being too general to use, while another 35 percent cite a lack of quantifiable ESG information in current firm sustainability reporting.

To summarize, many problems currently occur when attempts to integrate ESG data into the investment process. According to the IRRCi (2013), investors have to review large amounts of ESG data, and these data do not aid them in making informed decisions. Morgan Stanley (2018) finds that the lack of reliable data is a major problem for asset owners. In fact, three out of four of the top challenges that practitioners encounter involve integrating ESG metrics into asset valuation because of some form of informational inadequacy.

ESG DISCLOSURE AND ASSET MANAGER VALUATION METHODOLOGY

Bank Ki-moon, United Nations Secretary-General, identified sustainability as a global imperative and stated that ESG was his top priority in 2016. The United Nations–supported Principles for Responsible Investments (PRI) complement the UN Global Compact, which calls for firms to come to a national consensus in the areas of human rights, labor standards, the environment, and corruption. PRI also complements the UN Environment Programme Finance Initiative that encourages capital markets to consider ESG factors in their decision-making process. As of 2016, the Investor Responsibility Research Center Institute (2018) finds that PRI had more than 1,400 investment managers' signatures from over 50 countries with a combined asset value of more than $82 trillion.

Numerous motivations exist that may be driving both firms and asset managers to use ESG data. Deng, Kang, and Low (2013) find higher merger announcement returns and realized positive long-term stock returns. Also, firms with good ratings on "material" sustainability topics significantly outperform firms with poor ratings on these issues (Khan et al. 2016). Dhaliwal, Zhen, Tsang, and Yang (2011) find potentially lower costs of equity with higher ESG scores.

Khan et al. (2016) discover another critical factor driving the importance of ESG data, namely, that sophisticated asset managers of pensions, endowments, and foundations use this information in their investment analysis. Although academics continue to debate the relevance of ESG metrics and firm performance, over 82 percent of portfolio managers, in a recent survey by Amel-Zadeh and Serafeim

(2018), already incorporate ESG information in their investment decision-making, at least to some extent. They also find that an additional driver of ESG data is that some asset managers believe ESG information is material to their understanding of equity performance. Yet, only 32 percent of money managers indicate that they use ESG data because doing so is an ethical responsibility. Finally, only 25 percent of the respondents cite direct client mandates as a reason for considering ESG in their asset valuation process.

ESG DISCLOSURE LACKS USEFULNESS

The Investor Responsibility Research Center Institute (2013, p. 2) cites a recent report by an executive at Microsoft that adequately captured the most common problem that sustainable investors face today: "Despite the great volume of reporting available for investors, many contend that current reporting of ESG data is not offering the information they need to make informed decisions and to communicate a company's strategy effectively and means to generate value."

Conversely, firms have also increased disclosure of their voluntary nonfinancial (ESG) data. In a research study from the IRRCi (2013), 499 of the 500 firms in the S&P 500 index report some form of sustainability metrics. However, the data reported are not standardized across industries and tend to be ad hoc, which is not particularly helpful. The study also reports that only 7 out of 499 companies had fully integrated their financial and sustainability reporting into their required SEC filings. Finally, the IRRCi (2013) finds that the firms fully integrating their sustainability and financial reports provide complete information for asset managers, which leads to significantly lower volatility in earnings projections from sell-side analysts who incorporate ESG into their valuation models. In summary, asset managers are currently using ESG metrics in their equity valuation and firms are producing considerably more ESG data. Yet, academic research remains inconclusive about the relation between ESG metrics and firm performance.

METHODS FOR OPERATIONALIZING ESG ISSUES

Sustainable investing encompasses multiple strategies that attempt to maximize both societal good and financial returns. Although mainstream investors often use ESG integration to maximize risk-adjusted returns, others merely seek strategies that can create societal change by transferring investment capital from nonsustainable to sustainable firms. Since these methods for operationalizing ESG issues are not mutually exclusive, investors and practitioners often use them in combination. These methods can also be designed to accommodate more traditional investors who worry about maximizing risk-adjusted returns and more socially conscious investors who worry about making a difference.

Divestment

Divestment is the conscious act of removing specific stocks and entire industries from an investment portfolio based on objections to a firm's business practices. Divestment is a controversial decision that can have real ramifications for investors, practitioners, beneficiaries, firms, and even society. For example, Karmin (2008) finds that the California State Teachers' Retirement System (CalSTRS), the second-largest pension fund in the United States, announced that it was considering lifting a nearly eight-year ban on investing in tobacco securities. CalSTRS indicated that missing out on a "market weighting" in tobacco stocks between January 2000 and June 2008 cost the fund more than $1 billion in lost investment returns.

Divestment is a difficult choice because it involves possibly sacrificing investment returns. By not owning these firms, investors have no say in how these firms run their business and have no possibility of influencing them to make meaningful changes in their business practices. Instead, some socially conscious investors choose to use a best-in-class screening, in which firms, even if deemed to be operating in controversial industries, can be owned because they have improving ESG performance compared to their industry peers.

Negative (Exclusionary) Screening

Negative screening involves excluding specific holdings from any investment consideration based solely on ESG criteria and firms that are deemed objectionable to promote societal goals and norms. For example, the MSCI KLD 400 Social Index, launched in May 1990, is one of the first SRI indexes (KLD Index 2019). The index is maintained in two stages. First, analysts screen out securities of companies involved in nuclear power, tobacco, alcohol, gambling, military weapons, civilian firearms, genetically modified organisms (GMOs), and adult entertainment for the index. Then they make additions from the list of eligible companies based on considerations of ESG performance, sector alignment, and size representation. The academic literature on the performance of ESG investments widely cites the index because of its long track record.

Negative screening avoids specific securities of companies or countries based on many reasons, including religious beliefs, moral values, and societal norms. According to Humphrey and Tan (2014), some view exclusionary screening as the oldest form of sustainable investing. Also, using exclusionary screening reduces returns and increases risk. They also cite Fabozzi's dire warning to investors about negative screening. Fabozzi, Ma, and Oliphant (2008) strongly believe that trustees or fiduciaries who develop institutional investment policy statements should fully understand the economic consequences of screening out stocks of companies producing a product that is inconsistent with their value systems. Besides, they should question if the cost to uphold common social standards is worthwhile.

Positive/Best-in-class

Positive/best-in-class investing is a more modern adaption of SRI. It involves making investments in securities that previously would have been removed through negative (exclusionary) screening that demonstrates strong or improving ESG performance and is believed to be making a positive social impact. Positive/best-in-class investing is the opposite of divestment and seeks to reward firms for doing the right thing. It attempts to drive positive change through buying shares and being actively involved, instead of turning their back on certain industries. This investment approach allows investors to positively express their views on firm behavior by selecting stocks in which they believe, without sacrificing portfolio diversification or long-term performance.

Active Ownership

Active ownership involves engagement and communication techniques directed at large portfolio companies that hold a sizable percentage of shares in a stock allowing investors to have a direct dialogue. Active ownership is a long-term investment process that hopes to change a firm's direction and helps it to promote and develop key ESG issues and topics. Active ownership directly conflicts with traditional portfolio management best practices that call for removing a security from a portfolio that becomes unfavorable through investors' analysis. A wide range of active ownership strategies is available to promote change. They often involve some form of voting in general shareholder meetings, writing letters to the company, and possibly attempting to gain a seat on the firm's board. Active ownership differs from activist investing that is common in alternative investments, such as hedge funds, that often focus on short-term investing and is a much more controversial approach to effecting change in business. Many active ownership techniques involve the pooling of resources and cooperation related to advancing corporate engagement goals. Chapter 18 focuses on activist/impact investing.

Thematic Investing

Thematic investing refers to actions by investors who seek solutions for sustainability challenges, which include water scarcity, promoting health, food production, and energy efficiency. Thematic investing is not defined as including only ESG issues and can be based more on SRI and demographic trends.

Impact Investing

Impact investing can be distinguished from other forms of SRI by intentionally investing to generate and measure ESG performance and earn a minimum financial return that covers at least the cost of capital. Impact investing seeks to promote measurement and transparency. According to Hayat and Orsagh (2015), the practice of impact investing shares four core characteristics: (1) investors want to achieve ESG impact; (2) investments are expected to generate a financial return on capital and a return of capital; (3) investments must generate returns that range from below-market to the risk-adjusted market rate; and (4) investors are committed to measuring and reporting ESG impacts. Chapter 18 discusses impact investing.

FIDUCIARY DUTY AND ESG INVESTING

According to guidance offered by the U.S. Department of Labor (DOL) in 2015, ESG analysis is not in conflict with fiduciary duty and can even aid in the analysis (Hayat and Orsagh 2015). Unfortunately, Heim (2018) also finds that many investment practitioners and firms are still unaware of this DOL guideline and continue to be concerned that ESG analysis is an unreasonable practice and conflicts with fiduciary duties. Pension fund fiduciaries can consider ESG factors in their investment decisions without worrying about repercussions from the DOL (Bradford 2015).

ESG Integration

No standardized ESG integration process currently exists to guide investors and practitioners. Different styles of ESG investing are available, including considering ESG in the investing process from an active or indexed perspective. The question is, how should investors best integrate ESG data into an asset valuation model? Hayat and Orsagh (2015) find that despite the recommendation to include ESG data in asset valuation by asset managers, the CFA Institute acknowledges that difficulties still exist with using ESG data by asset managers for valuation because (1) assigning a monetary value to ESG issues is difficult; (2) ESG disclosures can be limited, unaudited, and nonstandardized; and (3) ESG issues tend to take time to appear in stock valuation.

ESG INTEGRATION FOR EQUITIES

According to Bos (2014a, 2014b), investors use several methods to apply ESG factors in equity valuations. One method is to adjust the discount rate for ESG factors using a discounted cash flow (DCF) valuation. Companies scoring high or low on ESG measurement receive a lower (higher) risk profile than the average firm in the industry. Bos (2014b) finds that adjusting the discount rate for ESG factors has potential problems. One problem is determining the number of basis points by which to adjust the firm's discount rate for ESG factors. Currently, no clear consensus exists about the magnitude of the discount rate adjustment for ESG considerations, making this an ad-hoc decision made arbitrarily by investment managers. Another problem involves double-counting a firm's ESG risks that are already widely known and reflected in the discount rate (Bos 2014b). Since more research is needed to support adjusting the discount rate for ESG measures, most practitioners do not recommend this method. Instead, Bos (2014b) contends that a better method is to force the investment manager to translate the ESG factor into direct cash flows and to focus only on "material" ESG factors that are likely to affect risk and return. Besides using a DCF, another widely used method is to value firms using multiples analysis and to integrate ESG data into target multiples. This way enables adding a premium to a firm's target multiple for firms showing strong ESG performance and penalizes a firm showing weak ESG performance.

CONSIDERATIONS FOR INTEGRATING ESG

Following a survey of global financial professionals as well as workshops with investors and analysts, the CFA Institute and the United Nations–supported Principles for Responsible Investment (PRI) suggest using the following considerations when integrating ESG factors in the investment process:

- No single agreed-upon definition of ESG or best practice for ESG integration is currently available. Each firm must integrate ESG data into its investment process and continue to meet the client's objectives and constraints.

- ESG integration looks at risks and opportunities revealed by the analysis of ESG issues that are "material" for a company or country. A good starting point to understanding materiality is to review the research by Khan et al. (2016), which finds that firms with good ratings on material sustainability issues significantly outperform firms with poor ratings on these issues. In contrast, firms with good ratings on immaterial sustainability issues do not significantly outperform those with poor ratings on the same issues. Another good source for the materiality of ESG metrics can be found at the Sustainability Accounting Standards Board (SASB), a U.S. private nonprofit organization based in San Francisco. Heim (2018) finds that the SASB's standards try to identify aspects of a firm's operations, leadership, and strategy that are financially material under U.S. securities requirements.
- Firms are predominately using ESG data to gain a better understanding of firm risk. However, the results of the survey and workshops show that few investors look at ESG analysis as a means of uncovering investing opportunities. ESG may also provide opportunities, but more research is needed to support this view.
- Investors should focus on ESG analysis, not ESG investing. Unfortunately, many firms appear to be trying to capitalize on ESG investing through marketing slogans, instead of using ESG analysis as a real component of the investment decision-making process. Eccles and Klimenko (2019) identify ESG as a fundamental change in the way investors evaluate companies. After interviewing 70 executives in 43 global institutional investment firms, the authors find that ESG is the top consideration for those executives. Also, corporations may ultimately lose the voluntary option to report on sustainability topics and be held accountable for their ESG performance.
- Buyers need to be aware of ESG investment products since firms are likely to define ESG differently and use different methods of operationalizing ESG data. Investors need to do their research when investing in anything called ESG or sustainable, to understand the product's ESG methodology, and to ensure that they agree with it.
- More transparency is needed among firms, investors, and investment professionals to do a better job of communicating with each other about their methods of integrating ESG data in the investment process. Also, more standardized reporting and audited data are needed than are being provided by firms in their sustainability reports.
- Heim (2018) finds that executives and consumers often have questions about sustainability, including how it is defined. He also finds that using buzzwords and catchphrases to summarize the ESG concept causes additional confusion. Additionally, both the CFA Institute and PRI find numerous concerns from investors worried about the quality, accuracy, and comparability of the ESG data they use in their analyses.

CASE STUDY

Apple is one of the world's largest manufacturers and designers of mobile communication and media devices. Several years ago, Apple's leading supplier, Foxconn, a Taiwanese multinational electronics contract manufacturing company operating in China, experienced an ethical issue involving the working conditions in the supplier's factories. The issue intensified in 2010 when workers jumped off the tops of company buildings, resulting in employee deaths. Some believe that employees working for the supplier committed suicide as a result of adverse working conditions. Their deaths attracted the attention of key global watchdog groups and negative media scrutiny. Apple and others conducted extensive investigations and found the following key points (Condliffe 2018):

- *Suicides*. A wave of suicides hit the subsidiary and other incidents occurred since the investigation started.
- *Wages and hours exploitation*. Authorities accused a subsidiary of forcing its employees to work excessive hours and paying them below the agreed-upon wages.
- *Poor employee livings standards*. The *New York Times* reported in 2012 that as many as 20 workers could be housed in a three-room staff apartment.
- *Serious accidents*. Many employees were seriously hurt by manufacturing equipment and fires that resulted from improper maintenance and training.

Apple has a history of healthy gross margins and its sales increased six-fold between 2009 and mid-September 2012 (Soranno 2015). Throughout this time, the company's Asian supply chains experienced multiple deadly events while assembling Apple's products. Unfortunately, most investors and analysts were unaware of these events. According to Soranno, Apple's shares have underperformed the S&P 500 index by more than 45 percent between 2012 Q1 and 2013 Q1. Since this event, Apple's management has addressed the supply chain weaknesses and spent millions to upgrade workers conditions and improve equipment safety.

SUMMARY AND CONCLUSIONS

Integrating ESG metrics into equity valuation is complex and lacks a common methodology and definitions. Despite these difficulties, many top firms are doing so. This investment method has far exceeded its original niche investment strategy that initially focused on exclusionary stock screens that negatively affected a portfolio's return and risk. Instead, top firms and institutional investors are using ESG metrics to identify both risks and opportunities better. This chapter focuses on the transition from traditional exclusionary screening SRI portfolios to the more common methodology that incorporates ESG integration in its equity valuation models, such as full integration.

Historically, SRI models concentrated on using ESG metrics to impact equities. Today, integrating ESG metrics in fixed income, real estate, and alternative investments is becoming common. During the financial crisis of 2007–2008, asset valuation models demonstrated poor performance in predicting the expected stock returns of equities. Today, ESG metrics are being standardized and best practices are being created to improve understanding of risk and return for assets during future periods of financial turmoil.

DISCUSSION QUESTIONS

1. Discuss why the lack of standardized guidelines regarding voluntary nonfinancial disclosure (ESG metrics) is such a critical problem for integrating ESG metrics into equity valuation.

2. Discuss the findings from academic research about the traditional SRI practice of negative screening.
3. To account for Apple's supply chain problems, discuss whether an analyst should consider adjusting the company's cost of capital upward to reflect the negative events associated with the global supplier.
4. Discuss how investors should consider the new types of risk that may affect brand value from negative events such as what Apple experienced with its supplier.

REFERENCES

Akben-Selçuk, Elif. 2019. "Corporate Social Responsibility and Financial Performance: The Moderating Role of Ownership Concentration in Turkey." *Sustainability* 11:13, 1–10.

Amel-Zadeh, Amir, and George Serafeim. 2018. "ESG Investing Moves to the Mainstream." *Financial Analysts Journal* 74:3, 87–103.

Bos, Jeroen. 2014a. "Integrating ESG Factors in the Investment Process." *CFA Institute Magazine*, January/February, 15–16.

Bos, Jeroen. 2014b. "Using ESG Factors for Equity Valuation." AJF Financial Services, September. Available at https://www.ajffinancial.com/using-esg-factors-for-equity-valuation-december-1-2014/.

Bradford, Hazel. 2015. "Department of Labor Opens the Door for ESG Considerations." *Pensions & Investments*, October. Available at https://www.pionline.com/article/20151022/ONLINE/151029940/department-of-labor-opens-the-door-for-esg-considerations.

Condliffe, Jamie. 2018. "Foxconn Is Under Scrutiny for Worker Conditions. It's Not the First Time." *New York Times*, June 11. Available at https://www.nytimes.com/2018/06/11/business/dealbook/foxconn-worker-conditions.html.

Deng, Xin, Jun-Koo Kang, and Buen Sin Low. 2013. "Corporate Social Responsibility and Stakeholder Value Maximization: Evidence from Mergers." *Journal of Financial Economics* 110:1, 87–109.

Dhaliwal, Dan, Oliver Zhen Li, Albert Tsang, and George Yang. 2011. "Voluntary Nonfinancial Disclosure and the Cost of the Equity Capital: The Initiation of Corporate Social Responsibility Reporting." *The Accounting Review* 86:1, 59–100.

Eccles, Robert, and Svetlana Klimenko. 2019. "The Investor Revolution: Shareholders Are Getting Serious about Sustainability." *Harvard Business Review*, May–June, 107–116.

Fabozzi, Frank J., K. C. Ma, and Becky J. Oliphant. 2008. "Sin Stock Returns." *Journal of Portfolio Management* 35:1, 82–94.

Filbeck, Aaron, Greg Filbeck, and Xin Zhao. 2019. "Performance Assessment of Firms Following Sustainalytics ESG Principles." *Journal of Investing* 28:2, 7–20.

Hayat, Usman, and Matt Orsagh. 2015. "Environmental, Social, and Governance Issues in Investing." CFA Institute, 1–43. Available at https://www.cfainstitute.org/en/advocacy/policy-positions/environmental-social-and-governance-issues-in-investing-a-guide-for-investment-professionals.

Heim, Lawrence. 2018. "Killing Sustainability." Amazon's Print-on-demand. Available at www.killingsustainability.com.

Humphrey, Jacquelyn E., and David T. Tan. 2014. "Does It Really Hurt to Be Responsible?" *Journal of Business Ethics* 122:3, 375–386.

Investor Responsibility Research Center Institute. 2013. "Integrated Financial and Sustainability Reporting in the United States." Available at https://www.iasplus.com/en/othernews/united-states/2013/integrated-reporting-in-the-us.

Investor Responsibility Research Center Institute. 2018. "State of Integrated and Sustainability Reporting." Available at https://www.weinberg.udel.edu/IIRCiResearchDocuments/2018/11/2018-SP-500-Integrated-Reporting-FINAL-November-2018-1.pdf.

Karmin, Craig. 2008. "Calstrs May Remove Ban on Tobacco Stocks." *Wall Street Journal*, June 5. Available at https://corpwatch.org/article/us-calstrs-may-remove-ban-tobacco-stocks.

Khan, Mozaffar, George Serafeim, and Aaron Yoon. 2016. "Corporate Sustainability: First Evidence of Materiality." *The Accounting Review* 91:6, 1697–1724.

KLD Index. 2019. "MSCI KLD 400 Social Index (USD)." November 29. Available at https://www.msci.com/documents/10199/904492e6-527e-4d64-9904-c710bf1533c6.

Laskar, Najul. 2018. "Impact of Corporate Sustainability Reporting on Firm Performance: An Empirical Examination in Asia." *Journal of Asia Business Studies* 12:4, 571–593.

Lu, Wenxiang, and Martin Taylor. 2016. "Which Factors Moderate the Relationship between Sustainability Performance and Financial Performance? A Meta-Analysis Study." *Journal of International Accounting Research* 15:1, 1–15.

Margolis, Joshua D., Hillary Anger Elfenbein, and James P. Walsh. 2008. "Do Well by Doing Good? Don't Count on It." *Harvard Business Review* 86:1, 19. Available at https://hbr.org/2008/01/do-well-by-doing-good-dont-count-on-it.

Morgan Stanley. 2018. "Sustainable Signals." Available at https://www.morganstanley.com/assets/pdfs/sustainable-signals-asset-owners-2018-survey.pdf.

Presler, Gabriel. 2019. "Sustainable Funds U.S. Landscape: 5 Takeaways from Our 2018 Report." *Morningstar*, February 19. Available at https://www.morningstar.com/blog/2019/02/19/esg-landscape.html.

Soranno, Steven. 2015. "Sustainable & Responsible Investing." Ameriprise Financial. Ameriprise Investment Research Group, May 27.

Schueth, Steve. 2003. "Socially Responsible Investing in the United States." *Journal of Business Ethics* 43:3, 189–194.

Wiengarten, Frank, Chris K. Y. Lo, and Jessie Y. K. Lam. 2017. "How Does Sustainability Leadership Affect Firm Performance? The Choices Associated with Appointing a Chief Officer of Corporate Social Responsibility." *Journal of Business Ethics* 140:3, 477–493.

CHAPTER 20

Pooled Investment Vehicles

Joseph McBride
Head of CRE Finance, Trepp LLC, Adjunct Assistant Professor of Finance,
Fordham University

Michael Pain
Managing Director, Arcview Capital, LLC, Independent Financial Consultant

Andrew C. Spieler
Robert F. Dall Distinguished Professor, Frank G. Zarb School of Business,
Hofstra University

INTRODUCTION

Pooled investment vehicles (PIVs) allow investors to aggregate investment funds to take advantage of the associated economies of scale in equity, fixed income, commodity, and derivative markets. Both active equity investors, looking to outperform a specific benchmark, and passive investors, simply tracking the return of an index, use PIVs. Many retail and institutional investors rely heavily on the almost endless combination of investment options provided by PIVs to meet their specific risk and return objectives. Today, PIVs cover virtually every conceivable style, factor, geography, company size, and management approach, as well as various environmental, social, and governance (ESG) matters.

According to the Investment Company Institute (2019a), equity PIVs experienced a global explosion in growth in recent years, from $11.9 trillion at the end of 2010 to $19.9 trillion by the end of 2018. Various long-term and cyclical macroeconomic factors such as increased competition, strong growth in passive investment management, and downward pressure on fees and expenses fueled this growth.

This chapter provides an overview of the most common PIVs dominating the market. The next section examines closed-end funds (CEFs), unit investment trusts (UITs), exchange-traded funds (ETFs), and open-end mutual funds (MFs). The chapter also explores various issues including comparative advantages and disadvantages, creation and redemption processes, liquidity, associated costs (implicit and explicit), leverage, and tax exposure.

OPEN-END MUTUAL FUNDS

As described by the Investment Funds Institute of Canada (2019), MFs have grown in popularity and provided investors with a cost-effective and relatively efficient way

TABLE 20.1   Net Assets in Investment Companies in the United States

This table displays the AUM in MFs, ETFs, CEFs, and UITs as of December 31, 2018. It demonstrates the market share dominance of MFs over all other fund structures, including ETFs. It does not, however, show the rate at which the gap between MFs and ETFs is narrowing.

Investment Vehicle	Assets in billions $	Percentage
Open-end mutual funds	17,707	82.8
Exchange-traded funds	3,371	15.8
Closed-end funds	250	1.2
Unit investment trusts	70	0.3
Total net assets	21,398	100.0

Source: Investment Company Institute (2019a).

of creating diversified portfolios since they were first created in 1924. MFs provide individual investors with an opportunity to access professional money managers that are otherwise unavailable to many individual investors. Although multiple PIVs are available to investors today, MFs continue to dominate this space in terms of assets under management (AUM). According to the Investment Company Institute (2019a), MFs accounted for about 83 percent of all pooled assets in the United States. Table 20.1 provides a breakdown of net assets across different PIVs in the United States.

Share Creation and Redemption Process

Understanding how MFs are formed and the process by which they issue and redeem shares is important to appreciate the risks and rewards associated with MF investing. The necessary process requires investors to invest directly with the MF company. The fund company accepts these investment dollars and issues new shares in the MF for the investor. The fund, in turn, invests the money received by purchasing more of the underlying assets of the MF, thereby providing the required equity exposure promised to the investor. Should investors need to sell/redeem their shares, the process is simply reversed. The fund liquidates the requisite amount of underlying assets to provide cash to the investor in exchange for the investors' shares in the MF. Because of this continual process across many investors, the fund is termed *open-end*.

MF shares trade only once per day after the market closes. Investors may place buy or sell orders with the fund at any point throughout the day, but they will not know the purchase or sale price of the shares in the fund until the market closes and the net asset value (NAV) at the close is calculated. Once the closing NAV per share is calculated, the MF executes all buy and sell orders at this NAV per share price.

Once-a-day trading has drawbacks for the investor and can create a cash drag on fund performance. The daily flow of cash into and out of the fund often results in the portfolio manager holding excess cash on hand to meet redemptions. The once-a-day trading of the shares also limits the portfolio manager from immediately investing cash received during the day. The cash drag imparts a countercyclical effect, dampening performance in rising markets and boosting performance in declining markets.

Costs Associated with Open-End Mutual Funds

Operating an MF involves a myriad of costs, including investment management/advisory fees, operational fees, custodial fees, marketing and distribution fees, and sales commissions/loads, to mention a few. Each MF's fee structure is different and must be fully disclosed in its prospectus. The fees charged affect both the fund's short- and long-term performance, so investors must clearly understand the total expenses and costs before investing in any fund. The following subsections explore a few of the main costs of MFs.

Sales Charges/Loads   *Loads* are effectively sales commissions paid to compensate the sales intermediary, such as a broker or investment advisor, for the time and expertise needed to select an appropriate fund for an investor. Loads fall into four main categories: (1) front-end load, (2) back-end load, (3) level load, and (4) no load.

1. *Front-end loads* are usually associated with "A-shares." Under this fee structure, an investor pays a sales charge when buying MF shares. This sales charge reduces the overall amount available to the portfolio manager to invest on behalf of the client. For example, an investor placing $10,000 in a fund with a 5 percent front-end load would end up paying $500 of that $10,000 as a sales commission up front. This reduction would leave $9,500 available to be invested in the fund at the NAV of the underlying securities. Front-end loads are generally unsuitable for investors with short-term investment horizons. Fund companies provide discounted sales loads as investors place more money with the fund. These discounts are commonly known as *breakpoints* and are simply the different dollar amounts at which an investor qualifies for a reduced sales charge. Breakpoints are specified in the fund's prospectus and determined by each fund individually. In the United States, the Securities and Exchange Commission (SEC) does not limit the sales load a fund may charge, but the Financial Industry Regulatory Authority (FINRA) does not permit mutual fund sales loads to exceed 8.5 percent. In practice, most sales charges fall well below this maximum level.

2. *Back-end loads*, also known as a *contingent deferred sales charge* (CDSC), are usually associated with "B Shares." Under this fee structure, investors pay no sales charge at the time of purchase. However, if they withdraw funds within a specified period, the fund assesses a charge on the full amount of principal withdrawn. The back-end sales charge can be a flat fee or, more commonly, a decreasing percentage over the years. For example, a fund with a 6 percent CDSC declining by 1 percent per year would charge a maximum sales load of 6 percent on any shares redeemed in the first year. In the second year, the sales load on redemptions would drop to 5 percent. This pattern would continue until no sales load would be charged on any redeemed shares after six years. The fund assesses a sales charge not only on the initial principal invested but also on any growth portion. This outcome could result in paying large commissions on shares that have performed well and are redeemed in the short run.

3. *Level loads* are usually associated with "C shares." Under this fee structure, the fund assesses a fixed sales charge on an annual basis. In the United States, this fee is capped at 1 percent annually. C shares often have a small, back-end load assessed on any redemptions that take place within the first year of share purchase. The level load structure is less suitable for both very-short-term and long-term investments. The level load structure is most appropriate for intermediate-term investments.
4. *No-load* funds are usually associated with index funds and do not have a sales charge levied on the purchase or sale of the MF shares. This situation does not mean that no-load funds do not have other fees or expenses.

Operating Expenses   Management fees are paid out of the fund's assets to the investment advisor/portfolio manager. The annual management fees vary substantially among funds depending on whether the fund is passively replicating an index or being actively managed to outperform a specific benchmark. The more actively managed the portfolio is and the greater the reputation of the manager, the higher the management fee is likely to be. High management fees come with the challenge for the portfolio manager to find and exploit market inefficiencies, to match and then outperform the fund's benchmark. Sharpe (1991) shows that the average return on actively managed assets underperforms the average return of passively managed assets due to the additional fees charged with active management. This finding is in line with reporting in March 2019 by S&P Dow Jones Indices, showing that the majority (64.5 percent) of large-cap funds underperformed the S&P 500 index (Soe, Liu, and Preston 2019).

The prospectus provides details of all fees and expenses but can still be confusing for many investors. Understanding the fund's expense ratio and comparing it to other funds can be helpful in the evaluation process. The annual *expense ratio* is simply the aggregation of all annual fees charged by the fund expressed as a percentage of the investment. The expense ratio does not factor in front- and back-end sales charges.

Fund Distributions   In most countries, including the United States, MFs receive special tax treatment. This treatment results in no taxes being assessed on the income earned or capital gains realized at the fund level. However, to qualify for this favored tax treatment, funds must distribute their income and realized capital gains to their shareholders. These distributions are then taxed at the shareholder level, at each shareholder's ordinary income and capital gains tax rates.

Distributions can affect after-tax returns and shareholder value. This relation increases the importance of understanding a fund's distribution schedule, turnover rate, as well as the nature and magnitude of the distributions. A fund's prospectus outlines its distribution schedule.

Distributions automatically reduce the fund's share price by the same amount as the distribution. However, the overall value to the shareholder remains the same as before the distribution. Despite the reduction in share price, this relation occurs because shareholders have now received a cash distribution equal to the exact amount of share price reduction. In a zero-tax world or tax-free account, the distribution would not affect the overall shareholder value. However, when considering taxes, the distribution creates a tax liability that the shareholder must pay, ultimately reducing overall shareholder value.

For example, if a shareholder owns 100 shares of a fund, each worth $100, the total value to the shareholder is $10,000. If the fund then distributes $5 per share, the share price drops to $95, and the total value to the shareholder is now 100 shares at $95 or $9,500. However, the shareholder has received a $5 cash distribution for each of the 100 shares held, resulting in a total cash distribution of $500. In a tax-free account, the total value to the shareholder is still $10,000. Taxing the distribution at 30 percent results in a tax liability of $150, which reduces the overall value to the shareholder from $10,000 to $9,850.

MFs generally distribute the net capital gains toward the end of each year. Existing shareholders are responsible for any associated tax liability at the time of capital gains distribution. Thus, shareholders can be exposed to unnecessary taxes if they buy a fund with considerable undistributed capital gains.

CLOSED-END FUNDS

According to the Investment Company Institute (2019b, 2019c, 2019d), assets held in CEFs totaled $270.17 billion across 499 CEFs at the end of the second quarter of 2019. However, the total investment in CEFs is relatively small compared to ETFs ($3.93 trillion) and MFs ($19.87 trillion). CEFs are investment companies that issue ownership shares initially through an initial public offering (IPO) and use the money raised to invest in equity, fixed income, and other investable assets (Closed-End Fund Association 2019). CEFs offer relatively liquid access to buy and sell pools of securities without having to trade the underlying assets in the pools (Cherkes, Sagi, and Stanton 2009). The major differences between CEFs and other PIVs stem from the structure of the funds, the mechanics of investing in them, their daily pricing, and the effect of investment flows on portfolio managers' investment decisions. Figure 20.1 summarizes the fund types of CEFs between 1996 and 2018. The overall invested funds have increased steadily since the financial crisis of 2007–2008.

Structure and Trading

The "closed-end" aspect of CEFs describes a key structural feature that differentiates them from MFs and ETFs. *Closed-end* means that the fund does not regularly issue new shares or redeem outstanding shares. At inception, a CEF issues a fixed number of shares to be sold to investors. Those shares then trade in the open market, most commonly on a stock exchange. Investors buy and sell the shares through brokerage accounts, just like buying and selling common equity stock, and the price of the CEF shares changes based on market supply and demand throughout the trading day (Closed-End Fund Association 2019). This process differs markedly from how investors access MFs. MFs calculate an execution price for all daily buys and sells based on the fund's end-of-day *net asset value* (NAV).

In the ordinary course of business, a CEF does not issue new shares or redeem outstanding shares. A mutual fund manager must issue new shares when buying activity outweighs selling activity and redeem, or buy back, shares when the reverse is true. Conversely, a CEF does not need to worry about liquidity logistics because the outstanding shares are freely tradable, and the funds are not required to redeem

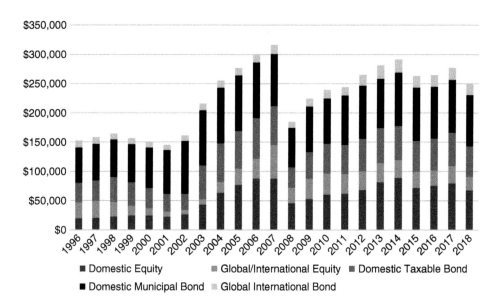

FIGURE 20.1   Closed-end Fund Asset Types

This figure provides the different types of CEFs in millions between 1996 and 2018.

Source: https://www.icifactbook.org/data/19_fb_data#section2.

shares from investors on demand (U.S. Securities and Exchange Commission 2019a). This structure leads to more liquidity for investors looking to buy or sell shares as well as more latitude in terms of the types of assets the fund can buy and sell. *Free-floating shares* mean an investor can buy or sell at any time during the trading day and that the price of the shares reacts quickly to market forces of supply and demand.

Further, because the fund itself has no obligation to redeem shares from sellers, it can enter less liquid and longer-term investments (U.S. Securities and Exchange Commission 2019a). Whereas MFs must have enough liquidity to pay for redemptions if and when they occur, CEF fund advisors are less influenced by the ebbs and flows of investor demand for their fund's shares. This arrangement allows them to invest in longer-term, less liquid assets, and, ideally, to maintain their investment strategy despite market turmoil.

Fund advisors are professional investment management firms that manage CEF activity. For this service, they collect a management fee that differs across CEFs. The fees are most often calculated as a percentage of total AUM, including the effect of leverage (Fidelity 2019). *Total assets* equal the total amount of equity capital invested in the fund plus any debt employed by the fund. Some CEFs employ debt to magnify returns and benefit from arbitrage opportunities. These funds benefit when their holdings appreciate more than unlevered funds that do not employ debt, but they also suffer greater losses when their assets lose value. Management fees in a leveraged fund are also higher as a percentage of *net assets*, the total capital invested by equity investors. This logic is similar to any company employing leverage, whether an investment or an operating company. Leverage magnifies the return on equity on both the upside and downside.

Although the general structure of CEFs is relatively simple, an often studied but not well-understood phenomenon occurs in the CEF market. Many CEFs trade at a discount to their NAV. *NAV* is calculated as the market value of the securities held less the liabilities, divided by the number of shares outstanding. For example, an investor can buy a share of a pool of securities worth $10 for less than $10. In a rational, no-arbitrage market, this pricing discrepancy technically should not exist. Researchers have extensively studied the discount between a CEF's share price and its NAV per share and attributed it to various causes such as management fees, investor liquidity, tax preferences, and finite individual investor time horizons (Dimson and Minio-Paluello 2002). None of these causes adequately explains this market anomaly. Some market watchers believe that buying funds that trade at a discount to their NAV should ultimately lead to outsized returns, while others are unconvinced that the discount is destined to shrink (Berk and Stanton 2004).

Sources of Return and Tax Implications

According to the Closed-End Fund Association (2019), CEF investors can realize a return in three ways: (1) income dividends, (2) capital gains distributions, and (3) gains on CEF share sales. Investment companies such as CEFs do not pay taxes on income or capital gains but rather pass them through to shareholders who pay tax. CEFs pay out income generated by fund holdings through interest or dividends to their shareholders, which can be paid monthly, quarterly, or annually depending on the CEF's structure. These cash flows are generally taxed at the investor's ordinary income tax rate. CEFs pay capital gains distributions usually once a year to shareholders. These gains are split between short- and long-term capital gains and shareholders are taxed on each portion differently depending on their tax bracket. Finally, an investor can generate returns simply by buying low and selling high. CEF prices usually appreciate along with their NAVs but can also benefit from increased investor demand.

In summary, CEFs offer individual investors access to pools of securities that would be difficult and costly for those investors to construct themselves. Individual investors benefit from professionally managed investment portfolios and a liquid market for buying and selling shares of those portfolios. Further, investors may benefit from buying into CEFs trading at a discount to their NAV. Although the CEF portion of the market is relatively small compared to MFs and ETFs, it offers a compelling proposition for investors seeking specific investment objectives and asset classes with increased liquidity.

UNIT INVESTMENT TRUSTS

A *unit investment trust* (UIT) is an investment company that issues shares once, holds a fixed portfolio of investment assets, and has a stated termination date when the trust sells any remaining assets and dissolves (U.S. Securities and Exchange Commission 2019b). As of year-end 2018, a total of 4,917 UITs existed with net assets of $70 billion outstanding, which is very small compared to ETFs, MFs, and CEFs (Investment Company Institute 2019a).

Structure and Trading

UITs have some structural similarities to MFs in that their shares are redeemable. However, UITs generally issue a fixed number of shares at inception, similar to CEFs. Unique to UITs is the concept of a fixed termination date or maturity, at which time the trust liquidates any remaining assets and distributes proceeds to UIT investors (Investment Company Institute 2019a). UITs are required by law to hold a mostly fixed portfolio with a clearly stated goal as detailed in the trust's prospectus. UITs can aim for a capital gain, income, or some combination of both through ownership of stocks, bonds, REITs, CEFs, or any other investable assets. The UIT's stated termination date often corresponds with its stated goals and portfolio mix. For example, a UIT that invests in long-term fixed-income assets typically has a longer stated life compared to a UIT seeking opportunistic capital appreciation (Investment Company Institute 2019a).

After issuing a fixed number of units at inception, trust sponsors often make a market by buying and selling trust units. Whether they make a market or not, trust sponsors must redeem units at the NAV upon investor request. In this way, UITs are similar to MFs. Both trust sponsors and brokers in commission or fee accounts sell UITs to investors (Mahn 2013). Unlike most other PIVs, UITs do not have a board of directors or an investment adviser because they hold a fixed pool of assets.

UITs are structured either as a Regulated Investment Company (RIC) or a Grantor Trust (BNY Mellon 2018). Both structures are alike from the investor's point of view, but structural differences exist. As an RIC, UIT holders are considered to own shares in the trust, not in the underlying securities. Conversely, investors in Grantor Trusts are viewed as holding a pro-rata share of each security in the trust. These differences can affect how investors are taxed on distributions and capital appreciation.

Sources of Return and Tax Implications

A UIT generates a return for unit owners based on the underlying assets the UIT holds. A fixed-income UIT tends to generate interest income, while an equity portfolio tends toward a mix of dividend income and capital appreciation. Of course, each UIT has specific investment goals and parameters that dictate the fixed pool of investments and the maturity of the trust.

UITs are structured as pass-through entities, so the trusts themselves are not subject to taxation. Holders of UIT units pay taxes on the income and realized capital appreciation. If the UIT is a RIC, taxes are determined at the level of the RIC units. An investor's cost basis is based on the purchase price of the UIT units, and taxes on dividend income and capital gains are calculated based on the UIT unit payouts. Conversely, in a grantor trust UIT, all calculations are done on a pro-rata basis at the underlying asset level. Because both trusts are priced at end-of-day NAV and tax reporting statements for each outline the proper categorizations of income types, these tax differences are less of an issue for the average investor. Figure 20.2 summarizes the fund types of UITs between 1996 and 2018. Aside from 1996, the majority of assets allocated to UITs are equity-based, followed by tax-free debt and taxable debt.

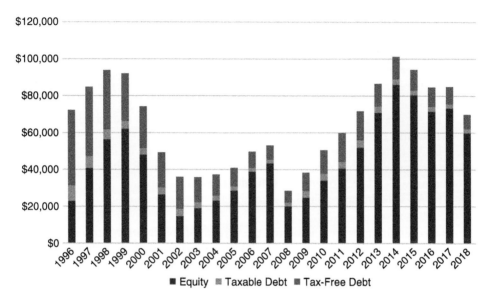

FIGURE 20.2 Unit Investment Trust Asset Types

This figure provides the total assets in millions of different types of UITs between 1996 and 2018.

Source: Investment Company Institute (2019b, 2019c, 2019d).

EXCHANGE-TRADED FUNDS

According to Vanguard (2019), the first ETF in the United States started trading in 1993. ETFs incorporate many of the same benefits of MFs such as providing investors with diversification and access to both active and passive professional money managers. ETFs have also improved on MFs in areas such as continuous trading, reduced administrative costs, greater transparency, and better tax efficiency. The structure of ETFs provides for new ways to manage risk and leverage returns in ways that MFs cannot. As with any PIV, ETFs also have drawbacks and risks associated with their structure such as market risk, trading costs on small positions, illiquidity, and composition risk.

ETFs have enjoyed a robust expansion in popularity and demand among both institutional and retail investors. According to the Investment Company Institute (2019a), ETFs accounted for almost 16 percent of all pooled assets in the United States. As mentioned previously, Table 20.1 provides a breakdown of net assets across different PIVs in the United States. The 16 percent ETF weighting is still a relatively small percentage by comparison to the almost 83 percent market share enjoyed by MFs. However, ETFs are continuing to rapidly acquire market share and narrow the gap in both domestic and international markets.

Basic Overview of ETF Share Creation and Redemption

To comprehend how ETFs work and their associated risks and benefits requires a clear understanding of the ETF share creation and redemption process. Once an ETF company establishes a fund and decides which underlying securities it wants to hold, it turns to institutional investors, known as *authorized participants* (APs), to begin the share creation process. The AP's role is to acquire the underlying securities that the ETF wants to hold.

The share creation process can be broken down into four steps:

1. The AP goes into the market and uses its capital to buy the securities that the ETF wants to hold.
2. The AP delivers these securities to the ETF.
3. In exchange for the securities received from the AP, the ETF company provides the AP with a block of equally valued ETF shares.
4. The AP sells the new ETF shares received in the open market to investors.

The redemption process is simply the reverse of the creation process. This creation/redemption process is ongoing and occurs repetitively as the demand and supply of ETF shares fluctuate.

Purchase/Sale of ETF Shares by Investors

Once ETF shares have been created, they trade on exchanges just like the shares of common stock. Investors can buy and sell shares continuously throughout the trading day, unlike MFs, which trade only once daily. Executing any ETF trades is subject to explicit trading costs such as commissions and exchange fees. Although ETFs are generally a cost-efficient way of acquiring the shares, the explicit costs can be a major burden for small value purchases. Executing ETF trades is also subject to implicit trading costs such as slippage, the bid–ask spread, and market impact. Buy and sell orders can be placed using both market and limit orders and their associated variations, thereby giving investors greater flexibility in determining the price at which they are willing to transact for a particular share.

Because ETFs trade on exchanges, they can trade at a premium or a discount to the NAV of their underlying securities. As net demand for shares increases, ETFs begin to trade at a premium. This premium signals the AP that more shares are needed in the market and that the opportunity to generate an arbitrage profit is now available to them. The AP takes advantage of this opportunity to profit by purchasing the underlying securities in the open market and delivering them to the ETF company in exchange for new ETF shares. The AP then turns around and sells these newly issued shares in the open market, at a premium to the NAV, generating a profit for itself and simultaneously driving the price of the ETF down closer to the NAV. The AP continues this process until the premium is eroded and the shares once again trade at or close to the NAV.

The reverse process is true if ETF shares are trading at a discount to the NAV. This situation indicates a decrease in net demand for ETF shares. The AP once again identifies the opportunity to make an arbitrage profit. In this situation, the AP buys ETF shares in the open market, driving the share price of the ETF back to the NAV. The AP then takes the ETF shares it just bought and returns them to the ETF fund company in exchange for the underlying securities. The AP then sells the underlying securities at their fair value in the open market, resulting in an arbitrage profit.

TABLE 20.2   Comparison of Open-End Mutual Funds and Exchange-Traded Funds

This table summarizes some of the primary differences between open-end mutual funds and exchange-traded funds.

Characteristic	Open-end Mutual Funds	Exchange-traded Funds
Share issuance and redemption	Directly from the MF company	Created using APs
Liquidity	Daily at the close of business	Continuously tradable during exchange operating hours
Share pricing	Always at the NAV	May trade at a premium, discount, or the NAV
Overall cost structure	Higher	Lower
Tax efficiency	Generally less tax-efficient	Generally more tax-efficient
Short positions of fund shares	Not permitted	Permitted
Margin	Not permitted	Permitted
Active/passive management	Both	Both but most ETFs are passively managed
Transparency	Lower	Higher

Normally an ETF has several APs associated with it. This situation creates competition and greater efficiency in the market. The ability for the AP to make an arbitrage profit is central to the share creation and redemption process and to keeping shares trading close to the NAV.

Related Benefits of the ETF Structure

The unique share creation and redemption process of ETF shares, along with the way ETFs trade in the secondary markets, provide benefits not only for the fund companies, APs, and exchanges, but also for the investor/shareholder. Some major shareholder benefits are discussed next. Table 20.2 provides a summary of the key differences between MFs and ETFs.

Transparency   According to ETF.com (2018), ETFs offer better transparency of their holdings than competing MFs. The holdings of almost all ETFs worldwide are available daily on websites such as www.ishares.com. The structure and share creation/redemption process of ETFs largely drive this transparency. In some cases, however, disclosure requirements are the driving force, as is the case with actively managed ETFs in the United States. This daily transparency differs substantially from MFs, which are only required to disclose their holdings quarterly and are afforded a 30-day delay in reporting these holdings. The benefit of having better transparency as with an ETF is that the investor can more effectively monitor and detect any style drift that may be taking place and evaluate the impact on the portfolio's overall asset allocation.

Tax Efficiency   According to Johnson (2019), ETFs tend to be more tax efficient than MFs. ETFs have historically had much lower capital gains distributions than MFs, which is partially the result of most ETFs being passively managed index funds with minimal turnover. However, when comparing index funds, ETFs are still more tax efficient due to the in-kind redemption process. When an MF has a redemption, fund managers must sell underlying fund shares to provide cash to pay to the shareholder. These sales create turnover and realized capital gains that the fund must distribute to shareholders. The process for ETFs is different. When investors want to sell their shares, they sell them on the exchange, having no impact on the turnover of the ETF's underlying portfolio. Besides, if ETF shares are returned in-kind to the AP as previously described, this situation avoids additional turnover and manufacture of capital gains that must be distributed. ETFs can still have some capital gains that must be distributed to shareholders occasionally, but the amount is a fraction of the gains incurred by MFs.

Short Positions   Unlike MFs, ETFs can be sold short with two key benefits to the investor. First, shorting the ETF provides the investor with the opportunity and ability to profit in a down market. Second, investors can use shorting as an effective risk management tool to help hedge their exposure. For example, an investor with a large restricted stock position in a single security could mitigate some downside risks by shorting an ETF concentrated in the industry in place of the restricted position.

Margin   Once again, unlike MFs, investors can buy ETF shares on margin, thus leveraging their returns. This situation differs from and should not be confused with ETFs and MFs, which can both use internal leverage to enhance their returns if designated by the fund's prospectus. Most MFs do not use internal leverage and are governed by strict rules regarding any leverage allowed within an MF. Leveraged ETFs often use both debt and derivatives to enhance their returns. Investors should be aware that internal leverage can also amplify any losses within the fund.

SUMMARY AND CONCLUSIONS

PIVs provide investors with the ability to pool their investment funds to take advantage of associated economies of scale while diversifying their holdings. With an already large and expanding universe of PIVs, the task of identifying, evaluating, and selecting the most appropriate vehicle for an investor becomes increasingly difficult and requires proper due diligence. Before engaging in the due diligence necessary to evaluate a PIV, the investor's investment risk and return objectives must be identified along with any investment constraints, such as time horizon, liquidity needs, tax exposure, legal issues, and any unique needs. Only after understanding these objectives and constraints should an investor begin the task of identifying and evaluating the merits of a MF, CEF, ETF, or UIT.

Understanding the features and associated implications of each PIV is critical to the overall investment due diligence process. Investors must, however, go further and remember that MFs, CEFs, ETFs, and UITs are simply wrappers around the underlying securities held. Investors need to evaluate these underlying securities in terms of their objectives, constraints, and overall portfolio.

As discussed throughout the chapter, PIVs can simplify an investor's investment process and provide a wide range of benefits. However, if not correctly understood and evaluated, PIVs can also result in a wide range of unintended negative consequences.

DISCUSSION QUESTIONS

1. Discuss the tax efficiency of ETFs relative to MFs.
2. Discuss the relative transparency of ETFs into the underlying assets and benefits to investors.
3. Discuss three benefits of ETFs.
4. Contrast the share creation processes of MFs and ETFs.
5. Describe the important differences between MFs and CEFs.

REFERENCES

Berk, Jonathan, and Richard Stanton. 2004. "A Rational Model of the Closed-End Fund Discount." Working Paper, Haas School of Business, University of California at Berkeley. Available at https://pdfs.semanticscholar.org/be92/cc469e372d7f5c358e9991b84860e4c98566.pdf.

BNY Mellon. 2018. "Unit Investment Trust General Information for Reporting." Available at https://www.invesco.com/static/us/investors/contentdetail?contentId=132182dd9ac12610VgnVCM1000006e36b50aRCRD.

Cherkes, Martin, Jacob Sagi, and Richard Stanton. 2009. "A Liquidity-Based Theory of Closed-End Funds." *Review of Financial Studies* 22:1, 257–297.

Closed-End Fund Association. 2019. "CEF Basics." August. Available at https://www.cefa.com/Learn/Content/CEFBasics.fs.

Dimson, Elroy, and Carolina Minio-Paluello. 2002. *The Closed-End Fund Discount*. Charlottesville, VA: The Research Foundation of the Association for Investment Management and Research.

ETF.com. 2018. "How Transparent Are ETFs?" Available at https://www.etf.com/sections/features-and-news/etf-education-how-transparent-are-etfs.

Fidelity. 2019. "Closed-End Fund Expenses." August. Available at https://www.fidelity.com/learning-center/investment-products/closed-end-funds/expenses.

Investment Company Institute. 2019a. *Investment Company Factbook, 59th Edition*. Available at https://www.icifactbook.org/ch2/19_fb_ch2.

Investment Company Institute. 2019b. "Closed End Fund Assets and Net Issuance Second Quarter, 2019." August. Available at https://www.ici.org/research/stats/closedend/cef_q2_19.

Investment Company Institute. 2019c. "ETF Assets and Net Issuance June 2019." August. Available at https://www.ici.org/research/stats/etf/etfs_06_19.

Investment Company Institute. 2019d. "Trends in Mutual Fund Investing June 2019." August. Available at https://www.ici.org/research/stats/trends/trends_06_19.

Investment Funds Institute of Canada. 2019. "The History of Mutual Funds." Available at https://www.ifca.ca/en/articles/.who-we-are-history-of-mutual-funds.

Johnson, Ben. 2019. "What Drives ETF Tax Efficiency?" Morningstar Research Services LLC, August 7. Available at https://www.morningstar.com/blog/2019/08/07/etf-tax-efficiency.html.

Mahn, Kevin. 2013. "Why Unit Investment Trusts Can Be a Good Investment Alternative." *Forbes*, April 22. Available at https://www.forbes.com/sites/advisor/2013/04/22/why-unit-investment-trusts-can-be-a-good-investment-alternative/#2c4371ce5bd7.

Sharpe, William 1991. "The Arithmetic of Active Management." *Financial Analysts Journal* 47:1, 7–9.

Soe, Aye, Berlinda Liu, and Hamish Preston. 2019. "SPIVA US Scorecard." S&P Dow Jones Indices. Available at https://us.spindices.com/documents/spiva/spiva-us-year-end-2018.pdf.

U.S. Securities and Exchange Commission. 2019a. "Closed-End Funds." August. Available at https://www.investor.gov/additional-resources/general-resources/glossary/closed-end-funds.

U.S. Securities and Exchange Commission. 2019b. "Unit Investment Trusts." August. Available at https://www.sec.gov/fast-answers/answersuithtm.html.

Vanguard. 2019. "What Is the History of ETFs?" Available at https://advisors.vanguard.com/VGApp/iip/site/advisor/etfcenter/article/ETF_HistoryOfETFs.

Special Equity Topics

CHAPTER 21

Investing in Private Equity

Gaurav Gupta
Analytics Consultant, SRNL International
Tianqi Jiang
PhD Candidate, University of Rhode Island
Zhao Wang
Assistant Professor of Finance, Capital University of Economics and Business

INTRODUCTION

Private equity (PE) is an alternative asset class of particular interest to institutional investors and family offices. PE investments, as opposed to public market investments, are private ownership interests in the equity of private companies or publicly listed companies (Hasan 2014). Investors in PE are typically invested for a 7- to 10-year time horizon. PE falls under a broader category of alternative investments, which also includes real estate, hedge funds, and commodities, among others. Only accredited investors, such as high-net-worth individuals (HNWI) or institutional investors, can participate in PE investments. Such investments are less liquid, require a longer capital commitment, and have a longer time-horizon than the traditional publicly listed asset classes such as equities and bonds. PE investments require more involvement in the invested business from the investor/PE firm. Additionally, an average commitment period is for five years, and an investor must keep cash readily available for any capital calls within this commitment period. A *capital call* is a request from a PE fund to the investor in a commitment period to advance cash. This capital call usually occurs when a potential deal can be closed or has been closed.

PE includes venture capital (VC), leveraged buyouts (LBOs), direct lending, distressed debt, and private investment in a public entity (PIPE) (Hasan 2014). PE can also include *equity bridge financing*, which is temporary financing given to a company until it acquires permanent financing through an initial public offering (IPO) or debt financing. VC is an early-stage investment in the startup phase of a company. A *buyout* occurs when a private entity buys a public company, removing it from the public markets. When buyouts are financed with debt, they are called *leveraged buyouts*. Smaller players who have limited or no access to the public markets for funding may need to borrow directly from PE firms. This form of funding is *direct lending*. PE firms also lend money to companies in bankruptcy proceedings. This form of investing is *distressed debt investing*. Instead of a complete buyout, PE can also buy a proportion of a publicly listed company, which is termed a PIPE.

Typically, annualized target returns in PE often range between 15 and 25 percent. To allow multiple investors to participate in PE investments, a pooled structure known as a PE fund can be established. A *PE fund* is a closed-end fund with an average time horizon of 7 to 10 years, which can be extended to an additional 1 to 5 years, if required (Yau, Schneeweis, Robinson, and Weiss 2017).

VC is an early-stage investment in a business. This investment can include seed money, startup financing, and equity bridge financing.

- *Seed money* refers to the financing made available to a business when it is in the idea phase, not the operational phrase. Since no real asset/business exists at this stage, a seed investor is also called an *angel investor* for taking a risk and supporting a company in the idea phase. Many consider this investment to be one of the riskiest investments.
- *Startup financing* refers to funds provided when a company has been formed and is now in the operational stage. The company needs this funding to start generating revenues.
- *Equity bridge financing* is temporary financing made available to the business before it can acquire other permanent financing from other sources such as IPOs and debt financing (Williams 2016).

A *buyout* (BO) is a transaction in which a buyer acquires a private or public company, restructures the firm, and resells it to make profits. When financed with debt, buyouts are known as LBOs.

The major investors in a PE fund are pension funds, endowments, foundations, and family offices. In assessing the appropriateness of a PE investment, an investor should consider five factors: (1) liquidity, (2) long-term capital commitment requirement, (3) relative risk compared to traditional publicly listed asset classes, (4) potential for portfolio diversification, and (5) required commitment (investment) amount.

The remainder of this chapter is organized as follows. The next section provides an overview of PE funds' performance evaluation to explain the importance of PE in a portfolio. The following section discusses PE returns and how PE can enhance portfolio returns, followed by a discussion on factors that drive PE investments. Next, the chapter provides a detailed discussion on the related risk factors such as liquidity risk, default risk, and capital risk. Finally, the chapter offers a summary and conclusions.

PERFORMANCE OF PE FUNDS

Investors expect fund managers to deliver returns appropriate to the risk level being taken. Not surprisingly, they also seek managers who can do a superior job. Therefore, evaluating the performance of PE funds is an essential task for investors who invest in PE.

One strand of literature documents that the returns on PE investments are no higher than those on public equity. For example, Moskowitz and Vissing-Jørgensen (2002) show that only 34 percent of PE firms survive 10 years after their inception. They also recognize that obtaining a precise measure of PE's mean return is difficult.

Phalippou and Gottschalg (2009) examine mature funds both net-of-fees and gross-of-fees, finding that the net-of-fees fund performance, on average, underperformed the S&P 500 index. The performance would be worse if they incorporated risk factors into the calculation. However, these funds outperformed the S&P 500 index gross-of-fees by 3 percentage points per year. Their sample selection aims to minimize the impact of self-reported net asset value (NAV) of the ongoing investments, and thus, performance can be evaluated on cash inflows and outflows only.

Their results show that funds still report large accounting valuations for their ongoing investments even when they have reached their normal liquidation age. This behavior biases performance estimates upward based on the internal rate of return (IRR). The authors also focus on the present value of investments and use it to weigh fund performance. Compared with the standard capital-committed weighting, this choice reduces performance by 2 percentage points. Further, adjusting for risk decreases performance by about 3 percentage points annually, leading net-of-fees alpha to –6 percentage points annually.

Given the differences between PE investments and public equities, one may expect different evaluation measures for PE funds. The most widely used measures are IRR and the multiple of invested capital (MOIC). Calculating IRR of PE funds is based on a set of cash flows, which include cash contributed, distributions, and unrealized investments. *MOIC* is a ratio of the sum of realized and unrealized value to the cash contributed. Each measure has advantages and limitations. For example, Ljungqvist and Richardson (2003) document that the illiquidity of PE funds could result in imprecise estimates of performance measures, such as IRR.

Compared with other approaches, the public market equivalent (PME) has the main advantage of being simple to calculate and apply. Sorensen and Jagannathan (2015) conclude that PME is a ratio in which the numerator is the discounted distribution and the denominator is the discounted capital call. A distribution represents a cash flow that goes to the limited partners (LP) from the PE fund after the fund successfully sells or recapitalizes a company. *Capital calls* are the investment of the LP. The authors show that the PME is valid under three unrestrictive conditions: (1) markets are frictionless and the "law of one price" holds; (2) the LP's preference can be measured by a logarithmic function; and (3) the return on the LP's total wealth portfolio equals the return on the public market. The authors show that the PME approach is equivalent to evaluating the performance of PE funds using Rubinstein's (1976) dynamic capital asset pricing model (CAPM). However, PME's main limitation is that it works well for evaluating past performance, but not as well for forecasting.

Kaplan and Schoar (2005) investigate PE performance using three methods: (1) IRR calculated by a data provider, (2) IRR calculated by the authors, and (3) PME. Their PME is based on fund cash flows and exhibits as a market multiple. To calculate the PME, they invest all cash outflows of a PE investment at the total return to a market index and compare the resulting value to the value of the cash inflows to the PE investment using the total return to the market index.

To illustrate, suppose PE Fund A invested $100 million in March 2015, and it grew to $120 million in three years. If this fund had invested the same amount of money in the S&P 500 index, the fund would have been worth $127 million at the end of the three years. The PME, in this case, is 0.95 (120/127), which means that the fund underperformed the market index. As another example, assume PE Fund B had a value of $100 million in February 2016 after an initial investment of $100 million in February 2015. However, the assets would have declined to $92 million if the fund invested $100 million in the S&P 500 index over the same period. In this case, the PME is 1.08 (100/92), which means that the fund outperformed the market index. The IRR in the first case is positive, and the IRR in the second case is zero.

Kaplan and Schoar (2005) find that the net-of-fees return to funds, on average, approximately equals that of the S&P 500 index, but substantial heterogeneity exists across funds. Weighted by committed capital, VCs outperform the S&P 500 index over their sample period between 1980 and 1997, but buyout funds do not. Additionally, the gross-of-fees return to both types of funds outperforms the S&P 500 index over the sample period.

Harris, Jenkinson, and Kaplan (2014) emphasize that high-quality data are essential for evaluating the performance of PE investments. They find that buyout funds outperform the S&P 500 index. Each dollar invested in the PE fund, on average, resulted in a gain of at least 20 percent more than a dollar invested in the S&P 500 index. This result is insensitive to benchmark selection and systematic risk. VC funds outperformed the public markets before the 2000s but have underperformed since then.

Phalippou (2014) uses a publicly available dataset for buyout fund cash flows to replicate the findings of Harris et al. (2014). Although the author finds that buyout funds outperform the S&P 500 index, Phalippou contends that buyout funds are primarily invested in small and value firms, thus, a large-cap index, such as the S&P 500 index, may be an inappropriate benchmark. Further, the author finds that the average buyout fund underperforms the public market if the benchmark is changed to small and value indices.

PERFORMANCE PERSISTENCE

Besides knowing whether funds outperform, a more critical question is whether they can consistently outperform. Specifically, can analysts or investors use the track record of funds to predict future performance? Continued outperformance does not necessarily reflect the superior skill of a PE fund's general partners (GPs), but random outperformance could be due to good luck only. This section reviews the empirical results of persistence in PE fund performance.

Kaplan and Schoar (2005) provide early evidence of performance persistence of PE funds. Their findings show that a 100 basis point (bps) increase in the fund's past performance is associated with a 54 bps higher performance of the current fund. They also consider two concerns that may weaken their findings. First, a particular GP may have some investments in common for the current and previous funds. Second, overlapping periods across funds may induce some persistence. After removing these two concerns and other potential drivers, Kaplan and Schoar find that GPs whose funds outperform the industry in one fund tend to outperform the industry in the next. The persistence exists between two consecutive funds and between the current fund and the second previous fund.

In a follow-up study, Phalippou (2010) revisits Kaplan and Schoar's (2005) investigation of return persistence. He finds that Kaplan and Schoar overstate the performance persistence of PE because they do not use an ex-ante performance measure of the earlier funds. Phalippou maintains that an investor's capital allocation is a one-time decision because the investor cannot continuously change the fund's capital allocation. In practice, an investor's allocation happens at the time of fundraising. Thus, ex-ante performance refers to the information on past performance at the time of fundraising. The author documents that unsophisticated investors mainly drive performance, despite the ex-ante measure used. Meanwhile, earlier funds' performance, sequence, and size do not help sophisticated investors to predict fund performance.

Harris, Jenkinson, Kaplan, and Stucke (2014) provide a new way to analyze the performance persistence of PE funds using a new dataset, Burgiss, of fund-level cash flows. They confirm the previous findings of the performance persistence of buyout funds and venture funds in the pre-2000 period. For the post-2000 period, the authors find little evidence of performance persistence for buyout funds, but VC funds remain as persistent as the pre-2000 period. Harris et al. provide two possible explanations. First, the buyout business could have changed after 2000. Second, GPs learned from their peers, reducing return persistence. For VC funds, their results indicate that investing in previously outperforming GPs remains a good strategy. Moreover, previous funds that are above the median show stronger persistence.

Some recent studies offer a more in-depth analysis of the performance persistence of PE funds. Braun, Jenkinson, and Stoff (2017) revisit the issue of performance persistence using a new dataset of buyout funds. The authors collect 13,523 investments made by 269 GPs and find that persistence declined. They document that the performance persistence of buyout funds is weaker when traditional analysis is used. They also contend that the mature market makes the privileged access to outperformed GPs less valuable so that GP performance persistence disappears. As the market matured, it becomes more competitive. Accordingly, the authors find that performance persistence exists during low-competition periods only. In line with Phalippou (2010), they claim that uninformed investors hold underperforming funds. Braun et al. find that bottom-quartile performing funds show persistence regardless of the market state (low competition or high competition).

In another recent study, Korteweg and Sorensen (2017) decompose the persistence of PE performance into long-term, investable, and spurious persistence. The authors define *long-term persistence* as the possibility that some PE funds persistently generate higher (or lower) expected net-of-fees returns. *Investable persistence* refers to the difficulty of identifying high-expected-return PE funds. *Spurious persistence* stands for a component that arises from the partial overlap of consecutive funds that are managed by the same GP. After conducting this decomposition, the authors find a high level of long-term persistence and low investable persistence. They also find that the long-term persistence of smaller funds is greater than that of larger funds.

FACTORS DRIVING PE PERFORMANCE

Fund-level studies explore the determinants of returns on PE investments. For example, Kaplan and Schoar's (2005) pioneering work, past returns, and fund size are primary drivers of fund performance. Phalippou and Zollo (2005) also focus on fund-level data and explore factors driving returns.

Phalippou and Zollo (2005) examine the impact of business cycles and stock market cycles on returns. Given the industry information and investment types, they compute the proxy for the CAPM beta for each investment based on the matching industry betas with certain leverage assumptions. They then aggregate investment betas at the fund level to obtain a fund beta. However, the authors do not find a significant association between fund beta and performance. Further, Phalippou and Zollo find that macroeconomic conditions significantly drive the performance of PE investments. Those factors are particularly important at the time of investment inception.

Moreover, public stock markets significantly affect PE investments. They find a positive relation between public market value-weighted returns and PE fund returns. When considering those two factors simultaneously, macroeconomic conditions are more influential when making investments, whereas public stock market returns are influential over the private investment's life.

Aigner, Albrecht, Beyschlag, Friederich, Kalepky, and Zagst (2008) extend prior literature and examine a set of potential determinants of PE fund performance by developing regression models that explain up to 64 percent of the variation in PE returns. After calculating the buyout ratio as the percentage of buyout deals in a PE fund, the authors find that the buyout ratio is positively related to fund performance, and the fund with more buyout deals is less likely to incur a deficit for one deal. Consistent with prior literature, they find that GPs' experience can improve a PE fund's performance. However, experienced GPs are more willing to invest in riskier projects, bringing a fund a higher possibility of losing money. Aigner et al. also show that microeconomic conditions affect fund performance. For example, interest rates negatively impact fund performance. Also, the average GDP growth rate of the targeted region for investment has a positive relation with fund performance. However, the average GDP growth rate during a fund's vintage years shows a negative relation with fund performance.

With a broader view on a stock market index, Aigner et al. (2008) find that average MSCI World Index returns positively affect PE fund returns measured by the gross IRR. Similar to the impact of GDP during a fund's vintage years, MSCI returns during the vintage year increases a portfolio firm's probability of having a negative IRR. Moreover, their evidence shows that fund length positively affects fund performance, and fund size is negatively associated with fund returns.

Nielsen (2007) provides a corporate angle for the determinant of PE performance. Institutional investors choose private firms that are likely to reduce expected agency costs. The author investigates the association between institutional ownership and performance measured by the industry-adjusted operating return on assets (ROA). He finds that institutional investors choose below-median-performing firms within an industry. Using a three-year average performance measure, he finds a decline in the relative performance subsequent to an investment. One possible explanation is that these firms need external funding to finance their growth.

Managerial incentives are also crucial for PE fund performance. Robinson and Sensoy (2013) document that managers with higher fees generate higher gross performance. They use novel data from the 1980s to 2010s to study the relation between the fund contract and fund performance. Their results do not show evidence supporting the argument that funds with higher fixed fees underperform lower-fee funds on a net-of-fee basis. This result indicates that relatively expensive PE funds earn sufficiently higher gross returns. Further, they do not find evidence that funds with low GP ownership underperform.

Gohil and Vyas (2016) examine how each factor accounts for the performance of PE funds measured by different proxies. For factors driving cash multiple, the authors find that some factors are significant. These factors include the type of exit route, holding period, investment year (the year of investment in the portfolio firm by the PE fund), entry in Nifty (the value of the S&P CNX Nifty index in the month of investment in the portfolio company), exit from Nifty (the value of the S&P CNX Nifty index in the month of exit from the portfolio company), and market returns. Conversely, the size of the investment, type of exit route, stage of investment, investment year, entry in Nifty, and market returns can affect IRR. Finally, the type of industry, type of sponsor, type of exit route, and stage of investment can affect the PME.

Unlike many studies focusing on the U.S. market, Diller and Kaserer (2009) examine mature European PE funds. Some contend that management teams in the United States have different skills compared with their colleagues in Europe. However, the authors test the money chasing deals hypothesis that total fund flows during the fund inception period determine fund performance. To test this hypothesis, they distinguish absolute and relative cash inflows into PE funds. For a given absolute cash inflow, the allocation of money to a particular fund type shows a negative association with fund performance. Specifically, this effect is more significant for VC funds than buyout funds. This result sends a signal that segmentation and stickiness play roles that are more important in the VC industry than in the buyout industry, and supports the money chasing deals hypothesis. Additionally, GP skills and the stand-alone investment risk of a fund show a positive association with fund returns. However, Diller and Kaserer do not find evidence to support the argument that stock market returns are related to PE fund performance.

RISK FACTORS OF PE FUNDS

The most fundamental strategy in finance is the return-risk tradeoff. Phalippou (2007) addresses the limitations of estimating the performance of PE funds. Analysts can use neither the IRR nor the *profitability index* (PI), which is the ratio of the present value of the distributed cash flows to the present value of the invested cash flows as input for expected returns. More importantly, a performance measure is hard to interpret without a risk measure. This section provides a literature review on risk factors related to PE investments.

A critical question in analyzing risk factors of PE funds is: What is the risk profile of PE investments? Additionally, what systematic and unsystematic risks are associated with PE investments? Ljungqvist and Richardson (2003) attempt to answer these questions and to obtain a PE fund's beta. They assume that the beta of each investment is equal to the average beta of publicly traded stocks in the same industry or the same as the leverage-adjusted average beta of publicly traded stocks in the same industry. Next, they calculate the average beta for all investments in a fund to obtain a fund beta. The average beta obtained is 1.08 using the first measure and around 1.30 using the second approach.

Bilo, Christophers, Degosciu, and Zimmermann (2005) construct representative portfolios from the 114 listed PE vehicles included in their sample to study risk characteristics of PE investments. The authors focus on three different portfolio strategies. The first strategy is a value-weighted portfolio with buy-and-hold returns. They determine the weights using the relative market capitalization of individual investments in the fund, partially rebalancing the portfolio. The second portfolio is equally weighted and rebalanced weekly. The final portfolio is equally weighted at the beginning of the sample period and partially rebalanced. The authors report standard deviations, Sharpe ratios, alphas, and CAPM betas. They find that betas for these three strategies are 1.20, 0.60, and 0.74, respectively. The performance also varies for different periods. Their evidence indicates that the selected investment style is important in studying the risk-adjusted performance of PE funds.

Cochrane (2005) also provides an early view on VC risk by assuming that the returns of VC funds are lognormally distributed. The author identifies several reasons VC funds differ from stocks. One is that PE is held in large chunks so that each investor may put a sizable fraction of his or her wealth in one investment. This fact implies that risk management in PE investments could be more important for investors than that in other investments. Cochrane measures the risk of VC funds using betas and standard deviations with correction for selection bias. He finds that this correction dramatically reduces high arithmetic average returns.

One caveat of Cochrane (2005) is that the risk discussed in his research is based on GPs. To estimate the risk faced by investors using cash flow data, an early study by Jones and Rhodes-Kropf (2004) uses venture fund data. The authors obtain alpha by regressing the expected market values on a set of risk factors. Their findings show that investors, on average, earn zero abnormal returns, but the relation between realized risk and returns is statistically significant.

Using market prices of publicly traded funds of funds holding unlisted PE funds and publicly traded PE funds, Jegadeesh, Kräussl, and Pollet (2015) estimate systematic risks for PE using the standard time-series regression approach. One advantage of this method is that the authors can observe the market prices directly. They find that returns on listed funds of funds and listed PE funds are related to the future self-reported returns on unlisted PE funds in the Private Equity Performance Index (PEPI). They also find that systematic risk is relatively smaller for PEPI, indicating that self-reported NAVs do not fully reflect valuation changes promptly.

Driessen, Lin, and Phalippou (2012) develop a new method to estimate risk exposure of nontraded assets from cash flows, which received little attention before this study. They explore whether the risk is time-varying and extend the standard IRR approach to a dynamic setting. That is, they base their method on the concept that investors of PE funds put their cash away at different points in time and receive dividends at another point of time during the fund's finite life. This study is the first to decompose PE returns into different parts from systematic risk and alpha, both before and after fees. The authors find that VC funds have a higher CAPM beta compared to buyout funds. Although the alpha of VC funds is significantly negative both before and after fees, it does not differ significantly from zero for buyout funds.

Some more recent studies report that PE funds suffer from exposure to liquidity risk. Franzoni, Nowak, and Phalippou (2012) quantify liquidity risk in PE and test whether the market prices this risk. The authors document that PE is significantly exposed to the same liquidity risk factor as public equity and other asset classes. Thus, PE's diversification benefits may be lower than previously thought, given the exposure to liquidity risk. They find that the unconditional liquidity risk premium is about 3 percentage points annually, the total risk premium is about 18 percent, and alpha (gross-of-fees) does not differ statistically from zero. These results suggest that different risk exposures can largely explain the high returns on PE funds, and liquidity risk seems to be an important source of risk premium.

SUMMARY AND CONCLUSIONS

PE serves as both a portfolio diversifier and a return enhancer. These characteristics of PE investments make them lucrative for HNWI (family offices) and institutional investors. PE remains a niche market, given that access is unavailable to all because of high barriers to entry. Liquidity remains a concern of PE managers. Although they can source good deals, a lack of liquidity can jeopardize such deals. These managers need to properly deploy *dry powder*, which is industry slang for undeployed cash, to make the best returns.

This chapter provides an overview of PE, factors affecting performance, and risk factors influencing returns. VC and buyouts remain the most common forms of PE. VC involves investing in a company's early stage to earn returns from the company's growth. By contrast, a buyout involves taking a public company private to earn returns from restructuring the company and reselling it (exiting). The high administration and incentive fees charged by PE funds remain a topic of debate. Although the gross returns are often high, fees and other expenses considerably reduce returns.

PEs have traditionally helped portfolio companies and investors alike. Apart from acquiring funds needed for the company's growth, portfolio companies (issuers who raise funds) have direct access to the expertise of the PEs. This access enables the portfolio companies to have an efficient channel to garner the maximum attention required to be successful. These companies sometimes lack expertise in running operations; PEs can help in optimizing the operational processes and running the companies efficiently. VCs help issuers finance their company even before they start generating any revenues. PE benefits from these investments when they do well, and the rewards can be high compared to other asset classes. PE can harvest fixed income in the form of interest payments/dividends over a company's life.

When investing in PE, investors should consider all the risk factors inherent in these investments. Any adverse investment can potentially be a substantial financial setback.

DISCUSSION QUESTIONS

1. Define PE and list its different types.
2. Define commitment period, capital call, seed money, and bridge financing.
3. Discuss the different types of risks involved with PE investments.
4. List the main factors that PE investors should consider before investing.
5. Discuss an investor's motivation to invest in VC versus a buyout and an issuer's motivation for PE financing over other sources of financing.
6. Define different measures of PE returns and discuss why they differ from conventional public market metrics.

REFERENCES

Aigner, Philipp, Stefan Albrecht, Georg Beyschlag, T. I. M. Friederich, Markus Kalepky, and Rudi Zagst. 2008. "What Drives PE? Analyses of Success Factors for Private Equity Funds." *Journal of Private Equity* 11:4, 63–85.

Bilo, Stephanie, Hans Christophers, Michel Degosciu, and Heinz Zimmermann. 2005. "Risk, Returns, and Biases of Listed Private Equity Portfolios." Working Paper, University of Basel.

Braun, Reiner, Tim Jenkinson, and Ingo Stoff. 2017. "How Persistent Is Private Equity Performance? Evidence from Deal-level Data." *Journal of Financial Economics* 123:2, 273–291.

Cochrane, John H. 2005. "The Risk and Return of Venture Capital." *Journal of Financial Economics* 75:1, 3–52.

Diller, Christian, and Christoph Kaserer. 2009. "What Drives Private Equity Returns? Fund Inflows, Skilled GPs, and/or Risk?" *European Financial Management* 15:3, 643–675.

Driessen, Joost, Tse-Chun Lin, and Ludovic Phalippou. 2012. "A New Method to Estimate Risk and Return of Nontraded Assets from Cash Flows: The Case of Private Equity Funds." *Journal of Financial and Quantitative Analysis* 47:3, 511–535.

Franzoni, Francesco, Eric Nowak, and Ludovic Phalippou. 2012. "Private Equity Performance and Liquidity Risk." *Journal of Finance* 67:6, 2341–2373.

Gohil, Raviraj Karmvir, and Vijay Vyas. 2016. "Factors Driving Abnormal Returns in Private Equity Industry: A New Perspective." *Journal of Private Equity* 19:3, 30–36.

Harris, Robert S., Tim Jenkinson, and Steven N. Kaplan. 2014. "Private Equity Performance: What Do We Know?" *Journal of Finance* 69:5, 1851–1882.

Harris, Robert S., Tim Jenkinson, Steven N. Kaplan, and Rüdiger Stucke. 2014. "Has Persistence Persisted in Private Equity? Evidence from Buyout and Venture Capital Funds." Working Paper No. 2304808, Darden Business School, University of Virginia.

Hasan, Rajibul. 2014. "Private Equity Investment Practices: A Comprehensive Study." *Journal of Private Equity* 18:1, 73–101.

Jegadeesh, Narasimhan, Roman Kräussl, and Joshua M. Pollet. 2015. "Risk and Expected Returns of Private Equity Investments: Evidence Based on Market Prices." *Review of Financial Studies* 28:12, 3269–3302.

Jones, Charles, and Matthew Rhodes-Kropf. 2004. "The Price of Diversifiable Risk in Venture Capital and Private Equity." Working Paper, Columbia University.

Kaplan, Steven N., and Antoinette Schoar. 2005. "Private Equity Performance: Returns, Persistence, and Capital Flows." *Journal of Finance* 60:4, 1791–1823.

Korteweg, Arthur, and Morten Sorensen. 2017. "Skill and Luck in Private Equity Performance." *Journal of Financial Economics* 124:3, 535–562.

Ljungqvist, Alexander, and Matthew Richardson. 2003. "The Cash Flow, Return and Risk Characteristics of Private Equity." Working Paper No. w9454, National Bureau of Economic Research.

Moskowitz, Tobias J., and Annette Vissing-Jørgensen. 2002. "The Returns to Entrepreneurial Investment: A Private Equity Premium Puzzle?" *American Economic Review* 92:4, 745– 778.

Nielsen, Kasper Meisner. 2007. "Institutional Investors and Private Equity." *Review of Finance* 12:1, 185–219.

Phalippou, Ludovic. 2007. "Investing in Private Equity Funds: A Survey." Working Paper, Research Foundation of the CFA Institute, Charlottesville, VA.

Phalippou, Ludovic. 2010. "Venture Capital Funds: Flow-performance Relationship and Performance Persistence." *Journal of Banking & Finance* 34:3, 568–577.

Phalippou, Ludovic. 2014. "Performance of Buyout Funds Revisited?" *Review of Finance* 18:1, 189–218.

Phalippou, Ludovic, and Oliver Gottschalg. 2009. "The Performance of Private Equity Funds." *Review of Financial Studies* 22:4, 1747–1776.

Phalippou, Ludovic, and Maurizio Zollo. 2005. "What Drives Private Equity Fund Performance?" Working Paper, Said Business School, University of Oxford.

Robinson, David T., and Berk A. Sensoy. 2013. "Do Private Equity Fund Managers Earn Their Fees? Compensation, Ownership, and Cash Flow Performance." *Review of Financial Studies* 26:11, 2760–2797.

Rubinstein, Mark. 1976. "The Strong Case for the Generalized Logarithmic Utility Model as the Premier Model of Financial Markets." *Journal of Finance* 31:2, 551–571.

Sorensen, Morten, and Ravi Jagannathan. 2015. "The Public Market Equivalent and Private Equity Performance." *Financial Analysts Journal* 71:4, 43–50.

Williams, James. 2016. "Equity Bridge Financing Solution Helps Improve IRR." *Hedgeweek*, July 11. Available at https://www.hedgeweek.com/2016/11/07/245476/equity-bridge-financing-solution-helps-improve-irr.

Yau, Jot K., Thomas Schneeweis, Thomas R. Robinson, and Lisa R. Weiss. 2007. "Alternative Investments Portfolio Management." In *Managing Investment Portfolios: A Dynamic Process*, edited by John L. Maginn, Donald L. Tuttle, Dennis W. McLeavey, and Jerald E. Pinto, 477–578. Hoboken, NJ: John Wiley & Sons.

CHAPTER 22

Investing in Emerging Markets

Xiaohua Diao
Professor of Finance, Chongqing Technology and Business University
Shantanu Dutta
Associate Professor of Finance, University of Ottawa
Peng Cheng Zhu
Associate Professor of Finance, University of San Diego

INTRODUCTION

Traditionally, emerging markets have offered both greater return potential and diversification opportunities than do purely domestic investments (Conover 2011). Since developed markets' asset returns show an increased level of co-movement over the years, investors have fewer opportunities to diversify their risks if they focus only on developed markets, making emerging markets particularly appealing to global investors. Although recent evidence shows that emerging market returns are converging to those of developed markets, Goetzmann, Li, and Rouwenhorst (2005) and Eun and Lee (2010) contend that emerging markets are still distinct from developed markets and provide a greater opportunity to invest in an expanded number of markets and diversify investment risk.

Although a large gap still remains between emerging markets' gross domestic product (GDP) share in the world and their market capitalization, this gap has decreased in recent decades. For example, in 1987, emerging market GDP represented only 16 percent of world GDP and less than 1 percent of world market capitalization. By 2016, these figures had changed to 40 percent of world GDP and 10.8 percent of world market capitalization (Bekaert and Harvey 2017). These statistics show that while emerging markets have experienced tremendous economic growth, they have not realized their full potential in terms of market capitalization and offer somewhat limited opportunities to international investors. In many emerging countries, banks provide the primary source of financing, and capital markets have a much lower proportion of free float compared to other developed economies. *Free float* is the portion of a corporation's shares that are held by public investors as opposed to locked-in stock held by promoters, company officers, controlling-interest investors, or governments. Therefore, investors need to realize that while emerging markets offer opportunities to invest in potentially higher-yielding assets, major challenges exist in identifying the most appropriate emerging markets and deciding on asset allocations.

This chapter provides a discussion of the various aspects associated with capital flows to emerging markets and important characteristics of capital markets in emerging economies. It also examines various investment strategies for better investment strategies, the influence of political connection and corporate governance on investments, and challenges associated with asset valuation in emerging markets.

CAPITAL FLOWS TO EMERGING MARKETS

International capital flows are important for global economic developments. Free capital movement can markedly affect the allocation of resources and economic productivity (Ahmed and Zlate 2014). Understanding the dynamics behind capital inflows to emerging markets is important, as emerging markets' economic growth largely depends on investments from other advanced economies.

The economics and finance literature discusses many factors that impact the capital flows to emerging market economies, generally from the perspective of three types of investment flows: (1) portfolio debt flow, (2) portfolio equity flow, and (3) banking flow. For example, Koepke (2019) discusses various factors such as global risk aversion, interest rate differential, and output growth that influence capital inflows to emerging markets.

Earlier studies report that an increased level of global risk aversion generally has a strong negative effect on portfolio and banking flows to emerging markets (Milesi-Ferretti, Tille, Ottaviano, and Ravn 2011; Broner, Didier, Erce, and Schmukler 2013; Bruno and Shin 2015). This aspect has received more attention from global fund managers since the global financial crisis of 2007–2008 (Koepke 2019). Another set of studies examines the impact of external interest rates in the context of capital inflows to emerging economies. These studies find that as the interest rate differential increases in favor of external countries, portfolio flows to emerging markets tend to decrease (Baek 2006; Fratzscher, Lo Duca, and Straub 2018). Ahmed and Zlate (2014) further report that during the post-financial crisis period, emerging market economies experienced a greater level of capital inflow sensitivity to interest rate differentials. Other factors, such as domestic output growth and domestic asset returns, also play an important role in capital inflows to emerging markets. For instance, Bruno and Shin (2013) and Herrmann and Dubravko (2013) find a strong positive relation between domestic growth and portfolio flows to emerging markets. According to Koepke (2019), some emerging economies tend to implement capital control policies to change the composition and volume of various fund flows, which yield limited success.

ISSUES RELATED TO CAPITAL MARKET INTEGRATION

Given the distinct features of emerging markets, investors need to understand the return characteristics, diversification opportunities through emerging market investments, co-movement of security returns, and access to different asset classes. This section provides a brief discussion of these issues.

Return Characteristics

Bekaert and Harvey (2017) find that emerging market stocks show much higher volatility than those in developed markets. Their Sharpe ratios, which indicate risk-adjusted stock return performance, are also higher. Despite the severe effect of the financial crisis of 2007–2008 on emerging markets, some of the larger markets such as Brazil, Russia, and South Africa continued to do well in terms of stock market performance. Some earlier studies also report that emerging market stock returns are not normally distributed and frequently show extreme positive and negative returns (Conover 2011). However, Bekaert and Harvey find that emerging market indices do not show substantially more nonnormalities than the MSCI World Index. Bae, Lim, and Wei (2006) report that stock returns show a more positive skewness in emerging markets. This finding could be attributed to managerial discretion to release good news immediately while delaying the release of bad news to dampen its negative effect. Chan and Hameed (2006) examine the relation between analyst coverage and synchronicity of stock returns and report a positive relation. They also find that prices of firms with higher analyst coverage in emerging markets reflect market information more quickly and experience higher stock returns than in developed markets.

Capital Market Integration

As Bekaert and Harvey (2017, p. 10) note, "From an investment perspective, the absolute risk of emerging markets is largely irrelevant. Investors in developed markets will invest only a portion of their portfolio in emerging markets, and therefore the correlation between developed markets and emerging markets will be an important driver of the ultimate risk borne." However, the correlation between an emerging market index and a world index has gradually increased from 0.40 in the 1990s to 0.80 by 2015, which makes the diversification argument less convincing. Bekaert and Harvey note that although the emerging and developed markets look more positively correlated in modern times, most emerging markets are still not fully integrated, primarily due to regulatory hurdles and an incomplete integration process. Political intervention, corruption, lack of transparency, and weaker corporate governance practices are other impediments in achieving greater market integration. Further, Bekaert and Harvey (p. 17) state that "despite the increase in correlations with world markets at the index level, the high individual country volatility and country factors create potentially useful investment opportunities for active asset managers."

Cultural Distance and Stock Market Returns

Individuals in similar cultures are likely to think and behave in a similar way, which may also influence their investment behavior (Adler 1997; Kim, Moshirian, and Wu 2005). Lucey and Zhang (2010) use the MSCI daily national stock market index for 23 emerging markets to examine the relation between cultural similarities/dissimilarities and stock market co-movements. They use two measures: (1) religious commonality and (2) a variant of Hofstede measures as used by Kogut and Singh (KS) (1988). The larger the KS measure, the greater the cultural distance between the two countries. Lucey and Zhan find that the smaller the cultural distance between two countries, the higher the levels of bilateral stock market co-movement.

Emerging Asset Classes

Besides a steady growth in the equity market, the corporate bond market has also experienced tremendous growth in recent years, which has expanded the investment opportunities in emerging market economies. About a decade ago, the corporate bond market was much smaller compared to sovereign issuance, which now represents 78 percent of new issuance of emerging market dollar bonds. At the same time, the local currency debt market also experienced rapid growth in emerging economies (Bekaert and Harvey 2017).

INSTITUTIONAL STRATEGIES FOR BETTER INVESTMENT DECISIONS

Emerging market economies are characterized by low to middle income of their citizens, high GDP growth, low GDP per capita, economic liberalization, gradual integration to global economies, and a strong focus on manufacturing activities (Hoskisson, Wright, Fitatotchev, and Peng 2000). By contrast, developing economies have a low per capita GDP, a high level of poverty and unemployment, and substantial bureaucratic barriers that restrict entrepreneurial activities, trade, and investment. Although the academic literature often refers to emerging markets as a homogeneous group, some differences exist among various emerging economies in terms of the process of attaining such labeling, which may affect their institutional process. For example, emerging economies in Asia, Latin America, Africa, and the Middle East have gradually transformed from developing country status. By contrast, former Soviet Union and Eastern European countries made their transition from centrally planned economies to market economies (Wright, Filatotchev, Hoskisson, and Pend 2005; Khanna and Palepu 2010). Although their transition process differs, they have moved toward a common set of characteristics of emerging market economies as mentioned previously. Despite their nature of political change and economic growth, Marquis and Raynard (2015, p. 297) note that the emerging economies "share a number of characteristics that not only differentiate them from the more traditionally studied developed markets but also create a set of general challenges for navigating their business environments."

As the characteristics of emerging market economies markedly differ from developed or developing economies, investors need to pay attention to various institutional, social, and cultural aspects of these markets to make more informed and educated investment decisions. In light of Marquis and Raynard (2015), the following discussion briefly examines three institutional aspects that are important for emerging market investment decisions: (1) understanding the value of a relational strategy, (2) being aware of the relevance of an infrastructure-building strategy, and (3) focusing on a sociocultural bridging strategy.

Understanding the Value of a Relational Strategy

In an emerging market, setup investors need to pay attention to how a firm maintains its relations with various stakeholders. An inability to address various stakeholder concerns can erode a firm's legitimacy and negatively affect its profitability and growth potential (Berman, Wicks, Kotha, and Jones 1999; Freeman, Wicks, and Parmar 2004). However, the nature of effective relational strategy can differ markedly between developed and emerging economies. For example, in developed economies, a firm may try to influence overall public policy to achieve specific gains. Such a move would also facilitate other firms in the same industry facing similar situations. Yet, given a generally nontransparent political and regulatory environment, such strategies are unlikely to reap benefits for a firm in emerging markets (Marquis and Raynard 2015). In emerging markets, instead of trying to alter public policy, firms are more likely to benefit by pursuing self-interests in terms of receiving various concessions such as government subsidies and tax benefits.

Further, earlier studies report that firms in emerging markets can gain from investing heavily in interpersonal networks, forming alliances with other partners, implementing interorganizational agreements to meet transactional goals, and maintaining close ties with local governments to have resource access and avoid government intervention in business and reduce the threat of government appropriation (Nee 1992; Peng and Luo 2000; Zhu and Chung 2014). Although the benefits of maintaining interpersonal networks and close relations with government and regulatory bodies are well documented, a set of other studies cautions that impending costs could exist for such reliance and association (Sun, Mellahi, and Thun 2010). Ties with the government, regulators, and other political actors may make a firm more vulnerable because such ties can exert pressure on a firm to channel its resources to unproductive sectors to advance a specific political agenda, which could be detrimental to the firm's future profitability (Okhmatovskiy 2010; Marquis and Qian 2014). Studies show that state-owned firms in emerging economies with strong ties to the government and political elites perform poorly, as they are required to maintain a higher employment level or follow inefficient policies (Fan, Wong, and Zhang 2007; Kozhikode and Li 2012). In summary, although firms in emerging economies are likely to gain from pursuing well-devised relational strategies, they should be careful about overreliance on government or political support.

Relevance of an Infrastructure-building Strategy

Another important concern for investors in emerging market economies is that prospective firms operate their businesses without proper infrastructural support. For example, emerging economies generally lack efficient telecommunication infrastructure and have inadequate physical transportation networks and distribution channels to support their supply chain–related operations (Hitt, Dacin, Levitas, Arregle, and Borza 2000). As Hoskisson, Wright, Fitatotchev, and Peng (2013) contend, the absence of a good transportation network hindered the progression of the Indian automobile industry. Investors need to pay attention to a firm's strategic location and see how it copes with the infrastructural challenges in emerging market economies. To overcome such challenges, many firms establish their distribution channels and formal/informal networks with other supply chain partners to ensure uninterrupted operation.

The other "soft" infrastructural challenge in the emerging markets, which surprisingly draws less attention, is the lack of well-established intellectual property protection regulation (Marquis and Raynard 2015). Because of this situation, many firms, especially those engaged in the high-tech industry, suffer from piracy and patent infringement, which can substantially reduce their revenue and profitability (Bird 2006). Although investors need to be aware of various infrastructural challenges in emerging markets, emerging economies are increasingly investing in physical infrastructural developments, adopting global standards, initiating credit agencies, and implementing patent and intellectual property protection laws to promote a better business environment and to alleviate investor concerns.

Focusing on a Sociocultural Bridging Strategy

In emerging economies, firms face two other important challenges in the context of a country's sociocultural characteristics. First, they face a complex demographic challenge. As emerging market economies tend to grow quickly and venture into diverse and complex manufacturing activities, they encounter the challenging problem of obtaining skilled workers. Proper employee identification, training, and retention become a priority for a firm trying to maintain its competitive edge (Hiatt and Sine 2014). Second, firms face the challenge of understanding the demographic disparity, prevalence of income inequality, employee unrest, and the possibility of politically motivated social unrest (James 2011). A main driving force in emerging markets is the emergence of an affluent middle class. But at the same time, a growing concern surfaces about income inequality, which can lead to social unrest, protests, and economic disruptions. To avoid such unnecessary situations, London and Hart (2004) advise firm managers to emphasize social embeddedness to have a better understanding of and integration with the local environment. Social embeddedness requires a deeper grasp of local sociocultural issues and values. Foreign firms that are interested in investing in emerging markets should focus on a sociocultural bridging strategy and investors should also look for firms that invest adequately to facilitate social embeddedness (Marquis and Raynard 2015).

POLITICAL CONNECTIONS, INVESTMENT DECISIONS, AND PERFORMANCE

As previously discussed, emerging market economies generally have a nontransparent political and regulatory environment. Also, government intervention in business is common in those markets. According to Bao, Johan, and Kutsuna (2016, p. 24), "Through taxation, regulation, policy and so forth, governments influence various aspects of business: from output, production processes, to input such as land, energy, infrastructure, and financing." Accordingly, some studies contend that political connections can benefit firms in emerging markets in various ways, such as accessing bank loans and long-term financing as well as successfully competing for government contracts (Faccio 2006; Fan et al. 2007). As Chen, Sun, Tang, and Wu (2011, p. 260) note, a common view is that "political connections are more important than operational efficiency in emerging markets such as those of Southeast Asian countries." Most of the bigger or economically influential firms in emerging markets tend to maintain a close relationship with ruling parties and the government.

Studies also show that political connections pay off in emerging market economies (Li, Mend, Wang, and Zhou 2008; Goldman, Rocholl, and So 2009). For instance, using a sample of 413 initial public offerings (IPOs) from 2009 to 2012, Bao et al. (2016) find that private firms with political connections have a lower risk of IPO rejection by regulatory bodies. Such connections also reduce an IPO's costs and increase profitability in the post-IPO period. Li et al. find that Chinese non-SOEs (i.e., non-state-owned enterprises) can get easier access to bank loans and other government loans if they are linked to the Communist Party. Faccio (2006) shows that in emerging markets, firms experience an increase in firm value if their executives join politics in anticipation of getting some getting exclusive benefits for the respective firms.

Similarly, Goldman et al. (2009) also show a positive connection between political connections and firm value. Chan, Dang, and Yan (2012) find that compared to non-politically-connected firms, politically connected firms show a lower level of financial constraints. Cull, Li, Sun, and Xu (2015) report similar results, showing that government connections are associated with less severe financial constraints. Using political connection indicators based on campaign contribution data, Claessens, Feijend, and Laeven (2008) show that Brazilian firms providing contributions around the 1998 and 2002 elections to elected federal deputies experience higher stock returns than firms that did not.

However, another strand of research shows that political connections do not always benefit a firm. Chen, Chen, and Wei (2011) find that government interference in state-owned enterprises (SOEs) through a majority of state ownership or appointing connected government managers or board members may induce a firm to take suboptimal investment decisions. More specifically, the authors use a sample of non-financial A-share firms in China from 2001 to 2006. China A-shares are only quoted in RMB, whereas B-shares are quoted in foreign currencies, such as the U.S. dollar, and are more widely available to foreign investors. By using ownership structure as a measure of government intervention, they find that compared to non-SOE firms, SOE firms have a lower sensitivity of investment expenditure to growth opportunity. They also find a similar result by using politically connected board members as a measure of government intervention.

With a sample of 779 newly partially privatized firms in China, Fan et al. (2007) examine how government connection or intervention affects these firms' future course of actions and profitability. They find that compared to the firms without any direct political connections, politically connected firms tend to underperform based on three-year post-IPO stock returns, sales growth, and earnings growth. Another risk of being politically connected is to get labeled as a close ally to a particular political party or ideology, which may prove counterproductive at the time of a power structure change in a country.

Fisman (2001) examines such possibilities and finds that Indonesian firms connected to President Suharto's family – who ruled the country for an extended period with a tight grip – faced financial instability as the president's health started to deteriorate. Using a data set between 2001 and 2011, Jackowicz, Kozłowski, and Mielcarz (2014) find that political connections lower firm profitability.

This discussion suggests that political connections are common in emerging markets and that such connections can generally be beneficial to firms. However, political connections can also have some drawbacks for firms. Accordingly, firms and investors need to be cautious about the pros and cons of maintaining close connections with political players.

CORPORATE GOVERNANCE AND PERFORMANCE

Emerging markets have weaker corporate governance practices and relatively more inadequate investor protections (Schacht, Allen, and Orsagh 2009). Bekaert and Harvey (2003) identify several weaknesses in terms of corporate governance practices in emerging markets. For example, entrenched managers and their inclination for perquisite consumption, pyramidal ownership structure, and creditor rights are detrimental to shareholder interests. A growing body of corporate governance literature examines the relation between governance practices as well as firm performance and stock returns from emerging country perspectives. For instance, by examining a sample of 1,433 firms from 18 emerging markets, Lins (2003) finds that when a management group's control rights exceed its cash flow rights, the firm's value decreases. At the same time, large non-management control rights block holdings are positively related to firm value. These results are more pronounced in countries with lower shareholder protection.

Lemmon and Lins (2003) find that during the East Asian financial crisis in the late 1990s, firms with disproportionate control rights vis-à-vis their direct ownership experienced significantly lower stock market returns. Morey, Gottesman, Baker, and Godridge (2009) report that better corporate governance practices by firms in emerging markets companies tend to have higher company value, as measured by Tobin's q and a higher market-to-book ratio. Chen, Chen, and Wei (2009, 2011) find that better corporate governance practice is associated with a lower cost of capital in 17 emerging markets. This effect is more pronounced in countries with weaker legal protection to investors and shareholders. In general, the literature shows that "improvements in corporate governance of emerging market companies increase shareholder wealth, company valuation, and investor interest" (Conover 2011).

VALUATION PRACTICES IN EMERGING MARKETS

Better valuation practices and methods are instrumental in attracting investors, enhancing the flow of funds to emerging economies, and allocating resources. Asset valuation can be challenging in emerging markets due to a lack of transparency as well as a higher level of uncertainty, corruption, transaction costs, and market illiquidity (Bruner, Conroy, Estrada, Kritzman, and Li 2002). Further, as these authors point out, unlike developed economies, emerging markets lack best-practice rules that are widely accepted by practitioners and scholars. Pereiro (2006, p. 106) observes that asset valuation techniques based on market efficiency theory are also questionable in emerging markets: "The existence of market efficiency in emerging markets is highly debatable since these markets are small, concentrated and prone to manipulation; as a result, the straight application of the classical CAPM for defining the cost of equity capital is controversial." The author conducts a survey of Argentine firms, which presents a useful summary of valuation practices in an emerging market.

Findings show that, like in developed countries, firms in emerging markets also use standard valuation techniques such as net present value (NPV), internal rate of return (IRR), and the payback period. The capital asset pricing model (CAPM) is also popular, and firms/investors tend to adjust the discount rate with a country risk premium. However, the study observes that in capital budgeting analysis, firms use U.S. dollars to forecast revenues and expenses, although their businesses are conducted in local currencies. Interestingly, firms tend to use comparable U.S. firm beta in their analysis and do not correct the values for country-specific differences. Finally, analysts of emerging market firms generally do not take into account some firm-specific risks such as size and illiquidity in their analysis.

García-Sánche, Preve, and Sarria-Allende (2010) further reflect on the implementation of the discounted cash flow (DCF) method in the context of emerging markets. In line with Pereiro's (2006) finding, they also observe that practitioners and academicians tend to adjust the discount rate to accommodate the unique features and market-specific risks in emerging markets. However, such an approach is flawed, and valuation in emerging markets needs a careful approach to make necessary adjustments to the predicted cash flows. To understand the rationale behind it, García-Sánchez et al. (p. 100) clearly identify the basic tenets of the DCF method: "the DCF method is based on the idea of discounting unconditional expected cash flows at a discount rate that reflects risk that is symmetric (or two-way) and cannot be hedged by holding a globally diversified portfolio – that is, global market- or economy-wide risk." Various methods proposed by academics and practitioners to adjust the discount rate or cost of capital to account for country-specific risks do not solve the problem. This approach of adding country risk to CAPM estimates violates the spirit of the model, according to which discount rates should reflect only "symmetric" (or two-sided), nondiversifiable risks. Country risk, however, is not symmetric and may be at least partly diversifiable. With respect to the latter, some models of dynamic correlations across countries give some support to the alternative view.

Further, this approach ignores an important aspect of risk adjustment – specifically, the effect of country-specific risk is not the same for all firms in a particular emerging market. Accordingly, the authors propose not adjusting the discount rate based on estimated country risk. Instead, they recommend trying to estimate the true unconditional cash flows to be used in the DCF model. Estimating the true expected cash flows is challenging. Thus, they recommend using simulation methods to estimate the cost of financial distress in light of a particular emerging market's country risk profile and to make necessary adjustments to the estimated cash flows.

SUMMARY AND CONCLUSIONS

Emerging markets present expanded investment opportunities to global investors. Emerging market returns are becoming more correlated with developed market returns, which reduces the attractiveness of diversification. Still, emerging markets are sufficiently distinct to appeal to global investors. These markets offer higher return potential. To realize better returns and manage associated risks, investors need to understand various factors associated with capital flows to emerging markets, various market characteristics, investment strategies, political dynamics, and valuation challenges. Further, investors should pay close attention to the legal protection, corporate governance, and regulatory environment that could influence investment returns. They should realize that due to a distinct market setup, potential political intervention, and vulnerability to the global/local financial crisis, valuing emerging-market assets is more challenging. Finally, investors need to formulate appropriate investment strategies for emerging market economies and understand the risk-return relation.

DISCUSSION QUESTIONS

1. Identify the factors affecting the capital flow to emerging markets.
2. Discuss how global investors can still benefit from investing in emerging markets given that these markets are becoming more integrated with developed markets.
3. Discuss some effective institutional strategies for making better investments in emerging markets.
4. Discuss whether political connections matter in investment decisions and performance in emerging markets.

REFERENCES

Adler, Nancy J. 1997. *International Dimensions of Organizational Behavior*. Cincinnati, OH: International Thomson Publishing.

Ahmed, Shaghil, and Andrei Zlate. 2014. "Capital Flows to Emerging Market Economies: A Brave New World?" *Journal of International Money and Finance* 48:B, 221–248.

Bae, Kee-Hong, Chanwoo Lim, and K. C. John Wei. 2006. "Corporate Governance and Conditional Skewness in the World's Stock Markets." *Journal of Business* 79:6, 2999–3028.

Baek, In-Mee. 2006. "Portfolio Investment Flows to Asia and Latin America: Pull, Push or Market Sentiment?" *Journal of Asian Economics* 17:2, 363–373.

Bao, Xiaolu, Sofia Johan, and Kenji Kutsuna. 2016. "Do Political Connections Matter in Accessing Capital Markets? Evidence from China." *Emerging Markets Review* 29: December, 24–41.

Bekaert, Geert, and Campbell R. Harvey. 2003. "Emerging Markets Finance." *Journal of Empirical Finance* 10:1–2, 3–55.

Bekaert, Geert, and Campbell R. Harvey. 2017. "Emerging Equity Markets in a Globalizing World." Working Paper, National Bureau of Economic Research. Available at https://papers.ssrn.com/sol3/papers.cfm?abstract_id=2344817.

Berman, Shawn L., Andrew C. Wicks, Suresh Kotha, and Thomas M. Jones. 1999. "Does Stakeholder Orientation Matter? The Relationship between Stakeholder Management Models and Firm Financial Performance." *Academy of Management Journal* 42:5, 488–506.

Bird, Robert C. 2006. "The Impact of Coercion on Protecting US Intellectual Property Rights in the BRIC Economies." In *Emerging Economies and the Transformation of International Business: Brazil, Russia, India and China (BRICs)*, edited by C. Jain Subhash, 431–451. Northampton: Edward Elgar Publishing.

Broner, Fernando, Tatiana Didier, Aitor Erce, and Sergio L. Schmukler. 2013. "Gross Capital Flows: Dynamics and Crises." *Journal of Monetary Economics* 60:1, 113–133.

Bruner, Robert F., Robert M. Conroy, Javier Estrada, Mark Kritzman, and Wei Li. 2002. "Introduction to 'Valuation in Emerging Markets.'" *Emerging Markets Review* 3:4, 310–324.

Bruno, Valentina, and Hyun Song Shin. 2013. "Capital Flows, Cross-border Banking and Global Liquidity." Working Paper No. w19038, National Bureau of Economic Research.

Bruno, Valentina, and Hyun Song Shin. 2015. "Capital Flows and the Risk-taking Channel of Monetary Policy." *Journal of Monetary Economics* 71:1, 119–132.

Chan, Kalok, and Allaudeen Hameed. 2006. "Stock Price Synchronicity and Analyst Coverage in Emerging Markets." *Journal of Financial Economics* 80:1, 115–147.

Chan, Kenneth S., Vinh Q. T. Dang, and Isabel K. M. Yan. 2012. "Chinese Firms' Political Connection, Ownership, and Financing Constraints." *Economics Letters* 115:2, 164–167.

Chen, Kevin C. W., Zhihong Chen, and K. C. John Wei. 2009. "Legal Protection of Investors, Corporate Governance, and the Cost of Equity Capital." *Journal of Corporate Finance* 15:3, 273–289.

Chen, Kevin C. W., Zhihong Chen, and K. C. John Wei. 2011. "Agency Costs of Free Cash Flows and the Effect of Shareholder Rights on the Implied Cost of Capital." *Journal of Financial and Quantitative Analysis* 46:1, 171–207.

Chen, Shimin, Zheng Sun, Song Tang, and Donghui Wu. 2011. "Government Intervention and Investment Efficiency: Evidence from China." *Journal of Corporate Finance* 17:2, 259–271.

Claessens, Stijn, Erik Feijend, and Luc Laeven. 2008. "Political Connections and Preferential Access to Finance: The Role of Campaign Contributions." *Journal of Financial Economics* 88:3, 554–580.

Conover, Mitchell C. 2011. "Investment Issues in Emerging Markets: A Review." *The Research Foundation of CFA Institute Literature Review* 6:1, 1–27.

Cull, Robert, Wei Li, Bo Sun, and Lixin Colin Xu. 2015. "Government Connections and Financial Constraints: Evidence from a Large Representative Sample of Chinese Firms." *Journal of Corporate Finance* 32:June, 271–294.

Eun, Cheol S., and Jinsoo Lee. 2010. "Mean-Variance Convergence Around the World." *Journal of Banking & Finance*, 34:4, 856–870.

Faccio, Mara. 2006. "Politically Connected Firms." *American Economic Review* 96:1, 369–386.

Fan, Joseph P. H., T. J. Wong, and Tianyu Zhang. 2007. "Politically Connected CEOs, Corporate Governance, and Post-IPO Performance of China's Newly Partially Privatized Firms." *Journal of Financial Economics* 84:2, 330–357.

Fisman, Raymond. 2001. "Estimating the Value of Political Connections." *American Economic Review* 91:4, 1095–1102.

Fratzscher, Marcel, Marco Lo Duca, and Roland Straub. 2018. "On the International Spillovers of US Quantitative Easing." *Economic Journal* 128:608, 330–377.

Freeman, R. Edward, Andrew C. Wicks, and Bidhan Parmar. 2004. "Stakeholder Theory and the Corporate Objective Revisited." *Organization Science* 15:3, 364–369

García-Sánchez, Javier, Lorenzo A. Preve, and Virginia Sarria-Allende. 2010. "Valuation in Emerging Markets: A Simulation Approach." *Journal of Applied Corporate Finance* 22:2, 100–108.

Goetzmann, William N., Lingfeng Li, and K. Geert Rouwenhorst. 2005. "Long-Term Global Market Correlations." *Journal of Business* 78:1, 1–38.

Goldman, Eitan, Jörg Rocholl, and Jonhil So. 2009. "Do Politically Connected Boards Affect Firm Value?" *Review of Finance Studies* 22:6, 2331–2360.

Herrmann, Sabine, and Mihaljek Dubravko. 2013. "The Determinants of Cross-border Bank Flows to Emerging Markets." *Economics of Transition* 21:3, 479–508.

Hiatt, Shon R., and Wesley D. Sine. 2014. "Clear and Present Danger: Planning and New Venture Survival Amid Political and Civil Violence." *Strategic Management Journal* 35:5, 773–785.

Hitt, Michael A., M. Tina Dacin, Edward Levitas, Jean-Luc Arregle, and Anca Borza. 2000. "Partner Selection in Emerging and Developed Market Contexts: Resource-based and Organizational Learning Perspectives." *Academy of Management Journal* 43:3, 449–467.

Hoskisson, Robert E., Mike Wright, Igor Fitatotchev, and Mike W. Peng. 2013. "Emerging Multinationals from Mid-range Economies: The Influence of Institutions and Factor Markets." *Journal of Management Studies* 50:7, 1295–1321.

Jackowicz, Krzysztor, Lukasz Kozłowski, and Paweł Mielcarz. 2014. "Political Connections and Operational Performance of Non-financial Firms: New Evidence from Poland." *Emerging Markets Review* 20:September, 109–135.

James, K. S. 2011. "India's Demographic Change: Opportunities and Challenges." *Science* 333:6042, 576–580.

Khanna, Tarun, and Krishna G. Palepu. 2010. *Winning in Emerging Markets: A Road Map for Strategy and Execution*. Boston, MA: Harvard Business Press.

Kim, Suk Joong, Fariborz Moshirian, and Eliza Wu. 2005. "Dynamic Stock Market Integration Driven by the European Monetary Union: An Empirical Analysis." *Journal of Banking and Finance* 29:10, 2475–2502.

Koepke, Robin. 2019. "What Drives Capital Flows to Emerging Markets? A Survey of the Empirical Literature." *Journal of Economic Surveys* 33:2, 516–540.

Kogut, Bruce, and Habir Singh. 1988. "The Effect of National Culture on the Choice of Entry Mode." *Journal of International Business Studies* 19:3, 411–432.

Kozhikode, Rajiv Krishnan, and Jiatao Li. 2012. "Political Pluralism, Public Policies, and Organizational Choices: Banking Branch Expansion in India, 1948–2003." *Academy of Management Journal* 55:2, 339–359.

Lemmon, Michael L., and Karl V. Lins. 2003. "Ownership Structure, Corporate Governance, and Firm Value: Evidence from the East Asian Financial Crisis." *Journal of Finance* 58:4, 1445–1468.

Li, Hongin, Lingsheng Meng, Qian Wang, and Li-An Zhou. 2008. "Political Connections, Financing and Firm Performance: Evidence from Chinese Private Firms." *Journal of Development Economics* 87:2, 283–299.

Lins, Karl V. 2003. "Equity Ownership and Firm Value in Emerging Markets." *Journal of Financial and Quantitative Analysis* 38:1, 159–184.

London, Ted, and Stuart L. Hart. 2004. "Reinventing Strategies for Emerging Markets: Beyond the Transnational Model." *Journal of International Business Studies* 35:5, 350–370.

Lucey, Brian M., and QiYu Zhang. 2010. "Does Cultural Distance Matter in International Stock Market Comovement? Evidence from Emerging Economies Around the World." *Emerging Markets Review* 11:1, 62–78.

Marquis, Christopher, and Cuili Qian. 2014. "Corporate Social Responsibility Reporting in China: Symbol or Substance?" *Organization Science* 25:1, 127–148.

Marquis, Chris, and Mia Raynard. 2015. "Institutional Strategies in Emerging Markets." *Academy of Management Annals* 9:1, 291–335.

Milesi-Ferretti, Gian-Maria, Cédric Tille, Gianmarco I. P. Ottaviano, and Morton O. Ravn. 2011. "The Great Retrenchment: International Capital Flows during the Global Financial Crisis." *Economic Policy* 26:66, 289–346.

Morey, Matthew, Aron Gottesman, Edward Baker, and Ben Godridge. 2009. "Does Better Corporate Governance Result in Higher Valuations in Emerging Markets? Another Examination Using a New Data Set." *Journal of Banking & Finance* 33:2, 254–262.

Nee, Victor. 1992. "Organizational Dynamics of Market Transition: Hybrid Forms, Property Rights, and Mixed Economy in China." *Administrative Science Quarterly* 37:1, 1–27.

Okhmatovskiy, Ilya. 2010. "Performance Implications of Ties to the Government and SOEs: A Political Embeddedness Perspective." *Journal of Management Studies* 47:6, 1020–1047.

Peng, Mike W., and Yadong Luo. 2000. "Managerial Ties and Firm Performance in a Transition Economy: The Nature of a Micro–macro Link." *Academy of Management Journal* 43:3, 486–501.

Pereiro, Luis E. 2006. "The Practice of Investment Valuation in Emerging Markets: Evidence from Argentina." *Journal of Multinational Financial Management* 16:2, 160–183.

Schacht, Kurt, James Allen, and Matthew Orsagh. 2009. *Shareowner Rights across the Markets: A Manual for Investors.* Charlottesville, VA: CFA Institute.

Sun, Pei, Kamel Mellahi, and Eric Thun. 2010. "The Dynamic Value of MNE Political Embeddedness: The Case of the Chinese Automobile Industry." *Journal of International Business Studies* 41:7, 1161–1182.

Wright, Mike, Igor Filatotchev, Robert E. Hoskisson, and Mike W. Peng. 2005. "Strategy Research in Emerging Economies: Challenging the Conventional Wisdom." *Journal of Management Studies* 42:1, 1–33.

Zhu, Hongjin, and Chi-Nen Chung, 2014. "Portfolios of Political Ties and Business Group Strategy in Emerging Economies: Evidence from Taiwan." *Administrative Science Quarterly* 59:4, 599–638.

CHAPTER **23**

Disclosure Regulations in Emerging Economies and Their Impact on Equity Markets

Xiaohua Diao
Professor of Finance, Chongqing Technology and Business University
Shantanu Dutta
Associate Professor of Finance, University of Ottawa
Peng Cheng Zhu
Associate Professor of Finance, University of San Diego

INTRODUCTION

Corporate disclosure and financial reporting convey valuable information to shareholders and market participants. A widely accepted view is that disclosure of financial information to investors is important to shareholders and other market participants (Lin 2009). Although corporations routinely engage in financial reporting, mostly in regular intervals according to regulatory requirements, corporate disclosures could be voluntary or mandatory depending on the nature of the information. Corporate disclosures on various aspects such as corporate social responsibility (CSR) initiatives, insider trading activities, and private meetings make investors and regulators better informed about a firm's operational strategies and increase informational transparency. Until the early 2000s, most corporate disclosure initiatives occurred in developed markets. However, given the shifting focus toward socially responsible investing (SRI), emerging markets have also taken active interests in promoting the notion of voluntary corporate disclosures in nonfinancial areas, as well as starting to introduce specific disclosure regulations to enhance transparency in terms of environmental issues, CSR expenditures, insider trading, and private meetings. A better corporate disclosure environment is likely to facilitate doing business, boost investor confidence, and improve security valuation. According to Lopes and Alencar (2010, pp. 443–444), "The basic idea is that higher levels of disclosure contribute to a reduction in information asymmetry between managers and investors and, consequently, cause a reduction in the idiosyncratic component of the cost of equity capital."

Despite these views that more efficient and transparent corporate disclosure practices and environments benefit firms and investors alike, Lin (2009, p. 14) finds that corporate disclosure quality in emerging markets suffers problems, including "a very limited amount of information; lack of comparability over the years and between companies; unbalanced disclosure, with a greater emphasis on good rather than bad news; and a lack of third-party auditing to assure information credibility."

This chapter focuses on various corporate disclosure policies and the state of the disclosure level in emerging market economies. More specifically, it discusses three important information disclosure regulations that are of particular interest among practitioners and academicians: (1) environmental and CSR disclosure regulation, (2) insider trading disclosure regulation, and (3) private meeting disclosure regulation. The chapter also highlights the important impact on equity markets in the context of these disclosure regulations.

VARIOUS DISCLOSURE REGULATION APPROACHES

According to Lin (2009), three distinct disclosure approaches are available in security regulation: (1) voluntary, (2) mandatory, and (3) comply or explain disclosure. Each approach is motivated by a country's institutional environment and has its strengths and weaknesses.

Voluntary Disclosure

In most emerging markets, corporate social and environmental disclosures remain voluntary. Voluntary disclosures depend on investor demand. Since investors in emerging markets are sometimes unsure about their information requirements, voluntary disclosure regulation may not be the best option to reduce information asymmetry between firm management and investors. Further, better-governed firms, which have lower informational asymmetry concerns, may make more voluntary disclosures.

Mandatory Disclosure

Another disclosure regime that has become more prominent in emerging markets is the mandatory disclosure regulation, which compels firms to disclose specific information about a firm's operation and policies. However, the success of mandatory disclosure regimes depends on the legal enforceability in a country and the true intention of regulatory bodies. Further, mandatory disclosure regulations could be costly for small and medium-sized enterprises (SMEs), which are generally resource-constrained.

Comply or Explain Disclosure

The third approach is a comply or explain disclosure regime, which requires a firm to disclose the required information or explain the reasons for nondisclosure. Although this approach appears optimal because it balances market power, informational demand, and regulatory requirements, the success of this approach depends on the legal enforceability and market pressures of emerging markets. These markets differ in terms of their choices concerning the disclosure regulation regime. For example, Lin (2009, p. 24) notes that "South Africa and Thailand both take a comply or explain approach embedded in the entire corporate governance scheme. Malaysia also adopts an approach that partly reflects the concept of complying or explaining. Both China and Taiwan adopt traditional mandatory disclosure in securities regulation, requiring the disclosure of information concerning certain topics."

ENVIRONMENTAL AND CSR DISCLOSURE IN EMERGING MARKETS

Development of effective disclosure regulations is a complex and time-consuming process (Situ and Tilt 2018). Such development depends on various factors such as the socioeconomic environment of a country, investor sophistication and activism, institutional pressure, and the extent of global integration. Although most emerging economies are adopting various disclosure regulations in light of developed market regulations, the lack of enforceability of such regulations undermines the effectiveness of disclosure regulations in those markets. Further, as Budsaratragoon, Hillier, and Lhaopadchan (2012) suggest, emerging markets should not blindly follow the disclosure regulations of developed economies, because such an approach may not yield desired results. The next two subsections examine environmental and CSR disclosure in China and other emerging markets.

Disclosure in China

Zheng, Xu, Dong, and Tam (2010) examine the nature of corporate environmental information disclosure (EID) for 871 Chinese manufacturing firms. *Corporate EID* refers to the information disseminated by a corporation about its activities related to the natural environment and its protection. This study reports that firms in environmentally sensitive sectors (e.g., paper manufacturing, food, drink, and metal), with more foreign and Chinese state ownership as well as with a larger asset base and market capitalization are more likely to have a higher level of EID. Liu and Anbumozhi (2009) report that the corporate EID level is marginal among Chinese firms. About 40 percent of firms do not disclose substantial environmental information to stakeholders. Further, the study reports that the disclosure level depends on a firm's geographical location and its economic performance. Firms with better economic performance and located in relatively developed cities tend to make more disclosures.

Liu, Yu, Zhang, Bi, Ge, Yuan, and Yu (2010) investigate the effectiveness of the GreenWatch program initiated by Chinese regulators in the late 1990s to identify and disclose the name of main polluting enterprises. In their survey of both participating and nonparticipating firms in the GreenWatch program, they find that participating firms tend to be more forthcoming in disclosing their environmental information. By following 497 firms in Jiangsu province that continuously participated in Green-Watch program for five years, Liu, Yu, Zhang, Bi, Ge, and Bu (2012) report that firms with poor initial ratings, wholly foreign-owned firms, and firms from densely populated areas are more likely to improve their environmental disclosure ratings over time. The study further finds that newly participating firms contribute more toward improving overall rating improvement. Liu, Yu, Zhang, et al. (2010) also report an overall improvement in rating for the participating firms in the GreenWatch program.

Liu, Yu, Fujitsuka, Liu, Bi, and Shishime (2010) examine the impact of government-initiated company environmental performance rating systems in China, which the government introduced in 1998. This program rates a company's environmental performance in five categories and discloses the results to the public. The authors find that companies with poor rating records are more likely to improve their environmental performance in subsequent years. Although this initiative had some positive impact on the overall environmental performance of Chinese companies, a lack of strong pressure from the classified stakeholders such as investors, business partners, and creditors undermines the success of this initiative to some extent.

Meng, Zeng, Shi, Qi, and Zhang (2014) explore how corporate environmental performance influences a firm's disclosure level and the nature of environmental disclosures. They find that compared to average environmental performers, both poor and good performers make more environmental disclosures. However, poor performers tend to make more "soft" disclosures, and good performers make more "solid" disclosures. Also, after being exposed as environmental violators, poor performers increase overall disclosure levels, but such disclosures lack substance.

Other studies focus on the impact of CSR reporting regulation. Kuo, Yeh, and Yu (2012) examine the CSR reporting behavior of Chinese firms and find that about 42 percent of them do not disclose any relevant information to their stakeholders, another 42 percent present description of their general CSR activities, and only 17 percent present proposer CSR statistics. The study further finds that environmentally sensitive firms and state-owned enterprises (SOEs) are more likely to make EID.

Similarly, Noronha, Tou, Cynthia, and Guan (2013) examine CSR reporting by Chinese firms. They find that despite the introduction of detailed CSR guidelines, CSR reporting was still quite limited among Chinese firms and is mainly exploratory. Further, the study observes that the Chinese Academy of Social Sciences (CASS), a national academic research institution, tends to give higher ratings for CSR reports issued by SOEs.

Xu, Zheng, and Tam (2012) explicitly examine stock market reactions to negative environmental events for Chinese firms. They find that market reaction is less pronounced in China compared to reactions to similar events in other countries. This finding implies that in China, market participants and stakeholders pay less attention to corporate environmental violation issues. Yu, Jian, and He (2011) explore the relation between a firm's economic information disclosure (EID) and its financial performance and report a significant positive association between EID and economic value-added. Similarly, Qi, Zeng, Ahi, Meng, Lin, Meng, and Yang (2014) also report a significantly positive association between a firm's environmental performance and financial performance.

Chen, Hung, and Wang (2018) investigate how mandatory CSR disclosure regulation of China that the government introduced in 2008 impacts firm performance and social externalities. The study finds that although the CSR disclosure mandate does not require a firm to invest additionally in CSR-related activities, mandatory CSR reporting firms experience a decrease in profitability after the mandate. However, this disclosure mandate has led to an improvement in water quality and SO_2 emission levels in the cities that are most impacted by this mandate.

Disclosure in Other Emerging Markets

A number of studies have also examined corporate disclosure environments in other emerging economies. These studies report that the level of corporate environmental and CSR disclosure depends both on firm characteristics and emerging markets' governance and legal environment. For example, Durnev and Kim (2005) find that a firm's disclosure level depends on its growth opportunities and external financing needs. This result is more relevant in emerging markets with weaker legal protection. Berglöf and Pajuste (2005) examine the determinants of disclosure level with a sample of central and Eastern European economies and find that higher transparency is associated with large controlling ownership, lower leverage, smaller firm size, and higher market-to-book ratios.

Similarly, Hanifa and Rashid (2005) find that the disclosure level of Malaysian firms depends on firm size, growth prospects, ownership concentration, and leverage. Bokpin (2013) reports similar results for the Ghanaian market. Using a sample of 145 companies from Croatia, Macedonia, Slovenia, and Serbia, Arsov and Bucevska (2017) find a positive relation between the level of transparency, company size, and the need for external financing, but a negative relation with ownership concentration. Using a sample of 216 annual reports for companies followed by Standard & Poor's/International Finance Corporation (S&P/IFC) and pertaining to 13 Middle Eastern and North African (MENA) emerging markets, Othman and Zeghal (2010) find that MENA companies from countries having historical links with Great Britain have substantially higher transparency and disclosure (T&D) scores than those from countries having historical links with France. The study further finds that the nature of business culture, company size, and the importance of intangibles affect positively the level of T&D scores in the MENA region.

INSIDER TRADING, DISCLOSURES, AND RELATED REGULATION

Insider trading and related disclosure regulations have drawn much attention from investors, market participants, and regulators. Although insider trading can contribute positively by improving information environment, facilitating the communication of private information and compensating managers for their entrepreneurial efforts (Roulstone 2003; Piotroski and Roulstone 2005; Dai, Fu, Kang, and Lee 2016), insiders can use their informational advantage for their personal benefit (Strudler and Orts 1999). The insider trading literature generally supports the view that senior executives and other insiders make abnormal profits through their trading activities in their own company (Seyhun 1998; Inci, Narayanan, and Seyhun 2017).

The relative costs and benefits of insider trading present a dilemma to the regulatory bodies: Should insider trading be extensively regulated? In general, regulators recognize the informational value of insider trading and presume that timely disclosure of insider trading activities could provide valuable information to market participants. Timely disclosure is also helpful in restricting the opportunistic behavior of insiders, as they are likely to be subject to tighter and earlier scrutiny (Bhattacharya and Daouk 2002; He and Rui 2016), which in turn would enhance investors' confidence (McGee 2008). Despite the prevalence of insider trading regulation, evidence shows that insiders continue to make substantial profits through insider trading activities around the world. The problem is more pronounced in emerging markets where legal enforcement is weaker. For example, Qiu, He, and Xiao (2018) observe that the legal environment in China is not effective enough to curb opportunistic insider trading.

Notwithstanding the opportunistic trading concerns, a benefit of insider trading is that these trades reveal important information to market participants. Chauhan, Kumar, and Chaturvedula (2016) contend that two important factors could have different effects on the informativeness of insider trading in emerging markets. First, emerging-market firms tend to have more concentrated ownership, which could negatively influence the information asymmetry between insiders and outsiders. Under such an environment, insider trading could convey more useful information. Second, emerging markets tend to have weaker regulatory restrictions on insider trading, which could encourage insiders to trade on private information more frequently.

To get a better insight into insider trading–related disclosures and restrictions, the following discussion involves insider trading regulations of three emerging markets. Evidence shows that although regulations may vary in terms of scope, most of the emerging markets are moving toward adopting stricter insider trading regulations and promoting a more transparent disclosure environment. However, legal enforcement remains a serious concern and opportunistic insider trading activities are rampant in emerging markets.

Insider Trading in China

Huang (2005, 2013) presents detailed discussions on the extent of insider trading, relevant laws, and enforcement in China. To illustrate the problem's importance, Huang (2005) mentions that about 80 percent of the securities cases in China concern insider trading activities. Huang (2013) contends that insider trading is a serious problem in China, even in the current period. Despite considerable effort from Chinese regulatory authorities, most insider trading activities go undetected. According to Huang (2013, p. 306), "the reported cases may just be the tip of the iceberg." Huang (2013, p. 306) further notes that "My 2003 study found that insider trading was widespread in China. Nine years on, the insider trading problem is likely to remain the same, and in fact, may be more severe than before as a result of the new developments of the markets."

Recognizing that insider trading is detrimental to developing a healthy financial market, China started developing its insider trading regulation in the early 1990s. The China Securities Regulatory Commission (CSRC) is the main national regulatory body that tracks insider trading activities and takes necessary actions. Based on other developed countries' experiences, China has created a relatively complete regulatory regime that includes severe penalties and punitive measures for insider trading activities (Huang 2013). In 1999, the SSE and the Shenzhen Stock Exchange (SZSE) coupled with the Chinese Securities Regulatory Commission (CSRC) and introduced the Securities Law of the People's Republic of China (known as the Securities Law), which includes various articles defining insiders, the nature of insider trading, and various liabilities. Authorities later updated relevant clauses in 2006 (Duan 2009; Tong, Zhang, and Zhu 2013). According to the Chinese Securities Law (Article 75), inside information is information concerning the business or finance of a company or may have a major effect on the market price of its securities without being publicized in securities trading. Article 75 also highlights the nature of material information by providing some examples such as earnings news, acquisitions, restructuring, and paying dividends. Nevertheless, the scope exists for some alternative explanations that may undermine the effectiveness of insider trading regulation.

Despite its efforts, the CSRC recognizes that insider trading remains a relevant issue in China (Huang 2013) and most of the cases do not face any legal penalties (Huang 2005). Various factors limit the effectiveness of insider trading regulation, including vagueness in defining insider information and insider group identification, diverging interests of the CSRC, resource constraints (Tong et al. 2013), and not allowing investors to file private litigation against insider traders (He and Rui 2016).

Insider Trading in India

To ensure a level playing field for all market participants regarding information accessibility, the Securities and Exchange Board of India (SEBI) introduced SEBI (insider trading) regulation in 1992. According to the SEBI regulation (section 13), any shareholder who holds more than 5 percent shares or voting rights, as well as any director or executive, is required to disclose that insider trading information to the firm within two days of trading activities. In turn, the firm must convey the information to the stock exchange within the next two days. To monitor insider trading activities, Indian firms are also required to have a compliance officer whose responsibility is to ensure that insiders do not trade on "price-sensitive information."

According to Chauhan et al. (2016, p. 67), Indian insider trading regulation differs from U.S. regulation as follows:

> *Unlike the U.S., trading on price-sensitive information is not a criminal offense in India. If the regulator suspects that any person has violated regulations, it may call for inquiries against the suspected person and the regulator may take any or all of the actions against the suspected person such as (1) Such person can be prevented from dealing in securities. (2) His trade can be declared as null and void. (3) Such a person can be asked to deliver the purchased stocks to the seller; if the buyer is not in a position to deliver such stocks, the current market price or purchase price, whichever higher, should be paid to the seller. And, (4) The regulator can impose a monetary penalty on such insider.*

In general, Indian insider trading regulations are not as stringent as those in the United States, which enables insiders to trade on private information and gives them an undue advantage (Beny 2005; Chauhan et al. 2016).

Insider Trading in Thailand

In 1992, Thailand adopted its insider trading regulation through Securities and Exchange Act B.E. 2535, which authorities developed in light of insider trading regulations from five countries (Australia, the United States, the United Kingdom,

Hong Kong, and Singapore) (Budsaratragoon et al. 2012). Like the insider trading regulations in other developed markets, Thai regulation also does not permit company directors and senior executives to trade on private information or around major corporate events. However, unlike those five countries, as mentioned earlier, Thai regulation does not precisely specify the trading ban periods around major corporate events. It vaguely states that insiders should not trade until outside traders get an opportunity to assess any new information or disclosure, which could vary from 24 to 48 hours. To discourage opportunistic insider trading, Thai regulation further mandates that companies should disclose any material information after trading hours and clearly outline their policies to restrict opportunistic insider trading or exploitation of private information by company insiders.

In their examination of the effectiveness of Thai insider trading regulations, Budsaratragoon et al. (2012) find that the regulations fail to deter insiders from pursuing opportunistic trades. Furthermore, Thai insiders appear to trade within trading ban periods with fewer legal consequences.

INFORMATION DISCLOSURE THROUGH PRIVATE IN-HOUSE MEETINGS

Investors, analysts, and other market participants gather firm-specific information from various publicly available sources, including annual reports, press releases, media reports, and other corporate documents. Besides these conventional public information channels, other private interaction events such as phone calls, conference calls, and private in-house meetings, including site visits, are available, through which investors and various market participants attempt to collect additional information from the firm's management itself. However, such private interactions could lead to selective disclosures of material information to a small group of market participants. Although all types of private interactions could give an undue informational advantage to select investors, private in-house meetings are more contentious because participants can directly meet the managers and engage in in-depth discussions (Chen and Matsumoto 2006; Soltes 2014; Solomon and Soltes 2015).

Private meetings are not unlawful. In fact, private meetings are encouraged in many countries to have a better informational exchange. For example, Article 41 of the "Guidelines of Investor Relations Management" issued in 2006 by the Shenzhen Stock Exchange (SZSE) – the second-largest stock exchange in China – encouraged companies to accommodate requests from investors and market participants to have private in-house meetings and site visits. Yet, regulators remain concerned about the possibility of material information leakage during these private in-house meetings, which in turn may facilitate informed trading activities.

Another plausible channel of informational gain by private meeting participants is the generation of "mosaic information." Even though a firm's management does not directly reveal any material information, sophisticated meeting participants still can build an useful information mosaic by putting together various signals derived from their interactions with firm management. Such possibilities are likely because information disclosure regulation around the world does not clearly specify what constitutes material nonpublic information.

Although regulators around the world are concerned about the unintended consequences of information leakage through private meetings, only SZSE in China has implemented specific disclosure regulations in this regard (Bowen, Dutta, Tang, and Zhu 2018). The next subsection discusses the relevant disclosure regulations and the impact on equity markets in the context of private meetings.

Regulatory Environment: Private In-house Meetings

A typical private in-house meeting in China lasts between one and two hours. It may also include site visits and question and answer sessions. Investors, fund managers, analysts, and other market participants attend these private meetings. Generally, some senior managers or public relations officers other than the chief executive officers (CEOs) and chief financial officers (CFOs) accompany the participants. Either firm management or investors/analysts can initiate these private in-house meetings. Also, once the investors or analysts know about the meeting dates, they can start trading on relevant stocks even before the scheduled meeting dates.

To prevent material information disclosure through private meetings and associated insider trading, SZSE, and the Chinese securities exchange commission have taken several steps. For example, in 2006, SZSE issued "Fair Disclosure Guidelines," stressing that firms should not disclose any material nonpublic information to participants during private in-house meetings. The fair disclosure guidelines are motivated by Reg FD as introduced by the U.S. Securities and Exchange Commission (SEC) in 2000. Prior studies, however, present a mixed view on the success of Reg FD in leveling the playing field for various investors (Koch, Lefanowicz, and Robinson 2013). One contentious issue involving Reg FD is that it does not specify what constitutes material nonpublic information (Bushee, Gerakos, and Lee 2018). Koch et al. report that after the introduction of Reg FD, U.S. firms expanded public disclosures, leading to an improvement in the informational environment in the marketplace. Yet, complete information available on small and technology-oriented firms has decreased.

SZSE intended to have a similar benefit when it introduced fair disclosure guidelines in 2006. Whether Reg FD is successful in China is a debatable issue. Although the authorities claim that Reg FD has been successful in curbing the material disclosure of nonpublic information, other evidence undermines such an assertion. Other investors and market participants have complained about the possible leakage of material information through private in-house meetings. Given that the Chinese legal environment is still evolving and corporate governance practices are not among the best in the world, one cannot rule out the possibilities of unfair disclosure in private meetings. Some recent steps undertaken by SZSE support this view. For example, since 2009, firms listed on SZSE are required to report private meeting information in annual reports. However, major concerns about information disclosure and insider trading surround these private meetings. No clear guidelines are available on what constitutes "material nonpublic information," which creates a severe obstacle to the regulatory bodies in curbing the unwarranted effects of private-in-house meetings. In July 2012, SZSE started requiring firms to publish a standard report on private meetings within two days of the meeting date through the stock exchange's online web portal.

Empirical Evidence: Private In-house Meetings

Bowen et al. (2018) examine insider trading activities around private in-house meetings by analyzing 17,000 private meeting summary reports of SZSE firms between

2012 and 2014. The study finds that private meeting reports are informative and corporate insiders make substantial profit around these private meetings. Cheng, Du, Wang, and Wang (2016) and Han, Kong, and Liu (2018) find that forecast accuracy increases for analysts who participate in private in-house meetings, which supports the informational advantage conjecture in the context of private in-house meetings. Cheng, Du, Wang, and Wang (2019) also find that private in-house meetings or site visits are highly informative, as the market reacts significantly to these meetings. Specifically, the market reacts more strongly for group visits, visits to firms with a poor informational environment, visits to manufacturing firms, and visits by mutual fund managers. The study further finds that stock returns around site visits are positively associated with firms' future performance. Gao, Cao, and Liu (2017) and Lu, Fung, and Su (2018) examine the relation between the frequency of private in-house meetings in a firm and the firm's future stock price crash risk. These studies report a significant association.

In general, a growing body of private in-house meeting literature indicates that these meetings are informative and may give some undue advantage to a select group of investors, analysts, and fund managers. Although disclosure regulation is supposed to mitigate the undue advantage of private in-house meetings, current empirical evidence questions the effectiveness of such regulations.

SUMMARY AND CONCLUSIONS

Although firms routinely engage in financial reporting, mostly in regular intervals according to regulatory requirements, corporate disclosures can be voluntary or mandatory depending on the nature of the information. This chapter primarily discusses three disclosure regulations: (1) environmental and CSR disclosure regulation, (2) insider trading disclosure regulation, and (3) private in-house meeting disclosure regulation. Evidence generally shows that emerging market economies have taken various initiatives to improve the disclosure environment for publicly listed firms, especially in the areas of the environmental and CSR-related disclosure environment. However, the effectiveness of such regulations remains questionable.

To introduce an in-depth view of various disclosure regulations and their effectiveness, this chapter focuses on various emerging markets, especially China, which have undertaken major steps to improve the disclosure environment over the past three decades. Following in the footsteps of developed economies, emerging market regulators have also started to introduce various disclosure regulations to reduce information asymmetry and ensure transparency in different capital markets. Although authorities introduced the regulations with good intentions, empirical evidence shows that the implementation of these regulations has not been particularly effective. In many instances, authorities fail to identify or take adequate actions against violators. Nonetheless, regulatory bodies have become more careful in recent years, which is likely to enhance the effectiveness of these disclosure regulations. Among the emerging markets, China has taken comprehensive steps to improve its disclosure environment on different fronts, such as environmental, governance and CSR disclosures, insider trading–related disclosures, and private meeting–related disclosures. The experience is extremely helpful for other emerging markets that want to implement similar regulations or intend to improve the existing ones.

DISCUSSION QUESTIONS

1. Discuss the pros and cons of various disclosure regulation approaches: voluntary, mandatory, and comply or explain options.
2. Elaborate on the challenges associated with environmental disclosure regulation in China.
3. Discuss the information mosaic argument in the context of private meetings.
4. Explain how insiders can make profits around private meetings in China.

REFERENCES

Arsov, Sasho, and Vesna Bucevska. 2017. "Determinants of Transparency and Disclosure – Evidence from Post-transition Economies." *Economic Research* 30:1, 745–760.

Beny, Laura Nyantung. 2005. "Do Insider Trading Laws Matter? Some Preliminary Comparative Evidence." *American Law and Economics Review* 7:1, 144–183.

Berglöf, Erik, and Anete Pajuste. 2005. "What Do Firms Disclose and Why? Enforcing Corporate Governance and Transparency in Central and Eastern Europe." *Oxford Review of Economic Policy* 21:2, 178–197.

Bhattacharya, Utpal, and Hazem Daouk. 2002. "The World Price of Insider Trading." *Journal of Finance* 57:1, 75–108.

Bokpin, Godred A. 2013. "Determinants and Value Relevance of Corporate Disclosure: Evidence from the Emerging Capital Market of Ghana." *Journal of Applied Accounting Research* 14:2, 127–146.

Bowen, Robert M., Shananu Dutta, Songlian Tang, and Pengcheng Zhu. 2018. "Inside the 'Black Box' of Private In-house Meetings." *Review of Accounting Studies* 23:2, 487–527.

Budsaratragoon, Pornanong, David Hillier, and Suntharee Lhaopadchan. 2012. "Applying Developed-country Regulation in Emerging Markets: An Analysis of Thai Insider Trading." *Accounting and Finance* 52:4, 1013–1039.

Bushee, Brian J., Joseph Gerakos, and Lian Fen Lee. 2018. "Corporate Jets and Private Meetings with Investors." *Journal of Accounting and Economics* 65:2–3, 358–379.

Chauhan, Yogesh, K. Kiran Kumar, and Chakrapani Chaturvedula. 2016. "Information Asymmetry and the Information Content of Insider Trades: Evidence from the Indian Stock Market." *Journal of Multinational Financial Management* 34:March, 65–79.

Chen, Shuping, and Dawn A. Matsumoto. 2006. "Favorable Versus Unfavorable Recommendations: The Impact on Analyst Access to Management-Provided Information." *Journal of Accounting Research* 44:4, 657–689.

Chen, Yi-Chun, Mingyi Hung, and Yongxiang Wang. 2018. "The Effect of Mandatory CSR Disclosure on Firm Profitability and Social Externalities: Evidence from China." *Journal of Accounting and Economics* 65:1, 169–190.

Cheng, Qiang, Fei Du, Brian Yutao Wang, and Xin Wang. 2019. "Do Corporate Site Visits Impact Stock Prices?" *Contemporary Accounting Research* 36:1, 359–388.

Cheng, Qiang, Fei Du, Xin Wang, and Yutao Wang, 2016. "Seeing Is Believing: Analysts' Corporate Site Visits." *Review of Accounting Studies* 21:4, 1245–1286.

Dai, Lili, Renhui Fu, Jun-Koo Kang, and Inmoo Lee. 2016. "Corporate Governance and the Profitability of Insider Trading." *Journal of Corporate Finance* 40:October, 235–253.

Duan, Liu. 2009. "The Ongoing Battle against Insider Trading: A Comparison of Chinese and U.S. Law and Comments on How China Should Improve Its Insider Trading Law Enforcement Regime." *Duquesne Business Law Journal* 12:1, 129–161.

Durnev, Art, and E. Han Kim. 2005. "To Steal or Not to Steal: Firm Attributes, Legal Environment, and Valuation." *Journal of Finance* 60:3, 1461–1493.

Gao, Shenghao, Feng Cao, and Xiangqiang Liu. 2017. "Seeing Is Not Necessarily the Truth: Do Institutional Investors' Corporate Site Visits Reduce Hosting Firms' Stock Price Crash Risk?" *International Review of Economics & Finance* 52:November, 165–187.

Han, Bing, Dongmin Kong, and Shasha Liu. 2018. "Do Analysts Gain an Informational Advantage by Visiting Listed Companies?" *Contemporary Accounting Research* 35:4, 1843–1867.

Hanifa, Mohamed Hisham, and H. Ab. Rashid. 2005. "The Determinants of Voluntary Disclosures in Malaysia: The Case of Internet Financial Reporting." *Unitar E-Journal* 2:January, 22–42.

He, Qing, and Oliver M. Rui. 2016. "Ownership Structure and Insider Trading: Evidence from China." *Journal of Business Ethics* 134:4, 553–574.

Huang, Hui. 2005. "The Regulation of Insider Trading in China: A Critical Review and Proposals for Reform." *Australian Journal of Corporate Law* 17, 281–322.

Huang, Hui. 2013. "The Regulation of Insider Trading in China: Law and Enforcement." In *Research Handbook on Insider Trading*, edited by Stephen M. Bainbridge, 303–326. Springfield, MA: Edward Elgar Publishing.

Inci, A. Can., M. P. Narayanan, and H. Nejat Seyhun. 2017. "Gender Differences in Executives' Access to Information." *Journal of Financial and Quantitative Analysis* 52:3, 991–1016.

Koch, Adam S., Craig E. Lefanowicz., and John R. Robinson. 2013. "Regulation FD: A Review and Synthesis of the Academic Literature." *Accounting Horizons* 27:3, 619–646.

Kuo, Lopin, Chin-Chen Yeh, and Hui-Cheng Yu. 2012. "Disclosure of Corporate Social Responsibility and Environmental Management: Evidence from China." *Corporate Social Responsibility and Environmental Management* 19:5, 273–287.

Lin, Li-Wen. 2009. "Corporate Social and Environmental Disclosure in Emerging Securities Markets." *North Carolina Journal of International Law & Commercial Regulation* 35:1, 1–32.

Liu, Xianbing, and V. Anbumozhi. 2009. "Determinant Factors of Corporate Environmental Information Disclosure: An Empirical Study of Chinese Listed Companies." *Journal of Cleaner Production* 17:6, 593–600.

Liu, Beibei, Qinqin Yu, Biang Zhang, Jun Bi, Junjie Ge, Zengwei Yuan, and Yang Yu. 2010. "Does the GreenWatch Program Work? Evidence from a Developed Area in China." *Journal of Cleaner Production* 18:5, 454–461.

Liu, Beibei, Qinqin Yu., Bing Zhang, Jun Bi, Junjie Ge, and Maoiang Bu. 2012. "A Study on the Short-term and Long-term Corporate Responses to the GreenWatch Program: Evidence from Jiangsu, China." *Journal of Cleaner Production* 24:March, 132–140.

Liu, Xianbing, Qinqin Yu, Tetsuro Fujitsuka, Beibei Liu, Jun Bi, Tomohiro Shishime. 2010. "Functional Mechanisms of Mandatory Corporate Environmental Disclosure: An Empirical Study in China." *Journal of Cleaner Production* 18:8, 823–832.

Lopes, Alexsandro Broedel, and Roberta Carvalho de Alencar. 2010. "Disclosure and Cost of Equity Capital in Emerging Markets: The Brazilian Case." *International Journal of Accounting* 45:4, 443–464.

Lu, Xian-Wei, Hung-Gay Fung, and Zhong-Qin Su. 2018. "Information Leakage, Site Visits, and Crash Risk: Evidence from China." *International Review of Economics & Finance* 58:C, 487–507.

McGee, Robert W. 2008. "Applying Ethics to Insider Trading." *Journal of Business Ethics* 77:2, 205–217.

Meng, X. H., S. X. Zeng, Jonathan J. Shi, G. Y. Qi, and Z. B. Zhang. 2014. "The Relationship between Corporate Environmental Performance and Environmental Disclosure: An Empirical Study in China." *Journal of Environmental Management* 145:1, 357–367.

Noronha Carlos, Si Tou, M. I. Cynthia, and Jenny J. Guan. 2013. "Corporate Social Responsibility Reporting in China: An Overview and Comparison with Major Trends." *Corporate Social Responsibility and Environmental Management* 20:1, 29–42.

Othman, Hakim Benand, and Daniel Zeghal. 2010. "Investigating Transparency and Disclosure Determinants at Firm-level in MENA Emerging Markets." *International Journal of Accounting Auditing and Performance Evaluation* 6:4, 368–396.

Piotroski, Joseph D., and Darren T. Roulstone. 2005. "Do Insider Trades Reflect both Contrarian Beliefs and Superior Knowledge about Future Cash Flow Realizations?" *Journal of Accounting and Economics* 39:1, 55–81.

Qiu, Ying, Hua He, and Gang Xiao. 2018. "The Information Content of Insider Trading: Evidence from China." *Finance Research Letters* 26:September, 126–131.

Qi, G. Y., S. X. Zeng, Jonathan J. Shi, X. H. Meng, H. Lin, and Q. X. Yang. 2014. "Revisiting the Relationship between Environmental and Financial Performance in Chinese Industry." *Journal of Environmental Management* 145:1, 349–356.

Roulstone, Darren T. 2003. "The Relation between Insider-Trading Restrictions and Executive Compensation." *Journal of Accounting Research* 41:3, 525–551.

Seyhun, H. Nejat. 1998. *Investment Intelligence from Insider Trading*. Cambridge, MA: MIT Press.

Situ, Hui, and Carol Tilt. 2018. "Mandatory? Voluntary? A Discussion of Corporate Environmental Disclosure Requirements in China." *Social and Environmental Accountability Journal* 38:2, 131–144.

Solomon, David H., and Eugene F. Soltes. 2015. "What Are We Meeting For? The Consequences of Private Meetings with Investors." *Journal of Law and Economics* 58:2, 325–355.

Soltes, Eugene F. 2014. "Private Interaction between Firm Management and Sell-side Analysts." *Journal of Accounting Research* 52:1, 245–272.

Strudler, Alan, and Eric W. Orts. 1999. "Moral Principle in the Law of Insider Trading." *Texas Law Review* 78:2, 375–438.

Tong, Wilson H. S., Shaoun Zhang, and Yanjian Zhu. 2013. "Trading on Inside Information: Evidence from the Share-structure Reform in China." *Journal of Banking & Finance* 37:5, 1422–1436.

Xu, X. D., S. X. Zeng, and C. M. Tam. 2012. "Stock Market's Reaction to Disclosure of Environmental Violations: Evidence from China." *Journal of Business Ethics* 107:2, 227–237.

Yu, Zhongfu, Jianhui Jian, and Pinglin He. 2011. "The Study on the Correlation between Environmental Information Disclosure and Economic Performance." *Energy Procedia* 5, 1218–1224.

Zheng, S. X., X. D. Xu, Z. Y. Dong, and Vivian W. Y. Tam. 2010. "Towards Corporate Environmental Information Disclosure: An Empirical Study in China." *Journal of Cleaner Production* 18:12, 1142–1148.

CHAPTER 24

Equity Crowdfunding Investments

Dianna Preece
Professor of Finance, University of Louisville

INTRODUCTION

In 2006, Jeffrey Howe coined the term *crowdsource* (Howe 2006). He believed that a group of individuals could achieve more, and in many cases, be faster, less resource-intensive, and achieve better quality than large organizations. Howe also believed that the crowd would reinvent the technological world.

Crowdsourcing can take many forms, ranging from putting up a suggestion box in a school cafeteria to soliciting ideas to figure out how to stop the increase of plastic nanoparticles in the world's oceans. However, crowdfunding, not crowdsourcing, is the focus of this chapter. The same year Howe coined the term crowdsourcing, an entrepreneur named Michael Sullivan created the term *crowdfunding* (Breedlove 2018). A modern example, and perhaps the start of crowdfunding, happened in 1997 when the British rock band Marillion let their fans know, via the internet, that they could not go on a reunion tour because the tour would lose money. Their fans responded, donating $60,000 online to fund the tour. Following Marillion's and others' success, Artistshare started in 2000 as the first rewards-based "fan funding" site. As evidence of the interest in and popularity of tapping the masses for ideas and funding, the members of LinkedIn's CrowdSourcing and CrowdFunding group numbered over 19,000 members in early 2013, whereas the initial public offering (IPO) group numbered only 1,400. Investors and firms alike have taken an interest in this new form of capital raising (Jacobs 2013).

This chapter proceeds as follows. The next section details the types of crowdfunding available to investors. The following section discusses the Jumpstart Our Business Startups (JOBS) Act of 2012, the kickoff to equity crowdfunding in the United States. Next, the advantages and disadvantages to both investors and capital raisers are discussed, followed by academic research on crowdfunding. Finally, the chapter provides a summary and conclusions.

TYPES OF CROWDFUNDING

Crowdfunding falls into four basic categories: (1) charitable giving, (2) rewards-based, (3) debt, and (4) equity crowdfunding. Popular sites like Indiegogo (www.indiegogo.com), founded in 2008, and Kickstarter (www.kickstarter.com), founded in 2009, are *rewards-based crowdfunding platforms*. Backers receive perks such as concert tickets, T-shirts, and experiences such as being an extra on a movie set, in exchange for funding, and the perks increase as the amount of funding increases. A donation-based crowdfunding site is an appropriate channel for those who want to support public initiatives such as public parks or private needs. An example of the latter is the response to the recent suicide/arson attack that killed 34 people at Kyoto Animation Studios in Japan; the campaign had an original goal of $500,000 and raised nearly $2,400,000 on the GoFundMe platform. GoFundMe (www.gofundme.com), launched in 2010, is the leader in donation-based crowdfunding.

The initial rewards-based crowdfunding efforts grew out of a regulated environment. Before the JOBS Act of 2012, federal securities laws prohibited companies from selling shares of stock directly to the public through *private placements*, without registering the securities with the Securities and Exchange Commission (SEC). Yet, some exemptions exist as specified in Regulation D. Thus, the initial crowdfunding efforts had to entice investors by offering them something that did not resemble a company's shares (Weitz and Halket 2015).

Firms found creative ways to bypass regulations by offering alternatives to shares of stock or anything tied to profits. Companies offer experiences and products instead. The perks were not tied to the firm's success. This situation is akin to the late 1970s and early 1980s when banks offered toaster ovens, sets of dishes, and airline tickets to entice individuals to open deposit accounts in the face of rising interest rates and interest rate regulation (Weisenthal 2009). Regulation Q, which prohibited banks from paying interest on checking accounts and set a maximum on the rate banks could pay on savings accounts, resulted in, at a time of high-interest rates, creative ways to sidestep regulation and "pay" customers a pseudo interest rate.

Many contend that those banking regulations were outdated, and they were rewritten in 1980 and 1982. Others might argue that securities laws are outdated and need to be written to allow the "common man" to take part in lucrative investments in startups and private equity. This situation is complicated because investments are risky, and many nonaccredited investors are unsophisticated.

Debt-based crowdfunding, also known as *peer-to-peer lending*, allows startups to borrow without having to seek funding from banks. Lenders receive interest payments in exchange for capital. The focus of this chapter is on the fourth type, equity crowdfunding. *Equity crowdfunding*, also called *investment crowdfunding, crowd equity, hyper funding*, and *crowd investing*, offers private company securities to individuals via online platforms. Equity crowdfunding has its own set of unique challenges and rewards, discussed later in this chapter. According to Weitz and Halket (2015, p. 522), U.S. securities laws have "largely acted as a brake on the ability of those seeking crowdfunding to issue stock or other securities in exchange for the funds raised."

Crowdfunding can also follow a profit-sharing model or some hybrid of debt and equity. Some smaller ventures may even give investors the product or other "prizes" instead of or in addition to firm shares. Because firms do not have to jump through the SEC hoops of IPOs, small businesses and startups may be able to raise equity capital faster or cheaper than through traditional routes. Typically, firms that are raising smaller amounts of equity funding are best able to use crowdfunding. As a firm grows and becomes more established, it often uses other sources of funds such as angel investors and venture capital (VC).

The United States is behind the Australian and European equity crowdfunding bandwagons. The first equity-based crowdfunding platform, the Australian Small Scale Offerings Board (ASSOB), which now trades as Enable Funding, started in 2007 in Australia (Best, Neiss, Swart, Lambkin, and Raymond 2013). The first U.S. crowdfunding platform, a U.S.-based company called Profounder, launched a model for startups to raise capital on the firm's website directly. Unfortunately, as Profounder launched before the JOBS Act was enacted, it failed due to regulatory reasons that prevented companies from raising capital. Some of the earliest U.K. crowdsource platforms include Crowdcube and Seedrs. Platform models vary. For example, the European firm Exorot.com invests its own money in each startup, on top of the funds raised on the platform. The JOBS Act of 2012 launched equity crowd investing in the United States.

THE JOBS ACT OF 2012

Although crowdfunding gained traction outside the United States as early as 2007 in Australia, the idea was more firmly established in the United States with the JOBS Act, which passed with bipartisan support in April 2012 (Congress.gov 2012). Former U.S. President Obama, who had been successfully raising money online for his campaign from "the crowd," saw a potential opportunity to help jumpstart the economy following the financial crisis of 2007–2008. Raising capital, especially equity capital, was challenging for most businesses in the years following the financial crisis, but was particularly difficult for smaller businesses, artisans, entrepreneurs, and early-stage businesses. Adding crowdfunding to the JOBS Act was initially intended to provide a path for early-stage companies to raise capital beyond friends and family networks, a compelling idea for politicians struggling with the economic realities of the financial crisis of 2007–2008.

One goal of the JOBS Act was to ease securities regulations and to help small businesses raise capital. Although Congress passed the Act, also known as the Crowdfund Act, which went into effect in September 2013, the SEC took years to develop the specific rules to regulate crowdfunding in the United States. Among the many critics of the JOBS Act was Mary Schapiro, then chairperson of the SEC (Protess 2012). Despite opposition, proponents could get an exemption to the registration provisions of the Securities Act of 1933.

The JOBS Act allows businesses to use crowdfunding to issue securities. Before the JOBS Act, a nearly-90-year ban existed on general solicitations from the public to raise equity capital (Breedlove 2018). The intent of the Securities Act of 1933 and the Securities Exchange Act of 1934 was to protect investors following the Great Depression (Weitz and Halket 2015). The JOBS Act enabled soliciting funding via online platforms from accredited investors. An *accredited investor* is a person or business entity who is permitted to deal in securities that may not be registered with financial authorities. The Crowdfund Act allowed startups and other companies to reach out to large numbers of investors. The Obama Administration's goal was to support small businesses in America. The JOBS Act was an important step in the government's embracing of financial technology (FinTech), specifically to increase small businesses' access to capital. In his address, when signing the bill into law, President Obama (2012) said:

> *And for start-ups and small businesses, this bill is a potential game-changer. Right now, you can only turn to a limited group of investors – including banks and wealthy individuals – to get funding. Laws that are nearly eight decades old make it impossible for others to invest. But a lot has changed in 80 years, and it's time our laws did as well. Because of this bill, start-ups and small businesses will now have access to a big new pool of potential investors – namely, the American people. For the first time, ordinary Americans will be able to go online and invest in entrepreneurs that they believe in.*

Of course, to avoid taking advantage of Americans, the websites where people go to fund these startups and small businesses are subject to rigorous oversight. The SEC played an important role in implementing this bill. Congress required the SEC to develop investment rules by the end of 2012 but the SEC did not complete its task in 2015. On May 16, 2016, the SEC's new investment crowdfunding rule, Regulation Crowdfunding (Regulation CF), went into effect.

According to Jacobs (2013), Senate amendments resulted in heavier regulatory, legal, and procedural burdens than proposed in the original bill. In essence, the increased burden, some believed, made the registration exemptions useless. Crowdfunding is, in essence, a private placement of securities. Regulation D, an SEC regulation governing private placements, requires that investors be accredited.

In fairness to the SEC, the regulation of an entirely novel approach to raising capital was a difficult task. Congress and the executive branch asked the SEC to provide rules to protect the most vulnerable of investors, namely, small, nonaccredited investors who are investing in the riskiest of investments such as startups and small businesses. Although the SEC did a good job of balancing the competing interests, it did not approve the rules, called Regulation Crowdfunding, until late 2015. These rules finally went into effect in May 2016 (Grills and Soroushian 2018). The intent of the JOBS Act was to allow startups and other businesses to raise money with fewer regulatory hurdles than IPOs. Firms could raise money through online portals, allowing them to raise capital without establishing relationships with angel investors or venture capitalists. The JOBS Act was also supposed to expand the pool of potential investors beyond accredited investors, as was required before the JOBS Act to raise funds privately.

Who Can Invest?

Accredited investors include institutional investors such as banks and trusts as well as some individuals. In terms of individuals, accredited investors have historically been defined based on an individual's assets and net worth (i.e., a person with $200,000 or more in income or $300,000 including a spouse's income or individual or joint net worth exceeding $1,000,000). The definition is crucial because only accredited investors had access to potentially lucrative investments in private equity and hedge funds. Thus, defining an accredited investor based solely on income and net worth limits the investment possibilities for numerous investors. As such, some in the financial industry wanted to widen the definition to consider a person's financial education, work experience, and sophistication in defining an accredited investor. JOBS 3.0 tackles the issue, enabling some investors, such as those licensed as a broker or those with job experience and/or education deemed by the SEC as sufficient, to be classified as an accredited investor. Nonetheless, the approval process is likely to be difficult, and how the SEC will monitor and enforce this process is unclear.

JOBS 3.0

This short history has led to the current state of crowd investing in the United States. In 2018, the U.S. House of Representatives passed, with a 406–4 bipartisan vote, a financial reform legislation entitled the JOBS and Investor Confidence Act of 2018, commonly called JOBS 3.0 (Grills and Soroushian 2018). Major policy challenges are associated with crowdfunding. Although the legislation easily passed the House of Representatives, it stalled in the U.S. Senate as members were facing mid-term elections. The Senate Committee on Banking, Housing, and Urban Affairs finally considered the Act in early 2019 (Britton 2019). To date, the Senate has not moved to pass it into law. JOBS 3.0 contains several important changes to make crowd-source investing more accessible and more efficient. JOBS 3.0 arose out of the original JOBS Act.

CROWDFUND INVESTMENT OPPORTUNITIES AND INCENTIVES

Advantages are available to crowdfund investors from both the investor's and the entrepreneur's perspectives. First, from the latter's perspective, crowdfunding widens the pool of potential investors beyond friends and family, angels, and venture capitalists to a world of investors. VCs, for example, set commitment expectations for funding. Using the crowd allows a firm to set its targets and commitments without the agreements required from VCs.

Additionally, in theory, the cost of capital may be lower relative to traditional sources such as friends and family, credit cards, home equity lines, VC or angel funding due to incentives for investing, and the expertise of the American people. This outcome is possible because, according to Agrawal, Catalini, and Goldfarb (2014), better matches may be available between entrepreneurs and investors (i.e., those who are interested in the product, not just a local pool of potential investors). The authors also contend that founders may be able to bundle a product or experience, as offered on rewards-based platforms, with equity, potentially lowering the cost of equity. Finally, they assert that an information advantage may be present, such as the interest in a product generated on an online platform that causes backers to be willing to pay more "to get in on it," lowering the cost of capital. Crowdfunding may also increase the competition to supply early-stage capital, currently the domain of friends and family, VCs, and angels.

Additionally, equity crowdfunding should reduce other costs of raising funds. First, the entrepreneur does not have to invest time and substantial resources in developing relationships with venture capitalists. Second, at least in theory, the regulatory burdens, such as SEC filing costs, should be lower under a crowdfunding model.

Compared to an IPO, the costs of hiring an investment banking firm to underwrite the securities offering should be much lower. To protect less sophisticated and vulnerable investors, the SEC has, at least until recently, imposed a regulatory burden that is greater than perhaps intended by the original JOBS Act.

One unexpected advantage of equity crowdsourcing involves female entrepreneurs. Although equity crowdfunding is alleged to deregionalize fundraising, providing capital-raising opportunities outside expected geographic areas such as Silicon Valley and New York City (NYC), data suggest it has actually "degenderized" equity fundraising. VC funding is still "a boys' club" (Hinchliffe 2019). In 2018, total VC funding to all female-founded companies was about 2.2 percent of the total. The numbers are slightly better for women on the "team" – between 10 percent and 18 percent of VC funding, depending on the study, go to companies with women on the startup team. Also, deal sizes are much larger for male-founded and/or -led firms. For example, the largest deal to a male-founded firm in 2018 was $12.8 billion for e-cigarette maker Juul.

In contrast, the largest deal to a female-led company was $208 million to Minted (Hinchliffe 2019). On equity crowdfunding platforms, 22 percent of the founders raising capital are women. Also, these women are raising only 3 percentage points less than men. Additionally, underrepresented groups such as black and Latino founders can raise funds via equity crowdsourcing. For example, Republic, a crowdfunding platform, reports that 25 percent of investments go to companies with black and Latino founders and 44 percent to businesses with female founders (Deutsch 2018).

Another advantage of funding through online solicitations is the actual investors attracted. In a study that combines crowdfunding data with survey data from founding entrepreneurs, Stanko and Henard (2017) find that the amount of funding a company raises on the Kickstarter platform does not predict the market success of the product being launched. Yet, the number of people who invest – the backers – correlate positively with future performance. The study focused on 1,000 successful Kickstarter campaigns and 224 full or partially completed surveys from entrepreneurs in the areas of product design, video games, technology, and hardware. According to Stanko and Henard, crowdfunding creates a community that raises product awareness. Founders and entrepreneurs benefit from this awareness in multiple ways, including feedback from backers about the product to serving as "evangelists," touting the product on social media, and through word of mouth. Feedback from backers allows for "radical innovation" by entrepreneurs. Funders often have ideas for project improvement that allow entrepreneurs to respond, innovating based on feedback. They also find that entrepreneurs who raise funds beyond their goal are less likely to innovate. The authors focus on a rewards-based platform for their analysis due to the slow establishment of equity crowdfunding in the United States. Stanko and Henard conclude that backers can play an important role "beyond their wallets" in helping a startup become successful.

CROWDFUND INVESTMENT CHALLENGES AND DISINCENTIVES

In 2013, securities lawyer Brian Korn, in a *Forbes* article, enumerated at least 10 reasons he believes crowdfunding is infeasible relative to alternative private placement options. He said, about the SEC's requirements regarding private placements, "These statutory requirements effectively weigh it down to the point of making the crowdfunding exemption under the JOBS Act utterly useless" (Jacobs 2013). One of his primary concerns is the $1 million cap that is imposed on issuers in 12 months. This cap makes taking advantage of online platforms to raise capital nearly impossible for faster-growing startups or later-stage firms, forcing them to seek funding from traditional sources such as private equity.

Several problems are associated with the original JOBS Act, and with crowdfunding in general, that creates problems for U.S. investors and U.S. companies to take advantage of the new mechanism for raising capital (Jacobs 2013). JOBS 3.0 addresses some of these issues. For example, one of the biggest criticisms of equity crowdfunding is that it excluded most investors (i.e., nonaccredited investors). Most marketing and advertising efforts directed at investors are targeted at Regulation D, the SEC regulation that governs private placement exemptions in securities regulations. From the perspective of individual investors, Reg D essentially limits private placements to a small group of sophisticated and wealthy individuals. Thus, it locks out the majority of investors instead of opening up investing to a broader audience, which was one of the key aims of the JOBS Act. According to Rosenberg (2018), individuals with income or net worth under $100,000 are prohibited, from investing, over 12 months, more than $2,000 in one or more businesses. In 2017, the SEC announced an increase to $2,200 per year for those making under $105,000. Although the Reg D exemptions have been revisited and may be modified in the latest round of changes to the JOBS Act, it has kept equity crowdfunding from taking off in the United States, despite heated interest from both investors and entrepreneurs.

According to Grills and Soroushian (2018), some concern still exists that policymakers are not fostering the crowdfunding market to the extent that they might. In theory, crowdfunding should deregionalize access to capital. For example, those seeking funds should not have to be in Silicon Valley or New York City. However, the authors discuss a study by the Small Business Administration's (SBA) Office of Advocacy, showing that equity crowdfunding is concentrated in specific geographic areas. For example, 35 percent of issuers are in California, and 9 percent are in Florida. Although not optimal, concentrations are in areas of the United States one might expect. Many perceive California, home to Silicon Valley, to be open to new ideas, and California businesses likely have greater access to capital than entrepreneurs in the "flyover" states of the Midwest. Florida ranks third overall for highest-growth-rate states based on population growth and growth in GDP using 2014 to 2017 data trends from the Bureau of Economic Analysis data (*U.S. News & World Report* 2018). Conversely, despite geographic concentration, Agrawal, Catalini, and Goldfarb (2011) find that funding is not geographically constrained for the entrepreneur. In an examination of Sellabond, a music-only platform created in 2006 in Amsterdam that offered royalty sharing with backers, more than 86 percent of investors were more than 60 miles away from the entrepreneur, and the average distance between the entrepreneur and the funder was more than 3,000 miles.

Another concern that many experts express is the challenges and costs of managing a large number of small investors. This situation also complicates the task of raising capital in subsequent rounds from VC firms. Yet, some momentum is underway to allow special purpose vehicles (SPVs) in which the investments of the crowd can be pooled and managed by an investment professional. This pooled investment is likely to show up as one investor on the startups' capitalization (cap) table, rather than hundreds of investors. This situation should increase the ease with which a firm can raise additional funding from VCs.

Entrepreneurs have to disclose their products in a public forum, which may be a disincentive for inventors/creators who are afraid their product may be imitated or copied. Suppliers can also see how much money an entrepreneur has raised on a public forum, giving them leverage in negotiating the prices of product inputs and supplies. Although disclosures and documentation are less than required for companies going public, they are still substantive and costly to startups that likely have little expertise in securities regulation and have to hire lawyers and accountants to assist, which can cost a young firm tens of thousands of dollars (Rosenberg 2018). Such costs can eat into the capital the startup raises via equity crowdfunding, which, as previously noted, is limited to $1 million per year. Additionally, these costs add a work burden to already stressed founders trying to run a new company. Another issue that hinders companies in their crowdfunding efforts and increases the number of small investors who must be managed is the cap on the amount a small investor may invest. As identified previously, this amount is $2,200 per year total across all investments for those earning less than $105,000.

Because some potential investors may be unsophisticated, a greater potential for fraud exists (Griffin 2012; Hazen 2012; Agrawal et al. 2014). Given that most investments are small relative to the funds provided by VCs and angels, the incentive to perform adequate due diligence is lower, increasing the likelihood that smaller, unsophisticated investors may not reap the rewards they may expect from startup investing. This situation enables free riders to take advantage of the efforts of those who do perform due diligence.

One disappointment regarding crowdfunding is that it has not appealed to the broad masses as expected and intended by the JOBS Act. Crowdfunding, according to former President Obama, was to appeal to this big new pool of investors, "the American people." According to Rosenberg (2018), approximately half of the investors in crowdfunding companies are the company's customers who want to support their favorite startup, whether it be a new brewery or clothes designer or music project. That makes equity crowdfunding more like rewards-based crowdfunding in spirit than the "let's open up startup investments beyond the rich, to the common man" idea espoused by its proponents and anticipated by those who expected it to be a bonanza. According to Nick Tommarello, CEO of Wefunder, the largest regulation equity crowdfunding portal, "There's not a lot of people out there saying, 'gee, we want to invest in startups'" (Rosenberg 2018). This situation surprised many who believed that a pent-up demand existed from the general public.

Some believe, though, that not having thousands or millions of unsophisticated, less financially sound individual investors jump on the equity crowdfunding bandwagon is best. Statistics show that 90 percent of startups fail (Patel 2015). Startups generally fail because they create a product that the market does not want or need. They also fail because the founder micromanages the business or the firm grows too fast, or the availability and timing of financing is difficult.

Not everyone is suited to investing in startups. Most people, including professional investors, are not great at picking the few winners out of the many startup firms. Despite the slower acceptance of equity crowdfunding in the United States than expected, many small companies, companies that were too small to raise funds in the private equity/VC market, have been able to successfully raise funds via equity crowdfunding and keep their businesses afloat (Rosenberg 2018). Many smaller firms bypass equity crowdfunding altogether and raise funds on crowdfunding platforms such as Indiegogo and GoFundMe. These sites are rewards-based and donation-based platforms that appeal to people who like the idea or product of the startup and want to support the effort. The real advantage of these sites relative to equity crowdfunding sites is that they impose no limits on the amount a company or individual can raise, unlike the $1 million caps on equity crowdfunding in a calendar year. These platforms also have less paperwork because this type of funding does not fall under SEC securities regulations. Nevertheless, some firms want actual investors who have a stake in the company, as they often act as brand ambassadors and can help firms in unexpected ways.

Another concern raised is that crowdfunding could lead to a startup bubble. Some expect crowdfunding to outstrip VC investments eventually. This situation could lead to overfunding of perhaps nondeserving, early-stage companies. In 2017, $1.4 billion of crowdsourced equity startup funding occurred in the United States and $8 billion worldwide. According to Statista's Alternative Financing, that number is expected to reach $5 billion in the United States by 2022 and $31 billion globally (Deutsch 2018). In an examination of the first 100 companies to get equity startup capital after the SEC rules went into effect, more than 60 percent of the businesses were less than one year old – much younger than businesses funded by angel investors and VC firms. Although crowdfunding may enable some firms to survive longer, it does not change the fact that most ultimately fail. Entrepreneurs should not view raising capital as the goal of the business.

ACADEMIC RESEARCH

Academic studies of equity crowdfunding are limited, especially using U.S. data, because the market started in May 2016. Little data are available on the successes and failures of firms that have received funding in this manner. Additionally, scant evidence is available on returns from these investments. Existing evidence mostly focuses on companies in the United Kingdom and Germany, as they got their start about five years sooner than U.S. equity crowdfunding. Academic studies tend to focus on the funding itself rather than investor outcomes. For example, studies often examine factors that increase the likelihood of full or overfunding. The following discussion offers a sampling of academic research related to equity crowdfunding.

To explain crowdfunding from an economic perspective, Agrawal et al. (2014) identify several features that distinguish crowdfunding from traditional funding sources. A particularly important feature that distinguishes equity crowdfunding is information asymmetry. At the point of publication, equity crowdfunding had not yet been launched in the United States, as the SEC was still formulating the governing rules. Yet, Agrawal et al. (2014, p. 68) contend that the "most critical differences between equity and non-equity crowdfunding will arise due to the amplification of information asymmetries." The founder no longer has to deliver a product, as is common in both donation- and rewards-based crowdfunding models, but now has to build a company and create wealth for its shareholders. Because reporting requirements, governance, accounting, and other requirements are lower for equity crowdfunding relative to publicly traded securities, equity crowdfunders are taking on inordinately more risk. Without data, the authors postulate that adverse selection, moral hazard, and collective action all pose threats to the market.

Herding behavior is particularly likely in a crowdfunding environment. Many studies suggest that crowds often exhibit herd-like behavior, and crowdfunders are no exception. Agrawal et al. (2014) suggest that investors rely on accumulated capital as a signal of the quality of the underlying firm or product. They base this assertion on economic fundamentals as well as previous research (Agrawal et al. 2011; Zhang and Liu 2012; Burtch, Ghose, and Wattal 2013).

In a more recent study of European equity crowdfunding platforms, Vulkan, Astebro, and Sierra (2016) find empirical evidence to support the claim. The study focuses on funding and the factors that support full funding for creators. Using data from the U.K. equity crowdfunding platform SEEDRS, the authors draw several conclusions. In examining the herding behavior of backers, the authors find that the more capital a campaign raises, the more investors are likely to contribute. The faster a campaign gets off the ground, the more investors are likely to invest. Also, large contributions from one or more investors increase the contributions of the herd. The authors note that herding is expected in a world with so much uncertainty. They also find that equity crowdfunders make a much higher contribution than donation- or rewards-based backers. Additionally, the campaign's goal is also much higher than the typical donation- or rewards-based drive. They find that firms raising capital through equity crowdfunding have a premoney valuation and that investors expect a monetary return on their investments.

Using data from four German equity crowdfunding portals, Hornuf and Schwienbacher (2018) examine four-fifths of the German crowdfunding volume and the number of startups being financed. The authors find the dynamics of equity funding to be more L-shaped than U-shaped. This means that while a small uptick in investments occurs in the last three days of a campaign, the bulk of the dollars raised are at the beginning of the campaign, supporting their contention that a collective attention effect exists. The authors also find evidence that entrepreneurs raise more capital after the initial funding goal is met. They infer that backers view passing through the funding threshold as a positive signal. This logic follows the work of Cumming, Leboeuf, and Schwienbacher (2019), who suggest that funders face much less risk when a campaign reaches its minimum goal.

Hornuf and Schwienbacher (2018) also examine the peer effect. They note that larger investments convey information to other investors in a market with substantial information asymmetries. Larger-sized investments may signal the involvement of more sophisticated investors. Also, greater due diligence may precede larger investments. This situation is of interest from a policy perspective, as regulators limit the amount individual investors may invest in equity crowdfunding sites. The authors, however, note that peer effects may not be as strong in the early days, as friends and family often invest in the campaign during the early stages. Agrawal, Catalini, and Goldfarb (2015) find that friends and family invest early and for varied reasons, not simply the expectation of a financial return. Hornuf and Schwienbacher conclude how securities are allotted to backers influence funding dynamics. Auction mechanisms induce investors to enter late, while a first-come-first-served portal encourages investors to invest early, in the first few days that the campaign is seeking funds.

Hornuf and Schmitt (2016) examine the relative success and failures of firms that have raised capital via equity crowdfunding in the United Kingdom and Germany. The two markets arose in 2011, several years before U.S. equity crowdfunding started. When examining insolvency rates of firms that have received funding, the authors find that equity crowdfunded businesses have a higher survival rate in the United Kingdom than in Germany. Yet, 70 percent of German campaigns funded between September 2011 and December 2015 were still operating four years after the campaign, and 85 percent were operational three years after the date of incorporation. Hornuf and Schmitt also find that firms unable to raise equity funding through crowdfunding were more likely to fail than those companies that ran successful campaigns. The result may be because the firms were, as a result of an unsuccessful campaign, undercapitalized and thus failed for that reason.

The question remains: Did the company not get funding because it was doomed to failure, or did it fail because it could not get funding? Hornuf and Schmitt (2016) do not answer that question but instead suggest that VC and angel investors may use equity crowdfunding as a mechanism to screen potential investments. Crowdfunding, in general, whether rewards-based or equity-based, can uncover future demand for a product. In the United Kingdom, a higher proportion of firms receive VC funding before launching an equity crowdfunding campaign. Hornuf and Schmitt assert that this fact may help explain the higher survival rates of funded firms in the United Kingdom. In contrast, German startups are more successful than U.K. startups, attracting VC and angel funding after a successful equity crowdfunding campaign. Exit opportunities are challenging for investors to identify.

Although studies that focus on the returns on equity crowdfunding investments are rare to nearly nonexistent, some evidence suggests that returns are limited given the risk of startup investment. Signori and Vismara (2016), examining 212 successfully funded startups on the Crowdcube site, find an expected annual rate of return of 8.8 percent. In contrast, Hornuf and Schmitt (2016) construct a naively diversified portfolio of all the companies in the German equity crowdfunding market and find that investors would have earned a negative 23.2 percent. Their analysis neither considers any interest payments investors may have received nor any perks (i.e., the products and experiences rewards-based crowdfunders receive), which, for some investors, may comprise a large portion of their expected return. The authors conclude that, ignoring interest and perks, the returns made from successful exits could not overcome the losses from insolvencies.

SUMMARY AND CONCLUSIONS

Evidence suggests that the United States has been slow to adopt equity crowdfunding, despite the enthusiastic acceptance of both donation-based and rewards-based models. For example, in 2016, equity crowdfunding totaled $233 million in the Eurozone. In the United States, those seeking crowdfunding raised a mere $30 million between May 2016 and May 2017 (Grills and Sorouschian 2018). As of May 2018, about 450 companies have raised approximately $105 million in total. Those supporting broader access to capital, including some members of Congress and the SBA Office of Advocacy, believe that the SEC rules are still too onerous. For example, the $1 million funding cap is limiting, especially for businesses that are growing quickly.

Even if they can use the crowdfunding market, the funding is likely insufficient. The businesses have to ultimately seek other funding sources, such as from angel investors or venture capitalists. Others contend that the market is likely to overtake the VC market soon, possibly leading to a startup bubble. Academic research is sparse due to the newness of equity crowdfunding. Additional research should focus on the risks and rewards to investors, as well as the true costs to entrepreneurs. Until the passage of JOBS 3.0, which should fix many of the current problems, growth is likely to be slow.

DISCUSSION QUESTIONS

1. Describe the slow growth of equity crowdfunding in the United States.
2. Identify four types of crowdfunding.
3. List two opportunities, relative to traditional sources of funding, for entrepreneurs and/or investors to participate in the equity crowdfunding market.
4. Identify two challenges faced by entrepreneurs and/or investors who participate in the equity crowdfunding market.

REFERENCES

Agrawal, Ajay, Christian Catalini, and Avi Goldfarb. 2011. "The Geography of Crowdfunding." National Bureau of Economic Research. Available at https://www.nber.org/papers/w16820.

Agrawal, Ajay, Christian Catalini, and Avi Goldfarb. 2014. "Some Simple Economics of Crowdfunding." National Bureau of Economic Research. Available at https://www.journals.uchicago.edu/doi/pdfplus/10.1086/674021.

Agrawal, Ajay, Christian Catalini, and Avi Goldfarb. 2015. "Crowdfunding: Geography, Social Networks, and the Timing of Investment Decisions." *Journal of Economics & Management Strategy* 24:2, 253–274.

Best, Jason, Sherwood Neiss, Richard Swart, Anthony Lambkin, and Sam Raymond. 2013. *Crowdfunding's Potential for the Developing World.* Washington DC: World Bank Group. Available at http://documents.worldbank.org/curated/en/409841468327411701/Crowdfundings-potential-for-the-developing-world.

Breedlove, Elizabeth. 2018. "The History of Crowdfunding." July. Available at https://enventyspartners.com/blog/the-history-of-crowdfunding/.

Britton, Diana. 2019. "Senate Committee Considers JOBS 3.0." February. Available at https://www.wealthmanagement.com/regulation-compliance/senate-committee-considers-jobs-act-30.

Burtch, Gordon, Anindya Ghose, and Sunil Wattal. 2013. "An Empirical Examination of the Antecedents and Consequences of Contribution Patterns in Crowd-Funded Markets." *Information Systems Research* 24:3, 499–519.

Congress.gov. 2012. "Jumpstart Our Business Startups Act." April. Available at https://www.congress.gov/112/plaws/publ106/PLAW-112publ106.pdf.

Cumming, Douglas J., Gael Leboeuf, and Armin Schwienbacher. 2019. "Crowdfunding Models: Keep-It-All vs. All-Or-Nothing." *Financial Management.* Available at https://onlinelibrary.wiley.com/doi/full/10.1111/fima.12262.

Deutsch, Waverly. 2018. "Equity Crowdfunding Is Inflating a Bubble: Millions of Small Investors Are Likely to Lose a Lot of Money." *Chicago Booth Review.* Available at https://review.chicagobooth.edu/entrepreneurship/2018/article/equity-crowdfunding-inflating-bubble.

Griffin, Zachary J., 2013. "Crowdfunding: Fleecing the American Masses." *Case Western Reserve Journal of Law, Technology & the Internet* 4:2, 375–410. Available at https://scholarlycommons.law.case.edu/jolti/vol4/iss2/5/.

Grills, Peter, and John Soroushian. 2018. "Equity Crowdfunding: Promises and Challenges." Bipartisan Policy Center. August. Available at https://bipartisanpolicy.org/blog/equity-crowdfunding-promises-and-challenges/.

Hazen, Thomas Lee. 2012. "Social Networks and the Law: Crowdfunding or Fraud Funding? Social Networks and the Securities Laws. Why the Specially Tailored Exemption Must Be Conditioned on Meaningful Disclosure." *North Carolina Law Review* 90:5, 1735–2162.

Hinchliffe, Emma, 2019. "Funding for Female Founders Stalled at 2.2% of VC Dollars in 2018." *Fortune*, January 28. Available at https://fortune.com/2019/01/28/funding-female-founders-2018.

Hornuf, Lars, and Matthias Schmitt. 2016. "Success and Failure of Crowdfunding." CESifo DICE Report, ISSN 1613-6373, ifo Institut – Leibniz-Institut fur Wirtschaftsforschung an der Universitat Munchen 14:2, 16–22. Available at https://www.econstor.eu/bitstream/10419/167259/1/ifo-dice-report-v14-y2016-i2-p16-22.pdf.

Hornuf, Lars, and Armin Schwienbacher. 2018. "Market Mechanisms and Funding Dynamics in Equity Crowdfunding." *Journal of Corporate Finance* 50:C, 556–574.

Howe, Jeffrey. 2006. "The Rise of Crowdsourcing." *Wired*, June 1. Available at https://www.wired.com/2006/06/crowds/.

Jacobs, Deborah L. 2013, "The Trouble with Crowdfunding." *Forbes*, April 17. Available at https://www.forbes.com/sites/deborahljacobs/2013/04/17/the-trouble-with-crowdfunding/#ec1033118bfc.

Obama, Barack. 2012. Remarks by the President at JOBS Act Bill Signing. April. Available at http://www.whitehouse.gov/the-press-office/2012/04/05/remarks-president-jobs-act-bill-signing.

Patel, Nick. 2015. "90% Of Startups Fail: Here's What You Need to Know About the 10%." *Forbes*, January 16. Available at https://www.forbes.com/sites/neilpatel/2015/01/16/90-of-startups-will-fail-heres-what-you-need-to-know-about-the-10/#3f3c11ef6679.

Protess, Ben. 2012. "Regulator Seeks Feedback on JOBS Act." *New York Times*, April 11. Available at https://dealbook.nytimes.com/2012/04/11/regulator-seeks-feedback-on-jobs-act.

Rosenberg, Joyce, 2018. "Why Equity Crowdfunding Is Not Living Up to the Hype." *Inc.*, May. Available at https://www.inc.com/associated-press/equity-crowdfunding-investing-business-not-working-hype-investors-regulations-sec.html.

Signori, Andrea, and Silvio Vismara. 2016. "Returns on Investments in Equity Crowdfunding." Available at https://papers.ssrn.com/sol3/papers.cfm?abstract_id=2765488.

Stanko, Michael A., and David H. Henard. 2017. "Toward a Better Understanding of Crowdfunding, Openness and the Consequences for Innovation." *Research Policy* 46:4, 784–798.

U.S. News & World Report. 2018. "Growth Rankings: Analyzing State Populations and GDP Trends." Available at https://www.usnews.com/news/best-states/rankings/economy/growth.

Vulkan, Nir, Thomas Astebro, and Manuel Fernandez Sierra. 2016. "Equity Crowdfunding: A New Phenomena." *Journal of Business Venturing Insights* 5:C, 37–49.

Weisenthal, Joe. 2009. "Why Banks Used to Give Out Toasters." *Business Insider*, March. Available at https://www.businessinsider.com/why-banks-used-to-give-out-toasters-2009-3.

Weitz, Theodore, and Thomas D. Halket. 2015. "State Crowdfunding and the Intrastate Exemption Under Federal Securities Laws – Less Than Meets the Eye?" *Review of Banking and Financial Law* 34:1, 521–564.

Zhang, Juanjuan, and Peng Liu. 2012. "Rational Herding in Microloan Markets." *Management Science* 58:5, 892–912.

Discussion Questions and Answers (Chapters 2–24)

CHAPTER 2 OWNERSHIP STRUCTURE AND STOCK CLASSES

1. Compare and contrast depositary receipts and cross-listed stocks.

   Depositary receipts and cross-listed stocks both enable investors to purchase shares of a foreign corporation in their home market. Both mechanisms facilitate ownership in foreign institutions for investors. Cross-listed stocks represent direct listings by the corporation on a foreign stock exchange. Depositary receipts represent certificates of ownership in a company, which correspond to shares held by an intermediary financial institution. Cross-listed shares are always sponsored by the listing entity, whereas depositary receipts may or may not have the corporation's sponsorship. A financial institution can create a depositary receipt against the shares of a corporation without consulting the corporation. Moreover, because the financial institution holds the shares directly and then sells receipts representing those shares, depositary receipts are an indirect ownership vehicle.

2. Discuss the benefits and drawbacks for investors in tracking stocks.

   Tracking stock allows a corporation to offer shares for subdivisions of the parent organization, thereby increasing investor choice. If a conglomerate has a mature, slow-growing division and a high-growth division, it may offer tracking stock for the high-growth division. Investors may then choose whether to invest in the parent organization or invest solely in the high-growth division. However, tracking stock does not have a legal claim on the assets of the subdivision because the parent company remains the legal owner. Although tracking stock seeks to mimic the financial performance of the subdivision, investors are shareholders in the broader corporation, not in the subdivision. Therefore, they are exposed to the liabilities of the entire corporation, not merely those attributed to the tracked subdivision. Furthermore, the corporation's board of directors is a fiduciary for the parent organization, thereby potentially acting disadvantageously for tracking stock shareholders.

3. Explain the three types of dual-listed company structures.

   The three types of dual-listed company structures are combined entities, separate entities, and stapled stock. In a combined entities structure, the two merging companies create an intermediary holding company that houses the assets of Company A and Company B, similar to a joint venture. In the separate entities structure, Company A and Company B retain ownership of their respective assets and maintain legal separation, but they operate as if they were a single company, as if an actual merger occurred. The separate entities' structure has been likened to a synthetic merger. Finally, the stapled stock structure involves combining the assets into a jointly held company while preserving Company A and Company B's separate stock listings, yet shares of Company A and Company B are stapled together and cannot be traded separately.

4. Identify what motivates companies to offer dual-class equity structures.

A company may issue dual-class equity for several reasons. These share structures enable insiders to control a company without having a proportionate amount of capital at risk. Additionally, because majority control is attained by super-voting shares, managers can focus on long-term value creation, without having to yield to market pressures or short-term-focused investors. Lastly, the founder's economic wealth and reputation are typically highly correlated with the firm's value and performance, aligning incentives with inferior voting shareholders.

CHAPTER 3 EQUITY MARKETS AND PERFORMANCE

1. Explain at least two ways to classify financial markets.

Several ways are available to classify financial markets. One way is to classify them based on the maturity of the issues involved in transactions – either the *money* market for short-term investments or the *capital* market for long-term investments. Capital markets consist of *debt* and *equity* markets. Debt markets include long-term notes payables, bonds, and debentures, and equity markets include common stocks and preferred stocks.

2. Discuss why the equity market is important to the economy.

The equity market is important to the economy for several reasons. First, stock markets provide a source of funding for business entities. Second, the equity market facilitates allocating money. Third, equity markets send credible signals to the marketplace through stock price movements, which have real effects on a country's economy.

3. Define and differentiate between at least two of the equity market indices used as market indicators.

Three popular stock indices for tracking the performance of the U.S. market are the Dow Jones Industrial Average (DJIA), the Standard & Poor's 500 (S&P 500) Index, and the NASDAQ Composite Index. The DJIA is an index that tracks 30 large, publicly-owned companies trading on the New York Stock Exchange

(NYSE) and NASDAQ. These stocks constitute about 25 percent of the total value of the U.S. stock market. Another market indicator is the S&P 500 Index, which comprises 500 of the largest companies in the U.S. market. The NASDAQ Composite Index is an index of equities listed on NASDAQ.

4. Explain the difference between liquidity and marketability for a financial market.

   Liquidity refers to the speed with which an asset can be converted into cash without a loss of value. *Marketability* refers to the level of ease or the ability of buyers or sellers of a security to create and complete a transaction. Generally, securities with better marketability are more liquid than those with poor marketability.

5. Define financial market efficiency.

   Financial market efficiency suggests that stock prices rapidly incorporate relevant information. In efficient capital markets, the prices of company stocks must be good, if not perfect, indicators of firm value because these prices incorporate all available information. On average, the returns earned in an efficient market should be commensurate with the level of risk taken.

6. Define and differentiate among the weak-form, semi-strong form, and strong form levels of market efficiency.

   Weak-form efficiency occurs if stock prices currently reflect all known market information, including stock prices and volume. Semi-strong form efficiency takes place if stock prices currently reflect all known public information, including all market information. Strong-form efficiency occurs if stock prices currently reflect all known information, including all public and private information.

CHAPTER 4 SECURITIES REGULATION

1. Explain the nature and function of trading rules on stock exchanges.

   Trading rules govern the permitted conduct of brokers and other market participants that trade securities on stock exchanges. The three main categories of trading rules are rules designed to: (1) mitigate insider trading, (2) lessen market manipulation, and (3) curtail broker-agent conflicts. Insider trading rules prohibit trading on information that is materially and not yet publicly disclosed. Insider trading includes specific types of activities such as front running and client precedence, where the inside information is the knowledge of the client's order. Market manipulation encompasses various types of price and volume manipulation. Broker conduct rules govern broker behavior such as trade-through rules. Trading rules are sometimes found on the stock exchange web page and other times regulated as securities laws in a country.

2. Differentiate between trading rules and surveillance.

   Trading rules are the rules pertaining to trading on an exchange. *Surveillance* refers to the enforcement of such rules. Surveillance also refers to automated computer algorithms that are used to detect manipulative trading patterns. Surveillance algorithms send messages called "alerts" to staff who work at securities commissions or the authority that governs the particular stock exchange. The alerts are in real time, meaning that market abuse is detected immediately. With one-time behavior, a manipulation might lead a surveillance authority to call the trader(s) involved for an explanation. Computer software providers, such as SMARTS Group, Inc., had provided software to over 50 exchanges around the world before being acquired by NASDAQ in 2010. Such software customizes its system to manage the type of alerts provided to surveillance staff. Such customization is necessary as each exchange or securities commission around the world differs in scope and requirements for surveillance. These alerts apply to both single-market manipulations and cross-market manipulations. *Cross-market* surveillance refers to surveillance across different products, such as an equity and a related option on the same underlying equity, and across markets or different exchanges or different countries. Cross-market surveillance is much more technical to perform and execute in terms of computing power. Moreover, cross-market surveillance requires information-sharing agreements across exchanges.

3. Identify the criticisms and benefits of securities regulation.

   Securities regulation and its enforcement enhance market efficiency and fairness or integrity. Market efficiency is important because it matters how often people trade on an exchange. An inefficient market has high bid–ask spreads, meaning it is expensive to trade on the market in terms of transaction costs. Also, inefficient markets are subjected to other costs of illiquidity and inefficient price discovery. Market integrity is also important to market participants, as it indicates a degree of fairness insofar as no one is likely to be unduly harmed or disadvantaged by participating in exchanges of securities. Markets without integrity are regularly manipulated and subjected to various problems of self-dealing.

4. Discuss how trading rules differ across countries.

   Some countries have specific rules for insider trading, market manipulation, and broker-agency conduct. Other countries have broad statements about not permitting market manipulation without much rule specificity. Still other countries have changed their rules over time. For example, a set of pan-European directives in the mid-2000s brought about improvements in rule specificity on trading. More developed countries typically have more detailed rules.

5. Discuss how trading rules and surveillance affect firm outcomes such as M&As and innovation.

   More detailed trading rules and better surveillance systems enhance market outcomes, including more efficient markets such as more liquid markets. Also, evidence suggests that more detailed rules enable better corporate outcomes. For example, mergers are less likely to be withdrawn in countries with better rules and surveillance, as less market manipulation occurs around mergers. With less market manipulation, investors are likely to pay larger premiums on stocks in mergers. Furthermore, other market outcomes are improved as well. Companies can more easily raise new capital in countries with less market manipulation, which enables more managerial focus on long-term value creation such as through innovation.

CHAPTER 5 INVESTOR PSYCHOLOGY AND EQUITY MARKET ANOMALIES

1. Discuss three conditions needed for market inefficiency and whether bounded rationality may address these conditions.

   Three conditions needed for market inefficiency include somewhat irrational investors, correlated biases among these investors, and inattentive or limited arbitragers. Market inefficiency is created by investor irrationality. This inefficiency is neither canceled out by the randomness of other investors' biases nor corrected by the purposeful actions of arbitragers. Although bounded rationality is usually used to address the first condition of investor irrationality at the individual level, it can also help shed light on the other two conditions. Bounded rationality maintains that investor behavior at the individual level, group level, and even arbitrage level may lead to mispriced stocks because it is limited by three factors: the information investors have, their cognitive abilities, and the time available to make a decision.

2. List three different effects that relate to PT and how each effect can cause investors to make irrational decisions.

   Three effects related to prospect theory (PT) include the certainty effect, reflection effect, and disposition effect:

   1. *Certainty effect.* The certainty effect highlights that investors often outweigh probable outcomes. Simply put, most investors are risk-averse and accept a certain outcome, even if less certain outcomes have higher probable payouts.
   2. *Reflection effect.* The reflection effect maintains that investors may have different preferences for gambles, depending on whether the outcome is a gain or a loss. In other words, investors are more likely to be risk-averse when they have something to gain and more likely to be risk-seeking when they have something to lose.
   3. *Disposition effect.* The reflection effect helps explain the *disposition effect*, which is the tendency for investors to cut short their profits and let their losses run, because most investors dislike losing money more than they enjoy gaining money. Thus, investors tend to sell investments that have gained value too soon because they want to avoid taking the chance of losing money. Likewise, they tend to hold onto investments that have lost value too long because they do not want to realize the loss.

3. List three violations of the weak form EMH and explain how they differ.

Three violations for the weak form EMH include calendar-related anomalies, the momentum effect, and the reversal effect. *Calendar-related anomalies*, such as the small-firm-in-January effect, represent recurring stock price patterns for different periods. The momentum and reversal effects are two different types of serial correlations. A *momentum effect* is a form of positive serial correlation where the stock's recent performance has a direct relation with its future performance. Thus, positive stock returns tend to follow positive stock returns. Conversely, the *reversal effect* is a type of negative serial correlation where the stock's recent performance has an inverse relation with its future performance. Thus, positive stock returns tend to follow negative stock returns.

4. List three announcement-related violations of the semi-strong form EMH and explain how they differ.

Three announcement-related violations of the semi-strong form EMH include the post-earnings announcement price drift, stock split effect, and merger-arbitrage effect:

   1. *Post-earnings announcement price drift* (PEAD). The PEAD is the tendency for a firm's stock price to continue to drift in the same direction as an earnings surprise for days, weeks, and even months after the announcement.
   2. *Stock split effect.* The stock split effect is a special conundrum because a stock price should not affect firm value. Nonetheless, a strong tendency exists for a firm's stock price to increase not only immediately after a stock split announcement, but also for days, months, and even years after a split.
   3. *Merger-arbitrage effect.* Firms can create a merger-arbitrage effect when they announce a merger or acquisition. This announcement tends to increase the value of the target firm's stock and decrease the value of the bidding firm's stock.

CHAPTER 6 FINANCIAL STATEMENT ANALYSIS AND FORECASTING

1. Explain the difference between forecasting based on technical analysis and fundamental analysis.

Technical analysis is typically limited to using past earnings. It uses historical data to fit well-known time-series models such as the random walk or ARIMA and then uses the model parameters to predict future earnings. In contrast, fundamental analysis uses the most recent reported accounting information from a cross-section of firms either for the entire market or for subsectors within the broader market to estimate parameter weightings on a set of variables. Analysts then use this information to predict subsequent period earnings or earnings changes. In a technical sense, technical analysis is a firm-specific time series–based approach, while fundamental analysis is a cross-sectional approach using a set of homogeneous or nonhomogeneous firms. However, engaging in firm-level fundamental analysis is also possible.

2. Discuss whether security analysts typically use information in financial statements in making their forecasts.

Limited evidence is available on whether security analysts use information from financial statements in making forecasts. Some evidence suggests that analysts' forecasts do not necessarily incorporate information contained in financial statement analysis. In other evidence, researchers document that a model of earnings increases based on financial statement information performs better than analysts' stock recommendations, suggesting that analysts do not fully incorporate the information in financial statements.

3. Discuss how analysts can use financial statements to improve their forecasts.

No definitive evidence is available on whether analysts can improve upon their forecasts by using information in financial statements. However, to the extent that combining multiple forecasts does better than the best individual forecasts, the possibility exists that security analysts can improve their forecasts. Thus, a simple average of earnings forecast based on financial statement analysis and the analysts' forecasts could be more accurate than either forecast individually.

4. Discuss the limitations of using financial statements for purposes of forecasting and how forecasters can overcome such limitations.

Financial statement analysis–based forecasting depends on information contained in financial statements. Thus, the limitations of financial statements such as conservatism in reporting, earnings management, and the absence of many tangible assets on the balance sheet are likely to affect the forecasts. However, forecasters, through careful analysis, can and should incorporate such information to the extent available and make appropriate adjustments.

5. Discuss whether technical and fundamental analysis can be combined to achieve superior forecasting.

The statistical literature suggests that combining forecasts can yield more accurate and hence superior forecasts than any single forecast. However, little evidence is available showing whether academics or practitioners engage in combining both types of analysis when forecasting.

CHAPTER 7 FUNDAMENTALS OF EQUITY VALUATION

1. Describe the major categories of equity valuation models and discuss the pros and cons of each.

The major categories of equity valuation models are free-cash-flow models and dividend discount models (DDMs). Although these models are more rigorous approaches because of their theoretical foundation, they require many assumptions about parameters such as the future growth rate, investment time horizon, and net income distribution rate. They also require calculating the risk-adjusted cost of capital using the CAPM or another model. A market-based valuation that compares firm ratios to others is popular and easier to implement. The analysis does not usually use real options models, which offer the possibility to consider flexibility or delays, because of their complexity.

2. Assume a stock is priced at $100; calculate its intrinsic value based on the Gordon growth DDM, with the following assumptions: $D_0 = \$3$, $g = 6$ percent, and $k = 10$ percent. Indicate whether investors should buy, hold, or sell the stock. Indicate your recommendation if $g = 7$ percent.

   Applying Equation 7.12, the stock's theoretical value is $\$3.00(1 + 0.06)/(0.10 - 0.06) = \$79.50$. This value is much less than the stock's market price of $100, suggesting that the recommendation should be to sell the stock. If $g = 7.00$ percent, the stock value is $107.00 and the recommendation should be to buy the stock given that its intrinsic value exceeds the market price of $100.

3. Explain the rationale for using price multiples to value equity, how the P/E and P/B multiples relate to fundamentals, and using multiples based on comparable firms.

   The rationale is to compare parameters or ratios for a peer group of firms. For example, considering two similar firms, the lower the P/B ratio, the more the firm equity can be considered as underpriced, other things being equal.

4. Explain why FCFF is discounted at the WACC.

   FCFF is the cash remaining to compensate those who finance the capital employed, namely the shareholders and creditors or bondholders. Hence, the discount rate that reflects their expectations about time and the risks they bear is the WACC.

5. Explain the main limitation of the P/E ratio.

   A main limitation of the P/E ratio is that it cannot be used for companies with negative earnings, such as startups. Another limitation is that earnings per share is open to manipulation. For example, buying back shares makes the stock appear "a good bargain." Lastly, what happens if the market is irrational when selecting the sample of comparable listed firms? This outcome results in an incorrect valuation of the security.

CHAPTER 8 COMPANY ANALYSIS

1. Describe the three steps linking business activities to equity prices.

   In step 1, the accounting process maps the company's transactions and events into financial statements. In step 2, investors, analysts, and others apply fundamental analysis techniques to the financial statements, mapping financial statement information into expectations of future earnings, cash flows, and dividends, and ultimately into share value estimates. In step 3, trading activities map investor information and value estimates in equity prices.

2. Discuss why the analysis of a company's accounting policies is an important part of company analysis.

Analysts use a company's financial reports to develop an understanding of a company's fundamentals. The financial statements provide useful information for evaluating a company's operating, investing, and financing activities and understanding how those activities generate profitability and growth. Accounting analysis provides analysts with a better understanding of how well the financial statements reflect the firm's true underlying business reality.

3. Explain how risk, economic rents, and accounting distortions affect ROA.

Risk shapes the return on the capital. If managers riskily deploy assets, for example, in developing markets or in more speculative projects, the expected return should be higher to compensate for the higher risk. Whereas risk shapes the competitive rate of return, a company can outperform by successfully executing a winning strategy or windfall gain. A company can also underperform due to competitive disadvantages and windfall losses. Outperformance or underperformance relative to a competitive or expected rate of return is termed *economic rent*.

Finally, the capital base in ROA is total assets, as measured on the balance sheet. Besides limitations from historical cost accounting, accounting rules prohibit capitalizing many expenditures that build intellectual capital (R&D), brand capital (advertising), and organization capital (training costs). These intangible assets have economic value that is likely to be realized through future streams of sales and earnings. Omitting these assets from the capital base of total assets results in chronically overstating ROA and, by extension, ROE and ROIC.

4. Discuss how ROA relates to ROE.

ROA focuses on the performance of the business. ROA can be decomposed into profit margin and total asset turnover. Profit margin reflects the cost structure on a company's income statement and provides insights into a company's operating activities. Asset turnover measures the sales generated from the asset base. Asset turnover thereby focuses on a company's investment activities. ROE is a measure of profitability for the owners. ROE reflects a company's operating, investing, and financing activities. In other words, the return to equity holders reflects the performance of the business and the choices a company makes about how the business is financed.

ROA relates to ROE through leverage multipliers. Earnings leverage describes how the owners and lenders of a business share the total accounting return for the period. Asset leverage relates the asset base to the equity base. Asset leverage indicates how many dollars a company invests in the business for each dollar invested by the owners. Profitability (measured by ROE) rises with greater assets per dollar of equity (asset leverage), greater sales that those assets generate (asset turnover), higher returns remaining for investors per dollar of sales (profit margin), and more of the return that the owners keep (earnings leverage).

CHAPTER 9 TECHNICAL ANALYSIS

1. Discuss the philosophical link between technical and fundamental investment strategies.

   Both schools of investing philosophically agree that fundamentals matter more than price itself. Without strong fundamental trends, no strong price trends are likely to occur. Both technical and fundamental investors believe that in the long term, the market is efficient, but in the short term, it can be random and inefficient.

   Dow Theory sets forth three time frames of trends: primary, secondary, and minor. Fundamentals drive the long-term primary trend and emotions and behavioral biases drive secondary and minor trends. These strategies differ in the process each follows to capture long-term trends driven by fundamentals. Fundamental investors typically try to find prices that differ from what they believe represent fair value. In essence, they search for situations in which they believe the market is wrong or is mispricing a security based on the premise that other investors will eventually come around to their view, resulting in the stock's trend inflecting from down to up. By contrast, technical investors assume the market is right, and that if a stock is trending in the primary time frame, it is doing so for fundamental reasons. Therefore, rather than forecasting a price change, technical investors wait for that change and then invest. Either way, both investors are attempting to invest in the same trend.

2. Explain the importance of properly defining the market's primary trend as a first step toward building a portfolio.

   All stocks typically go down in a bear market but up in a bull market. Being aware of the market's primary trend is important because that condition plays a vital role in determining the success or failure of one's stock selection at the port-folio level. In cases when the primary trend is bearish, investors can either raise cash, engage in short positions, or rotate into defensive holdings that are likely to go down less than the market. In cases when the primary trend is bullish, investors should be fully invested with low short exposure, using relative per-formance, be it relative strength comparative or cross-sectional momentum, to ensure that they are buying the best stocks in the best sectors and industries.

3. Identify the three phases that both primary bull and bear markets undergo and explain how changing economic and fundamental trends and investors' behaviorally biased perceptions are driving forces.

A primary bull market undergoes three stages: accumulation, public participation, and speculation. During accumulation, informed investors begin buying inexpensive stocks from panicking uninformed sellers in the late stages of a primary bear market. During public participation, individual investors begin buying with increased confidence. In the final stage of a primary bull market – speculation – a euphoric public begins aggressively buying expensive equities, often using margin.

The subsequent primary bear market begins with distribution, as informed investors begin selling their expensive stocks to unformed investors. The next phase is liquidation, as public investors begin selling in response to clearly worsening economic conditions. The bear market ends in panic, with public investors aggressively selling stocks despite inexpensive valuations.

4. Discuss the similarities and differences between trend following and cross-sectional momentum strategies.

Trend following is based on the principles of Dow theory, including higher highs and lows measured over three time frames, as well as moving averages and relative strength comparative. Guided by these tools and strategies, trend-following investors either use their discretion to make buy and sell decisions or develop models based on these inputs to more systematically identify opportunities. The idea is to buy stocks with positive trend structures (e.g., higher highs and lows and short- and medium-term averages above longer-term averages) during primary bull markets, using relative strength comparative to ensure that investors are buying not only attractive absolute trend structures but also stocks that are outperforming the broader market. In instances of primary bear markets, trend followers can either raise cash due to a lack of positive trends and build short exposure due to increased negative trends, or favor stocks with positive relative performance trends to at least ensure that holdings are going down less than the broader market.

Investors using cross-sectional momentum are purely systematic, shunning discretion and visual chart reviews in favor of models that quantitatively rank a universe of stocks based on their performance over the prior 12 months. Investors should buy the top decile and short the bottom decile, without regard for the market's broader primary trend.

Despite having advantages and disadvantages, each approach tends to share more traits than not. Indeed, trend-following investors can use cross-sectional momentum ranks to ensure that they are buying the best absolute price structure with prospects for future top decile momentum.

CHAPTER 10 DISCOUNTED DIVIDEND VALUATION

1. Discuss the advantages and limitations of the Gordon model.

The main advantage of the Gordon model is that it is simple to calculate and easy to understand. This model is useful for companies that have reached the maturity stage in their life cycle and are growing at a rate less than or equal to the growth rate of the economy in which they are operating. However, the model also has several limitations. First, the assumption of constant growth into perpetuity is unlikely to hold for many companies, which limits the model's applicability. Second, the model is susceptible to the values chosen for the growth rate and cost of equity. If they are chosen incorrectly, the model can give misleading results such as extremely high stock values (if the cost of equity and growth rate are close) or negative values (if the growth rate is higher than the cost of equity). Finally, as in all dividend discount models (DDMs), the formula is only applicable to firms that currently pay dividends.

2. Explain the life-cycle stages followed by firms constituting the basis of multi-stage DDMs.

Many firms are likely to follow three stages of growth throughout their life cycle. In the first stage, often called the "supernormal growth stage," firms are growing at a rate that is faster than that of the general economy in which they are operating. During that first stage, firms have high needs for funds to finance their investments, and hence they distribute a lower portion of their earnings as dividends. This fast-growth stage is usually followed by a "transition phase," in which the growth rate is lowered to converge to that of the general economy, funds needed for investment are lowered, and dividend payout ratios start to increase. Finally, the last stage in a firm's life cycle is the "mature phase," in which the growth rates and dividend payout ratios reach their steady-state levels. Thus, the Gordon model can be successfully applied to calculate a common stock's fair value.

3. Identify in which company types the classical two-stage DDM is likely to work best to estimate common stock value.

Since the classical version of the two-stage DDM assumes that a firm grows at an above-normal rate for a determined amount of time and then reaches its steady-state rate of growth to infinity, the model works best for firms that currently expect a high growth rate, which is due to factors that are expected to end in the future. One such example would be patent holders that are currently growing at above-normal rates but are expected to go into average growth once the patent expires. Another example would be firms benefiting from a first-mover advantage, which disappears once new firms enter the industry resulting in slower growth.

4. Explain the basic features of stochastic DDMs and compare them to traditional constant growth and multi-stage models.

Traditional constant growth and multi-stage DDMs operate in a deterministic setting that does not allow probabilities. Stochastic DDMs introduce the probability by which dividends are expected to change or remain constant into the equation. Two versions of stochastic DDMs are binomial models, which assume that dividends either increase or remain constant, and trinomial models, which assume that dividends can increase, remain constant, or decrease. Both of these versions can be additive (i.e., dividends are assumed to change at a predetermined dollar amount) or geometric (i.e., dividends are assumed to change at a predetermined percentage rate). Stochastic DDMs are useful in overcoming major limitations of the traditional models in which analysts can provide an estimated stock price, but they cannot specify their degree of confidence in their estimation. Stochastic models allow analysts to generate a probability distribution for a stock's price, which reflects the degree of confidence in the estimation.

5. Discuss the uses of DDMs.

The main output of DDMs is the fair price per share of common stock given expected dividends, growth rates, and the required rate of return. Although the DDM does not tell when the actual price is likely to reach the fair price, investors can use the output to identify overvalued (i.e., the actual or market price is more than the stock's intrinsic value or fair price) or undervalued (i.e., the actual or market price is less than the stock's intrinsic value or fair price) stocks and take action accordingly. Another way of using DDMs is to calculate expected returns, which can be defined as the discount rate that equates the stock's actual price to the present value of expected future dividends. Investors then use this expected return to identify any mispriced securities by comparing it to the required rate of return. If the expected return is higher than the required rate of return, the stock is undervalued; if the expected return is lower than the required rate of return, the security is overvalued. Finally, investors can use the equations provided by DDMs to establish relations between stock prices or price multiples such as the price-to-earnings ratio or price-to-book value ratio and the company's fundamental characteristics. Based on these derived equations, the price per share is positively related to dividend payout ratio, growth rate, book value per share, and return on equity and negatively related to cost of equity. The price-to-earnings ratio is positively related to the dividend payout ratio and the growth rate and negatively related to the required rate of return. Price-to-book value ratio has a positive relation with dividend payout, return on equity, and growth rate, and a negative relation with the cost of equity.

CHAPTER 11 FREE CASH FLOW VALUATION

1. Articulate the advantages and disadvantages of FCF valuation analysis relative to DDM analysis.

DDM analysis involves assumptions about the timing, magnitude, and growth rate of dividends. This type of analysis can be challenging when a firm does not pay dividends. An advantage of FCF valuation is that it allows analysts to make more specific decisions about the accounts that affect the computation of the cash flows, which is more extensive in scope than using a DDM. A disadvantage is the added level of complexity that is involved in forecasting more accounts.

2. Define what is meant by FCFF and FCFE.

   Free cash flow to the firm (FCFF) is the amount of cash generated from the business operations that is available for the company's use, after deducting investments to sustain its ongoing operations, both long-term (fixed assets) and short-term (working capital). Free cash flow to equity (FCFE) adjusts FCFF by subtracting after-tax interest expenses and adding increases in debt.

3. Explain why growth patterns are important in modeling FCFs.

   If the growth rate for a firm's earnings is higher than the discount rate, a firm's valuation does not converge to a finite number. Hence, modeling higher growth rates for a limited time period is important, before recognizing a long-term stable growth rate (lower than the discount rate).

4. Discuss the choice of an FCF method that would be most suitable for the valuation of: (1) a venture capital investment, (2) a mature manufacturing firm, (3) an acquisition through an LBO, and (4) a commercial bank.

   A venture capital investment can be modeled using an FCFE approach and may be all equity financed. A mature manufacturing firm can be modeled with a WACC approach, assuming a constant target debt-to-equity ratio. An acquisition using an LBO can be modeled with an APV approach, assuming changing dollar levels of debt over time. A commercial bank can be modeled with a CCF approach if interest income and interest expense can be explicitly computed as part of the cash flow.

5. Summarize the alternative uses of a DCF model besides valuing a company.

   A DCF model can also be used to back out a company's WACC or long-term stable growth rate if its price per share is observed and assumed to be a company's "true" intrinsic value per share.

CHAPTER 12 MARKET-BASED VALUATION

1. Give several examples of widely used valuation multiples and discuss how to estimate the target's value using these multiples.

   Two widely used groups of valuation multiples are (1) equity-related multiples such as P/E, P/B, P/S, and P/CF and (2) EV-related multiples such as EV/EBIT, EV/EBITDA, EV/Sales, and EV/CF.

   An example of a target valuation using the P/E multiple:

   ■ The estimate of the target's stock price = P/E × EPS of the target

An example of target valuation using EV/EBITDA:

- The estimate of the target's EV = EV/EBITDA × EBITDA of the target
- The estimate of the target's stock price = Estimated EV/Number of shares outstanding for the target

2. Identify the main factors proposed in academic research to determine the values of different multiples.

Academic researchers propose using industry classification, size, growth rate, leverage ratio, and market risk to determine the values of different multiples. Also, exchange listing status and accounting methods may influence the multiples.

3. Discuss the major advantages and disadvantages of using the multiple valuation method.

The market-based multiple approach of valuation has distinctive advantages over a more complicated intrinsic valuation, such as the DCF approach. It is quick and easy to apply and does not require estimating future cash flows and the discount rate, which may contain added biases due to arbitrary assumptions on the growth rate and the weighted average cost of capital. The disadvantages of the multiples approach include the difficulty of selecting closely matching comparable firms; needed adjustments on market sentiment, control premium, and liquidity premium; and the unavailability of multiples due to negative cash flows or earnings.

4. Discuss the main reasons that researchers and practitioners use forecasted values rather than historical values for the value drivers.

Historical values sometimes reflect transitory earnings or margins, which would be corrected in the future. Analysts' consensus of forecasted values or forward earnings should account for the possible distortion brought from the transitory performances into the estimated values.

5. Discuss using the harmonic mean as a normalizing method for different multiples drawn from different comparable firms.

Researchers and practitioners propose using the harmonic mean to calculate the average of various estimates of multiples from a portfolio of comparable firms. It penalizes large values and also aggravates the bias from small values. Since the multiple valuation method uses only positive numbers, the harmonic mean reduces the potential bias from outliers with a large number. The harmonic mean can be calculated using three P/E ratios as follows:

- $P/E_1 = 15$, $P/E_2 = 20$, and $P/E_3 = 10$
- Harmonic mean = $3/(1/15 + 1/20 + 1/10) = 13.85$
  Arithmetic mean = $(15 + 20 + 10)/3 = 15$

CHAPTER 13 RESIDUAL INCOME VALUATION

1. Define RI and discuss how to measure it.

   Residual income (RI) is a method for investors to assess the profitability of an investment project after explicitly accounting for the opportunity cost of the capital invested in the project. Accounting-based measures of profitability, such as net income, usually incorporate revenues and expenses associated with the project but exclude the cost of equity. RI addresses this shortcoming of traditional profitability measures. Measuring RI begins with adjusting numbers reported in financial statements to remove potential distortions in revenues and expenses reported in conformity to generally accepted accounting principles (GAAP). After obtaining a relatively unbiased measure of profits, a capital charge computed as book value times, the cost of equity is subtracted from the adjusted net income to yield RI. The computation of RI can be represented as follows:

   $$RI_t = NOPAT_t - (WACC_t \times TIC_{t-1})$$

   where $NOPAT$ is net operating profits after tax (earnings before interest and taxes, EBIT, adjusted for taxes); $WACC$ is the weighted average cost of capital (a weighted average of the costs of debt and equity, where the cost of debt is computed on a post-tax basis); and TIC is the total invested capital (sum of debt and equity). The equation can be alternatively expressed as:

   $$RI_t = NI_t - (k_t \times BV_{t-1})$$

   where NI is net income; BV indicates the book value of equity; and k is the cost of equity. Because NI accounts for the cost of debt, subtracting the cost of equity from NI also yields RI. Therefore, these equations represent two alternative approaches to calculate RI.

2. Discuss the types of adjustments to reported financial statement numbers needed when calculating RI, and why such adjustments are needed.

   Financial statements such as the balance sheet and the income statement are prepared in conformity with GAAP. Accounting rules require specific treatment of various revenue, expense, asset, and liability items that may not always reflect their true economic value. For example, U.S. GAAP requires full expensing of research and development (R&D) expenditures, rather than capitalizing and amortizing R&D, even though R&D expenditures may lead to long-term future benefits. Advocates of RI suggest making adjustments to reported financial statement numbers so they reflect a firm's economic resources and opportunities more accurately. For example, RI practitioners recommend capitalizing R&D expenditures and amortizing them over time, as in the case with long-lived assets. Other suggested adjustments include adding back accounting depreciation and subtracting "economic" depreciation instead, capitalizing operating leases, and accounting for income taxes on a cash basis rather than an accrual basis. Such adjustments are meant to remove potential distortions and biases from financial statement numbers so they can form inputs to computing RI.

3. Discuss how RI is applied to equity valuation.

   Traditional finance theory uses the discounted dividends model (DDM) to value firms. The DDM involves summing up the discounted present value of expected dividends to yield firm value. RI-based valuation replaces dividends in the DDM with current book value and discounted future RI estimates. The RI valuation model can be expressed as:

   $$V_t = BV_t + \sum_{n=1}^{n=\infty} RI_{t+n}/(1+k)^n$$

   where V is the market value of equity; BV represents the book value of equity; RI indicates residual income; and k is the cost of equity capital.

4. Explain the advantages of RI valuation over traditional approaches such as the DDM.

   Although RI valuation involves several adjustments to financial statement amounts and estimation of the opportunity cost of capital, it has several advantages over traditional valuation approaches such as DDM. First, RI is an intuitive approach based on the concept of opportunity cost. RI valuation can be applied in settings in which traditional valuation approaches cannot be used, including for new or growth firms that do not pay dividends. Also, RI valuation can better explain the observed volatility in stock prices since book values and RI exhibit a greater degree of variation compared with cash dividends that tend to be constant and persistent. Finally, the RI model focuses on value creation (excess profits) rather than value distribution (dividends). Therefore, RI can have powerful incentive effects for managers to create shareholder value.

5. Explain the disadvantages of RI valuation compared with traditional approaches such as the DDM.

   RI valuation is not without weaknesses. Some scholars raise concerns over the construct validity of the RI model and its correspondence with other valuation frameworks such as the DDM. By contrast, practitioners criticize the RI model over implementation difficulties such as choosing an appropriate cost of capital and the necessary accounting adjustments. Despite its intuitive appeal, empirical studies find that when using the RI model for equity valuation, it provides only minor improvements in explanatory power over the traditional approaches. Moreover, key inputs to RI valuation, such as future expected abnormal earnings, are forecasts, not past realizations of earnings. This limits the role of past financial statements in developing expectations of future abnormal earnings. RI valuation also imposes data requirements that are difficult to meet in real-life settings. As a result, many empirical studies result in implementing the model with potential internal inconsistencies. Finally, practitioners find the wide variety of accounting adjustments required under different variants of RI to be arbitrary, burdensome, and sometimes in conflict with one another.

CHAPTER 14 PRIVATE COMPANY VALUATION

1. Discuss some limitations of the DCF valuation method and the comparable firm valuation method in private company valuation.

   Although the DCF approach has a firmer theoretical foundation than any other approach, early-stage private companies typically forecast a period of negative cash flows with uncertain but potentially large future rewards. This cash flow profile rests on the valuation assumptions made. Therefore, the reliability of DCF in the setting of private company valuation depends on using accurate cash flow projections and appropriate discount rates. The comparable firms approach works best in private company valuation when a highly comparable group is available. Although this approach can reduce the probability of improperly valuing a firm relative to others, it provides no safeguard against an entire sector being undervalued or overvalued.

2. Discuss the justifications for using high target rates of returns (discount rates) in the VC valuation method.

   Although requiring a liquidity premium for private company investments may have some validity, the estimated premium may be too large. Further, venture capitalists harvest a large part of the returns on their investments in exit transactions in which the firm goes public or is acquired by another public company so that their shares become fully liquid. Additionally, many private equity investors have long-term time horizons, including endowments, foundations, and wealthy individuals. Second, instead of adjusting the discount rate for services provided by the venture capitalist, these services can be easily valued, and shares equal to this value could be given as explicit compensation to the venture capitalist. Finally, instead of using high discount rates to compensate for inflated cash flow projections by entrepreneurs, building uncertainty into the cash flow estimates using scenario analysis is much more effective and appropriate. The correct approach is to obtain unbiased estimates of the company cash flows by determining the possible values of various future scenarios and the probability of occurrence.

3. Discuss the accuracy of calculating the post-money valuation in the VC method as an estimate of the implied enterprise value of a private company.

   In the standard application of the VC method, a private company's implied enterprise value equals the company's post-money valuation in the current financing round. The post-money valuation equals the venture capitalist's investment amount scaled by the venture capitalist's required equity stake. It is also defined as the purchase price per share in a financing round multiplied by the fully diluted share count. For example, if a venture capitalist pays $6 million to purchase a convertible preferred stock that would convert to one-third of the common stock, then the company's post-money valuation would be $18 million. The pre-money valuation is calculated as the difference between the post-money valuation and the new investment, which in this case would be $12 million. However, these simple calculations do not provide an accurate estimate of a company's enterprise value. This lack of accuracy is because the standard VC method does not account for the special features of preferred stock issued to investors, and instead treats all VC investments as though they were common stock.

4. Identify the role of capital structure in private company valuation.

In applying DCF valuation methods in private company valuation, estimating the discount rate as if the company is an all-equity firm is reasonable. To the extent that debt financing plays a much more minor role in the financing of many entrepreneurial private firms, a reasonable assumption is that the discount rate applied to interest tax shields equals the cost of the assets. The capital structure of many entrepreneurial private firms involves hybrid securities, which are not easily classified as debt or equity, making estimating a private firm's target debt-to-value ratio in the long run challenging. Both the CCF and APV methods are more flexible than DCF methods that avoid this complexity by better accommodating dynamic capital structure features of private companies.

CHAPTER 15 EQUITY INVESTING STRATEGIES

1. Explain how technical analysis and fundamental analysis differ.

Technical analysis relies on past market data, including volume, price, and spreads. Technical analysis also uses historical trends to predict future stock prices. In contrast, fundamental analysis relies heavily on analyzing financial statements, company, and industry-specific performance and efficiency as well as macroeconomic factors. Fundamental analysts also forecast future free cash flows for discounted cash flow methods and consider relative pricing multiples such as P/E and P/B.

2. Describe how to assess a stock's intrinsic value.

The first and most important step is understanding the core business of the company and the industry in which it operates. Porter's five forces analysis can be used to assess long-term profitability and industry structure, including a firm's market share, products, cost structure, capital structure, margin stability, and profitability in comparison to its peer group.

The next step is choosing the appropriate valuation model. The most common model to use is the DCF model, which discounts future cash flows at an appropriate cost of capital. Additionally, other types of valuation models are available such as multiplier models and asset-based valuation models. Multiplier models are a relative valuation approach. The analyst uses multiples such as price-to-sales, price-to-earnings, price-to-book value, and enterprise value-to-EBITDA ratios to value a company relative to its peer group or industry. Holding all other necessary factors constant, if a firm's multiples are below (above) its peer group, the company maybe be undervalued (overvalued).

3. Identify some key characteristics of a growth stock.

   A *growth stock* is a stock of a company that can sustain an above-average sales growth rate compared to its industry. Its valuation often involves carefully analyzing a company's management and research and development department. Both strong and effective management and an innovative R&D department can indicate a company's ability to create new products once old products have reached the end of their life cycle. If a company cannot successfully innovate, then it may experience a rapid sales decline and a loss of market share to competitors.

4. Discuss the basics of income investing using equities.

   Income investing is an investment strategy that seeks to increase holding period returns above a security's capital appreciation. Investors purchase stocks with high dividend yields rather than high expected growth rates. Investors purchase these stocks in anticipation of the predictable stream of dividends.

5. Describe the trend in ESG investing.

   ESG is becoming more popular in the investment landscape because new and evolving types of risks exist, including cybersecurity, data, climate change, and carbon emission risks. Another reason for ESG's increased popularity is the desire for investors to try to affect society positively. This last point is particularly important for millennials and younger investors who are more interested in the social impact of their investing than any previous generation.

CHAPTER 16 FACTOR INVESTING

1. Define the term *factor*.

   A factor is a measurement of systematic risk, typically measured using a long-short, market-neutral framework to isolate its specific risk–return profile. Empirical research and economic intuition, usually in a risk-based or behaviorally based context, support the factors. Factors are associated with the cross-sectional performance of stocks and explain the performance within an equity market or portfolio.

2. Identify and discuss the four most prominent factors in academic literature.

   The four most prominent factors include the market factor (CAPM beta), value (HML), size (SMB), and momentum (WML). The market factor is the tendency for stocks to outperform the risk-free rate. The premise behind this factor is that an investor who takes on the risk of owning stocks, rather than holding a portfolio in risk-free assets, should be compensated for taking on that additional risk. The factor HML is the tendency for relatively cheap stocks to outperform relatively expensive stocks. The level of cheapness is measured by a ratio of the stock's market value to a fundamental value on that company's financial statements. The SMB factor is the tendency for smaller companies to outperform larger companies, as measured by market capitalization. The WML factor is the tendency for recent relative winners to outperform recent relative losers, as measured by stock price performance.

3. Identify and discuss two distinct arguments for why factor performance is robust over time.

The risk-based framework assumes that investors are rational, and investors bear risk premiums for taking the opposite side of a factor trade. The behavioral framework assumes that investors are human and hence sometimes irrational, which leads to market dislocations, creating factor premium opportunities. The risk-based framework follows the ideals of the efficient market hypothesis in that stocks with higher levels of risk should outperform stocks with lower levels of risk. For example, risk-based theorists contend that cheap stocks are riskier than expensive stocks. That is, stocks are cheap for a reason. Therefore, the value factor works because value investors are being compensated for taking additional risk. The behavioral-based framework focuses on investor psychology and investor irrationality. For example, behavioral-based theorists maintain that cheap stocks are cheap due to a short-term, often transitory, event, but market participants are pricing the stock as if it may not recover. Investors in the company should be rewarded when the market revalues that company.

4. Discuss why combining multiple factors into a portfolio can be beneficial to investors.

True factors draw performance from differentiated sources of risk and return. Therefore, they should have low correlations with other factors. If a factor is rewarded over time, combining factors can increase diversification.

5. Discuss how and why an investor could use factors to benchmark fundamental active managers.

Most active managers use factors in some way. Using factor benchmarks can help set expectations for manager performance and hold managers more accountable to their specific style. For example, a fundamental manager's stated strategy might be to buy relatively cheap companies with attractive balance sheets and high profitability. From a benchmarking standpoint, benchmarking this manager to a value/profitability factor benchmark rather than to a capitalization-weighted index might be appropriate. Two reasons exist for this conclusion: (1) if the manager is underperforming his or her benchmark, this underperformance may be partially due to the factor being out of favor, and (2) a factor benchmark can help better explain returns. Perhaps the manager is not earning a true alpha and is instead loading up on a factor that is in favor.

CHAPTER 17 SMART BETA STRATEGIES VERSUS ALPHA STRATEGIES

1. Distinguish between factor investing and smart beta.

   Unlike pure factor investing, smart beta is generally a long-only investment approach. Thus, smart beta can be implemented via ETFs to individual investors and financial advisors. Factor investing normally adopts a long/short strategy, most commonly employed by hedge funds and investment bank trading desks. Also, factor investing is typically benchmarked to a value-weighted index. Conversely, most smart beta strategies weight security holdings using company fundamental data (e.g., low volatility and high dividends). Thus, the differences in relative performance often depend on the benchmarking scheme. Finally, some view smart beta as simply a marketing strategy to promote factor investing for ETF providers.

2. Differentiate between smart beta and alpha-seeking strategies.

   Alpha and beta are common investment metrics. Beta is a historical measure of volatility and measures how an asset such as a stock, ETF, or portfolio moves relative to a benchmark such as the S&P 500 Index. In contrast, alpha is a historical measure of an asset's return in excess of the risk-free rate regardless of the benchmark return. One approach to separating these investment strategies is the concept of "portable" beta, which seeks to separate these two components of investment returns. Because factor exposure is more limited and specific in smart beta strategies, smart alpha strategies have better diversification potential.

3. Explain the performance of smart beta strategies between 1967 and 2010 and between 2009 and 2018.

   The most plausible explanation of the difference in performance is that while smart beta may have previously been an unexploited anomaly in the earlier period, the proliferation of smart beta ETFs have contributed to investor "herding" into this sector that has suppressed further returns to this strategy during the latter period. Furthermore, markets are quick to exploit any apparent pricing inefficiencies. Although smart beta strategies have outperformed in earlier periods, this outperformance has probably been noted by market participants and it may not be as effective as previously. Thus, as investors exploit these inefficiencies, no guarantees exist that smart beta approaches will continue to be profitable.

4. Discuss whether the various investment strategies described in this chapter experience similar levels of volatility between 2009 and 2018.

   According to the analysis of variance in Table 17.4, the variances of each group are statistically significantly different. However, the vastly higher variance of the smart alpha funds entirely drives this difference. The variance of the smart beta funds and the S&P 500 Index are not significantly different. This result indicates that smart beta strategies are perhaps no longer able to generate significant risk-adjusted outperformance to naïve index strategies, but they are still superior to alpha-seeking strategies, as currently constituted. Sharpe ratios for the smart beta funds are significantly higher than those of alpha-seeking funds, although not for naive value- and equal-weighted indices. This result indicates that the effectiveness of the smart beta paradigm may have attenuated.

CHAPTER 18 ACTIVIST AND IMPACT INVESTING

1. Discuss the effectiveness of activist investing and identify its limitations.

   Activist investing refers to an individual or group that purchases a significant stake in a public company's shares and tries to obtain seats on the board of directors to influence or change company decisions. Because of headline risk (negative attention) that can quickly arise, activism is effective in getting the attention of both company management and shareholders. Although activism is effective through shareholder proxies that allow shareholders to vote on corporate decisions, such proxies are not binding.

2. Describe the most common hedge fund activist approaches.

   Hedge fund activist approaches include the following:

   - *Engage management.* The hedge fund goes directly to management to effect the change it believes is necessary.
   - *Capital structure.* The hedge fund proposes a change to the target. The hedge fund tries to alter the capital structure by forcing the company to sell off a major asset of the target company.
   - *Block merger.* The hedge fund attempts to block a merger that it views as a poor strategic fit.
   - *Financing and bankruptcy.* The hedge fund provides financing for a company that needs the capital to sustain operations.

3. Describe the key differences between individual and institutional activists.

   Institutional investors and individual activist investors are similar in their approaches and goals. However, a key difference between them is that individual investors are generally focused on short-term and immediate changes, while endowments/foundations and other institutional investors focus on changes that can bring about both short-term and long-term results.

4. Compare and contrast the differences between SRI, ESG, and impact investing approaches and the associated asset class investments.

   - SRI is an approach mostly found in publicly traded portfolios that avoids companies generating revenues from what could be considered objectionable sectors.

- ESG is an approach usually found in publicly traded portfolios that integrates ESG factors during investment selection.
- Impact investing is an approach typically found in private equity and venture capital portfolios that seeks investments having measurable social and environmental benefits alongside a financial return.

5. Discuss the challenges in measuring impact and ESG investing. Describe the tools that are currently available.

Impact Reporting and Investment Standards (IRIS) and the UN Sustainable Development Goals (SDGs) are examples of measurement frameworks. The challenge with measuring ESG and impact investing is a lack of standard metrics. Moreover, low correlation exists among ESG scores across data providers, which prevents a meaningful comparison of ESG scores.

CHAPTER 19 SOCIALLY RESPONSIBLE INVESTING

1. Discuss why the lack of standardized guidelines regarding voluntary nonfinancial disclosure (ESG metrics) is such a critical problem for integrating ESG metrics into equity valuation.

Although the increased transparency currently being reported by many firms is important, much of this data is not audited, lacks consistency from firm to firm, and frequently uses different methods that can result in reporting differences from similar firms. These data quality problems make integrating ESG metrics into the equity valuation process with any consistency difficult. Therefore, ESG metrics, in their current form, are not generally helpful for practitioners who want to integrate ESG information into their asset valuation methods.

2. Discuss the findings from academic research about the traditional SRI practice of negative screening.

Research evidence shows that excluding "sin stocks" (e.g., negative screening) from a portfolio reduces portfolio performance and increases risk. Evidence also shows no difference in the return or risk of screened (e.g., positive/best-in-class) and unscreened portfolios.

3. To account for Apple's supply chain problems, discuss whether an analyst should consider adjusting the company's cost of capital upward to reflect the adverse events associated with the global supplier.

Best practices do not dictate adjusting Apple's cost of capital to reflect the negative ESG material data. Instead, analysts should either adjust future cash flows of Apple or integrate ESG factors by adjusting target multiples using multiples analysis.

4. Discuss how investors should consider the new types of risk that may affect brand value from adverse events such as what Apple experienced with its supplier.

   Analysts should consider how to integrate the new risks identified through ESG analysis into their valuation models. After the incident with Foxconn, Apple experienced large fines that led to more restrictive regulatory oversight disrupting its operations. These impacts negatively affected Apple's future cash flows, which can be modeled using a discount cash flow (DCF) model during the equity valuation process.

CHAPTER 20 POOLED INVESTMENT VEHICLES

1. Discuss the tax efficiency of ETFs relative to MFs.

   ETFs tend to be more tax-efficient than MFs due to the ETF redemption process. The redemption process allows for the in-kind return of shares, which reduces the taxable capital gains distributions to shareholders. In contrast, MFs must sell underlying securities to meet the share redemptions, thereby incurring capital gain/loss distributions ultimately taxable to the shareholder.

2. Discuss the relative transparency of ETFs into the underlying assets and benefits to investors.

   Investors can publicly view the holdings of most ETFs. This availability is in stark contrast to MFs that are only required to disclose their holdings every quarter. The added transparency of ETFs allows investors to more quickly and precisely identify and evaluate any style drift of the fund and, if necessary, make adjustments to the portfolio's overall asset allocation.

3. Discuss three benefits of ETFs.

   Three benefits of ETFs include the following:

   1. ETFs have continuous trading throughout the trading day, meaning that investors do not have to wait for the end of the day. The NAV may be higher or lower than when the investor made the buy or sell decision. This relation can affect the trade's overall profitability in a trending market.
   2. ETF shares are marginable, which provides investors with the opportunity to leverage return.
   3. Investors can short ETF shares, which enables them to profit on downside movements and gives additional choices for hedging other equity positions.

4. Contrast the share creation processes of MFs and ETFs.

   Investors can buy MF shares directly from the fund company once daily at the NAV. This opportunity contrasts with shares in ETFs, which investors can buy and sell in the secondary market. APs previously created the shares trading in the secondary market by purchasing the underlying securities that the fund company wants to hold and then exchanging them with the fund for shares in the ETF. The AP then sells those shares on the open market.

5. Describe the important differences between MFs and CEFs.

CEFs trade freely (intraday) on the open market, usually on a stock exchange. When a CEF holder wants to sell shares, the CEF issues do not redeem the shares, but instead, other independent investors buy the shares. In this way, the market sets CEF prices like other traded equity security. Conversely, the MF buys and sells its shares directly from the fund at the end of the day at the NAV. Additionally, CEFs may trade at prices other than the NAV, whereas MFs trade at the NAV based at the end-of-day closing prices.

CHAPTER 21 INVESTING IN PRIVATE EQUITY

1. Define PE and list types of PE.

PE investments are private ownership interests in the equity of private companies or publicly listed companies. PE includes VC, LBOs, direct lending, distressed debt, and PIPE. VC is an early-stage investment in a company's startup phase. Buyouts occur when a private entity buys a public company and removes it from the public markets. When buyers finance these buyouts with debt, those buyouts are known as leveraged buyouts. Smaller players who have less or no access to the public markets for funding may need to borrow directly from PEs. This form of funding is *direct lending*. PE firms also lend money to companies in bankruptcy proceedings. This form of investing is called *distressed debt investing*. Instead of a complete buyout, PEs can also buy a proportion of a publicly listed company; this arrangement is termed a PIPE. PE firms can also participate in *equity bridge financing*, which is temporary financing given to a company until it acquires permanent financing through an IPO or debt financing.

2. Define commitment period, capital call, seed money, and bridge financing.

The *commitment period* refers to the period during which a PE fund can request capital from an investor. Usually, this period is five years. The request for capital to the investor is known as a *capital call*. An investor must honor this call. *Seed money* is an early-stage investment in a startup that is still in the idea phase. Since seed money is distributed while the company is still only an idea and is not generating any cash flows, the investor funding the seed money is often called an *angel investor*. *Bridge financing* is temporary funding provided before the company can acquire permanent funding through an IPO or debt financing.

3. Discuss the different types of risks involved with PE investments.

Liquidity risk, capital risk, and default risk are common risks involved in PE:

- *Liquidity risk* can be interpreted in two ways: (1) the risk that assets are unlikely to be sold at fair value and (2) the risk that funding is likely unavailable to make investments. PE investments may remain for many years before realizing a return on the investment.
- *Capital risk* is the risk that a part or all of the capital invested can evaporate and not be recovered. A capital call may not be fulfilled because an investor does not have cash available and therefore the deal cannot be closed.
- *Default risk* is the risk that the issuer company may default (i.e., the company cannot grow enough to recover the entire initial capital).

4. List the main factors that PE investors should consider before investing.

PE investors should consider several factors before investing:

- *Lack of a secondary market.* Since these deals are private, no secondary market exists for these investments, which also makes valuing the investment difficult.
- *Time horizon.* PE typically has a *time horizon* of 7 to 10 years before an investment can be realized. Therefore, investors should ensure that they can keep their liquidity tied up for that long and not need cash.
- *Possibility of default.* Since PE investment issuer companies can default at a higher rate than other relatively more established companies, they carry more risk.
- *Risk level.* PE often requires investments in hundreds of million dollars in the deals. Investors should ensure that they have sufficient risk tolerance to take on this risk.
- *Diversification effects.* PE acts as portfolio diversifiers having a lower correlation with other asset classes.

5. Discuss an investor's motivation to invest in VC versus a buyout and an issuer's motivation for PE financing over other sources of financing.

The motivation behind investing in VC is that the issuer company is likely to experience future growth and provide above-normal returns. The motivation behind investing in a buyout is that the acquired company can have its operations improved to achieve efficiencies that enable the buyout firm to sell the company at a higher price. An issuer's motivation behind obtaining PE financing is to leverage the PE fund's expertise.

6. Define different measures of PE returns and discuss why they differ from conventional public market metrics.

Since analysts do not value PE investments in the same way as other traditional asset classes, their performance calculations differ. The most widely used performance measures are IRR and MOIC. Calculating the IRR of PE funds is based on a set of cash flows, which includes cash contributed, distributions, and unrealized investments. MOIC is a ratio of the sum of realized and unrealized value to the cash contributed. Analysts use a measure called PME to enable comparing public markets by converting a PE return measure into the PME.

CHAPTER 22 INVESTING IN EMERGING MARKETS

1. Identify the factors affecting the capital flow to emerging markets.

   The economics and finance literature discuss various factors such as global risk aversion, the interest rate differential, and the output growth rate in domestic markets that influence capital inflow to emerging markets. Generally, an increased level of global risk aversion has a strong negative effect on portfolio and banking flows to emerging markets. This aspect has received more attention from global fund managers since the global financial crisis of 2007–2008. Another set of studies examines the impact of external interest rates in the context of capital inflows to emerging economies. These studies find that as the interest rate differential increases in favor of external countries, portfolio flows to emerging markets tend to decrease. Other factors, such as domestic output growth and domestic asset returns, also play an important role in capital inflows to emerging markets. Relevant studies report a strong positive relation between domestic growth and portfolio flows to emerging markets. Some emerging economies tend to implement capital control policies to change the composition and volume of various fund flows. However, their policies yield limited success.

2. Discuss how global investors can still benefit from investing in emerging markets given that these markets are becoming more integrated with developed markets.

   Although recent evidence shows that emerging economy capital market returns are converging to those of developed economies, studies contend that emerging markets are still quite distinct from developed markets and provide a greater opportunity, mainly due to country-specific variations, to invest in an expanded number of markets and diversify investment risk. Since developed markets' asset returns have been showing an increased level of co-movement over the years, investors have less opportunity to diversify their risks if they only focus on developed markets. This situation makes emerging markets more appealing to global investors.

   However, the correlation between the emerging market index and the world index has gradually increased from 0.40 in the 1990s to 0.80 by 2015, which makes the diversification argument less convincing. Although the emerging and developed markets look more correlated in modern times, most of the emerging markets are still not fully integrated primarily due to regulatory hurdles, and the integration process is far from complete. Political interventions, corruptions, lack of transparency, and weaker corporate governance practices are other impediments in achieving greater market integration. Further, some recent influential studies observe that country factors still dominate cross-country valuations, and despite the increase in correlations with world markets, emerging markets still present good opportunities to achieve higher returns and diversification opportunities because of the high individual country volatility and country-specific factors.

3. Discuss some effective institutional strategies for making better investments in emerging markets.

As the characteristics of emerging market economies markedly differ from developed or developing economies, investors need to pay adequate attention to various institutional, social, and cultural aspects of these markets to make a more informed and educated investment decisions. Three institutional strategies are important for emerging market investment decisions: (1) understanding the value of relational strategy, (2) adopting a relevant infrastructure-building strategy, and (3) focusing on a sociocultural bridging strategy.

1. *Understanding the value of relational strategy.* In emerging markets, investors need to understand how a firm maintains its relations with key stakeholders. Failing to do so, a firm may lose investors' trust and confidence, which may negatively affect its growth potential and profitability.
2. *Relevance of infrastructure-building strategy.* Emerging markets often lack adequate infrastructure such as a telecommunication network and transportation network. Therefore, firm location becomes critical in emerging markets. Investors should pay attention to how a prospective firm plans to cope with infrastructural challenges.
3. *Focusing on a sociocultural bridging strategy.* Investors should try to identify which firms have invested adequately to attain greater social embeddedness. In emerging economies, firms may face two types of challenges in the context of sociocultural aspects. First, a fast-developing country often faces a shortage of skilled workers. To maintain a competitive edge, a firm must have adequate skilled workers and plan for their training. Second, a firm has to be cautious about social inequality and possible unrest, which can hinder its productivity and future growth prospect.

4. Discuss whether political connections matter in investment decisions and performance in emerging markets.

Emerging market economies generally have a less transparent political and regulatory environment than do developed economies. Also, government intervention in business is common in those markets. A common view is that political connections are more important than operational efficiency in emerging markets. Thus, most large or economically influential firms in emerging markets tend to maintain a close association with ruling parties and the government. Studies show that political connections pay off in emerging market economies. Politically connected firms get more investment opportunities and tend to perform better in these economies. However, another strand of research shows that political connections do not always benefit a firm. Politically connected firms may need to accommodate undue pressure from political parties or government, which could negatively affect their performance.

CHAPTER 23 DISCLOSURE REGULATIONS IN EMERGING ECONOMIES AND THEIR IMPACT ON EQUITY MARKETS

1. Discuss the pros and cons of various disclosure regulation approaches: voluntary, mandatory, and comply or explain options:

   - *Voluntary disclosure.* Voluntary disclosures depend on investor demand. Since investors in emerging markets are sometimes unsure about their information requirements, voluntary disclosure regulation may not be the best option to reduce information asymmetry between firm management and investors. Also, better-governed firms, which have lower informational asymmetry concerns, usually make more voluntary disclosures in emerging markets. Further, some studies find that since retail investors dominate emerging markets, additional information disclosure could attract more noise traders.
   - *Mandatory disclosure.* The success of a mandatory disclosure regime depends on the legal enforceability in a country and the true intention of regulatory bodies. Further, mandatory disclosure regulations could be costly for small and medium-sized firms, which are generally resource-constrained.
   - *Comply or explain.* A comply or explain disclosure regime requires a firm to disclose required information or to explain the reasons for nondisclosure. Although this approach may appear optimal because it balances market power, informational demand, and regulatory requirements, the success of this approach depends on the legal enforceability and market pressures of emerging markets.

2. Elaborate on the challenges associated with environmental disclosure regulation in China.

   Although regulations in China led to tremendous progress in enacting various laws and regulations to facilitate environmental information disclosure and transparency, their effective implementation remains a serious concern. Many polluting companies refuse to disclose environmental information, citing article 8 of Open Government Information Regulation (OGIR), which allows companies to withhold information on the grounds of national security, public security, economic security, or social stability. Also, few instances of sanctioning firms are available that violate the environmental information disclosure provisions. These instances undermine the effective implementation of Chinese environmental disclosure requirements.

3. Discuss the information mosaic argument in the context of private meetings.

   In the United States and in other markets, managers are not required to reveal any material information during private meetings due to the restrictions imposed by Reg FD or similar regulations. Yet, investors can still become more informed by interacting with firm management. Using various legitimate sources, sophisticated investors generally gather information about a firm and develop their insights to carry out future trades. These investors can derive valuable information from the nonmaterial disclosures made by the firm's management during the private meetings. Sophisticated investors have the ability to put together the shared information, albeit nonmaterial, with their preexisting information "mosaic" that can eventually increase the quality of their trading decisions and informed trading activities. The situation becomes more delicate as the Reg FD or similar regulations do not specify what constitutes material nonpublic information. Firm management has considerable flexibility on the nonmaterial information that can be shared with investors and analysts. For instance, management can review an analyst's model and recommend changes if these corrections are matters of historical fact. Thus, meeting participants, especially sophisticated investors, can gain an informational advantage that leads to more informed trading.

4. Explain how insiders can make profits around private meetings in China.

Insider trading is a serious problem in China. Despite implementing strong regulation, CSRC still faces a challenge of fighting insider trading as the Chinese market becomes more complex and the insider trading becomes more sophisticated. Also, ambiguous restrictions on insider trading activities around private in-house meeting dates encourage executives to make a profit through insider trading activities. Evidence shows that private in-house meetings are normally associated with positive market reactions. Insiders can take advantage of this timing and participate in informed trading activities. They can buy stocks beforehand and make a profit from price increases around meeting dates. Alternatively, executives can use positive market sentiment around meeting dates to sell their own holdings. Many SZSE-listed firms are young and characterized with high insider ownership. Therefore, executives and their associates can potentially use the positive environment surrounding private in-house meeting dates to cash out their own holdings.

CHAPTER 24 EQUITY CROWDFUNDING INVESTMENTS

1. Describe the slow growth of equity crowdfunding in the United States.

Equity crowdfunding has been slow to ignite in the United States because it took the Securities and Exchange Commission years, not months, to establish the rules to govern equity crowdfunding. The rules were stricter than perhaps intended by the original JOBS Act of 2012, making investment more difficult for Americans.

2. Identify four types of crowdfunding.

Crowdfunding falls into four basic categories: (1) charitable giving, (2) rewards-based, (3) debt, and (4) equity crowdfunding. Hybrids also exist. Investors may combine lending and taking a stake in a company, or they might receive perks and shares of stock in the startup.

3. List two opportunities, relative to traditional sources of funding, for entrepreneurs and/or investors to participate in the equity crowdfunding market.

Opportunities available to equity crowdfunders and investors include the following:

- A wider pool of investors from which to raise capital.
- No need to establish relationships with angel investors and venture capitalists (VCs). Also, the entrepreneur can set specific targets, rather than having to meet targets set by VCs.
- A possible reduction in the cost of equity.
- More funding available to women and minorities relative to VC funding.
- Investors who are interested and want to support the product or idea.

4. Identify two challenges faced by entrepreneurs and/or investors who participate in the equity crowdfunding market.

Challenges related to equity crowdfunding include the following:

- The difficulty of raising capital due to more SEC regulations. A $1 million cap exists on the amount that can be raised, and caps exist on how much nonaccredited investors may invest, which is about $2,200 per year.
- The costs associated with managing many small investors.
- The need for entrepreneurs to divulge their ideas and products in a public forum to raise capital.
- The presence of unsophisticated investors, which creates a greater potential for fraud.

Index

Note: Page references in *italics* refer to figures and tables.